The World in 1938

ARCTIC OCEAN

OCEAN

Severnaya Zemlaya

Novo Sibirskie

LAPDEV SEA

Ostrova

EAST SIBERIAN SEA

Wrangel

Prince Patrick

Banks
Victoria

BEAUFORT SEA

ALASKA

CANADA

Great Bear Lake

Great Slave Lake

SOVIET SOCIALIST REPUBLICS

BERING SEA

Gulf of Alaska

Bering Strait

SEA OF OKHOTSK

Kamchatka Peninsula

Aleutian Is

L Baikal

MONGOLIA

MANCHURIA

Amur

Sakhalin

Kurile Is

USA

CHINA

Balkhash

KOREA

SEA OF JAPAN

JAPAN

PACIFIC

Yangtze Kiang

YELLOW SEA

Ryukyu Is

Midway

TIBET

NEPAL BHUTAN

Ganges

Bonin Is

Hawaiian Is

INDIA

BURMA

FRENCH INDO-CHINA

TAIWAN

Hong Kong

Hainan

Marianas

Wake I

Bay of Bengal

SIAM

SOUTH CHINA SEA

PHILIPPINE IS

Guam

Andaman Is

Gilbert Is

OCEAN

Nicobar Is

CEYLON

MALAYA

Sarawak

Palau Is

Caroline Is

Sumatra

Borneo

Celebes

Halmahera

New Ireland

ELLICE IS

ago Archipelago

Java

PAPUA NEW GUINEA

New Britain

SOLOMON IS

Phoenix Is

DUTCH EAST INDIES

Timor

New Britain

Santa Cruz

Tokelau Is

DIAN

CORAL SEA

NEW HEBRIDES

Samoan Is

OCEAN

Samoan Is

AUSTRALIA

New Caledonia

FIJI

TONGA

Tahiti

elen Is

Norfolk I

Lord Howe I

Kermadec Is

Great Australian Bight

TASMAN SEA

NEW ZEALAND

Tasmania

Chatham Is

Auckland Is

Antipodes Is

D1123606

ANTARCTICA

Britain, British Empire and Commonwealth

United States of America and Mandated Territories

Soviet Union

Germany

Japan and Japanese Empire

Netherlands, Dutch East Indies and Guiana

France and French Colonial Empire

China

Belgium and Belgian Congo

Italy and Italian Empire

SUMMIT
BOOKS

THE
Month-by-Month
ATLAS OF
WORLD WAR II
BARRIE AND FRANCES PITT

SUMMIT BOOKS

New York   London   Toronto   Sydney   Tokyo

SUMMIT BOOKS

Simon & Schuster Building
Rockefeller Center
1230 Avenue of the Americas
New York, New York 10020

Copyright © 1989 by Barrie and Frances Pitt

All rights reserved
including the right of reproduction
in whole or in part in any form.

SUMMIT BOOKS and colophon are trademarks
of Simon & Schuster Inc.

Manufactured in Spain

10 9 8 7 6 5 4 3 2 1

Library of Congress Cataloging in Publication Data

Pitt, Barrie.
  The month-by-month atlas of World War II.

  Shows the war month-by-month, 1940–1945.
  Copublished with Macmillan London Ltd.
  1. World War, 1939–1945 — Maps.   2. World War,
1939–1945.   I. Pitt, Frances, 1948–
II. Title.   III. Title: Atlas of World War II.
G1038.P6   1989   940.53'0223   89–675257

ISBN 0–671–68880–4

This atlas is dedicated
to
the Director and Staff of
THE IMPERIAL WAR MUSEUM
in gratitude for the unstinting help
they give to all who ask for it

Contents

Authors' Note

The idea behind this book was conceived at an informal meeting of over a dozen people at FitzHead; some had fought during World War II, many had served at some time in one service or another, and all had a deep interest in military history, particularly that of World War II. Each of us had a fairly detailed knowledge of one campaign or another, or one particular aspect of the conflict, in one case of artillery and in another of guerrilla campaigns.

Talk had been wide-ranging for some time, when one member remarked that it had only been in the last few days that he had realised that D-Day had coincided with the last stages of the Battle of Kohima.

Further investigations into the chronology of that month revealed other lapses in knowledge among the group. Few had realised, for instance, that on the day Montgomery moved his headquarters to the Normandy bridgehead, the US Pacific Fleet had opened its attack on Guam, Saipan and Tinian, and the US Fifth Army was consolidating its hold on Rome, while the Eighth was capturing Pescara and the Red Army was driving into the Karelian Isthmus. A few days later when the first flying bombs landed on London, Chindits and Merrill's Marauders were attacking Mogaung, the first Super-Fortress Raid took place on Tokyo, and the naval and air battle known as the 'Great Marianas Turkey Shoot' occurred.

Again, most people knew that at the same time that the Battle of Alamein was being fought, the Torch convoys were sailing from the east coast of America, and the Battle of Stalingrad was reaching a bitter climax; but few present also realised that the Australians were beginning the drive over the Owen Stanley Range in Papua, the US Marines had at last secured all vital positions on Guadalcanal, and British brigades were driving south on Madagascar.

It was quite astonishing to find how many of us had detailed knowledge of specific events, but had never seen how each event occurred in an overall historical picture; then it became evident that the whole geographical picture had never been presented to them, either. One member was a cartographer who had drawn several maps of both *Operation Market Garden* and the Battle of the Bulge but had not realised that it is possible to drive from Arnhem to Bastogne in a morning; only one person knew that when the Guards Armoured Division had driven from Douai to Brussels on September 3, 1944, they had completed the longest opposed advance that any division, in any army, had ever before undertaken in a single day.

It was the same with the sizes of armies or fleets. Alamein was fought by 23 assorted British, Commonwealth, German and Italian divisions; when *Barbarossa* opened, 117 German divisions and 14 Rumanian divisions drove forward into a front held by 132 Soviet divisions. Over 700 ships of the US Pacific Fleets fought off the Japanese attacks at Leyte on October 20, 1944 – and over 5,000 ships of one sort or another took part in *Operation Overlord.*

The problem posed soon crystallised during the resultant discussion. How – for the first time – could the whole panorama of the war be presented so that not only could the progress of each individual campaign and battle be followed, but also their relationship to the whole global conflict?

This atlas attempts to solve the problem.

Each month appears as a double-page spread, the background of which is constant: the world in simple outline, pale blue sea, white land with a darker blue outline. Upon this outline are shown the areas held at the end of each month by the original aggressors, Germany and Japan – illustrating their initial rapid expansion and their subsequent contraction as the Allies pressed in on them until they were defeated. The main efforts of the bombing campaigns, small actions such as commando raids, and small naval actions which do not warrant more detailed maps are shown on these world maps, as are the sites of the various important conferences.

Linked by numbering to the main areas of conflict are larger-scale, detailed maps which show the progress of the battles – troop movements, armoured thrusts, battle-fleet manoeuvres. As a general rule, only the axes of the advances are shown, and the line of advance reached at the end of each month: where large-scale sweeping advances were maintained throughout the whole month – as often happened on the Russian Front – these are shown as blocks of national colour with arrows picked out in ground colour showing the direction of troop movements; where the battles were fought through difficult terrain to secure focal points – as in Burma or New Guinea – the movements are shown in arrows of national colour. Narrative essays accompany the maps when necessary.

There were certain highly significant occurrences during the war which merited extended and more detailed treatment –

Barbarossa and *Overlord* are examples – and these have received it in the form of longer essays and larger maps, and double-page spreads to themselves. An attempt has also been made to present the political geography of the world immediately before and after the war.

No project such as this can succeed without the help of others. To the original group among whom the idea was generated, all of whom have been generous with their advice and encouragement, we would both like to express our gratitude – as to all the other fellow historians, archivists and friends who have helped us. In particular, like any other writers attempting to portray the enormous conflict on the Eastern Front, we must express our indebtedness to Professor John Erickson, and in this instance also to Mr Carl van Dyke, who clarified for us the complications of the ever-changing Red Army Fronts. The staffs of the Admiralty and the Wiener Libraries have also earned our gratitude.

We would also like to thank Kyle Cathie for her attention and encouragement, Kate Jones, Amanda Batten and Serena Dilnot for their constant checking of myriad detail, Dick Vine for his very real assistance during a crucial period – and all the other members of Macmillan's staff who have helped us.

Finally we would like to thank Martin Blumenson for his stimulating and generous Foreword. Regard from such an authority as he, is regard indeed.

Barrie Pitt, Frances M. Pitt
FitzHead, Somerset, 1989

Foreword

Martin Blumenson

War is a political act. It is organized violence waged by adversaries, each seeking to gain power at the expense of the other or to deny to the other the extension of power. Generally it is the last resort of diplomacy at an impasse over resolving serious international problems or of domestic argument related to stability and change. The prosecution of war encompasses a vast sub-culture of practices, habits, and customs, including leadership, training, doctrine, technology, logistics, and many other compartments of knowledge and tradition. All these have evolved over the course of history.

The heart of warfare is the battle, the active confrontation between the opponents. The outcome of a clash usually has a bearing on the eventual result, the success or the failure of the war to attain the objectives sought.

A battle takes place in a specific geographical setting and time sequence. Although the site may be described by words, a photograph, or a drawing, it is best demonstrated by a map. A diagrammatic representation of the earth's surface, a map shows the relationship of a certain point to other features. It does so by means of its direction and distance from other geographical points.

A series of hostile meetings in a certain region over the course of a segment of time is a campaign, and normally it determines the ultimate consequence of the warfare: victory, defeat, or a draw. A series of maps showing a series of consecutive battles in a particular area indicates how a campaign developed.

World War II was the greatest single event of the 20th century. The military action, called operations, flared in far-flung areas spread over the globe. Most of the fighting was conventional and linear warfare. The uniformed combatants faced each other across a well-defined front, a position displayed by an imaginary line traced on a map.

During the war, the people at home followed the course of the conflict in their newspapers. In accounts filed by war correspondents near the front, they learned what their warriors on land and sea and in the air were doing and whether their exertions were leading to triumph or setback. But the best way of determining how the struggle was going was to glance at the map, to see where the front was, and to note which way the front had moved since the last reading.

Whether the front inched forward or backward at a snail's pace or bounded either way at an accelerating rate was also significant in judging the progress of the war. For the geographical position of the front also showed how much territory on land and sea each belligerent controlled. Over a period of time, the changing location of the front marked the expansion or contraction of that realm of control, and that too meant winning or losing.

The demands of security and secrecy sometimes inhibited the accuracy of war maps in the newspapers. Also, the lack of precise information often caused mistakes. Now, more than forty years after the end of the contest, these conditions no longer apply.

The maps here presented by Barrie and Frances Pitt give a marvelous panorama of the struggle. Above all else, they are correct. The pictures of the ongoing combat are precise and true. They are expert representations of how the conflict evolved.

Barrie Pitt was among the earliest and also among the leading interpreters of World War II. From the first, his mastery of the materials of the war has marked his distinguished career. His flair was perhaps nowhere better displayed than in his brilliant and conspicuously successful publication for Purnell. His wide-ranging knowledge and his ability to transform that knowledge into readable prose are at their best in the lucid text accompanying the battle and campaign maps.

His essays here perform two functions. They explain the cartography of the war. They also make clear those aspects of warfare that cannot be represented graphically, for example, the political aims of the belligerents, the leadership on both sides, and the like.

Frances Pitt is a portrait painter here turned cartographer. Her drawings and use of color render the ebb and flow of the war with a clarity and simplicity that evoke on every page the skill and understanding of the artist.

Together they have performed a valuable function. They have chosen to break the war into monthly segments, and these pieces, individually and together, show, as nothing quite like them in existence, how the war developed and how all the parts fit together into one seamless whole. They have made it easy for all their readers to understand how World War II happened during the course of its existence and over the face of the globe. Their accomplishment is nothing less than dazzling.

The World in Summer 1939

By August 1939 the world's attention was focused on one man – Adolf Hitler, Chancellor and President of Germany, Führer of the Third Reich. He had become Chancellor in early 1933, combining the position with that of President upon the death of President Hindenburg in August 1934. Since then Hitler had consolidated his position into one of unchallenged dictatorship inside Germany, and immense, if sinister, influence and prestige throughout the rest of the world. It is arguable that in no other country and in no other combination of circumstances could so meteoric a rise of an individual have taken place.

At the end of World War I, the German people as a whole were in a state of shock. This had not been due to the enormous tribulations and losses they had suffered throughout the war years, but because of the fact that, only five months before the end, German armies had pushed the line of the Western Front back to within forty miles of Paris, and it had seemed to the average German citizen that the victory which his country's revered leaders had promised him for the last four years was now imminent.

Then suddenly came the announcement of the abdication of the Kaiser, the mutiny of the High Seas Fleet, the surrender of the armies – and in the months immediately after the Armistice, chaos, starvation, and a sudden upsurge of splinter parties of such extreme views that political murders were of almost daily occurrence. In due course the terms of the Treaty of Versailles were announced, and under these, if Germany did not herself suffer a great deal of territorial loss she was certainly humiliated, while the empire of her closest ally, Austria–Hungary, was dismembered.

The motives behind the men who drew up those terms were mixed. Lloyd George for England was concerned that Britain's naval supremacy should be preserved and her links with her Empire secured, while Clemenceau, the French representative, who would seem to have regarded the whole process with deep cynicism – as he did the setting up of the League of Nations – was determined to make Germany pay in the form of massive reparations for the damage and losses the war had caused France. President Wilson for the United States was probably the man inspired by the highest motives though perhaps not with the strongest degree of political realism. His guiding principle was that all peoples should have the right of self-determination – which, when put into practice, redrew the map of Europe.

From the Austro-Hungarian Empire were carved the new states of Czechoslovakia and Hungary, while much of Austria's south-western provinces was combined with Serbia to make up Yugo-Slavia. In the north, Estonia, Latvia and Lithuania were brought back into existence, Poland was reinstated as a nation in such a manner as to cut East Prussia off from the rest of the Reich, while in the west the Saar and the Rhineland were demilitarised to form a buffer zone between France and Germany, thus stripping Germany of her most concentrated industrial region, and for the foreseeable future occupied by Allied troops.

Whatever justice may or may not have lain behind the terms of the Treaty of Versailles, they left the German people bitter and angry – especially the Army which had for so long embodied the national pride and was, indeed, a central and essential core of the people. They all believed that the German forces had been beaten, not by military skill, but by a combination of overwhelming numbers and material possessed by the enemy, and betrayal at home. Despite the surrender which had followed the Armistice, the armies had marched back into their own country – whose borders had never been breached by the enemy – with flags flying and bands playing, to discover that sailors, a few civilians and a

group which soon became known as the 'November criminals' had been carrying on a semi-revolution which had effectively 'stabbed them in the back'.

The legends grew. In the chaos of the early post-war years ex-soldiers banded together to form small armies in support of many political principles, from the Spartacists who wished to follow the lead of the Bolshevik movement in Russia (and at times seemed likely to succeed: a Communist government was formed in April 1919 in Bavaria, which for a month was one of the Soviet Republics) to the Freikorps which fought to retain the gains won during the war in the east.

One of the political groupings which emerged from the chaos as early as 1919 became known as the National Socialist German Workers' Party (abbreviated to 'Nazi'), its fifth member, soon to become its unchallenged leader, Adolf Hitler. The basic Nazi creed was that the German peoples had been – and were still being – seduced from their natural patriotism by foreign, and especially Jewish, left-wing agitators; these must be defeated by recourse to their own methods. Hitler quickly developed his own natural talents into those of a mass orator, purveying slogans not arguments, issuing orders not discussing principles. His targets were the workers not the bourgeoisie, his appeal to their emotions, not their intellects.

During the years from 1925 to 1929 the Nazi Party remained very much in the shadows, even in Bavaria, for by this time economic reality had forced America to extend vast credits to support German industry, not only to dispel the appalling inflation but also to provide some financial stability throughout central Europe. Unemployment fell, living standards rose to pre-war levels and the conditions in which revolution is traditionally fostered faded away. Then, in 1929 Wall Street crashed, in due course the 'Great Depression' began – and now were to be attracted to Hitler's Party not only the unemployed German workers, but also the German middle class who had seen their savings disappear in the financial maelstrom.

By this time Hitler had not only stamped his own extreme right-wing nationalistic Leadership Principle upon his Party and imbued it with his own hate-filled philosophy, he had also recruited armed thugs into his 'Sturmabteilung' (the SA), dressing them in para-military uniform and employing them to beat up his enemies on the streets and to eject hecklers with the maximum brutality from his meetings.

However, during the years since he had first taken over the Party he had learned one important lesson. In 1923 he had attempted a *coup d'état* in Munich which had failed miserably and led to his incarceration for thirteen months in Landsberg gaol – a respite from political activity of the more violent kind during which he not only wrote his autobiography and polemic *Mein Kampf*, but also had time to reflect upon events. His attempt to overthrow the Weimar Republic had been defeated to a great extent by the loyalty of the German Army to the existing government; and that loyalty would be transferred to his own government – more importantly to himself personally – only if he attained the office of Chancellor by legal means. Once he had done that, of course, the Army would stand by and watch him destroy democracy throughout Germany – and indeed throughout the rest of the world if he had his way – with folded arms.

To this end he began a process of flattering the rich (and thus ensuring a flow of money into the Party coffers) and frightening the uninfluential into agreement – presenting himself on the one hand as the only true bulwark against Communism, but on the other doing nothing to curb the violence of his stormtroopers. Even by these means, however, in 1928 the Nazi Party only polled 800,000 votes out of 31 million cast in the

election, and thus had only 12 seats out of 491 in the Reichstag.

Then Wall Street crashed, an economic storm swept through Europe and the rest of the world, millions were suddenly out of work – and Hitler's hour had come. On January 30, 1933, he became Chancellor. Germany's fate from that day on would be his own.

From the beginning of his political life, Hitler had made it quite clear that his ambition was boundless. Mastery of Europe was his first aim followed by domination of the world – both aims to be secured by armed force. Only days after taking office as Chancellor of Germany he gave a talk to a gathering of Nazi Party officials and officers of the Army and Navy, in which he announced the absolute necessity of occupation by force of western Russia at least as far as the Urals, and its subsequent 'unqualified Germanisation' – to the astonishment and considerable discomfiture of many of his listeners. During the months which followed it seemed that every event, however minor, aided his plans.

Three weeks after this speech the German Parliament building, the Reichstag, was burnt out – by whom has never been satisfactorily established, but it gave Hitler the excuse to suspend all civil liberties in Germany, start a witch-hunt against the Communists and, at the end of the following month, pass the 'Enabling Acts' which gave him dictatorial powers. During the year which followed he turned his attention to internal party affairs and tackled the problem of members who felt that they deserved more recognition of the part they had played in his rise to power – particularly the leaders of the stormtroops whose violence had taken him to the office of Chancellor. There were also some members who felt that as much attention should be paid to the 'Socialist' claims in the Party's title as to the 'National', and these, together with certain other elements in both party and influential circles must be eliminated.

On June 30, 1934 occurred the 'Night of the Long Knives', when Himmler's black-uniformed SS – in fact Hitler's Praetorian Guard – eliminated the SA Brownshirts, shooting all the leaders and hundreds of the rank and file together with any other potential opponents to Hitler's rise to untrammelled power. By the end of the week hardly a critic in party or German political society still lived, and the German people as a whole had been stunned into incredulous acquiescence; from now on they would certainly do as they were bade, with varying degrees of enthusiasm depending upon how long they had been exposed to the Party's increasingly effective propaganda.

A vitally important section of the community was also to be wooed by significant improvements in its standing. Having proclaimed himself Führer of the German Reich and assumed the Presidency on Aug 2, on Oct 1 Hitler ordered the creation of the German Air Force (expressly forbidden under the Versailles Treaty) and the swift expansion of the German Army and Navy, to provide him with the divisions and battle fleets he would need to realise his ambitions. Not only would the armed services of the Reich now be committed by loyalty to a legally elected government, but the holders of the highest ranks would be grateful to him for their increased responsibilities and the perquisites of rank which would go with them. Their indebtedness was underlined when he personally assumed Supreme Command of the German Armed Forces.

But the expanded armed forces (the Wehrmacht) would need weapons, and the traditional industrial heart of Germany lay in the Saar and the Rhineland, areas only recently vacated by Allied occupation troops and still part of the 'demilitarised zone'. The Saar region he regained by organising a plebiscite asking whether the inhabitants wished to be considered part of

1

Germany; as the vast majority were of German birth he gained overwhelming support, then presented the region's nomination as part of his Reich as a *fait accompli* to a world as yet unsuspicious of his motives. Encouraged, his next step in March 1936 was to send his troops into the Rhineland itself – to the extremely nervous apprehension of most of his military advisers who were certain that both Britain and France would react with superior forces against his as yet untried battalions. But the democracies did nothing – except argue amongst themselves and eventually excuse their own inaction with such casuistries as, 'After all, he is only walking into his own back yard!' If Hitler's overweening ambition was the main cause of the dreadful war which was to engulf Europe, the pusillanimity and lack of vision of other European leaders was by no means blameless.

It was an encouragement to others as well: while the German divisions were making their presence felt in their newly occupied territories, Mussolini sent out his blackshirted Fascist Legions on large-scale depredations into Africa, and shortly after Hitler had gone into the Rhineland Il Duce proclaimed Ethiopia an Italian colony. Two months later – on July 18 – the Spanish Civil War broke out, within months both Führer and Duce had placed themselves unreservedly alongside General Franco, the right-wing rebel leader, and for the remainder of the conflict Spain provided an excellent training ground for Italian – and especially German – pilots and tank crews. It was bombers of the Luftwaffe Condor Legion which carried out the destruction of Guernica, giving the world its first glimpse of the horrors of war to be expected in any future conflict.

Nevertheless, by 1937 Britain and France were beginning to sense the dangers arising around them and to take steps to provide themselves with better protection. France began the construction of an extension to the Maginot Line, the system of fortifications she had built in the immediate post-World War I period as a safeguard against possible future German aggression, while Britain went so far as to pass an Air Raids Precaution Bill through Parliament. The possibility of much further military preparation by Britain, however, was to a great extent negated by the succession to Mr Stanley Baldwin in the office of Prime Minister of Mr Neville Chamberlain, who soon became convinced that fate had cast him in the role of Saviour of Peace. Thus believing, he sent his Foreign Secretary, Lord Halifax, to Berlin to enquire of Hitler the grounds upon which the latter was basing his sudden and inexplicable claims to the Sudetenland, the western and most highly industrialised province of Czechoslovakia.

For Hitler's eyes had now turned for the moment to the east. Czechoslovakia in his opinion was an anachronistic product of the hated Treaty of Versailles, and as such must cease to exist and instead become part of his own Reich. He did not go so far as to state this baldly to Halifax – or anyone else for the time being – perhaps because it might have been pointed out to him that as the Czechoslovakian provinces had in fact been parts of the old Austro-Hungarian Empire, they had never been governed from Berlin anyway. Such irrelevancies need not be discussed, only the subject of an apparently downtrodden Sudeten-German population proclaimed to a puzzled but acquiescent British Foreign Secretary; in any case, Hitler had plans for the immediate future which would render any arguments on the subject null and void.

On March 12, 1938, having by then taken personal command of German forces in the field, Hitler sent them across the border with Austria and into Vienna where they received a rapturous welcome from a population well prepared by Nazi propaganda, and deeply penetrated by an indigenous Austrian Nazi Party. The following day he arrived in Vienna himself and after a triumphant parade through the capital, announced the 'Anschluss' – the indissoluble union of Austria and Germany into a 'Greater German Reich'.

This demonstration of *force majeure* coupled with almost hysterical joy on the part of the Austrians should, he felt, be sufficient to persuade the Czechs of the enormous advantages to be gained from Nazi rule – or at least of its inevitability; and he was both disappointed and frustrated when the Czechs continued to object to his proposed annexation of their most valuable lands. In fury, he announced on May 30, 1938 his 'irrevocable decision to destroy Czechoslovakia', mobilised again what had become 'his' Wehrmacht, and during the days which followed observed with detached scorn the excited flurryings taking place amongst the chancelleries of the rest of Europe.

Throughout that summer the Nazi press continually informed the world of the humiliations and atrocities suffered by the Sudeten Germans, while the Czechoslovak Government itself and especially its President, Dr Benes, was the butt of a stream of insults and threats. Such was the power of the Nazi propaganda machine that by late summer Chamberlain had concluded that the only hope for the preservation of peace was concession by Benes to Hitler's demands for the granting of complete autonomy to the Sudetenland.

By early September Chamberlain had decided that the best way in which he could bring calm to a troubled scene was by a personal visit to Hitler, and he arrived at Munich airport on the afternoon of Sept 15, having travelled by air for the first time in his life. There he was met by embassy officials who told him that since the announcement of his visit, Hitler's appetite had increased; now Sudetenland's complete incorporation into the Reich was to be the price of peace, and at the subsequent interview with the Führer not one millimetre was yielded in this demand. Nevertheless, Chamberlain's impression of Hitler was favourable. He might be hard, perhaps even ruthless, but he had assured Chamberlain that he had no further territorial ambitions in Europe and as Chamberlain announced upon his return, the Führer was a man 'who could be relied upon when he had given his word'. Herr Hitler was a gentleman.

There followed a series of talks between British and French ministers – not about whether to accede to Hitler's demands, but only on the form in which they would be presented to the Czech Government; and on Sept 22 Chamberlain again flew to Germany to meet the Führer, who this time graciously travelled some way to meet him in a hotel in Godesberg. There Chamberlain's announcement that Britain and France had recommended Czechoslovakia's total acceptance of Hitler's demands was met with courteously expressed thanks, tinged with a degree of sad regret. The Führer explained that now this was not enough. As Sudetenland was to be handed back to Germany, the eastern Czechoslovakian provinces containing Polish and Hungarian populations must also be handed back to *their* parent countries who were – and Hitler sympathised with them – demanding the same treatment as he had secured for the Reich.

It seemed briefly that Hitler had overplayed his hand, for Chamberlain returned to England, a decision was taken in both Whitehall and Paris to reject all Hitler's demands, and little occurred during the days which immediately followed other than the mobilisation of the Czech army. Then on Sept 28 Hitler himself sent a message inviting Chamberlain and the French Premier, Daladier, to Munich for a third conference, to be attended this time also by Mussolini; and at it, presumably overawed by circumstance or persuaded by oratory, Prime Minister and Premier signed the agreement under which Sudetenland would become German by Oct 10, and an International Commission appointed to resolve the Polish and Hungarian claims. The Czech delegation who had been kept waiting outside the conference room were then coldly informed of their country's immediate future – and then another agreement was signed by Hitler and Chamberlain, signifying a desire 'that our two peoples never go to war with one another again'. Chamberlain then flew home, happily waving the piece of paper when he arrived in Whitehall, saying, 'This is the second time in our history that there has come back from Germany to Downing Street peace with honour. I believe it is peace for our time!'

By the end of the year most of the Czech defences in the Sudetenland had been dismantled and transported west where they were installed in the Siegfried Line – Germany's answer to the Maginot – Hungary had occupied a large part of southern Czechoslovakia and Poland had grabbed Teschen . . . while somewhat to Chamberlain's surprise, civilians were digging trenches in Hyde Park and building air-raid shelters in their gardens, and volunteers were flocking to join auxiliary services such as the Royal Naval Volunteer Reserve, the Territorial Army or the Royal Air Force Volunteer Reserve. It seemed they no longer shared the Prime Minister's faith.

In 1939, democracy's chicken came home to roost. General Franco's armies defeated the Loyalists and so began over thirty-five years of Falangist dictatorship in Spain, placing, it seemed at first, a third powerful right-wing partner at the apex of a triangle which contained the European democracies of France, Belgium, Holland, Luxembourg and Switzerland. But by then Chamberlain had had to face a bitter realisation: on March 15 German troops had driven east out of Sudetenland, occupied Prague and then the whole of Bohemia and Moravia, allowing Hitler blatantly to proclaim that, as he had promised, 'Czechoslovakia had ceased to exist!' He had broken his word. He was not a gentleman, after all.

Within a matter of days it became obvious that there was now another intended target for Hitler's 'territorial ambition' – Poland. In view of Poland's recent rapacity with respect to the Czechoslovakian eastern provinces, a fairly detached view of her plight might have been taken in Britain and France; but it would seem that a realistic appreciation of Hitler's motives and principles of action was being adopted at all levels of European life. In both Britain and France it became evident that the people as a whole were beginning to accept that something must be done to stop the expansion of Fascist dictatorship, and that despite their experiences of twenty-five years before they must again brace themselves to face the rigours of war. At a higher level there were hurried consultations between embassies in an effort to cobble together a credible opposition to Hitler's ambitions, and in Britain conscription was introduced for men aged 20–21.

Throughout April and May the scurrying between embassies continued (with a flourish of satisfaction Führer and Duce announced the formation of a treaty which bound Italy and Germany for ever in a 'Pact of Steel') and in August at the suggestion of Winston Churchill but with the greatest reluctance on the part of both Chamberlain and Lord Halifax, a mission was sent to Moscow to explore the possibilities of an alliance with the only state already in possession of an army of comparable size to that of Germany. Such an alliance had previously been suggested by the Soviet Union herself, but been rejected with an almost insulting brusqueness by Foreign Office officials who sympathised with the deeply religious Lord Halifax.

Nevertheless, the members of the mission still felt that they could accommodate the Soviet Union – and especially the Red Army – into their international consortium against Hitler, so it was with some discomfiture and astonishment that they – and the rest of the world – learned of the newly agreed non-aggression pact between Germany and Russia (with secret clauses only too soon to become evident). In a spirit of outraged defiance, Chamberlain now announced that any move by either Germany or Russia against Poland would meet immediate counter-measures from Britain who, with France, would guarantee Poland's independence.

Many people wondered how, but not for long. On Aug 31 Hitler ordered the invasion of Poland and his troops crossed the frontiers. The next day both Britain and France demanded their instant withdrawal and, in the face of the contemptuous silence from Berlin which followed, consulted upon how best to implement their guarantee. It is a question which was not resolved then, and has remained unresolved ever since.

An ultimatum was sent to Berlin from Paris and London – and ignored. At 1100 on Sunday, September 3, 1939, Chamberlain broadcast the news that Great Britain was now at war with Germany. We could all imagine, he suggested, what a bitter blow it was to him.

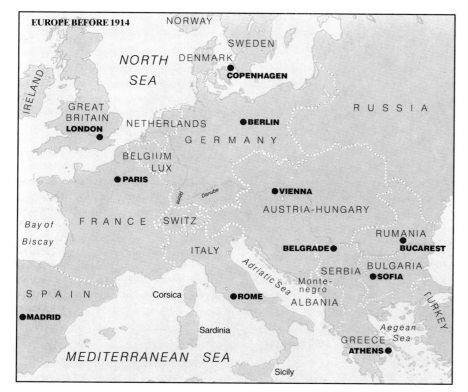

EUROPE BEFORE 1914

EUROPE AFTER 1919

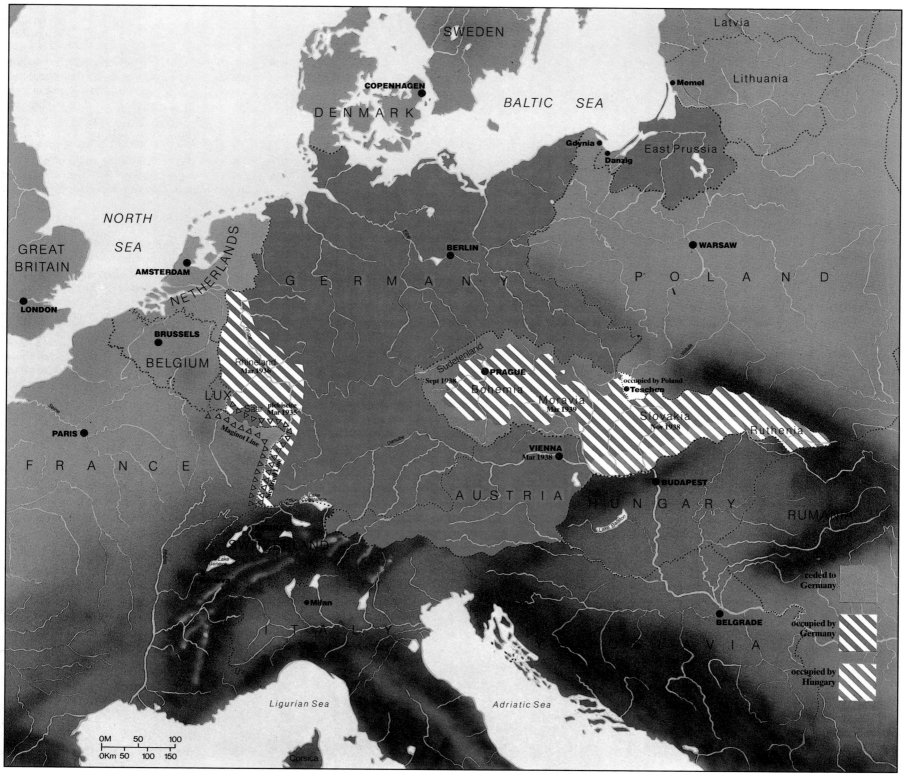

3

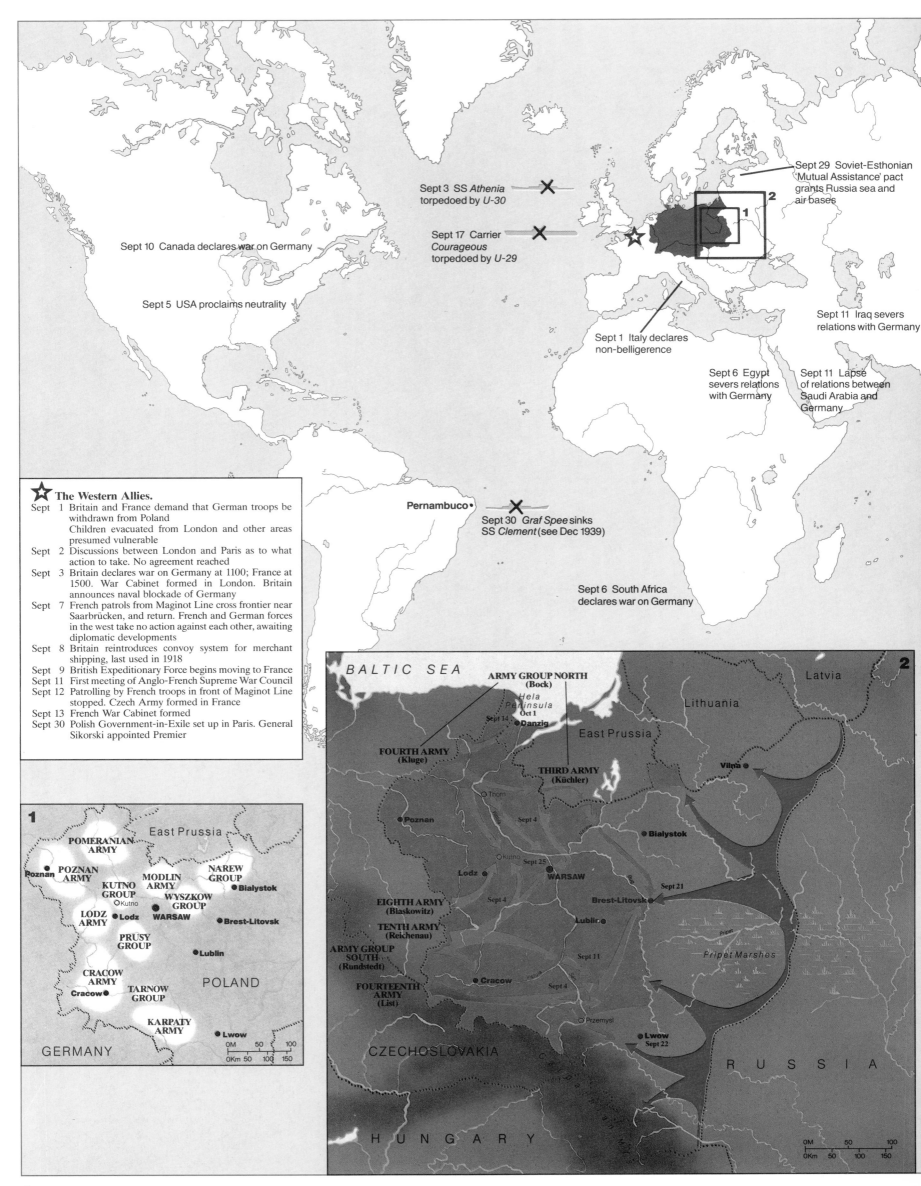

Sept 3 SS *Athenia* torpedoed by *U-30*

Sept 17 Carrier *Courageous* torpedoed by *U-29*

Sept 10 Canada declares war on Germany

Sept 5 USA proclaims neutrality

Sept 29 Soviet-Esthonian 'Mutual Assistance' pact grants Russia sea and air bases

Sept 11 Iraq severs relations with Germany

Sept 1 Italy declares non-belligerence

Sept 6 Egypt severs relations with Germany

Sept 11 Lapse of relations between Saudi Arabia and Germany

Pernambuco•

Sept 30 *Graf Spee* sinks SS *Clement* (see Dec 1939)

Sept 6 South Africa declares war on Germany

☆ The Western Allies.

Sept 1 Britain and France demand that German troops be withdrawn from Poland
Children evacuated from London and other areas presumed vulnerable

Sept 2 Discussions between London and Paris as to what action to take. No agreement reached

Sept 3 Britain declares war on Germany at 1100; France at 1500. War Cabinet formed in London. Britain announces naval blockade of Germany

Sept 7 French patrols from Maginot Line cross frontier near Saarbrücken, and return. French and German forces in the west take no action against each other, awaiting diplomatic developments

Sept 8 Britain reintroduces convoy system for merchant shipping, last used in 1918

Sept 9 British Expeditionary Force begins moving to France

Sept 11 First meeting of Anglo-French Supreme War Council

Sept 12 Patrolling by French troops in front of Maginot Line stopped. Czech Army formed in France

Sept 13 French War Cabinet formed

Sept 30 Polish Government-in-Exile set up in Paris. General Sikorski appointed Premier

1

East Prussia

POMERANIAN ARMY

Poznan• POZNAN ARMY

KUTNO GROUP
Kutno○

MODLIN ARMY

NAREW GROUP
•Bialystok

WYSZKOW GROUP

LODZ ARMY
•Lodz

WARSAW

•Brest-Litovsk

PRUSY GROUP

•Lublin

CRACOW ARMY

TARNOW GROUP

POLAND

Cracow•

KARPATY ARMY
•Lwow

GERMANY

0M 50 100
0Km 50 100 150

2

BALTIC SEA

ARMY GROUP NORTH (Bock)

Hela Peninsula Oct 1

Sept 14 •Danzig

Latvia

Lithuania

East Prussia

FOURTH ARMY (Kluge)

THIRD ARMY (Küchler)

•Vilna

○Thorn

Sept 4

•Poznan

•Bialystok

○Kutno Sept 25

•Lodz

WARSAW

Sept 21

Sept 4

Brest-Litovsk

EIGHTH ARMY (Blaskowitz)

Lublin•

TENTH ARMY (Reichenau)

ARMY GROUP SOUTH (Rundstedt)

Sept 11

Pripet Marshes

FOURTEENTH ARMY (List)

•Cracow

Sept 4

○Przemysl

•Lwow Sept 22

CZECHOSLOVAKIA

R U S S I A

H U N G A R Y

0M 50 100
0Km 50 100 150

4

SEPTEMBER 1939

Sept 4 Japan declares her neutrality; her involvement in China since 1937, a 'domestic incident'

Sept 3 India declares war on Germany

Sept 3 Australia and New Zealand declare war on Germany

1 & 2 **The First Blitzkrieg.** Early in the morning of Sept 1, squadrons of Luftwaffe bombers and fighters took off from airfields in Pomerania and East Prussia to fly over Poland and commence the destruction of Polish communication centres, airfields and aircraft, and all identifiable centres of command or troop concentration. One hour after the first airstrikes the armoured and infantry divisions of two large German Army Groups moved forward to thrust over the Polish borders in an operation based upon speed and manoeuvrability.

The flat – and at this time of year, hard and dry – countryside of Poland was ideally suited to this form of attack, and as it happened her defences were sited and deployed in such a way as to render them extremely vulnerable. Poland's western frontiers were really too long for the forces available to defend them, and in any case she was flanked by her enemy on two sides – East Prussia to the north and the newly occupied Czechoslovakian territories to the south. Crucially, the most valuable industrial areas lay between those flanks, protruding into danger like a tongue, and here of necessity her armies were deployed.

Such a disposition of forces would probably have spelt disaster anyway, but in fact Poland's greatest weakness lay in the composition of her forces, for her 30 divisions of infantry were supported only by 11 brigades of horsed cavalry and 2 motorised brigades. Against them were launched 27 infantry divisions, whose task would be to hold the Polish infantry in place while 6 German armoured divisions and 8 motorised divisions carried out wide-sweeping encircling movements.

From the German point of view everything worked perfectly. By Sept 4, spearheads of Tenth Army of Army Group South were 50 miles into Poland and curving up towards Warsaw at a speed no Polish formation could match, cutting off the Polish Lodz and Poznan Armies from their supplies, while Fourteenth Army panzers were at Przemysl. At the same time, Army Group North had struck down from East Prussia, one army along the line of the Vistula towards Warsaw, another down the line of the Bug, aiming for eventual junction with Fourteenth Army coming up from Przemysl.

Two huge encirclements were therefore planned, that along the line of the Bug intended to block escapees from the one closing at Warsaw. It was soon obvious that a considerable measure of success had been achieved, but summer dust and the confusion of battle caused doubt in German HQ – and allowed some hope amongst the Polish Command. But this was ill-based. Despite the desperate gallantry of the Polish infantry, despite the ferocity of a two-day battle fought west of Warsaw, the Poles were fighting with antiquated weapons against an army with modern equipment, who had by then been given time to organise defences against an enemy now fighting in reverse. Very few of the Poles reached Warsaw – then to find themselves cut off from escape by the outer encirclement.

And even those few who managed this were then confounded when on Sept 17 the contents of the secret clauses of the Russo-German Pact signed in August were revealed, and the Red Army closed in to take their share of the spoils.

Once again Poland as a nation disappeared, and again there was a common frontier between Russia and Germany – this time running from East Prussia, past Bialystok, Brest-Litovsk and Lwow as far as the Carpathians.

How long would this one last?

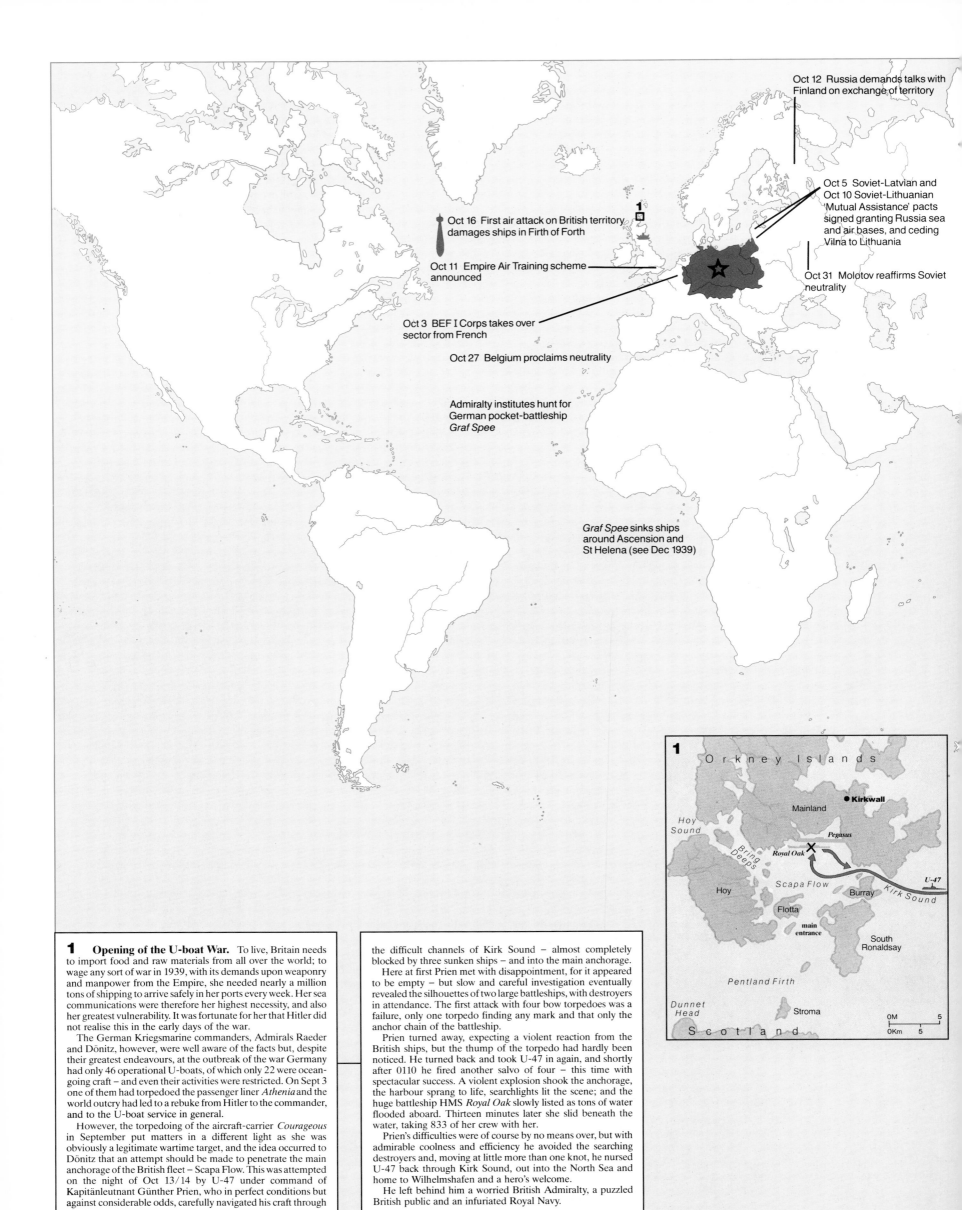

Oct 12 Russia demands talks with Finland on exchange of territory

Oct 5 Soviet-Latvian and Oct 10 Soviet-Lithuanian 'Mutual Assistance' pacts signed granting Russia sea and air bases, and ceding Vilna to Lithuania

Oct 16 First air attack on British territory damages ships in Firth of Forth

Oct 31 Molotov reaffirms Soviet neutrality

Oct 11 Empire Air Training scheme announced

Oct 3 BEF I Corps takes over sector from French

Oct 27 Belgium proclaims neutrality

Admiralty institutes hunt for German pocket-battleship *Graf Spee*

Graf Spee sinks ships around Ascension and St Helena (see Dec 1939)

1

O r k n e y   I s l a n d s

● Kirkwall

Mainland

Hoy Sound

Pegasus

Royal Oak X

Scapa Flow

Burray

U-47

Kirk Sound

Hoy

Flotta

main entrance

South Ronaldsay

Pentland Firth

Dunnet Head

Stroma

S c o t l a n d

0M 5
0Km 5

1   Opening of the U-boat War. To live, Britain needs to import food and raw materials from all over the world; to wage any sort of war in 1939, with its demands upon weaponry and manpower from the Empire, she needed nearly a million tons of shipping to arrive safely in her ports every week. Her sea communications were therefore her highest necessity, and also her greatest vulnerability. It was fortunate for her that Hitler did not realise this in the early days of the war.

The German Kriegsmarine commanders, Admirals Raeder and Dönitz, however, were well aware of the facts but, despite their greatest endeavours, at the outbreak of the war Germany had only 46 operational U-boats, of which only 22 were ocean-going craft – and even their activities were restricted. On Sept 3 one of them had torpedoed the passenger liner *Athenia* and the world outcry had led to a rebuke from Hitler to the commander, and to the U-boat service in general.

However, the torpedoing of the aircraft-carrier *Courageous* in September put matters in a different light as she was obviously a legitimate wartime target, and the idea occurred to Dönitz that an attempt should be made to penetrate the main anchorage of the British fleet – Scapa Flow. This was attempted on the night of Oct 13/14 by U-47 under command of Kapitänleutnant Günther Prien, who in perfect conditions but against considerable odds, carefully navigated his craft through

the difficult channels of Kirk Sound – almost completely blocked by three sunken ships – and into the main anchorage.

Here at first Prien met with disappointment, for it appeared to be empty – but slow and careful investigation eventually revealed the silhouettes of two large battleships, with destroyers in attendance. The first attack with four bow torpedoes was a failure, only one torpedo finding any mark and that only the anchor chain of the battleship.

Prien turned away, expecting a violent reaction from the British ships, but the thump of the torpedo had hardly been noticed. He turned back and took U-47 in again, and shortly after 0110 he fired another salvo of four – this time with spectacular success. A violent explosion shook the anchorage, the harbour sprang to life, searchlights lit the scene; and the huge battleship HMS *Royal Oak* slowly listed as tons of water flooded aboard. Thirteen minutes later she slid beneath the water, taking 833 of her crew with her.

Prien's difficulties were of course by no means over, but with admirable coolness and efficiency he avoided the searching destroyers and, moving at little more than one knot, he nursed U-47 back through Kirk Sound, out into the North Sea and home to Wilhelmshafen and a hero's welcome.

He left behind him a worried British Admiralty, a puzzled British public and an infuriated Royal Navy.

6

OCTOBER
1939

☆ **Inside the New Reich.**

Oct 1 Three Polish destroyers and three submarines escape from the Baltic to British ports

Oct 6 Addressing the Reichstag, Hitler proposes a Peace Plan, rejected on Oct 11 by France and on Oct 12 by Britain

Oct 8 Evacuation of 'Reich' Germans from Latvia begins

Oct 19 Hitler incorporates western Poland into the Reich, proclaims the new State of Poland between that area and the line of the Soviet occupation, and establishes the first Jewish ghetto, in Lublin

Oct 23 Papal protest against treatment of the Catholic Church in Poland

Oct 24 Polish patriots smuggle 70 tons of gold from Warsaw to Paris

Oct 28 Czech Independence Day celebrations suppressed by Gestapo

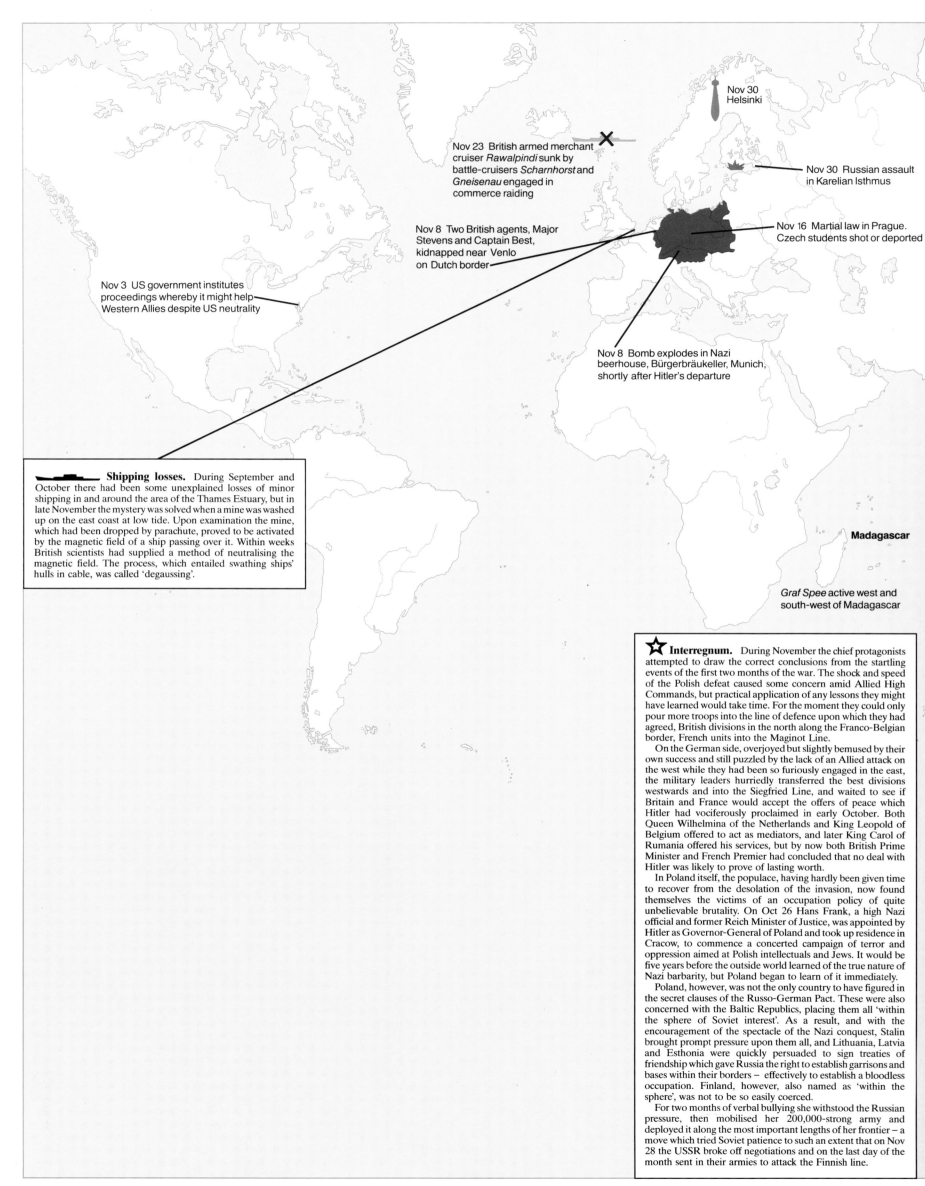

Nov 30 Helsinki

Nov 23 British armed merchant cruiser *Rawalpindi* sunk by battle-cruisers *Scharnhorst* and *Gneisenau* engaged in commerce raiding

Nov 30 Russian assault in Karelian Isthmus

Nov 8 Two British agents, Major Stevens and Captain Best, kidnapped near Venlo on Dutch border

Nov 16 Martial law in Prague. Czech students shot or deported

Nov 3 US government institutes proceedings whereby it might help Western Allies despite US neutrality

Nov 8 Bomb explodes in Nazi beerhouse, Bürgerbräukeller, Munich, shortly after Hitler's departure

Shipping losses. During September and October there had been some unexplained losses of minor shipping in and around the area of the Thames Estuary, but in late November the mystery was solved when a mine was washed up on the east coast at low tide. Upon examination the mine, which had been dropped by parachute, proved to be activated by the magnetic field of a ship passing over it. Within weeks British scientists had supplied a method of neutralising the magnetic field. The process, which entailed swathing ships' hulls in cable, was called 'degaussing'.

Madagascar

Graf Spee active west and south-west of Madagascar

Interregnum. During November the chief protagonists attempted to draw the correct conclusions from the startling events of the first two months of the war. The shock and speed of the Polish defeat caused some concern amid Allied High Commands, but practical application of any lessons they might have learned would take time. For the moment they could only pour more troops into the line of defence upon which they had agreed, British divisions in the north along the Franco-Belgian border, French units into the Maginot Line.

On the German side, overjoyed but slightly bemused by their own success and still puzzled by the lack of an Allied attack on the west while they had been so furiously engaged in the east, the military leaders hurriedly transferred the best divisions westwards and into the Siegfried Line, and waited to see if Britain and France would accept the offers of peace which Hitler had vociferously proclaimed in early October. Both Queen Wilhelmina of the Netherlands and King Leopold of Belgium offered to act as mediators, and later King Carol of Rumania offered his services, but by now both British Prime Minister and French Premier had concluded that no deal with Hitler was likely to prove of lasting worth.

In Poland itself, the populace, having hardly been given time to recover from the desolation of the invasion, now found themselves the victims of an occupation policy of quite unbelievable brutality. On Oct 26 Hans Frank, a high Nazi official and former Reich Minister of Justice, was appointed by Hitler as Governor-General of Poland and took up residence in Cracow, to commence a concerted campaign of terror and oppression aimed at Polish intellectuals and Jews. It would be five years before the outside world learned of the true nature of Nazi barbarity, but Poland began to learn of it immediately.

Poland, however, was not the only country to have figured in the secret clauses of the Russo-German Pact. These were also concerned with the Baltic Republics, placing them all 'within the sphere of Soviet interest'. As a result, and with the encouragement of the spectacle of the Nazi conquest, Stalin brought prompt pressure upon them all, and Lithuania, Latvia and Esthonia were quickly persuaded to sign treaties of friendship which gave Russia the right to establish garrisons and bases within their borders – effectively to establish a bloodless occupation. Finland, however, also named as 'within the sphere', was not to be so easily coerced.

For two months of verbal bullying she withstood the Russian pressure, then mobilised her 200,000-strong army and deployed it along the most important lengths of her frontier – a move which tried Soviet patience to such an extent that on Nov 28 the USSR broke off negotiations and on the last day of the month sent in their armies to attack the Finnish line.

8

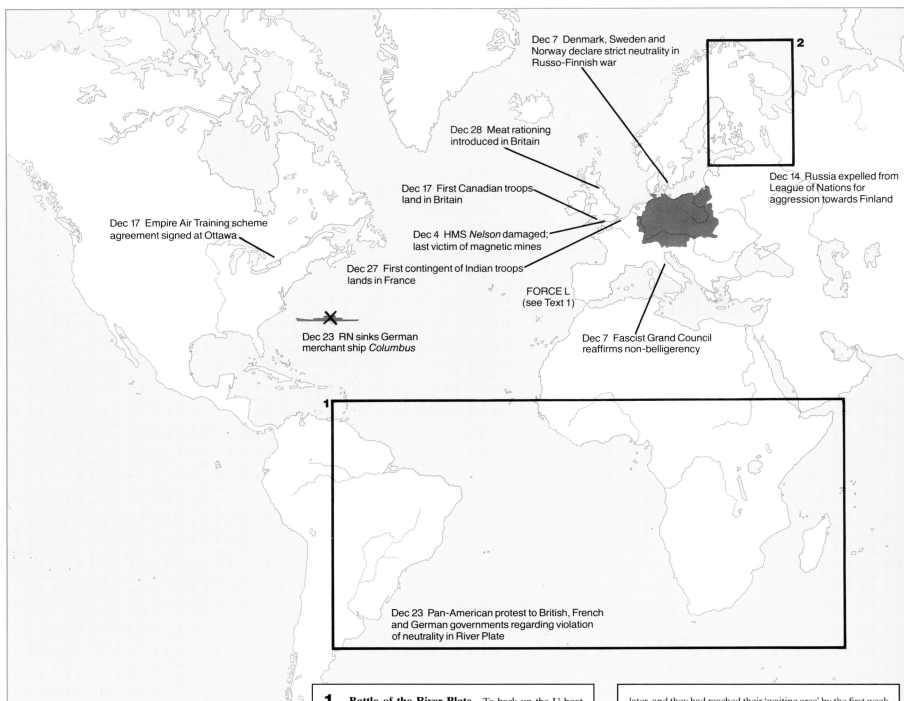

Dec 7 Denmark, Sweden and Norway declare strict neutrality in Russo-Finnish war

Dec 14 Russia expelled from League of Nations for aggression towards Finland

Dec 28 Meat rationing introduced in Britain

Dec 17 First Canadian troops land in Britain

Dec 17 Empire Air Training scheme agreement signed at Ottawa

Dec 4 HMS *Nelson* damaged; last victim of magnetic mines

Dec 27 First contingent of Indian troops lands in France

FORCE L (see Text 1)

Dec 23 RN sinks German merchant ship *Columbus*

Dec 7 Fascist Grand Council reaffirms non-belligerency

Dec 23 Pan-American protest to British, French and German governments regarding violation of neutrality in River Plate

1 Battle of the River Plate. To back up the U-boat threat to Britain's lines of supply, Germany had in the 1930s built three 'pocket-battleships' – the *Graf Spee*, the *Deutschland* and the *Admiral Scheer*. They were 12,000-ton battle-cruisers, fast enough to leave well astern the heavy battleships which were the only vessels capable of sinking them, but with 11-inch guns which would sink anything fast enough to catch them.

With a range of 12,500 miles without refuelling they were indeed a grave threat to Britain's supply lines, and at the outbreak of war two of them were already at sea. *Graf Spee* had left Wilhelmshafen on Aug 21 and *Deutschland* three days later, and they had reached their 'waiting area' by the first week of September, *Graf Spee* south of the equator, *Deutschland* to the north.

They were to wait until Sept 23 before they received permission to commence their operations against British shipping, and although *Deutschland* was recalled to Germany after sinking only two ships, *Graf Spee* in the southern hemisphere carried out a successful raiding foray for over two months, which spread considerable alarm among the Allies.

Her first victim had been the SS *Clement* off Pernambuco on Sept 30; during October she sank four more merchantmen, then sailed east into the Indian Ocean where she sank the tanker *Africa Shell* off Lourenço Marques. Her commander, Kapitän zur See Langsdorff, who acted throughout with scrupulous care and indeed chivalry to the crews of his victims, then decided to return to the Atlantic where between Dec 2 and 7 he sank three more ships before deciding to head towards what were probably the richest hunting grounds for him – the shipping lanes leading up from the river Plate.

Unfortunately for Captain Langsdorff, the probability that he would eventually arrive there had been foreseen by Commodore H.H. Harwood, commanding Force G, one of seven squadrons the Allied navies had spread through the Atlantic to search for the pocket-battleships. Commodore Harwood's squadron was, compared with the formidable armament at Captain Langsdorff's disposal, under-gunned. Two light cruisers, HMS *Ajax* and HMNZS *Achilles* were armed with only 6-inch guns, the *Exeter* and the *Cumberland* having 8-inch (though Harwood had been forced to detach *Cumberland* to the Falkland Islands for a refit). Thus he had only one medium and two light cruisers on the morning of Dec 13, when *Graf Spee* was sighted due west of the Plate estuary.

It seems probable that Langsdorff mistook the cluster of masts over the horizon for those of an escorted convoy, and he immediately headed in to attack it. By the time he realised his mistake, it was too late, for he was himself under attack according to a plan which had long been worked out by Harwood and his staff.

Exeter and *Graf Spee* first exchanged fire at 0620, while *Ajax* and *Achilles* crammed on speed to take *Graf Spee* in flank. Within minutes *Exeter* had been badly hit several times, many of her crew had been killed or wounded, she was afire and

10

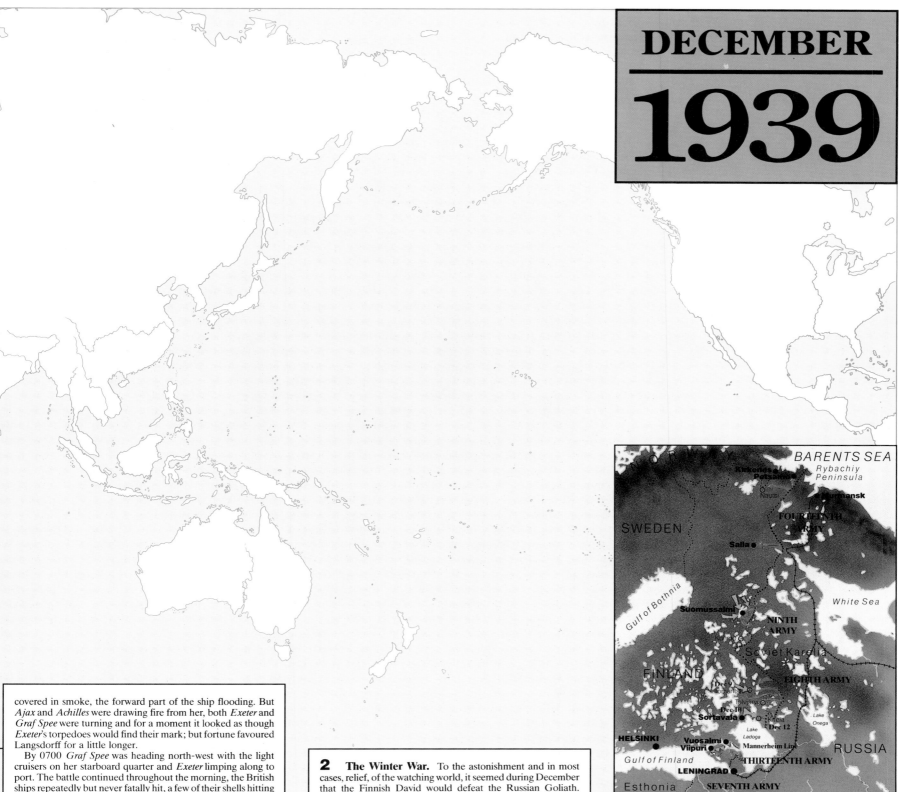

covered in smoke, the forward part of the ship flooding. But *Ajax* and *Achilles* were drawing fire from her, both *Exeter* and *Graf Spee* were turning and for a moment it looked as though *Exeter's* torpedoes would find their mark; but fortune favoured Langsdorff for a little longer.

By 0700 *Graf Spee* was heading north-west with the light cruisers on her starboard quarter and *Exeter* limping along to port. The battle continued throughout the morning, the British ships repeatedly but never fatally hit, a few of their shells hitting the *Graf Spee*; and despite their losses, the cruisers hung on. In due course it became evident that Langsdorff had decided to run for port – for Montevideo, where he could shelter for the moment in neutral waters. *Graf Spee* arrived there at 0500 on Dec 14, the two British light cruisers took station outside the port, *Exeter* was making her painful way back to the Falklands and *Cumberland* was on her way up to take her place.

For three days Montevideo was the scene of a flurry of diplomatic activity, and of a remarkable epic of propaganda and bluff. The British bought up every light aircraft in the vicinity so that no one except themselves could observe the sea approaches, while radio broadcasts told of the rapid approach of a mighty fleet of British capital ships. By the afternoon of Dec 16 only *Cumberland* had, in fact, arrived, but Langsdorff – in common with the rest of the world – believed that beyond the eastern horizon from Montevideo awaited a fleet of battleships, aircraft-carriers and destroyers sufficient to blow *Graf Spee* out of the water.

There was a last exchange of signals with Berlin and then, in the late afternoon of Dec 17, *Graf Spee* accompanied by a German merchantman crept out of harbour into the main channel of the Plate estuary and, at sunset – 2054 – having disembarked the crew on to the merchantman, Langsdorff saluted, gave the order and the demolition charges were fired to blow the bottom out of his ship.

Out at sea, reaction among the British was mixed, though subsequent reflection revealed that relief was the correct one. *Graf Spee* could easily have escaped, probably sinking one, if not more, of the waiting squadron. And they were all saddened by the news, three days later, that Kapitän zur See Langsdorff had committed suicide in a Buenos Aires hotel room.

2 **The Winter War.** To the astonishment and in most cases, relief, of the watching world, it seemed during December that the Finnish David would defeat the Russian Goliath. Despite the fact that at its peak the Finnish Army could produce only 16 divisions – and those short of all types of military equipment from signal sets to heavy artillery, and with no armour at all – they successfully held their positions in the Mannerheim Line from the Gulf of Finland to the Vuoksi river. Moreover, from the Vuoksi to Lake Ladoga, they held the Russian attack *in front* of their own defensive line, their accurate rifle and machine-gun fire and their gallant attacks with petrol bombs on the Russian tanks proving so successful that on Dec 22 the Russian Seventh and Thirteenth Armies broke off the action and retired – evidently to regroup.

To the north of Lake Ladoga, fortunes were mixed. Six Red Army divisions had crossed the border and driven inexorably forward as far as the Finnish defences between Kitelä and Ilomantsi, but there they found that their lines of supply were at risk from the highly trained and motivated Finnish ski-troops. Small Russian formations were cut off and decimated, some completely destroyed.

Further north, the picture was similar. At Suomussalmi a complete Red Army division was surrounded and subjected to such continuous harassment by small-arms and mortar fire that on Dec 29 it broke, the survivors fleeing back into Soviet Karelia leaving behind tanks, guns and 150 lorries.

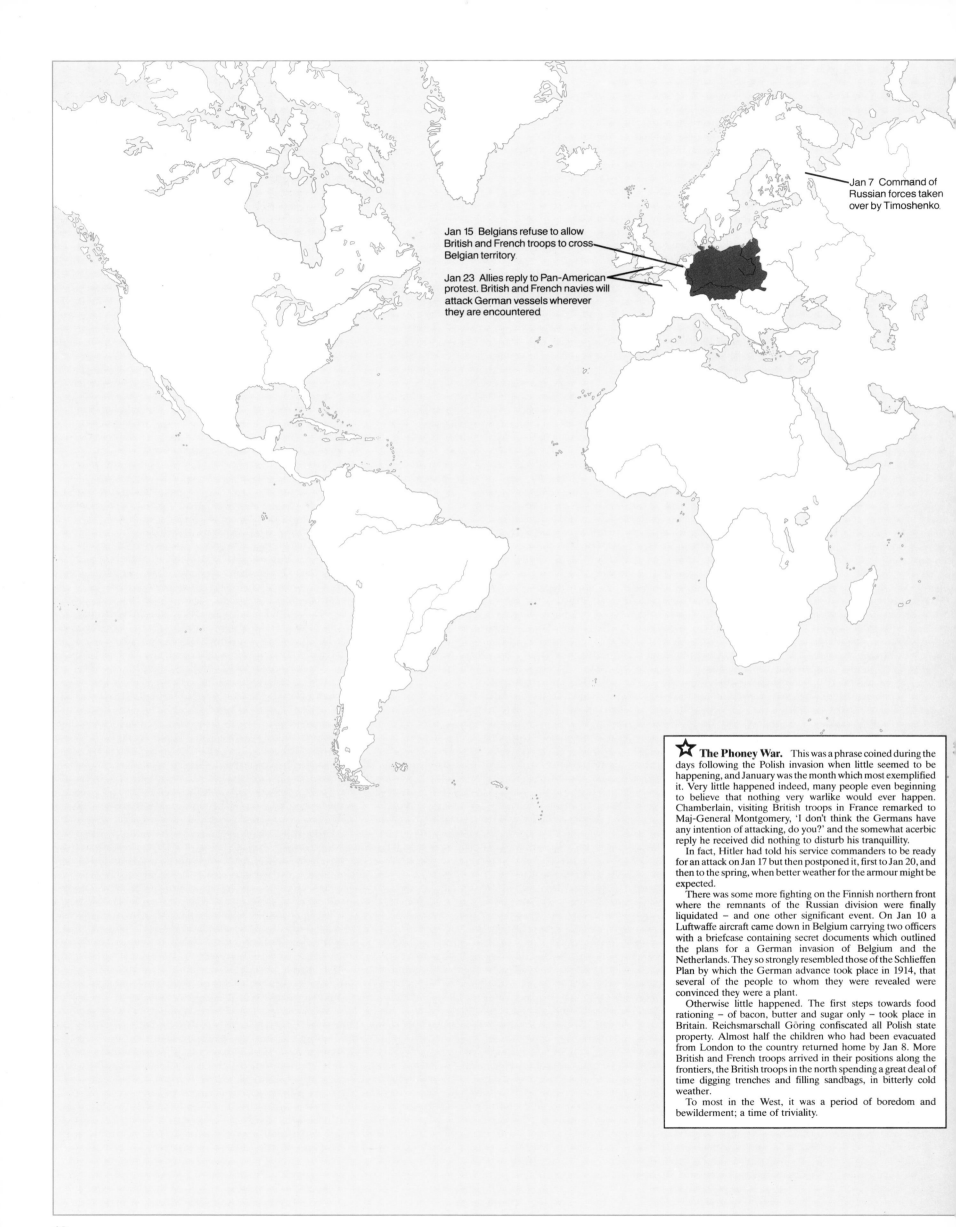

Jan 7 Command of Russian forces taken over by Timoshenko.

Jan 15 Belgians refuse to allow British and French troops to cross Belgian territory.

Jan 23 Allies reply to Pan-American protest. British and French navies will attack German vessels wherever they are encountered.

The Phoney War. This was a phrase coined during the days following the Polish invasion when little seemed to be happening, and January was the month which most exemplified it. Very little happened indeed, many people even beginning to believe that nothing very warlike would ever happen. Chamberlain, visiting British troops in France remarked to Maj-General Montgomery, 'I don't think the Germans have any intention of attacking, do you?' and the somewhat acerbic reply he received did nothing to disturb his tranquillity.

In fact, Hitler had told his service commanders to be ready for an attack on Jan 17 but then postponed it, first to Jan 20, and then to the spring, when better weather for the armour might be expected.

There was some more fighting on the Finnish northern front where the remnants of the Russian division were finally liquidated – and one other significant event. On Jan 10 a Luftwaffe aircraft came down in Belgium carrying two officers with a briefcase containing secret documents which outlined the plans for a German invasion of Belgium and the Netherlands. They so strongly resembled those of the Schlieffen Plan by which the German advance took place in 1914, that several of the people to whom they were revealed were convinced they were a plant.

Otherwise little happened. The first steps towards food rationing – of bacon, butter and sugar only – took place in Britain. Reichsmarschall Göring confiscated all Polish state property. Almost half the children who had been evacuated from London to the country returned home by Jan 8. More British and French troops arrived in their positions along the frontiers, the British troops in the north spending a great deal of time digging trenches and filling sandbags, in bitterly cold weather.

To most in the West, it was a period of boredom and bewilderment; a time of triviality.

12

JANUARY
1940

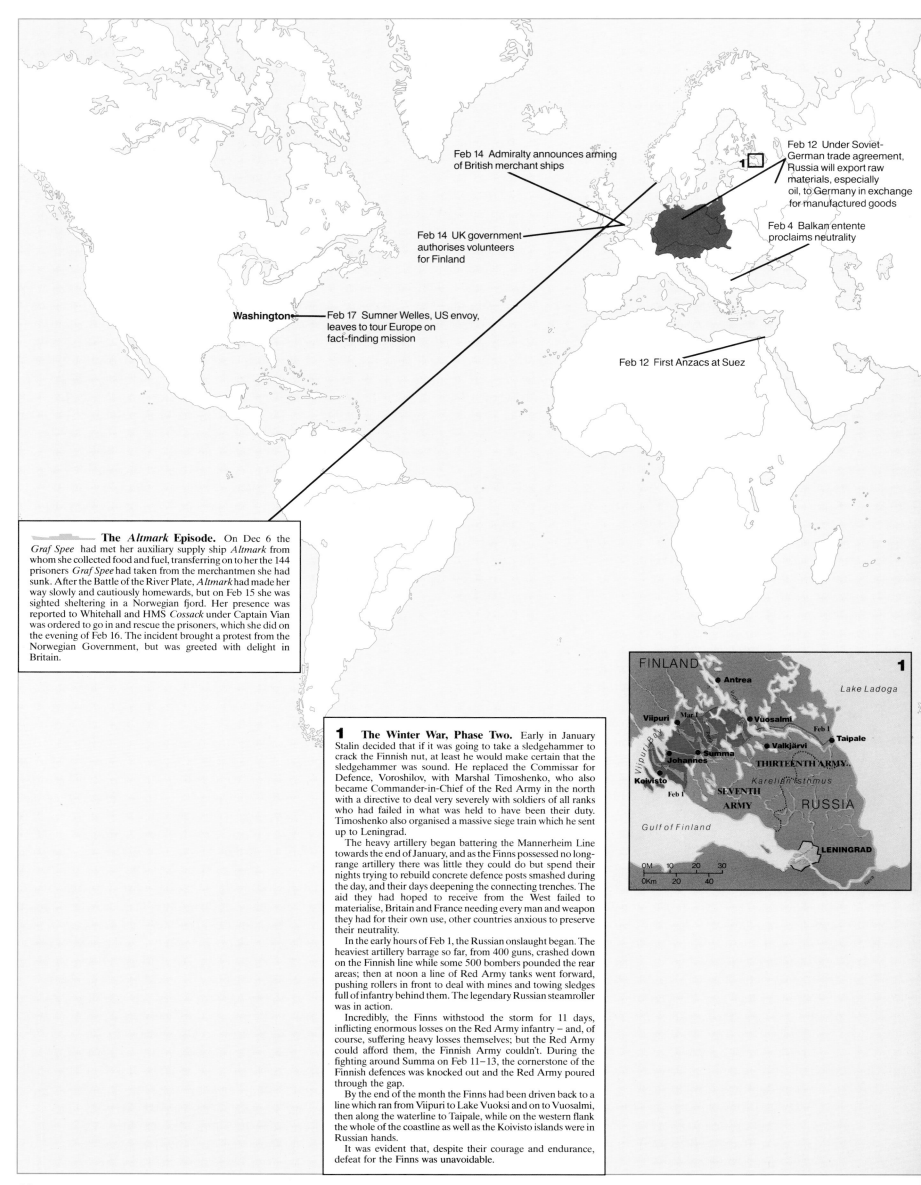

Feb 14 Admiralty announces arming of British merchant ships

Feb 14 UK government authorises volunteers for Finland

Feb 12 Under Soviet-German trade agreement, Russia will export raw materials, especially oil, to Germany in exchange for manufactured goods

Feb 4 Balkan entente proclaims neutrality

Washington — Feb 17 Sumner Welles, US envoy, leaves to tour Europe on fact-finding mission

Feb 12 First Anzacs at Suez

The *Altmark* Episode. On Dec 6 the *Graf Spee* had met her auxiliary supply ship *Altmark* from whom she collected food and fuel, transferring on to her the 144 prisoners *Graf Spee* had taken from the merchantmen she had sunk. After the Battle of the River Plate, *Altmark* had made her way slowly and cautiously homewards, but on Feb 15 she was sighted sheltering in a Norwegian fjord. Her presence was reported to Whitehall and HMS *Cossack* under Captain Vian was ordered to go in and rescue the prisoners, which she did on the evening of Feb 16. The incident brought a protest from the Norwegian Government, but was greeted with delight in Britain.

1 The Winter War, Phase Two. Early in January Stalin decided that if it was going to take a sledgehammer to crack the Finnish nut, at least he would make certain that the sledgehammer was sound. He replaced the Commissar for Defence, Voroshilov, with Marshal Timoshenko, who also became Commander-in-Chief of the Red Army in the north with a directive to deal very severely with soldiers of all ranks who had failed in what was held to have been their duty. Timoshenko also organised a massive siege train which he sent up to Leningrad.

The heavy artillery began battering the Mannerheim Line towards the end of January, and as the Finns possessed no long-range artillery there was little they could do but spend their nights trying to rebuild concrete defence posts smashed during the day, and their days deepening the connecting trenches. The aid they had hoped to receive from the West failed to materialise, Britain and France needing every man and weapon they had for their own use, other countries anxious to preserve their neutrality.

In the early hours of Feb 1, the Russian onslaught began. The heaviest artillery barrage so far, from 400 guns, crashed down on the Finnish line while some 500 bombers pounded the rear areas; then at noon a line of Red Army tanks went forward, pushing rollers in front to deal with mines and towing sledges full of infantry behind them. The legendary Russian steamroller was in action.

Incredibly, the Finns withstood the storm for 11 days, inflicting enormous losses on the Red Army infantry – and, of course, suffering heavy losses themselves; but the Red Army could afford them, the Finnish Army couldn't. During the fighting around Summa on Feb 11–13, the cornerstone of the Finnish defences was knocked out and the Red Army poured through the gap.

By the end of the month the Finns had been driven back to a line which ran from Viipuri to Lake Vuoksi and on to Vuosalmi, then along the waterline to Taipale, while on the western flank the whole of the coastline as well as the Koivisto islands were in Russian hands.

It was evident that, despite their courage and endurance, defeat for the Finns was unavoidable.

FINLAND

Antrea
Lake Ladoga
Viipuri • Mar 1 • Vuosalmi
Feb 1 • Taipale
Valkjärvi
Summa THIRTEENTH ARMY
Johannes Karelian Isthmus
Koivisto
SEVENTH
Feb 1 ARMY RUSSIA
Gulf of Finland
LENINGRAD

0M 10 20 30
0Km 20 40

FEBRUARY
1940

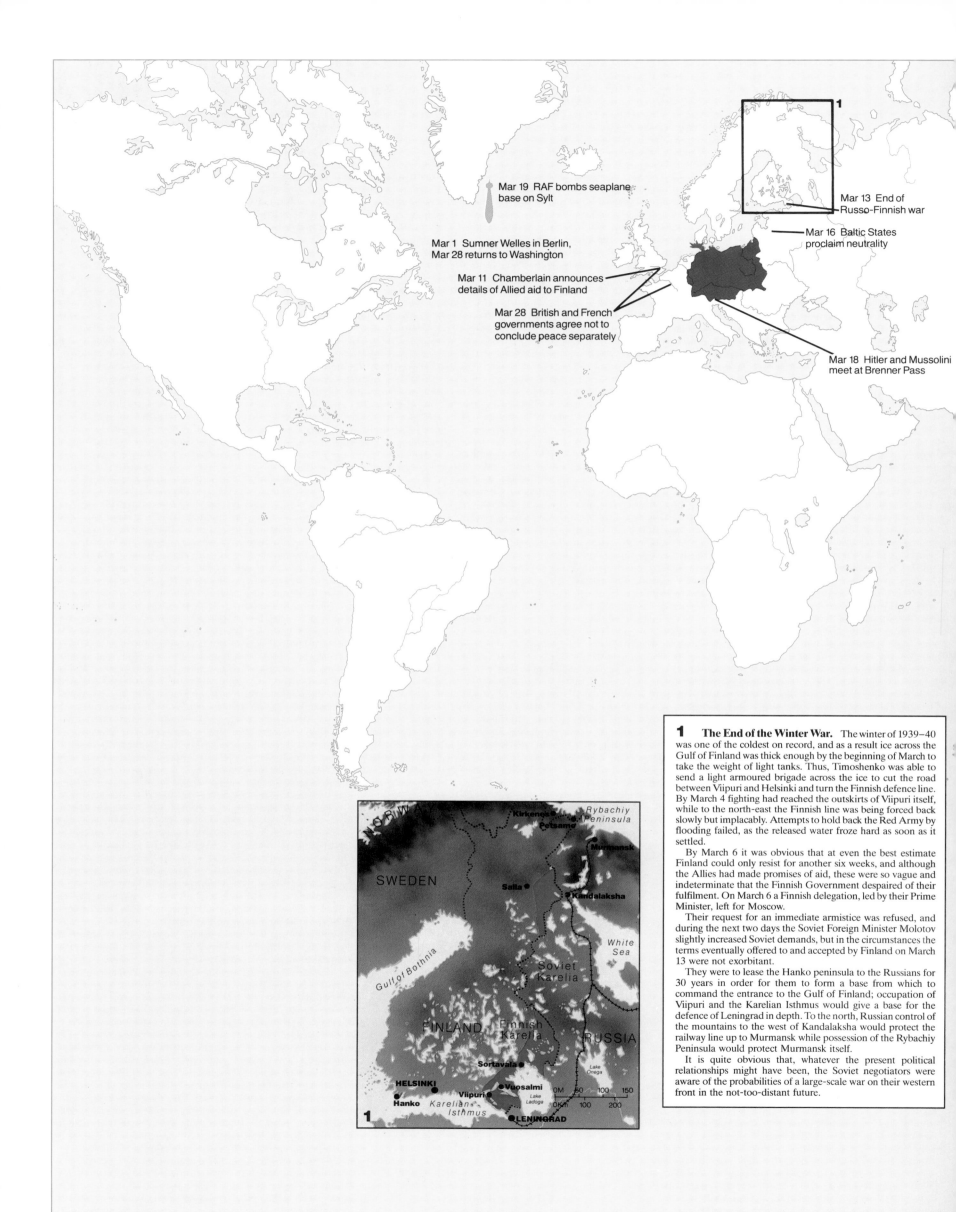

Mar 19 RAF bombs seaplane base on Sylt

Mar 1 Sumner Welles in Berlin, Mar 28 returns to Washington

Mar 11 Chamberlain announces details of Allied aid to Finland

Mar 28 British and French governments agree not to conclude peace separately

Mar 13 End of Russo-Finnish war

Mar 16 Baltic States proclaim neutrality

Mar 18 Hitler and Mussolini meet at Brenner Pass

1 **The End of the Winter War.** The winter of 1939–40 was one of the coldest on record, and as a result ice across the Gulf of Finland was thick enough by the beginning of March to take the weight of light tanks. Thus, Timoshenko was able to send a light armoured brigade across the ice to cut the road between Viipuri and Helsinki and turn the Finnish defence line. By March 4 fighting had reached the outskirts of Viipuri itself, while to the north-east the Finnish line was being forced back slowly but implacably. Attempts to hold back the Red Army by flooding failed, as the released water froze hard as soon as it settled.

By March 6 it was obvious that at even the best estimate Finland could only resist for another six weeks, and although the Allies had made promises of aid, these were so vague and indeterminate that the Finnish Government despaired of their fulfilment. On March 6 a Finnish delegation, led by their Prime Minister, left for Moscow.

Their request for an immediate armistice was refused, and during the next two days the Soviet Foreign Minister Molotov slightly increased Soviet demands, but in the circumstances the terms eventually offered to and accepted by Finland on March 13 were not exorbitant.

They were to lease the Hanko peninsula to the Russians for 30 years in order for them to form a base from which to command the entrance to the Gulf of Finland; occupation of Viipuri and the Karelian Isthmus would give a base for the defence of Leningrad in depth. To the north, Russian control of the mountains to the west of Kandalaksha would protect the railway line up to Murmansk while possession of the Rybachiy Peninsula would protect Murmansk itself.

It is quite obvious that, whatever the present political relationships might have been, the Soviet negotiators were aware of the probabilities of a large-scale war on their western front in the not-too-distant future.

16

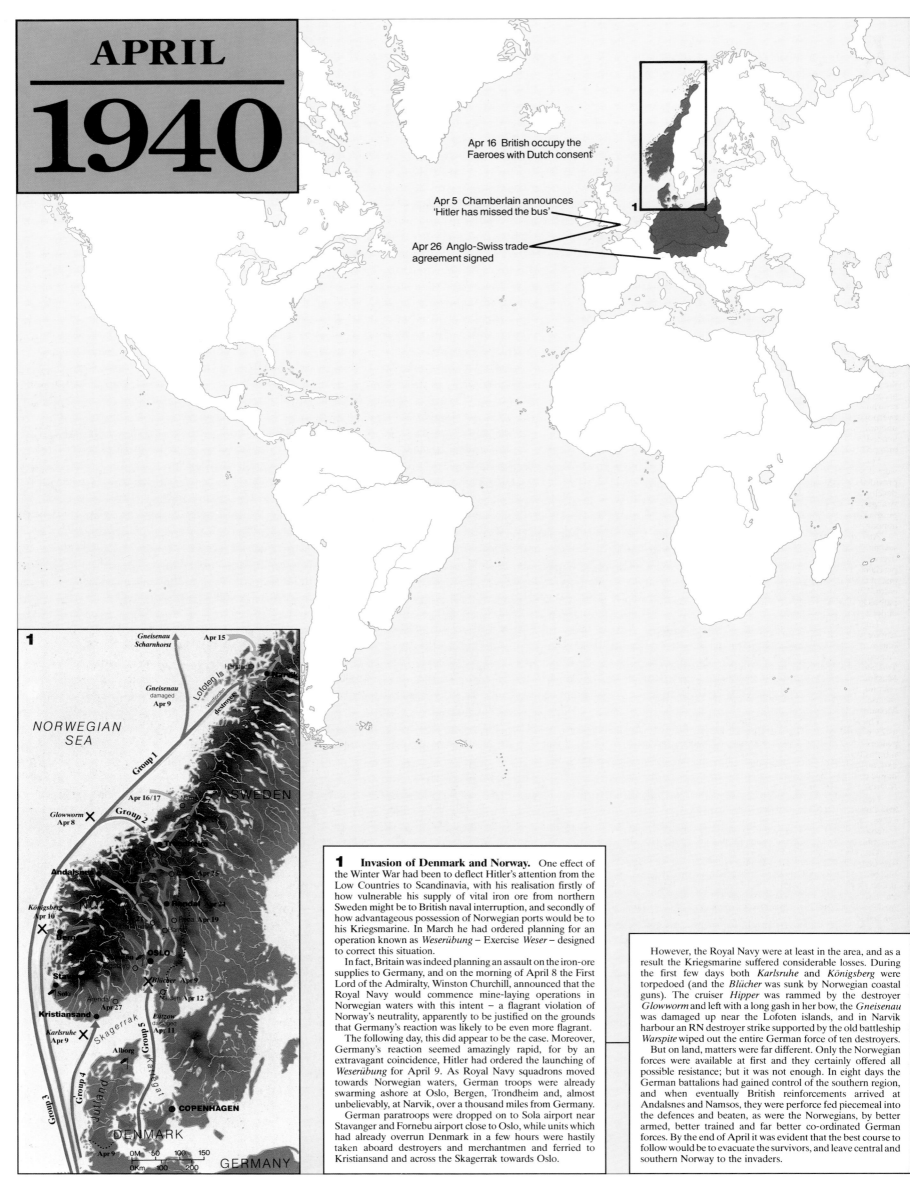

APRIL
1940

Apr 16 British occupy the Faeroes with Dutch consent

Apr 5 Chamberlain announces 'Hitler has missed the bus'

Apr 26 Anglo-Swiss trade agreement signed

Map 1 (inset)

Gneisenau Scharnhorst — Apr 15

Gneisenau damaged Apr 9

NORWEGIAN SEA

Group 1

Apr 16/17

Glowworm Apr 8 ✕ Group 2

Andalsnes

Königsberg Apr 10 ✕

Bergen ✕

OSLO

Stav ✕ Blücher Apr 9

Sola

Kristiansand ✕ Lützow damaged Apr 11

Karlsruhe Apr 9 ✕ Skagerrak

Aalborg

Group 3 Group 4 Group 5 Jutland Kattegat

COPENHAGEN

DENMARK

Apr 9 — 0M 50 100 150 / 0Km 100 200

GERMANY

1 Invasion of Denmark and Norway. One effect of the Winter War had been to deflect Hitler's attention from the Low Countries to Scandinavia, with his realisation firstly of how vulnerable his supply of vital iron ore from northern Sweden might be to British naval interruption, and secondly of how advantageous possession of Norwegian ports would be to his Kriegsmarine. In March he had ordered planning for an operation known as *Weserübung* – Exercise *Weser* – designed to correct this situation.

In fact, Britain was indeed planning an assault on the iron-ore supplies to Germany, and on the morning of April 8 the First Lord of the Admiralty, Winston Churchill, announced that the Royal Navy would commence mine-laying operations in Norwegian waters with this intent – a flagrant violation of Norway's neutrality, apparently to be justified on the grounds that Germany's reaction was likely to be even more flagrant.

The following day, this did appear to be the case. Moreover, Germany's reaction seemed amazingly rapid, for by an extravagant coincidence, Hitler had ordered the launching of *Weserübung* for April 9. As Royal Navy squadrons moved towards Norwegian waters, German troops were already swarming ashore at Oslo, Bergen, Trondheim and, almost unbelievably, at Narvik, over a thousand miles from Germany.

German paratroops were dropped on to Sola airport near Stavanger and Fornebu airport close to Oslo, while units which had already overrun Denmark in a few hours were hastily taken aboard destroyers and merchantmen and ferried to Kristiansand and across the Skagerrak towards Oslo.

However, the Royal Navy were at least in the area, and as a result the Kriegsmarine suffered considerable losses. During the first few days both *Karlsruhe* and *Königsberg* were torpedoed (and the *Blücher* was sunk by Norwegian coastal guns). The cruiser *Hipper* was rammed by the destroyer *Glowworm* and left with a long gash in her bow, the *Gneisenau* was damaged up near the Lofoten islands, and in Narvik harbour an RN destroyer strike supported by the old battleship *Warspite* wiped out the entire German force of ten destroyers.

But on land, matters were far different. Only the Norwegian forces were available at first and they certainly offered all possible resistance; but it was not enough. In eight days the German battalions had gained control of the southern region, and when eventually British reinforcements arrived at Andalsnes and Namsos, they were perforce fed piecemeal into the defences and beaten, as were the Norwegians, by better armed, better trained and far better co-ordinated German forces. By the end of April it was evident that the best course to follow would be to evacuate the survivors, and leave central and southern Norway to the invaders.

Rise of Mussolini

Benito Mussolini became Prime Minister of Italy in 1922 and unchallenged dictator by the end of 1926, using methods later to be copied by Hitler. Mussolini's equivalent of the German 'Enabling Acts' had been a decree passed in December 1925 considerably extending the existing powers of the prime minister, removing the prerogative of the king to choose or dismiss ministers and authorising the prime minister to issue decrees with the force of statute law. The Fascist emblem was embodied in the national insignia, the Fascist Grand Council stood higher in the state than the Council of Ministers, and all opposition activities in politics or the press were prohibited. It had taken Mussolini 25 years of varied political life, and 7 years as head of the Fascist Party, to become Il Duce – leader of the Italian nation.

As in Germany, violence and political murder played a significant part in the rise of Fascism; as in Germany, the success of the tactics owed much to dissatisfaction with the terms of the Treaty of Versailles, and to the fluidity of the world economic situation. The Treaty of Versailles had failed to satisfy Italian ambitions regarding both the port of Fiume and the redistribution after 1918 of German East African colonies, all of which had been mandated to other countries. As for the economic consideration, for many years as many as half a million Italians had emigrated every year, mostly to North or South America, and their dutiful remittances home had done much to help with Italy's foreign currency problems. But with the tightening of controls on immigration everywhere which accompanied the various financial crises, more Italians were returning home than were leaving, so problems of both overpopulation and the balance of international debts arose. So did unemployment – and the attraction of a fervently patriotic party headed by a dominant, authoritarian personality swept the Fascists into power.

For Mussolini was spectacularly authoritarian. His uniforms were designed and tailored to portray a bull-like strength, he was provided by nature with the profile of a Roman emperor, and he developed a compelling style of oratory, delivering his speeches in a strangely emotive voice with, at the height of his powers, a persuasive charm which gave him in the late 1920s and early 1930s a national popularity to rival that of any opera singer or film star.

At the beginning of his rule, Mussolini was undoubtedly sustained by great self-confidence, but soon this became an overweening arrogance which allowed him, for instance, to proclaim, 'When I die, I want this epitaph on my grave: "Here lies one of the most intelligent animals ever to appear on the face of the earth."' But behind the imposing façade, Mussolini was unstable and pathologically egotistic, concealing a basic ignorance of reality under a cloak of bombast.

This was palpably obvious in his attitude to Italy's colonial empire and his ambitions to see it expanded. Libya had been under Italian domination since 1912 (as had the Dodecanese in the Aegean), Turkey having ceded sovereignty at the close of the Italo-Turkish war. Greatly to Italian surprise, the Libyans preferred Muslim rule from Istanbul to Catholic rule from Rome and continually rebelled against Italian government, declaring themselves a republic under the rule of the Senussi leader, Mohammed Idris.

This had resulted in continuous though sporadic fighting, and in 1923 Mussolini sent General Graziani to Libya with increased powers and military force. Tripolitania was under control within months, the Fezzan by 1929, after which by ruthless use of armoured cars, automatic weapons and bombs, Cyrenaica was 'pacified' – and in due course a triple wire fence erected running from Sollum down to Jarabub to prevent dissident Senussi escaping into Egypt.

Here was one possible solution to Italy's population problem, and during the late 1930s over 50,000 Italian settlers arrived in Libya, to form farming communities around Tripoli and in Cyrenaica. Few of them ventured far south, for the Libyan desert was inhospitable, as were the Bedouin tribesmen who inhabited it.

The other two areas of East Africa which fell under Mussolini's rule from the start were Eritrea and Italian Somaliland. The former had been an Italian colony since 1889 when the sovereignty of the Italian king had been recognised by Menelik, Emperor of Ethiopia; but Italian attempts to expand into the Emperor's realm had been met by an army of tribesmen who administered a crushing defeat on the Italian forces at Adowa in 1896. Mussolini, who was 13 at the time, later wrote that the facts of the disaster 'were still hammering in his skull'. He nursed the national grievance as a young man and as dictator eventually developed the means for revenge.

As for Italian Somaliland, it had fallen under Italian rule almost by default during the latter years of the nineteenth century when Britain, France and Italy had been jockeying for position around the Horn of Africa coast. For many years all three colonies – British, French and Italian Somaliland – had been the scene of sporadic but bitter fighting between the colonial powers and the followers of the Somali Sayid, Mohammed bin Abdullah Hassan; but by 1920 administrative control had been established, and in 1923 a Fascist governor was sent out to bring force to bear upon what rebellious elements still remained. Italian settlements sprang up, the port of Kismayu further developed, and, possibly with an eye to the future, a policy of gradual encroachment northwards into Ethiopia was encouraged.

By the early 1930s Mussolini was facing the problem which comes to all demagogues who sweep to power by spectacular but insubstantial means: once the honeymoon is over, new spectacles must be provided. He had by now run out of propaganda stunts to occupy the population at large, the artificial value of the lira had driven away foreign trade and the world depression was having a disastrous effect upon the precarious Italian economy. In these circumstances a solution might be found in an expanding empire, the expansion not only occupying Italian attention to the exclusion of all else, but perhaps also going some way towards gratifying his greatest wish – to leave a deeper imprint upon history than any previous Italian leader.

What better target for such intentions than Ethiopia, already sandwiched between Italian possessions? Certain treaties existed which might be thought to inhibit aggressive action, but treaties, he considered, were not 'eternal' and were bound to be 'revised'. And the memory of the defeat at Adowa was far more compelling than any words on paper, irrespective of whose signature was at the bottom.

By 1935 the vision of a great colonial empire occupied his mind to the exclusion of everything else – the rise of Hitler, the pledge that Italy had given to abide by the rulings of the League of Nations, or even the possibility that Italy's finances might not be sound enough to support a long campaign waged 3,000 miles from Rome.

A small incident in December 1934 at an insalubrious waterhole called Walwal in the already encroached area of southern Ethiopia provided the trigger. Brushing aside all protests, from whatever direction, Mussolini announced the despatch of army and blackshirt divisions to Eritrea and Somaliland, and replied to a warning that the Emperor of Abyssinia seemed unlikely to provide him with a genuine excuse for invasion of his country, 'If the Negus does not intend to attack us, we ourselves must take the initiative.'

Two hundred thousand men, 7,000 officers, 6,000 machine-guns, 700 guns, 150 tanks and 150 aircraft arrived in East Africa during the next few months, mostly into Eritrea though some went to General Graziani's command in Somaliland. General Emilio de Bono was appointed Commander-in-Chief, and on Oct 2 Il Duce broadcast yet another of his thundering rodomontades to the Italian people, a large proportion of whom welcomed it with enthusiasm. They had yet to learn the realities of warfare.

The legions duly crossed the borders and began their separate advances towards Addis Ababa. Despite delays caused by poor organisation and the resistance of Ethiopian tribesmen far stronger than had been expected, there was never any doubt as to the eventual outcome; against machine-guns, artillery, aerial bombardment and at times, poison gas, Haile Selassie could put little but the bravery of his men. His only other comfort was the sympathy of most of the rest of the world, and the fact that on Oct 19 the League of Nations called for sanctions to be imposed against Italy.

In the event, both comforts proved cold indeed. The Italian legions lurched heavily forward, Gondar was reached from the north on April 1, Harar from the south by April 30 and on the afternoon of May 5, de Bono drove into Addis Ababa. Mussolini had declared Ethiopia a part of the Italian Empire two days before.

He had also of late become more conscious of events to the north and had had to face the bitter realisation that as a right-wing dictator he had been overtaken and surpassed in renown by another. Il Duce was now in second place to the Führer.

There was little he could do to redeem the situation, but he did find that whereas his recent colonialisation of Ethiopia had made him unpopular in many parts of the world, Germany was more than ready to extend the hand of friendship. On Oct 25, 1936, Führer and Duce announced the 'Rome–Berlin Axis' and went further the following month with a joint recognition of General Franco's Government in Spain, despite the fact that the civil war there was by no means over.

Nevertheless, Hitler's successes in absorbing Austria and Czechoslovakia into his Reich necessitated some comparable Italian achievement on the European mainland, so on April 7 (Good Friday, to the shocked surprise of the Vatican which had until now given tacit approval to most of Mussolini's actions), he invaded Albania on the most transparent of excuses, sending 100,000 troops backed by naval and air support into a totally unprepared country. Within weeks Albania was little but an Italian province, with Victor Emmanuel III proclaimed king.

On the day that German armies invaded Poland, Mussolini announced that he would remain neutral; Italy would not intervene. But when such spectacular success was achieved by German arms, and when it became evident that not only Hitler's Reich but the rest of the world too were taking little account of Italy's attitude or his own opinion, he began to worry that when peace came (he was quite sure that the Allies would be quickly beaten) there would be no place for him at the resulting conference table.

Then in April, when German troops flooded into Denmark and across into Norway to stamp the swastika across the face of yet another subjugated country, his exasperation grew, his anti-British pronouncements became more impassioned, and it was obvious that another development, however minor, would tip Italy over the edge into the conflict. Il Duce's thirst for glory was to be paramount.

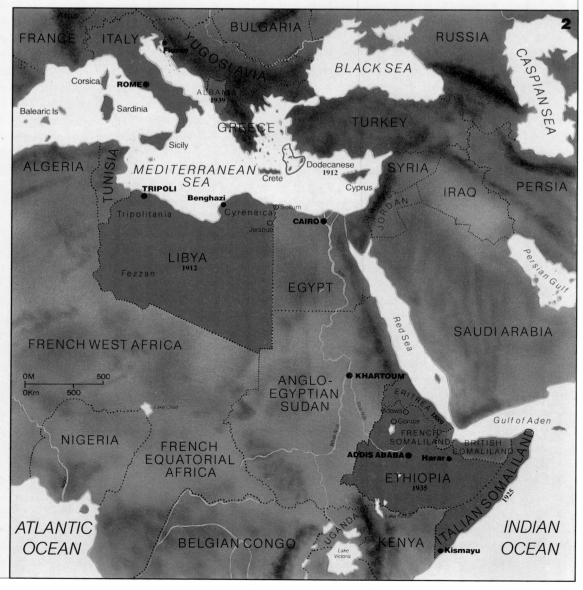

19

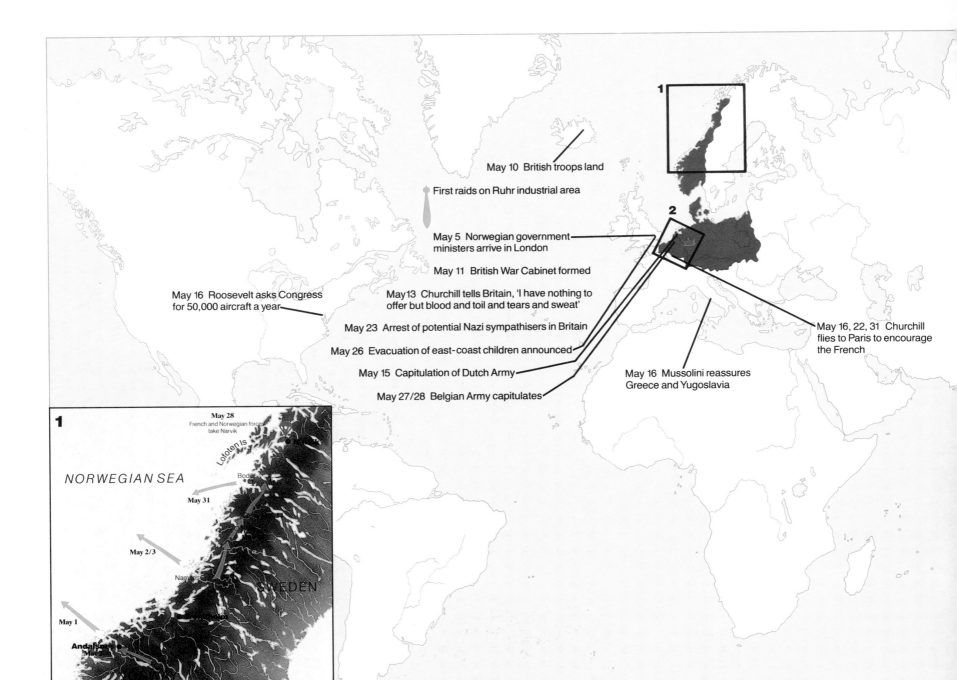

1 Norway. Rapid and efficient military manoeuvres supported by excellent air cover had given the Germans southern and central Norway during April. In the north, their success was not so sure. General Dietl's force of some 2,000 mountain troops, plus the survivors from the Kriegsmarine flotilla which had brought them to Narvik, found themselves first isolated by the destruction of the German destroyers, then penned into Narvik itself as British, French, Polish and Norwegian units combined to bring increasing pressure to bear from north, south and west.

Airborne reinforcements were dropped to Dietl, but on May 28 a concentric attack by men of the French Foreign Legion and a Norwegian battalion forced the Germans out and for a time it looked as though they would either have to retreat across the border into Sweden and internment – or die of exhaustion and cold in the icy conditions which still reigned.

But events elsewhere saved them. German forces had been making their way north throughout the month and by May 30 had reached Bodö, where the remainder of a hurriedly despatched British force was re-embarked with equal speed; even more crucially, events in the Low Countries had now reached such a crisis that the British Cabinet decided it must abandon its commitments in Norway.

Ironically, on the very day that Narvik was taken, orders arrived to evacuate all Allied forces, bringing with them as many Norwegian soldiers as chose to come.

☆ The Fall of Chamberlain. The Norwegian campaign was undoubtedly a set-back for the Allied military forces; it was a disaster for Mr Chamberlain. Now indeed the results of his policies, first of appeasement, then after the war had started of empty optimism, became evident; the whole country was bewildered, and on the afternoon of May 7 the packed House of Commons was furious. Never before, in the memory of one member of the House, had such a bitter attack been made upon a policy and a prime minister responsible for it.

It reached its peak when one of Chamberlain's oldest friends and supporters in the House turned on him and quoted Cromwell's indictment of his leaders some three hundred years before. 'You have sat here too long for any good you have been doing,' he proclaimed. 'Depart I say, and let us have done with you! In the name of God, go!' – and, accompanied by cries from the backbenchers on both sides of the House of 'Go! Go! Go!', Chamberlain left the House.

Even now he seemed unable to believe that he was not still to be the Saviour of Peace and the Nation, but two days of discussion and argument at last persuaded him that the country no longer wished to follow his lead. Two possible successors occurred to him – Winston Churchill whom he disliked rather, and certainly distrusted; and Lord Halifax who would be his preferred choice. Even in this Chamberlain's grasp on reality was weak; as a member of the House of Lords, Halifax would be unable to debate in the Commons the major decisions which a state of war would undoubtedly require, for these were the days before a peer could disclaim his title.

As a result, reluctantly, Chamberlain called upon His Majesty King George VI, and recommended that he ask Mr Churchill to form a new Government with which to lead the British people through the war.

The announcement was made the following morning, but by that time events elsewhere were commanding the world's attention and Churchill's appointment – 'arguably the most crucial in Britain's history' – passed almost unnoticed.

2 Onslaught in the West. The war began for the armies of the Western Allies on the morning of May 10, and its disastrous course for them during the following weeks owed as much to Hitler's continuing good fortune as to Allied military mismanagement.

The plans which had fallen into Allied hands in January had, in fact, been genuine, and the fact that they had now been displayed to the enemy made Hitler amenable to the idea of changing them. As a result, he was in a receptive frame of mind when visited – on a different matter – by General Erich von Manstein, who left with him his own plans for an entirely different form of offensive. Some days later, to the annoyance of several of the High Command staff, they received instructions to abandon *Fall Gelb* – the original plan – and draw up orders for the execution of *Fall Sichelschnitt, Operation Sickle*.

As a result, when news came of the air bombardment of Rotterdam, of the descent of German paratroops at various points in Holland, of a glider-borne assault of Fort Eben Emael in Belgium and of the crossing of the Dutch border by German divisions, the 5 British divisions and 15 French divisions along the Belgian border left the defensive positions they had been so arduously building during the freezing winter months, and moved forward to join the Belgian armies in a series of positions along the Dyle and Meuse rivers.

The fact that those defensive positions were meagre in the extreme compared with those they had left behind was, in fact, tactically of no great account. The military threat they were advancing to meet – that of General von Bock's Army Group B – was little but the waving of 'the matador's cape'. The real attack came from the panzer group of Army Group A to the south, aimed to crash through the Ardennes (long proclaimed impassable to armour by Anglo-French military staff), split the Anglo-French armies and cut those in the north off from their supplies.

It is probable that even Manstein was surprised at the success of his plan. By May 14 Guderian's panzer corps were at Sedan on the Meuse and the next day across it; Hoth's panzer corps was at Dinant to the north, with General Rommel's 7th Division already holding a bridgehead on the far bank. The next day

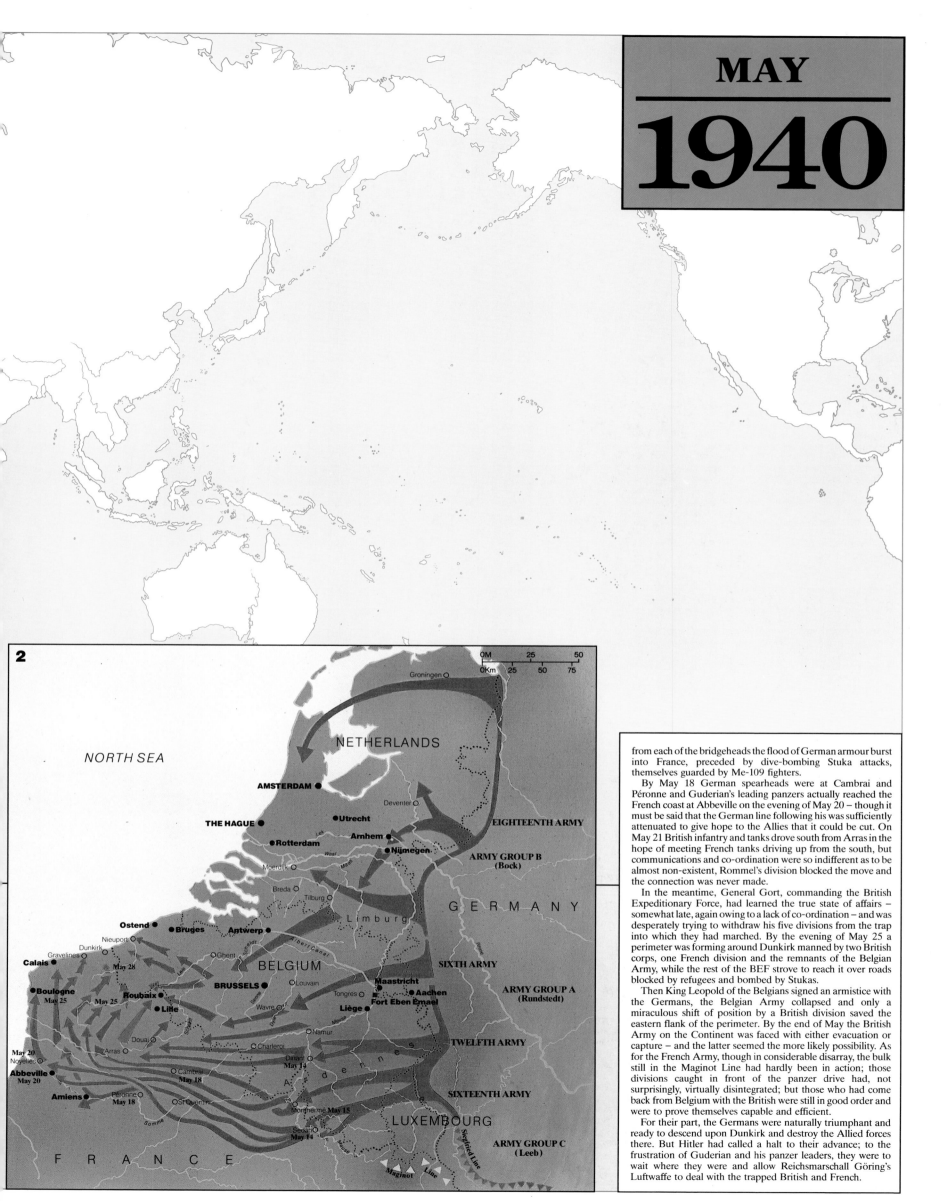

MAY
1940

from each of the bridgeheads the flood of German armour burst into France, preceded by dive-bombing Stuka attacks, themselves guarded by Me-109 fighters.

By May 18 German spearheads were at Cambrai and Péronne and Guderian's leading panzers actually reached the French coast at Abbeville on the evening of May 20 – though it must be said that the German line following his was sufficiently attenuated to give hope to the Allies that it could be cut. On May 21 British infantry and tanks drove south from Arras in the hope of meeting French tanks driving up from the south, but communications and co-ordination were so indifferent as to be almost non-existent, Rommel's division blocked the move and the connection was never made.

In the meantime, General Gort, commanding the British Expeditionary Force, had learned the true state of affairs – somewhat late, again owing to a lack of co-ordination – and was desperately trying to withdraw his five divisions from the trap into which they had marched. By the evening of May 25 a perimeter was forming around Dunkirk manned by two British corps, one French division and the remnants of the Belgian Army, while the rest of the BEF strove to reach it over roads blocked by refugees and bombed by Stukas.

Then King Leopold of the Belgians signed an armistice with the Germans, the Belgian Army collapsed and only a miraculous shift of position by a British division saved the eastern flank of the perimeter. By the end of May the British Army on the Continent was faced with either evacuation or capture – and the latter seemed the more likely possibility. As for the French Army, though in considerable disarray, the bulk still in the Maginot Line had hardly been in action; those divisions caught in front of the panzer drive had, not surprisingly, virtually disintegrated; but those who had come back from Belgium with the British were still in good order and were to prove themselves capable and efficient.

For their part, the Germans were naturally triumphant and ready to descend upon Dunkirk and destroy the Allied forces there. But Hitler had called a halt to their advance; to the frustration of Guderian and his panzer leaders, they were to wait where they were and allow Reichsmarschall Göring's Luftwaffe to deal with the trapped British and French.

21

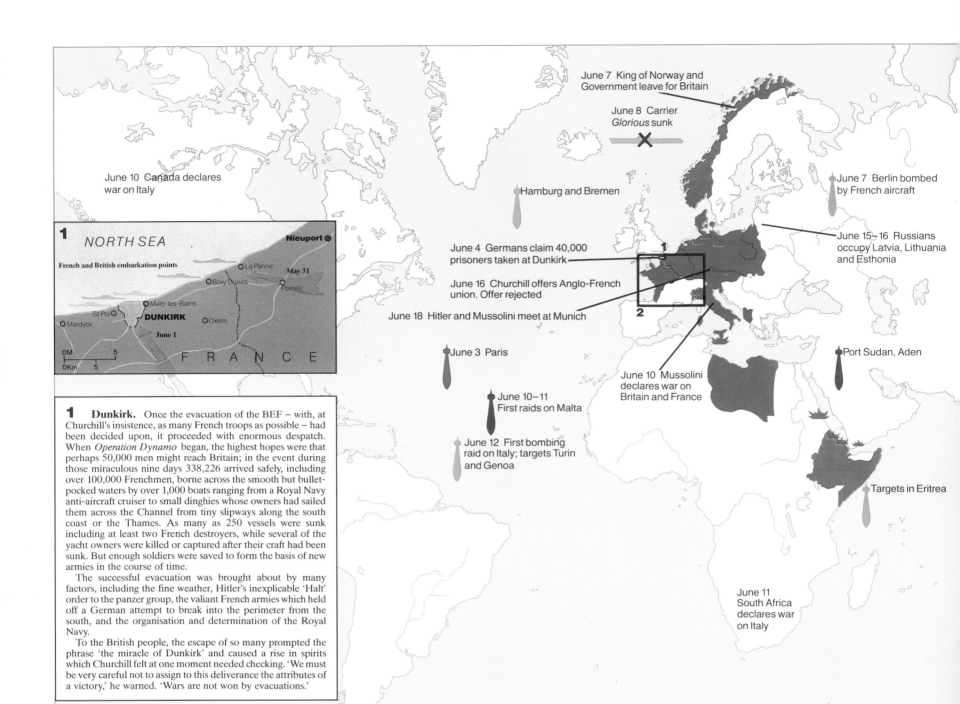

June 7 King of Norway and Government leave for Britain

June 8 Carrier *Glorious* sunk

June 10 Canada declares war on Italy

Hamburg and Bremen

June 7 Berlin bombed by French aircraft

June 4 Germans claim 40,000 prisoners taken at Dunkirk

June 16 Churchill offers Anglo-French union. Offer rejected

June 18 Hitler and Mussolini meet at Munich

June 15–16 Russians occupy Latvia, Lithuania and Esthonia

June 3 Paris

June 10 Mussolini declares war on Britain and France

Port Sudan, Aden

June 10–11 First raids on Malta

June 12 First bombing raid on Italy; targets Turin and Genoa

Targets in Eritrea

June 11 South Africa declares war on Italy

1 NORTH SEA Nieuport

French and British embarkation points

La Panne May 31

Bray Dunes Furnes

Malo-les-Bains St Pol

Mardyck DUNKIRK Oxem

June 1

0M 5 0Km 5

F R A N C E

1 Dunkirk. Once the evacuation of the BEF – with, at Churchill's insistence, as many French troops as possible – had been decided upon, it proceeded with enormous despatch. When *Operation Dynamo* began, the highest hopes were that perhaps 50,000 men might reach Britain; in the event during those miraculous nine days 338,226 arrived safely, including over 100,000 Frenchmen, borne across the smooth but bullet-pocked waters by over 1,000 boats ranging from a Royal Navy anti-aircraft cruiser to small dinghies whose owners had sailed them across the Channel from tiny slipways along the south coast or the Thames. As many as 250 vessels were sunk including at least two French destroyers, while several of the yacht owners were killed or captured after their craft had been sunk. But enough soldiers were saved to form the basis of new armies in the course of time.

The successful evacuation was brought about by many factors, including the fine weather, Hitler's inexplicable 'Halt' order to the panzer group, the valiant French armies which held off a German attempt to break into the perimeter from the south, and the organisation and determination of the Royal Navy.

To the British people, the escape of so many prompted the phrase 'the miracle of Dunkirk' and caused a rise in spirits which Churchill felt at one moment needed checking. 'We must be very careful not to assign to this deliverance the attributes of a victory,' he warned. 'Wars are not won by evacuations.'

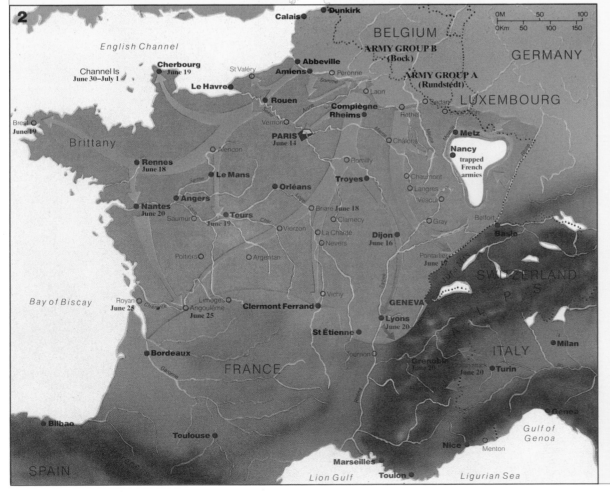

2 English Channel

Calais Dunkirk

BELGIUM GERMANY

0M 50 100 0Km 50 100 150

ARMY GROUP B (Bock)

Cherbourg June 19 St Valéry Abbeville Amiens Péronne ARMY GROUP A (Rundstedt) Sedan LUXEMBOURG

Channel Is June 30–July 1 Le Havre Rouen Compiègne Rheims Laon Metz

Brest June 19 Vernon Nancy trapped French armies

Brittany PARIS June 14 Alençon Romilly Chaumont

Rennes June 18 Le Mans Orléans Troyes Langres

Angers Briare June 18 Gray

Nantes June 20 Saumur Tours June 19 Vierzon La Charité Dijon June 16 Belfort

Poitiers Nevers Basle

Bay of Biscay Argentan SWITZERLAND ALPS

Limoges Vichy GENEVA

Royan June 25 Angoulême June 25 Clermont Ferrand Lyons June 20

Bordeaux St Étienne Grenoble June 20 Turin

ITALY Milan

FRANCE

Bilbao Gulf of Genoa

Toulouse Nice Menton

SPAIN Marseilles Toulon Ligurian Sea Lion Gulf

2 The Fall of France. The freeze Hitler had placed on Guderian's panzer group had been cancelled on May 29, but his orders were that now both Rundstedt and Bock must direct their attention to the defeat of the French armies, leaving Britain's fate still to the Luftwaffe.

Bock therefore left one of his infantry armies to settle affairs in Belgium while the rest of Army Group B moved to the line of the Somme between Péronne and the sea, and Rundstedt's armies deployed on the left as far as Sedan. By June 5 ten panzer divisions had been lined up for attack and early that morning, preceded as usual by swarms of Stuka dive-bombers, they burst out of two bridgeheads they had formed across the river and drove for the Seine.

'The second great offensive is starting today,' Hitler announced, 'with formidable new resources.'

By June 11, despite fierce though sporadic resistance from French troops assembled into 'hedgehogs', Hoth's XV Panzer Corps had reached the line of the Seine from Vernon to the coast, while two of Rundstedt's corps were cutting between Rheims and the Aisne as his Ninth Army drove straight for Paris. The following day German armies controlled the whole area between the Meuse and the Seine and on June 14 they drove into Paris, hastily declared an Open City by the French Government as it decamped for Bordeaux.

By this time the French Commander-in-Chief, General Gamelin, had been replaced by General Weygand, though it cannot be said that any firmer grip on the situation developed. Perhaps it was too late; about this time General Sir Alan Brooke, who had been sent back by Churchill to try both to put new heart into the French Army and to evacuate some 200,000 British line-of-communication troops who had all been stationed well to the west of Dunkirk, became convinced that the French Army was close to disintegration. Not only did they lack firm leadership, but, as so often happens to a losing side, fortune deserted them. On one occasion French armour battled their way successfully through to rescue an infantry regiment,

22

June 24 Japan asks Britain
to close the Burma Road

June 11 Australia and
New Zealand declare war on Italy

only to run out of petrol and find themselves in turn encircled.

As the panzers drove deeper and deeper into French territory and the grey-clad columns, generally singing and laughing as they marched, followed, French morale plummeted. As early as June 9 Weygand had announced that defeat was almost upon them, and two days later he moved to Briare on the Loire with his staff, there to meet Churchill who had flown over (for the third time; he had gone to France twice during May in the hope of putting some iron into the spirit of the French leadership), but after three hours of discussion it was evident that there was little hope in his mind for anything less than capitulation.

He would not even consider the idea of leaving France with the Government and going to North Africa with the French Navy and remnants of their Air Force, there to continue the struggle alongside Britain. 'I cannot think of such an ignominious proposal without a shiver of disgust!' he wrote later, though only eight days were to pass before he was to order 400,000 French troops in and behind the Maginot Line to 'ask for a cessation of fighting, with war honours', a proposal which would in itself seem to contain an appreciable element of ignominy.

By June 20 German troops were lining the Swiss border to the east, along the Biscay coast to the west down as far as Royan, and at Lyons and Grenoble in the south; and the following day a downcast French delegation trooped into the railway carriage at Compiègne in which the 1918 Armistice had been signed, where they were awaited by a triumphant Führer and his staff.

By 1900 on June 22, the Armistice had been signed and the limits of German occupation agreed. The French battle fleet would remain in Toulon under French command, which presumably gave some grounds for the proclamation made three days later by Marshal Pétain, who had taken over as head of the Government. 'Honour is saved!' he announced. 'We must now turn our efforts to the future. A new order is beginning!'

There is little doubt that France had been badly served by her generals. Afterwards there were to be attempts to blame the defeat on social causes which had sapped the morale of her servicemen. But it had been Napoleon who said, 'There are no bad soldiers; only bad officers.'

There had been a further development from Rome as the German armies drove south into France. If the events of April had exasperated Mussolini, those of May and June reduced him to a frenzy.

'We Italians are already sufficiently dishonoured,' he declared on May 13. 'Any delay is inconceivable. We have no time to lose. Within a month I shall declare war. I shall attack France and Great Britain in the air and on the sea!' And when his military advisers pointed out to him that the lack of almost every sort of military equipment made the carrying out of this declaration difficult if not impossible, he muttered, gloomily but defiantly, 'Then we will do what we can!'

May had passed in a flurry of conferences and correspondence (that with Hitler had remained curiously unanswered; but of course, the Führer was very busy), but after due preparation in the press and radio, on the evening of June 10 Mussolini read a speech from the balcony of the Palazzo Venezia, to a markedly unenthusiastic crowd, detailing the enormous provocations to which their country had been subjected by both Great Britain and France, and declaring war on them.

He had already sent another 80,000 men to Libya to confront the British, but now his immediate concern was to prod his army over the border into France and capture Nice before the Germans reached it, with Briançon and Grenoble further north as possible improvements.

To his fury, the Armistice was signed before any of his divisions got very far, at which point he received a message from Hitler suggesting that he call a halt to all further movement. The Führer's recent agreement with the French must be honoured at all costs.

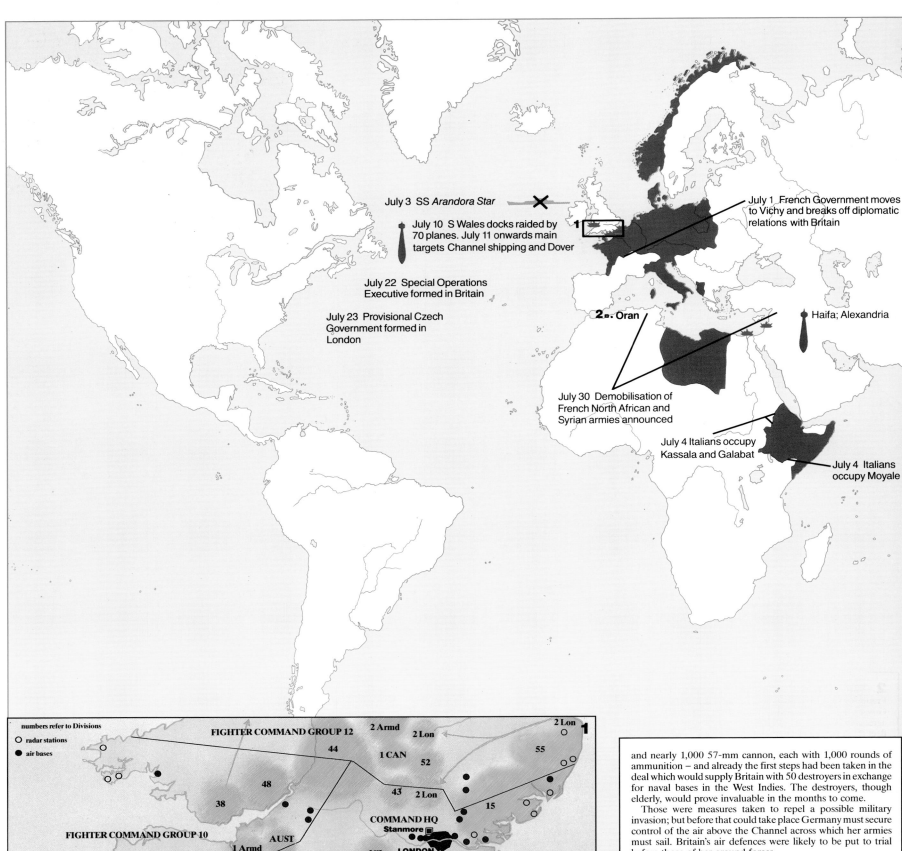

July 3 SS *Arandora Star*

July 10 S Wales docks raided by 70 planes. July 11 onwards main targets Channel shipping and Dover

July 22 Special Operations Executive formed in Britain

July 23 Provisional Czech Government formed in London

1

July 1 French Government moves to Vichy and breaks off diplomatic relations with Britain

2 ■ Oran

Haifa; Alexandria

July 30 Demobilisation of French North African and Syrian armies announced

July 4 Italians occupy Kassala and Galabat

July 4 Italians occupy Moyale

---

numbers refer to Divisions
○ radar stations
● air bases

FIGHTER COMMAND GROUP 12

2 Armd
2 Lon
2 Lon **1**
1 CAN
52
55
44
48
43 2 Lon
38
15
COMMAND HQ
Stanmore
FIGHTER COMMAND GROUP 10
AUST
1 Armd
NZ **LONDON**
1 Lon
FIGHTER COMMAND GROUP 11
50
23 4
Southampton
3
45
Plymouth
I of Wight

0M   25   50   75
0Km 25 50 75 100

1 'The Battle of Britain is about to begin.' So announced Winston Churchill in one of his most famous speeches, made at the end of June, going on to spur the British people to defend themselves against the onslaught to come. Some may have wondered at the time, 'What with?'

As the bone-weary survivors from Dunkirk struggled ashore during those chaotic days of early June, observers said many of them moved like sleepwalkers. They were amongst Britain's most highly trained and experienced soldiers, but their equipment – tanks, transport, guns and light weapons – was still on the roads to Dunkirk, or on the beaches from which the men had been snatched. There were now not enough weapons in Britain to re-equip them, let alone arm the Local Defence Volunteers – soon to be rechristened the Home Guard – who were flocking forward to help.

Yet by mid-July southern Britain resembled an armed camp.

Divisions which had not gone to France were brought down from the north, those which had returned in fair order – such as the 3rd Division under Maj-General Montgomery – posted in the more vital sectors and hastily made up to strength either with reservists or new conscripts.

As for the weapons, though many were scraped from armouries and rifle clubs, and Britain's factories were working day and night to produce aircraft, guns, tanks and ammunition as fast as they could, the needs were of the hour, not of the month, and could only be filled from existing arsenals; and the only ones available were in America.

Now the long friendship between Churchill and Roosevelt was to prove crucial. The need was obvious and urgent; red tape was quickly cut and by the end of the month half a million rifles had arrived (most of them packed in 1918 in grease which had become so hard that the rifles had to be boiled to clear them)

and nearly 1,000 57-mm cannon, each with 1,000 rounds of ammunition – and already the first steps had been taken in the deal which would supply Britain with 50 destroyers in exchange for naval bases in the West Indies. The destroyers, though elderly, would prove invaluable in the months to come.

Those were measures taken to repel a possible military invasion; but before that could take place Germany must secure control of the air above the Channel across which her armies must sail. Britain's air defences were likely to be put to trial before those of her ground forces.

In the coming battle, Britain held three advantages. Her fighter strength lay in the Spitfire and the Hurricane, the former marginally faster and more manoeuvrable than the Luftwaffe's Me-109; secondly, although she was desperately short of pilots, at least a reasonable proportion of those shot down during the forthcoming battle might land comparatively unhurt on British soil; most importantly, she had the most advanced radar screen in the world which would pick up enemy bomber or fighter formations before they left the French coast. This was backed up by a remarkably efficient Observer Corps to track the enemy fleets inland, thus avoiding the necessity for standing patrols which could prove fatally expensive in both men and machines.

During July, the Luftwaffe mounted several bombing attacks on widely separated targets in England, but it seems that most of them were mounted more to give the crews experience in night operations than actually to carry out bombing operations. Hitler still hoped for a favourable reaction to what he called his 'Last appeal to reason and common sense in Britain' – but this was curtly rejected within 48 hours and so he ordered his service chiefs to continue with plans for *Operation Sea-Lion,* the invasion of Great Britain.

Interestingly enough, on July 21 he also ordered selected members of the Wehrmacht Staff to begin preliminary preparations for an attack on Russia.

And on the last day of the month, as a token of what was to come, 15 more ships packed with war materials left American ports for Britain.

24

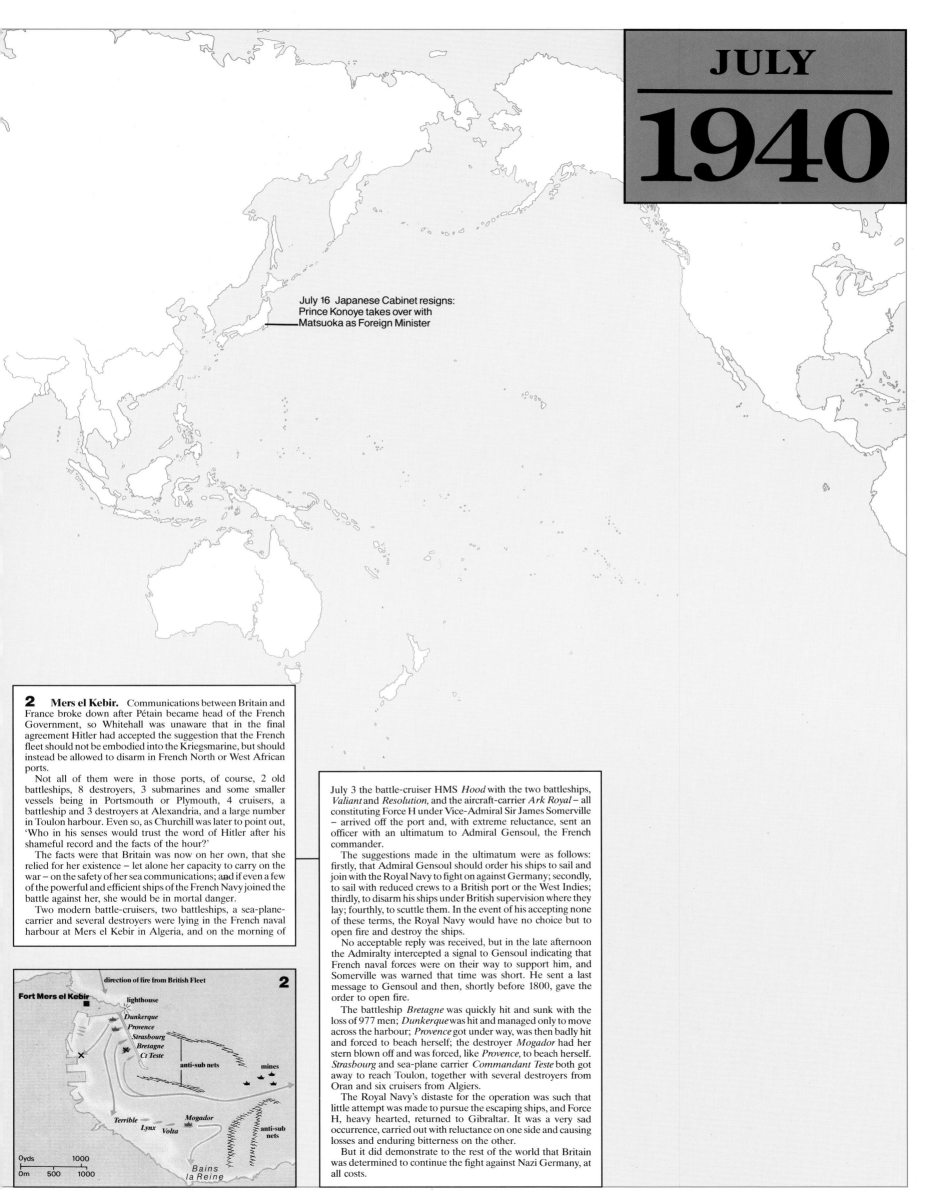

July 16 Japanese Cabinet resigns:
Prince Konoye takes over with
Matsuoka as Foreign Minister

2 **Mers el Kebir.** Communications between Britain and France broke down after Pétain became head of the French Government, so Whitehall was unaware that in the final agreement Hitler had accepted the suggestion that the French fleet should not be embodied into the Kriegsmarine, but should instead be allowed to disarm in French North or West African ports.

Not all of them were in those ports, of course, 2 old battleships, 8 destroyers, 3 submarines and some smaller vessels being in Portsmouth or Plymouth, 4 cruisers, a battleship and 3 destroyers at Alexandria, and a large number in Toulon harbour. Even so, as Churchill was later to point out, 'Who in his senses would trust the word of Hitler after his shameful record and the facts of the hour?'

The facts were that Britain was now on her own, that she relied for her existence – let alone her capacity to carry on the war – on the safety of her sea communications; and if even a few of the powerful and efficient ships of the French Navy joined the battle against her, she would be in mortal danger.

Two modern battle-cruisers, two battleships, a sea-plane-carrier and several destroyers were lying in the French naval harbour at Mers el Kebir in Algeria, and on the morning of

July 3 the battle-cruiser HMS *Hood* with the two battleships, *Valiant* and *Resolution,* and the aircraft-carrier *Ark Royal* – all constituting Force H under Vice-Admiral Sir James Somerville – arrived off the port and, with extreme reluctance, sent an officer with an ultimatum to Admiral Gensoul, the French commander.

The suggestions made in the ultimatum were as follows: firstly, that Admiral Gensoul should order his ships to sail and join with the Royal Navy to fight on against Germany; secondly, to sail with reduced crews to a British port or the West Indies; thirdly, to disarm his ships under British supervision where they lay; fourthly, to scuttle them. In the event of his accepting none of these terms, the Royal Navy would have no choice but to open fire and destroy the ships.

No acceptable reply was received, but in the late afternoon the Admiralty intercepted a signal to Gensoul indicating that French naval forces were on their way to support him, and Somerville was warned that time was short. He sent a last message to Gensoul and then, shortly before 1800, gave the order to open fire.

The battleship *Bretagne* was quickly hit and sunk with the loss of 977 men; *Dunkerque* was hit and managed only to move across the harbour; *Provence* got under way, was then badly hit and forced to beach herself; the destroyer *Mogador* had her stern blown off and was forced, like *Provence,* to beach herself. *Strasbourg* and sea-plane carrier *Commandant Teste* both got away to reach Toulon, together with several destroyers from Oran and six cruisers from Algiers.

The Royal Navy's distaste for the operation was such that little attempt was made to pursue the escaping ships, and Force H, heavy hearted, returned to Gibraltar. It was a very sad occurrence, carried out with reluctance on one side and causing losses and enduring bitterness on the other.

But it did demonstrate to the rest of the world that Britain was determined to continue the fight against Nazi Germany, at all costs.

Fort Mers el Kebir

direction of fire from British Fleet

2

lighthouse
Dunkerque
Provence
Strasbourg
Bretagne
Ct Teste
anti-sub nets
mines
Terrible
Lynx Volta
Mogador
anti-sub nets

0yds 1000
0m 500 1000

Bains la Reine

25

1 **The Battle of Britain.** On Aug 1 Hitler issued the order 'The German air force is to overcome the British air force with all means at its disposal, and as soon as possible.' His peace proposal had been rejected by Churchill and *Operation Sea-Lion*, the invasion of Britain, was to go ahead. D-Day was set for Sept 15, and the German Army and Navy would need ten days' notice of confirmation of date, by which time the RAF must have ceased to exist as a force to be reckoned with.

In the opinion of the head of the Luftwaffe, Reichsmarschall Hermann Göring, his fighters and bombers had ample time for the task. Four days would be enough to smash all fighter defences south of the line London–Gloucester, four weeks for the complete elimination of the Royal Air Force; *Adler Tag* – Eagle Day – would be as soon after Aug 10 as weather would allow.

For the task the Luftwaffe had three Luftflotten – air fleets. Luftflotte II under Field Marshal Kesselring was deployed in northern Germany, Holland, Belgium and north-east France, Luftflotte III under Field Marshal Sperrle in northern and western France, and to threaten northern England and Scotland Luftflotte V under General Stumpff was in Denmark and Norway. Between them they had over 3,000 aircraft of which just over one-third were fighters, mostly Me-109s, though the fighters attached to Luftwaffe V were Me-110s which, though not so agile as the Me-109s, had the necessary range to take them across the North Sea.

The bombers were mainly Heinkel 111s with some Dornier 17s, together with a large number of Junkers 87s and 88s. These should be enough to bomb the airfields, radar stations and aircraft factories out of existence while the fighters dealt with the RAF Spitfires and Hurricanes in the air.

Those Spitfires and Hurricanes had almost doubled in number during the last month, for as the head of Fighter Command, Air Chief Marshal Dowding pointed out, aircraft were leaving the factories faster than pilots could be trained to fly them. The lack of skilled fighter pilots was to be his chief concern during the weeks to come, not shortage of aircraft.

Fighter Command was now divided into four groups – 10, 11, 12 and 13 – deployed respectively in the South-west, South-east, Midlands and the North. Obviously to start with Group 11 would be the most heavily engaged and here the sector stations, fighter bases and radar stations were thickest; Dowding's Fighter Command HQ was itself in this area, at Stanmore, north-west of London.

As the opening of the assault drew near – and all Britain knew that it must come – the Royal Air Force waited with confidence, relying not only upon the skill and courage of the young pilots, but also on the experience, technical knowledge and foresight of their commanders. Between July 10 and Aug 10 they had already seen some results of their expertise: the RAF had shot down 217 German aircraft for the loss of only 96 of their own.

Aug 11 was a cloudy day and little happened, but on Aug 12 the assault really opened, with hundreds of Luftwaffe aircraft

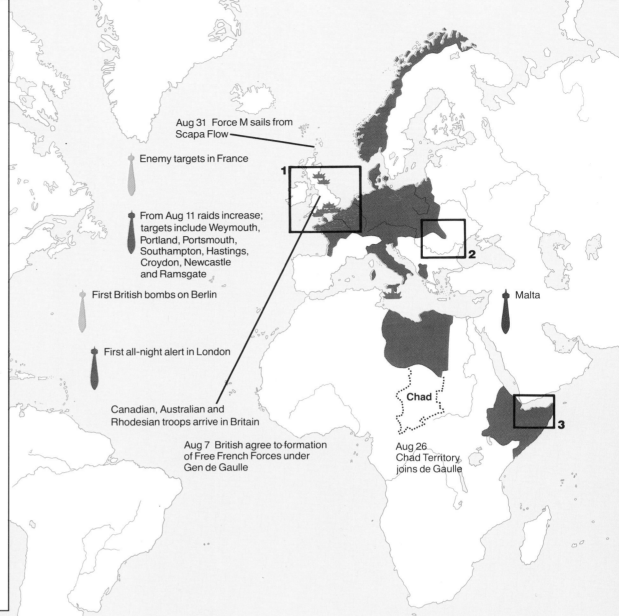

Aug 31 Force M sails from Scapa Flow

Enemy targets in France

From Aug 11 raids increase; targets include Weymouth, Portland, Portsmouth, Southampton, Hastings, Croydon, Newcastle and Ramsgate

First British bombs on Berlin

First all-night alert in London

Canadian, Australian and Rhodesian troops arrive in Britain

Aug 7 British agree to formation of Free French Forces under Gen de Gaulle

Chad

Malta

Aug 26 Chad Territory joins de Gaulle

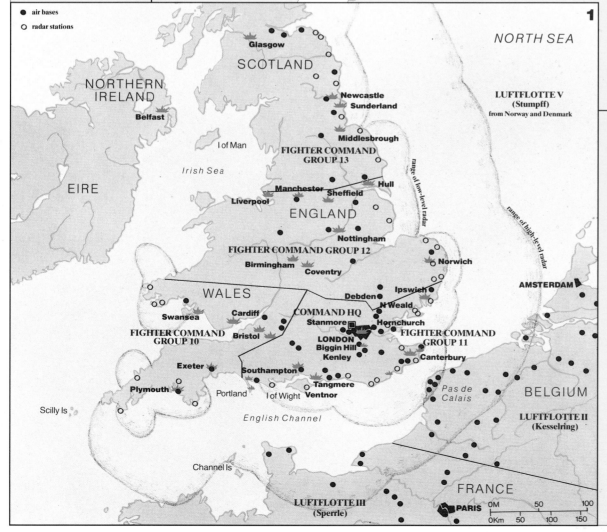

- ● air bases
- ○ radar stations

1

NORTH SEA

Glasgow

SCOTLAND

NORTHERN IRELAND

Belfast

Newcastle
Sunderland

LUFTFLOTTE V (Stumpff) from Norway and Denmark

I of Man

Middlesbrough

FIGHTER COMMAND GROUP 13

Irish Sea

EIRE

Manchester
Sheffield
Hull
Liverpool

ENGLAND

range of low-level radar

range of high-level radar

Nottingham

FIGHTER COMMAND GROUP 12

Birmingham
Coventry

Norwich

WALES

Ipswich
Debden
N Weald

AMSTERDAM

Swansea
Cardiff

COMMAND HQ Stanmore
Hornchurch

FIGHTER COMMAND GROUP 10
Bristol

LONDON
Biggin Hill
Kenley

FIGHTER COMMAND GROUP 11

Canterbury

Exeter
Southampton

Tangmere
Plymouth
Portland
I of Wight
Ventnor

Pas de Calais

BELGIUM

Scilly Is

English Channel

LUFTFLOTTE II (Kesselring)

Channel Is

FRANCE

LUFTFLOTTE III (Sperrle)

PARIS

0M 50 100
0Km 50 100 150

striking at airfields and radar stations – and knocking out the important one at Ventnor; at the end of the day 31 German aircraft had been shot down, 22 British.

Aug 13 was officially *Adler Tag* and in all 1,485 German sorties were flown, culminating in a successful night attack on a Spitfire factory near Birmingham; but for 45 German aircraft lost, only 13 of Fighter Command went down and of these 6 of the pilots were saved.

The following day only 500 German sorties were flown, but on Aug 15 – regarded by some as that vital 'fourth day' – they mounted seven major raids using all three Luftflotten. They were so timed that there were Luftwaffe squadrons over some part of Britain throughout the entire day in the hope of over-stretching the defences, and certainly all raids were fiercely challenged. But the Group system worked well and the attacks were dealt with within their areas. The raids mounted by Luftflotte V from Norway and Denmark found themselves especially hard hit, for this was Group 13's first taste of major action and they met the Luftwaffe out over the North Sea, thoroughly outmanoeuvring the Me-110s and shooting down 8 bombers and 7 fighters at no cost to themselves. Altogether on this day – when the area under attack was the most extensive of the whole Battle of Britain, with assaults from Dorset to Northumberland – the Germans lost 77 aircraft against 34 British; the following day with an effort almost as large – 1,700 sorties – they only lost 45 aircraft against 21 British. This was the day they concentrated with some success against airfields, damaging many and putting Tangmere virtually out of action.

As German Intelligence now put the total fighter strength of the RAF at 300, the Luftwaffe leaders decided that one more day's powerful assault would be needed, so on Aug 18 another series of full-force attacks was launched. But they suffered even higher losses than before and were forced to the conclusion that perhaps their figures were wrong as, quite evidently, RAF Fighter Command was still in existence. A change of plan seemed advisable.

The new plan came so close to success, and was foiled by so apparently trivial an occurrence, that one wonders if this was the time when Hitler's luck began to change.

From Aug 24 the Luftwaffe struck at airfields further inland than before, escorting their bombers with stronger fighter cover. Biggin Hill, Debden, Kenley, North Weald and Hornchurch were hit again and again, and although the losses suffered by the Luftwaffe were heavier than those by the RAF, the Luftwaffe could afford them. By now a large and ever-

Tientsin

Shanghai

Aug 18 British troops withdrawn from Tientsin,
Aug 21–25 from Shanghai

3 **Italian Victory.** Il Duce's thirst for military glory had hardly been satisfied by the events of the weeks immediately following his proclamation from the Palazzo Venezia. His attempts to accelerate the fall of France had been curtailed by the Führer, his armies in both Albania and Libya seemed curiously unwilling or unable to take punitive action against either the Greek or the British enemy, and despite the removal of the French Navy from the Mediterranean chessboard, the Italian fleet in general remained in port.

But as July ended and the enormous heat of Equatorial Africa built up, it occurred to both Il Duce and his commander-in-chief in Ethiopia, the Duke of Aosta, that one small enclave of British dominion was now surrounded on three sides by Italian or French possessions, and in view of the events at Mers el Kebir in July, all could be considered hostile to British interests. It should be comparatively easy, between them, to expel the British through the fourth side of British Somaliland and into the Gulf of Aden.

For this purpose the Italian Force commander, General Nasi, assembled 26 Italian and colonial battalions, 21 batteries of artillery, several squadrons of tanks and armoured cars, and 5 groups of 'irregulars', who might or might not fight well, depending upon their opportunities for loot.

On Aug 3 these forces crossed the British border in the form of a trident, the left-hand column driving for Zeila, the main, central column for Hargeisa and the right-hand column for Odweina. All objectives were reached with little opposition, but now the main force and the right-hand column faced the problem of driving through a pass through the ridge of hills between them and the only port, Berbera. The pass was called Tug Argan, and here was posted the only force the British commander had at his disposal – 5 infantry battalions, 4 3.7-inch howitzers . . . and the 3-pounder saluting gun lent them by HMAS *Hobart* of the naval contingent, standing by to aid the inevitable evacuation.

The action opened on the afternoon of Aug 11, and Maj-General A.R. Godwin-Austen, who had been hastily sent down to take command, found his forces all in action when he arrived.

For four days they held back the Italian columns, but slowly their positions were outflanked, their guns ran out of ammunition and the plight of the wounded in the stunning heat became unbearable. On Aug 15 he gave the order for withdrawal, first through a screen of Black Watch, then down into Berbera from which all British civilians had already been loaded on to the waiting ships.

British and Australian naval units moved in to use their guns in the final perimeter battles, the last survivors were picked up at 1400 on Aug 18 and the ships moved away – though HMAS *Hobart* remained until the morning of Aug 19 in case any lone individual arrived, and also to greet the first Italians with a final salvo as they entered the port.

The defence had cost the British 260 casualties, and when Mussolini trumpeted the news of his great victory, which meant, he claimed, that his forces now exercised a 'total blockade' of all British possessions in the Mediterranean and in Africa, he said it was owed to 2,052 glorious dead and/or wounded heroes.

increasing number of the most highly skilled RAF pilots were being lost – not only by the law of averages but also through cumulative exhaustion. Fighter Command was being worn down, and at an increasing rate.

But on the night of Aug 24/25, owing to faulty navigation, a Luftwaffe bomber dropped – or jettisoned – bombs over central London. They were the first of what was later to become many, but Churchill felt that retaliation was justified so for several of the following nights RAF bombers arrived over Berlin and inflicted a certain amount of damage – little compared with what was to follow. But just the fact that they could penetrate so far into his Reich infuriated Hitler, and he ordered the Luftwaffe to change targets.

The Blitz on London was about to begin; but RAF Fighter Command was, as a result, to be given the chance to regain its strength.

2 **The Vienna Award.** In the speed and violence of events in France and Britain, it is hardly surprising that the world scarcely noticed the dismemberment of one of the Balkan countries. Rumania had sided with the Western Allies during the First World War and after it she reaped her reward – some 60,000 square miles of territory which for centuries she had disputed with her neighbours, Hungary, Bulgaria and Russia. Now, with her traditional protectors apparently facing defeat, came the time of reckoning.

Russia moved first. On June 26 the Soviet representative in Bucarest presented a demand for the return to Russia of the lands she had lost in 1918 – Bessarabia and northern Bukovina. In a frantic attempt to win powerful intercession, King Carol announced his great admiration for Hitler and his Reich and pointed out that Rumania's Iron Guard were now free to march around again.

Hitler, of course, held an inborn distaste for territorial aggrandisement by anyone except himself, but for the moment his attentions were engaged elsewhere and in any case he regarded the whole matter as irrelevant. Whoever held those

territories for the moment would yield them all to him in the comparatively near future, so he instructed Carol to hand over the disputed region without further ado.

This, of course, prompted the Bulgarians to put in their claim to southern Dobruja, and then the Hungarians arrived to press their claim to Transylvania – again with reference to the most potent figure then in European politics. Hitler's patience with the affair was running out but on the other hand he knew that in the near future the Ploesti oilfields were going to be vital to his plans. Moreover, Hungary was already so much under his domination as to be almost a part of his Greater Reich, so he instructed all parties concerned to send delegations to Vienna where Count Ciano and Ribbentrop would adjudicate.

It did not take long. After less than 48 hours the two delivered their judgement; Rumania would hand over an area of about 17,000 square miles of the richest part of Transylvania, including the city of Cluj, to Hungary, and to Bulgaria whatever part of the Dobruja she required. That should teach Rumania to choose her friends more carefully in the future.

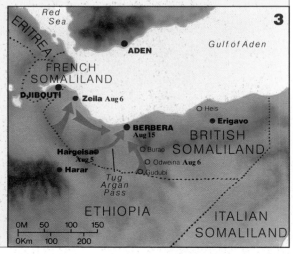

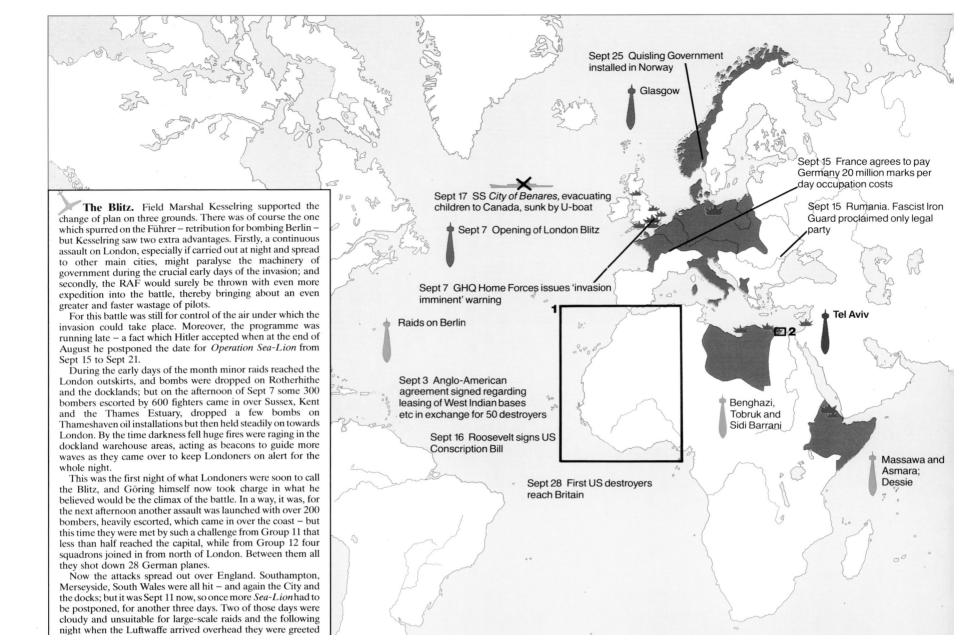

Sept 25 Quisling Government installed in Norway

Glasgow

Sept 15 France agrees to pay Germany 20 million marks per day occupation costs

Sept 15 Rumania. Fascist Iron Guard proclaimed only legal party

Sept 17 SS *City of Benares*, evacuating children to Canada, sunk by U-boat

Sept 7 Opening of London Blitz

Sept 7 GHQ Home Forces issues 'invasion imminent' warning

Raids on Berlin

Tel Aviv

Sept 3 Anglo-American agreement signed regarding leasing of West Indian bases etc in exchange for 50 destroyers

Sept 16 Roosevelt signs US Conscription Bill

Benghazi, Tobruk and Sidi Barrani

Massawa and Asmara; Dessie

Sept 28 First US destroyers reach Britain

The Blitz. Field Marshal Kesselring supported the change of plan on three grounds. There was of course the one which spurred on the Führer – retribution for bombing Berlin – but Kesselring saw two extra advantages. Firstly, a continuous assault on London, especially if carried out at night and spread to other main cities, might paralyse the machinery of government during the crucial early days of the invasion; and secondly, the RAF would surely be thrown with even more expedition into the battle, thereby bringing about an even greater and faster wastage of pilots.

For this battle was still for control of the air under which the invasion could take place. Moreover, the programme was running late – a fact which Hitler accepted when at the end of August he postponed the date for *Operation Sea-Lion* from Sept 15 to Sept 21.

During the early days of the month minor raids reached the London outskirts, and bombs were dropped on Rotherhithe and the docklands; but on the afternoon of Sept 7 some 300 bombers escorted by 600 fighters came in over Sussex, Kent and the Thames Estuary, dropped a few bombs on Thameshaven oil installations but then held steadily on towards London. By the time darkness fell huge fires were raging in the dockland warehouse areas, acting as beacons to guide more waves as they came over to keep Londoners on alert for the whole night.

This was the first night of what Londoners were soon to call the Blitz, and Göring himself now took charge in what he believed would be the climax of the battle. In a way, it was, for the next afternoon another assault was launched with over 200 bombers, heavily escorted, which came in over the coast – but this time they were met by such a challenge from Group 11 that less than half reached the capital, while from Group 12 four squadrons joined in from north of London. Between them all they shot down 28 German planes.

Now the attacks spread out over England. Southampton, Merseyside, South Wales were all hit – and again the City and the docks; but it was Sept 11 now, so once more *Sea-Lion* had to be postponed, for another three days. Two of those days were cloudy and unsuitable for large-scale raids and the following night when the Luftwaffe arrived overhead they were greeted by strong anti-aircraft fire from newly arrived guns. Sept 14 came and went, and another postponement of three days put D-Day for the invasion at Sept 27 – and soon after that, according to the Kriegsmarine, tide and weather would make invasion difficult if not impossible.

There was another cause for worry about the feasibility of an invasion. During the first week of September, RAF reconnaissance planes had brought back photographs revealing an immense build-up of barges and landing-craft in ports and harbours along the Belgian and French coasts, and Bomber Command together with Coastal Command began night attacks on them, with particular success on Sept 13/14. Now the Kriegsmarine were worried that even if the Luftwaffe assured them of ten days' non-interference from the RAF, they would lack the craft to take the army across to Britain.

Sunday, Sept 15, was thus a crucial day for *Operation Sea-Lion*. The RAF had to be destroyed or the invasion might well have to be postponed until 1941 – and Hitler knew that by that time he would have other plans for the Luftwaffe and, indeed, the whole Wehrmacht.

By noon mass formations of escorted bombers were crossing the coast *en route* for London. They were met by Group 11 fighters before they reached Canterbury, then more squadrons challenged them on the close approach, while over London itself five squadrons from the Duxford Wing of Group 12 were waiting. Few of that first wave of bombers got past south London before they turned back, many of them jettisoning their bombs over the open countryside – over which they were again challenged by the refuelled Group 11 squadrons.

Two hours later, radar warned Fighter Command HQ of another mass build-up over the Pas de Calais, and within another hour the earlier events were being repeated. Again Group 11 fighters challenged the Luftwaffe all the way to London, again Group 12 were waiting for them, again the bombers were turned away before they could wreak the havoc they intended. Other Luftwaffe formations attacked Portland and Southampton, and that night Manchester, Cardiff, Liverpool and Bristol. But the RAF were now scenting victory, for they were rested after the exhausting days of late August, and Spitfires and Hurricanes were still pouring from the factories. New squadrons were being formed every day, the callow recruits of the opening days of the battle, if still alive, were hardened, skilful and experienced.

On Sept 17 Hitler postponed *Sea-Lion* indefinitely, and a few days later he agreed to the dispersion of the fleet of invasion barges before they were all destroyed. Though the Blitz would continue for some time yet, and be repeated during the years to come, the invasion threat was over. The RAF had won.

1 **Operation Menace.** Since the fall of France, General de Gaulle had been gathering his Free French forces together, and by August was convinced that the French colonies in West, North and Equatorial Africa were anxious to join him. When he proposed to Churchill that an expedition should be mounted to land himself and a Free French contingent at Dakar, where the garrison would be invited to welcome him as a liberator, he gained an enthusiastic supporter. Dakar safely in Allied hands would safeguard the sea passages in the south Atlantic, the French colonial empire on the Allied side would bring solid help and prestige.

Force M consisted of 11 merchantmen with 4 battalions of Royal Marines and 2,700 Free French troops aboard, with an escorting force drawn from the Home Fleet, from Force H at Gibraltar and from the south Atlantic. It left Great Britain on Aug 31, bound first for Freetown where they were to refuel before sailing north again to Dakar. Such an impressive show of strength, it was felt, should help to swing French opinion in the expedition's favour, a point which in the event was negated by their arrival off Dakar in dense mist which thickened as the morning passed.

The whole enterprise was plagued with such circumstances, the chief being the despatch, by pure coincidence, of 3 French cruisers and 3 fast destroyers from Toulon to Dakar on Sept 11, bound eventually for Libreville. After Mers el Kebir the Royal Navy had no wish to become embroiled again in a battle with the French squadron and the resulting signals, arguments and pleas to the French ships to turn back to Casablanca, though successful, bordered at times on the farcical.

The greatest setback to *Operation Menace*, however, was the revelation that despite de Gaulle's opinion, Dakar and its garrison were solidly loyal to Vichy, and the Governor informed de Gaulle's envoys that any attempt to land would be most vigorously opposed. Moreover, if any of the British fleet came within range of the Dakar shore batteries they would be shelled, and French submarines in the harbour sent out to launch torpedo attacks against them.

Despite this, unsuccessful attempts were made to land some

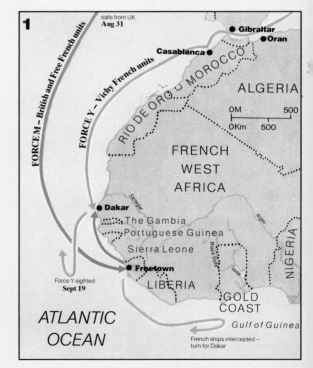

1 FORCE M – British and Free French units

FORCE Y – Vichy French units

sails from UK Aug 31

Gibraltar
Oran

Casablanca

RIO DE ORO MOROCCO

ALGERIA

0M 500
0Km 500

FRENCH WEST AFRICA

Dakar

The Gambia
Portuguese Guinea
Sierra Leone

Freetown

LIBERIA

Force Y sighted Sept 19

NIGERIA

GOLD COAST

ATLANTIC OCEAN

Gulf of Guinea

French ships intercepted – turn for Dakar

of the Free French, and on Sept 25 when at last the mist dispersed, the fleet moved in to engage the fortresses. The results of that unfortunate day were that HMS *Resolution* was hit by a torpedo amidships which caused serious flooding, HMS *Barham* was hit by shellfire, HMS *Australia* was hit twice, and then *Resolution*, listing badly, was attacked by French air patrols, fortunately unsuccessfully.

By noon sanity had returned to the Allied command and, despite Churchill's disappointment, the force withdrew to Freetown. Thus ended an ill-starred venture, based upon unfounded optimism, inadequate political, and almost non-existent military, intelligence.

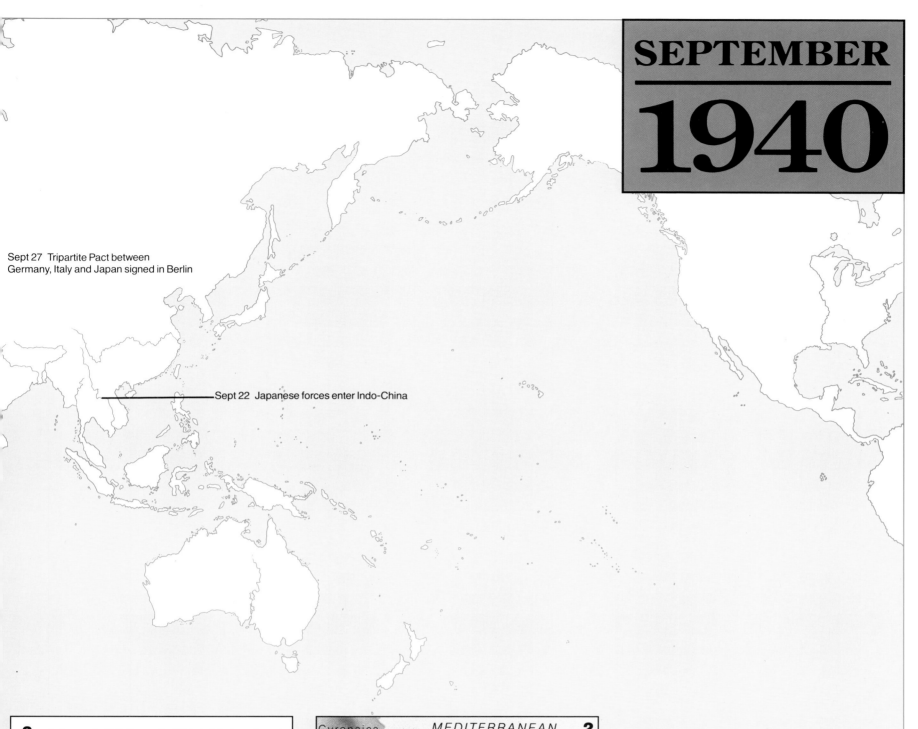

Sept 27 Tripartite Pact between
Germany, Italy and Japan signed in Berlin

Sept 22 Japanese forces enter Indo-China

2 **Advance to Sidi Barrani.** With the 'glorious victory' of British Somaliland behind him, Mussolini now demanded further onslaughts on the British – especially as he expected to hear any day of the successful German invasion of Britain. 'On the day on which the first platoon of German soldiers touches British territory, you will simultaneously attack,' he wrote to Marshal Graziani, now commanding Italian forces in Libya. '. . . there are no territorial objectives, it is not a question of aiming for Alexandria, nor even for Sollum. I am only asking you to attack the British forces facing you.'

As the forces Graziani was massing at the frontier comprised 3 infantry divisions, 2 motorised divisions and a mobile group sufficiently large to be commanded by a lieutenant-general, and the only forces which General Wavell on the British side could put against him consisted of 4th Indian Division, short of one complete brigade and much of its artillery, and the 7th Armoured Division with only 65 of its complement of 220 tanks, Mussolini's request does not seem to have been unreasonable. Nevertheless, Graziani produced so many excuses for non-action and demanded so much more in the way of reinforcement and supply, that eventually Mussolini lost patience and roundly instructed him to drive into Egypt not later than Sept 9.

So on Sept 13, after a spectacular bombardment of the empty barracks at Musaid, the whole panoply of the Italian Tenth Army threaded its way through the triple wire fence (through gaps made by British reconnaissance cars), then one half descended the escarpment immediately down to Sollum, the other half making their way along the top towards Halfaya Pass where they intended to descend.

They were watched all the way with some curiosity by a single platoon of the Coldstream Guards who, once the Italians had reached Halfaya, closed down their signals net, activated the mines left in Sollum, and withdrew along the coast. As the Italian forces began the two descents, British artillery began shelling the passes, and RAF Gladiators and Blenheims machine-gunned and bombed the slow-moving columns.

By the morning of Sept 14 the mass of the Italian Tenth Army was down the escarpment and moving cumbersomely along the coastal road, immutably pushing back the British lines of

infantry and artillery ranked in front of them. The British force was commanded by Lt-General Richard O'Connor and his plan was to hinder the Italian advance as much, but as cheaply, as possible by use of infantry and artillery, until the head of the Italian forces reached Mersa Matruh, at which point he would launch 7th Armoured Division up from the south to drive to the coast and cut the Italian supply lines. He would then release the brigades of 4th Indian Division to attack the forward Italian formations.

All through Sept 15 the Italian advance continued, the British roadblocks systematically withdrew, the 7th Armoured Division watched and waited. Then at dusk on Sept 16 the Italians reached Sidi Barrani, probed on a little farther towards Maktila, then began preparations for a long stay. Apparently they had no intention of going any further. 'It was all', wrote General O'Connor, 'rather a disappointment.'

According to Rome radio, however, Tenth Army had achieved another fine victory against fanatical but out-manoeuvred British forces. 'All is now quiet in Sidi Barrani,' the panegyric ended, 'the shops are open and the trams are running again' – which must have come as a surprise to the inhabitants, most of whom had never seen a tram in their lives.

29

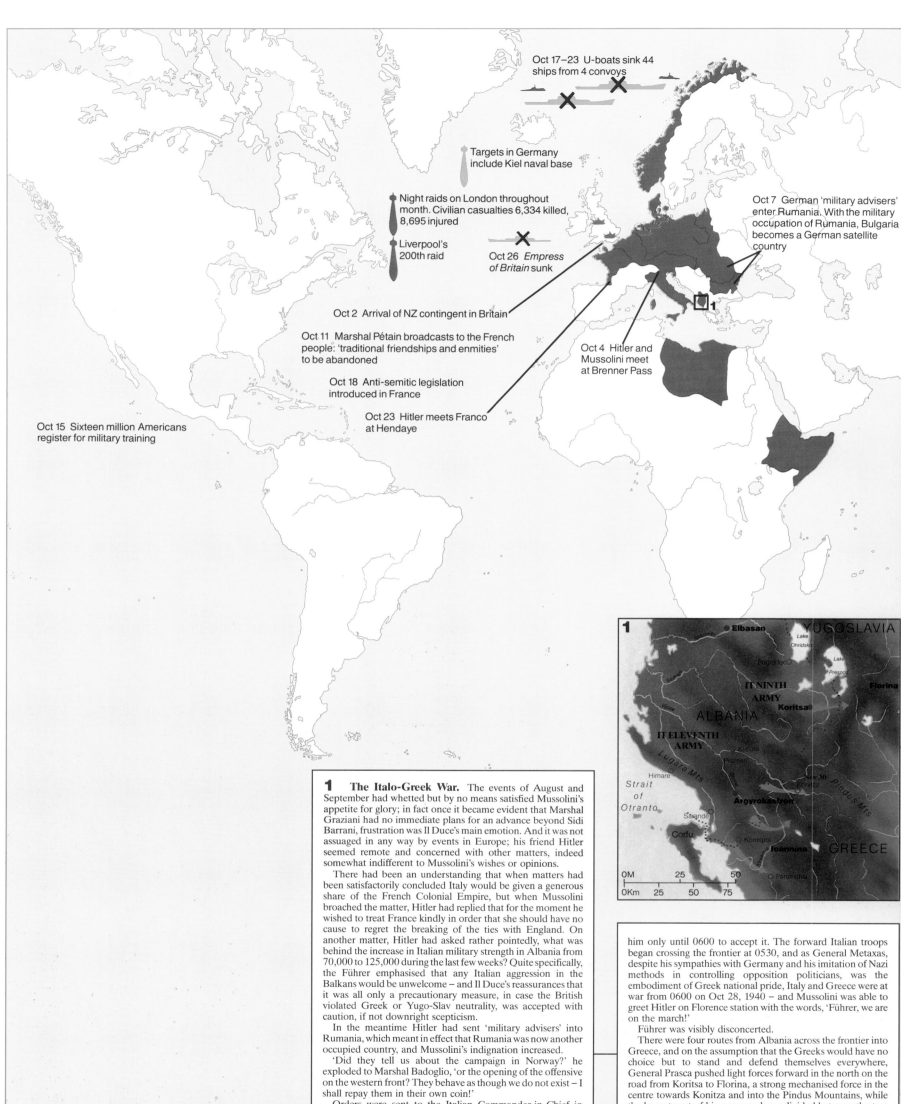

Oct 17–23 U-boats sink 44 ships from 4 convoys

Targets in Germany include Kiel naval base

Night raids on London throughout month. Civilian casualties 6,334 killed, 8,695 injured

Liverpool's 200th raid

Oct 26 *Empress of Britain* sunk

Oct 7 German 'military advisers' enter Rumania. With the military occupation of Rumania, Bulgaria becomes a German satellite country

Oct 2 Arrival of NZ contingent in Britain

Oct 11 Marshal Pétain broadcasts to the French people: 'traditional friendships and enmities' to be abandoned

Oct 4 Hitler and Mussolini meet at Brenner Pass

Oct 18 Anti-semitic legislation introduced in France

Oct 23 Hitler meets Franco at Hendaye

Oct 15 Sixteen million Americans register for military training

1 **The Italo-Greek War.** The events of August and September had whetted but by no means satisfied Mussolini's appetite for glory; in fact once it became evident that Marshal Graziani had no immediate plans for an advance beyond Sidi Barrani, frustration was Il Duce's main emotion. And it was not assuaged in any way by events in Europe; his friend Hitler seemed remote and concerned with other matters, indeed somewhat indifferent to Mussolini's wishes or opinions.

There had been an understanding that when matters had been satisfactorily concluded Italy would be given a generous share of the French Colonial Empire, but when Mussolini broached the matter, Hitler had replied that for the moment he wished to treat France kindly in order that she should have no cause to regret the breaking of the ties with England. On another matter, Hitler had asked rather pointedly, what was behind the increase in Italian military strength in Albania from 70,000 to 125,000 during the last few weeks? Quite specifically, the Führer emphasised that any Italian aggression in the Balkans would be unwelcome – and Il Duce's reassurances that it was all only a precautionary measure, in case the British violated Greek or Yugo-Slav neutrality, was accepted with caution, if not downright scepticism.

In the meantime Hitler had sent 'military advisers' into Rumania, which meant in effect that Rumania was now another occupied country, and Mussolini's indignation increased.

'Did they tell us about the campaign in Norway?' he exploded to Marshal Badoglio, 'or the opening of the offensive on the western front? They behave as though we do not exist – I shall repay them in their own coin!'

Orders were sent to the Italian Commander-in-Chief in Albania, General Visconti Prasca, to be ready to move, and when Hitler, who was visiting Pétain at Montoire, suggested a meeting in Florence on Oct 28, Mussolini sent the signal. At 0300 on that morning the Greek dictator, General Metaxas, was awoken by the Italian representative in Athens with an ultimatum couched in vague but menacing language and giving

him only until 0600 to accept it. The forward Italian troops began crossing the frontier at 0530, and as General Metaxas, despite his sympathies with Germany and his imitation of Nazi methods in controlling opposition politicians, was the embodiment of Greek national pride, Italy and Greece were at war from 0600 on Oct 28, 1940 – and Mussolini was able to greet Hitler on Florence station with the words, 'Führer, we are on the march!'

Führer was visibly disconcerted.

There were four routes from Albania across the frontier into Greece, and on the assumption that the Greeks would have no choice but to stand and defend themselves everywhere, General Prasca pushed light forces forward in the north on the road from Koritsa to Florina, a strong mechanised force in the centre towards Konitza and into the Pindus Mountains, while the largest part of his command was divided between the two coastal routes.

Despite the weight, despite the mechanisation – far greater than anything the Greeks possessed – in two days the coastal thrusts had only advanced six miles each; in the Pindus Mountains they had reached and taken, unopposed, Konitza; while in the north they had hardly crossed the frontier.

30

Oct 8 Britain refuses Japan's request
to close the Burma Road

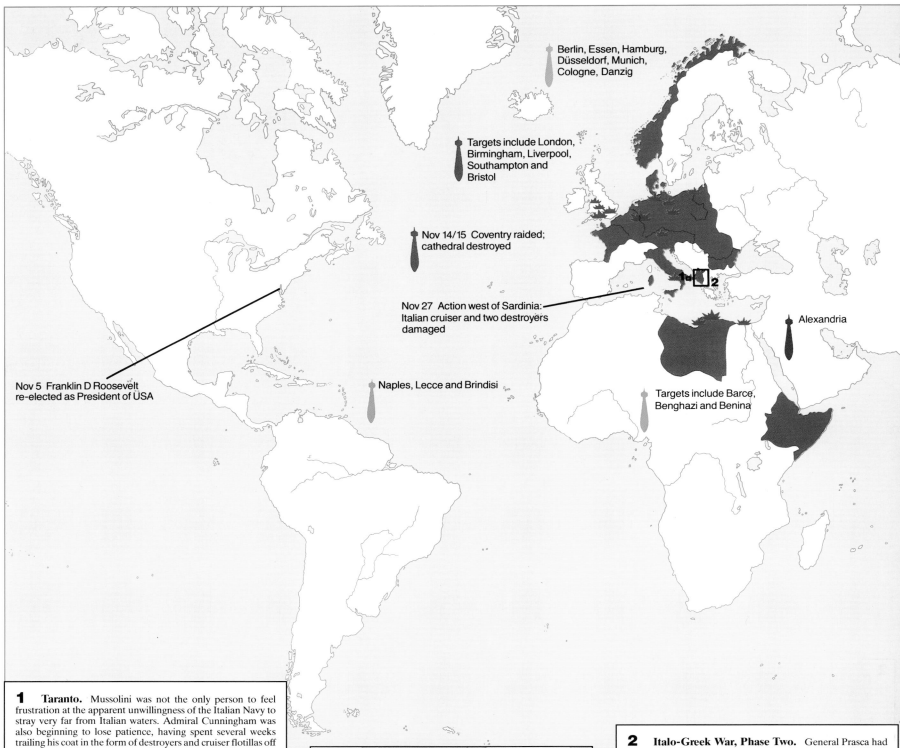

Berlin, Essen, Hamburg, Düsseldorf, Munich, Cologne, Danzig

Targets include London, Birmingham, Liverpool, Southampton and Bristol

Nov 14/15 Coventry raided; cathedral destroyed

Nov 27 Action west of Sardinia: Italian cruiser and two destroyers damaged

Alexandria

Nov 5 Franklin D Roosevelt re-elected as President of USA

Naples, Lecce and Brindisi

Targets include Barce, Benghazi and Benina

1   Taranto. Mussolini was not the only person to feel frustration at the apparent unwillingness of the Italian Navy to stray very far from Italian waters. Admiral Cunningham was also beginning to lose patience, having spent several weeks trailing his coat in the form of destroyers and cruiser flotillas off the various Italian ports, to no effect. By the end of October he had concluded that as the Italian ships seemed reluctant to come out and meet him, he must go in to them.

At Taranto the two anchorages of Mare Grande and Mare Piccolo make up one of the finest harbours in the Mediterranean, and by the early evening of Nov 11 Cunningham knew that six of the most powerful Italian battleships together with several cruisers and destroyers were at anchor in Mare Grande, while more cruisers were in Mare Piccolo, itself surrounded by oil storage depots, repair sheds and aircraft hangars. Many very valuable Italian eggs were in one basket – and an augmented Royal Naval force which included the aircraft-carrier *Illustrious* was only 200 miles away, having just delivered a convoy to Malta.

Shortly before 2100, 12 Swordfish aircraft – 'Stringbags' as their crews derisively called them – climbed awkwardly off *Illustrious*'s flight deck. Six had torpedoes slung beneath them, 4 had six 250-pound bombs, 2 had four bombs and heavy illuminating flares. They had all been given extra fuel tanks, either in the rear cockpits or slung on the outside.

By 2250 they were approaching Taranto, the sirens were screaming, searchlights from the ships below were searching the skies, already anti-aircraft- and machine-guns were firing at them. Just off Cape San Vito the two aircraft with flares aboard swung away to starboard, while the first wave of torpedo-bombers lined up to attack through the line of barrage balloons. As they flew in across the bay, the flares burst behind the harbour, silhouetting immediately below and in front the spectacular outline of the battleship *Cavour*.

One member of the first wave had lost his way in and so swung around in a huge curve to attack from over Taranto town, and the second wave which arrived an hour later swung in over Cape Rondinella – but by 0300 all except two aircraft were safely back aboard *Illustrious*.

They left behind them scenes of devastation and chaos. The battleships *Cavour*, *Littorio* and *Duilio* had all been successfully torpedoed; *Cavour* was out of action for ever, the

other two for many months. Moreover, behind Mare Grande an aircraft hangar had been left blazing and a cruiser damaged by bombs from the Swordfish dropping the flares. Two Swordfish failed to return though the crew of one – the first torpedo-dropping plane to attack – had been taken prisoner.

For the loss of two elderly aircraft and two crew members killed, the naval balance of power in the Mediterranean had been altered. Later the same night a force of cruisers and destroyers which Cunningham had detached and sent up through the Strait of Otranto caught an Italian convoy of four merchantmen with two escorts. They chased away the escorts and sank the merchantmen, together totalling 17,000 tons.

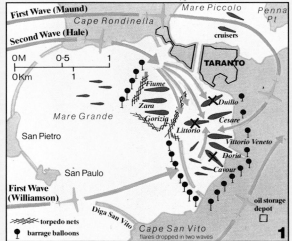

First Wave (Maund)
Second Wave (Hale)
First Wave (Williamson)
Mare Piccolo
Penna Pt
Cape Rondinella
cruisers
TARANTO
Fiume
Zara
Gorizia
Duilio
Littorio
Cesare
Vittorio Veneto
Doria
Cavour
Mare Grande
San Pietro
San Paulo
Diga San Vito
Cape San Vito
oil storage depot
torpedo nets
barrage balloons
flares dropped in two waves

2   Italo-Greek War, Phase Two. General Prasca had been right in his assumption that he would find Greek formations on every line of his advance, but wrong in the belief that they would stand on the defensive.

General Papagos, the Greek Commander-in-Chief, appreciating the fact – which would seem to have escaped Prasca – that the most dangerous threat lay in the north where Italian success in the drive on Florina could reach Salonika and cut western Thrace off from the body of Greece, flung five divisions across the country from the Bulgarian borderlands and into a powerful counter-attack. On Nov 2 to the astonishment and delight of the outside world (including some circles in Berlin) news came that Greek forces were inside Albania, on Nov 5 that they had cut the road leading north-west out of Koritsa, and the next day that they were shelling the town from both sides.

Moreover, in the centre, by using the mountains which they knew and leaving the valleys to the Italians, a reinforced Greek division had surrounded the 'Julia' Division which had taken Konitza and so threatened it with artillery and machine-gun fire that even the much-vaunted Alpini had panicked and fled back into Albania in near rout, sweeping away the reinforcements which Prasca had hastily sent up.

On the coast, the Italian advance had continued for a few more days and by Nov 8 they reached and crossed the Thyamis river, only then to become aware of the fact that to the north their compatriots were retreating into Albania. By Nov 13 cool logic had prevailed and they began to withdraw themselves.

By the end of the month, no Italian soldiers remained on Greek soil. Koritsa in the north was in Greek hands with quite a considerable harvest of war material, in the centre Greek forces were driving up the valley of the Vijose, while on the coast the main Italian force was anxiously trying to reach Sarandë before they were cut off by a possible Greek drive to the coast.

But Mussolini now had other matters to give him cause for concern. If his army was taking unexpected punishment, it paled into insignificance compared with what had happened to his navy.

NOVEMBER
1940

2

YUGOSLAVIA

Elbasan
Lake Ohridsko
Lake Prespos

Florina

Meskopolis
Koritsa
Nov 22

ALBANIA

Nov 18

Premet
Dec 4

Lugara Mts

Himare
Strait of Otranto

Argyrokastron

Koniza

Pindus Mts

Vouvousa
Nov 3

Sarande
Déo 4
Corfu

Konispol

Ioannina

Paramithia

GREECE

0M   25   50
0Km 25   50   75

Düsseldorf, Mannheim

Sheffield, London

Dec 29 Roosevelt announces USA 'must be the arsenal of democracy'

Dec 29/30 Heavy incendiary raid on London. Guildhall and eight Wren churches destroyed or damaged

Dec 6 Luftwaffe units to operate in Italy

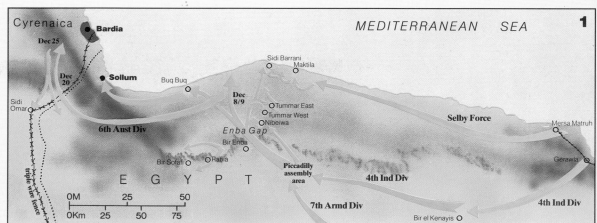

1 **Operation Compass.** The Italian Tenth Army, having reached Sidi Barrani in September, spent the next few weeks laying a road and pipe-line up from Sollum, and constructing five camps in a rough quadrant curving south-west from between Sidi Barrani and Maktila on the coast, back to Sofafi on the escarpment south of the Enba Gap: Tummar East, Tummar West, Nibeiwa – Enba Gap – Rabia, Sofafi. They were held by five divisions with one blackshirt division in reserve at Buq Buq, and another four divisions back behind the frontier at Sollum, Bardia and Tobruk; on the night of Dec 8/9, General O'Connor launched the two divisions of his Western Desert Force – 4th Indian and 7th Armoured – through the Enba Gap on *Operation Compass,* a raid intended to destroy the Italian camps and drive the garrisons back into Libya.

By 0200 the armoured brigades were through the gap and knifing up towards the coast to cut Italian communications and guard the rear of the Indian infantry who would be attacking the camps, while the Royal Navy bombarded Maktila and Tummar East, and the RAF created as much noise as possible above Nibeiwa; Camerons and Rajputana Rifles, with Matilda tanks of 7th Royal Tank Regiment, waited for the barrage about 700 yards west of the rear entrance to Nibeiwa.

The barrage opened, the tanks rumbled forward, the Camerons and Rajputs charged – and suddenly the Italian garrison, shocked out of sleep and in all stages of undress, found themselves surrounded by the chaos and confusion of battle, the skirl of pipes, the battle-cries of the Rajputs, and the tanks roaming everywhere 'like iron rods probing a wasps' nest'.

It was all over in a couple of hours. The Tummar camps were occupied before noon the following day, and such was the violence and surprise of the attacks that three days later all Italian garrisons in Egypt had been routed – five reinforced divisions in all – and were either fleeing back across the frontier, or marching glumly towards Egyptian prison-camps.

With the realisation of the extent of their victory, both General O'Connor and the Commander-in-Chief, Middle

East, General Wavell, saw the opportunity of invading Cyrenaica and capturing Bardia – perhaps even Tobruk. It would all depend upon the speed with which the infantry and armour could move and be supplied.

Unfortunately, General Wavell had made plans for the employment of the 4th Indian Division in a proposed action in the south against Eritrea and Ethiopia, so time was wasted bringing up the comparatively untrained 6th Australian Division to take their place.

Nevertheless, by Christmas Day the Australians and the Support Group of the 7th Armoured Division had invested Bardia, while one brigade of 7th Armoured had turned back from the escarpment and captured the Italian camp at Sidi Omar, thus clearing the northernmost stretch of the Wire.

34

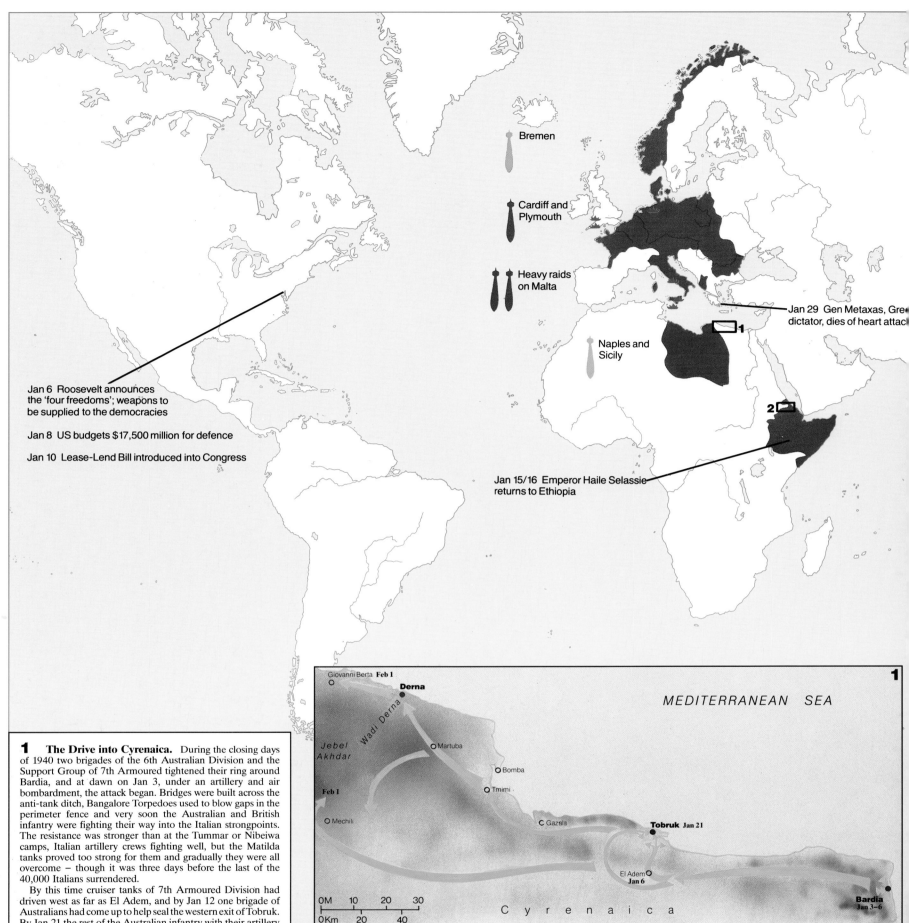

Bremen

Cardiff and
Plymouth

Heavy raids
on Malta

Naples and
Sicily

Jan 29 Gen Metaxas, Gre[e]
dictator, dies of heart attac[k]

Jan 6 Roosevelt announces
the 'four freedoms'; weapons to
be supplied to the democracies

Jan 8 US budgets $17,500 million for defence

Jan 10 Lease-Lend Bill introduced into Congress

Jan 15/16 Emperor Haile Selassie
returns to Ethiopia

1 **The Drive into Cyrenaica.** During the closing days of 1940 two brigades of the 6th Australian Division and the Support Group of 7th Armoured tightened their ring around Bardia, and at dawn on Jan 3, under an artillery and air bombardment, the attack began. Bridges were built across the anti-tank ditch, Bangalore Torpedoes used to blow gaps in the perimeter fence and very soon the Australian and British infantry were fighting their way into the Italian strongpoints. The resistance was stronger than at the Tummar or Nibeiwa camps, Italian artillery crews fighting well, but the Matilda tanks proved too strong for them and gradually they were all overcome – though it was three days before the last of the 40,000 Italians surrendered.

By this time cruiser tanks of 7th Armoured Division had driven west as far as El Adem, and by Jan 12 one brigade of Australians had come up to help seal the western exit of Tobruk. By Jan 21 the rest of the Australian infantry with their artillery had arrived and Tobruk was sealed off; at 0540 the heaviest barrage the Western Desert had known so far crashed out along a 2,500-yard stretch of the perimeter. Infantry and Matilda tanks had now worked together so many times that they made an almost irresistible force against the Italians. By nightfall the attacking formations had reached the centre of the garrison area and the following morning, as they drove on towards the sea, they captured the commanding General; shortly afterwards they drove into the port itself and took the surrender of the Admiral.

By now O'Connor had discussed the situation again with Wavell and they agreed to attempt a raid on Benghazi. The Australians would drive around the bulge containing the Jebel Akhdar, the 7th Armoured, one brigade having helped the Australians as far as Martuba, would concentrate at Mechili, carry out what had become urgent maintenance on their tanks, and prepare to drive direct for the Gulf of Sirte. By the end of the month, both moves were in progress, with the Australians, after a brisk battle for Derna, finding little or no resistance, for it seemed that General Graziani had ordered a complete withdrawal westwards of his forces.

MEDITERRANEAN SEA

Giovanni Berta **Feb 1**
Derna
Martuba
Jebel Akhdar
Wadi Derna
Bomba
Tmimi
Feb I
Mechili
Gazala
Tobruk Jan 21
El Adem
Jan 6
Bardia Jan 3–6
C y r e n a i c a

0M 10 20 30
0Km 20 40

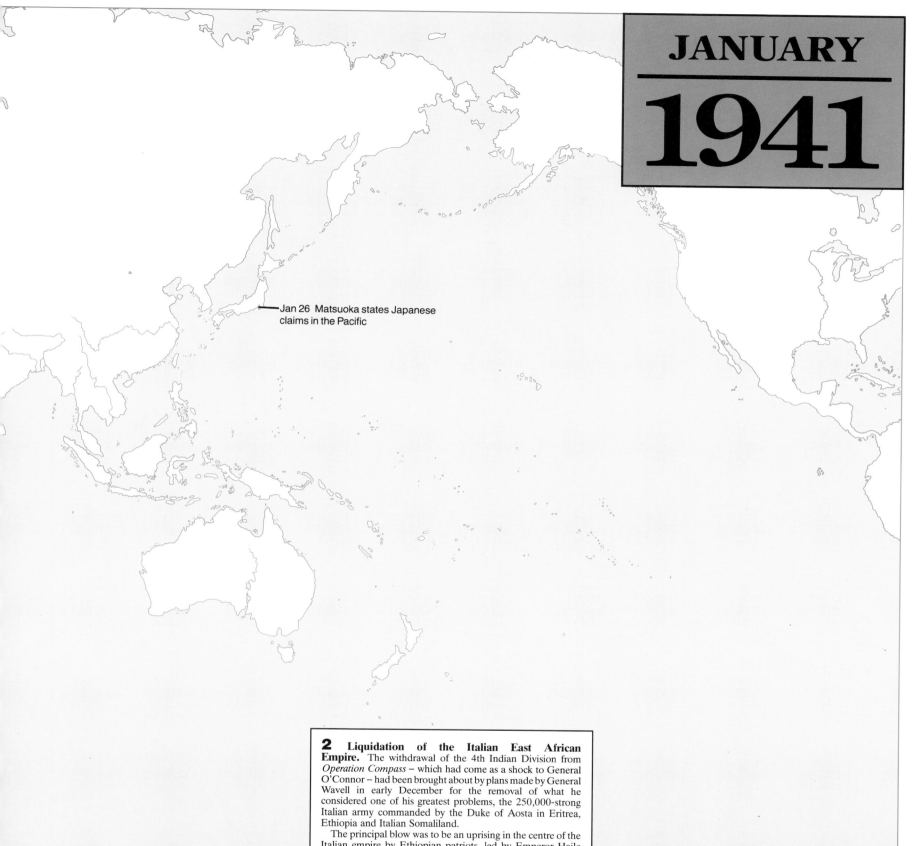

Jan 26 Matsuoka states Japanese claims in the Pacific

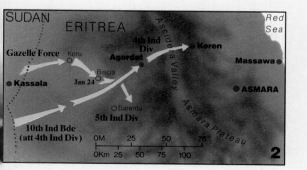

2 **Liquidation of the Italian East African Empire.** The withdrawal of the 4th Indian Division from *Operation Compass* – which had come as a shock to General O'Connor – had been brought about by plans made by General Wavell in early December for the removal of what he considered one of his greatest problems, the 250,000-strong Italian army commanded by the Duke of Aosta in Eritrea, Ethiopia and Italian Somaliland.

The principal blow was to be an uprising in the centre of the Italian empire by Ethiopian patriots, led by Emperor Haile Selassie who was flown back into his country by the RAF, organised by a Colonel D.A. Sandford who had farmed in Ethiopia before the war, and guided by a young and eccentric British officer named Orde Wingate.

This central uprising was to be assisted by a pincer movement from both north and south – into Eritrea from the Sudan, and into Italian Somaliland from Kenya. In the north, Lt-General W. Platt was to have both 4th and 5th Indian Divisions and with the latter had already so threatened the forward Italian position at Kassala, that when they advanced against it on Jan 19 they found that it had been vacated the day before. The first contact they had with the Italians was at Keru, 40 miles inside Eritrea, where to their astonishment they found themselves attacked from half a mile away by a cavalry charge by Askari natives led by Italian officers, all on small, shaggy ponies from which the riders hurled percussion grenades.

Once the attacked recovered from their surprise, the result was foregone. Riflemen, machine-gunners and even light artillerymen were in action before the cavalry were able to inflict the smallest damage on them, and within ten minutes the survivors were fleeing back into the scrub leaving the battlefield strewn with dead or wounded men and horses.

Meanwhile, one brigade of 4th Indian Division had driven across the frontier some 20 miles south of 'Gazelle Force', as the 5th Indian force was dubbed, herded some Italian colonial formations northwards into the Gazelle Force net, joined Gazelle at Biscia and with them drove on towards Agordat, one 5th Indian brigade having detached towards Barentu. The

Battle of Agordat lasted three days from Jan 28, was fought on both sides with vigour which had been lacking on the Italian side in previous encounters, and was in the end won by 4th Indian with the arrival of four of the implacable Matilda tanks against which the defenders had no counter.

On the last day of the month the leading squadron of the 4th Indian's reconnaissance regiment reached the Ascidera Valley and saw in front of them a steep, narrow gorge from which came the sounds of explosions as the retreating Italians blew in the sides. Keren and the Asmara plateau lay beyond.

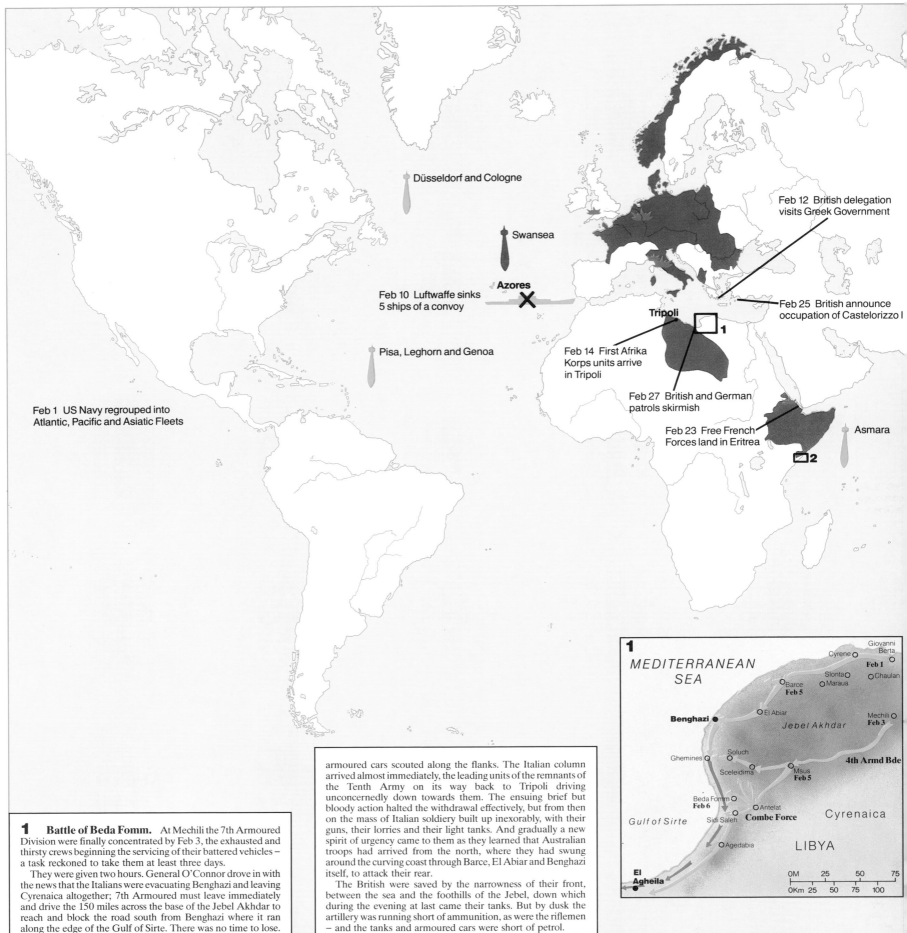

Düsseldorf and Cologne

Swansea

Azores

Feb 10 Luftwaffe sinks
5 ships of a convoy

Pisa, Leghorn and Genoa

Feb 1 US Navy regrouped into
Atlantic, Pacific and Asiatic Fleets

Feb 12 British delegation
visits Greek Government

Feb 25 British announce
occupation of Castelorizzo I

Tripoli

Feb 14 First Afrika
Korps units arrive
in Tripoli

Feb 27 British and German
patrols skirmish

Feb 23 Free French
Forces land in Eritrea

Asmara

1

MEDITERRANEAN
SEA

Giovanni
Berta

Cyrene **Feb 1**

Slonta Chaulan
Barce Maraua
Feb 5

Benghazi El Abiar Jebel Akhdar Mechili
Feb 3

Ghemines Soluch **4th Armd Bde**
Sceleidima Msus
Feb 5

Beda Fomm Antelat Cyrenaica
Feb 6 Sidi Saleh **Combe Force**
Gulf of Sirte

Agedabia LIBYA

El
Agheila

0M   25   50   75
0Km 25 50 75 100

---

1 **Battle of Beda Fomm.** At Mechili the 7th Armoured Division were finally concentrated by Feb 3, the exhausted and thirsty crews beginning the servicing of their battered vehicles – a task reckoned to take them at least three days.

They were given two hours. General O'Connor drove in with the news that the Italians were evacuating Benghazi and leaving Cyrenaica altogether; 7th Armoured must leave immediately and drive the 150 miles across the base of the Jebel Akhdar to reach and block the road south from Benghazi where it ran along the edge of the Gulf of Sirte. There was no time to lose.

The armoured cars got away first, followed by 50 cruiser and 90 light tanks with all the ammunition available, and enough water, petrol and food for two days. Behind them followed the artillery, and the troop carriers of one battalion of the support group – the only vehicles still mobile, carrying all the infantry that could be crammed into them.

The country through which they had to move was completely unknown to them, and very rough indeed. Huge rocks threatened the tank tracks, ditches and small chasms the sumps of the cars and lorries; and the bitter night air froze the faces of the tank commanders who had to travel standing in their hatches in order to look out for rocks. Later a fierce wind sprang up which brought torrential rain; and 'Thermos' bombs strewn across the track wrecked five vehicles before dawn.

But the leading armoured cars reached Msus on the evening of Feb 4 and the first tanks came in the next morning, guns and infantry raced on down to Antelat, then across the vital road to the coast at Beda Fomm. By 1400 on Feb 5 one company of infantry was in position across the road, two more formed a protective screen around the gun positions to the rear, while the

armoured cars scouted along the flanks. The Italian column arrived almost immediately, the leading units of the remnants of the Tenth Army on its way back to Tripoli driving unconcernedly down towards them. The ensuing brief but bloody action halted the withdrawal effectively, but from then on the mass of Italian soldiery built up inexorably, with their guns, their lorries and their light tanks. And gradually a new spirit of urgency came to them as they learned that Australian troops had arrived from the north, where they had swung around the curving coast through Barce, El Abiar and Benghazi itself, to attack their rear.

The British were saved by the narrowness of their front, between the sea and the foothills of the Jebel, down which during the evening at last came their tanks. But by dusk the artillery was running short of ammunition, as were the riflemen – and the tanks and armoured cars were short of petrol.

The night passed with little sign of movement among the packed ranks of the Italian columns, but when dawn came it revealed that during the night they had brought a dozen M13 tanks to the front – and these drove through the British forward infantry positions before the guns could register on them. The next half hour was filled with vicious hand-to-hand fighting, but when at last the sand and smoke cleared the watchers saw the 12 tanks smoking and stationary, tracks blown off by grenades, petrol tanks holed and set alight by rifle bullets, and one stopped by the last shell of the last anti-tank gun left in action.

The battle had been watched by both British and Italians, and when it ended an uncanny silence followed. Then, according to one tank commander, 'Gradually I became aware of a startling change. First one and then another white flag appeared amid the host. More and more became visible, until the whole column was a forest of waving white banners.'

The remnants of an army of ten whole divisions was surrendering to a force of less than one complete infantry division, two artillery batteries and one incomplete armoured squadron.

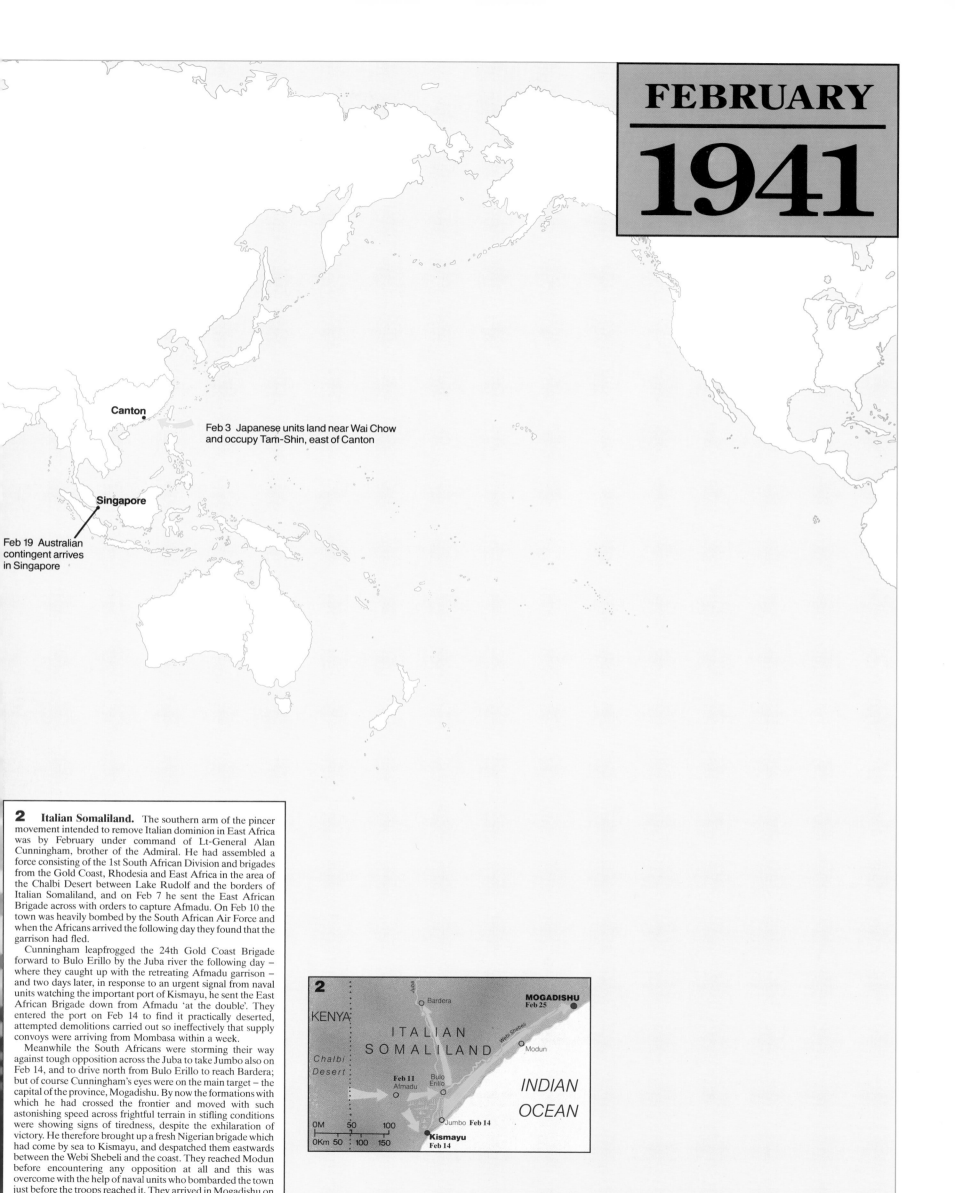

Feb 3 Japanese units land near Wai Chow and occupy Tam-Shin, east of Canton

Canton

Singapore

Feb 19 Australian contingent arrives in Singapore

2   Italian Somaliland. The southern arm of the pincer movement intended to remove Italian dominion in East Africa was by February under command of Lt-General Alan Cunningham, brother of the Admiral. He had assembled a force consisting of the 1st South African Division and brigades from the Gold Coast, Rhodesia and East Africa in the area of the Chalbi Desert between Lake Rudolf and the borders of Italian Somaliland, and on Feb 7 he sent the East African Brigade across with orders to capture Afmadu. On Feb 10 the town was heavily bombed by the South African Air Force and when the Africans arrived the following day they found that the garrison had fled.

Cunningham leapfrogged the 24th Gold Coast Brigade forward to Bulo Erillo by the Juba river the following day – where they caught up with the retreating Afmadu garrison – and two days later, in response to an urgent signal from naval units watching the important port of Kismayu, he sent the East African Brigade down from Afmadu 'at the double'. They entered the port on Feb 14 to find it practically deserted, attempted demolitions carried out so ineffectively that supply convoys were arriving from Mombasa within a week.

Meanwhile the South Africans were storming their way against tough opposition across the Juba to take Jumbo also on Feb 14, and to drive north from Bulo Erillo to reach Bardera; but of course Cunningham's eyes were on the main target – the capital of the province, Mogadishu. By now the formations with which he had crossed the frontier and moved with such astonishing speed across frightful terrain in stifling conditions were showing signs of tiredness, despite the exhilaration of victory. He therefore brought up a fresh Nigerian brigade which had come by sea to Kismayu, and despatched them eastwards between the Webi Shebeli and the coast. They reached Modun before encountering any opposition at all and this was overcome with the help of naval units who bombarded the town just before the troops reached it. They arrived in Mogadishu on Feb 25 – having advanced some 240 miles in three days.

2

KENYA

ITALIAN SOMALILAND

Chalbi Desert

Juba

Bardera

MOGADISHU Feb 25

Webi Shebeli

Modun

Feb 11 Afmadu

Bulo Erillo

INDIAN OCEAN

Jumbo Feb 14

Kismayu Feb 14

0M   50   100

0Km 50   100   150

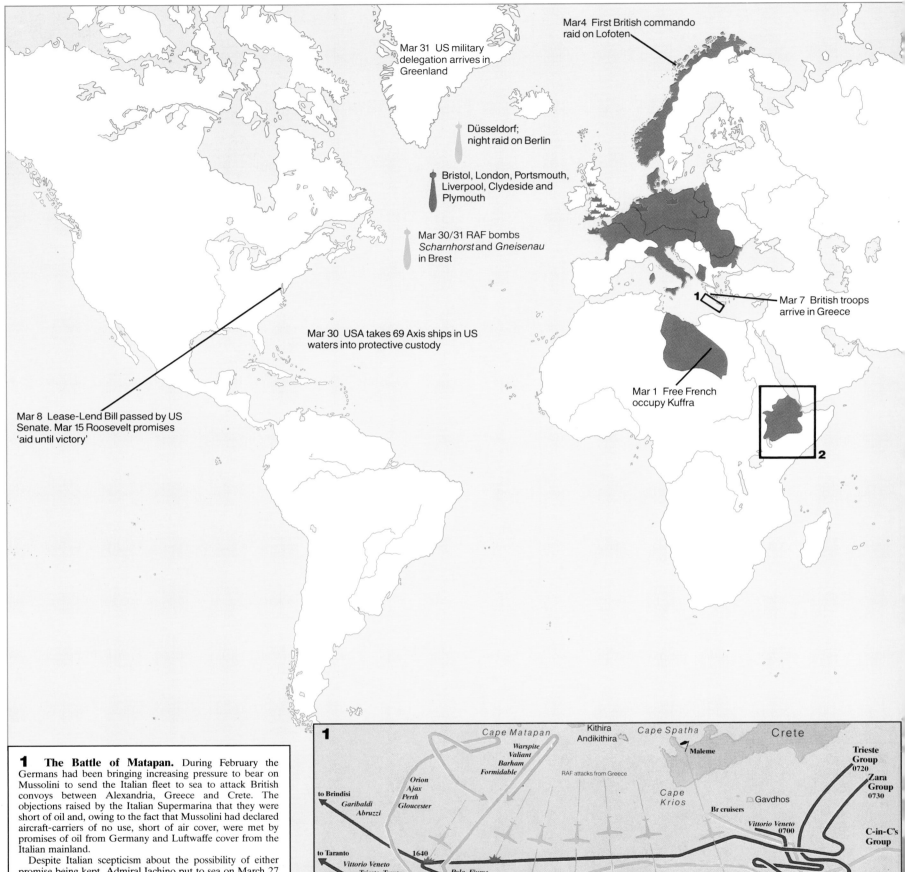

Mar 31 US military delegation arrives in Greenland

Mar4 First British commando raid on Lofoten

Düsseldorf; night raid on Berlin

Bristol, London, Portsmouth, Liverpool, Clydeside and Plymouth

Mar 30/31 RAF bombs *Scharnhorst* and *Gneisenau* in Brest

Mar 30 USA takes 69 Axis ships in US waters into protective custody

Mar 8 Lease-Lend Bill passed by US Senate. Mar 15 Roosevelt promises 'aid until victory'

Mar 7 British troops arrive in Greece

Mar 1 Free French occupy Kuffra

1 The Battle of Matapan.

Cape Matapan
Kithira
Andikithira
Cape Spatha
Crete

Warspite
Valiant
Barham
Formidable

RAF attacks from Greece

Maleme

Orion
Ajax
Perth
Gloucester

to Brindisi

Garibaldi
Abruzzi

Cape Krios

Gavdhos

Br cruisers

Trieste Group 0720

Zara Group 0730

to Taranto

1640

Vittorio Veneto
Trieste, Trento
Bolzano

Pola, Fiume
Zara

Zara Fiume

Pola
night battle 2227-2232 Mar 28

1900

Vittorio Veneto hit 1530

Vittorio Veneto 0700

C-in-C's Group

cruiser battle 0812-1130 Mar 28

0 NM — 50

1 **The Battle of Matapan.** During February the Germans had been bringing increasing pressure to bear on Mussolini to send the Italian fleet to sea to attack British convoys between Alexandria, Greece and Crete. The objections raised by the Italian Supermarina that they were short of oil and, owing to the fact that Mussolini had declared aircraft-carriers of no use, short of air cover, were met by promises of oil from Germany and Luftwaffe cover from the Italian mainland.

Despite Italian scepticism about the possibility of either promise being kept, Admiral Iachino put to sea on March 27 with the biggest of his remaining battleships, the *Vittorio Veneto*, six 8-inch-gun cruisers, two 6-inch-gun cruisers and nine destroyers.

Three of the cruisers with a destroyer escort were intended to steam north of Crete as far as the eastern end of the island, the rest to keep south of Crete as far as the island of Gavdhos, after which both forces would turn and go back home.

By the evening, though there had been no sign of the Luftwaffe cover, the RAF had shown up in the form of a single Sunderland flying-boat, which promptly signalled the presence of the northern force to Alexandria. That night Admiral Cunningham put to sea with the battleships *Warspite, Barham,* and *Valiant,* the aircraft-carrier *Formidable* and an escort of nine destroyers, in the hope of catching the Italians despite the distance he would have to travel.

He was unexpectedly helped by a force of British cruisers which had been covering a convoy to Crete, and which was sighted by the cruisers of the Italian northern force who had been instructed to join the main force at Gavdhos as soon as Supermarina had heard the Sunderland's signals. As the Italian cruiser force was obviously stronger than the British force, there was no trouble in luring them towards the British battleships as the British cruisers apparently fled.

Behind the Italian cruisers came the *Vittorio Veneto* at full speed, until Iachino became nervous, at which all ships reversed course and the British became the pursuers. Cunningham by now was 65 miles astern, so he sent five torpedo-bombers from *Formidable* in the hope of slowing the Italians and in the first attack *Vittorio* was hit on her port quarter, bringing her first to a dead stop; when she got under way again it was at only 20 knots – surrounded by five columns of protective escorts, including the *Zara* group which had turned back to help. RAF bombers from Crete and more aircraft from *Formidable* were effectively kept away from their main target, but they torpedoed the cruiser *Pola.*

By this time darkness had fallen, the Italian fleet was escaping but the British battleships were following hard. However, a little after 2000, Admiral Iachino suddenly discovered that *Pola* had been hit and left well behind, so he ordered the cruisers *Fiume* and *Zara* with four destroyers back to rescue her; and shortly after 2220 they steamed unknowingly across the path of the British battleships and only some 4,000 yards in front of them.

But one of the British ships – *Ajax* – had radar, and all had alert officers of the watch with excellent night vision. In four and a half minutes the cruisers and one destroyer were dead in the water and *Fiume* was sinking – and the other destroyers, after a gallant attempt to torpedo *Warspite,* were retiring fast with the British battleships in pursuit again.

The rest of the Battle of Matapan consisted of a vain attempt to catch the *Vittorio Veneto* and her escorts, and the final sinking of the damaged cruisers. A boarding party sent to the *Pola,* which had been stationary since being hit during the evening, found most of the crew drunk and quite amenable to being captured, but the possibility of Luftwaffe attacks once daylight came put an end to the chances of towing the cruiser back to Alexandria, so she was torpedoed after her crew had been taken off.

2 Into Ethiopia. Just before General Cunningham had sent the Nigerians off to Mogadishu, he had cabled General Wavell asking if it would be possible for a force from Aden to take the port of Berbera, thus considerably shortening his lines of communication should the momentum he might gather on the way to Mogadishu take him very far northwards. Astonishingly, his optimism proved to be justified.

The country to the north of Mogadishu, up as far as Jijiga, is flat Somaliland lava and bush plain providing no supplies of any kind. Everything including water had to be carried, and the withdrawing Italian forces were far too concerned with this aspect of their movement to organise any form of resistance. In fact, the 11th African Division which Cunningham sent after them had some difficulty in keeping up, and when they arrived at Jijiga on March 17 they found it abandoned.

The day before, troops from Aden had been landed at Berbera, to cross British Somaliland back through Tug Argan to Hargeisa by March 20, and on to join 11th African at Jijiga as they drove on westwards, first through two easily defensible passes, Marda Pass and Babile Pass, which between them held them up less than 12 hours. They were met 12 miles short of Harar by Italian officials with the news that Harar had been declared an Open Town in which they would be welcome, and short of Diredawa, 50 miles on, by agitated city officials begging them to hurry as the garrison had withdrawn leaving the civilians unprotected; the place was now at the mercy of gangs of armed Ethiopian deserters engaged on a rampage of looting, rape and murder. It was part of the somewhat fantastical atmosphere of this campaign that the South Africans could only move to the rescue by foot, as Italian demolitions on the road to Diredawa proved to be the most effective so far encountered.

In the north, however, Italian demolitions in the Dongolaas Gorge leading up to Keren and the approaches to Asmara, their roadblocks and at times spirited resistance painted a very different picture. The 4th Indian Division had arrived at the

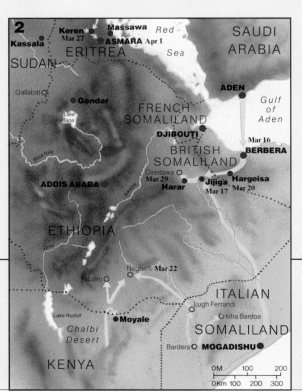

bottom of the Gorge by Feb 4, but it was not until late March, after they had been joined by 5th Indian Division, by a build-up of RAF fighter and bomber strength to give them cover during the fierce fighting in the Gorge itself, reminiscent according to some of the older participants of the worst battles fought for the Passchendaele ridge 24 years before – and the approach from the north-east of a brigade group containing Free French troops, Foreign Legionnaires and a battalion from the Chad Regiment – that they managed to break out of the Gorge into Keren and on to Asmara by April 1. The British had lost 536 killed in the battles for Keren, the Italians over 3,000.

Almost a thousand miles to the south, a third campaign had opened at the end of February, almost completely divorced from the other two. Once the fall of Kismayu had revealed the weakness of the Italian control in Ethiopia, two South African brigades were sent north from Kenya across the border, aiming first for Yaballo with a small force detached to retake Moyale. It had the unforeseen effect of drawing a whole Italian division from the main front towards Neghelli, but once the movement was observed, West African troops moved up from Bardera and they and the South Africans were in Neghelli by March 22 before the Italians were anywhere near.

1 Invasion of Yugoslavia and Greece. Hitler's plans for the invasion of Russia had long been laid, and they had included a directive for *Operation Marita*, a precautionary measure to clear his southern flank by a drive down through Bulgaria 'to occupy the north-east coast of the Adriatic . . . and, should this be necessary, the entire mainland of Greece.'

He thought he could deal with the problem posed by Yugoslavia, lying as she did between Germany, Hungary, Rumania and Bulgaria – by now virtually all members of his 'Greater Reich' – and his objective, Greece, by diplomatic means; in reality, by bullying. As early as November 1940 he had summoned the Yugoslav Foreign Minister to Berchtesgaden to suggest he place his country unreservedly on the side of the Axis. The Minister temporised – after all, Prince Paul, the Regent of the country, was related to the British Royal Family and had been educated at Oxford – but reality had to be faced and by the spring of 1941 Hitler, as undoubtedly the most powerful man in Europe, was not to be trifled with.

On March 19, 1941 Hitler gave Yugoslavia five days in which to sign a pact guaranteeing her frontiers and giving her use of the port of Salonika (which he intended to control quite soon) and made it clear that if she failed to sign, she would quickly be given cause to regret the decision. On March 25, the pact was signed and Hitler could turn his attention to other, more pressing matters.

But to the Führer's astonishment, the Serbian people who made up the larger – and certainly the most influential – part of the Yugoslav population refused to accept the new pact. On March 27 the Yugoslav Army with the enthusiastic support of the people of Belgrade executed a Palace coup, exiled Prince Paul, put young King Peter on the throne, and proclaimed the start of a new regime under the slogan 'Better war than pact; better grave than slave!'

Apr 12 US troops land in Greenland

Targets include Portsmouth, Bristol, Coventry, Birmingham and Plymouth

Apr 13 Soviet-Japanese neutrality pact signed

Apr 25 Germans occupy Lemnos

Apr 23 King George of Hellenes and Greek Government evacuated to Crete

Brest, Sofia, Kiel, Berlin and Bremen

Apr 16/17 St Paul's damaged in heavy raid on London. Two nights later another raid causes 2,300 deaths

Malta

Apr 3 Pro-Axis *coup d'état* in Iraq

Apr 16 Axis convoy of 5 supply ships and 3 destroyers sunk by RN

Apr 20 RN shells Benghazi

2 Enter Rommel. Shortly after the collapse of the Italian Tenth Army, General O'Connor's forces, newly christened XIII Corps, deployed themselves in new positions. But on Feb 12 Generalleutnant Erwin Rommel arrived at Castel Benito airfield near Tripoli with orders from Hitler to stop the Italian rot in North Africa, and if possible to throw the British back into Egypt. He was to be greatly aided by events.

First of all, the condition of 7th Armoured Division's tanks was now so deplorable that the whole division was recalled to Cairo, and the newly arrived 2nd Armoured Brigade sent up to defend the Jebel Akhdar. Then developments in Greece stirred Churchill to order that the most experienced division in the Middle East be sent to Greece's support, which meant the departure from Cyrenaica of the 6th Australians. Perhaps most favourable for Rommel and fatal for Great Britain, General O'Connor was taken ill and went into hospital in the Delta, and his place was taken by Lt-General Philip Neame, VC, who possessed neither O'Connor's experience nor his imagination. In late March, Wavell, whose attention had been diverted from Libya by many matters including the situations in Greece and Ethiopia, visited Neame and was astonished by the unsound deployment of the new XIII Corps.

So was Rommel when he found out about it. He returned to Berlin to put forward his ideas for an immediate offensive and was given orders to proceed very carefully, which he disobeyed with a Nelsonian zest. On March 31 he sent forward units of his Light Division in a probing reconnaissance towards Mersa el Brega, and by the end of the day was not only in control of the position, but had gained a clear insight into the mediocrity of the opposition. He ordered the 5th Light Division onwards to Agedabia where he set up his headquarters on April 2, and with complete disregard for established principles, he split his already tenuous force into three. One group he sent in a drive straight for Bir Tengeder and then up to Mechili, the bulk of his force up through Antelat and Msus with the same immediate objective, while he himself accompanied his reconnaissance units first up to Soluch and Ghemines and then, learning that the British were hurriedly evacuating Benghazi, straight for the port which they entered on April 4.

Two days before, Wavell had flown up to Benghazi and

Within hours General Halder, Chief of the German General Staff, received a new directive. Yugoslavia was to be destroyed as a military and as a national unit. 'Politically it is important that the blow against Yugoslavia is carried out with pitiless harshness.' Belgrade was to be destroyed. *Operation Strafgericht* (Punishment) was to begin as quickly as possible (the invasion of Russia could be postponed for up to four weeks) and might just as well be combined with *Operation Marita*. Yugoslavia and Greece would be dealt with in a joint blow, and what better day than April 6, Palm Sunday?

The citizens of Belgrade were awoken by the sounds of aircraft circling above them at 0530 and by 0600 bombs were falling on the railway station, the Royal Palace and the Zemun airfield where most of the pitifully few Yugoslav Air Force planes were caught on the ground. That day, 17,000 people were killed and the centre of Belgrade was reduced to rubble.

Five hundred miles to the south the scenes of ruin and chaos were duplicated. Piraeus harbour was full of shipping, some of which had brought parts of the 6th Australian Division after their triumphs in Cyrenaica, and by 2100 that Sunday mines were being parachuted down from Luftwaffe planes to seal the harbour, then the bombers followed. Shortly before 2200 one bomb burst aboard the SS *Glen Fraser* and the 250 tons of explosive in her hold blew up with a shattering roar.

From Bulgaria XXX Corps of the German Twelfth Army had driven south over the border into Thrace and reached Alexandroupolis and Xanthi, their 2nd Panzer Division hooking down through both Yugoslav and Greek borders to reach Salonika in three days, having cut off the Greek Eastern Macedonian Army. To the north XL Panzer Corps had reached Skopje by April 8 and swung down through the Monastir Gap the next day, with the whole of Greece before it.

The German conquest of Yugoslavia took only 12 days. Kleist's First Panzer Army had driven up from Bulgaria past Nis and along the Morava river to reach Belgrade, while Weichs's Second Army drove down from the north, through Zagreb (on April 10), one division having veered west to Ljubljana, and another crossing the Drava from Barcs to join the main force and arrive at Belgrade on April 12. Two days later a truce was requested; it took four days to arrange, by which time German and Italian units had overrun the whole country.

In Greece, there was little the Greek Army, outflanked by the panzers, could do. As for the British units which had been sent to help, they could do no more than try to hold gaps open for refugees to escape to the south. By April 21 the Greek Army was finished, and by the end of the month those British and Commonwealth units which had reached the southern ports were being hastily evacuated, mostly to Crete.

☆ **The Raschid Ali revolt.** At the outbreak of war the King of Iraq was only four years old, his uncle, the pro-British Amir Abdul Illah, acting as Regent. But the Prime Minister was Raschid Ali el Gailani, strongly pro-Italian and a confrère of the violently anti-British Grand Mufti of Jerusalem, in exile from Palestine. On April 3 Raschid Ali staged a *coup d'état* and as a result the position of British civilians in Baghdad became critical, the majority taking refuge in the British Embassy.

Far more exposed, however, were the RAF personnel, families and civilian support staff at the cantonment of Habbaniyah where there was a flying school, aircraft depot with repair shops, fuel and ammunition stores and a hospital. At the end of April about 1,000 airmen, 1,200 Iraqi and Assyrian levies, 300 men of the King's Own Royal Regiment and about 9,000 civilians were quartered there; and on the morning of April 30 came news that large bodies of Iraqi troops were leaving Baghdad in their direction.

Shortly afterwards an Iraqi officer arrived at Habbaniyah with a demand that all flying from the base should cease forthwith and that no one should attempt to leave, and by the afternoon it was evident that an attempt would soon be made to occupy – and certainly to place under siege – the entire station.

3 Collapse of Italian Resistance. With Diredawa in South African hands the next Italian resistance could be expected along the line of the Awash river, the only obstacle before the Ethiopian capital, Addis Ababa. Two brigades, one South African, the other East African, took up the pursuit of the Diredawa garrison, and moved so fast that they got there first. It took the East Africans a day to cross the river – one of the widest in the country, but the engineers quickly threw a bridge across – and now Addis Ababa was only 150 miles away.

At this point the Duke of Aosta decided not to defend the capital, though he left the city himself with the bulk of the garrison, to move to Amba Alagi in the mountains to the north where he intended to set up a fortress. As a result, on April 5 a frantic police messenger arrived at advanced South African positions with an urgent appeal that they move to Addis Ababa immediately. They were there to take control the following morning, having advanced 1,700 miles in 8 weeks across some of the most difficult terrain in the world.

In the meantime, the forces under Major Wingate and Colonel Sandford, who had brought the Emperor, Haile Selassie, into the country in January, were operating in the bend of the Blue Nile south of Lake Tana. 'Gideon Force' as it was called consisted mostly of Ethiopian and Sudanese troops, and Wingate's achievement in keeping them together and fighting was remarkable.

In late March the Italian commander in the area saw that he had a considerable force under his command in Debra Markos and two more brigades in Bahrdar Giorgis; and the Emperor and Gideon Force were somewhere between them. He therefore ordered a converging attack, to be supported by several thousand fierce Ethiopian warriors under a rebellious chieftain, Ras Hailu. In the circumstances, the wise course for Wingate to have followed would have been to retreat as quickly as possible. Instead, he split his force into two and attacked the Italian columns. By April 4, the Italians were in total disarray, Ras Hailu's warriors had returned precipitately to their villages, and Gideon Force took Debra Markos. A month later the Emperor re-entered his capital almost exactly five years after he had left it.

By then, the last stages of the Ethiopian campaign were in progress. Among mountain peaks between 10,000 and 12,000 feet high, in bitter cold and rain in some of the most spectacular scenery in Africa, two thrusts were converging on the Duke of Aosta's last stronghold, at Amba Alagi. In Eritrea, the vital port of Massawa had been occupied on April 8, and then 5th Indian Division left Asmara and began the drive south; from Addis Ababa the 1st South African Brigade Group moved north through an 11,000-feet-high pass, down again into the Great Rift Valley and almost immediately up towards Dessie which they took after a brisk fight on April 26. The country between both thrusts, however, was now to slow them down far more than any opposition the Italian forces were likely to put up.

Far to the south, a similar convergence of thrusts was taking place, as South African forces drove up from Neghelli and down from Addis Ababa to meet at Shashamanna. Though large areas of this immense and mountainous country would remain for months beyond British or South African control, it was now evident that all the main communication and supply routes were in their hands. Haile Selassie's empire had been returned to him.

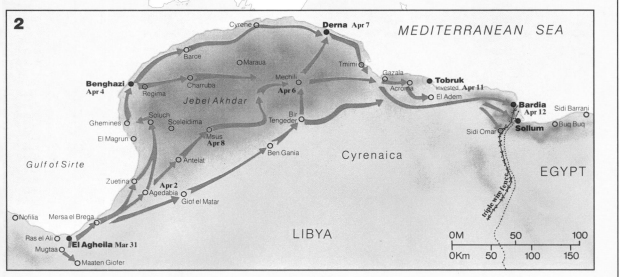

Apr 21 Japanese occupy Foochow
Foochow

Apr 27 British, Dutch and US conference in Singapore

quickly concluded that the battle was out of British control, most of XIII Corps being either left behind or about to be cut off between Rommel's three prongs. He sent for O'Connor to come out and try to exercise some control, left to return to Cairo but was forced down in the desert and eventually arrived more by luck than good judgement.

In the meantime, Rommel had driven around the coast to take Derna on April 7, and with Mechili also taken sent his forward units in a drive aimed south of Tobruk. By April 9 they were past El Adem, and at Bardia by April 12 with Halfaya Pass, Sollum, the Wire, and the Italian camps which *Operation Compass* had reduced in December, only a few miles ahead.

But behind lay Tobruk, a haven in which the retreating and disordered British forces congregated and which very soon became a fortress. Rommel attacked it with the bulk of his forces on April 12, but ran into a barrage of accurate and heavy artillery fire which, combined with his first sandstorm, persuaded him that he must wait for more panzer strength to arrive. But he could console himself with the facts of a remarkable advance, and one vital gain. In the shambles of the British retreat General O'Connor had been taken prisoner by one of his columns.

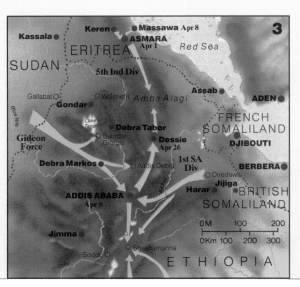

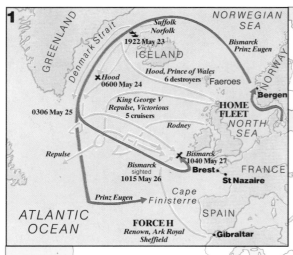

Map 1 labels: GREENLAND / NORWEGIAN SEA / Denmark Strait / Suffolk Norfolk / 1922 May 23 / ICELAND / Bismarck Prinz Eugen / ×Hood 0600 May 24 / Hood, Prince of Wales 6 destroyers / Faeroes / NORWAY / King George V Repulse, Victorious 5 cruisers / Bergen / HOME FLEET / NORTH SEA / 0306 May 25 / Rodney / Repulse / Bismarck sighted 1015 May 26 / ×Bismarck 1040 May 27 / Brest / St Nazaire / FRANCE / Prinz Eugen / Cape Finisterre / ATLANTIC OCEAN / SPAIN / FORCE H Renown, Ark Royal Sheffield / Gibraltar

1 The Cruise of the Bismarck. On the night of May 18 the most powerful ship of Germany's Kriegsmarine, the battleship *Bismarck*, accompanied by the heavy cruiser *Prinz Eugen*, left Gdynia for a raiding cruise into the Atlantic. As the British Admiralty had been expecting the move, it was not surprising that by the time the German ships were through the Skagerrak, the Commander-in-Chief of the Home Fleet at Scapa Flow, Admiral Sir John Tovey, had been informed and was making his dispositions.

Obviously, *Bismarck* and *Prinz Eugen* would have to sail up the Norwegian coast and reach the Atlantic either through the Denmark Strait or between Iceland and the Faeroes, and already there were cruisers up there on patrol. The first sighting – by HMS *Suffolk* – was at 1922 on May 23 in the Denmark Strait, and as a result two powerful forces – the battleship *Prince of Wales* with the battle-cruiser *Hood* and six destroyers, and Tovey's main force of the battleship *King George V* and the aircraft-carrier *Victorious* with a full cruiser and destroyer escort – put on speed to race across, south of Iceland, to intercept their quarry.

Shortly after 0530 on the morning of May 24, Vice-Admiral Holland aboard HMS *Hood* reported that the German ships were in sight and at 0552 *Hood*'s guns fired the first salvo, joined minutes later by those of the *Prince of Wales*. Two minutes later, *Bismarck* and *Prinz Eugen* replied; both ships' fire concentrated on *Hood* which was hit by a shell on the upper deck, starting a fire which enveloped the midship section in smoke.

The fifth salvo from *Bismarck* also hit the *Hood*, at a range of 19,000 yards with such a steep angle of descent that the salvo crashed through *Hood*'s deck, burst in a magazine and caused an explosion which blew the ship apart. Within minutes there was nothing to show of *Hood*'s existence but a cloud of smoke over the sea, and three survivors swimming below.

Prince of Wales turned away, as she had been hit, joined the shadowing cruisers and reported to Admiral Tovey, still some 300 miles away. By this time the Admiralty had ordered Force H at Gibraltar to join the search, and the aircraft-carrier *Ark Royal* with HMS *Renown* and HMS *Sheffield* were on their way up.

Aboard *Bismarck* the commander, Admiral Lütjens, now decided that his only course was somehow to throw off the shadowers and make for Brest, where it would be possible to repair some of the damage his ship had suffered from three hits during the action. During the night which followed, *Bismarck* was found by Swordfish aircraft from the *Victorious* and hit again, amidships, by a torpedo. This confirmed Lütjens in his resolution, so he detached *Prinz Eugen* with orders to turn back northwards, and himself took *Bismarck* on to the south.

By 0605 on the morning of May 25, to the frustration and fury of the British, it looked as though Lütjens's tactics had succeeded for the German ship had disappeared from their radar screens. A wide net was spread and every Allied ship in the vicinity was called upon for help, but had it not been for a long signal sent by Lütjens to Hitler, describing his action against the *Hood*, he might well have escaped. As it was, his position was at last pinpointed, though both Tovey's force and Force H seemed too far away to catch her.

The night of May 25/26 was spent by both sides in some anxiety, but in the morning RAF Coastal Command joined the search and at 1036 *Bismarck* was seen by a Catalina, and a few minutes afterwards a flight of Swordfish from *Ark Royal* found her too – and they were never to let her go. All day they shadowed her, reporting her position and speed to both Tovey and Admiral Somerville with Force H, now between *Bismarck* and the French coast. That evening at 1910, 15 torpedo-carrying Swordfish took off from *Ark Royal* and delivered an attack on the *Bismarck*, scoring two hits; one was not serious but the other on the starboard quarter wrecked her steering-gear, jammed her rudders and sealed her fate.

All night long, in a howling gale, *Bismarck*'s crew laboured to repair the damage, but when morning came the British battleships were closing in. HMS *Rodney* had joined the force and at 0847 fired the first salvo, which was followed minutes later by those of *King George V. Bismarck*'s crew fought while they could, but by 1000 her main armament was silent, and torpedoes finally sunk her at 1040. Of her crew of 2,300 only 115 survived.

Map (Europe, box 1) labels: Kiel, Hanover, Hamburg, Cologne, Bremen and Mannheim; Brest / May 10/11 Rudolf Hess, Hitler's deputy, flies to Scotland / Liverpool, Belfast, Clydeside, Hull and London (Houses of Parliament) / Malta constantly bombed / May 6 US Secretary for War advocates naval protection for supplies to Britain / May 25 Italian E-boats penetrate Gibraltar harbour / Derna and Benghazi / May 4 Hitler proclaims 'Reich to last a thousand years' / May 31 Growing German infiltration into Syria evident / May 25 Greek Government and King reach Egypt

Map 2 labels: Peloponnese / Milos / Stampalia / Nisiros / Cape Matapan / Thera / Anafi / Tilos / Kithira / May 22 German convoy attacked / Dodecanese / Khalki / Greyhound and Gloucester May 22 / Sea of Crete / Cape Spatha / May 21/22 German convoy attacked / Scarpanto / Imperial May 29 / Kastello / Canea / Suda Bay / Kasos / Maleme / Retimo / HERAKLION / Kastellion / Hereward May 29 / Sfakia / Crete / Cape Lithinon / 0M 50 100 / 0Km 50 100 150 / Fiji May 22 / Kashmir and Kelly May 23 / Gavdhos / to Alexandria / May 19 last fighters withdrawn / to Alexandria / Juno May 21

2 The Battle for Crete. Once the last survivors of the retreat through Greece had arrived, preparations began for the defence of Crete, as it was obvious to everyone that the island would be the next target of Hitler's aggression. Wounded, unfit and non-combatant were evacuated to Egypt, and Maj-General Bernard Freyberg, VC, deployed his forces.

Two brigades of his own New Zealanders he posted around the vital airfield at Maleme with three Greek battalions in support; in the Suda Bay area he sent a British, an Australian and a Greek battalion to support the existing Naval Defence Party; to Retimo he sent 5 battalions – 2 Greek and 3 Australian – with their machine-gunners; and to Heraklion he sent 2 British battalions, 2 Greek, 1 Australian and the men of an artillery regiment but with only their rifles. By May 7 15,000 British, 6,500 Australian, 7,750 New Zealanders and 10,200 Greeks were in position, training – and digging. From Egypt towards the end of the month one more British battalion, 22 tanks and 49 guns were sent to aid the defences at Heraklion.

Operation Merkur was launched at dawn on May 20, after a thorough strafing of all Allied positions by the Luftwaffe. The waiting defenders saw a huge fleet of transport planes coming towards them and as they arrived overhead, thousands of parachutes blossomed in the sky above Maleme and Canea; the battle for Suda Bay began. During the afternoon a second wave dropped over Retimo and Heraklion, seaborne forces were due to arrive off Maleme that evening in support and more the

following morning off Heraklion. The German plan called for a drive from both directions to take control of Suda Bay, after which panzers would flood ashore. Some 22,750 élite German troops were to go to Crete, mostly by air.

Although the airborne landings went well, by the end of the day it seemed to General Student, their commander, that his men were being beaten – almost solely by the remarkable shooting of the New Zealand and Australian infantry, many of them farmers who had used rifles and shot-guns since childhood. Only the parachute units who had been dropped away from the main targets were landing safely, the rest being decimated before they reached the ground.

One such lucky unit had been dropped so far west of Maleme that none of the parachutists even came under fire, so they assembled and marched towards the sound of battle, arriving at the edge of Maleme after dark and just in time to help fight off a New Zealand counter-attack. Their success put new heart into the German paratroops on the airfield, and worried the New Zealand battalion commander, Lt-Colonel Andrew, VC, DSO, whose radio set had broken down. Realising that a strong enemy force was close, and unable to make contact with two of his companies or with HQ, he withdrew in order to be in a sound position to beat off the attack which he was sure would come with dawn. In doing so, he left unoccupied a corner of Maleme airfield.

It is not too much to say that this tiny movement lost the

MAY
1941

4 Defeat of Raschid Ali. Despite the inexperience of the pupils at the Habbaniyah flying school, by the evening of May 1 they had carried out sufficient reconnaissance to be able to report the presence in the surrounding desert of at least two Iraqi infantry battalions, with supporting artillery. At dawn on May 2 the heavier machines, augmented by eight Wellingtons flown up from Shaiba, were out bombing and strafing Iraqi positions, to be met by scattered rifle and machine-gun fire which was later followed by sporadic shelling of the cantonment.

During the afternoon and the next two days the pattern was similar, but planes of the Iraqi Air Force joined in to shoot down and kill five of the flying school pupils. The investing force had now been brought up to brigade strength.

But each night the men of the King's Own Royal Regiment had gone out on wide-ranging patrols, and had not been in any way weakened or deterred by their encounters with the Iraqi Army. They were not very surprised when at dawn on May 6 they discovered that a large part of the brigade had disappeared, leaving the ground dotted with abandoned equipment which was dragged into Habbaniyah and put to good use.

That afternoon they chased and caught up with Iraqi columns streaming back towards Baghdad, and helped them on their way in two brisk actions, so by evening it was evident that the siege was over.

But Habbaniyah was still an isolated garrison 200 miles inside Iraq, and British civilians were still penned inside the embassy buildings in Baghdad. Two brigades of 10th Indian Division were despatched to Basra by sea, and a flying column hastily cobbled together in Palestine under Brigadier J.J. Kingstone to go to their relief. The column crossed the Iraqi frontier on May 13, was attacked by German fighters, diverted by floods caused by the destruction of bunds as they approached Lake Habbaniyah, and slowed by deep and soft sand out of which they had to dig their heavy lorries, often in temperatures as high as 120 degrees Fahrenheit.

Nevertheless, they reached Fallujah on May 19, by which time the 10th Indian brigades were at Basra, and during the next few days details of advances on Baghdad from both west and south-east were worked out. However, during this phase rumours reached Baghdad grossly exaggerating the size of the approaching forces, both of which were reported as containing an unknown but vast number of the latest British tanks – at which Raschid Ali's nerve broke and he and his supporters fled to Persia.

The Allied troops arrived on May 31, the Armistice was signed the same day and Amir Abdul Illah flew back to be reinstated as Regent. The Raschid Ali revolt was over.

May 14 Large British contingent arrives at Singapore

3 Operation Brevity. Reaction in Berlin to Rommel's remarkable advance was mixed. Hitler was delighted, General Halder, Chief of the General Staff, sceptical – to the point where he sent an emissary, Generalleutnant Friedrich Paulus, to observe and report. In due course Paulus signalled back to Berlin that Rommel's forces were grossly over-stretched, that they should concentrate further back, aim at holding the Jebel Akhdar country only as far forward as Gazala or even Mechili, and make no great effort to hold Sollum, Bardia or even Tobruk.

As the Ultra decoding organisation at Bletchley Park read this signal almost as soon as did Wehrmacht HQ, the British reaction was predictable. If the German Command felt that Rommel's forces were too far east, then the lightest push should be enough to send them back far enough for the ring around Tobruk to be removed, and the garrison brought out.

Operation Brevity began at dawn on May 15, and it soon became evident that neither Rommel nor his local commander, Oberst von Herff, were either aware of or in agreement with the conclusions drawn by Paulus.

The British attack was commanded by Brigadier Gott, who sent an infantry battalion supported by artillery along the coast

road to take the post at the bottom of Halfaya Pass, then to push along to Sollum and up the pass there to take Musaid Barracks at the top.

Along the top of the escarpment infantry of 22nd Guards Brigade were to march parallel, accompanied by 24 Matilda tanks with which they would take the post at the top of Halfaya, capture Fort Capuzzo and drive towards Bardia, while outside them and forming a shield to the south an Armoured Brigade Group would cross the Wire, drive over Hafid Ridge and make for the area of Sidi Azeiz, perhaps to exploit even further towards Tobruk.

The two infantry columns ran into trouble from the start. It took the coast group practically all day to capture their first objective at the bottom of Halfaya, and the battle which developed around Fort Capuzzo reached a pitch of intensity new to that particular area. By 0200 on May 16 the Guards Brigade and their remaining Matildas were back on the Halfaya Pass line, those infantry who had reached Capuzzo had been driven back with heavy loss to Musaid, and Gott was well aware of the vulnerability of all his forces above the escarpment

Allies the Battle of Crete. By noon on May 21 so many more German paratroops had dropped safely, so many gliders come in, so many Ju-52s had crash-landed on the slowly expanded space, that overwhelming strength had been packed into it. In the afternoon it burst out, and the Fallschirmjäger could follow Student's orders to 'Roll up Crete from the west.'

Five days of bitter action were to follow, but Freyberg soon realised that whereas German reinforcements and supplies were flooding in, his own strength was being inexorably whittled away. On May 26 he gave orders for a withdrawal across the mountains to the south coast, asking the navy to stand by to evacuate all who could reach the village of Sfakia.

A commando battalion was landed there to form a perimeter through which the exhausted survivors of Freyberg's command made their painful way, and between May 27 and 31 the navy lifted off nearly 14,000 men. But the navy paid a high price for their co-operation in the Battle of Crete, losing altogether 3 cruisers and 6 destroyers, two of the ships on a further evacuation from Retimo and Heraklion.

For the German forces, it proved a somewhat Pyrrhic victory. Of the 8,500 paratroops dropped, 3,764 had been killed, mostly on the first day, and so many aircraft had been shot down or crash-landed that Hitler declared that the Wehrmacht could never afford such an operation again.

should Herff receive armoured reinforcement.

This appeared at Sidi Azeiz a few hours later, its mere presence enough to cause the withdrawal of the Armoured Brigade Group, many of whose elderly cruiser tanks had already broken down, even more showing signs of being about to do so.

By the morning of May 17, the Afrika Korps had cleared the area west of a line running south from Sollum to Sidi Suleiman then across to Sidi Omar, and although the British now held Halfaya Pass, their grasp did not seem unbreakable. On May 27 Herff sent panzers and infantry out from both Sollum and Capuzzo and retook both upper and lower Halfaya posts.

Generalleutnant Rommel and his forces had to be taken much more seriously.

45

Barbarossa

The German invasion of the Soviet Union in June 1941 presented the most dramatic military spectacle the world had seen since the events of August 1914, and its intention was of even wider scope than that behind the Schlieffen Plan which had thrown the Kaiser's armies into Belgium and France.

'When Barbarossa is launched,' Hitler declared, 'the whole world will hold its breath!' – and the forces he assembled along the Russian frontier from the Baltic to the Black Sea during that early summer of 1941 represented the greatest concentration of military force in history.

Nearly 3,000,000 men, 3,200 tanks and 7,500 guns formed the 75 infantry divisions, 17 panzer divisions and 13 motorised divisions which would comprise the first wave, while 26 more infantry, another motorised and 2 more panzer divisions waited in immediate reserve. Stretching back in a band 100 miles wide along the whole length of the front were stores dumps, fuel and ammunition reserves calculated to feed the huge force over a 400-mile advance, while 500,000 lorries waited in massed parks from East Prussia down to Rumania – augmented by 600,000 horses and all their accoutrements and stabling – to rush it forward on demand.

This monumental military assembly was divided into three Army Groups, each with a distinct target and operational axis. Their deployment was dictated by one inescapable geographic factor – the Pripet Marshes, a vast and apparently bottomless swamp nearly 100 miles from north to south and 300 miles from east to west, which divides Belorussia from the Ukraine, and thus formed a formidable barrier almost in the middle of the invasion front.

The Barbarossa planners, therefore, had had to accept that there could be little or no contact during the early stages of the operation between the two Army Groups in the northern sector of the attack front, and Army Group South aimed into the Ukraine. It was with the two northern groups that the main weight of Barbarossa lay, Army Group North aimed up through the Baltic states of Lithuania, Latvia and Esthonia – which only the previous year had been occupied by Russia – first to Lake Peipus and then on towards Leningrad, Army Group Centre aimed due east through Belorussia first to Smolensk, and then (at least in the minds of the military) at Moscow.

Army Group North under Field Marshal von Leeb consisted of two infantry armies, the Sixteenth and the Eighteenth (17 divisions between them) and the 4th Panzergruppe with 3 panzer divisions, 3 motorised divisions and 3 infantry divisions, with 3 more infantry divisions held in reserve. Army Group Centre under the icily aristocratic Field Marshal von Bock also consisted of 2 infantry armies, the Ninth and the Fourth, but these held between them 23 divisions and were supported by 2 Panzergruppen, the 2nd and the 3rd, between them deploying 9 panzer divisions, 7 motorised and 7 infantry divisions, the 2nd Panzergruppe also contained a cavalry division. These were the units whose commanders intended to reduce Napoleon's feat of 129 years before to historical obscurity, for their leaders – especially General Heinz Guderian commanding 2nd Panzergruppe – intended to reach Moscow in eight weeks, annihilating the Soviet Army in the process.

Army Group South was commanded by Field Marshal Gerd von Rundstedt – 'der Alte' (the Old One) as Hitler respectfully referred to him even in the days of his later enforced retirement – and considering the enormous width of the Front this was the weakest of the groups. Along the northern 600 miles, von Rundstedt had the 18 infantry, 5 panzer and 3 motorised divisions of Sixth and Seventeenth Infantry Armies and First

Panzergruppe, with 5 more infantry divisions in reserve. Further south lay the 7 infantry divisions of the Eleventh Army, flanked by 14 Rumanian divisions, an Hungarian army corps and an Italian army corps – the latter all armed with almost obsolete rifles and machine-guns and equipped with the barest minimum of artillery and transport.

The Ukraine was Army Group South's immediate target with an advance on the far right through Bessarabia – also recently occupied by the Red Army – and on the far right along the Black Sea coast towards the Crimea. The flat rolling wheatlands before the main advance would make the task relatively easy, only the huge distances to be covered by the marching infantry posing difficulties, but the prime task – in the eyes of the Wehrmacht planners – would be to keep up with the central thrust north of the Pripet, to guard their right flank.

Above and in front of the three Army Groups would fly the fighters, bombers and reconnaissance aircraft of three Luftflotten – 775 bombers, 310 dive-bombers, 830 single-engined and 90 twin-engined fighters, 710 reconnaissance aircraft and 55 seaplanes to operate on either flank.

One of the tasks assigned to a few selected aircrews was to drop highly trained saboteurs and assault paratroops into the Soviet rear. Operating close behind the Soviet Front, they would create havoc and confusion amongst Soviet signal and command centres, some of them dressed in Russian uniforms establishing themselves at crossroads to add to the chaos by mis-directing traffic. With them would arrive the 'Brandenburg Units' who were to be shunted behind Soviet lines on the Bug river hidden in rail-trucks carrying gravel to attack special targets such as bridges, blow in tunnels, rip up railway lines. Operating with them would be a regiment of anti-Communist Ukrainians in the south, while up in the Baltic States so recently occupied by the Soviets, several resistance groups had been set up by German intelligence and were waiting to co-operate with them as soon as Army Group North moved forward.

Far more sinister than any of these formations, however, were those of the SS which had been the recipients of the 'Instructions on Special Matters' issued on March 13, 1941. This laid down the areas of activity wherein Reichsführer Himmler's edicts would run with complete freedom – in order 'finally to settle the conflict between the two opposing political systems'. For Operation Barbarossa was not merely an invasion of another country's land space; it was Hitler's personal 'crusade against Bolshevism' in which no hint of chivalry or compassion may alleviate the brutalities of warfare – a deliberate war of extermination of political opposition, together with the reduction of the surviving mass of Slav Untermenschen to a condition of slavery subject to bestial exploitation.

The notorious Commissar Order by which all Bolshevik Commissars and Communist intelligentsia would be shot out of hand was promulgated in a speech by Hitler on March 30, and would be carried out by specially appointed SS murder squads – later of course to continue their activities as the dreaded Einsatzgruppen who combed the prison camps for Jews, 'political enemies' and 'undesirables' – consisting of four groups of about 800 'specialists'. For the exploitation of all captured Russian industrial or agricultural resources, several agencies – and their executive forces – were set up as a result of competition between the various Nazi satraps. Göring, Rosenberg and Himmler to name but three, organised teams ranging from 1,000 to 10,000 'economic specialists' whose duties would be ruthlessly to dismantle every Soviet organisation capable of production of any type of useful material and tranship it

back to Germany if possible, or otherwise simply destroy it.

But these latter, of course, were not the strike elements of Operation Barbarossa. These were the massed forces of the German Wehrmacht now concentrated along the Soviet border, the hammer with which Hitler intended to smash Bolshevism – prodigious in size, formidable in technique, as experienced as any fighting force in the Western world.

There was another factor to help Operation Barbarossa on its way. It would be launched against forces badly deployed, of uncertain morale, ineptly commanded in vital areas – and totally unaware of its peril.

On paper, 132 divisions manned the defences opposite the three German Army Groups – 77 rifle divisions, 13 motorised divisions, 34 tank divisions and 8 cavalry divisions.

They were held in four 'Special Military Districts'. Baltic District consisted of three armies – Eighth, Twenty-seventh and Eleventh – with 17 rifle, 3 motorised and 6 tank divisions; Western District (facing Army Group Centre) consisted of four armies – Third, Fourth, Tenth and Thirteenth – with 20 rifle, 3 motorised, 10 tank and 3 cavalry divisions; Kiev District consisted of 5 armies – Fifth, Sixth, Twelfth, Eighteenth and Twenty-sixth – with 31 rifle, 6 motorised, 16 tank and 3 cavalry divisions; while Odessa District consisted of just one army – Ninth – 9 rifle, 1 motorised, 2 tank and 2 cavalry divisions.

Had all these divisions been up to strength, nearly 2,000,000 Russian soldiers, some 20,000 tanks and at least 12,000 aircraft would have been in position to repel the German invaders, but despite warnings from Britain and the United States, Stalin refused to believe in the possibility of Hitler breaking the non-aggression pact signed in 1939 (or at least, not so soon) and on his orders the Red Army in the west was specifically deployed not to offer the slightest provocation to the Germans. Thus many of the advanced formations were as much as 40 miles from the border, while one entire corps in the Brest-Litovsk area was scattered in summer training camps throughout Belorussia, some of its units separated by 200 miles and with only rudimentary communications.

Moreover, the army in what would prove to be the most vital sector in the days to come – the Tenth, in Western District – was deployed in a manner almost to invite encirclement. It was crammed up in a salient jutting into German-occupied Poland west of Bialystok in such a manner that when caught in the pincers of von Bock's Panzergruppen it would have no room for manoeuvre in any direction.

But Stalin's responsibility for the imminent destruction of such a large part of the Soviet forces was not confined just to the errors of their local deployment. Over the past four years he had deliberately weakened the Red Army, reducing it from a condition in 1936 when it could fairly claim to be one of the finest armies in the world, to one bereft of first-class military talent in its higher echelons and dominated by a fear throughout all its ranks which bred apathy, inertia and avoidance of any vestige of responsibility; for in 1937 it had appeared to Stalin's assuredly distorted vision as the only possible curb to his assumption of total power.

During 1935 and 1936 he had ruthlessly and methodically removed from power – most often with the rifle – all those old Bolshevik comrades whose reputations as important figures in the Revolution competed with or overshadowed his own. Piatakov, Radek the Marxist theoretician, and many others had been shot after patently rigged public trials, and other famous Bolsheviks had disappeared including Bukharin, a former Secretary-General of the Communist

International and close associate of Lenin, Rykov, Lenin's successor as Premier, and even Yagoda who for years had been the People's Commissar for Internal Affairs – Supreme Head of the NKVD, today's KGB. (They were all to be shot after another series of ludicrous public trials in 1938.)

In 1937 he had turned his attention to the Red Army. In the early years of the Revolution, Stalin had himself been connected with the Red Army's First Cavalry Army, and the men who had led them – ex-Sergeant-Major of Dragoons Budenny, Commissar Voroshilov, Marshal Timoshenko – were his men, men who owed something of their prestige to his patronage. But the younger, more progressive and scientific soldiers who since then had converted the Red Army from a swashbuckling force to keep Kulaks in their place into a formidable army to face such foreign threats as that posed by the German Wehrmacht, had risen by their own merits and had at times cast doubt upon his own military expertise and even his right to exercise it.

Men like Marshals Tukhachevsky and Blyukher – ex-Tsarist officers of professional standing – and Generals Alksnis, Yakir and Uborevich, had studied the works of theorists of tank warfare and in that light had developed a concept of a modern mechanised army, with tank divisions acting in concert with their own artillery and close air support; and they owed nothing to Stalin. They were thus the objects of his deep suspicion, and were among the first to be charged with a long catalogue of ludicrous crimes ranging from gross inefficiency and corruption to running an espionage network of devilish ingenuity for all the Western governments, and after the briefest of trials, found guilty and shot.

During 1937 and 1938 three of the five Marshals of the Soviet Union, 11 deputy commissars of defence, 13 out of 15 army commanders and all the military district commanders were shot or disappeared without trace . . . and some 35,000 officers of lesser rank were dismissed, imprisoned or executed. Thus by 1941, every serving officer had seen comrades vanish without warning or trial, and knew it could happen to him; the only hope of survival for any of them lay in slavish obedience to orders and the avoidance of any display of enterprise or initiative.

It was this abnegation of the prime military virtues that had brought about the dire performance of the Red Army during the Winter War against Finland, and this itself had produced even worse conditions by 1941. In the aftermath of the débâcle, Stalin had laid the blame entirely on the army and insisted on a new draconian code of discipline reminiscent of that in the old Imperial Army which increased even further the atmosphere of fear and dread. He appointed Marshal Timoshenko as Commissar for Defence with orders to institute throughout all Soviet forces a system of absolute obedience based on absolute fear. In such circumstances, only time-servers and sycophants could rise to the top, and genuine talent – and time was to prove that the Red Army was by no means short in this regard – was in hiding.

Nevertheless, some of the more glaring faults in the system had been recognised during the Finnish conflict, and Timoshenko was attempting to put them right. The establishment of armoured divisions was to replace the practice of parcelling out tank formations among rifle divisions, and the formation of 'artillery divisions' – concentrations of guns of all calibres at the disposal of front-line commanders for special tasks – was being considered. These were changes which should have been made over a two or three year period – but some had been started only a few months before, thus adding to the confusion and disarray of the army which had now to withstand the greatest onslaught in history.

Even though the Soviet Union possessed almost limitless manpower and her factories could certainly produce simple and robust weapons by the million, it is almost impossible to see how her armies could have been less prepared for the trials immediately ahead.

Hitler's declaration 'We have only to kick in the front door and the whole rotten Russian edifice will come tumbling down!' seemed only too well justified.

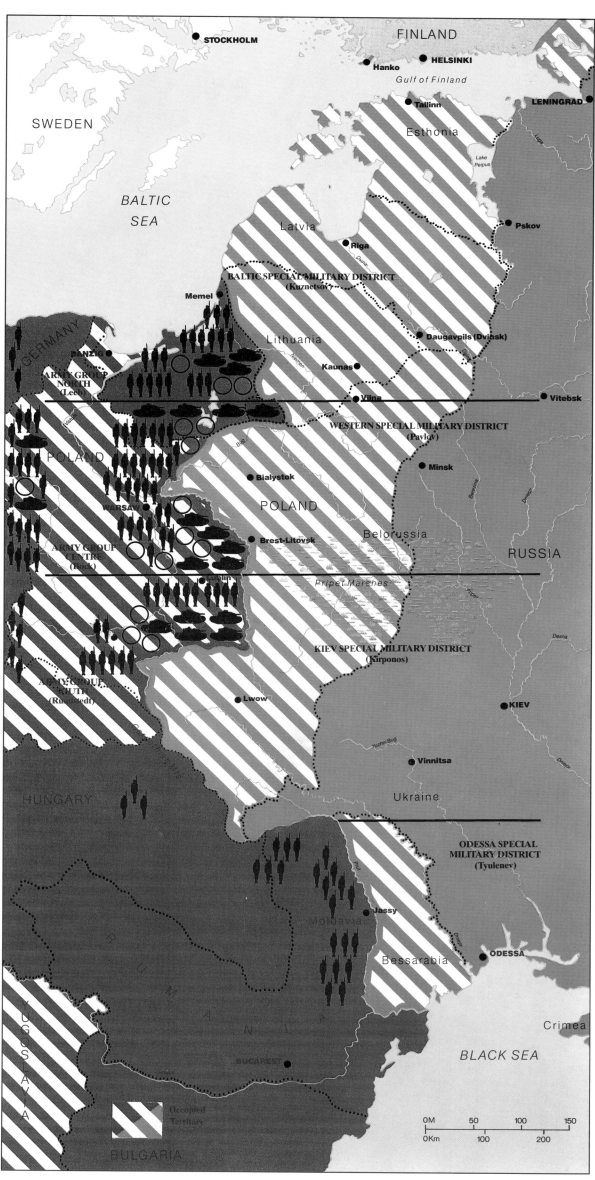

47

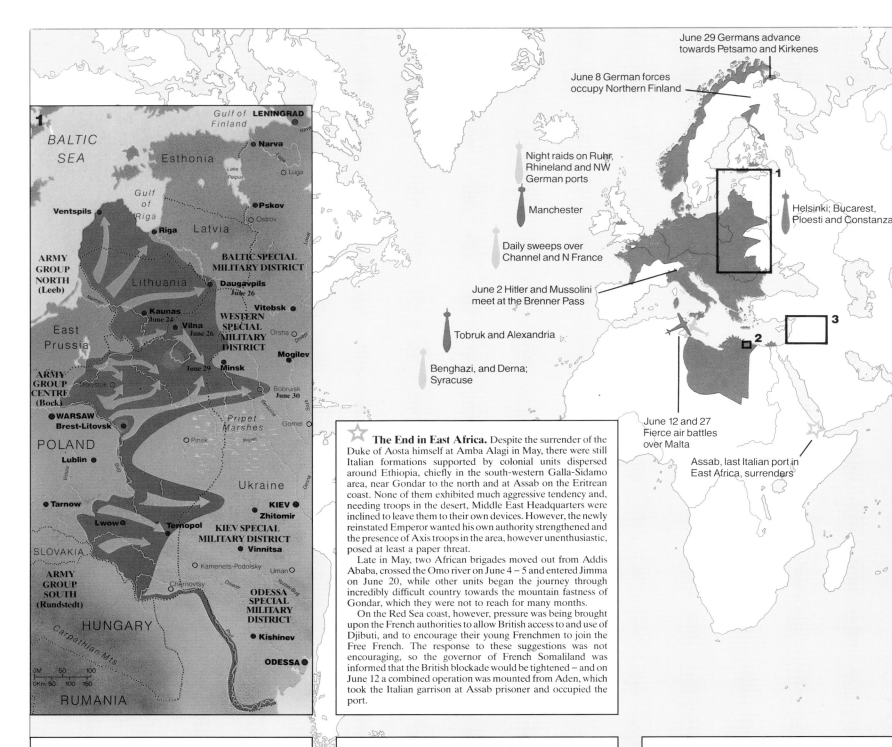

June 29 Germans advance towards Petsamo and Kirkenes

June 8 German forces occupy Northern Finland

Night raids on Ruhr, Rhineland and NW German ports

Manchester

Daily sweeps over Channel and N France

June 2 Hitler and Mussolini meet at the Brenner Pass

Tobruk and Alexandria

Benghazi, and Derna; Syracuse

Helsinki; Bucarest, Ploesti and Constanza

June 12 and 27 Fierce air battles over Malta

Assab, last Italian port in East Africa, surrenders

Map 1 labels: Gulf of Finland, LENINGRAD, BALTIC SEA, Esthonia, Narva, Luga, Ventspils, Gulf of Riga, Pskov, Ostrov, Riga, Latvia, ARMY GROUP NORTH (Leeb), Lithuania, Daugavpils June 26, Vitebsk, Kaunas June 24, WESTERN SPECIAL MILITARY DISTRICT, Vilna June 26, Orsha, East Prussia, Mogilev, ARMY GROUP CENTRE (Bock), June 29, Minsk, Bobrusk June 30, Gomel, WARSAW, Brest-Litovsk, Pripet Marshes, Pinsk, Pripet, POLAND, Lublin, Ukraine, Tarnow, KIEV, Zhitomir, Lwow, Ternopol, KIEV SPECIAL MILITARY DISTRICT, Vinnitsa, SLOVAKIA, Kamenets-Podolsky, Uman, Chernovtsy, ARMY GROUP SOUTH (Rundstedt), ODESSA SPECIAL MILITARY DISTRICT, HUNGARY, Carpathian Mts, Kishinev, ODESSA, RUMANIA, 0M 50 100, 0Km 50 100 150

☆ **The End in East Africa.** Despite the surrender of the Duke of Aosta himself at Amba Alagi in May, there were still Italian formations supported by colonial units dispersed around Ethiopia, chiefly in the south-western Galla-Sidamo area, near Gondar to the north and at Assab on the Eritrean coast. None of them exhibited much aggressive tendency and, needing troops in the desert, Middle East Headquarters were inclined to leave them to their own devices. However, the newly reinstated Emperor wanted his own authority strengthened and the presence of Axis troops in the area, however unenthusiastic, posed at least a paper threat.

Late in May, two African brigades moved out from Addis Ababa, crossed the Omo river on June 4–5 and entered Jimma on June 20, while other units began the journey through incredibly difficult country towards the mountain fastness of Gondar, which they were not to reach for many months.

On the Red Sea coast, however, pressure was being brought upon the French authorities to allow British access to and use of Djibuti, and to encourage their young Frenchmen to join the Free French. The response to these suggestions was not encouraging, so the governor of French Somaliland was informed that the British blockade would be tightened – and on June 12 a combined operation was mounted from Aden, which took the Italian garrison at Assab prisoner and occupied the port.

1 Barbarossa – The Shock. At 0135 on the morning of Sunday, June 22, the giant arc of the Soviet land frontier from East Prussia down through the Ukraine to the Black Sea burst into rippling flame and thunder as massed German batteries opened fire on the Soviet defences. To the unfortunate rank and file in the Soviet forward positions it might not have come as a total surprise for they had watched the preparations over the last weeks. Although much of the details of the Wehrmacht preparation had been well concealed, staff officers had been reporting events to their seniors in increasingly worried tones – to be told that they must not panic and at all costs, under threat of condign punishment, to avoid 'provocation'. No advancing German soldiers were to be fired on, no Luftwaffe plane shot at, no artillery barrage replied to. On that fateful morning Red Army communications were prime targets for artillery fire, Luftwaffe bombing and especially sabotage by the Brandenburger Regiment's 800 men; so it was not until nearly 0600, after Foreign Minister Molotov had read the missive just handed to him by the German ambassador to Moscow, von Schulenburg, that full realisation of the Soviet plight was accepted by Stalin and his henchmen.

In the meantime, Timoshenko could only read what signals were arriving with a mixture of horror and incredulity. Neither he nor Stalin as yet appreciated the extent of the havoc on their frontiers; there the commanders of formations as high as corps or even armies could do nothing but watch the destruction and chaos, occasionally getting through to some higher formation to receive back the single order, 'Wait!'

At last, at 0715, a directive was issued from Moscow. It informed the Red Army that an 'unjustified attack' had been made upon them by Germany, and ordered the soldiers to attack the enemy with all means at their disposal and to drive them back over the frontier. They were not themselves to cross the frontier line.

Having issued it, and then at noon authorised a limping announcement of the situation to the Russian people as a whole, Stalin removed himself from the public gaze for 11 days.

In that time the progress of the Wehrmacht on every front had been so spectacular that even the wary and sceptical Chief of

the Army General Staff, General Halder, expressed admiration and surprise.

Army Group North had brushed aside all opposition met on the first day and advanced 37 miles into Lithuania by evening. By early morning on June 26 7th Panzer Division had reached the Dvina river on both sides of Daugavpils, captured the two river bridges there intact and by evening the city itself was in their hands. This first objective of Army Group North had therefore been achieved in five days, and by the end of the month the entire XLI Panzer Corps had arrived to the north of Daugavpils to link up with 7th Panzer Division to form a bridgehead across the river. The supply base for the next bound forward was thus secure.

On the left flank of this dramatic advance, Eighteenth Army was doing just as well. Roads through the Baltic States were in better condition than those in Russia itself and both Ventspils and Riga were taken by June 29, giving the Wehrmacht control of the Baltic coast as far east as the mouth of the Dvina and the length of the river across the whole of Latvia itself.

Army Group Centre was enjoying a success just as spectacular, if not more so. The first task for Guderian's Second Panzergruppe had been to cross the Bug on both sides of the fortress of Brest-Litovsk, to capture it and then drive forward towards the city of Minsk, curving up to it from the south to meet the spearheads of Hoth's Third Panzergruppe coming down from the north. Thus would the Soviet forces – especially the Tenth Army in the Bialystok salient – be trapped and forced to surrender in due course.

Guderian himself crossed the Bug river before dawn on June 22, his XXIV Corps captured all the necessary bridges intact, Brest-Litovsk was encircled (although its garrison held out resolutely for some days) and Guderian's tanks sped on 30 miles into Belorussia during that first day. By June 24 they were over 100 miles from the frontier and Guderian himself only avoided capture by his driver's swift acceleration through a group of bewildered and surprised Red Army troops. Five days later 17th Panzer Division tanks met those of Hoth's Panzergruppe just short of Minsk, and the link-up, after only five days and some 200 miles into Soviet territory, aroused

visions of Smolensk in their hands by mid-July and Moscow a month later.

But behind them they had left pockets of Soviet troops showing unprecedented reluctance to admit defeat. There were in all 27 Red Army divisions plus the Brest-Litovsk garrison now coalescing into resistance pockets between the frontier and Minsk, and in both Guderian's and Hoth's opinions the task of destroying these was assigned to the infantry of Fourth and Ninth Armies, trudging up stolidly behind them. Unfortunately, as a result of the speed of the panzers, the infantry were quite a long way behind – and the panzer specialists pleaded in vain for permission to race further on ahead.

Rundstedt's Army Group South had made as promising a start as the other two groups, although as their objectives were less prestigious they did not for the moment rivet the world's attention quite so closely. Along the southern edge of the Pripet Marshes, von Kleist's First Panzergruppe ripped through the frontier defences and then for the rest of the month had only piecemeal resistance to overcome. General Kirponos, commanding Kiev Special Military District, was concerned to block the advance as far west as possible but in order to do so had to transfer troops from all corners of his vast command, with the result that no powerful formations arrived together. With Stalin's directive in mind and the consequences of an accusation of cowardice only too clearly evident, troops were sent into action off the march – many to be killed or taken prisoner immediately, the rest to be shouldered aside into the marshes where at least the panzers could not follow them.

To Kleist's south, Stulpnagel's Seventeenth Army had driven forward across the frontier, isolated Lwow (which finally fell on June 30), then driven on to reach the outskirts of Ternopol. For marching infantry this was a remarkable feat, only made possible by the dry, hard roads in this southern sector.

Even further south, down to the Black Sea coast, Eleventh Army with the Rumanian, Hungarian and Italian formations made little attempt to do more than occupy the opposing forward defence posts, organise the advance towards Odessa, and ensure that they were at least strong enough to protect the vital Ploesti oilfields behind them.

48

JUNE
1941

Chungking

2 Battleaxe. Churchill's response to the misfortunes which dogged *Operation Brevity* had been generous; gone was the nagging which had followed the retreat into Egypt, only enquiries came as to what help he could send to the hard-pressed army in the desert. The answer was obvious and drastic; over-riding the apprehensions of his military advisers in England, he stripped the Home Defence of every tank and aeroplane which could be spared and, despite the warnings from the Admiralty, rushed them by the fast Mediterranean route to Alexandria. His courage was rewarded by the safe arrival of four out of the five transports, carrying between them 238 tanks and 43 Hurricanes. How soon could they attack Rommel's forces and drive them back, first to Tobruk and then – reinforced by the Tobruk garrison – on and deep into the Jebel Akhdar?

Despite Churchill's urging, it was not until the morning of June 15 that two brigades of 4th Indian Division accompanied by Matildas as infantry support, advanced along the top and bottom of the Escarpment to attack both ends of the Halfaya Pass; to their south, two brigades of 7th Armoured Division – many in the new Crusader tanks – advanced in a swing to the north-west to attack Fort Capuzzo and then a known defensive

position at Hafid Ridge. This was the first time the two divisions had been together since the victorious days of *Operation Compass* the previous December; but now they were fighting against Rommel's Afrika Korps, not Graziani's army.

They were also facing for the first time the remarkable 88 mm anti-tank gun well sited in deeply dug and protected positions. By 0730, 16 of the 19 Matildas accompanying the 4th Indian infantry had been blown apart and the infantry pinned down, while at Hafid Ridge the British armour was experiencing their first taste of the German armoured tactics which were to decimate them for months.

The ridge consists of three gentle crests and between them lay the German anti-tank guns, and shortly after 0900 the first wave of British tanks – elderly A-9s and A-10s – breasted the first rise to meet a blast of fire which blew up two of them and sent the rest scuttling backwards. Nearly an hour passed while a more powerful thrust was organised, and RAF reports came in of German armour streaming towards the battle area – but also of German armour on the ridge pulling back, presumably to consolidate. The Crusaders were sent forward to take advantage of this situation, and as they swept over the first crest they saw exactly what they hoped – German lorries and towed guns moving up and over the crest beyond.

In less than five minutes, the Crusaders were topping the second crest, to be met by a storm of fire from 37mm and 50mm as well as from the 88mm guns – and within seconds 11 had been destroyed and 6 more badly damaged. They had in fact been neatly ambushed by the German tactic of luring enemy armour forward on to a line of concealed anti-tank guns.

This tactic was repeated time after time, and by the end of the first day of battle British armour had been reduced to 50% of its strength.

During the following two days, although Fort Capuzzo was captured by 22nd Guards Brigade and held against all attempts by 15th Panzer Division to recapture it, the British armour to the south was continually outfought by the Panzer divisions, who either sidestepped and outmanoeuvred them, or ambushed them as before. By the evening of June 17 it was obvious that hardly sufficient armour remained to protect the surviving British and Indian infantry who must now withdraw or be captured.

The following day, Churchill received a cable from Wavell beginning 'I regret to report the failure of "Battleaxe" ', and later came the news that 122 officers and men had been killed, 588 wounded and 259 were missing. The RAF had lost 36 aircraft and 4 guns had been destroyed; and of the tanks stripped from the Home Defence, 91 had been destroyed and half of the remainder so badly damaged as to be unusable for many weeks.

It was a grievous disappointment, and it confirmed Churchill in his opinion that Wavell was not the right man for the Middle East Command. He must go – back to India where he had spent so much of his military life; his place would be taken by the present Commander-in-Chief there, General Auchinleck, for whom Churchill had great admiration.

3 Operation Exporter. Under the terms of the Armistice made with Vichy France, an Italo-German Commission had arrived in Syria charged with the task of disarming the 120,000-strong French Army of the Levant. By mid-1941 it had succeeded to the extent that the Levant Army now consisted of some 35,000 officers and men charged with keeping order and security, under the command of the violently anti-British General Dentz.

The official British position regarding Syria was simple; although Britain was not at war with Vichy France she could not allow Syria to become the centre of activities, either covert or direct, against her. Drastic plans in Whitehall for dealing with the problem by invasion and occupation of the country were given added impetus by followers of General de Gaulle, who claimed that the bulk of the Army of the Levant were eager to join the Free French. They later strengthened their case by claiming that their intelligence sources had informed them that Dentz was about to withdraw all his forces into Lebanon and hand Syria over to a German occupation force.

As a result, and despite his strongest objections, Wavell was instructed to launch Operation Exporter. On June 8 a force consisting of Australian, Indian and Free French infantry, plus two regiments of British cavalry still on their horses and a battalion of Special Service troops crossed the Palestine border and advanced towards Damascus and Beirut. Other troops in Iraq moved towards the Syrian border, but it soon became obvious that little sympathy for Free French or British intentions existed among the defending troops. These were in fact well placed to withstand the advances and the fighting was bitter, especially between French troops when they met. Nevertheless, by the end of the month, Damascus was in British hands, Beirut under threat from Australians, and troops from Iraq ('Habforce') were driving west towards Palmyra.

49

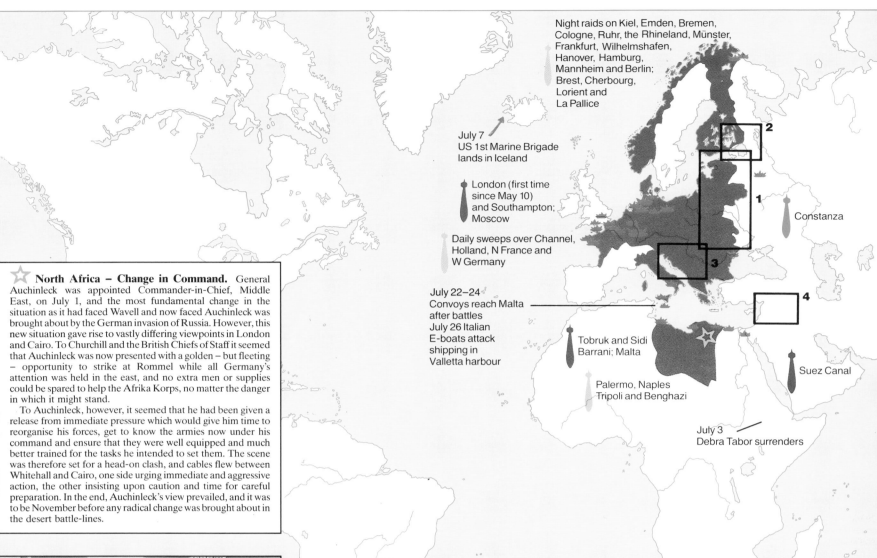

Night raids on Kiel, Emden, Bremen, Cologne, Ruhr, the Rhineland, Münster, Frankfurt, Wilhelmshafen, Hanover, Hamburg, Mannheim and Berlin; Brest, Cherbourg, Lorient and La Pallice

July 7
US 1st Marine Brigade lands in Iceland

London (first time since May 10) and Southampton; Moscow

Daily sweeps over Channel, Holland, N France and W Germany

July 22–24
Convoys reach Malta after battles
July 26 Italian E-boats attack shipping in Valletta harbour

Constanza

Suez Canal

Tobruk and Sidi Barrani; Malta

Palermo, Naples Tripoli and Benghazi

July 3
Debra Tabor surrenders

☆ **North Africa – Change in Command.** General Auchinleck was appointed Commander-in-Chief, Middle East, on July 1, and the most fundamental change in the situation as it had faced Wavell and now faced Auchinleck was brought about by the German invasion of Russia. However, this new situation gave rise to vastly differing viewpoints in London and Cairo. To Churchill and the British Chiefs of Staff it seemed that Auchinleck was now presented with a golden – but fleeting – opportunity to strike at Rommel while all Germany's attention was held in the east, and no extra men or supplies could be spared to help the Afrika Korps, no matter the danger in which it might stand.

To Auchinleck, however, it seemed that he had been given a release from immediate pressure which would give him time to reorganise his forces, get to know the armies now under his command and ensure that they were well equipped and much better trained for the tasks he intended to set them. The scene was therefore set for a head-on clash, and cables flew between Whitehall and Cairo, one side urging immediate and aggressive action, the other insisting upon caution and time for careful preparation. In the end, Auchinleck's view prevailed, and it was to be November before any radical change was brought about in the desert battle-lines.

1 **Barbarossa – the 'Front Door' Kicked In.** All through July the flooding success of *Barbarossa* continued to astonish the world. In the north, von Leeb's panzers had already crossed the Dvina and established a wide bridgehead from which, on July 2, the entire Panzergruppe set out on a 155-mile race to the Ostrov–Pskov area south of Lake Peipus. Within three days, Ostrov was in their hands and support columns were pouring in, so when a counter-attack was mounted by reserve Russian armour it was annihilated and by the evening of July 6 only the wrecks of 140 Soviet tanks lay between the Panzergruppe and Pskov.

On the left flank Eighteenth Infantry Army had been making excellent progress on the good roads of Lithuania, Latvia and Esthonia, and by July 7 Riga and the Dvina had been left far behind and German artillery was shelling Tallinn and Narva, while four infantry divisions had been detached to drive for the southern end of Lake Peipus and to join the Fourth Panzergruppe. Here fresh orders reached them; they were to become part of the Panzergruppe and take Pskov themselves, leaving the panzers free to race ahead towards the Luga river, only 60 miles from Leningrad. Here, however, a halt was called; in the eyes of Wehrmacht HQ far too many large pockets of Russian soldiers remained both behind them and on their flanks for such a headlong advance to be safe.

Army Group Centre's advance had continued – and was as alarming as Army Group North's to the High Command. On July 1 both Hoth and Guderian released panzer formations to race towards the Berezina river, and both were threatened with courts martial by General von Kluge for doing so; but on July 3 the release order was given and Hoth in the north and Guderian in the south were free to race ahead again, Hoth for Vitebsk (July 9), and Guderian first for the Dniepr (July 10/11) then on, against growing and fierce opposition from Russian infantry and artillery, with three objectives in mind. First, once they had circled around Smolensk on July 16, they had to hang on there until Hoth's panzers joined them from the north-west; second, they had to bar the escape to the south or east of Soviet forces they had by-passed on the way – and third, and most important from Guderian's point of view, they had to widen their hold on the land east of Smolensk (towards Roslavl and the Desna river at Yelnya) into a solid bridgehead for the final thrust to the great goal, Moscow.

But on July 29 Hitler's adjutant, Colonel Schmundt, arrived to present Guderian with the Oak Leaves to the Knight's Cross – and bring him fresh and direct orders. Hitler had decreed that the rolling wheatlands of the Ukraine and the Baku oilfields were now the vital objectives; Moscow could wait. Guderian for the moment must go no further east.

Army Group South had also made good progress. Far to the south, Eleventh Army and its conglomerate allies, having ensured the safety of the Ploesti oilfields, then moved forward slowly but surely (the Rumanian formations through what had been their own province of Bessarabia) and by the end of July had reached the mouth of the Dniepr, with Odessa just beyond.

Further north, on the left flank, First Panzergruppe had shouldered aside the Russian Fifth Army into the Pripet Marshes where they could not be followed – and as a result were themselves nearly cut off in mid-July when a powerful drive south-west from Korosten threatened to link up with a drive up from Berdichev by Sixth Army. This Russian move was only thwarted by German expertise coupled with uncertain Red Army planning, but for the next six weeks Army Group South commanders were always conscious of the threat hanging over their north-west shoulder.

The main drive down between the Bug and the Dniepr plunged implacably onwards, Kleist's Panzergruppe with Sixth Army in attendance driving towards Kiev and Zhitomir on the northern swing and down the bank of the Yuzhni Bug to the south. Here they would meet Seventeenth Army which had marched parallel, between the Bug and the Dniestr, and between them they would soon take control of the entire Ukraine – except, of course, for the pockets.

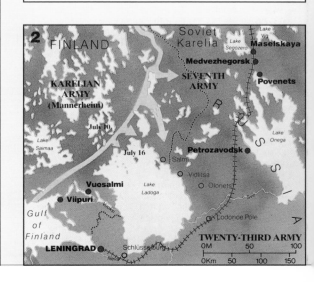

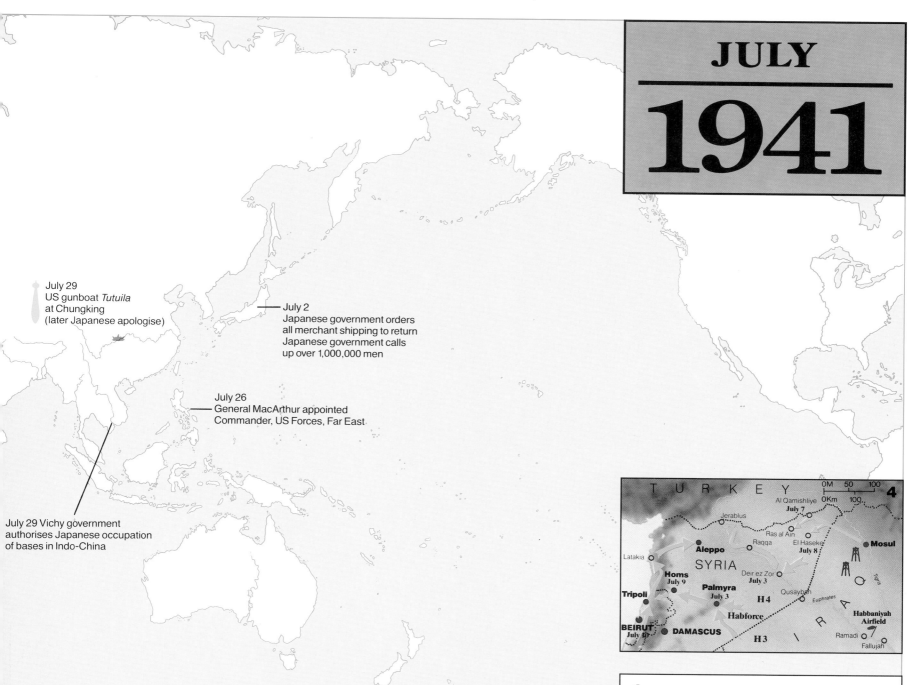

July 29
US gunboat *Tutuila*
at Chungking
(later Japanese apologise)

July 2
Japanese government orders
all merchant shipping to return
Japanese government calls
up over 1,000,000 men

July 26
General MacArthur appointed
Commander, US Forces, Far East

July 29 Vichy government
authorises Japanese occupation
of bases in Indo-China

2 Finland – the Reluctant Partner. From the moment the planning for *Barbarossa* started, Hitler assumed that Finland would be an ally, with Finnish and German troops holding the northern flank. Since the end of the Winter War he had been making covert advances to the Finnish government, firstly because he wished to ensure rights to the vital nickel deposits in northern Finland, second because he knew that sooner or later he would need to threaten Murmansk and its rail link back into Russia.

Finland had little choice but to accept these advances, so as early as June 8 German troops were moving north along the Gulf of Bothnia coast to Kemi [see August map] and the northern half of the country. As for the Finnish Army, a general mobilisation began on June 16 but it was not until early July that the Karelian Army was deployed along the new frontier, facing south-east towards their 1939 border with Russia.

On July 10 the two left-hand corps drove forward against two Russian divisions whose commanders dare not withdraw to make use of the open space behind them, and who thus became isolated. On the left flank the Finnish IV Corps reached the line of the old border within a few days and there halted on Mannerheim's orders. To their right VII Corps reached Lake Ladoga on July 16 and then drove down the eastern shore towards Vidlitsa by the end of the month.

3 Dismemberment of Yugoslavia. Hitler's hatred of Yugoslavia sprang from far deeper sources than just the necessity to change his plans and postpone *Barbarossa* in order to launch *Operation Punishment* against the recalcitrant Balkan state. Yugoslavia was a country created by the detested Treaty of Versailles; and he had hated the Serbs ever since the First World War. 'Belgrade must be destroyed by continuous day and night air attacks!' he demanded. 'Yugoslavia must cease to exist!' – and having subjected the country to a devastating military Blitzkrieg he then commenced its political dismemberment.

An independent state of Croatia which included most of Bosnia-Hercegovina was proclaimed under the puppet rule of Ante Pavelic. Slovenia in the north-west corner was divided in half, Germany annexing the northern half, Italy the southern. Italy also took part of the Dalmatian coast including the offshore islands, Montenegro, a large part of Kosovo-Metohija and a part of Macedonia, while Bulgaria was given the rest of

4 Exporter Completed. With the conclusion of *Operation Battleaxe*, two fighter and three bomber squadrons could be released to give more air cover to the Australians, the British and Free French formations now driving north from Sidon, and the 10th Indian Division moving westwards along the valley of the Euphrates from Baghdad, to take Deir ez Zor and threaten Aleppo. Meanwhile a second force, 'Habforce', took Palmyra and drove on to reach Homs by July 9, and on the same day, after a fierce battle, the Australians finally burst through the last Vichy French resistance to reach the outskirts of Beirut by the evening of July 10.

On July 11, General Dentz asked for an armistice, and terms for surrender were agreed by next morning – Allied occupation of the country, the handing over intact of ships, aircraft, naval and air establishments, the release of all British, Indian and Free French prisoners; and the choice to be given to the officers and men of the Levant Army either to be repatriated to France or to stay and join the Free French. Of the 37,736 officers and men offered this choice, only 5,668 opted to join De Gaulle's forces, and of these the majority were men of the Foreign Legion (mostly German or Russian), North Africans or Senegalese. The rest chose to go home to occupied France.

Macedonia and large areas of South Serbia. Hungary also was to be rewarded for her participation in *Barbarossa:* she was given areas on her own borders in the north – Prekomurje, Medjumurje, the Backa and neighbouring Baranja, while the Banat north of Belgrade was put under the rule and administration of the local German inhabitants.

As for the heart of the country – certainly the heart of any resistance to Germany – Serbia, this was given a puppet government under the quisling General Milan Nedić, whose rule would be maintained by a permanent German military occupation.

Though this division did not appear to give the real conquerors of the country the lion's share of the spoils, Germany nevertheless now controlled not only the areas producing coal, copper, chrome and bauxite, but also the vital Danube route to Rumania and her oilfields.

What opportunity the occupying forces would be given to enjoy their gains, however, only time would tell.

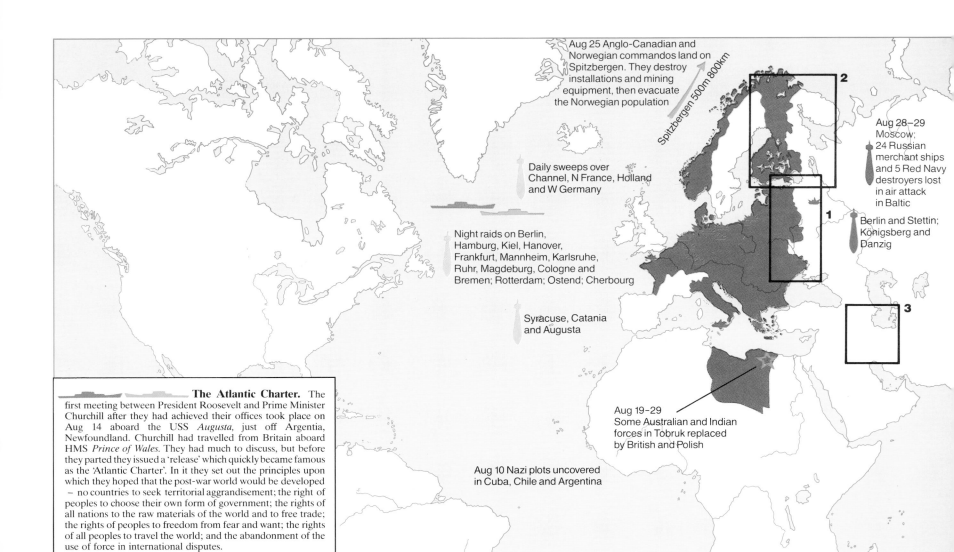

Aug 25 Anglo-Canadian and Norwegian commandos land on Spitzbergen. They destroy installations and mining equipment, then evacuate the Norwegian population

Aug 28–29 Moscow; 24 Russian merchant ships and 5 Red Navy destroyers lost in air attack in Baltic

Berlin and Stettin; Königsberg and Danzig

Daily sweeps over Channel, N France, Holland and W Germany

Night raids on Berlin, Hamburg, Kiel, Hanover, Frankfurt, Mannheim, Karlsruhe, Ruhr, Magdeburg, Cologne and Bremen; Rotterdam; Ostend; Cherbourg

Syracuse, Catania and Augusta

Aug 19–29 Some Australian and Indian forces in Tobruk replaced by British and Polish

Aug 10 Nazi plots uncovered in Cuba, Chile and Argentina

The Atlantic Charter. The first meeting between President Roosevelt and Prime Minister Churchill after they had achieved their offices took place on Aug 14 aboard the USS *Augusta,* just off Argentia, Newfoundland. Churchill had travelled from Britain aboard HMS *Prince of Wales.* They had much to discuss, but before they parted they issued a 'release' which quickly became famous as the 'Atlantic Charter'. In it they set out the principles upon which they hoped that the post-war world would be developed – no countries to seek territorial aggrandisement; the right of peoples to choose their own form of government; the rights of all nations to the raw materials of the world and to free trade; the rights of peoples to freedom from fear and want; the rights of all peoples to travel the world; and the abandonment of the use of force in international disputes.

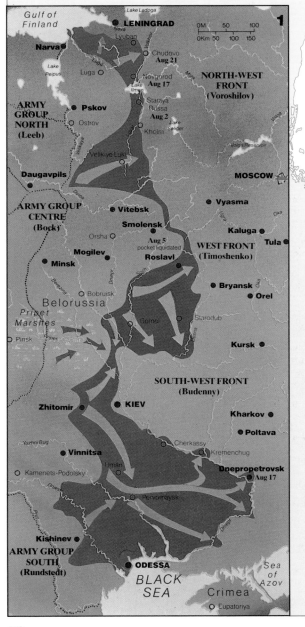

1 Barbarossa – the Change of Direction. By August two factors were beginning to affect the progress of *Barbarossa.* The heat and their own enormous exertions were slowing the pace of the German soldiers, while the swelling pockets of Russian soldiers still behind the prongs of the advance and the widening gaps between the main thrusts were straining the nerves of the German High Command.

The gap between Army Group North and Army Group Centre especially provoked alarm so despite anguished pleas from the Fourth Panzergruppe commanders, Rheinhardt and Manstein, to be allowed to thrust immediately into the heart of Leningrad a complete corps of Sixteenth Army was in fact diverted on the right wing and into the gap, well south of the agreed dividing line between North and Centre.

The capture of Pskov had been followed by a further infantry advance towards Lake Ilmen; here exhaustion brought the advance to a halt until Hitler decreed that Novgorod and Chudovo were the next essential objectives and that Manstein's panzers must go across to help there. The next major Army Group North attack began, in pouring rain, in the early morning of Aug 8, and consisted of drives north from the Luga bridgehead and north-east from the newly won ground west of Lake Ilmen; but the assault on the left ran into an attack planned by the Red Army on the Panzergruppe for exactly the same moment, and the storm of fire which blanketed the area stunned even the most experienced soldiers on each side.

Eventually, however, German training and efficiency told, the panzers broke through and in theory were clear for a drive into Leningrad - except for five Red Army infantry divisions just north of Luga which refused to surrender and proved almost impossible to move. In the end, the panzer divisions had to loop back and join a concentric assault which left all units engaged weakened and exhausted.

At least Manstein was now free to drive for Novgorod, which fell after a fierce fight on Aug 17, then on and past Chudovo to Lyuban by the end of the month. Moreover, on his right wing one of Hoth's panzer corps had by now been directed by Hitler – to their commander's intense fury – along the west bank of the Volkhov to swing in to aid in the last stage of the encirclement of Leningrad. By the end of August only those few miles between Lyuban and the mouth of the Neva were still open for either supplies into or escape from the old Tsarist capital.

Third Panzergruppe commander, Hoth, was by no means the only senior commander of German armoured troops in the area to be infuriated by his orders from the Führer's headquarters. Despite his recent decorations, despite the renaming of his command from Second Panzergruppe to Panzergruppe Guderian, the Oberstgeneral was still highly incensed at the attempted halting of his drive to Moscow, and severely critical of the strategic reasons he had been given by Colonel Schmundt. Like many soldiers before him, he felt that politicians should stick to politics and leave the military autocracy to deal with all matters pertaining to the battlefield; but being well aware of the power at Hitler's command and the ruthlessness with which it could be wielded, he proceeded with some caution.

Inventing the danger of a threat from Russian positions grouped around the small town of Roslavl, on Aug 1 Guderian launched his Panzergruppe forward in the hope that the resultant battle would be so engulfing that his command would be unable to disengage until it had at least 'eaten' its way much nearer to Moscow. He fell victim to his own competence as a commander. Far from being blocked by well sited defences manned by stubborn Russian infantry and gunners, his panzer units swept past and between what obstacles to their progress did exist, over-ran the Russian artillery and drove into Roslavl on Aug 3, then on to cross the Desna a few days later.

On Aug 4 it looked as though he was going to get away with it, for on that day Hitler visited the front and seemed for the

Chungking

3 Persia – the Pawn in the Game.

Maps labelled:

2 NORWAY, BARENTS SEA, Kirkenes, Petsamo, Murmansk, AOK NORWEGEN (Falkenhorst), Salla, Kandalaksha, Kemi, Kemijarvi, Loukhi, Kestenga, Yhta, Kem, Belomorsk, Oulu, German Command, Finnish Command, White Sea, SWEDEN, Gulf of Bothnia, KARELIAN ARMY (Mannerheim), Soviet Karelia, Lake Jlg, Medvezhegorsk, Povenets, FINLAND, Petrozavodsk, Lake Onega, Hanko (Russian), HELSINKI, Vuosalmi Aug 11, Vidlitsa, Viipuri, Lake Ladoga, Lodonoe Pole, Gulf of Finland, LENINGRAD, RUSSIA

3 RUSSIA, Baku, Maku, Khuoi, Ardebil, CASPIAN SEA, TURKEY, Lake Urmia, Tabriz Aug 26, Rasht, Bandar-Shah, Qazvin, TEHERAN, Shahrud, Mosul, Sinneh, Semnan, Kirkuk, Hamadan, Khanaqin, Kermanshah, Sultanabad, BAGHDAD, PERSIA, Masjid-i-Suleiman, Ahwaz, Haft Khel, IRAQ, Basra, Abadan Aug 26, Bandar Shahpur, Bandar Shiahpur, Persian Gulf, Aug 25

moment impressed by Bock's and Guderian's arguments, on the necessity of maintaining the impetus towards the Russian capital. But on Aug 24 Hitler sent for Guderian and told him that the prerequisites for an advance on Moscow were the securing of both flanks of Army Group Centre. Hoth must detach forces to go north to help von Leeb; Guderian must swing his Panzergruppe through 90° and drive down along the west bank of the Desna to make contact with Kleist's armour which would curve up to meet him, thus encircling the vast Russian armies in the Ukraine.

There is some irony in the fact that by August Hitler had decided the Southern Front was the most important for undoubtedly von Rundstedt had originally been given the least significant part to play in *Barbarossa* and therefore the weakest forces. By the end of July Kleist's armour and Stulpnagel's infantry were racing towards each other, and on Aug 3 they met, sealing into pockets behind them the Russian Sixth and Twelfth Armies and part of the Eighteenth. As Stalin refused permission for any of them to break out, they were all subjected to intense artillery bombardment (part of Schobert's Eleventh Army joined Stulpnagel at this point) and on Aug 10 they capitulated; 103,000 Red Army prisoners began their march to prison-camps and the awful fate which awaited them there.

To the south, the Rumanian divisions had also moved on and Odessa was completely encircled by early August. Although its siege was to last 64 days and inflict heavy casualties on the Rumanians, the huge Russian garrison there was tied up and unable to play any part in the drama unfolding to the north. By Aug 7 Pervomaysk was occupied, ten days later Kleist's armour was threatening both Kremenchug and Dnepropetrovksk and gathering itself for the turn north and the drive up to meet Guderian.

The greatest disaster of all was about to fall upon the Red Army.

2 Finland. Although General Mannerheim had no intention of Finnish troops taking part in any vast invasion of Russian domains, he realised the vulnerability of the old Russo-Finnish border and the desirability of establishing defences slightly beyond it. He therefore chose a Stop-line and authorised VI Corps to move up to it during the last days of August.

On Aug 1, he had ordered formations to the west of Lake Ladoga to advance, II Corps into the gap on the right of VII Corps so that between them they held all the ground up the north shore of the lake, then on down the west coast as far as the line of the Vuoksi river.

Then on Aug 23, IV Corps on the right flank of the Karelian Army drove down between the Vuoksi and the coast to clear the area to and around Viipuri, while seaborne troops also crossed the Gulf of Viipuri. The Russian garrison in Viipuri withdrew, and VI Corps and II Corps troops then linked up and drove straight down the Karelian Isthmus to reach the northernmost pre-1939 Leningrad fortifications by Aug 31.

At the far northern end of the front, on Aug 1 aircraft of the Fleet Air Arm and the Red Air Force together attacked the harbours of Kirkenes and Petsamo.

3 Persia – the Pawn in the Game. Once Germany had invaded Russia, the invasion of Persia by one or the other of the combatants became inevitable. Russia and her new ally Britain needed to ensure a supply route from the Persian Gulf to the Caspian Sea – and they needed to do so immediately. On the other hand, if Germany reached the Caucasus in the foreseeable future, an invasion of Persia by the Wehrmacht would menace the Russian rear and place Axis troops astride the British routes to India, Australia and the Far East. Perhaps more important, whoever controlled the Persian oilwells and those of neighbouring Iraq would have at their disposal the largest supply of fuel outside the United States.

Allied pressures on Persia to join them – or even to allow 'peaceful penetration' of certain key points – were understandably rejected by Reza Shah at a time when Germany appeared to be winning on all fronts. However, faced with British control of Iraq and knowledge of the movements of Russian forces along the Persian border with Azerbaijan, he concluded that an Allied invasion was inevitable, and the long-term interests of his country would best be served by nothing but a token resistance. Thus when General Novikov's mechanised columns crossed into Persia at Maku and Ardebil they met little but rifle-fire from rapidly disintegrating formations, reached Khuoi and Tabriz within two days, linked up and then drove on through Rasht and were close to Qazvin – only 100 miles from Teheran – by the end of the month. From the eastern side of the Caspian, another column crossed the border and took Bandar-Shah, then hooked across to Shahrud (both places railheads) and down to Semnan.

At the same time, two British columns drove in from Iraq. From Khanaqin a mechanised force under Maj-General Slim crossed the border early on the morning of Aug 25, and after meeting sporadic but at times fierce resistance were in sight of Kermanshah by the morning of Aug 28 when the Persian commander received orders to cease fighting. By Aug 31, Slim's forces had reached Hamadan and there they split, one column going north-west to Sinneh, Slim himself turning south-east to Sultanabad.

Down in the south, the vital oilfields at Abadan, Bandar Shahpur, Ahwaz, Haft Khel and Masjid-i-Suleiman had all by this time been occupied by the troops of two Indian brigades striking up from the head of the Persian Gulf and across from Basra. At least for the time being, the Allies would not be short of fuel.

53

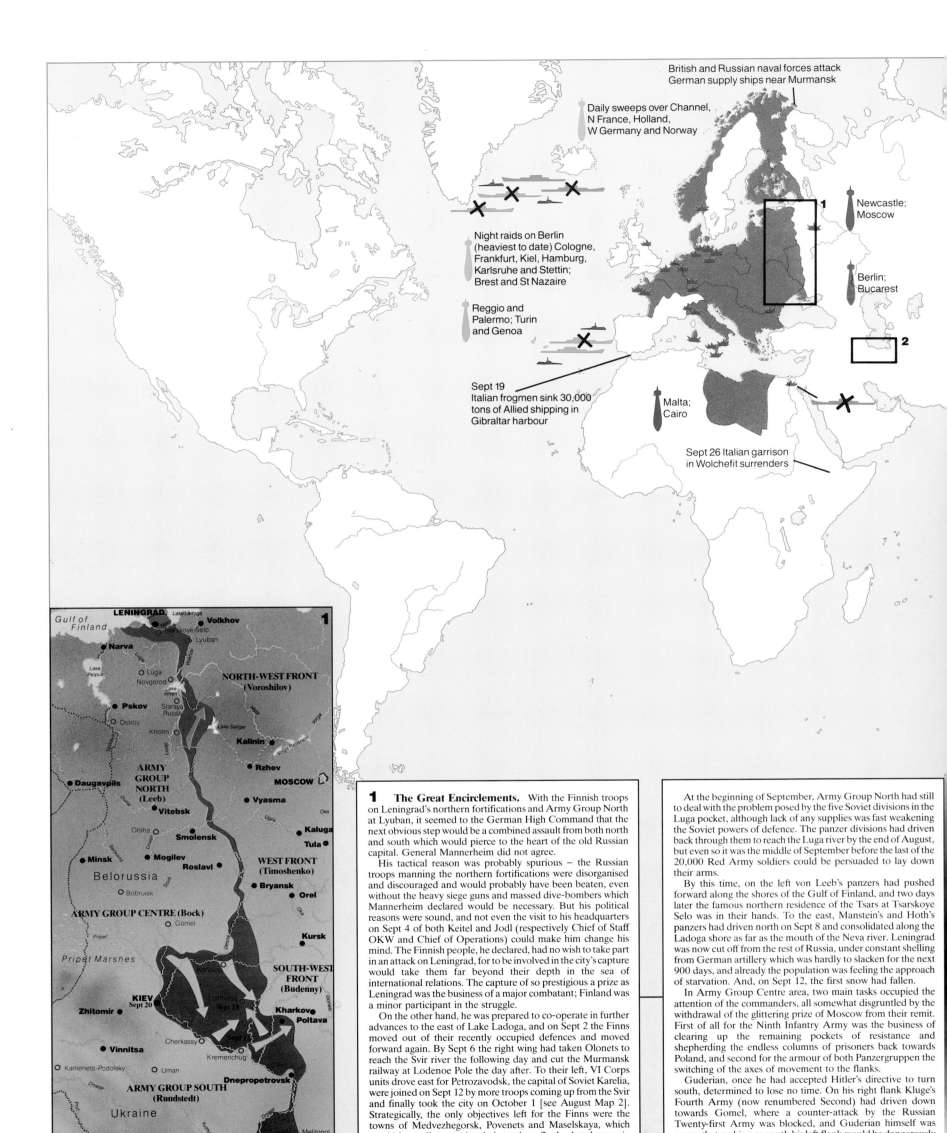

British and Russian naval forces attack German supply ships near Murmansk

Daily sweeps over Channel, N France, Holland, W Germany and Norway

Night raids on Berlin (heaviest to date) Cologne, Frankfurt, Kiel, Hamburg, Karlsruhe and Stettin; Brest and St Nazaire

Reggio and Palermo; Turin and Genoa

Sept 19 Italian frogmen sink 30,000 tons of Allied shipping in Gibraltar harbour

Newcastle; Moscow

Berlin; Bucarest

Malta; Cairo

Sept 26 Italian garrison in Wolchefit surrenders

1 **The Great Encirclements.** With the Finnish troops on Leningrad's northern fortifications and Army Group North at Lyuban, it seemed to the German High Command that the next obvious step would be a combined assault from both north and south which would pierce to the heart of the old Russian capital. General Mannerheim did not agree.

His tactical reason was probably spurious – the Russian troops manning the northern fortifications were disorganised and discouraged and would probably have been beaten, even without the heavy siege guns and massed dive-bombers which Mannerheim declared would be necessary. But his political reasons were sound, and not even the visit to his headquarters on Sept 4 of both Keitel and Jodl (respectively Chief of Staff OKW and Chief of Operations) could make him change his mind. The Finnish people, he declared, had no wish to take part in an attack on Leningrad, for to be involved in the city's capture would take them far beyond their depth in the sea of international relations. The capture of so prestigious a prize as Leningrad was the business of a major combatant; Finland was a minor participant in the struggle.

On the other hand, he was prepared to co-operate in further advances to the east of Lake Ladoga, and on Sept 2 the Finns moved out of their recently occupied defences and moved forward again. By Sept 6 the right wing had taken Olonets to reach the Svir river the following day and cut the Murmansk railway at Lodenoe Pole the day after. To their left, VI Corps units drove east for Petrozavodsk, the capital of Soviet Karelia, were joined on Sept 12 by more troops coming up from the Svir and finally took the city on October 1 [see August Map 2]. Strategically, the only objectives left for the Finns were the towns of Medvezhegorsk, Povenets and Maselskaya, which would form a line securing their northern flank – but the terrain was bad for offensives, and the Finnish Army was weary, cold, and the soldiers could see little point in advancing further away from their own homeland. Ominous signs of incipient mutiny appeared, and although progress could be made when little or no opposition was encountered it was to be December before Finnish troops reached Povenets.

At the beginning of September, Army Group North had still to deal with the problem posed by the five Soviet divisions in the Luga pocket, although lack of any supplies was fast weakening the Soviet powers of defence. The panzer divisions had driven back through them to reach the Luga river by the end of August, but even so it was the middle of September before the last of the 20,000 Red Army soldiers could be persuaded to lay down their arms.

By this time, on the left von Leeb's panzers had pushed forward along the shores of the Gulf of Finland, and two days later the famous northern residence of the Tsars at Tsarskoye Selo was in their hands. To the east, Manstein's and Hoth's panzers had driven north on Sept 8 and consolidated along the Ladoga shore as far as the mouth of the Neva river. Leningrad was now cut off from the rest of Russia, under constant shelling from German artillery which was hardly to slacken for the next 900 days, and already the population was feeling the approach of starvation. And, on Sept 12, the first snow had fallen.

In Army Group Centre area, two main tasks occupied the attention of the commanders, all somewhat disgruntled by the withdrawal of the glittering prize of Moscow from their remit. First of all for the Ninth Infantry Army was the business of clearing up the remaining pockets of resistance and shepherding the endless columns of prisoners back towards Poland, and second for the armour of both Panzergruppen the switching of the axes of movement to the flanks.

Guderian, once he had accepted Hitler's directive to turn south, determined to lose no time. On his right flank Kluge's Fourth Army (now renumbered Second) had driven down towards Gomel, where a counter-attack by the Russian Twenty-first Army was blocked, and Guderian himself was aware that on his way south his left flank would be dangerously exposed to any major force grouped around Bryansk – though he need not have worried. The Bryansk Front commander, General Yeremenko, was in receipt of conflicting orders from Stalin and the Stavka Chief of Staff, Shaposhnikov, and in the resulting shambles he lost the essential concentration of force necessary to check Panzergruppe Guderian.

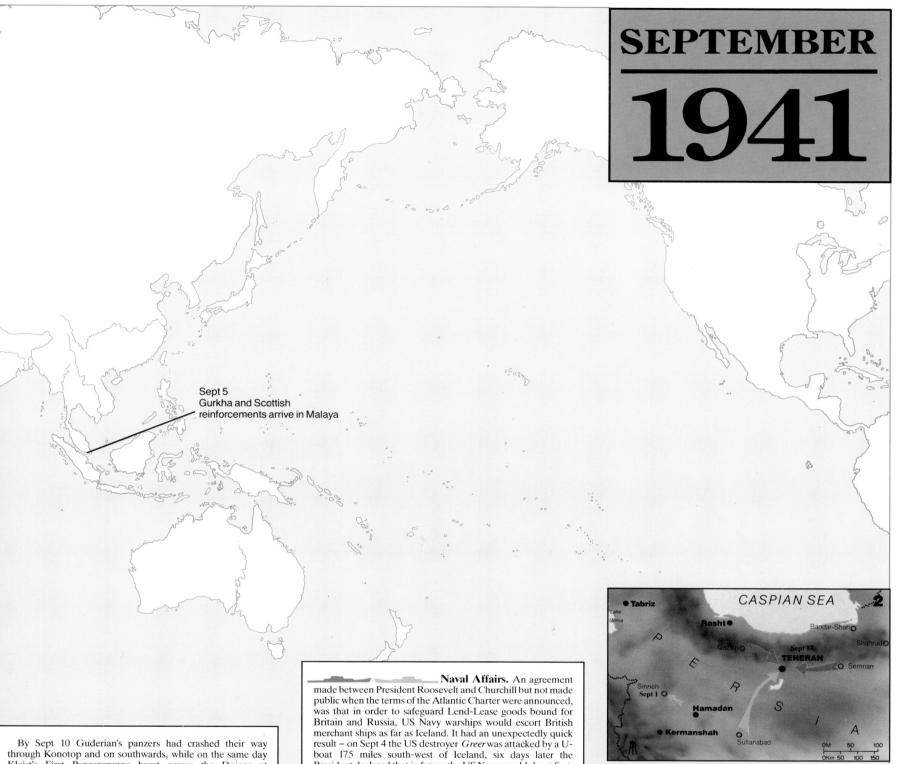

Sept 5
Gurkha and Scottish
reinforcements arrive in Malaya

CASPIAN SEA

Tabriz
Lake Urmia
Rasht
Bandar-Shah
Shahrud
Qazvin
Sept 17
TEHERAN
Semnan
Sinneh
Sept 1
Hamadan
Kermanshah
Sultanabad

P E R S I A

0 Km 50   100   150
0 M   50   100

By Sept 10 Guderian's panzers had crashed their way through Konotop and on southwards, while on the same day Kleist's First Panzergruppe burst across the Dniepr at Kremenchug and drove north to meet them, the outer armoured wings of a vast encirclement. Within hours the Russian commander, Marshal Budenny, and his political commissar, Khrushchev, were begging Stalin for permission for their still large but disintegrating forces to be allowed to escape through the rapidly narrowing gap; Stalin first temporised, then sought the views of General Kirponos still in the Kiev pocket. Kirponos echoed Budenny's thoughts, but Stalin then rejected them, dismissed Budenny and appointed Timoshenko to preside over the ensuing havoc, insisting through Shaposhnikov during the few days left before the gap closed, that all fronts, all armies, all divisions should stand fast where they were.

Guderian's panzers met Kleist's at Lokhvitsa on Sept 15, and infantry and guns from Second Army to the north and from Seventeenth to the south came up to harden the ring. By the evening of Sept 17 the biggest encirclement of the entire Barbarossa campaign – perhaps of history – had been formed; and this time hardly anyone would escape. That night permission at last arrived for the remnants of the Soviet armies to attempt to break out to the east, but most of them had too far to go and lacked the heavy guns and armour to smash through the waiting German ring.

Budenny and Khrushchev were flown out, Bagramyan brought out about 50 men, but Kirponos and most of the staffs of South-west Front and of five Soviet armies – 5th, 21st, 26th, 37th and 40th – were killed as they tried to escape, or rounded up and captured. With them into graves or prison-camps of the most appalling nature went at least half a million Russian soldiers, making this in terms of numbers the biggest military catastrophe in Russian history.

The only gleam of light in the whole sorry débâcle was that by the end of the month events had brought some sense of reality to the men in the Kremlin. On Sept 30 Stalin permitted the Odessa garrison to be evacuated to the Crimea, where their experience could be put to good use in the defence of Sebastopol.

Naval Affairs. An agreement made between President Roosevelt and Churchill but not made public when the terms of the Atlantic Charter were announced, was that in order to safeguard Lend-Lease goods bound for Britain and Russia, US Navy warships would escort British merchant ships as far as Iceland. It had an unexpectedly quick result – on Sept 4 the US destroyer Greer was attacked by a U-boat 175 miles south-west of Iceland, six days later the President declared that in future the US Navy would shoot first, and on the same day the US merchantman Montana was torpedoed and on Sept 19 the US steamer Pink Star met the same fate, both off Iceland. In addition, the USS Steel Seafarer was bombed and sunk in the Gulf of Suez early in the month.

There was little doubt that as far as US naval and merchant fleets were concerned, their country was at war with the Axis powers, and further authority was given to the feeling by the official announcement on Sept 16 that from then on the US Navy would give full protection to all Allied convoys as far east as 26° west.

This was certainly a development which brought relief to the hard-pressed Royal Navy, for convoys were now under increasing attack from U-boat packs. From Sept 9-19 Convoy SC42 of 70 ships was attacked by 15 U-boats, losing 18 ships (2 U-boats sunk), while off Cape St Vincent Convoy HG33 lost 10 out of 25 merchantmen, and late in the month 3 U-boats between them sank 7 out of the 11 ships of Convoy SL87.

In the Mediterranean, however, the Royal Navy had had a success – though at a cost. On Sept 24, 9 ships of the 'Halberd' convoy, escorted by 3 battleships, 5 cruisers, 18 destroyers and the aircraft carrier Ark Royal left Gibraltar for Malta. HMS Nelson was hit by a torpedo from an Italian aircraft and had to turn back, and on the afternoon of Sept 27 the remaining battleships plus 2 cruisers and 2 destroyers were detached to drive off an Italian fleet of 2 battleships, 4 cruisers and 16 destroyers. The Italian fleet withdrew before evening, however, but after dark torpedo-bombers attacked the convoy and damaged the Imperial Star so badly that she had to be sunk. But the following day all the remaining ships arrived safely in Valletta harbour, delivering 50,000 tons of supplies – enough essentials to last the beleaguered island until May 1942.

In the Baltic, however, German dive-bombers attacked the Russian ships in Kronstadt harbour to such effect that 2 battleships – Marat and Oktyabrskaya Revolutsia – and 2 destroyers capsized, and others were badly damaged.

2   Allied Success in Persia. As one of General Slim's columns arrived in Sinneh at midnight on Aug 31, they met a Russian column who had arrived earlier and roamed the surrounding countryside distributing propaganda material and pictures of Stalin. Courtesies were exchanged and the Russian column withdrew to Qazvin, the agreed limits of the Soviet occupation area.

In Teheran the situation was delicate. Although Reza Shah had ordered the end of resistance on Aug 28, high-ranking Persian Army and Air Force officers were on the verge of mutiny and martial law had therefore been declared in Teheran itself.

Wavell flew into Teheran for a meeting with the Soviet commander, and as a result of the conferences and arguments which followed Reza Shah abdicated in favour of his son Crown Prince Mohammed Reza Pahlavi who, educated in Europe and of pro-western views, set up a government pledged to the support of the Allies. British and Soviet troops entered the capital on Sept 17, and General Slim arranged for the policing of British lines of communication across Persia (now threatened by Kurdish and Luri tribesmen intent upon loot) by one Indian and one armoured brigade, and in conjunction with the Russian commander the preparation of defensive positions in north-west Persia against any possible German threat from the Caucasus.

However morally dubious the Allied action had been, it saved Persia from Axis domination and secured not only the sources of oil at the head of the Gulf but also the supply route from the Gulf to the Caspian along which would in the end be sent 5,000,000 tons of arms, aircraft and ammunition from Britain and the USA to Russia, together with nearly 250,000 lorries. It was thus quite a significant factor in the defeat of the Axis powers.

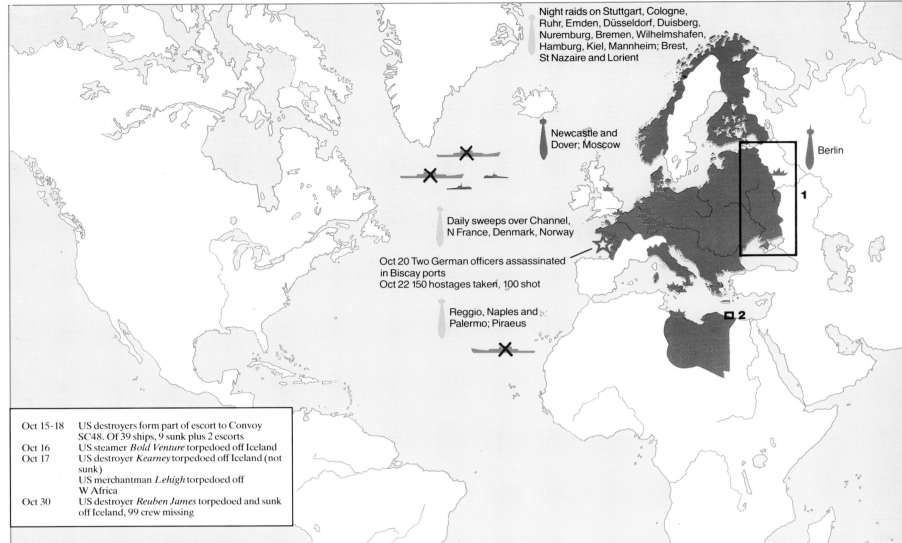

Night raids on Stuttgart, Cologne, Ruhr, Emden, Düsseldorf, Duisberg, Nuremburg, Bremen, Wilhelmshafen, Hamburg, Kiel, Mannheim; Brest, St Nazaire and Lorient

Newcastle and Dover; Moscow

Berlin

1

Daily sweeps over Channel, N France, Denmark, Norway

Oct 20 Two German officers assassinated in Biscay ports
Oct 22 150 hostages taken, 100 shot

□ 2

Reggio, Naples and Palermo; Piraeus

Oct 15-18	US destroyers form part of escort to Convoy SC48. Of 39 ships, 9 sunk plus 2 escorts
Oct 16	US steamer *Bold Venture* torpedoed off Iceland
Oct 17	US destroyer *Kearney* torpedoed off Iceland (not sunk)
	US merchantman *Lehigh* torpedoed off W Africa
Oct 30	US destroyer *Reuben James* torpedoed and sunk off Iceland, 99 crew missing

1 The Drive to Moscow. By October, Army Group North's role in *Operation Barbarossa* had been reduced to little more than that of a besieging army. Hitler had decided that the capture of Leningrad was unnecessary; it should instead be cut off from the rest of Russia, its population starved to death, its buildings bombed and shelled to ruins. Peter the Great's masterpiece was to be allowed to disintegrate into rubble.

There was still some clearing up to be done in the 'Volkhov corner', but the devaluation of the whole Northern Front was indicated by the removal of all the armour except one panzer corps. On Sept 17 command of the Leningrad operations had been taken over by Eighteenth Army, and Fourth Panzergruppe had begun its move to the south. So during October Army Group North did little but consolidate its position around Leningrad itself, and down the line of the Volkhov river to Lake Ilmen and then on south-east to Lake Seliger and the junction with Army Group Centre.

In Army Group Centre, morale was at its peak; orders for *Operation Typhoon* – the capture of Moscow – had been received at the end of September. Hoth's Third Panzergruppe had been reconstituted and waited with Ninth Army on the left flank, Fourth Army and now Fourth Panzergruppe were concentrated around Roslavl; Second Army held the ground south almost as far as Starodub, while Panzergruppe Guderian – to its commander's immense satisfaction – had turned north-west to aim up towards Orel. As he would have farther to go before he joined the main battle in front of Moscow, he would begin to advance two days before the others.

On the last day of September, Panzergruppe Guderian plunged forward and in brilliantly sunny weather drove for the Oka river, diverting the left wing northwards, however, to aim for Bryansk which they reached on Oct 6. Three days later, Second Army units drove in from the west and trapped the Third and Thirteenth Soviet Armies within the pocket thus formed. The positions of the Fiftieth Army lay to the north of Bryansk, threatened both by Guderian's left wing to the south and the main bulk of Second Army driving for Kaluga.

Further north, the infantry and armour of Fourth Army and Fourth Panzergruppe had broken out on Oct 2 from their concentrations north of Roslavl, the bulk driving straight for Moscow, the left wing curling north-east for Vyasma. On the northern side of Smolensk Third Panzergruppe and Ninth Army drove forward in a converging movement with the forces to the south, and on Oct 7 after violent fighting the spearheads of Fourth and Third Panzergruppen met near Vyasma closing the ring around the Soviet 19th, 24th, 29th, 30th, 32nd and 43rd Armies. It seemed that the triumphs of the frontier battles and of Kiev were about to be repeated.

While the encircling forces were engaged in tightening the rings and mopping up operations, their motorised forces on the flanks pushed through the wide gaps which had been torn in the Russian defences, reached Rzhev in the north and then pushed on to Kalinin, reached Mozhaysk in the centre as early as Oct 18 and Volokolamsk by the end of the month.

Meanwhile, to the south, Panzergruppe Guderian's armour had reached and taken Orel, then pressed on towards Tula along the line of the Orel-Moscow railway, with orders to continue on north towards – and perhaps into – the southern suburbs of the Russian capital.

It seemed on Oct 12 that nothing could keep the victorious Army Group Centre from winter quarters in Moscow, and thus the ultimate triumph of Hitler's Eastern Campaign. But on Oct 8 it had begun to rain and by Oct 13 the headlong rush had been slowed to a dogged trudge. Mud was engulfing everything which moved on wheels and much on tracks; and the men were close to exhaustion and, as supply convoys could not get through, hungry as well and with fast-emptying ammunition pouches. Nonetheless, hope and their own confidence in victory kept them going; by the end of the month they had consolidated a line which ran east from Lake Seliger and their junction with Army Group North, to Kalinin, south through Volokolamsk past Mozhaysk and Kaluga to Tula and down to Kursk and Army Group South.

Of all the Wehrmacht commanders on the Eastern Front, it would seem that Kleist was the one most conscious of the lack of time before the Russian winter would freeze them all into immobility. Once the Kiev pocket had been sealed and eliminated, he had withdrawn his Panzergruppe with admirable speed south into the area around Dnepropetrovsk, and on Sept 30 it erupted from a bridgehead over the Samara and drove down to the Sea of Azov, neatly trapping yet another three Soviet armies. Meanwhile Manstein's Eleventh Army had driven along the coast, detached one corps through the Perekop Isthmus to invade the Crimea and reach the outskirts of Sevastopol by the end of the month, the bulk meeting Kleist's panzers on the Azov coast. Kleist immediately took the advantage of infantry close behind to launch further eastwards to Taganrog and Stalino (Donetsk).

But again, rain, wind and the first snow flurries were bringing a hint of the white chaos which would engulf the whole Russian Front, and the panzer drives were slowing down; Rostov, Kleist's main objective, remained still just beyond his grasp.

Kharkov, however, Russia's third city, had been captured – by infantry of Reichenau's Sixth and Stulpnagel's Seventeenth Armies. They had crossed the Psel on Oct 1 and marched due east, at first rapidly but when the rains came the pace slowed. Wheeled vehicles were bogged down, the Soviet Air Force killed their horses, while the emergence of partisans on their flanks foreshadowed immense problems for the future.

But the Soviet defences had been so weakened during the previous months that they could not stop the advance. Rundstedt's armies edged their way forward, took bridgeheads over the river both north and south of Kharkov – and then suddenly found that only rearguards stood between them and the city. They entered it on Oct 24 – but there was a difference in this victory, for behind them was no bagful of Soviet armies. Stalin and STAVKA had learned the lesson – to trade space for time and men; the main armies at Kharkov had been pulled back.

56

2 MEDITERRANEAN SEA

Alexandria 360 m 575 km
beach hospital
caves
TOBRUK
'Bomb Alley'
to Derma
water-distilling plant
White Knoll
fig tree
Pilastrino
Bianca
Carrier Hill
BLUE LINE
to Bardia
concertina wire
RED LINE
mines
anti-tank ditch
0M 2·5 5
0Km 5
to El Adem

The Defence of Moscow. When *Operation Typhoon* was launched three Russian fronts barred the way to Moscow; Western Front under General Koniev with six armies, Reserve Front under Marshal Budenny (he was an old comrade of Stalin's and had thus been allowed reinstatement) with another six armies, and General Yeremenko's Bryansk Front with three armies. They had between them a total of 800,000 men, 770 tanks and 364 planes; almost half of the entire Red Army strength on the Eastern Front, a third of the tanks and guns. Within six days these armies had been torn to shreds by the Panzergruppen and the German infantry were pouring through the vast gaps – and both Stalin and Shaposhnikov were unwilling or unable to accept the disaster which threatened them.

On the morning of Oct 5, a pilot's report that a massive column of German vehicles including armour was approaching the Ugra river north of Kaluga was dismissed as false, so was a second report to the same effect, and a third – and the Moscow district fighter commander, Colonel Sbytov who forwarded all reports, was interrogated as a 'panic-monger' by no less an official than Beria; but then at last came the realisation that in fact at least nine Soviet armies had been obliterated and others were in danger of a similar fate.

It was time for rapid and drastic action. By Oct 7 Stalin was throwing into the defence of Moscow some 14 rifle divisions, 16 new tank brigades, over 40 artillery regiments supported by 10 flame-thrower companies, while from behind Moscow, from central Asia and the Urals and from the Far Eastern fronts were drawn more divisions, more regiments; the message of the brilliant Soviet spy in Tokyo, Richard Sorge, that Japan was planning to move south into the Pacific and not north against Russia, was at last believed.

Perhaps the most important step of all was taken on Oct 10, when General Zhukov was brought down from Leningrad and put in charge of the defence of Moscow.

He had some 90,000 men under his command – the remnants of the fronts through which the Germans had raced, but many more were to make their way back in time to join him, though on Oct 11 this was by no means certain. Stalin also gave him the population of Moscow (75% women), who were rushed out to the perimeter of a huge semi-circle which ran from the Moscow Canal in the north near Krasnaya Polyana, around to the line of the Oka river to the south-east of the capital. Nearly a million Muscovites dug ditches during those frantic days, buried tanks to make anchor defence points for lines of trenches, erected pickets and strung miles of barbed wire between them. After Oct 13, they worked in snow – but they were all used to it. Few realised it was their saviour.

On Oct 15, Molotov warned the British and American ambassadors to be ready to move to Kuibyshev as the Soviet government intended to depart and wage the war from there. The news leaked out and for a few hours Moscow panicked. The railway stations were crowded with people trying to flee; officials used their cars to escape and the roads east jammed. But the NKVD (the precursor of the KGB) moved fast and the rout was abruptly stopped. Moscow was saved – by harsh discipline and the onset of the Russian winter.

2 **Tobruk.** By October Tobruk had been under siege for six months and life for the garrison had settled into a routine. Some 23,000 men, all armed and capable of fighting, now held the port, of whom 15,000 were Australian, 500 Indian and the rest British. The Australians were men of the 9th Division – 20th, 24th and 26th Brigades – plus those of the 18th Brigade from 7th Division, together with divisional engineers and some gunners. The British were the tank crews, the majority of the field and anti-aircraft gunners, a third of the anti-tank gunners plus a battalion of machine-gunners.

Spirits had been somewhat cast down by the failures of the *Brevity* and *Battleaxe* operations, so to reinforce morale the commander, Maj-General Leslie Morshead, instituted a programme of intensive fortification and patrolling. The original Italian complement for each concrete-lined post in the outer defences had been two officers and 25 men with an orthodox scale of weapons; now the posts were meticulously cleaned of all debris and manned by half that number, but with their fire-power doubled and sometimes trebled by captured, reserviced and constantly maintained Italian weapons. This was the Red Line, held by fire-power, constantly strengthened by the construction of new intermediate posts, and covered by an ever-widening band of mines.

Two miles behind it was the Blue Line, a series of platoon-held strongpoints with heavier weapons including mortars, each surrounded by an anti-tank ditch and a zareba of barbed wire, its fire covering dense minefields which by now extended almost to the Red Line. Behind them were the main field artillery batteries which it was their principal duty to protect, while the guns in their turn would protect the infantry from any panzer attack which might reach this far.

Life was rougher for the Australians and Indian infantry around the perimeter than for the British gunners or tank crews, but on the other hand the gunners – especially those around the harbour – were bombed and shelled much more often. There was no refuge at all from Rommel's heavy artillery, and his airfields were so close that often his bombers would be heard from take-off until they dropped their load over the harbour. There was little the troops could do to protect themselves except dig fox-holes, reinforce shelters with concrete slabs or steel beams from wrecked buildings, or stake out claims in some of the deep caves the Italians had quarried out of the cliffs.

They were, of course, dependent on the Royal Navy for all their supplies, and the destroyers of the Inshore Squadron carried out the greater part of what became known as the 'Spud Run'. Their speed could take them quickly in and out of the danger zones and their fire-power was protection while they were in them; but there was also a whole flotilla of smaller craft – lighters, South African whalers, captured Italian schooners – all making their vital contributions. Every ship which visited Tobruk took in stores and took men out and by this time nearly 40,000 had been evacuated and replaced by 30,000, while 30,000 tons of stores had been brought in. But at some cost; 34 warships and merchantmen had been sunk and 33 damaged, and Tobruk harbour itself was dotted with wrecks which made navigation in the dark and under fire even more hazardous. Some of the wrecks, however, were adapted into landing stages

or anti-aircraft gun platforms and thus helped the rapid unloading and turn-around operations.

It was the aggressive patrolling by the Australians and the Indians which dominated the epic of the Tobruk siege. Some nights small patrols of just an officer or sergeant with ten men would go out and raid a gun position, shoot up the crew and wreck the gun with a grenade down the barrel; sometimes a whole company would go out in carriers accompanied by tanks, to destroy a known German or Italian post. The Indian troops specialised in the small patrols, moving in bare feet or home-made sandals soled in strips of old tyres, moving down like ghosts on their unsuspecting prey. One night a patrol found three Italians asleep by their gun ... and cut the throats of the two outside, deliberately leaving the one in the middle to a dire awakening.

The Italians were in general regarded with amused affection and left alone unless they came too close, but the atmosphere along the German sectors was different. Growing pro-fessionalism on both sides fostered a competition which added relentlessly to the casualty lists – but on the other hand efficiency bred respect, and the adversity in which both sides dwelt produced a degree of fellow-feeling. Wounded were fetched in and treated impartially by both sides, and the bearers not fired upon.

In some parts of the German sector, especially across and east of the El Adem road, a virtual armistice existed for two hours every night while men climbed out of their trenches to stretch their aching limbs, while water and food was brought up, the debris and filth of the day was cleaned up and some relief from the heat enjoyed during the blessed cool of the first few hours of darkness; there would be little firing, and that generally vague and unaimed, and an unspoken agreement existed that the time should not be used for patrolling. That should await the signal which ended the nightly truce – a burst of tracer fired vertically into the sky, usually at midnight.

By midsummer, however, the Australian government was suggesting that their men would have had enough of life under siege and demanding that they be replaced. In the end they insisted and the replacement by men of the British 70th Division and the 1st Polish Carpathian Brigade began in the dark period of August and September, and was practically completed in October – though one complete Australian battalion and two companies remained until the end of the siege.

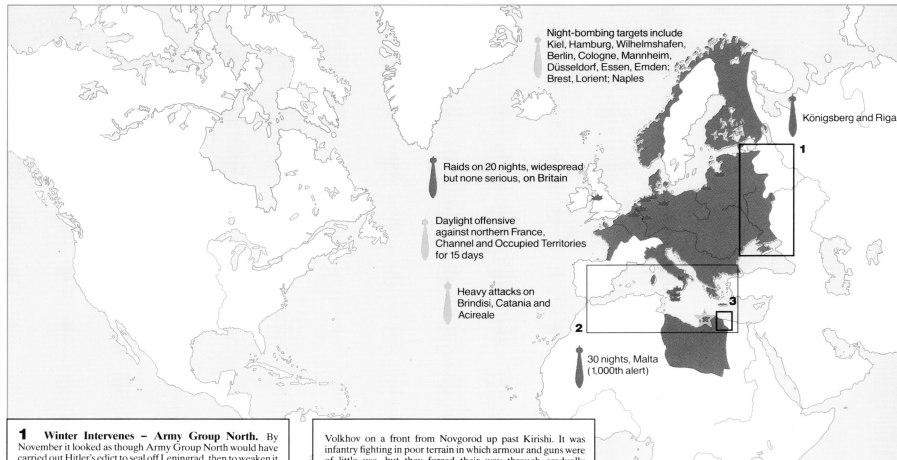

Night-bombing targets include Kiel, Hamburg, Wilhelmshafen, Berlin, Cologne, Mannheim, Düsseldorf, Essen, Emden; Brest, Lorient; Naples

Königsberg and Riga

Raids on 20 nights, widespread but none serious, on Britain

Daylight offensive against northern France, Channel and Occupied Territories for 15 days

Heavy attacks on Brindisi, Catania and Acireale

30 nights, Malta (1,000th alert)

1 Winter Intervenes – Army Group North. By November it looked as though Army Group North would have carried out Hitler's edict to seal off Leningrad, then to weaken it by terror and starvation. The temperatures were now dropping, and although equally badly affected, the German troops encircling Leningrad were at least much better fed than those inside.

Then on Nov 9 Army Group North delivered yet another blow. At the end of October they had begun a drive across the

Volkhov on a front from Novgorod up past Kirishi. It was infantry fighting in poor terrain in which armour and guns were of little use, but they forced their way through gradually weakening resistance until they finally reached Tikhvin, thus cutting the only rail link to the east and Moscow. As Lake Ladoga was becoming unnavigable through block-ice but was not yet sufficiently frozen to take traffic, the Leningraders' plight was now critical.

Army Group Centre. To the Wehrmacht leaders the situation at the beginning of November offered a choice: either they could accept that the weather combined with the lack of warm clothing made it necessary for them to withdraw to the line they held at the beginning of October, or they could succeed in taking Moscow. The nearer they got to Moscow the more exposed became their condition in the face of an enemy as yet unbeaten and showing every sign of recovery and reinforcement.

Then, as November began, the temperature sank below zero and – ironically in view of the lack of proper winter clothing and equipment – conditions immediately improved. The mud froze, the roads hardened, transport could move again.

But as a relief it was shortlived. Plans for the final drive to capture Moscow allowed for Army Group Centre to begin the assault on Nov 15 and over the next three days the move forward began – Ninth Army and Third Panzergruppe on the left driving through Klin towards the Volga Canal. To the south, Panzergruppe Guderian edged forward from Tula down to Tim, into a bulge which took it through Stalinogorsk to Mikhaylov and Gorlovo in the north, and Yefremov and Yelets in the centre; but they could go no further, for the temperature suddenly plummeted to 30° of frost, cold tore larger gaps in their ranks than enemy fire, while machine-guns, motor engines and tank engines froze solid.

Army Group South. Eleventh Army under Manstein continued its invasion of the Crimea during the early days of November, taking Simferopol on Nov I, Feodosia three days later, and by the middle of the month driving to the eastern end of the peninsula and occupying Kerch.

To their east, First Panzer Army now drove for Rostov, but not only did mud and bad roads pose problems but the Soviet Ninth Army had had time to build three defensive belts around the approaches to the city. By Nov 14 the panzers had reached the south bank of the Tuzlov river, and here Rundstedt held them back for two days for redeployment.

When the main assault began on Nov 17, it blasted its way into the northern edges of Rostov with ease, but the SS Viking Division on the left flank reported growing pressure from the direction of Novoshakhinsk. Two days later, with the bulk of the German armour well into Rostov, the weight of the Soviet Thirty-seventh Army fell on them and Rundstedt realised that for the first time the initiative lay with the Red Army. His forces had been led into a trap.

Three strong Soviet infantry armies were now grouped to deliver their first properly planned assault of the war. Ninth and Thirty-seventh Armies from the north and north-east, and Fifty-sixth Independent from the south, began their recapture of Rostov on the night of Nov 27–28, and with little hesitation the panzer army withdrew through a narrow corridor to the Mius river line, abandoning both Rostov – after only eight days – and Taganrog.

Hitler, of course, had ordered cancellation of Rundstedt's authorisation for the withdrawal immediately he heard of it – at which Rundstedt promptly resigned his command. Surprisingly, Hitler accepted it without comment and Germany's most eminent soldier left the Russian theatre, probably thankfully, for good.

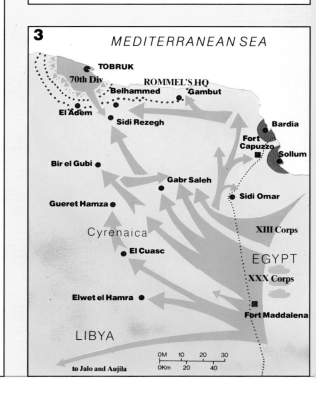

⭐ **Keyes Raid.** On the night of Nov 13/14 a small commando of about sixty men was landed from two submarines on to the Jebel Akhdar coast north of Cyrene. Their targets were enemy intelligence and communication centres near Cyrene and a German HQ at nearby Beda Littoria. Appalling weather hindered progress and some men were lost, but on the night of Nov 16 two attacks were made, a signal pylon was blown down and the HQ building was attacked and partly wrecked. Several Germans were killed and so was Keyes. Other commandos were wounded, and although most of the men made their way back to the coast, all except two were then captured. After 41 days the remaining two reported back to British lines.

58

NOVEMBER 1941

USA orders evacuation of
marines from Shanghai, Peking
and Tientsin

Peking

Tientsin

Japanese troops close
around Hong Kong

Shanghai

Hong Kong

Nov 25–26 Japanese Fleet movements
into Central Pacific and
towards Gulf of Thailand

3 Operation Crusader. By mid-November, General Auchinleck had sufficient men and arms to launch an offensive against Rommel's Panzergruppe Afrika, aimed first at the relief of Tobruk and then at the occupation of Cyrenaica. The force consisted of three divisions of infantry (New Zealand, 4th Indian and 1st South African Divisions), a Guards Brigade, 7th Armoured Division, 4th Armoured Brigade and 1st Army Tank Brigade (of mixed infantry support tanks). Altogether some 100,000 men, 600 tanks and about 5,000 assorted trucks, lorries and staff cars made up the two corps – XIII and XXX – of the newly formed Eighth Army, under command of Lt-General Sir Alan Cunningham.

They were opposed by the original divisions of the Afrika Korps – 15th and 21st Panzer Divisions and the 90th Light Division – and two Italian corps, one of five infantry divisions and one of the two Italian mobile divisions, Ariete Armoured and Trieste Motorised. Nominally under command of General Ettore Bastico, they were in fact at the disposal of General Rommel, who at that time was intent upon a massive attack on the Tobruk garrison from positions between Belhammed and Gambut. His intention was to smash through the perimeter with 15th Panzer and 90th Light Divisions, holding the Italian armour to the south of Tobruk in case the British should attempt to come to the garrison's rescue, and keeping 21st Panzer as reserve in the HQ area.

The Eighth Army crossed the frontier early on the morning of Nov 18, after two astonishing days of torrential rain which had reduced large areas of the desert to bog. Infantry and tanks of XIII Corps drove north once they had crossed the Wire in order to isolate the forward Axis garrisons between Sidi Omar and the coast, while the more mobile armour of XXX Corps on their left drove north-west, first for Gabr Saleh and then for Bir el Gubi and Tobruk.

By evening one brigade from 7th Armoured Division and its Support Group had reached Sidi Rezegh, two South African brigades were deployed south of Bir el Gubi, while the New Zealand and Indian troops had blocked off the Axis frontier positions. Elements of 21st Panzer, however, were probing between the two corps, while Italian artillery had beaten off an armoured assault on Bir el Gubi.

During the following day (Nov 19) the opposing formations skirmished and attempted to consolidate, but Rommel was still intent upon his plans to break into Tobruk and refused to take into account reports of large British forces to the south. The old and well-worn tanks of 7th Armoured Brigade pushed on past Sidi Rezegh to try to make contact with the forces inside Tobruk, but their armour was not strong enough to brush aside the fortified Italian positions in between. Back at the frontier, XIII Corps infantry and its support tanks kept German reconnaissance units at bay while further sealing in the Axis forward posts.

Nov 20 passed mainly in the same indecisive fashion, for Rommel still refused to be deflected from his own plans and Cunningham had not exerted a firm enough grip on his own forces. Then at 2100 hrs the BBC announced that a powerful

armoured force was advancing victoriously towards Tobruk; the scales fell from Rommel's eyes and he swiftly turned his attention to defeating yet another British assault.

The following morning he consolidated both 21st and 15th Panzer Divisions into one armoured hammerhead and sent it down into the gap between the two British corps, where they swept the space clean and severely depleted the tank strength of 4th Armoured Brigade. They then abruptly turned north-west and streamed back towards Sidi Rezegh, 7th Armoured Brigade and the Support Group.

Thirty old cruiser tanks and 20 Crusaders of 7th Hussars barred the way before the concentrated strength of the Afrika Korps; but not for long. All the Crusaders and all but ten of the cruiser tanks were pounded into scrap metal in the battle which followed, and only the guns of the Support Group, together with shortage of petrol in the panzer fuel tanks, saved the airfield at the top of Sidi Rezegh valley from being taken by the Germans that evening. But the following morning Rommel looped 5th Panzer Regiment around to the bottom of the valley and then drove on to the British positions from both sides. That day the Victoria Cross was won by Brigadier Jock Campbell in one of the most gallant actions of the war, but on the evening of Nov 22 the weight of the German armour crushed the last resistance and the airfield fell into German hands.

The following day, Sunday, Nov 23 – 'Totensonntag' – the Afrika Korps fought another battle of annihilation, and this time its prey was the 5th South African Brigade, laagered just east of Bir el Gubi. The two panzer divisions were now augmented by the lighter armour of the Ariete Division on their left flank, and at 1400 hrs the combined force moved implacably forwards towards the static mass of artillery and infantry defences in front of it. There followed one of the fiercest battles the Afrika Korps was ever to fight. By dark it was over; the South African Brigade no longer existed – and, although the Eighth Army had obviously suffered a grievous blow, the cost to the Panzergruppe was in the end to prove heavy.

XXX Corps had undoubtedly suffered severe losses, but XIII Corps was still virtually unscathed, and now the New Zealanders were driving along the coast road from the frontier towards Tobruk; the battlefield therefore began to resemble a multi-layered cake, with strong mobile elements of both armies driving to and from Tobruk in alternate sectors. On Nov 24, however, Rommel decided to resolve the situation, believing that the Eighth Army was in such a state of disorganisation that a rapid and vigorous thrust might totally unhinge British dispositions and prove decisive.

So, on Nov 24 Rommel set out on his 'Dash to the Wire'. Placing himself at the head of the combined armour of 21st and 15th Panzer Divisions, with Ariete collected en route, he led a 60-mile dash through Gabr Saleh to the frontier; it was to constitute one of the most spectacular events of the North African Campaign. The scenes which resulted as the panzers roared through the British dumps, supply echelons, armoured and infantry units and field medical centres between Sidi

Rezegh and the Wire live in legend – mostly hilarious. However, even though the Afrika Korps cut through the remains of XXX Corps like a hot knife through butter, the butter coalesced again when the knife had passed.

By nightfall Rommel was himself well into Egypt with the few panzers which had not broken down or run out of petrol – but he was isolated there. To his north 4th Indian Division was still inviolate, while behind him XXX Corps was reorganising rapidly and the New Zealanders were forcing their way through Italian infantry positions along the coast road towards Tobruk. They broke through on Nov 26, linked up with the Tobruk garrison and then turned to fight off a desperate onslaught as Rommel, realising that his eye-catching manoeuvre had in fact been a mistake, returned to rectify it.

In the meantime, Auchinleck felt it necessary to appoint a new commander of Eighth Army. General Cunningham had been unable to assert himself in the pattern of events, and had watched the progress of Rommel's 'Dash to the Wire' from a small aircraft flying above. He had not, therefore, seen the healing process that was going on behind it, and arrived back at his HQ profoundly depressed and talking of drawing back his forces. Auchinleck was there at the time and immediately realised that Cunningham was no longer the man to lead Eighth Army. Two days later Maj-General Neil Ritchie came out to take his place, though at that stage there was little a new commander could do but hold the army together and keep it fighting.

For the remainder of November the battle raged around Tobruk: twice the Allied corridor was cut, but the garrison and especially the New Zealanders – whose epic battle this was – fought like tigers to reopen it. All the time they had to beat off furious and increasingly desperate attacks by Rommel's armour, plus more and more of the Italian infantry which he insisted be fed into the conflict.

But by now Rommel's expenditure of fuel and ammunition was causing deep concern at his HQ. The Royal Navy and the Royal Air Force had been doing as much to defeat Rommel above the battlefield as the Eighth Army had on it; fourteen ships had been sent to the bottom since the battle began, taking 60,000 tons of Rommel's supplies, and only 2,500 tons of the vital fuel had arrived. When in addition to this the cost of Totensonntag in terms of senior officers and experienced NCOs was appreciated, an atmosphere of severe depression developed.

It affected even Rommel. By the end of the month he could see that his forces had been pressed back from the frontier to a line running south of Tobruk, and his intelligence staff was telling him that the new Eighth Army commander had consolidated in the lost space and now had the whole of the Tobruk garrison at his disposal, and that another new reserve division was coming up. Moreover, a strong British raiding group had taken Jalo and was threatening Aujila, well in his rear.

Despite its efforts and spectacular achievements, Panzergruppe Afrika was being forced back.

Japanese Onslaught

Japan had already been waging a major war for two years when the European conflict began in September 1939; what her leaders called the 'China Incident' had been launched in July 1937.

China had been the target of Japanese colonial ambitions ever since the mid-19th century when, under the rule of the powerful Emperor Meiji, Japan began to turn herself from a feudal state run by hereditary Shoguns into a highly industrialised and modern one, run at first by business interests and then, reverting to previous history, by military overlords.

By the end of the 19th century, Japan had successfully annexed the Kuriles, the Ryukus and Taiwan (Formosa) plus important areas of Chinese coastal territory – and she was bitterly angry when pressure from Russia, France and Germany forced her to hand back the Chinese territory. The attack on the Czar's Far Eastern Fleet in Port Arthur in 1904, followed in May 1905 by the stunning victory at Tsushima against the same enemy's Baltic Fleet, went some way towards calming the anger – and also gave to the Japanese the southern half of Sakhalin. They certainly established Japan as a power to be reckoned with in all Far Eastern affairs; but they did not supply her with the much larger markets she needed for her rapidly growing industries, nor overseas possessions to satisfy her engulfing national pride, based as it was on a semi-religious belief that it was the Japanese destiny to rule the world.

The youth of the country were now inculcated in this belief from their earliest years, accepting that the Japanese Emperor was divine and that the highest honour any of them could achieve would be to die in battle for him, and if in the early years of the 20th century there was little chance for such sacrificial devotion – compared with later years – at least the businessmen and politicians could exercise their talents in expanding the Emperor's domains. By the outbreak of World War 1, Korea had fallen totally under Japan's economic control, and as a result of Japan's entry into the war on the side of the victorious Allies at the end of it Tokyo was awarded mandate over the previous German possessions in the Pacific – the Marshall Islands, the Marianas and the Carolines, and the Kiaochao Peninsula in the Shantung Province of China. Japan was also by this time exercising almost complete economic control over Manchuria, an area which by 1932 she felt was so much a part of the Japanese Empire that she renamed it Manchukuo.

But the financial crash of 1929 had hit Japan at least as badly as it hit Europe, and by the early 1930s she was in an economic and political situation not dissimilar to the one in Germany – with similar results. By 1932, liberal politicians had all been discredited – some assassinated – and right-wing nationalists had taken their places, strongly backed by militarists including a large faction of young and ambitious army officers.

At first their yearnings for military glory and colonial expansion were satisfied by the annexation of Manchukuo and its occupation by the divisions of their Kwantung Army, but when the League of Nations refused to recognise the new state, Japan left the League and the concept of a 'Greater East Asia Co-Prosperity Sphere' was born within her ruling circles. At first this meant, in effect, Japanese domination of East Asia and the Western Pacific, but during the months that followed even this scenario for expansionism did not satisfy its creators' mounting ambition. With the lack of concerted opposition from Britain, France, Holland, or even from America, and with the example of Nazi Germany's successful aggression before them, Japanese militarists were soon envisaging Japanese hegemony over the entire Far East with all Europeans driven out. This was the ultimate strategic aim which was to underlie every Japanese tactical and strategic move during the decade and a half to come, and the main process began in July 1937 when, under the most spurious pretext, the Japanese armies began their invasion of North China.

But the 'China Incident' did not go quite as had been expected. The War Minister, General Sugiyama, had assured Emperor Hirohito that it would all be over within a few weeks, and at first the speed of the Japanese advance seemed to bear this out. By the end of that first month they had captured Tientsin, and during the first week of August the Chinese forces defending Peking seemed to melt away. They eluded the Japanese forces whenever they pushed forward – and the Japanese armies followed, drawn all the time deeper and deeper into China, whose rulers, disappointingly, showed not the slightest inclination to surrender. And every Japanese advance exacted its price in manpower. By the end of 1937 nearly 700,000 Japanese troops had followed the first invasion, of whom 75,000 had been killed or wounded – and if Chinese casualties were calculated at over five times that number it seemed that China could afford them.

China could also afford space. The Chinese leader, Chiang Kai Shek, having for the moment arranged a truce with the Communist forces under Mao Tse Tung, eventually removed his capital to Chungking, the eastern end of the 'Burma Road' along which Britain was sending what supplies she could spare. Needless to say, Japan found this support for China from Britain offensive, but for the moment there was little she could do about it, for both Britain and America were her chief suppliers of oil – and as month followed month and the Japanese armies moved farther and farther away from their homeland their transport, armour and air support gulped oil as fast as it could be supplied, while their military machine as a whole also devoured metal and rubber – of which Japan had little or no reserves within her own borders – with that voracity which war demands.

Then came 1939, and if European affairs diverted the world's attention from Japanese depredations and atrocities in China, they also diverted those essential supplies, for Britain now needed every ounce of war material she could produce for her own struggle against Germany, while America's industry was reorganising to aid Britain as far as neutrality would allow.

Thus it was evident that as Japanese need for war material grew her sources of supply would contract . . . and even while this lesson was being digested, Russian moves on the far side of the Amur river necessitated counter-manoeuvres and extra supplies to the Kwantung Army. Calculations would reveal that without a continual and ample supply of oil from outside the borders of her empire, Japan's reserves would be used up long before China could be subjugated, and her armies would have no choice but to retreat.

Early in 1940, Japan seemed suddenly to be presented with a golden opportunity. Two of the colonial powers which barred the way to Japanese domination of the Far East – France and Holland – lay shattered by Hitler's Blitzkrieg, and the third, Britain, was evidently close to defeat; the way was surely open to seize their colonies – Malaya, Burma, French Indo-China and the Dutch East Indies. Between them, these areas could easily provide all the oil and rubber Japan would need, first for the subjugation of China, and then for the foundation of a 'New Order' in the Far East which would result in that visionary 'Co-Prosperity Sphere'.

Faced with the choice of either seizing that opportunity, or of abandoning the hard-won conquests of nearly three years' fighting – and a consequent loss of face that no Eastern race could survive – it is hardly surprising that the gamble of military expansion was accepted.

Planning began immediately, but until it was complete and the necessary military and naval forces assembled and trained, diplomatic pressure would surely reap some rewards against such weakened opposition? So it proved. By the end of August 1940, Vichy France had agreed that Japanese troops and air squadrons could be stationed in northern Indo-China, and in the face of such a close threat Britain had little choice but to close the Burma Road. Moreover, Britain's need for troops elsewhere made her accept with little argument the Japanese insistence on the withdrawal of British garrisons from Shanghai and Tientsin. As for Holland, her representatives in Batavia were abruptly faced with demands for huge supplies of oil on long-term contracts, and the necessity for immediate agreement was underlined by the announcement on Sept 27, 1940, of the Tripartite Pact between Japan, Italy and Germany. Pressure, it was hinted, would be brought to bear on Amsterdam from Berlin if Batavia did not accede to Japanese demands.

But the reaction to the pact was not quite as Japanese leaders expected. America immediately promised the Chinese a $100 million loan and assured the Dutch that they could rely upon help from the United States in any confrontation with any aggressor nation – which, in American eyes, the signatories of the Tripartite Pact undoubtedly were. And Britain reacted by re-opening the Burma Road.

Nevertheless, by the end of 1940, Japan was in a strong position. Oil was still arriving from America and the Dutch East Indies and thus the reserves were rising; metal and rubber could still be bought. Moreover, diplomacy in the early months of 1941 brought other advantages for on April 13 the Foreign Minister, Matsuoka, signed a non-aggression pact with Russia which took some of the pressure off the Kwantung Army, which could therefore release troops for the China Front to the south.

Then on July 18, intent on seeing how far diplomacy would take them, Matsuoka's successor, Admiral

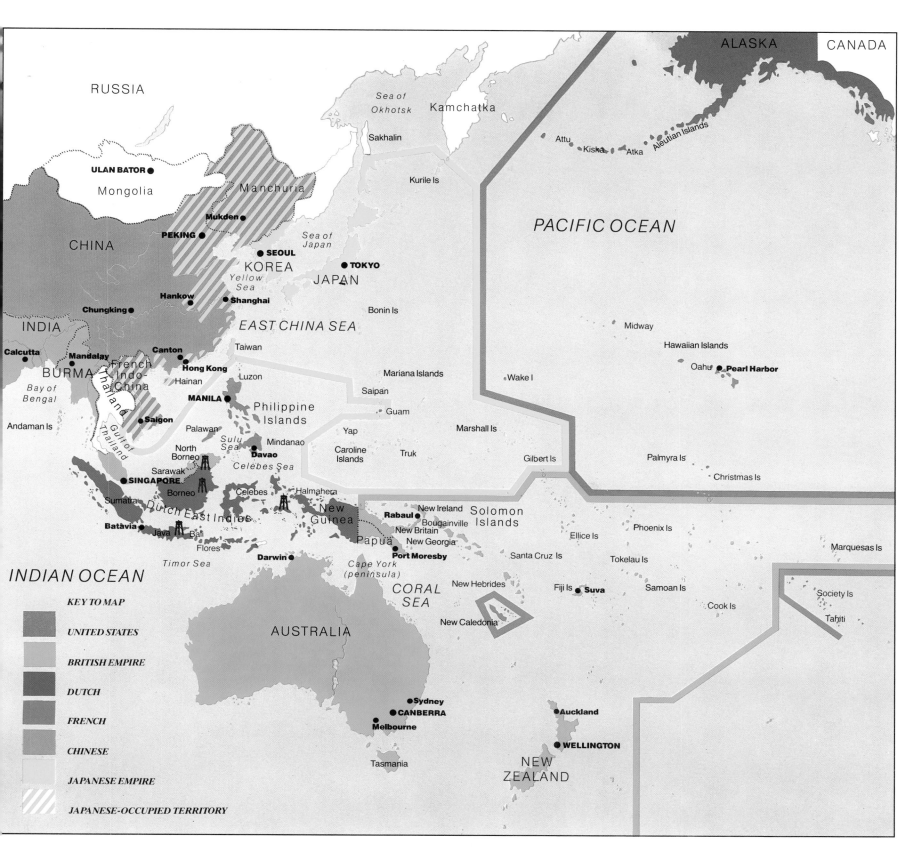

KEY TO MAP

UNITED STATES

BRITISH EMPIRE

DUTCH

FRENCH

CHINESE

JAPANESE EMPIRE

JAPANESE-OCCUPIED TERRITORY

Toyoda, presented France with demands for air, land and sea bases in southern Indo-China which would put Singapore within bombing range, and when Vichy France acceded on July 24, President Roosevelt decided that enough was enough.

Two days later all Japanese assets in America were frozen, the next day Britain and Holland followed Roosevelt's example, and at a stroke, the expected crisis was precipitated and all Japanese supplies of oil and most of her supplies of rubber were cut off. Now only military action was left: to the doubting Emperor Hirohito who recognised the possibility – indeed probability – that Japan could not win a long war against a nation with the vast industrial resources of America, the Chief of the Japanese Naval Staff, Admiral Nagano, declared 'Japan is like a fish in a pond from which the water is gradually being drained away'. Reluctantly, the Emperor listened to the plans.

The task of securing the most convenient areas producing oil and rubber – the Dutch East Indies – would pose no insuperable problems to a few divisions of an efficient battle-hardened army. The main problem would then be that of getting the war materials back to

the Japanese homeland through waters flanked by the British-controlled Malay States and Singapore, and the American-controlled Philippines with their naval base at Manila; for there could be no doubt as to the reaction of Britain and America to a *coup de main* against the Dutch possessions.

Both Singapore and Manila must be neutralised, and the only certain way would be occupation of all surrounding spaces. Luzon and Mindanao must therefore be conquered – obviously by forces direct from Japan or Taiwan; Malaya by forces operating from French Indo-China through Thailand – and if these proved quickly successful they could then drive up into Burma where yet more oil and rubber awaited collection. But the major threat to successful completion of such manifold and complex operations lay hundreds of miles away to the east across the international dateline; the American Pacific Fleet operating from Pearl Harbor, its base on the island of Oahu in the Hawaiian Islands.

As for the timing of the launch, this seemed almost preordained by Fate. Japan's oil reserves would fall past the crisis point at the end of December 1941. The 11 divisions which the army could spare for this entire

sequence of operations (35 remained in China and Manchukuo) would not be ready and in position until November; the navy required specific conditions of moonlight and weather for the approach to Pearl Harbor which would be best satisfied during the hours before dawn on Sunday, Dec 8.

Thus, during those fateful days at the beginning of December 1941, six gigantic military operations were launched into an area stretching a quarter of the way around the world, to open almost simultaneously on both sides of the dateline.

History had seen nothing to compare with it.

1 Red Army Counter-attacks. Encouraged by the recent developments around the mouth of the Don, on Dec 5 Stalin instructed the commanders of both Kalinin and West Fronts to take the offensive to push Army Group Centre back from Moscow, and on the following day they were joined by South-west Front – 15 armies altogether. Gradually but remorselessly, the German armies were levered away from the outskirts of Moscow, the pincers on each side bent back, Kalinin and Yolokolamsk retaken in the north, while to the south Guderian's recent gains were wiped out and the Russians began a drive from Tula up towards Kaluga. On the Northern Front armies from the Leningrad, Volkhov and North-western Fronts combined to try to break the iron circle around Leningrad, and at least they managed to regain Tikhvin and so re-open the rail link. As Lake Ladoga was fast freezing solid, convoys could begin crossing from the mouth of the Volkhov river, and the famous 'Ladoga Road' opened.

Far to the south, armies from the Caucasus Front followed up their recapture of Rostov and advance to the Mius river by large-scale operations on the southern side of the Sea of Azov. From Novorossiysk 14 transports set out across 100 miles of the Black Sea in a Force 8 gale, carrying 20,000 men who were landed on the Kerch Peninsula and at Feodosia, where they drove out elements of Manstein's Eleventh Army and posed a severe threat to the rest of it around Sevastopol. Much of the Red Army's success was undoubtedly due to the lessons its commanders had learned over the last dreadful months, together with the organisation of new armies from reserves – and several experienced armies had been brought from Siberia once Stalin had accepted that Russia was in no danger from Japan. Another key factor was the exhaustion of the German troops after their immense advances, augmented by their commanders' strong belief that the prudent course would be to withdraw to safe winter lines and prepare for a spring offensive.

Hitler, however, would have none of this, and was furious at both the suggestion and then the fact of any withdrawal at all. Faced on the maps with the results of the December fighting, he took instant revenge. On Dec 19 he himself took over the post of Commander-in-Chief of the army, and then a grand purge of the senior officers took place. Leeb was sacked, Bock sent home to hospital (he had been suffering from stomach cramps – as were so many of his army). Rundstedt had already gone. Thirty-five army, corps and divisional commanders, including Guderian, were relieved of their commands and one was court-martialled and dismissed from the Wehrmacht.

☆ **Commando Raids.** Dec 26/27. Large-scale commando raids on Vaagso and a smaller one on the Lofoten Islands. Destruction of fish-oil factories carried out, German garrisons killed or captured, gun batteries wrecked, Norwegian quislings and young volunteers brought away. These raids caused Hitler to reinforce the German Army in Norway.

Continual RAF daylight offensive against NW Germany

No serious Luftwaffe raids on Britain

Night raids on Aachen, Cologne, Wilhelmshafen, Bremen, Düsseldorf, Huls, Emden, Brest, St Nazaire and La Pallice

Damaging attacks on *Scharnhorst* and *Gneisenau* in Brest harbour

Fierce convoy battle off Portugal; 5 U-boats sunk, 1 aircraft-carrier, 1 destroyer and 3 merchantmen sunk

Desert Air Force bomb Benghazi and Tripoli

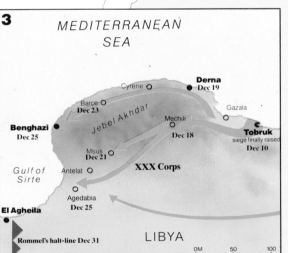

2

night Dec 12 — 2 It cruisers sunk — Palermo — Cape Bon — MEDITERRANEAN SEA — Dec 17 1st Battle of Sirte — Dec 18 Tripoli — Br Force K sustains losses in It minefield — Dec 15 Br cruiser torpedoed — Alexandria — Dec 19 2 Br battleships damaged by It frogmen

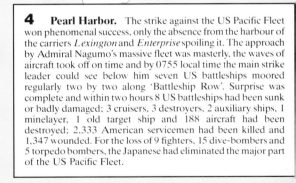

3 MEDITERRANEAN SEA — Cyrene — Derna Dec 19 — Barce Dec 23 — Jebel Akhdar — Mechili — Gazala — Benghazi Dec 25 — Dec 18 — Tobruk siege finally raised Dec 10 — Msus Dec 21 — Gulf of Sirte — Antelat — XXX Corps — Agedabia Dec 25 — El Agheila — Rommel's halt-line Dec 31 — LIBYA — 0M 50 100 / 0Km 50 100 150

1 Lake Ladoga — Volkhov — Tikhvin Dec 8 — LENINGRAD — NORTH-WEST FRONT (Kurochkin) — Lake Ilmen — Staraya Russa — Demyansk — Lake Seliger — Kholm — Yaroslavl — Velikiye Luki — Kalinin Dec 15 — Volga — Dec 15 — Klin — MOSCOW — Rzhev — Istra — Dec 11 — Vyasma — Serpukhov — WEST FRONT (Zhukov) — Orsha — Smolensk — Kaluga Dec 30 — Kozelsk — Tula — Roslavl — Dec 31 — BRYANSK FRONT (from Dec 18) (Yeremenko) — ARMY GROUP CENTRE (Kluge) — Bryansk — Orel — Yelets Dec 9 — Gomel — Kursk — Voronezh — Stary Oskol — KIEV — Lokhvitsa — Kharkov — SOUTH-WEST FRONT (Timoshenko) — Poltava — ARMY GROUP SOUTH (Reichenau) — Dnepropetrovsk — Ukraine — Taganrog — Rostov — Mariupol — Azov — ODESSA — Sea of Azov — CAUCASUS FRONT — BLACK SEA — Crimea — Dec 30 Kerch — Krasnodar — Eupatoriya — Dec 30 Feodosia — Novorossiysk — Maikop — Sevastopol — Yalta — Tuapse

3 Tired Crusader. The battle around Tobruk was still being fought on Dec 1, and to the hard-pressed New Zealanders it was by no means obvious that they were winning. They were still under violent attack from 15th Panzer Division and the remains of the Afrika Korps artillery train, and to them the link with the Tobruk garrison seemed tenuous indeed. So desperate did their situation look to their commander, Maj-General Bernard Freyberg, that he sent a message in clear to XXX Corps HQ saying that he intended to break out and race back into Egypt – and the interception of the signal was enough to send Rommel's hopes soaring once more.

But on the evening of Dec 5 a senior staff officer arrived from Supreme HQ in Libya and told Rommel bluntly that he could expect no early replacements for the 142 panzers, 25 armoured cars, 83 guns or 60 mortars he had lost, and, even worse, for the 16 commanding officers or the 4,000-odd other ranks now dead, badly wounded or missing.

Twenty-four hours later it became obvious that the British in front of him were about to launch another powerful drive forwards, and their heavy artillery hammered all the Axis forward positions. Reluctantly, Rommel accepted the situation and gave orders for a withdrawal as far as Gazala, and then, as there was no real defence line there, that the retreat must go back as far as the Gulf of Sirte.

As the Axis forces went back, the British followed up – cautiously, for experience had taught them of the efficacy of Panzergruppe rearguards. As they closed down through the Jebel Akhdar towards Antelat the combined remains of 15th and 21st Panzer turned sharply and struck at the following British armour, reducing it by 37 tanks. They all then carried on towards El Agheila.

4 Pearl Harbor. The strike against the US Pacific Fleet won phenomenal success, only the absence from the harbour of the carriers *Lexington* and *Enterprise* spoiling it. The approach by Admiral Nagumo's massive fleet was masterly, the waves of aircraft took off on time and by 0755 local time the main strike leader could see below him seven US battleships moored regularly two by two along 'Battleship Row'. Surprise was complete and within two hours 8 US battleships had been sunk or badly damaged; 3 cruisers, 3 destroyers, 2 auxiliary ships, 1 minelayer, 1 old target ship and 188 aircraft had been destroyed; 2,333 American servicemen had been killed and 1,347 wounded. For the loss of 9 fighters, 15 dive-bombers and 5 torpedo bombers, the Japanese had eliminated the major part of the US Pacific Fleet.

5 Malayan Peninsula. Matters went just as well elsewhere. Landings had taken place along the Thai coast from Prachuab in the north down to Khota Bharu, and from French Indo-China units would drive west to Bangkok and control the whole of northern Thailand by the end of the month.

From Singora and Patani, the Japanese 5th and 18th Divisions drove south towards the western coast of Malaya, reaching Penang by Dec 16, the Perak river-line and defences by Dec 17, broke through these and reached Ipoh by Dec 26. From Khota Bharu on the eastern coast, forces under General Takumi broke the British defences on the frontier just to the south, and then pushed on down the coast road as far as Kuantan, which they reached on Dec 31.

Off the east coast of Malaya, Japanese carrier-borne aircraft scored another striking success. The two British battleships *Repulse* and *Prince of Wales* had sailed from Singapore at 1735 on Dec 8 as soon as reports of Japanese landings on the Kra Isthmus were received. They were seen by two Japanese reconnaissance aircraft on the evening of Dec 9, four hours later Admiral Phillips received erroneous reports of Japanese landings at Kuantan and by morning was off the otherwise empty coast. Shortly after 1100 as the ships steamed southwards Japanese aircraft flew in from the north-west, by 1200 *Repulse* was under attack and hit, then a second wave of torpedo-bombers arrived and attacked the *Prince of Wales*. Two torpedoes ripped open her stern and within minutes it was obvious that she was doomed. She was a big ship, however, and it was not until 1320 that she eventually rolled over and sank.

Repulse had gone down, 'her bows sticking up into the air like a church steeple', at 1233. With them the two ships took 840 men of their joint complement of 2,921.

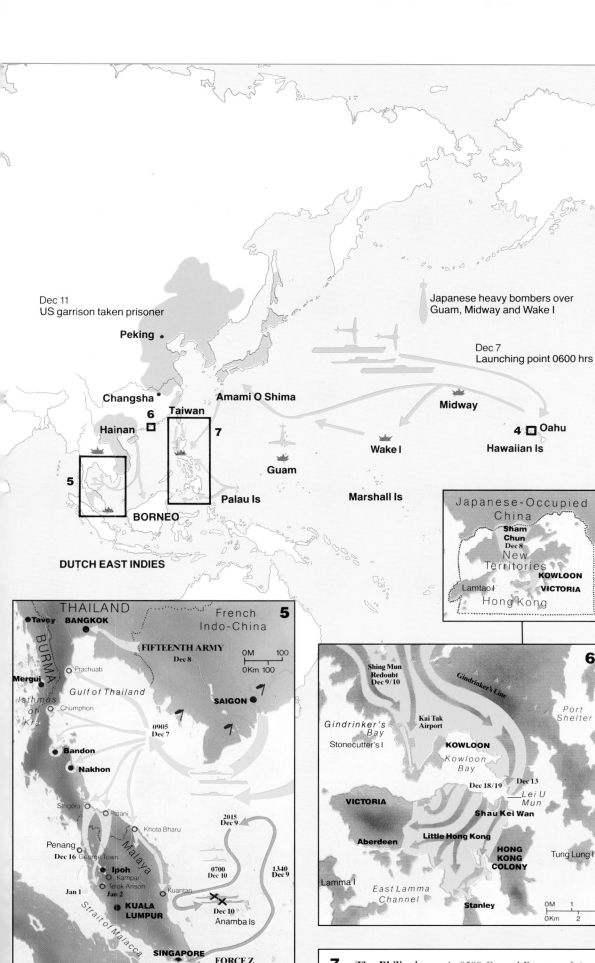

DECEMBER 1941

Dec 11
US garrison taken prisoner

Peking

Japanese heavy bombers over
Guam, Midway and Wake I

Dec 7
Launching point 0600 hrs

Changsha

Amami O Shima

6 Taiwan

Hainan

7

5

BORNEO

DUTCH EAST INDIES

Midway

Wake I

Guam

Palau Is

4 Oahu

Hawaiian Is

Marshall Is

4

1st attack   2nd attack

PACIFIC OCEAN

Oahu

43 fighters
54 high-level bombers
36 fighters
80 dive bombers
51 dive bombers
70 torpedo bombers
50 high-level bombers

Wheeler Airfield

Kaneohe Airfield

HONOLULU

Ewa Airfield   Hickham Airfield

Pearl Harbor

0M 5
0Km 5

Japanese-Occupied China

Sham Chun
Dec 8

New Territories

KOWLOON

Lamtao I   VICTORIA

Hong Kong

5

THAILAND   French Indo-China

Tavoy BANGKOK

BURMA

FIFTEENTH ARMY
Dec 8

0M 100
0Km 100

Mergui

Gulf of Thailand

Prachuab

Isthmus of Kra   Chumphon

SAIGON

Bandon

Nakhon

0905 Dec 7

Singora   Patani

2015 Dec 9

Penang   Khota Bharu

Dec 16 George Town

Malaya

0700 Dec 10   1340 Dec 9

Ipoh Kampar

Telok Anson Jan 2   Kuantan

Jan 1

KUALA LUMPUR

Strait of Malacca

Dec 10   Anamba Is

SINGAPORE   FORCE Z

Sumatra   1735 Dec 8

6

Shing Mun Redoubt Dec 9/10

Gindrinker's Line

Gindrinker's Bay

Kai Tak Airport

Port Shelter

Stonecutter's I   KOWLOON

Kowloon Bay

Dec 18/19   Dec 13

Lei U Mun

VICTORIA   Shau Kei Wan

Aberdeen   Little Hong Kong

HONG KONG COLONY

Tung Lung I

Lamma I   East Lamma Channel

Stanley

0M 1 2
0Km 1 2

7

Taiwan

Bashi Channel

Batan Dec 8

FOURTEENTH ARMY (Homma)

from Amami O Shima

Fuga   Camiguan

Laoag

Vigan Dec 10   Aparri Dec 10

Luzon

PHILIPPINE SEA

Dec 22   Lingayen Gulf

MANILA   Dec 24

Manila Bay   Lamon Bay   San Miguel Bay

Tayabas Bay   Dec 12

Mindoro   Legazpi

Mindoro Strait   Dec 20

Tablas   Masbate   Samar   from Palau

Palawan   Panay   Leyte

Cebu   Dinagat

Negros   Bohol

PHILIPPINE ISLANDS

Mindanao

Sulu Sea   DAVAO Dec 20

Moro Gulf

Dec 25

Jolo   from Palau

Borneo   Sulu Archipelago

0M 100 200
0Km 100 200 300

6 **Hong Kong.** Five hours after the attack on Pearl Harbor the Japanese attacked across the Sham river, their aircraft first destroying RAF planes at Kai Tak airfield. By the morning of Dec 10 they had captured the Shing Mun Redoubt in the 'Gindrinker's Line' and only a rapid retreat on to Hong Kong Island remained for the defenders.

Demands for the surrender of the island were at first rejected, but by Dec 17 the entire island was within range of Japanese artillery, which had already hit and wrecked many of the defences along the northern shore. During the night of Dec 18/19 Japanese infantry crossed the Lei U Mun Strait, and drove into the central part of the island against desperate resistance. But the end was inevitable; by Christmas morning only eight guns and a little ammunition was left. At 1515 the Governor, Sir Mark Young, surrendered to General Sakai in the Peninsula Hotel, and some 6,500 British and Indian soldiers went into Japanese captivity. Japanese casualties amounted to 2,750.

7 **The Philippines.** At 0500 General Brereton of the USAAF heard the news from Pearl Harbor and immediately began to organise bombing attacks on airfields in Taiwan, but it was 1215 before the aircraft were ready to take off and at that moment 108 Japanese bombers and 84 fighters arrived overhead. In the violence that followed, and during the next two days, US air power in the Philippines – at Clark Field, Nichols Field and three fields around Manila – was wiped out.

By then, elements of General Homma's Fourteenth Army had landed on Batan island, at Aparri, and at Vigan on the west coast of Luzon, to drive quickly down to the area covering Lingayen Gulf. Here, on Dec 22 the bulk of Homma's army went ashore and began their drive down towards Manila. Meanwhile, an infantry division had arrived at Lamon Bay from Amami O Shima and a smaller detachment from Palau at Legazpi, thus isolating south Luzon from Manila and the north.

Japanese advances in both directions were rapid and irresistible, by Dec 31 General MacArthur and his HQ had withdrawn on to Corregidor, and only the Bataan Peninsula was still in US hands.

Small Japanese detachments had also landed at Davao to occupy Mindanao, and on Dec 25 they sailed around and took Jolo, thus establishing control of the outer islands.

1 Russian Counter-attack. With the December successes to hearten his armies, Stalin summoned a meeting of STAVKA on Jan 5 and ordered an all-out offensive along the entire length of the front from the Baltic to the Black Sea. The main blow was to be delivered by the armies of North-west, Kalinin and West Fronts against Army Group Centre, but the Leningrad Front, aided by the Baltic Fleet and the right wing of North-west Front, was to defeat Army Group North and relieve Leningrad. In the south the Crimea was to be liberated by Caucasus Front and the Black Sea Fleet, while Army Group South was to be flung out of the Don basin (Donbass) by South-western and Southern Fronts.

In the circumstances, results were better than could have been expected. Between Lake Ilmen and just north of Orel some 17 Soviet armies pushed forward and from the North-west Front the Fourth Shock Army drove down between Army Groups North and Centre to Demidov, and towards Smolensk – though awkward salients reached up each side of the penetration, on the north to Kholm and on the east to Rzhev. On the West and Bryansk Fronts progress was made too, aided by large pockets of partisans to whom airborne reinforcements were dropped.

Further south, the armies of Marshal Timoshenko's South-west Front attacked over the Donets and drove forward 60 miles to form what was called the Izyum Bulge. Reaching Lozovaya, they raised hopes of a further drive to the South-west towards Dnepropetrovsk and the vital German supply lines through Zaporozhye, or one to the north to retake Kharkov. By Jan 31, however, Army Group South had shored up the defences along each side of the bulge and blocked it solidly in front.

In the Crimea more reinforcements were landed from Caucasus Front on the Kerch Peninsula, and these drove forward to link up with the Feodosia bridgehead, thus controlling the eastern end of the Crimea and the causeway that stretches across from the neck to the mainland. However, an attempt to break the siege of Sevastopol by a powerful drive westwards, aided by seaborne landings, was easily beaten off by the experienced formations of Manstein's Eleventh Army. By the end of January it was becoming increasingly evident that the huge Russian counter attack was losing momentum as too many men were lost through inexperience and lack of training, as ammunition stocks dwindled and as German technique solidified their defences.

Night-bombing targets: Emden, Hamburg, Bremen, Münster, Hanover, Brest, St Nazaire, Cherbourg, Boulogne, Le Havre, Rotterdam, Naples, Sicily

No serious Luftwaffe raids on Britain

Daylight bombing western Europe and English Channel 10 days

Malta bombed frequently

Middle East Air Force bomb Salamis, Heraklion, Tripoli

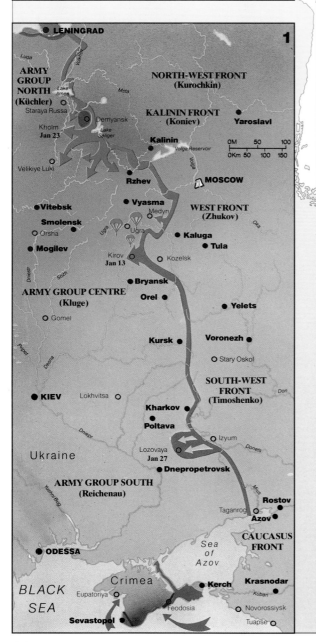

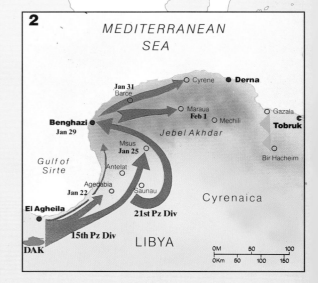

2 North Africa – Lightning Riposte. For an army which had just advanced from Egypt to the Gulf of Sirte, Eighth Army was in considerable disarray. Forward elements between Agedabia and El Agheila watched enemy units in front with little enthusiasm, while behind them other formations came up to complete the occupation of Benghazi, Barce and Derna, and further back still XXX Corps troops took the surrender of the isolated German garrisons at Bardia, Sollum and Halfaya. Many of the troops in the Jebel Akhdar area were newly arrived replacements for the Crusader casualties, and the remainder were tired after the stresses of the advance. Panzergruppe Afrika (about to be rechristened Panzerarmee Afrika), however, was in far better condition than could have been expected. Not only were their lines of communication much shorter than previously, but supplies were arriving in Tripoli at a hitherto unknown rate, owing much to the losses suffered during December by the Royal Navy. Of the five capital ships in the Mediterranean when Crusader was launched, only one was still afloat, and in addition two Royal Navy cruisers had been sunk, two badly damaged and one withdrawn by the Australian government for service nearer home.

Rommel struck early on the morning of Jan 21 and within two days had smashed through to Agedabia, thoroughly routed a British armoured brigade on Jan 24 to reach Msus in the evening, and by the next day had chased all the remaining British armour back to Charuba. By Jan 28 German units were closing on Benghazi, where a single Indian brigade was carrying out rapid demolitions and organising for itself a narrow, risky escape route. During those last days of January, under heavy rain and in appalling wind and sandstorms, the British withdrew in scattered, isolated columns as far as Gazala. The jubilant Panzergruppe followed, some through Mechili and some around the coastal route, at their own pace and convenience. Tobruk seemed, once again, almost within their grasp.

3 Malaya. General Yamashita's forces were now driving forward relentlessly; whenever an assault against defensive positions was mounted, only one-third of the force would make a frontal attack, while two-thirds swept around the flank to the rear positions. Time and time again the tactic worked and the British were pushed even further down towards their last defences and Singapore. By Jan 2 they were back on the Slim river and here on Jan 7 they suffered a really disastrous defeat, which reduced one brigade to one-third of its strength and totally destroyed another.

On Jan 11 the Japanese 5th Division reached Kuala Lumpur with its vast warehouses of military stores and equipment, and seaborne forces looped out from Kuala Selangor and took Port Swettenham. Gemas and Malacca fell to the advance on Jan 25, and then Yamashita's and Takumi's men where driving down on the last stretch to Johore Bahru. Churchill had sent a message to the Singapore commander, Lt-General A. E. Percival, which read: 'I want to make it absolutely clear that I expect every inch of ground to be defended . . . and no question of surrender to be entertained until after protracted fighting among the ruins of Singapore City.'

Part of 44th Indian Division – some 7,000 men – were landed on Jan 22, followed the next day by the main body of the British 18th Division plus some 1,900 Australian troops – and by the end of the month survivors of the fighting on the mainland were streaming back across the causeway. By Jan 31 all British and Indian forces were back on the island, and General Percival had at his disposal for the defence of Singapore nearly 85,000 men.

4 Dutch East Indies and the Pacific Area. With Malaya and the Philippines well within its grasp by the end of the year, the Japanese Command could now turn its attention to its chief target. On Jan 1 troops from the Western Force began their occupation of Sarawak and British North Borneo, and by the end of the month had pushed seaborne forces around to Pontianak in the south and Sandakan in the north. Then on Jan 11 they landed seaborne forces from Davao at Tarakan on Borneo and Manado on Celebes, then looped one force down the Strait of Makassar to Balikpapan and another through the Molucca Passage to Kendari, and yet another direct from Davao to Ambon on Ceram.

It was then that the first big naval battle of the Pacific theatre occurred, when 16 Japanese transports, escorted by a light cruiser and 9 destroyers, were attacked in the Strait of Makassar off Balikpapan by 4 US destroyers and a group of submarines. Four of the transports and 1 destroyer were sunk, and 1 US destroyer was damaged – but nonetheless Balikpapan fell the same day.

Further east, Rabaul in New Britain and Kavieng in New Ireland were bombed on Jan 20, and on Jan 24 troops were landed on both islands. In Rabaul they took 1,400 Australians prisoner after a short battle, but Kavieng was undefended, as was Bougainville in the Solomon Islands.

Realising the dangers in which its forces now stood, the Australian government withdrew them from Lae and Salamaua on the east coast of New Guinea, but reinforced the garrison at Port Moresby on the south coast.

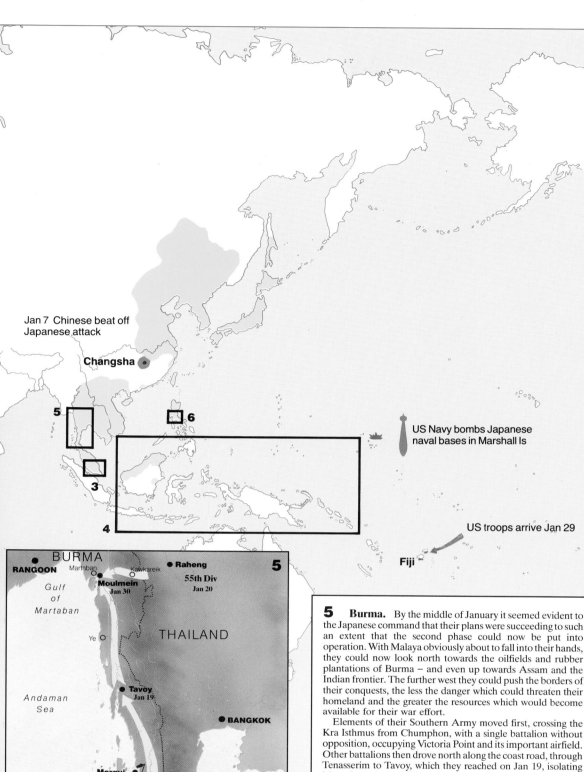

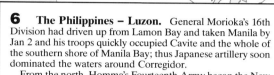

Jan 7 Chinese beat off Japanese attack

Changsha

US Navy bombs Japanese naval bases in Marshall Is

US troops arrive Jan 29

Fiji

6 **The Philippines – Luzon.** General Morioka's 16th Division had driven up from Lamon Bay and taken Manila by Jan 2 and his troops quickly occupied Cavite and the whole of the southern shore of Manila Bay; thus Japanese artillery soon dominated the waters around Corregidor.

From the north, Homma's Fourteenth Army began the New Year by breaking through a thin defence line at Porac and by Jan 6 they were pressing down into the Bataan Peninsula on each side of the central mountains, on the west aiming for Moron, on the east for the flat country leading down to the Orion–Bagac road, where they expected the main US defence line to lie. They suffered heavy casualties on the night of Jan 10/11 in the foothills of Mount Santa Rosa, but in the end the American and Philippino troops had to fall back. On the west side of the peninsula General Wainwright's I Corps were savagely attacked in the positions between Mount Natib and the coast from Jan 18 to Jan 25, and as exhaustion and shortage of ammunition became crucial they were forced to drop back behind the last defence line in the northern foothills of the Mariveles, where at least they were well covered by strong and dominating artillery positions on the slopes.

5 **Burma.** By the middle of January it seemed evident to the Japanese command that their plans were succeeding to such an extent that the second phase could now be put into operation. With Malaya obviously about to fall into their hands, they could now look north towards the oilfields and rubber plantations of Burma – and even up towards Assam and the Indian frontier. The further west they could push the borders of their conquests, the less the danger which could threaten their homeland and the greater the resources which would become available for their war effort.

Elements of their Southern Army moved first, crossing the Kra Isthmus from Chumphon, with a single battalion without opposition, occupying Victoria Point and its important airfield. Other battalions then drove north along the coast road, through Tenasserim to Tavoy, which they reached on Jan 19, isolating Mergui and its airfield.

The next day the Japanese 55th Division left Raheng in North Thailand and drove west over the Burmese border to Kawkareik, where it thoroughly routed the British 16th Brigade and sent its survivors staggering back towards Moulmein. The Japanese followed them, and a race developed between the forward elements of the 55th Division and those of the Southern Army, by now up past Ye and also heading for Moulmein. Both arrived on Jan 30 and the next day were already threatening Martaban and the road to Sittang and Rangoon, both places by now under heavy Japanese air raids.

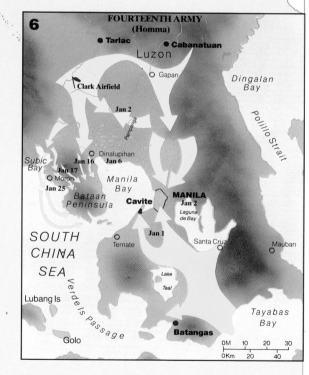

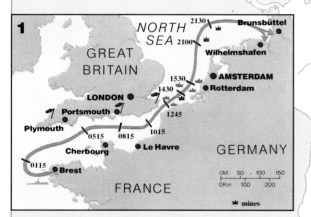

The Bruneval Raid. On the night of Feb 27/28, 118 men of the Parachute Regt and an RAF technician dropped into France near the village of Bruneval, close to Le Havre. They first attacked an isolated house and cleared it, then the technician and a small party raced across to a pit near the cliff-top containing part of the German radio-location chain. Flt-Sergeant Cox dismantled it and removed the main component, then he and his party ran down the cliff-path to the beach, defended by the remaining paratroops. Royal Navy landing-craft picked them up, then transferred them to fast motor gun-boats; within 24 hours the dismantled equipment was being examined by British scientists.

Stalemate Ruled on the Russian Front. The great counter-offensive ordered by Stalin had used up all available supplies of fuel and ammunition long before any significant breakthrough could have occurred, and neither Red Army communications nor their command control were as yet sound or experienced enough to sustain operations on such a vast scale. The drive down from between Lake Ilmen and Orel did manage to struggle a few miles nearer to Smolensk, but the main effect of this was to lengthen and make more dangerous the long German salient running up from Vyazma to Rzhev. As for the Germans, they had effectively halted the Russian counter-offensive and were recovering from their efforts, gradually accustoming themselves to the below-freezing temperatures and learning how to cope with them, while their new commanders studied their problems and planned for a Spring Offensive designed finally to annihilate the Red Army.

Feb 1 Puppet government set up in Norway under Quisling

Night raids on Kiel, Bremen, Mannheim, Cologne and Wilhelmshafen; Brest, Le Havre, Ostend and St Nazaire

No serious raids on Britain

Daylight bombing against France and Occupied Territories for 10 days

Malta bombed frequently

Middle East Air Force bombs Sicily, Tripoli, Benghazi and shipping in Mediterranean. Ten Axis ships sunk or damaged

1 The Channel Dash. Since March 1941 the two German battlecruisers *Scharnhorst* and *Gneisenau* had been sheltering in Brest harbour, and in June they had been joined by the heavy cruiser *Prinz Eugen*. All three ships had suffered some damage during the intervening months, enough to keep them in Brest harbour – and at the end of the year Hitler decided that they would risk much graver harm if they remained there, so on Jan 12, 1942, he ordered either that they return to home waters or that they be decommissioned. Admiral Ciliax, commanding the German squadron, knowing that the main weight of the British Home Fleet based on Scapa Flow, lay well to the north, laid plans for an audacious escape straight up the English Channel.

Not only were the plans detailed and soundly based, but the operation – code-named 'Cerberus' – was attended by excellent fortune. Escorted by six destroyers and a small fleet of support craft, the three ships formed up in the roadstead outside Brest at 2245 hrs on Feb 11, under heavy low cloud and shrouded in swirling mists. A British submarine on spotter duty outside the harbour had abandoned watch ten minutes before, as the Admiralty considered that any escape attempt would plan to pass through the Dover Straits in darkness which would necessitate leaving harbour much earlier. Radar equipment in aircraft overhead failed on two vital occasions, and it was 0830 hrs on Feb 12 before information of 'unusual activity' in the Channel reached RAF HQ. Even then it was 1020 before any special reconnaissance was ordered.

By this time the German ships were well past the Isle of Wight and about to enter the Dover Straits, and now continuous Luftwaffe fighter cover was available. By noon they had passed through a minefield and were able to steam at full speed, taking them beyond the range of coastal guns at Dover and enabling them to brush aside attacks by RN motor torpedo-boats. The only serious threat came at 1230 hrs from a squadron of six torpedo-carrying Swordfish under Lt-Commander Esmonde, but these were shot down by Luftwaffe fighters, all but five of the crews being killed (Esmonde received a posthumous Victoria Cross) and none of the torpedoes finding their targets.

Later attempts to co-ordinate an RAF bombing attack broke down through poor communications, and although both *Scharnhorst* and *Gneisenau* suffered damage from mines during the last phase of their voyage, they were back in home waters by dawn on Feb 13. Ironically, their return home released Royal Navy ships from watching the entrance to Brest for more pressing duties in the Atlantic.

2 North Africa. Though the British were mainly back in the Gazala Line positions by the beginning of February, for a variety of reasons, Panzerarmee Afrika, as it was now renamed under its newly promoted commander Col-General Rommel, did not immediately follow too closely. First, Rommel was still nominally under an Italian Commander-in-Chief who had been appalled at Rommel's impetuosity in the early days of the recent advance, and now insisted that Axis forward positions should be no further east than Maraua with only reconnaissance units between there and Gazala. Moreover, although the supply position had improved greatly of late, there was still a shortage of petrol; and also the pleasant but time-consuming duties of allocating to the most deserving of his forces some of the luxuries found in the abandoned British storehouses in Benghazi – including 7,000,000 cigarettes and several lorry-loads of rum. By the end of the month, only the original Afrika Korps units were in the Jebel Akhdar, the Italian divisions deployed around Benghazi and Antelat and forming a blocking force in the Agheila positions. But on Feb 13 a meeting took place in Berlin which was to have immediate effects in North Africa, for at it Hitler became aware that if Britain's main oil supplies at the head of the Persian Gulf could be captured, Britain could be knocked out of the war. If, therefore, a greatly reinforced drive by the Afrika Korps across the Nile and into Palestine met a powerful Spring Offensive on the Russian Front aimed down through the Caucasus into Persia, overwhelming victory might be his. Rommel's command must therefore be extended, his forces expanded and his supply position vastly improved; but one obstacle to this latter objective was the island of Malta, lying flat across the vital supply routes.

Two plans were evolved – *Operation Herkules*, for the invasion of Malta to be carried out by a German parachute division; *Operation Aida* for the drive to the Nile. In order to soften up the Malta defences, Marshal Kesselring was ordered to direct his Luftflotte 2 in a series of heavy attacks on the island.

3 The Sittang Bridge. By the beginning of the month, Maj-General Smythe, VC, commanding the 17th British Division in front of the advancing Japanese columns, knew that he must get his exhausted and inexperienced units first back behind the Bilin river and then – even more importantly – back over the Sittang; otherwise they would be trapped. But his first requests to do so were refused by an inexperienced command staff and as a result his troops had to fight desperately on the Bilin and suffer heavy losses, only then to have to withdraw 30 miles along a dusty track under pressure from two Japanese divisions provided with excellent air cover.

By the morning of Feb 21, although the rearguards had kept the 33rd Japanese Division at bay, other Japanese forces were outflanking them in the race to the Sittang bridge. By evening Smythe's HQ had reached the bridge, set up defence posts and the transport of the division was streaming across, while three battalions of Gurkha troops fought off ferocious attacks by Japanese forces closing in from all sides. Then intelligence reports warned of a possible Japanese parachute attack from behind, the main Gurkha force was cut off and Smythe was faced with the dreadful decision to blow the bridge and leave them behind. There was no doubt that this was the correct course, and the bridge was blown at 0530 on the morning of Feb 23.

In fact, the effects were not so disastrous as they might have been, for the Japanese immediately switched their attention to finding a crossing-point higher up the river, thus allowing the fit survivors of the rearguard battalions time to reach and swim the river. But they had had to leave behind all their equipment – and the wounded, who were all butchered as soon as they were found.

5 Struggles for the Java Sea. Timor was the next target after Ambon for the Japanese eastern thrust. Heavy bombing for six days, an airborne drop near Kupang and two landings on the west coast secured the island by Feb 22. On the Celebes, the Kendari force looped forward to take Makassar on Feb 9, then took Bali on Feb 19. During the following night in the Battle of Lombok Strait a Dutch destroyer was sunk and a light cruiser hit at a cost of two Japanese destroyers and a transport damaged – and no delay suffered in Japanese operations.

Meanwhile, Central Force consolidated at Balikpapan, then moved south by sea to take Bandjermasin and its airfield, thus securing air domination over the Java Sea and all nearby straits. Now Western Force left Camranh Bay in Indo-China, to land troops on Banka Island on Feb 14 and occupy Muntok airfield. The next day troops sailed up the Musi river into Sumatra to join 700 paratroops dropped near Palembang, and on Feb 16 the town was taken with its oilfields intact. Attacks by the Allied fleet against Western convoys were again ineffective.

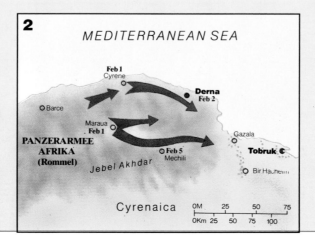

Rangoon; Andaman Is

Wake I
Feb 24

Marshall Is

Surprise US naval attacks
on Japanese air bases
Feb 1

Rabaul and Gasmata
(New Britain)

Gilbert Is

Sourabaya and Batavia (Java);
Palembang (Sumatra);
Port Moresby (Papua)

Darwin
Feb 19

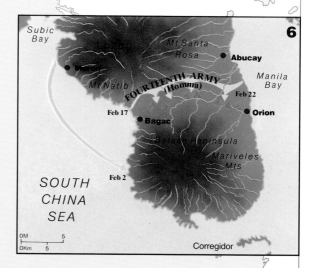

6

Subic Bay · Luzon · Mt Santa Rosa · Mt Natib · **FOURTEENTH ARMY (Homma)** · Bagac · Bataan Peninsula · Mariveles Mts · **SOUTH CHINA SEA** · Abucay · Manila Bay · Feb 22 · Feb 17 · Orion · Feb 2 · Corregidor

3
B U R M A
BURMA ARMY (Hutton) · THAILAND · Papun · Sittang · Pegu · Bilin · Feb 19 · Thaton Feb 15 · Martaban Feb 10 · **RANGOON** · Moulmein · Kawkareik · Gulf of Martaban · **FIFTEENTH ARMY (Iida)**

4
5th & 18th Divs Feb 8/9 · Feb 9/10 · **Johore Bahru** naval base · Johore State · Feb 7 **Imperial Guards** · Kranji · Mandai · Nee Soon · Pulau Ubin · **Tengah** Feb 9 · Changi · Feb 11 · Bukit Timah · Paya Lebar · Jurong · Feb 15 · Bedok · **SINGAPORE** · Johore Strait

4 Fall of Singapore. By Feb 1 the Japanese forces under command of General Yamashita had closed down to the Singapore Island defences and were ready to attack. On the night of Feb 8/9, Imperial Guard regiments made a feint at the eastern end of the Johore Strait, while 5th and 8th Divisions crossed at the western end under heavy artillery cover. By mid-morning of Feb 9 they had reached Tengah airfield to find it abandoned, but still with neatly parked British aircraft on the runways, meals cooking, tables laid – all the classic signs of panic and confusion caused by shock. By Feb 13 they had pinned inside a 28-mile perimeter the remaining 80,000 British defenders, who now found themselves with no plans for a counter-attack, no morale and no confidence whatsoever in their leadership.

In this they were undoubtedly justified. On Feb 15, despite Churchill's direct instructions, General Percival ordered a white flag to be hoisted and in due course he met General Yamashita in the Ford factory at Bukit Timah and surrendered un-conditionally – presumably in order to avoid a 'bloodbath'.

Had he or his troops foreseen their suffering as prisoners of the Japanese during the next four years they might well have chosen the 'bloodbath' with its possibility, however remote, of victory – and its certainty of avoiding the humiliation they now suffered.

6 Stalemate on the Bataan Peninsula. By the beginning of February General Homma's Fourteenth Army were finding themselves in unexpected difficulty. As they closed up to the Orion-Bagac line they came under heavy and increasingly accurate artillery fire poured down by the US gunners from dominating positions on the Mariveles. They were to suffer 2,700 killed and over 4,000 wounded during the month, and in addition the Japanese troops were no more immune to malaria and other tropical diseases than their enemies. Nearly 12,000 of Homma's men went sick before the beginning of March, and at one moment he could hardly raise enough fit men to muster 3 effective battalions. But if his men lacked numbers, they made up for it in aggression and ingenuity. Patrols probed forward into the American and Philippino lines every night, keeping the defences awake, irritable and nervous. Isolated shots rang out all the time, every one from a different angle, every one more threatening to the exasperated defenders. Loudspeakers would suddenly boom out like barrage or bombardment, then a voice would proclaim news of the latest Japanese victory, the latest disaster to Allied arms – followed shortly by recordings of Bing Crosby or Judy Garland crooning out nostalgic lullabies to remind the listeners of the peace and comforts of home. The Japanese seemed to have an unlimited supply of fire-crackers and a device for hurling long strings of them up into trees behind the defence lines; suddenly it would seem to the tiring American and Philippino soldiers that they were being attacked from every direction at once.

All the time, Japanese reinforcements were arriving to replace Fourteenth Army casualties and, more important, as repairs were carried out on Clark and the other airfields, Japanese twin-engined bombers were flying in and preparing for the final liquidation of American strength in the Philippines. Crucially, from General Homma's point of view, time was on his side. There was not the smallest possibility of the opposing forces being either reinforced or evacuated in the face of Japanese control of the air above and the seas around; he could wait until his strength was enough to guarantee success.

With the capture of Bali and the eastern end of Sumatra, the Dutch East Indies government at Batavia and the Allied (ABDA) HQ nearby on Java were now cut off from Australia, so in an attempt to delay the invasion of Java, an Allied fleet of 4 cruisers, 12 destroyers and an aircraft-carrier with 32 fighters aboard sailed to intercept the Japanese Eastern Force.

The Battle of the Java Sea cost the Japanese one minesweeper and a transport sunk, three destroyers damaged, three transports beached – after their troops and equipment had landed. The Allies lost the aircraft-carrier and all its planes before contact with the Japanese had been made, and the bulk of their fleet during the two days of battle. Only four US destroyers remained afloat to get back to Australia – and now the whole island barrier of the Dutch East Indies was at Japanese command.

On Feb 19, waves of Japanese aircraft from Timor, Kendari and from four aircraft-carriers bombed Port Darwin killing 240 people and injuring 150 more.

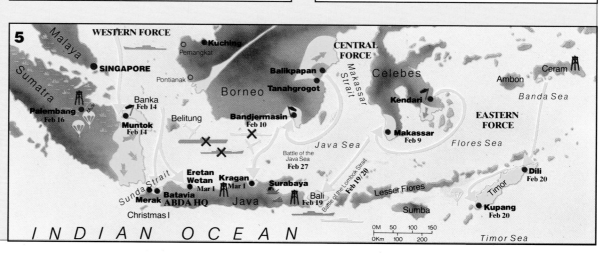

5 · Malaya · **WESTERN FORCE** · Kuching · **CENTRAL FORCE** · Pemangkat · Ceram · **SINGAPORE** · Balikpapan · Celebes · Ambon · Sumatra · Pontianak · Tanahgrogot · Makassar Strait · Banda Sea · **Palembang** Feb 16 · Banka · Belitung · Borneo · Kendari · **EASTERN FORCE** · **Muntok** Feb 14 · Feb 14 · **Bandjermasin** Feb 10 · **Makassar** Feb 9 · Flores Sea · Java Sea · Battle of the Java Sea Feb 27 · **Eretan Wetan** Mar 1 · **Kragan** Mar 1 · **Surabaya** · Bali Feb 19 · Lesser Flores · **Dili** Feb 20 · Sunda Strait · **Merak** **Batavia** **ABDA HQ** · Christmas I · Battle of the Lombok Strait Feb 19/20 · Timor · Sumba · **Kupang** Feb 20 · **I N D I A N   O C E A N** · Timor Sea

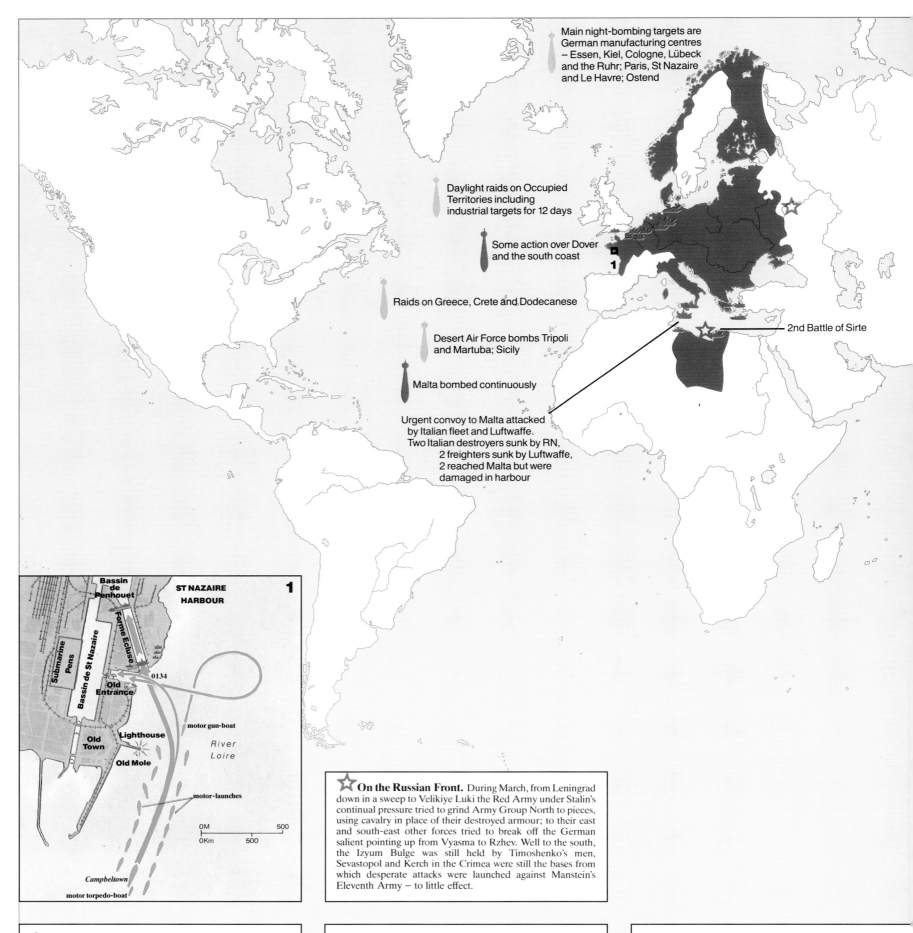

Main night-bombing targets are German manufacturing centres – Essen, Kiel, Cologne, Lübeck and the Ruhr; Paris, St Nazaire and Le Havre; Ostend

Daylight raids on Occupied Territories including industrial targets for 12 days

Some action over Dover and the south coast

Raids on Greece, Crete and Dodecanese

Desert Air Force bombs Tripoli and Martuba; Sicily

Malta bombed continuously

Urgent convoy to Malta attacked by Italian fleet and Luftwaffe. Two Italian destroyers sunk by RN, 2 freighters sunk by Luftwaffe, 2 reached Malta but were damaged in harbour

2nd Battle of Sirte

ST NAZAIRE HARBOUR — 1

Bassin de Penhouet
Submarine Pens
Forme Ecluse
Bassin de St Nazaire
Old Entrance
0134
Lighthouse
Old Town
Old Mole
River Loire
motor gun-boat
motor-launches
Campbeltown
motor torpedo-boat

0M 500
0Km 500

☆ **On the Russian Front.** During March, from Leningrad down in a sweep to Velikiye Luki the Red Army under Stalin's continual pressure tried to grind Army Group North to pieces, using cavalry in place of their destroyed armour; to their east and south-east other forces tried to break off the German salient pointing up from Vyasma to Rzhev. Well to the south, the Izyum Bulge was still held by Timoshenko's men, Sevastopol and Kerch in the Crimea were still the bases from which desperate attacks were launched against Manstein's Eleventh Army – to little effect.

1 **The Raid on St Nazaire.** By March 1942, from the point of view of observers in the Admiralty, it seemed that Britain stood in great danger of losing the war. Some 250 U-boats were now in commission, 15 new ones were joining Admiral Dönitz's striking force every month, and the most powerful battleship in the world, the *Tirpitz,* was now completing her sea-trials in Norwegian waters. Should she break out through the North Sea and the Denmark Strait, the havoc she would wreak among the Atlantic convoys could be enough to seal Britain's fate.

But *Tirpitz* could not operate in the Atlantic without a base in which she could be maintained and repaired – and only one base existed outside German waters with a large enough dry dock to accommodate her. At St Nazaire lay the *Forme Ecluse,* 380 yards long, 55 yards wide and deep enough to take a ship of 85,000 tons. In 1942 it was therefore a crucial factor in the Battle of the Atlantic, and on the afternoon of March 26, a force consisting of 3 Royal Navy destroyers accompanied by a motor torpedo-boat, a motor gun-boat and 15 motor-launches carrying in all 611 sailors and commandos between them, left Falmouth on *Operation Chariot* intending to wreck it.

By dawn on March 27 the expedition was well out into the Atlantic to the west of St Nazaire. They moved in towards the French coast under darkening afternoon skies, and at 2200 the striking force passed their guiding submarine at the mouth of the Loire. At 0128 on the morning of March 28 their presence was realised by the enemy and every German gun in the port defences opened up on them, and at 0134 with half the men on board dead or wounded, HMS *Campbeltown* ripped through an anti-torpedo net and crashed full tilt into the outer gate of the *Forme Ecluse,* buckling back 35 feet of her bows and hull, and finally coming to rest with the vast concrete block in her mid-hull hard against the lock gate. Her captain had brought her to the target just four minutes late.

Meanwhile, the motor gun-boat had circled and run in towards the swing bridge across the entrance gate to the main *Bassin de St Nazaire* to land the headquarter team of the commandos, the survivors of the main body of whom were now leaping ashore from the *Campbeltown* to carry out sabotage on the dock installations. At the same time the motor torpedo-boat raced in alongside the motor gun-boat and torpedoed the entrance gate beyond. Sabotage teams now ranged the dock

area, blowing up shipping, storming and destroying gun and searchlight positions, blowing up the pump- house installations, wrecking the winding-house at the southern end of the lock, then the gate and winding-house at the northern end.

But the price they paid was high in killed and wounded, and by 0230 they knew they had little hope of escape; practically all their motor-launches were in flames or had been sunk.

The survivors ashore split up into small parties and tried to escape into the countryside, but few reached it. The captain of the *Campbeltown,* Lt-Commander Beattie, was caught just before 1000 and was interrogated by his captors, one of whom commented that the gate upon which Beattie had hurled his ship was much stronger than it looked, and that it would not be long before the wreck would be dragged away and the *Forme Ecluse* back in operation again.

At that moment, there was an enormous explosion as the charges concealed in the huge block of concrete blew up, the lock gate disintegrated and a huge wave swept the remains of the *Campbeltown* halfway along the length of the dock. It was still there at the end of the war – and the *Tirpitz* never ventured into the Atlantic to threaten the vital convoys.

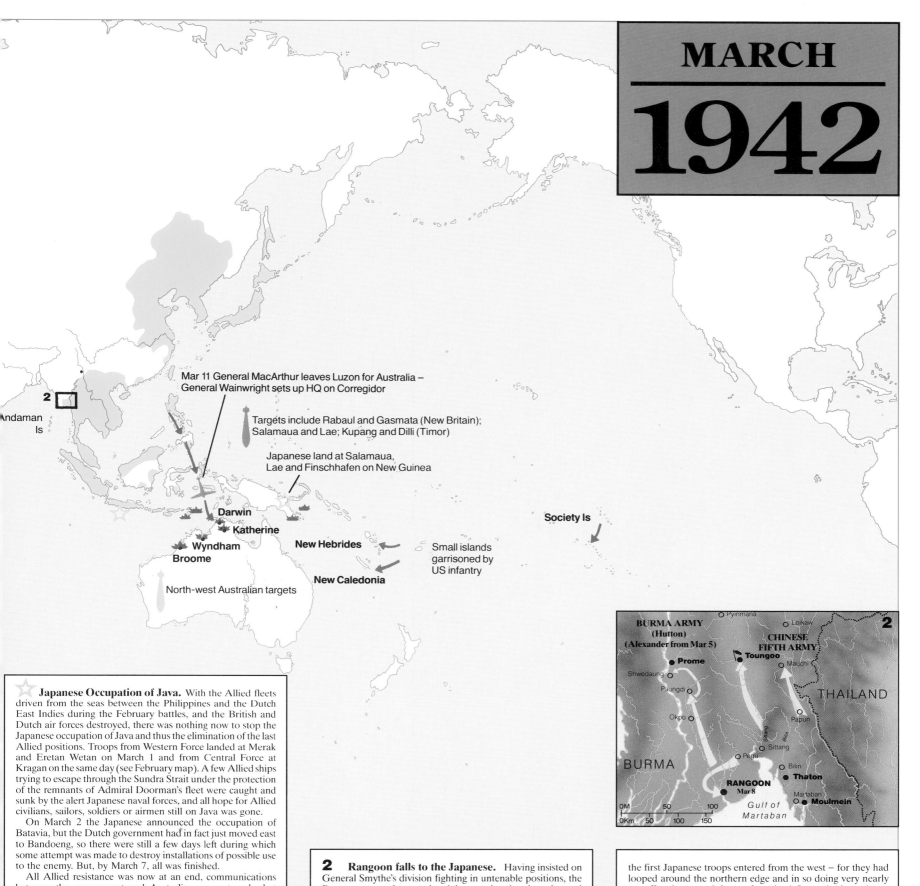

Mar 11 General MacArthur leaves Luzon for Australia – General Wainwright sets up HQ on Corregidor

Targets include Rabaul and Gasmata (New Britain); Salamaua and Lae; Kupang and Dilli (Timor)

Japanese land at Salamaua, Lae and Finschhafen on New Guinea

Andaman Is

2

Darwin

Katherine

Wyndham

Broome

North-west Australian targets

New Hebrides

New Caledonia

Society Is

Small islands garrisoned by US infantry

BURMA ARMY (Hutton) (Alexander from Mar 5)

CHINESE FIFTH ARMY

Pyinmana

Loikaw

Prome

Toungoo

Mauchi

Shwedaung

Paungdi

THAILAND

Okpo

Papun

BURMA

Pegu

Sittang

Bilin

RANGOON
Mar 8

Thaton

Martaban

Moulmein

0M · 50 · 100

0Km · 50 · 100 · 150

Gulf of Martaban

☆ **Japanese Occupation of Java.** With the Allied fleets driven from the seas between the Philippines and the Dutch East Indies during the February battles, and the British and Dutch air forces destroyed, there was nothing now to stop the Japanese occupation of Java and thus the elimination of the last Allied positions. Troops from Western Force landed at Merak and Eretan Wetan on March 1 and from Central Force at Kragan on the same day (see February map). A few Allied ships trying to escape through the Sundra Strait under the protection of the remnants of Admiral Doorman's fleet were caught and sunk by the alert Japanese naval forces, and all hope for Allied civilians, sailors, soldiers or airmen still on Java was gone.

On March 2 the Japanese announced the occupation of Batavia, but the Dutch government had in fact just moved east to Bandoeng, so there were still a few days left during which some attempt was made to destroy installations of possible use to the enemy. But, by March 7, all was finished.

All Allied resistance was now at an end, communications between the government and Australia were cut and what remained of the Dutch garrisons under General Poorten were forced to surrender.

2 Rangoon falls to the Japanese. Having insisted on General Smythe's division fighting in untenable positions, the Burma command now ordered them to abandon the only good defensive position they had occupied behind the Sittang river.

The 17th Division itself was now down to less than half its infantry strength and had lost the bulk of its guns and transport, but the survivors reached Pegu where it was reinforced by the 7th Armoured Brigade (7th Hussars and 2nd Royal Tank Regiment), and re-equipped from the storehouses of Rangoon. Moreover, some realisation of the weaknesses of the Burma command had percolated the higher levels in Delhi and London, and Lt-General Sir Harold Alexander was on his way to take overall command with Lt-General William Slim commanding the re-formed Burma Corps. Fortunately, at the very end of February, the few remaining RAF fighters together with the men of the American Volunteer Group had caught the Japanese Air Force by surprise and shot down some 170 bombers and fighters; thus gaining command of the air above Rangoon while another Indian brigade and three more infantry battalions were brought in.

Nevertheless, it was obvious that Rangoon would soon be in Japanese hands. Evacuation of all British civilians and army and RAF administration troops was begun, together with demolition of docks, oil installations and any workshops or factories likely to be of use to the enemy. By the afternoon of March 7, the city was burning as a result both of demolitions and a wave of incendiarism, the last train-load had pulled out to the north and the last transports had left for Calcutta. On March 8

the first Japanese troops entered from the west – for they had looped around the northern edge and in so doing very nearly cut off and captured the newly arrived General Alexander.

As soon as General Sakurai realised the British had left Rangoon, he ordered pursuit up the Prome road – the only route for wheeled traffic out of the city. But despite the tribulations the men of Burma Corps had suffered they were now under firm command and capable of strong rearguard resistance, and Japanese progress was as a result slow and cautious. Moreover, on the eastern flank, in their drive along the banks of the Sittang, they had been abruptly stopped at Toungoo by the 200th Chinese Division which from the middle of March held all approaches to the town and the vital bridge.

By March 26, however, Chinese casualties were so great that it became obvious that they must soon pull back so, to relieve pressure on them, General Slim ordered 17th Division to turn in its tracks and drive their pursuers back at least as far as Okpo. They were almost there when it was realised that the Japanese were again using outflanking tactics and had cut the road behind them at Shwedaung, so they turned again to fight their way back into Prome by the end of the month. They arrived on March 30, and on the same day the last Chinese units pulled out of Toungoo without, unfortunately, destroying the bridge.

Once Rangoon was firmly in Japanese hands it was realised that the British and Gurkha garrisons on the Andaman Islands were completely exposed, so on March 12 they were flown out by sea-plane. On March 23 Japanese troops arrived and took over what remained of the bases.

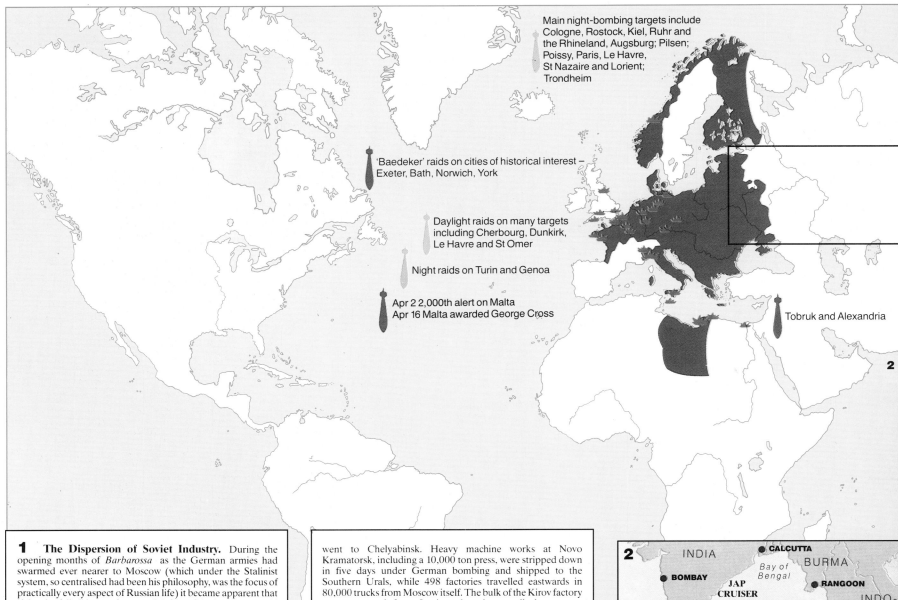

Main night-bombing targets include Cologne, Rostock, Kiel, Ruhr and the Rhineland, Augsburg; Pilsen; Poissy, Paris, Le Havre, St Nazaire and Lorient; Trondheim

'Baedeker' raids on cities of historical interest – Exeter, Bath, Norwich, York

Daylight raids on many targets including Cherbourg, Dunkirk, Le Havre and St Omer

Night raids on Turin and Genoa

Apr 2 2,000th alert on Malta
Apr 16 Malta awarded George Cross

Tobruk and Alexandria

1 **The Dispersion of Soviet Industry.** During the opening months of *Barbarossa* as the German armies had swarmed ever nearer to Moscow (which under the Stalinist system, so centralised had been his philosophy, was the focus of practically every aspect of Russian life) it became apparent that if the city fell all hope of eventual defeat of the invaders would go too. As a result, though Stalin himself never left the capital, the main departments of the chief Commissariats and especially of the People's Commissariat for Defence were transported eastwards by an enormous feat of logistics. Some went as far as Krasnoyarsk, nearly 3,000 miles from Moscow, well behind the Urals.

Just as essential and even more spectacular had been the transportation in the same direction of as much of Soviet industry as could be saved from the engulfing Wehrmacht advance. By the end of November 1941, the area of the Soviet Union already occupied or under threat contained over half the pre-war coal-mines, two-thirds of the heavy metal production plant and over 300 ammunition factories. Had all this fallen into German hands, *Barbarossa* might well have brought the successes dreamed of in Berlin.

Appreciation of the danger came early, and quite astonishing feats of reorganisation were launched. Vast armour plate mills were shifted bodily from Mariupol to Magnitogorsk; entire steel mills from Zaporozh'ye and the tube-rolling plant from Dniepropetrovsk were transported beyond the Urals, while Kharkov's tank-engine plant, its last mammoth jigs loaded on to the trains while German shells crashed around the railhead,

went to Chelyabinsk. Heavy machine works at Novo Kramatorsk, including a 10,000 ton press, were stripped down in five days under German bombing and shipped to the Southern Urals, while 498 factories travelled eastwards in 80,000 trucks from Moscow itself. The bulk of the Kirov factory was evacuated from Leningrad and sent all the way to Sverdlovsk, a further 92 plants had been brought out during August and September and, on Stalin's direct orders, more was ferried across Lake Ladoga and so to the east even after Leningrad had been virtually sealed in.

Between July and October 1,500,000 trucks and 915,000 railway wagons had shifted over 1,000 plants eastwards – 455 to the Urals, 210 to western Siberia, 200 to the Volga and over 250 to Kazakhstan and Central Asia, together with the men to rebuild the factories, instal the machinery and then run it. From Leningrad nearly 20,000 scientists and technicians were flown out to Sverdlovsk, Chelyabinsk and Kazan; in all over 100,000 men accompanied this diaspora of Soviet industry.

Their achievements were prodigious. Aircraft factories in Saratov began production even before the roofs were on, and 14 days after the last jigs were in place the first MiG fighter rolled out; ten weeks after the last teams of engineers left Kharkov the tank works produced the first 25 T-34s. By April 1942, the corner had been turned.

Despite the biting cold and rudimentary shelter the new factories produced over 4,500 tanks, some 3,000 aircraft, 14,000 guns and over 50,000 mortars during those winter months. They were to play a vital part in the battles immediately ahead.

2 **The Ceylon Raid.** At the beginning of the month a Japanese carrier fleet of 5 carriers, 4 battleships, 4 cruisers and 8 destroyers moved into the Indian Ocean. Between April 5 and 9 their aircraft bombed both Colombo and Trincomalee harbours with great effect, sinking several ships. They also sank the British destroyers *Cornwall* and *Dorsetshire*, the aircraft carrier *Hermes* and an escorting destroyer, while a cruiser force also penetrated the Bay of Bengal and wrought havoc among commercial shipping. Japanese losses amounted to 17 aircraft.

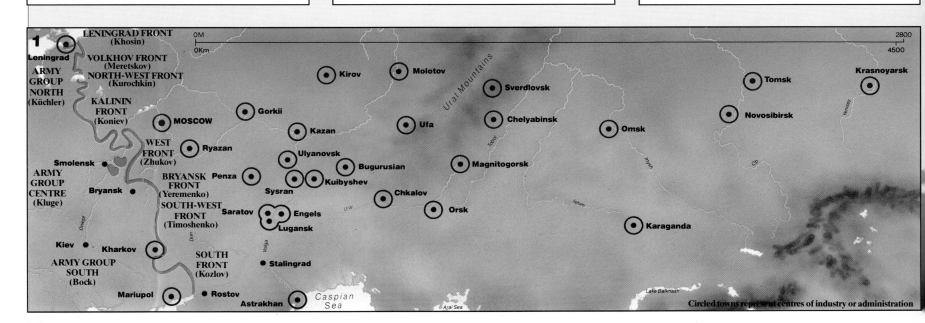

First raids on India at Coconada and Vizagapatan; Trincomalee (Ceylon); Mandalay and Lashio (Burma)

Apr 18 'Doolittle' raid. Sixteen B-25 bombers took off from US carrier *Hornet* and bombed Tokyo, Kobe, Yokohama, Nagoya and Yokosaka, then flew on to crash land in China

Andaman Is; Rangoon

Rabaul and Gasmata; Salamaua and Lae; Kaveing (New Ireland)

Port Moresby and Darwin

Sorong

Apr 6
Hollandia

Kupang (Timor)

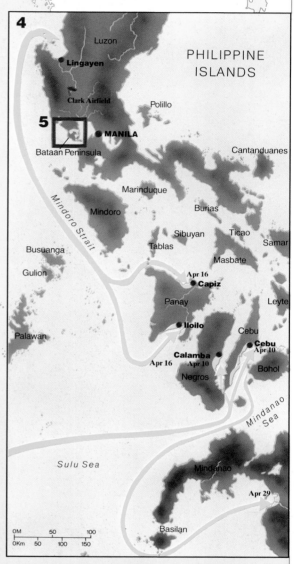

PHILIPPINE ISLANDS

Luzon, **Lingayen**, Clark Airfield, Polillo, **MANILA**, Bataan Peninsula, Cantanduanes, Marinduque, Mindoro, Burias, Sibuyan, Ticao, Samar, Busuanga, Tablas, Masbate, Gulion, Panay, Leyte, Palawan, **Iloilo**, Cebu, **Cebu** Apr 10, **Calamba** Apr 16, Apr 10, Negros, Bohol, Mindanao Sea, Sulu Sea, Mindanao Apr 29, Basilan

3 **Allied Collapse in Burma.** With Toungoo in Japanese hands, the army commander, General Iida, planned the advance northwards along three rivers – along the Irrawaddy against the British 'Burcorps', the Sittang against the Chinese Fifth Army, and the Salween against the Chinese Sixth Army. Iida's immediate aim was to cut the Burma Road – the only line of supply and communication for the Chinese armies – in the vicinity of Lashio, and eventually to encircle the British and Chinese around Mandalay and trap them against the Irrawaddy.

By the beginning of April his forces on the eastern flank had taken Mauchi and were soon driving up towards Bawlake and Loikaw beyond. They outflanked and then scattered the Chinese 55th Division by the middle of the month, cut the escape routes behind the remnants by racing along narrow tracks across the Salween, and on April 21 reached and occupied Hopong. By this time the Chinese Sixth Army was itself disintegrating, and its commander, General Kan, took the sorry collection of random units and demoralised soldiers first eastwards and then, once news of further Japanese advances reached him, north and back into China. The road to Lashio was now open.

For some time Alexander and Slim and the American general, 'Vinegar Joe' Stilwell, had been unaware of developments on their left flank, and Slim was preparing for a strong defence of the country east of Magwe, covering the valuable oilfields at Chauk and Yenangyaung. His land forces were now well organised and under firm control, but the RAF and AVG had been withdrawn northwards and Japanese planes dominated the skies. General Iida's forces closed up with their usual efficiency and then attacked; on April 16 Slim was forced to begin withdrawal after first ordering the destruction of millions of gallons of oil, which converted Yenangyaung's complex of installations and storehouses into one vast sheet of flame.

For ten days, assisted by the Chinese Sixty-fifth Army, Burcorps held the Japanese south of Mandalay, but when Alexander realised that Lashio was about to fall he decided that his main task must be the defence of India. He ordered Slim to withdraw across the Irrawaddy to Kalewa, and after some problems getting the main force across the Ava bridge all went well until on April 29 they learned not only that the Japanese were at Lashio, but that they had outflanked Burcorps as well. They would obviously capture Monywa by May 1.

What should have been a controlled retirement now became a harried retreat which could easily develop into a disaster.

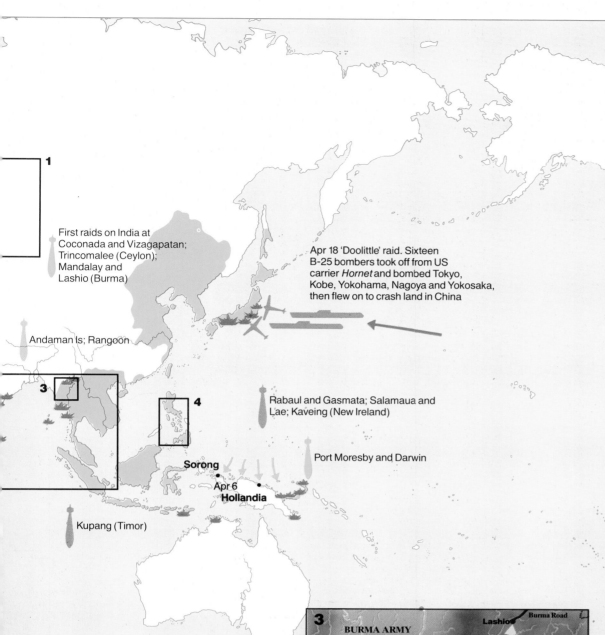

BURMA ARMY (Alexander) — Monywa, MANDALAY, Ava, **Lashio**, Burma Road, **CHINESE SIXTH ARMY (Kan)**, BURMA, Meiktila, Taunggyi, Hopong, Chauk, Yanangyaung, Magwe, Puinmana, Loikaw, Prome, **Toungoo**, Bawlake, Taungup, Mauchi, **SOUTHERN ARMY (Iida)**

5 **American Collapse in Bataan.** On April 5 a heavy Japanese bombardment opened on the US defensive positions on the eastern half of the Orion-Bagac Line, augmented by 60 tons of bombs dropped by newly arrived aircraft from Clark Field. By evening Japanese infantry were through the line in most places and 1,000 yards on, and the following day General Homma repeated the pattern. His 65th Brigade smashed through the central positions, so by dawn on April 7 they were commanding the northern slopes of the Mariveles, and the US 11 Corps began to disintegrate.

Wainwright suggested to the commander of the Luzon defences that 1 Corps be thrown into a flank attack, but the US forces on Bataan were by now in a condition not far from rout. They knew that they could not be reinforced or evacuated, they had watched the implacable advance of the Japanese with the same resignation as had overcome the Dutch in Java and the British in Singapore, and as they had no conception of the treatment they would receive as prisoners in Japanese hands, they lacked the desperation which might still have thrown the Japanese back. On April 9, the surrender of Bataan was agreed. Some 2,000 men escaped to Corregidor – for the moment – and 78,000 men of a demoralised army went into a dreadful captivity from which few would return. At their peak, General Homma's forces had never exceeded 30,000.

4 **The Japanese Occupation.** With the capitulation of the Dutch East Indies and the conquest of all of Luzon except for Corregidor, there was nothing to stop Japanese forces landing anywhere their transports could take them. On April 10 infantry and artillery arrived on Negros and Cebu Islands from Borneo, on April 16 more arrived on Panay from Lingayen Gulf, and on April 29 small detachments were landing on Mindanao to link up with forces already there since December.

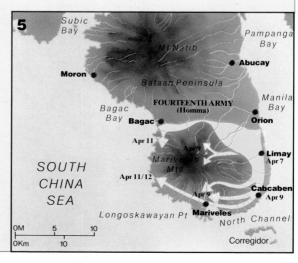

Subic Bay, **Mt Natib**, Pampanga Bay, **Moron**, **Abucay**, Bataan Peninsula, Bagac Bay, **FOURTEENTH ARMY (Homma)**, Manila Bay, **Bagac**, **Orion**, Apr 11, Mariveles Mts, SOUTH CHINA SEA, Apr 11/12, **Limay** Apr 7, Apr 9, **Cabcaben** Apr 9, **Mariveles**, Longoskawayan Pt, North Channel, Corregidor

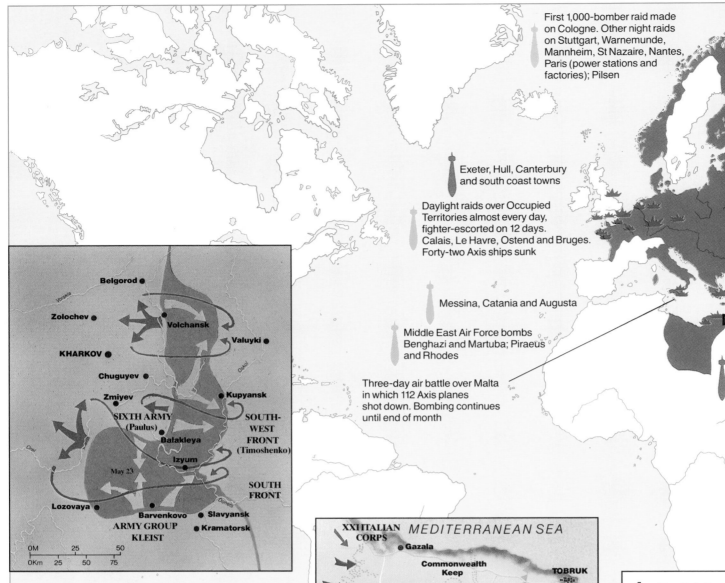

First 1,000-bomber raid made on Cologne. Other night raids on Stuttgart, Warnemunde, Mannheim, St Nazaire, Nantes, Paris (power stations and factories); Pilsen

Exeter, Hull, Canterbury and south coast towns

Daylight raids over Occupied Territories almost every day, fighter-escorted on 12 days. Calais, Le Havre, Ostend and Bruges. Forty-two Axis ships sunk

Messina, Catania and Augusta

Middle East Air Force bombs Benghazi and Martuba; Piraeus and Rhodes

Three-day air battle over Malta in which 112 Axis planes shot down. Bombing continues until end of month

May 11 RN destroyers *Lively*, *Kipling* and *Jackal* sunk by Luftwaffe

Alexandria

1 Battle of the Izyum Bulge. By the beginning of May, under pressure from Stalin, STAVKA (Russian High Command) had produced plans for another Soviet offensive, albeit on a small scale compared with the January all-out attacks. South-west Front under Marshal Timoshenko was to mount two converging thrusts, north-west out of the Izyum Bulge by Sixth Red Army, and west then south-west by Twenty-Eighth Army from the Volchansk areas – the two armies to meet west of Kharkov, thus liberating the city.

On May 12 the opening phase was launched and within two days both thrusts were over 15 miles ahead, but now inexperience at staff level and shortages of ammunition and fuel stalled the advances. And on May 17 the great Summer Campaign of the Wehrmacht was launched.

The primary objectives of Hitler's 1942 Summer Campaign were the oilwells of Baku and the southern Caspian shore-line, with the wheatlands of the Caucasus an added bonus and the possibility of a continued advance down through Persia to the head of the Persian Gulf – a distant but enticing prospect. But first it was necessary to clear the Don basin (the Donbass) to open the way south, and also to drive a protective shield eastwards from the Kharkov area, across the Don to the Volga, in the general area of Stalingrad.

By May 23 Kleist's Army Group had smashed across the rear lines of Sixth Red Army to meet Paulus's men driving down from the Balakleya area thus cutting off Timoshenko's thrust out of the Izyum Bulge, while to the north the main bulk of Paulus's Sixth Army drove due east for Kupyansk and the river Oskel while their left flank units swept down from north of Kharkov and the Volchansk area, to cut off the Russian northern thrust. Stalin repeated his old mistakes of refusing Timoshenko permission to reverse the Soviet thrusts until far too late, and when the columns eventually turned to fight their way out of the traps, they were soon cut into small groups, short of fuel and ammunition, out of contact with headquarters and each other.

By the end of May, Paulus's Sixth Army and Kleist's Army Group held the line of the Oskol as far north as Kupyansk and then on in a curve further north, in solid positions and under skies securely dominated for them by the Luftwaffe. There they waited, blocking all but a very few attempts by the Russian units to escape, massing their strength for the great offensive which would open up for them the riches of the Caucasus.

Further to the south, Manstein had also launched the bulk of his Eleventh Army against the Russian forces of the Crimean Front. Again under skies dominated by the Luftwaffe, three German divisions drove east into the Kerch Peninsula and by May 20 a large-scale Russian evacuation across the straits to the Taman Peninsula was under way. By the end of May, only the fortress at Sevastopol was still in Russian hands.

2 Gazala. During March and April both armies at Gazala had been building up their strength for the forthcoming battle, Eighth Army under General Ritchie determined to press forward at least as far as El Agheila and perhaps to Tripoli, Rommel and his Panzerarmee with their sights on Cairo, the Nile Delta, Palestine and the Persian Gulf oilwells beyond.

Rommel struck first. On the evening of May 26 he led the 10,000 vehicles of his original panzer divisions, with Italian armoured divisions on his left and 90th Light on his right, south in a gigantic hook around the desert fortress of Bir Hacheim (held by Free French troops), then up towards the heart of the Eighth Army defences.

The British command was deeply divided in tactical opinion, some of the top commanders bitterly antagonistic between themselves and thus uncooperative. As a result, Rommel's forces were able to drive over unprotected infantry 'boxes', destroy armoured brigades which should have united but instead remained separate, and by the end of the month despite several tactical errors which in the face of a co-ordinated enemy could have been fatal, Rommel had established a powerful position in the centre of the British defences. He had in the process completely annihilated one British infantry brigade which occupied what should have been an impregnable position, and sewn doubt and mistrust throughout the ranks of his enemies. An overwhelming victory seemed within his grasp.

4 The Epic Retreat. General Stilwell's forces from the Chinese 5th Army had held the Japanese central thrust during the last days of April – indeed, led personally by 'Vinegar Joe' they had at one point re-occupied Taunggyi, driven eastwards and threatened the Japanese advance on Lashio. But Stilwell's forces became attenuated and as administration broke down the Chinese 5th Army disintegrated as had the 6th. Stilwell himself got back to Shwebo, but then, with just his own headquarters party, was forced to walk to the Chindwin, and on through the hills to Imphal and the safety of Assam.

On the western flank the Japanese drive continued, along the coast to Akyab and along the line of the Chindwin to Shwegyin and Kalewa, driving Burcorps back towards Assam. Then on May 12 the monsoon broke with all its fury, and although it turned the retreat into a misery of soaking, mud-caked, bone-chilling discomfort, it also stopped the Japanese pursuit dead in its tracks.

Some transport struggled out from India to meet Slim's columns of exhausted and fever-ridden troops and at least had room for the very sick and most of the wounded, and for three days the survivors of Burcorps struggled back across the Burma–India frontier, after an epic retreat of nearly one thousand miles. It was the longest in British history, had lasted five and a half months and had caused the loss of 10,036 British, Indian and Gurkha soldiers.

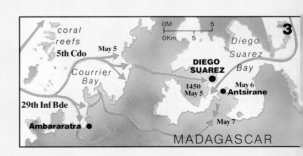

3 Madagascar. The Japanese naval raid into the Indian Ocean in April raised fears in Allied minds that Madagascar, still loyal to Vichy France, might become an Axis base which would threaten Allied supply lines. Force 121 arrived off the coral reefs protecting Courrier Bay at 0235 on the morning of May 5 and within three hours the bulk of 29th Infantry Brigade and all of No 5 Commando were ashore. The following day, Royal Marines landed at Antsirane and after two days of sporadic fighting, French resistance ended.

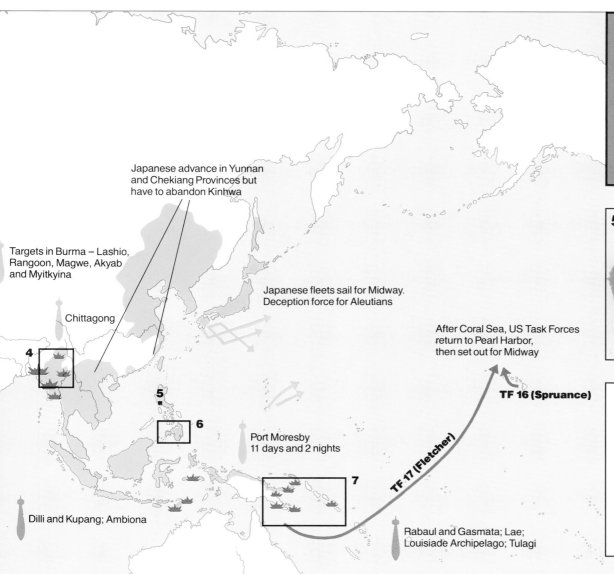

Japanese advance in Yunnan and Chekiang Provinces but have to abandon Kinhwa

Targets in Burma – Lashio, Rangoon, Magwe, Akyab and Myitkyina

Chittagong

Japanese fleets sail for Midway. Deception force for Aleutians

After Coral Sea, US Task Forces return to Pearl Harbor, then set out for Midway

TF 16 (Spruance)

TF 17 (Fletcher)

Port Moresby 11 days and 2 nights

Dilli and Kupang; Ambiona

Rabaul and Gasmata; Lae; Louisiade Archipelago; Tulagi

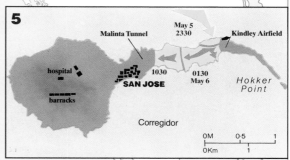

5

Malinta Tunnel

May 5 2330

Kindley Airfield

hospital

1030 SAN JOSE

0130 May 6

Hokker Point

barracks

Corregidor

0M 0·5 1
0Km

5 **Corregidor.** At 0725, April 29, the barrage opened and during the hours which followed bombers from Clark Field added to the chaos, though no one on Corregidor noticed. The din was indescribable, steel and concrete flew through the air, trees were flung about like rushes, and for days there was not a minute's break. Then on May 2 a time-fused 240-mm shell crashed through weakened concrete into a magazine, and to the watchers it seemed as though Corregidor itself blew up.

On the evening of May 5 Japanese troops began landing against little resistance, and by the following morning they had both tanks and light artillery support ashore – unnecessarily for the garrison surrendered before noon. Corregidor was finished and the Japanese conquest of Luzon – and the Philippines – was complete.

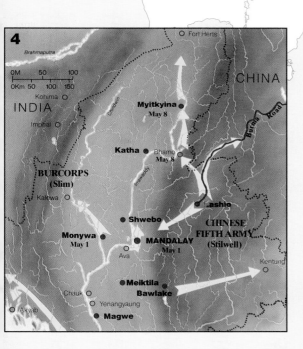

4

Brahmaputra

Fort Herts

0M 50 100
0Km 50 100 150

Kohima

INDIA

Imphal

Myitkyina
May 8

CHINA

Katha

Bhamo
May 8

BURCORPS (Slim)

Kalewa

Shwebo

Monywa
May 1

Lashio

MANDALAY
May 1

Ava

CHINESE FIFTH ARMY (Stilwell)

Kentung

Chauk

Meiktila
Bawlake

Yenangyaung

Akyab

Magwe

Burma Road

6 **Mindanao.** While General Homma had been massing his men and guns for the assault on Corregidor, Japanese naval forces had been occupying – generally unopposed – the eastern chain of Philippine islands. Mindoro, Panay, Negros, Cebu and Bohol were all in Japanese hands by the end of April, leaving only Mindanao still with possibility of some resistance to conquer.

This was, however, minimal. Japanese forces had been at Davao since December, and when troops were put ashore at Cotabato at the beginning of May, they quickly linked up. Then on May 5 more units came ashore at Cagayan and Misamis, and with the surrender of Corregidor the local commander ordered his men to lay down their arms. From then on only guerrilla action posed a threat to the Japanese.

6

Negros

Bohol

Cebu

Sulu Sea

Cagayan

Misamis

Mindanao

Illana Bay

Moro Gulf

Cotabato

Basilan

DAVAO

Davao Gulf

0M 50 100
0Km 50 100 150

7 **The Battle of the Coral Sea** was noteworthy on two counts. It was the first naval battle in which the opposing fleets were never in sight of each other as all attacks were carried out by aircraft; and it was also the first occasion upon which the American commanders benefited from the cracking of Japanese naval codes by their cryptographers. Admiral Chester Nimitz knew every detail of Japanese intention.

As a result, on May 7 and 8 Dauntless and Devastator squadrons from Task Forces 17 and 11 under Rear-Admirals Fletcher and Fitch respectively fought it out with dive-bombers and fighters of Rear-Admiral Goto's covering group and Vice-Admiral Tagaki's striking force, and turned the Japanese fleets back from their objective – Port Moresby. The US carrier *Lexington* was sunk and the *Yorktown* damaged (and sent back to Pearl Harbor for repair); Admiral Goto's light carrier *Shoho* was sunk and the *Shokaku* damaged and sent back to Truk. The Japanese lost 43 aircraft and their pilots, the Americans 33 of each – but as the US training and industrial programmes were gathering pace, their losses were much easier to accept.

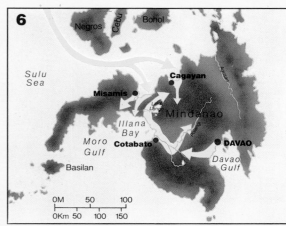

7

Bismarck Sea

Rabaul

PORT MORESBY INVASION GROUP

Bougainville

JAPANESE CARRIER FORCE (Takagi)

NEW GUINEA

New Britain

Gasmata

Lae

Salamaua

Huon Gulf

SOLOMON SEA

Choiseul

Santa Isabel

New Georgia

Rendova

landings May 3

PACIFIC OCEAN

Solomon Islands

PAPUA

Woodlark

Tulagi

Malaita

PORT MORESBY

Guadalcanal

San Christobal

1135 May 7
Shoho bombed

Louisiade Archipelago

0630 May 4

Rennell

1930 May 5

0M 50 100 150
0Km 100 200

Tagula

1400 unsuccessful air attack

0900 May 8

1127 May 8
Lexington hit

YORKTOWN (Fletcher)

CORAL SEA

0816 May 5

2000 May 8
Lexington sinks

May 11
tanker damaged *Neosho* scuttled

1200 May 7
Neosho & *Sims* bombed

Sims sunk

LEXINGTON (Fitch)

AUSTRALIA

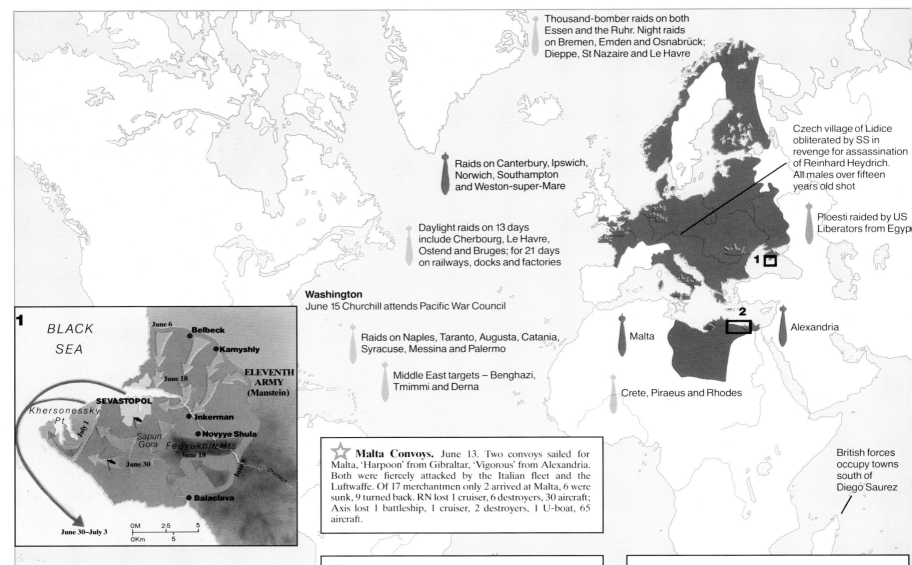

Thousand-bomber raids on both Essen and the Ruhr. Night raids on Bremen, Emden and Osnabrück; Dieppe, St Nazaire and Le Havre

Czech village of Lidice obliterated by SS in revenge for assassination of Reinhard Heydrich. All males over fifteen years old shot

Raids on Canterbury, Ipswich, Norwich, Southampton and Weston-super-Mare

Ploesti raided by US Liberators from Egypt

Daylight raids on 13 days include Cherbourg, Le Havre, Ostend and Bruges; for 21 days on railways, docks and factories

Washington
June 15 Churchill attends Pacific War Council

Raids on Naples, Taranto, Augusta, Catania, Syracuse, Messina and Palermo

Malta

Alexandria

Middle East targets – Benghazi, Tmimmi and Derna

Crete, Piraeus and Rhodes

British forces occupy towns south of Diego Saurez

Inset 1 – BLACK SEA

1 BLACK SEA

June 6 — Belbeck
Kamyshly
June 18
ELEVENTH ARMY (Manstein)
SEVASTOPOL
Khersonessky Pt
July 1
Inkerman
Sapun Gora
Novyye Shula
Fedyukhin Hts
June 30
June 18
Balaclava
June 30–July 3

0M   2·5   5
0Km   5

Malta Convoys. June 13. Two convoys sailed for Malta, 'Harpoon' from Gibraltar, 'Vigorous' from Alexandria. Both were fiercely attacked by the Italian fleet and the Luftwaffe. Of 17 merchantmen only 2 arrived at Malta, 6 were sunk, 9 turned back. RN lost 1 cruiser, 6 destroyers, 30 aircraft; Axis lost 1 battleship, 1 cruiser, 2 destroyers, 1 U-boat, 65 aircraft.

1 Fall of Sevastopol. Sevastopol's fate in June was similar to Corregidor's in May, though on a larger and more desperate scale. Manstein's plan to crack the huge armoured nut of the Sevastopol defences envisaged a pre-attack bombardment lasting five days, using the largest engines of destruction ever built. *Big Dora* threw her shells from 30 miles away, *Karl* hurled 2-ton mortar bombs, and a host of similar and only slightly smaller weapons added their quota to the weight of steel and explosive which crashed down on the Sevastopol defences. It is still a matter for wonder that when, on June 7/8, Manstein sent in his infantry and armour, they were met by a furious defence amid the ruined forts and emplacements. Every remaining building, together with the labyrinthine passages which connected them all, had to be cleared of Soviet marines and riflemen, gas-masked in the smoke and stench, but after 10 days Soviet ammunition was running low and their losses in men were astronomical. The Black Sea Fleet brought in some supplies and reinforcements, but at a terrible price in ships and after June 27 only submarines could approach the port. On the night of June 30, the crew of the last battery blew up themselves and their guns, and the Germans reached the Khersonessky Point: Sevastopol had fallen.

2 Retreat to Alamein. During the first days of June General Ritchie endeavoured to organise a series of attacks on Rommel's positions behind the centre of what had been the British defence line running south from Gazala, but the attacks were badly coordinated and, although fierce enough to earn the title of 'Cauldron Battles', totally ineffective; and reinforcement and supplies were now reaching the Panzerarmee through the gap left by the destruction of 150th Infantry Brigade.

Rommel now decided to clear his southern flank by the destruction of the Free French post at Bir Hacheim, and the ring around the fortress was closed by June 5. The battle raged for nearly six days, all attempts by Eighth Army to break the siege failed and by the morning of June 11 Rommel was inspecting the captured fort and equipment.

The confusion among the British commanders remained unresolved. Another 'Cauldron Battle' was fought at the Guards Brigade positions at Knightsbridge, again German efficiency won, and on June 14 it was decided that the South African Division and the two remaining British brigades holding the northern end of the Gala Line must be withdrawn – at least as far as Tobruk. The South Africans did not stop there but continued on into Egypt, and the advance of the Panzerarmee seemed both to themselves and the watching world inexorable.

Tobruk, having held out for nine months in 1941 against Rommel's most furious onslaughts, fell in two days (Rommel was promoted Field Marshal on June 21 as a result, though when the news reached him he commented caustically that he would much prefer another panzer division). Within hours 15th and 21st Panzers with 90th Light Division were pressing eastwards again towards the Egyptian border. In this pursuit they were aided all the time by the swift capture of enormous British supply dumps, especially of petrol, and the luck which goes to the victorious. Even when the British set their fuel dumps alight, it seemed that the wind blew the flames out, or at least away from the main tanks. By June 23 the panzer spearheads were across the frontier and the following day they had curved up to reach the coast 50 miles east of Sidi Barrani – well over a hundred miles into Egypt.

By this time, the British retreat had become little more than a rout, and Auchinleck had decided he must take command of Eighth Army himself, for Ritchie's plans for the immediate future envisaged a totally impractical attempt to hold Mersa Matruh – as evidently untenable as Tobruk, Bardia and the other recent victims of Rommel's ambition. Certainly some defence must be staged at Mersa Matruh, but more in the nature of a holding operation while more effective defences were consolidated further back. For there was one last position, before the Nile Delta, where the Panzerarmee might be held.

Throughout the entire course of the Desert War, an open flank had existed to the south around which every attacker had swung, but now to the south lay the Qattara Depression, a deep wide cleft in the desert surface, with cliff-like sides and a swampy bottom which in places might support small vehicles, but nowhere would take the weight of a tank. About a hundred miles east of Mersa Matruh was the narrowest neck between the Depression and the coast – a 30-mile-wide gap through which any force invading the Nile Delta from the west must pass.

Here, obviously, lay the best hope of stopping Rommel, and a series of defensive positions had already been laid out and occupied, the chief being the box around the small railhead of El Alamein on the coast. This was now held by a brigade of South African troops, while 18th Indian Brigade held the ground immediately to the south – and in a long arc to the south-east from the box Auchinleck now massed all the artillery he could collect, both from the Delta and from the retreating columns.

Rommel's reconnaissance units arrived there at dawn on June 29 and the leading units of 90th Light were close behind them – well mixed with the rear columns of the British retreat. By the last day of June, Panzerarmee formations were at Tel el Eisa, the panzer divisions out to the south and Rommel's plans laid for the last battle before victorious entry into Alexandria. Mussolini was so excited by the prospect that he had flown to Derna, taking a white charger with him, upon which he intended to lead the victory parade.

Inset 2 – Retreat to Alamein

2

MEDITERRANEAN SEA

Gazala
TOBRUK
1900 June 20
Bir Hacheim
June 1
DAK (Rommel)
June 21
Bardia
Sollum
Sidi Barrani
Sidi Omar
June 24
Mersa Matruh
June 27
Fuka
June 23
Fort Maddalena
Sidi abd el Rahman
LIBYA
June 29
El Alamein
June 30
EIGHTH ARMY
E G Y P T
Qattara Depression

0M   25   50   75
0Km 25 50 75 100

74

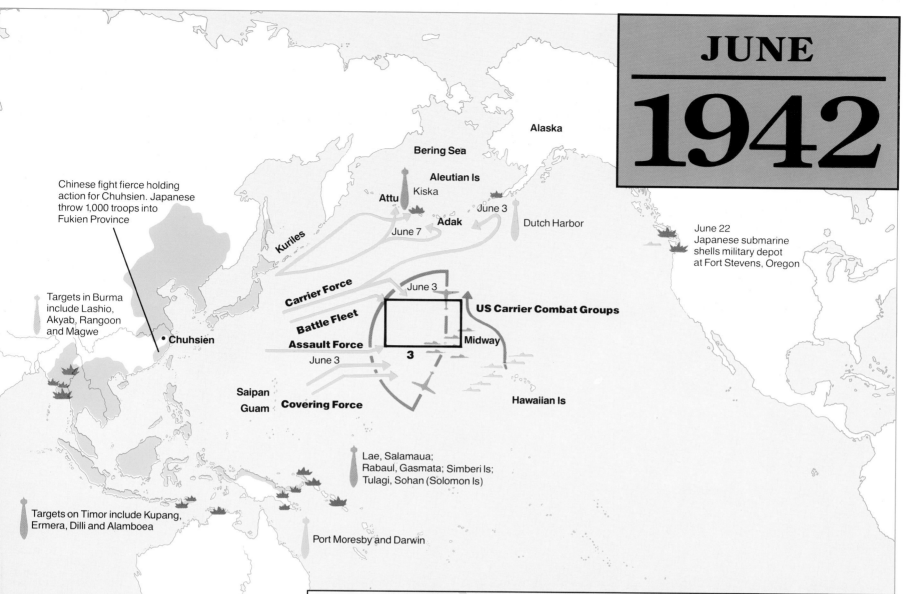

Chinese fight fierce holding action for Chuhsien. Japanese throw 1,000 troops into Fukien Province

Targets in Burma include Lashio, Akyab, Rangoon and Magwe

• Chuhsien

Targets on Timor include Kupang, Ermera, Dilli and Alamboea

Alaska

Bering Sea

Aleutian Is
Kiska
Attu
June 3
Adak
Dutch Harbor
June 7

June 22 Japanese submarine shells military depot at Fort Stevens, Oregon

Kuriles

Carrier Force

June 3

US Carrier Combat Groups

Battle Fleet

Assault Force

June 3

3

Midway

Saipan
Guam

Covering Force

Hawaiian Is

Lae, Salamaua; Rabaul, Gasmata; Simberi Is; Tulagi, Sohan (Solomon Is)

Port Moresby and Darwin

3 The Battle of Midway. The set-back to his plans at Coral Sea did not unduly concern Admiral Yamamoto. Believing that both *Lexington* and *Yorktown* had been sunk, he was now so sure of Japanese naval supremacy that he immediately began planning for a confrontation which would give him overwhelming victory.

He sent off a carrier fleet under Vice-Admiral Nagumo comprising four large carriers, two battleships and three cruisers, to arrive off Midway at dawn on June 4. There they were to deliver a heavy bombardment of the American base as prelude to the arrival, two days later, of an assault force under Admiral Kondo, a move which he considered would bring the strongest force Admiral Nimitz could muster from Pearl Harbor, passing over two lines of Japanese submarines on the way. The survivors would then have to face not only the combined squadrons of Nagumo's carrier fleet, but also the huge guns and torpedoes of the 5 battleships, 4 cruisers and over 30 destroyers of his own Battle Fleet, which would have been waiting over the horizon.

Yamamoto was not to know that his battle plans were being studied by the Americans almost as soon as he issued them. As a result, by June 3 the US carrier fleet, divided into two task forces under Rear-Admirals Fletcher and Spruance was cruising some 200 miles north of Midway, secure in the knowledge that the approaching enemy were completely unaware of their presence.

Nonetheless, the first phase of Yamamoto's plan seemed to achieve gratifying success. Kates and Vals from Nagumo's forces arrived unhindered and on time over Midway, and their protecting Zero fighters shot the US Brewster Buffaloes out of the sky as soon as they appeared. An attack on Nagumo's fleet at 0710 by aircraft from Midway was easily beaten off, as was a heavier one by dive-bombers and Flying Fortresses half an hour later.

Then at 0745 one of Nagumo's scouting planes suddenly reported the presence of the US task forces, and Nagumo promptly ordered a change of course to parry the new threat. The immediate result of this was that three separate US attack groups comprising altogether 49 bombers and fighters arrived over empty seas, and had either to return to the fleet or ditch as fuel ran out, and although three more squadrons did find the Japanese fleet they were beaten off. Then, just after 1000, fortunes abruptly changed.

The Zeros, Kates and Vals were back aboard their carriers, the majority refuelled, re-bombed and reammunitioned, all effort concentrated on getting the planes back into action. Suddenly, attention was jerked upwards by the high-pitched, rising scream of dive-bombers, and 35 Dauntlesses from

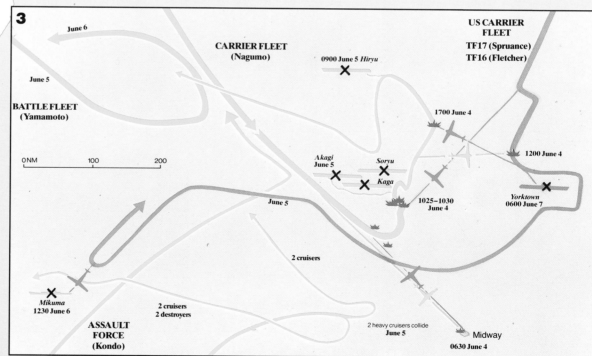

3

June 6
June 5

CARRIER FLEET (Nagumo)

0900 June 5 *Hiryu*

US CARRIER FLEET
TF17 (Spruance)
TF16 (Fletcher)

BATTLE FLEET (Yamamoto)

1700 June 4

0 NM   100   200

Akagi June 5
Soryu
Kaga

1200 June 4

1025–1030 June 4

Yorktown 0600 June 7

June 5

2 cruisers

Mikuma 1230 June 6

2 cruisers
2 destroyers

2 heavy cruisers collide June 5

Midway

0630 June 4

ASSAULT FORCE (Kondo)

Enterprise and *Hornet* swept down upon them, 1,000-pound bombs swinging away underneath.

Akagi was hit first, amidships with a bomb which exploded next to a torpedo store, then with another amid assembled Kates whose petrol-tanks blew apart in vast sheets of flame; within minutes Nagumo's flagship was doomed, though she remained afloat for some hours. Four bombs hit *Kaga* with similar results, though she too remained afloat long enough to be found and torpedoed by a US submarine, but *Soryu* was hit three times by *Yorktown*'s bombers and went down 20 minutes later. In five violent minutes half Japan's carrier force was thus eliminated, together with the most experienced crews in the world.

Before the day was out, American pilots also found *Hiryu* and damaged her so badly that the following morning her crew scuttled her – though she had exacted a price. Her aircraft had found *Yorktown* just before noon and started internal fires

which *Yorktown*'s crew fought with some success until early afternoon. But then Kates arrived from *Hiryu* and their torpedoes put an end to her; she finally sank on the morning of June 7.

It was not only the Japanese carrier fleet which suffered off Midway. During the morning of June 5 the heavy cruisers *Mikuma* and *Mogami* collided while taking avoiding action on sighting a US submarine and were so badly damaged that they were ordered back to Truk, and the following day *Mikuma* was found by aircraft from *Enterprise*. One plane crashed on her deck, petrol fumes were sucked down into an engine-room and exploded, and *Mikuma* sank just after noon.

Thus by the evening of June 4 the smoking hulls of four Japanese aircraft-carriers had marked the turning of the Pacific war. Though it was not realised at the time – or for some time afterwards – the Battle of Midway was one of the truly decisive battles of history.

75

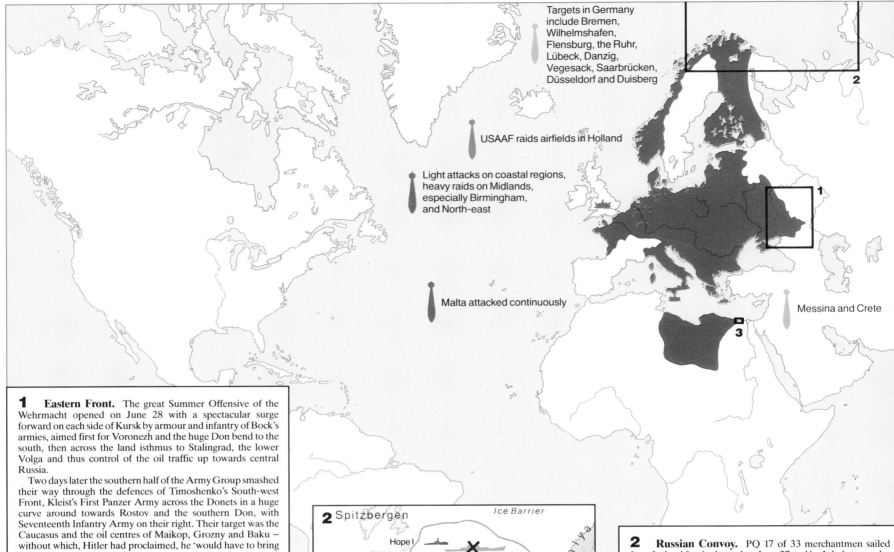

Targets in Germany include Bremen, Wilhelmshafen, Flensburg, the Ruhr, Lübeck, Danzig, Vegesack, Saarbrücken, Düsseldorf and Duisberg

2

USAAF raids airfields in Holland

1

Light attacks on coastal regions, heavy raids on Midlands, especially Birmingham, and North-east

Malta attacked continuously

Messina and Crete

3

1 Eastern Front. The great Summer Offensive of the Wehrmacht opened on June 28 with a spectacular surge forward on each side of Kursk by armour and infantry of Bock's armies, aimed first for Voronezh and the huge Don bend to the south, then across the land isthmus to Stalingrad, the lower Volga and thus control of the oil traffic up towards central Russia.

Two days later the southern half of the Army Group smashed their way through the defences of Timoshenko's South-west Front, Kleist's First Panzer Army across the Donets in a huge curve around towards Rostov and the southern Don, with Seventeenth Infantry Army on their right. Their target was the Caucasus and the oil centres of Maikop, Grozny and Baku – without which, Hitler had proclaimed, he 'would have to bring the war to an end'.

It seemed at first that the days of easy victory had returned, for the Wehrmacht legions swept ahead through the open rolling corn and steppe grass. Voronezh was reached by July 7, a slight hesitation about his left flank by Bock was brushed aside (and Bock dismissed) and then the whole power and thrust of two infantry armies (Second and Sixth) and one panzer army (Fourth) was directed down through the Donets Corridor to fill the Don bend.

There was a certain amount of administrative chaos caused by the excitement which gripped the German High Command, and Hoth's Fourth Panzer Army was directed further south than originally intended to help in the Caucasus drive, leaving only the Sixth Army under General Paulus to occupy the easternmost curve of the bend and threaten Stalingrad; but in July Stalingrad was just another Russian city to be despoiled in due course.

The main target was the oil, and by the end of the month panzers from the newly formed Army Group A under Field Marshal List had reached Proletarskaya and Salsk, the great prizes by the Caspian now surely within their grasp.

2 Spitzbergen

Ice Barrier

Hope I
2205 July 4

PQ 17

Bear I

Cruiser & destroyer escort

14 sunk by July 5

7 sunk or run aground July 6–8

2130 July 5

2 sunk July 10

Banak
Tromso
Narvik
Kirkenes
Petsamo
Murmansk

SWEDEN   FINLAND   RUSSIA

0M 100 200
0Km 100 200 300

Novaya Zemlya

2 Russian Convoy. PQ 17 of 33 merchantmen sailed from Iceland for Archangel on June 27 and by July 1 was under attack from eight U-boats. The close escort of corvettes, trawlers and minesweepers was enough to hold the U-boats off for a while, but two days later one ship was lost to a torpedo bomber, and during the following days the Luftwaffe pressed home their attacks relentlessly.

On the evening of July 4, the Admiralty concluded that strong German naval forces, possibly including the battleship *Tirpitz*, were closing on the convoy and that neither the close escort nor the distant escort of four cruisers could fight them off. They therefore ordered the escort to withdraw and the convoy to scatter in the hope that some individual ships might get through. During the next 24 hours U-boat and Luftwaffe attacks sank 12 ships, and the onslaught continued until July 10. Only 10 of the 33 merchantmen and their cargoes got through.

3 Panzerarmee Falters. Rommel at the beginning of July was coming face to face with one of the immutable laws of warfare. The more rapid an advance, the quicker the lines of communication become attenuated, the farther behind are left your own sources of supply – though for a limited period it may be possible to live off captured enemy supplies. The enemy forces, however, unless they are destroyed, are retreating upon their own bases where weapons, ammunition and reinforcements may be awaiting them.

By the end of June, the panzer divisions had but 55 panzers between them, the Ariete and Trieste Armoured Divisions but 30 M13s. There were sufficient men to crew the tanks and the artillery, but infantry strength was ominously low. In morale, of course, no army in history could have been better founded than Panzerarmee Afrika at that moment; however hungry, thirsty, dirty or exhausted the men were, their spirits were exalted, the confidence in their leader and quick victory sublime.

Opposite them in the Alamein positions were men less tired, better fed and, as the days passed, better equipped – and much more heavily armed. As a result, when the panzer divisions and the 90th Light moved off on the morning of July 1 to attempt to outflank Alamein itself and reach the coast road which would lead to Alexandria, on the right flank the panzers came up against well-conducted defences by South African and Indian troops along Ruweisat Ridge – and on the left 90th Light ran into a 'Trommelfeuer' from the waiting guns which shook even the men old enough to remember the barrages of the First World War. For the first time ever, the Afrika Korps War Diary reports panic in their own ranks.

Moreover, to their ordeal was now added the weight of heavy bombing from the Desert Air Force, now operating from nearby airfields and under protection of fighter patrols which had swept the Luftwaffe from the skies. By July 3 it was evident that even Rommel's toughest and most experienced troops were too exhausted for further prolonged effort; the first stage of the First Battle of Alamein was at an end.

The following stages were to last the rest of July, and consisted of Auchinleck's attempts to smash the Panzerarmee. But like so many attacks by Eighth Army at this time, they lacked firm direction, co-operation, even competent planning.

By the end of the month Rommel was short of ammunition, and Auchinleck again short of men so heavy had been his casualties. The fighting had produced one success and one failure for each side; Auchinleck had halted Rommel's drive to the Nile – but the Panzerarmee was still in existence and until Eighth Army could solve its problems of technique and efficiency, the danger of the Nile Delta falling to German aggression would still exist.

1

BRYANSK FRONT
(Golikov)

Orel

Yelets

VORONEZH FRONT
(formed July 7)
(Vatutin)

Kursk

Voronezh
July 7

ARMY GROUP B
(Weichs)

Stary Oskol

SOUTH-WEST FRONT
(Timoshenko)

Belgorod

Rossosh
July 10

Kletskaya   Kachalinskaya

KHARKOV

Poltava

STALINGRAD

Izyum

Donets Corridor

Morozovsk

Kalach

STALIN-GRAD FRONT
(Gordov)

ARMY GROUP A
(formed July 13)
(List)

Tsimlyansky
July 18

Rostov
July 24

Azov

Taganrog

Proletarskaya
July 29

Salsk
July 31

Sea of Azov

Tikhoretsk

0M 50 100
0Km 50 100 150

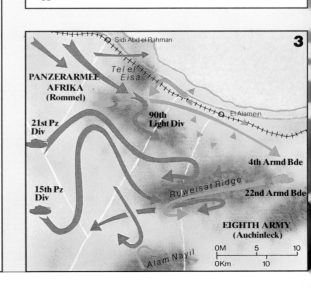

Sidi Abd el Rahman

PANZERARMEE AFRIKA
(Rommel)

Tel el Eisa

El Alamein

21st Pz Div

90th Light Div

15th Pz Div

Ruweisat Ridge

4th Armd Bde

22nd Armd Bde

EIGHTH ARMY
(Auchinleck)

Alam Nayil

0M 5 10
0Km 10

3

76

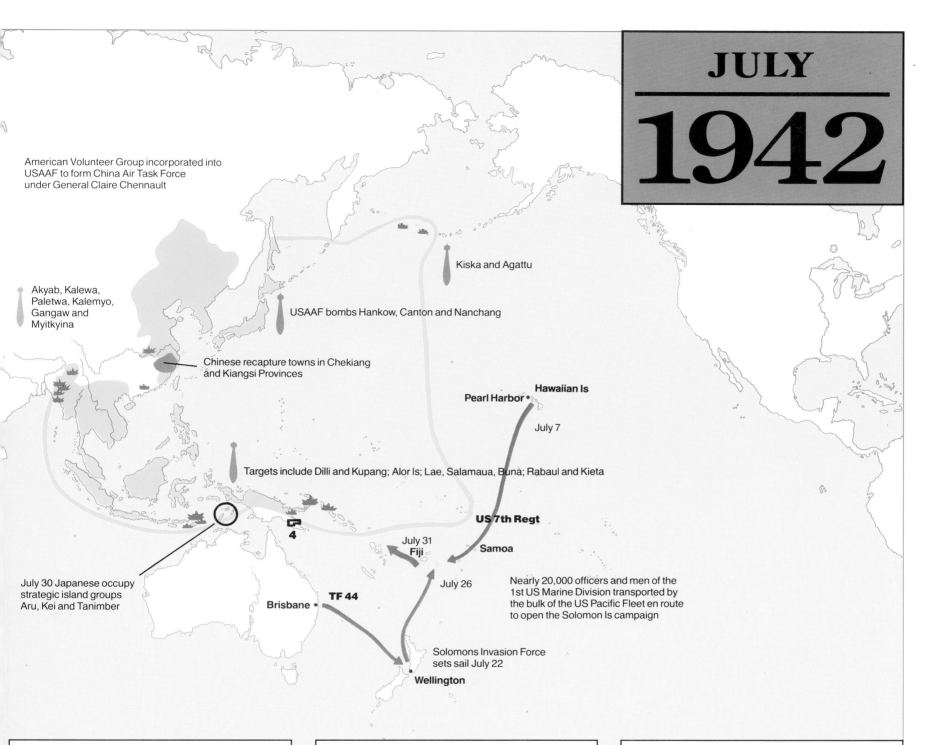

American Volunteer Group incorporated into USAAF to form China Air Task Force under General Claire Chennault

Kiska and Agattu

Akyab, Kalewa, Paletwa, Kalemyo, Gangaw and Myitkyina

USAAF bombs Hankow, Canton and Nanchang

Chinese recapture towns in Chekiang and Kiangsi Provinces

Hawaiian Is

Pearl Harbor

July 7

Targets include Dilli and Kupang; Alor Is; Lae, Salamaua, Buna; Rabaul and Kieta

US 7th Regt

4

July 31
Fiji

Samoa

July 30 Japanese occupy strategic island groups Aru, Kei and Tanimber

July 26

Nearly 20,000 officers and men of the 1st US Marine Division transported by the bulk of the US Pacific Fleet en route to open the Solomon Is campaign

Brisbane

TF 44

Solomons Invasion Force sets sail July 22

Wellington

4 Papua and New Guinea. The main drive of the Japanese offensive during the months immediately after Pearl Harbor had been south-westwards from the home islands, towards the oil and mineral targets of Burma and the Dutch East Indies. The Japanese commanders, however, were well aware that sooner or later they would have to defend themselves against American and Australian attack from the east, and that they must quickly form a shield against this. The island chains of the Marianas and the Carolines – and especially the deep harbour at Truk – would be essential, and further to the south-east they should try to obtain control of first the Solomons and then of Papua and New Guinea.

As early as March they had landed troops unopposed at Salamaua and Lae on the north coast of New Guinea, and these had quickly built up a base with stores, workshops and an airfield nearby, confident that once the Japanese Navy had landed more troops and taken control of Port Moresby it would be possible for both Japanese forces to expand and meet each other, and thus control the entire peninsula.

But the reverse suffered by the navy in the Coral Sea necessitated a change in emphasis. Now the forces in the north must undertake the task on their own, themselves take Port Moresby, crossing the formidable Owen Stanley Range on the way; but first, there was a local matter which had to be cleared up. The base and airfield had since April been subject to harassment and sabotage by Australian commandos, and now it seemed that these were being reinforced; two Australian infantry brigades had arrived at Port Moresby to establish a larger base there, and on July 2 a pair of infantry battalions had been despatched up the Kokoda Trail across the range towards Buna, where it was intended to build an airfield from which the Japanese further along the coast could be attacked. The battalions reached Kokoda on July 2 and pressed forward, though progress was slow due to the rudimentary nature of the track and the fact that in places it had risen over 1,000 feet in less than three miles, while between the top of the peak and Kokoda it dropped 5,000 in five!

Japanese reaction to this threat was rapid. On July 21 they put 2,000 men ashore at Buna (the Australians were still on

their way), following them by the end of the month with another 11,000 men of General Hyakutake's Seventeenth Army from Davao and Rabaul. The first units ashore drove south to meet the Australians – who had had no warning of their presence – sweeping up commando units on their way. By July 28 they were themselves at Kokoda and by July 31 they had reached Isurava, with their forward patrols at the 'Gap' on the very peak

of the ridge overlooking the Australian position and the route down to Port Moresby and the sea.

It seemed that their confidence had been justified, their reputation for invulnerability strengthened and their present opposition no more worthy of their respect than that against which they had fought in Burma, Bataan or the Dutch East Indies.

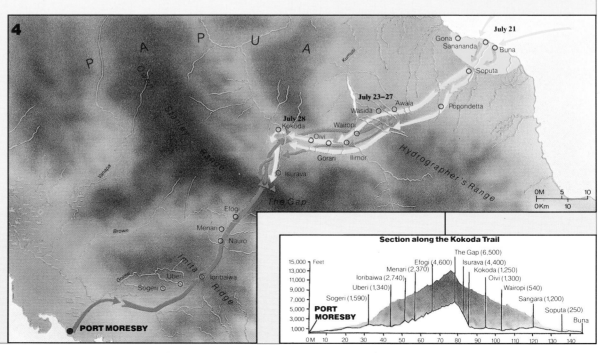

Section along the Kokoda Trail

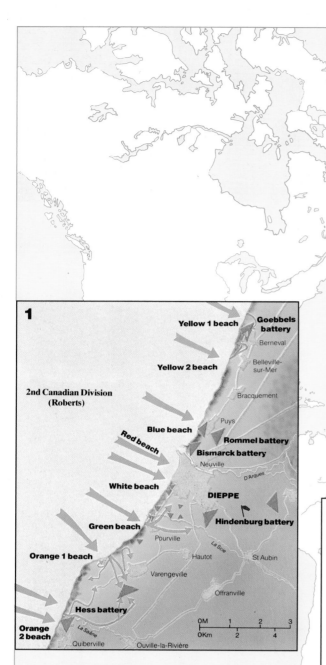

Night targets include Duisberg, Osnabrück, Mainz, Flensburg, Frankfurt, Wiesbaden, Nuremberg and Saarbrücken; Cassel, Gdynia

Continuous bombing of industrial and communications targets

Mainly coastal areas of the UK

Königsberg, Danzig; Warsaw and Berlin

Raids by Flying Fortresses. Rouen hit

Targets include Crete, Rhodes, Navarino; Sicilian airfields; Tobruk, Mersa Matruh and shipping

1 The Dieppe Raid was mounted to discover if it would ever be possible to capture a French port. On the night of Aug 18, nine infantry landing ships carrying four battalions of Canadian infantry and one of tanks, escorted by nearly 250 naval vessels some of which bore the men of 3 and 4 Army Commandos and of Royal Marine A Commando, left south coast ports and by 0540 the next morning 3 and 4 Commandos were ashore on the flanks of the attack, successfully neutralising the menacing gun positions. But between these assaults, disaster struck the Canadians, for the Germans had planned efficient beach defences. Machine-gun fire swept the approaches, wire entanglements blocked the beach and mortar fire covered every dip in the shingle. By 0900 it was evident that the attack was a failure, and by early afternoon the last attempt to lift off survivors was abandoned. Of the 7,000 officers and men who had landed, 4,384 were killed, wounded or taken prisoner.

2 Approach to Stalingrad. Throughout August, List's Army Group A flooded south. Stavropol fell to them on Aug 5, Armavir on the 7th and Maikop and the first oilwells were reached on the 9th. On the right flank Seventeenth Infantry Army marched down the rail-line towards Krasnodar to be joined by units from Manstein's Eleventh Army which crossed the Straits from the Crimea into the Kuban. By the end of the month Mozdok was in German hands and the swastika was flying from the peak of Mount Elbruz, the highest in the Caucasus.

But to List's north, matters did not proceed so satisfactorily for General Paulus. As his divisions had filled the Don bend his thoughts had centred on the idea of taking Stalingrad 'on the march', but he had lost Hoth's Fourth Panzer Army, and with only Weitersheim's panzer corps, he felt that he could not force the Don crossing in the necessary strength. However, Paulus was one of Hitler's favourites, so Hoth's panzers were soon driving back north-east on the far side of the Don to join him and take the southern flank of his advance on Stalingrad, Weitersheim's panzer corps on the northern, the nine infantry divisions between.

By Aug 20 Paulus's command was across the Don and driving east; by the evening of the 23rd, Weitersheim's forward thrust had lanced across the city's northern suburbs to reach the Volga, and on the night of 23/24th the Luftwaffe mounted its heaviest raid since June 1941 and burned the sprawling wooden shopping and housing blocks to ashes. All that was left to do, apparently, was to 'roll the city's defences up from the north'. But by the end of the month it was beginning to dawn on the men of the Sixth Army that it might not be as easy as that. Stalingrad was about to assume an epic status in the history of the Second World War which would compel the world's attention.

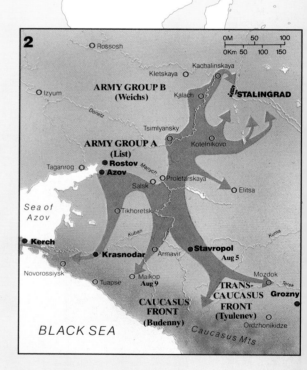

3 Malta Convoy. After the comparative failure of the June convoys to relieve Malta it became imperative to try again with even stronger escort forces. The 'Pedestal' convoy of 14 merchantmen, including the *Ohio* carrying 12,000 tons of oil, passed Gibraltar early on Aug 10, accompanied by 3 aircraft carriers with 72 fighters aboard, 2 battleships, 3 light cruisers, 3 6-inch cruisers, an anti-aircraft cruiser and 24 destroyers.

By noon, Aug 11 they were under continual observation from enemy aircraft, at 1315 the carrier *Eagle* was torpedoed and sank in eight minutes, and that evening the bombing attacks

began. Nevertheless, another 24 hours were to pass before further serious loss, when a destroyer and another aircraft carrier were put out of action. But that evening the main strength of the escort had to return to Gibraltar, only cruisers and destroyers remaining. From then on U-boats, MTBs and bombers attacked continuously and with some success. At 1800 Aug 13, one more followed an hour later and early on the 15th the vital tanker *Ohio* was nursed into the harbour with destroyers lashed alongside to keep her afloat.

☆ North Africa. Mr Churchill was with President Roosevelt in Washington when he learned of the fall of Tobruk. Mr Roosevelt's immediate reaction was 'What can we do to help?' and as a result within days 300 Sherman tanks and 100 self-propelled 105mm guns were on their way to Egypt in six fast American ships.

Mr Churchill returned to London on June 27, throughout July dealt with the political consequences of the reverses in the desert – and shortly after dawn on Aug 3 he and General Sir Alan Brooke arrived in Cairo to conduct investigations on the spot. It did not take them long to decide that sweeping changes must be made. General Auchinleck was relieved of the Middle East command and his place taken by Lt-General the Hon. Sir Harold Alexander, and command of the Eighth Army went to Lt-General Sir Bernard Law Montgomery, who immediately set about reshaping it in accordance with his own ideas.

More men and more equipment – including the Shermans – began arriving in the Delta, but most important of all a feeling spread throughout the formations in both armies that a new element had arrived in the Middle East theatre. Much later a German officer summed it up. 'The war in the desert ceased to be a game when Montgomery took over.'

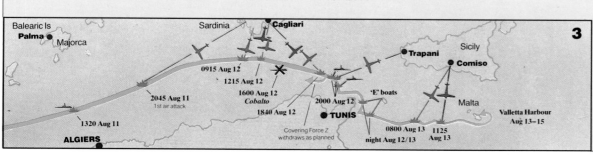

Cruisers and destroyers shell Kiska

Chinese claim recovery of all positions in Kiangsi recently lost, and all important Japanese strongholds in South Chekiang

Rabaul, Kavieng, Gasmata, Lae, Salamaua and Kei Is

US Marines raid Makin

Aug 23–25 Battle of the E Solomons

Targets in Burma include Myitkyina, Akyab; Kalewa, Homalin, Lashio and Magwe

The picture was different on Tulagi and the other Florida Bay islands. On Tulagi itself the 1st Marine Raiders went ashore successfully, but then ran into stiff Japanese resistance. During the night of Aug 7/8 they had to fight off four separate attacks, then spend the next few days hunting down and killing the Japanese survivors; it was the first time the marines met the phenomenon of Japanese fanaticism in defence. On the neighbouring islands, too, it took naval bombardment and heavy air strikes from the US carriers before the marines were in control.

On Guadalcanal, 1st US Marine Division held the airfield by the morning of Aug 9 (they christened it Henderson Field) and were rapidly consolidating, but suddenly found that their position had become critical. During the previous night the Allied naval forces guarding the northern entrance around Savo Island to Ironbottom Sound (the 'Slot') had been virtually wiped out by a Japanese cruiser force in a brilliant night action. Moreover, to the south the three aircraft carriers of Admiral Fletcher's Task Force, which had been providing them with air cover, had already been withdrawn for service elsewhere, and in the circumstances the admiral commanding the ships of the original landing force decided that he too must withdraw. By Aug 10 the 1st US Marines were on their own.

The Japanese did not intend to leave them so. On Aug 18 the first echelon of an attack force was landed at Taivu under Colonel Ichiki, who despite his experience held his enemy in such contempt that, without waiting for more support, he mounted a brief mortar bombardment of the Henderson Field defences on the morning of Aug 21 and then sent his men – who had already marched five miles and waded two rivers that morning – into a frontal bayonet charge. They ran into deadly fire from well placed positions, suffered heavy casualties and when a second attempt failed, Ichiki withdrew back across the Ilu river.

But the day before Ichiki's attack, 19 Wildcats and 12 Dauntlesses had flown into Henderson Field, and during the next two days they gave the marines air cover to launch a flanking attack between the Ilu and the Tenaru which annihilated the remaining Japanese and caused Ichiki to commit hara-kiri. The US marines had won the first round of the Battle for Guadalcanal.

The next attempt by the Japanese to land more troops was blocked when the Japanese fleet, which included three aircraft carriers, was driven back on Aug 23 by aircraft from Admiral Fletcher's carrier force in the Battle of the Eastern Solomons. One Japanese carrier and one destroyer were sunk for no American losses.

5 Guadalcanal. Japanese forces had moved down into the Solomons by the end of May, first occupying Tulagi and neighbouring islands off Florida Island, then putting small forces ashore on the north coast of Guadalcanal. Although reports of these movements reached Allied HQ in Australia and Washington, nothing was done immediately as men and materials were in demand elsewhere. But when Japanese engineers began building an airfield near Lunga Point – virtually the only piece of flat ground in the Solomons – action became necessary; whoever held that field would dominate the whole area.

In size, the operation now mounted by the US Command constituted the most powerful amphibious attack force ever assembled to that date, though in training and experience it was woefully inadequate. Fortunately, when the first waves of the 1st US Marine Division went ashore early on Aug 7 just to the west of Lunga Point they met no opposition, and the chaos and confusion of the landing did not end in the disaster which might have been expected. Nevertheless, it took them until the evening of Aug 8 to advance less than five miles and occupy the half-constructed airfield – still against no opposition.

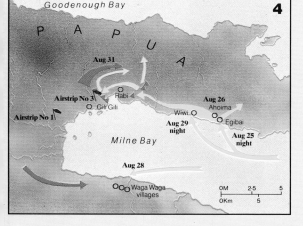

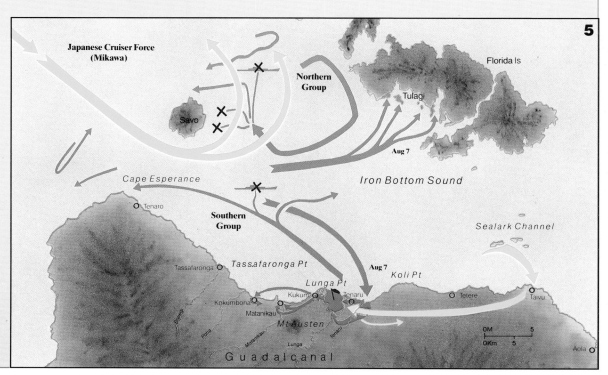

4 Papua/New Guinea. Though by the end of July Japanese troops had reached the 'Gap' at the top of the Owen Stanley Range, they had also reached the end of their present lines of communication and supply, and had for the moment to stay where they were. But General Hyakutake had always envisaged a two-pronged attack, and on the morning of Aug 26 he put ashore some 2,000 troops on the northern shore of Milne Bay under the impression that they would be opposed by a mere two or three companies of Australian infantry, based there to defend an airstrip holding 20 to 30 fighters.

In fact, two brigades of Australian troops were there, and under protection of Kittyhawk squadrons were soon engaged in bitter infantry fighting against some of the most experienced jungle fighters of the day. A few Japanese light tanks gave the Japanese some advantage as the Australians were without anti-tank guns, but as August ended the Kittyhawk squadrons were bombing Japanese landing points, destroying barges, fuel and stores dumps, and the Australian infantry were learning the crafts of night fighting. The myth of Japanese invincibility was being seriously challenged for the first time.

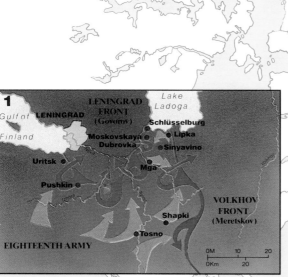

1
LENINGRAD FRONT (Govorov)
Lake Ladoga
Gulf of Finland
LENINGRAD
Schlüsselburg
Moskovskaya
Dubrovka
Lipka
Sinyavino
Uritsk
Mga
Pushkin
Shapki
VOLKHOV FRONT (Meretskov)
Tosno
EIGHTEENTH ARMY
0M 10 20
0Km 20

PQ 18 arrives Murmansk with only small losses

Light raids on coastal areas of UK

Daytime raids on Le Havre, Rouen, Abbeville, St Omer; Utrecht and Rotterdam

Twelve Bomber Command night raids on Germany, 5,000 tons of bombs dropped in first ten. Targets include Saarbrücken, Karlsruhe, Bremen, Duisberg, Frankfurt, Dusseldorf, Wilhelmshafen, Essen and the Ruhr, Flensburg, Munich and the Saar

Coastal Command raid Cherbourg and Bordeaux

Fewer raids on Malta

Night raids on Warsaw, Budapest, Vienna, Königsberg, Bucarest and Ploesti

Main targets in the Mediterranean are N African ports, Crete and shipping. Some activity over Sicily and Italy

1 & 2 Eastern Front. Once it became clear to STAVKA that the greatest danger lay at Stalingrad, it was decided to increase pressure all along the Northern and Central Fronts in order at least to tie up German forces there, possibly even to attract some from the danger area. They were to some extent aided by Hitler's decision in August to proceed with Operation *Nordlicht* – the plan to seize Leningrad and link up with the Finns, from whom he had long hoped for closer cooperation. As a result, he had ordered Manstein's Eleventh Army up from the far south, to launch the main attack on Sept 14.

By that time, however, the Red Army's Operation *Sinyavino* had been launched by both Leningrad and Volkhov Fronts under Generals Govorov and Meretskov respectively, Govorov driving south-west over the Leningrad perimeter towards Uritsk, south between the rivers Izhora and Tosna, and south-east towards Mga and Sinyavino. From his front, Meretskov would drive west to meet Govorov at Sinyavino, and further to the south, towards Shapki.

The first of Manstein's divisions arrived just in time to shore up Eighteenth Army's broken front south of Lake Ladoga, and Manstein's detailed plans for the reduction of Leningrad were never put into action. Neither, of course, were STAVKA's hopes for any relief of Leningrad realised, for the forces were equally balanced and neither side was to predominate. By the end of the month both Russian fronts had retired behind their original start lines, Manstein's Eleventh Army, its manpower and stocks of ammunition severely depleted, limped back to Vitebsk while the remnants of the once mighty Army Group North resigned itself to more months of deadlock – with yet another Russian winter immediately ahead.

To the south of these operations North-western Front continued attempts to clean out the Demyansk pocket, while further south still and immediately west of Moscow, continued Soviet pressure in the Rzhev sector made small advances to recapture some 25 villages.

Kleist's Army Group A were still driving down between the Black Sea and the Caspian, aided at first by units from Manstein's command crossing from Kerch to the Taman peninsula to take Novorossiysk during the first week of September. Further to the east the oil-derricks of Grozny came into view – but so did the first snows . . . and soon came orders for Manstein's men to move north; and with those orders a diminution of supplies, a redirection of reinforcements and a virtual cessation of encouragement or attention from the Führer's HQ, which had just moved east from Rastenburg to Vinnitsa.

For now the Battle for Stalingrad was the focus of all attention – not only in Germany, but around the world.

Paulus had but one objective – to amass the greatest power at his command along the Stalingrad perimeter and smash it forward, first across what open ground still separated his armies from the Stalingrad suburbs, then through the fire-blackened waste of the city's domestic quarters, and finally through the huge complex of steel and concrete factories along the Volga bank. A German 'steamroller' would crush Stalingrad and drive its inhabitants into the river.

The first massive attack was launched on Sept 12 by 11 infantry and 3 panzer divisions, which split apart the two defending Soviet armies, 62nd and 64th, at Kuporosnoye, then drove north along the river bank gradually forcing up towards No 1 Station opposite Krasnaya Sloboda. Red Army units hung grimly on to the slopes of Mamayev Kurgan for some days, but on Sept 26 a second vast onslaught fell upon them, a converging attack was launched at the northern end on the Orlovka Salient and by the end of the month the German line was closing around the Tractor, Barrikady and Krasny Oktyabr factories, by now focal centres of the defence.

But nearly 20 miles of the Volga bank was still in Red Army hands. In addition, moreover, General Chuikov was now in command of the city's defences while General Zhukov had come south to direct the strategic battle. Neither had yet lost a battle and they had no intention of starting now.

2
Orlovka
Rynok
Sept 26
Sept 26
Gorodishche
Sept 26
tractor factory
SIXTH ARMY (Paulus)
Sept 26
Barrikady factory
Krasny Oktyabr factory
Mamayev Kurgan
Sept 12
hospital
62nd ARMY (Chuikov)
Krasnaya Sloboda
Sept 12
FOURTH PANZER ARMY (Hoth)
Sept 12
STALINGRAD
Yelshanka
SOUTH-EAST FRONT (Yeremenko)
Sept 12
Kuporosnoye
64th ARMY (Shumilov)
0M 2·5 5
0Km 5

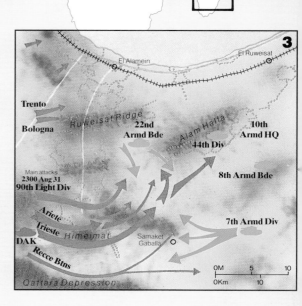

3
El Alamein
El Ruweisat
Trento
Bologna
Ruweisat Ridge
22nd Armd Bde
Alam Halfa
44th Div
10th Armd HQ
Main attacks 2300 Aug 31 90th Light Div
8th Armd Bde
Ariete
Trieste
Himeimat
Samaket Gaballa
7th Armd Div
DAK
Recce Btns
Qattara Depression
0M 5 10
0Km 10

3 The Battle of Alam Halfa. By the end of August Rommel knew that time was running out for him. Every morning his intelligence staff warned him of the exhaustion and sickness now racking Panzerarmee Afrika, and the inexorable build-up of forces opposite. A convoy bearing 100,000 tons of supplies for Eighth Army would arrive at Suez soon, whereas supplies for his own army were hardly enough to sustain it in position, let alone build up reserves for a battle.

But speed, surprise and German tactical skill might still win the opening stages of a breakthrough – and if reaction to events of the new Eighth Army commander was as slow as that of his predecessors, Rommel could yet lead his men to the Nile.

As darkness fell on Aug 30, the leading panzers edged forward into the gap just north of Himeimat, reconnaissance battalions on the right, Italians and 90th Light on the left. But as they reached the edge of the minefields, RAF bombers arrived overhead and the night became a calvary of explosions, of burning lorries and panzers; obviously there had been no element of surprise. Dawn brought the realisation that the day's objectives must be curtailed, and instead of driving far to the east, the axis of attack must curl northwards and break through the British positions along the Alam Halfa Ridge.

But soft sand slowed them and the bombing increased with daylight, as did the shelling when the panzers drew nearer to the Ridge; and nowhere did the British armour allow itself to be tempted into killing range, acting instead as mobile artillery behind their anti-tank screen. When darkness fell on that second day there was still no pause in Panzerarmee's ordeal, for all night long the desert floor shook as the bombs plummeted down, wrecking more vehicles and stretching taut nerves towards breaking-point.

Panzerarmee was in a trap. Alam Halfa Ridge had been firmly buttressed with extra guns, infantry and a brigade of armour, two more brigades waited to the east while 7th Armoured Division sealed the southern line. All the time, the RAF bombers cruised overhead, and now for the first time among them appeared Mitchells and Liberators of the USAAF. The Luftwaffe was almost non-existent.

By Sept 3, Rommel knew he must pull back his forces. Not only were the Eighth Army and the Desert Air Force inexorably destroying the Panzerarmee, but the Royal Navy was at work too, and of 5,000 tons of petrol he had been promised for the battle 2,600 tons had already been sunk between Italy and Benghazi. Gradually, the survivors of the two panzer divisions drew back, and on the night of Sept 3/4, German and Italian infantry along the northern edge of the gap above Himeimat fought off fierce attempts to close it. By the evening of Sept 6 what was left of the army which had advanced so spectacularly from Gazala during the last three months was back behind the minefields it had penetrated a week before.

80

Series of raids launched on Kiska from newly constructed airstrip on Adak, 250 miles away

Japanese retaliate with nuisance raids

Small aircraft launched from a submarine drop incendiary bombs near Brookings, Oregon

Sept 21 14th Indian Div leave Chittagong on first stage of attempt to recover Arakan

Lae, Salamaua, Rabaul, Gasmata Buna, Buka and Kieta

Targets in Burma include Akyab, Rangoon, Mandalay, Prome and Mogaung

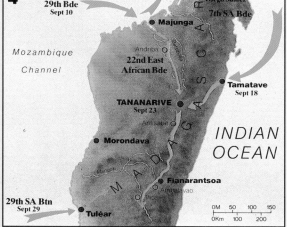

4

29th Bde Sept 10

re-embarks for Tamatave

from Diego Suarez

7th SA Bde

● Majunga

Mozambique Channel

Andriba

22nd East African Bde

● Tamatave Sept 18

TANANARIVE Sept 23

Antsirabe

INDIAN OCEAN

● Morondava

MADAGASCAR

● Fianarantsoa

Ambalavao

29th SA Btn Sept 29

● Tuléar

0M 50 100 150
0Km 100 200

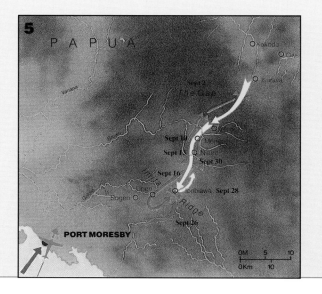

5

P A P U A

○ Kokoda

○ Gona

Sept 2

The Gap

○ Isurava

Sept 13

Sept 10

Sept 14 Nauro

Sept 16

Ioribawa Sept 28

Sogeri

Imita Ridge

Sept 26

Sept 30

PORT MORESBY

0M 5 10
0Km 10

5 Papua/New Guinea. During August the Japanese positions at the 'Gap' had been strengthened and their supply position improved to some extent, so at the beginning of September they again took up their apparently inexorable advance across the Owen Stanley Range. By Sept 6 they had forced the Australian militia battalions in front of them back some 15 miles to Efogi, where there was another pause while 1,000 fresh Japanese troops with engineers and two mountain guns joined the forward units. Thus strengthened, the Japanese pushed on further, now against seasoned Australian Imperial Force units who, though they were retreating, exacted a heavy price for each step back. By Sept 23 the Japanese were facing the Australians on the Imita Ridge at Ioribawa and here they were held. By now tropical diseases were taking as great a toll of Japanese strength as the growing Australian expertise, and their lines of supply were lengthening while Australian supplies were closer at hand. The next day, the leading Australian battalions moved forward and by the end of the month the Japanese were a few miles back on a retreat which would end eventually on the northern coast.

6

Iron Bottom Sound

Lunga Pt

Pt Cruz ○ Kukum   **1st Marine Div**

Matanikau

Henderson Field

Sept 14   *Bloody Ridge*

Mt Austen

Sept 12–14

Lunga

G u a d a l c a n a l

0M 1 2 3
0Km 2 4

6 Guadalcanal. After the repulse of Colonel Ichiki's force, Japanese High Command sent in the original 2nd echelon followed by a complete infantry brigade under General Kawaguchi. On his part, General Vandergrift, commanding the US marines, brought over the Raiders and paratroops from Tulagi and, correctly guessing his enemy's intentions, stationed them along a ridge to the south of Henderson Field.

At noon on Sept 12, Japanese bombers pounded the ridge, during the afternoon a cruiser and three destroyers shelled it and after dusk three battalions of infantry charged up the slope with the same fanaticism as that shown by Ichiki's men – and with the same results. Machine-gun, rifle and mortar fire decimated their ranks and the attack was stopped dead; but Kawaguchi was undaunted and during Sept 13 more furious onslaughts were launched while two more battalions circled around to the south and attacked US defences west of Kukum.

But shortly before – and despite the loss during the convoy of the carrier *Wasp* and the destroyer *O'Brien* – 4,000 Marine reinforcements had been landed, and with their help all attacks were held, though the fighting was bitter. Sometimes the marine line bent, but it never broke.

A week's pause gave both sides time to regroup, and Vandergrift a chance to expand his bridgehead. On Sept 26/27 he sent one battalion west from Kukum towards the mouth of the Matanikau river, the Raiders on a circular approach from the south, and a third battalion by sea around past Point Cruz in an effort to outflank the Japanese defences. Though the operation was only partly successful, by the end of September the marines were on the river-line with a firm base for defence, or for a further advance in due course.

4 Allied Occupation of Madagascar. The collapse of Vichy French resistance at the end of May had not, of course, removed all danger of Japanese occupation of Madagascar, so during August it was decided to move forces down from the Diego Suarez district into the central and southern areas of the island. Three operations were mounted: 7th South African Brigade drove down from Diego Suarez, 29th Brigade landed at Majunga where they quickly overcame a single French battalion and then handed over to 22nd East African Brigade which drove south towards Tananarive, while 29th Brigade hastily re-embarked and sailed around to Tamatave where they landed and raced the East Africans to the capital. They lost the race but both brigades, after meeting little resistance, arrived on Sept 23, to be greeted with flowers and applause. On Sept 29 a South African battalion landed at Tuléar and although negotiations were still to take place, these were but a formality. Free French forces took over the island in December and the bulk of the Vichy forces, which had on occasion fought the British, joined them. The occupation had in all cost the British and African forces 33 killed and 96 wounded, though malaria had also caused as many deaths.

El Alamein

There is no doubt – even discounting General Montgomery's conviction that troops suffering the grievous disability of not having been trained under his personal direction would be unlikely to withstand the rigours of battle – that Eighth Army in August 1942 lacked certain military qualities essential for victory against so skilful a foe as the Afrika Korps, in any area of the desert and especially in the Alamein positions.

So far as the armoured forces were concerned, not only was there the problem of co-operation between them and the infantry to solve, but with the arrival of the Shermans many of the tank crews had now to learn to take fullest advantage of a tank whose armament, power and reliability were well above anything they had previously experienced. Though this would undoubtedly be a positive factor in the battle to come, it was nevertheless a task to be tackled before the battle began – and a less favourable factor was that they would be required to advance at night, and a specially chosen, moonless night at that. As recently as July, one armoured commander had refused to allow his tanks to move to support a New Zealand brigade in severe trouble, as 'Tanks can't be expected to move about in darkness!'

There were also both general and particular aspects of infantry fighting in need of improvement, not least because among the divisions which had been out in the desert for some time was a deep conviction that 'the best training is fighting'. As they had seen so much of it they must therefore already be well trained – a dictum which might have held greater validity had more of Eighth Army's fighting in recent weeks been successful. Moreover, they had also lost a number of experienced officers and NCOs during the retreat from Gazala and the replacements needed grooming for their new responsibilities; it takes more than just a period of time as a good rifleman to make a satisfactory corporal, or as a subaltern to make a good captain.

But there was an added reason for re-training the desert army, as a totally new approach to battle was now necessary. For the first time in the desert fighting there was no open flank for the attacking force to hook around – no Bir Enba Gap as for 7th Armoured and 4th Indian in 1940, no wide space as for XXX Corps during *Crusader* or for Rommel's armour during the Gazala battles. By September 1942 the defences of both armies stretched the whole way from the sea at Tel el Eisa down to the Qattara depression south of Himeimat, and every day that passed saw the thickening of those defences. There was no open flank, and even the gap which had existed below Alam Halfa had now been sealed from both sides.

The keynotes of the sealing were minefields and deep-dug gun positions, and if shortage of barbed wire did not allow entanglements of quite the complexity of the Western Front in 1918, the situation would nevertheless demand an attack of 1918 style. Massive artillery bombardment would be followed by direct infantry assault, and the mathematics of the battle would have to be based upon the cold, grim facts of attrition. One of these was that the assaulting force 'at the sharp end' would need to be numerically three times as strong as the defenders and to be prepared to suffer casualties in the same proportion. One of General Montgomery's first directives stressed this aspect of affairs. 'This battle will involve hard and prolonged fighting. Our troops must not think that, because we have a good tank and very powerful artillery support, the enemy will all surrender. The enemy will NOT surrender, and there will be bitter fighting. The infantry must be prepared to fight and kill, and to continue doing so over a long period . . .'

But first of all, the infantry with its supporting armour would have to cross the enemy minefields, some of them hundreds of yards deep and all of them covered by enemy artillery or machine-gun positions. Nearly half a million mines had now been sewn by the indefatigable German engineers, at least 90% of which were anti-tank mines which would not necessarily destroy a tank but would cripple it, probably by blowing off a track; and it would certainly wreck a wheeled vehicle and kill the majority of its occupants. Fortunately for the attacking infantry, a much smaller proportion of the mines were anti-personnel – though even this proportion was enough to make the task of walking across a minefield one of particular sensitivity; 'walking' was essential, no one ran.

Through these 'Devil's Gardens' as the Germans rather picturesquely called the minefields, three corridors had to be cleared during the opening hours of the attack, wide enough to allow two tanks abreast through – more practically, to allow following tanks to edge past one broken down or brewed up. A special School of Mine-clearance was set up, and during the weeks between mid-August and the end of October, hundreds of men were trained in the techniques of mine-detection, mine-clearance, and the accurate but concealed signposting of the edges of the cleared lanes so that only those following could see them. As an indication of the size of the operation, 88,755 lamps were positioned and lit on the night; the number of mines found, lifted, 'de-loused' (to use the Australian sappers' jargon) and piled along the edges of the corridors seems never to have been established.

If the task of mine-clearance constituted one separate operation in the preparations for the Battle of Alamein, another was the concealment of the area and date of the major assault. From the outset, General Montgomery knew that nothing could hide the enormous build-up of men and material pouring into the Suez ports, obviously intended for use against the Panzerarmee at Alamein, but if he could not disguise the strategy, he was determined at least to extract what element of surprise he could in regard to tactics; as his main stroke would fall in the northern half of the line, everything must be done to give the impression that it would fall in the south.

From the twin peaks of Himeimat, which had deliberately been left in German hands after Alam Halfa, a great deal of activity could be seen, and Axis reconnaissance aircraft were also given much opportunity to observe and report back the continual bustle and movement down there. But the majority of this was around dummy administration camps dotting the area south of Ruweisat Ridge, or existing supply dumps which were grossly expanded with empty cases and tentage. A dummy freshwater pipe was laid complete with three dummy pump-houses, leading from the coast down towards Gaballa in the south – an objective which at the maintained steady rate of progress would not be reached until early November.

But the main deception operation was mounted in the north. From the beginning it was decided that every evidence of concentration of force would be openly displayed as soon as possible so that, when no assault immediately followed, the enemy would grow used to its existence and notice no difference when fact replaced fiction.

Slit-trenches were dug in advanced positions and then left unused. Thousands of dummy vehicles, guns, tanks and dumps were positioned early in September – but either remained static or were occasionally moved around to give the impression of occupation by the

deception staff. Meanwhile the real tanks, guns and lorries arrived, were tested and their crews trained; and when the time came, they moved up under cover of darkness and took the place of the dummies, all trace of movement swept away before it could be detected by enemy observation. A whole system of bogus signal traffic was instigated with continuous routine messages passing between the HQs of non-existent units, or ones which had moved elsewhere and were observing signal silence – very strictly enforced.

A dummy railhead was set up well behind Alamein with a dummy oil-discharging point nearby, and around them were piled inflammatory materials with remotely controlled igniters; when the Luftwaffe bombed them, the igniters were fired, and following Luftwaffe waves dumped their bombs on what appeared to be worthwhile targets. Alongside the oil-jetty, a convertible tanker was moored, which one day would present to the observers the picture of a one-funnelled ship, the next day two funnels and a mast on a lengthened hull with derricks or some other variation. One new installation was not camouflage, however, and every stage of its progress was carried out at night, every vestige of the work scrupulously removed from sight every morning; this was the replacement of the main water pipe-line from Alexandria to Alamein by one of much larger bore, with a new water-point concealed in El Imayed station.

All the time this activity was taking place, the bulk of Eighth Army were holding the line – at times spread very thinly – and taking part in the training exercises. One essential aspect of this was brought about by Montgomery's realisation that, although the sun had burned them to an impressive shade of mahogany, thus giving them an appearance of physical well being, too many of them had spent too much time of late in static posts on guard, or travelling to and fro in trucks or lorries.

This battle for which we are preparing – he wrote in one of his directives – will be a real rough house and will involve a great deal of very hard fighting . . . The battle may go on for many days, and the final issue may well depend on which side can best last out and stand up to the buffeting, and ups and downs, and the continuous strain, of hard battle fighting.

There will be no tip and run tactics in this battle; it will be a killing match; the German is a good soldier and the only way to beat him is to kill him in battle.

During the next month, therefore, it is necessary to make our officers and men really fit; ordinary fitness is not enough, they must be made tough and hard.

As a result, in addition to special skills they were now called upon to learn, Eighth Army throughout September and the early part of October marched further than most of them had since their recruit days, carrying ever-heavier loads across sand under a hot sun. Shell-shock would undoubtedly claim many victims once the battle opened but on the Allied side true battle-fatigue would not prove a great problem.

By the end of September, the re-training was in full spate and Montgomery had laid his plans. XXX Corps, consisting of Australian, Scottish, New Zealand and South African infantry divisions, would mount the main attack in the north where two wide corridors through the minefields would be cleared through which the armour of X Corps would pass. XIII Corps infantry down in the south would mount two attacks, but these would be mainly holding attacks to disguise where the main weight was and to hold the Axis divisions down there in place. They would be supported by light tanks of 7th

82

Armoured Division, moving up through the third cleared lane.

Once X Corps were through the minefields and the main enemy infantry positions in the north, they were to deploy to prevent the German and Italian armour coming to the defence of their own infantry who would then be destroyed piecemeal by the XXX Corps infantry, reinforced as necessary by XIII Corps infantry brought up from the south. The battle would begin on the evening of Oct 23.

The main tasks for the commanding generals was completed by Oct 20, but from then on the lives of the staff officers were ones of immense concentration, constant activity and, for some of them, nightmarish worry. Theirs was the responsibility of ensuring that by the morning of Oct 23, over 2,000 guns, 1,000 tanks and some 220,000 men were all in their assigned positions, and that everything that the soldiers would require, from ammunition to drinking-water, to fight a 12-day battle would be available to them when and where required. And in order that the enemy should be given no inkling of the imminence of the first attack, at least 60% of all these men and all this material had to be moved during four successive nights, and in such a manner that no trace of its passing would remain on the desert floor to be observed by hostile eyes during the hours of harsh desert light in between.

Its successful execution in broad daylight would rank as a feat of organisation to compare with any; its successful completion at night is a near miracle, especially when the matter of concealment is taken into consideration. Every track made by a vehicle was brushed away before daylight, every picket holding guiding lights snatched away, and every fence-line or dummy hut which had been moved a few hours before carefully replaced.

By dawn on Friday, Oct 23, the Eighth Army was in position. All along the Front soldiers lay in their slit-trenches, sweating, roasting in the concentration of heat from which they might not escape for any reason at all, plagued the whole day by flies. Behind them, the artillery banged away occasionally, maintaining the weight of fire which had been thrown at the Axis positions during the past few weeks.

Then, at last, the sun began to sink, the heat drained from the sky. Suddenly, the flies were gone, the stars were out; it was dark. Out of the ground climbed the Eighth Army, stretching its limbs, coughing, swearing, still keeping voices low. Rifles clunked on the ground, webbing creaked, cooking-pots clanked as hot food arrived; out in front the forward patrols moved cautiously back, passing as they did so hurrying figures laying out the white tape start and guiding lines. Those who possessed watches glanced repeatedly at them and wondered about the state of the men opposite.

The condition of Panzerarmee by this time was serious. There had been no alleviation of the strains which had so exhausted them during August and September, and although extra formations had arrived to fill some of the gaps in their ranks – including units of 164th Division and the Ramcke Parachute Brigade – these had arrived in North Africa by air and thus had brought no transport with them. As a result, their supplies had to be brought from Tripoli and Benghazi in the now badly worn trucks and lorries which were barely enough to maintain the original Afrika Korps formations.

An extra cause for depression was the absence of their heroic commander, whose health had recently deteriorated even more than that of his men. Rommel was far older than they were, had been out longer than most of them and had been subject to far more serious mental strain. A series of fainting fits coupled with the discovery that he had been concealing severe stomach and intestinal troubles from his doctor, caused an upheaval at his headquarters, cables to Berlin from the doctor and eventually an order that he should proceed to Wiener-Neustadt for treatment and extended leave.

His replacement was General der Kavallerie Georg Stumme, lately commander of a panzer division on the Eastern Front, who did little to commend himself to old Afrika hands with his announcement that, after the

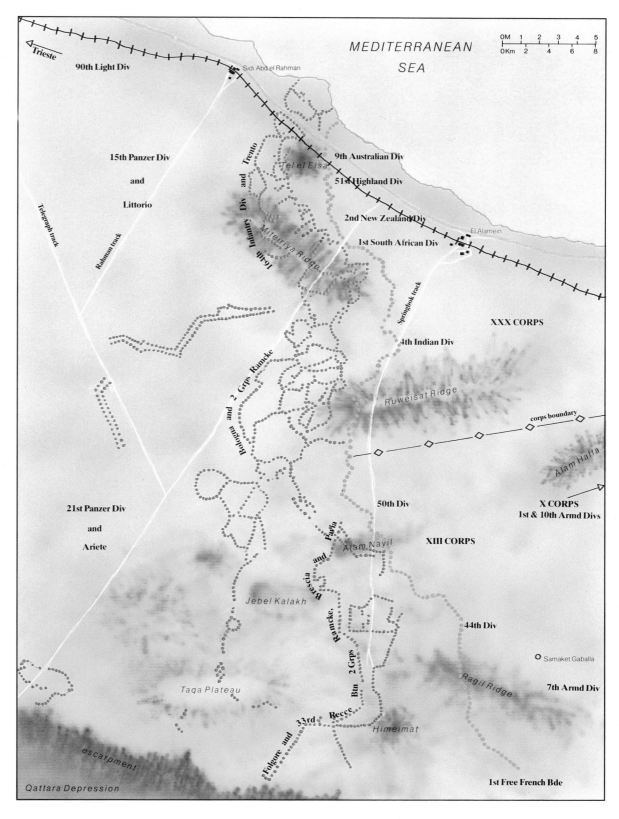

rigours of a Russian winter, he positively relished the climatic conditions in the desert. He found little to criticise in the disposition of forces now under his command or with the proposals for fighting the battle which all indications confirmed would begin some time in November, but his position was not made easier by Rommel's announcement, just before he left, that the moment the battle commenced he would abandon his cure and return to take command.

But Stumme was a large, cheerful man, and as the days passed some of his optimism began to lift the spirits of all. More armour was arriving at the front, as rear workshops repaired and serviced those perforce abandoned since Gazala; the Italian artillery – always their strongest arm – had been augmented, and although it would obviously never reach the power and weight of the enemy, it might well block Eighth Army tanks unless these showed far more expertise than ever before. And perhaps by November their 'Devil's Gardens' might be so wide and thick that no force, however determined, could pass through them without such severe casualties as to render it ineffective in any breakout.

So, as the October weeks passed, the 50,000-odd Germans and the 62,000 Italian soldiers at Alamein were

not particularly anxious about their immediate future. Oct 23 was exactly like every other day, and like the men a few thousand yards away to the east those at the Front watched the sun go down with relief, climbed out of their trenches, stretched luxuriously, consumed their evening meals and went about their allotted night-time duties. They too occasionally glanced at their watches, but only to see how much of their guard remained.

Just after eight o'clock there were sounds of gun-fire at the northern end of the line, those up there cursed the Australians who were apparently about to launch one of their raids, those to the south blessed their good fortune. Like the day, the night promised to be an ordinary one.

Forty minutes later, the eastern horizon suddenly turned pink and for a few seconds an astonished silence gripped the world.

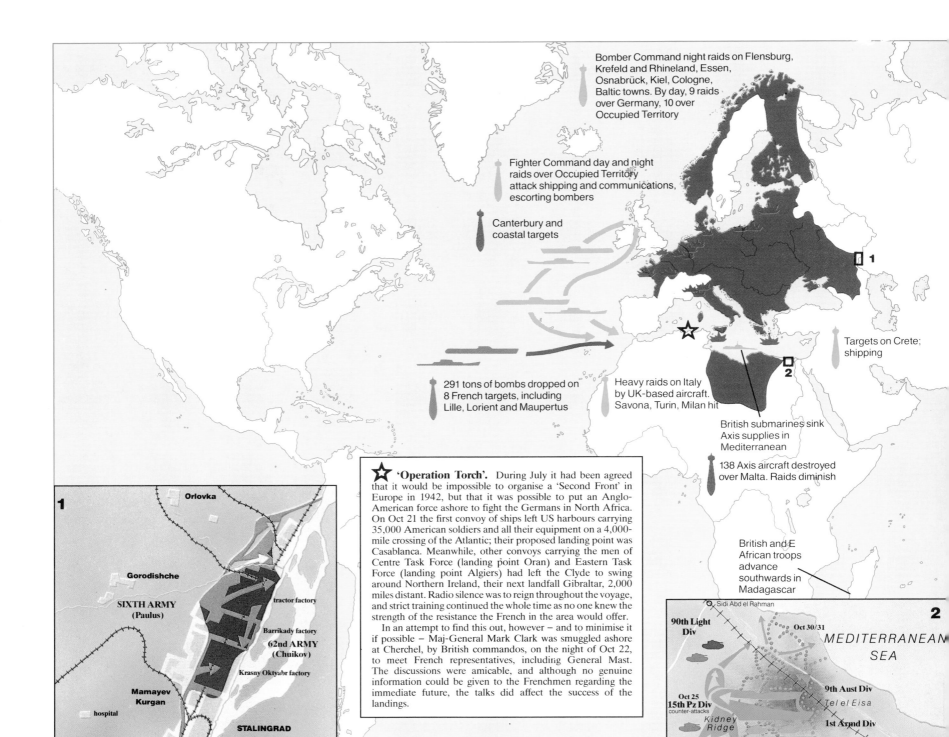

Bomber Command night raids on Flensburg, Krefeld and Rhineland, Essen, Osnabrück, Kiel, Cologne, Baltic towns. By day, 9 raids over Germany, 10 over Occupied Territory

Fighter Command day and night raids over Occupied Territory attack shipping and communications, escorting bombers

Canterbury and coastal targets

Targets on Crete; shipping

291 tons of bombs dropped on 8 French targets, including Lille, Lorient and Maupertus

Heavy raids on Italy by UK-based aircraft. Savona, Turin, Milan hit

British submarines sink Axis supplies in Mediterranean

138 Axis aircraft destroyed over Malta. Raids diminish

British and E African troops advance southwards in Madagascar

Map 1 (Stalingrad):
Orlovka
Gorodishche
SIXTH ARMY (Paulus)
tractor factory
Barrikady factory
62nd ARMY (Chuikov)
Krasny Oktyabr factory
Mamayev Kurgan
hospital
STALINGRAD
Krasnaya Sloboda
0M 1 2 3
0Km 2 4

Map 2 (Alamein):
Sidi Abd el Rahman
90th Light Div
Oct 30/31
MEDITERRANEAN SEA
Oct 25 15th Pz Div counter-attacks
Kidney Ridge
9th Aust Div
Tel el Eisa
1st Armd Div
51st Highland Div
10th Armd Div
2nd NZ Div
1st SA Div
Miteiriya Ridge
Oct 27 21st Pz Div comes up from south
Oct 25 15th Pz Div counter-attacks
0M 1 2 3
0Km 2 4

☆ **'Operation Torch'.** During July it had been agreed that it would be impossible to organise a 'Second Front' in Europe in 1942, but that it was possible to put an Anglo-American force ashore to fight the Germans in North Africa. On Oct 21 the first convoy of ships left US harbours carrying 35,000 American soldiers and all their equipment on a 4,000-mile crossing of the Atlantic; their proposed landing point was Casablanca. Meanwhile, other convoys carrying the men of Centre Task Force (landing point Oran) and Eastern Task Force (landing point Algiers) had left the Clyde to swing around Northern Ireland, their next landfall Gibraltar, 2,000 miles distant. Radio silence was to reign throughout the voyage, and strict training continued the whole time as no one knew the strength of the resistance the French in the area would offer.

In an attempt to find this out, however – and to minimise it if possible – Maj-General Mark Clark was smuggled ashore at Cherchel, by British commandos, on the night of Oct 22, to meet French representatives, including General Mast. The discussions were amicable, and although no genuine information could be given to the Frenchmen regarding the immediate future, the talks did affect the success of the landings.

2 The Battle of Alamein. During the evening of Oct 23, the opening barrage of the Battle of Alamein from over 1,000 guns shook even the men who were expecting it; its immediate effect upon the men of the Panzerarmee was shattering – to such effect that within hours their temporary commander, General Stumme, was dead of a heart attack. It took all the superb efficiency of the German Staff to prevent a total collapse.

During the night that followed, Eighth Army infantry and engineers began the nerve-racking job of punching two corridors through the defended minefields at the northern end of the line, all peppered with enemy machine-gun posts and under registered artillery fire. The plan called for both corridors to be completed by dawn for the armour to pass through, but, as Montgomery later admitted, he was perhaps asking too much of the infantry. The corridors were not clean through by morning, and bitter fighting raged in the minefields all next day and the following night, by which time Rommel had returned to Egypt to resume control of the Panzerarmee.

After three days of gruelling battle, the divisions of XXX Corps – 9th Australian, 51st Highland, 2nd New Zealand and 1st South African – had forced a deep bulge into the German positions, four miles deep along the northern flank, bulging further forward in the centre, then running back along the line of the Miteiriya Ridge. However, such had been the confusion of battle within the bulge that neither of the two armoured divisions of X Corps had been able to break out past the forward infantry, despite the most stringent orders of the army commander.

In the circumstances, Montgomery decided upon a change of plan. The first stage was carried out by the 9th Australians, who turned north from the tip of their salient and drove up towards the railway line and the coast, thus drawing upon themselves desperate attempts by the German forces in the area to keep an escape route open for their own forces still at the top of the original line. The 'crumbling' battles which now followed were fierce and unremitting, battles of attrition which the Australians won in the end, not only because of their efficiency, but also because there were many more of them – a full-strength division against two under-strength brigades.

1 Stalingrad. Towards the end of October a panzer officer wrote 'Stalingrad is no longer a town . . . when night arrives, one of those scorching, howling, bleeding nights, the dogs plunge into the Volga and swim desperately to gain the other bank. The nights of Stalingrad are a terror for them. Animals flee this hell; the hardest stones cannot bear it for long; only men endure.'

The first half of October was used by Paulus to draw even tighter the line around the factory district and then to marshal the forces for the great assault. At 0800 on Oct 14 it opened – 3 infantry and 2 panzer divisions with 300 panzers and blanketing air and artillery support – in a storm of fire aimed for the Volga through the three great factory complexes. The battle raged for three weeks, each section of each factory changing hands constantly, each room of each building fought for in hand-to-hand fighting of unimaginable ferocity; and in this type of fighting the Russian soldier proved himself the more adept. Were it not for the fact that Zhukov's deliberate policy was being followed of feeding into the defence the *minimum force necessary* and not the *maximum force possible* – which was what Paulus was doing – the whole factory complex would probably have been held and the perimeter pushed westwards instead of gradually edging towards the Volga bank. By the end of the month, although Paulus's Sixth Army units had reached the Tractor and Barrikady factories' embankments along over four miles, bitter fighting still raged inside the buildings themselves and although much of the Krasny Octyabr factory was also penetrated, 16 miles of river bank and areas to a depth of 3,000 yards or more still lay firmly in Red Army hands. The swastika did not yet fly over Stalingrad.

Meanwhile, to the south of the Australian sector Montgomery sent out strong infantry detachments with supporting screens of anti-tank guns and some armour to secure certain areas, fortify them and thus draw upon themselves more German and Italian armoured units, for he knew that Rommel could not afford to leave these strongpoints unchallenged. The most famous of these actions was fought on Oct 26/27 on Kidney Ridge by the men of the 2nd Battalion the Rifle Brigade, with attached anti-tank companies, and earned for the commander a Victoria Cross.

Behind these screens, utilising the time saved for him by the Australians and the detachments, Montgomery withdrew the bulk of the armour blocked in the bulge, brought 7th Armoured Division up from the south with some of the XIII Corps infantry, and prepared another powerful armoured thrust intended to break out along the northern line of the original Australian salient. Another heavy artillery bombardment would be organised to precede it, an engineer team would again be available for mine-clearance – though not on the same scale as on the outbreak of the battle – and the Desert Air Force would lay another carpet of bombs. This operation would be called *Supercharge* and be launched early on the morning of Nov 2.

84

OCTOBER
1942

Targets in Burma include Akyab, Mandalay and Myitkyina

Santa Cruz

Vice-Admiral Halsey replaces Vice-Admiral Ghormley in command of US Pacific Fleet

The Battle of Santa Cruz. In the expectation that General Maruyama's attack would succeed, the Japanese Combined Fleet under Vice-Admiral Kondo was cruising north of the Solomons waiting to fly off aircraft to take over Henderson Field. On Oct 25 US Catalinas from US Task Forces 16 and 17 sighted two Japanese aircraft carriers.

By 0710 65 Japanese aircraft, half of them Zeros, were on their way to attack – and as they cleared the decks and another wave began their lift from the hangars, two US dive-bombers from *Enterprise* dropped out of the skies and put *Zuiho* out of action for the day. But this was almost the last US tactical success; Avengers, Dauntlesses and Wildcats in separate groups from *Enterprise* and *Hornet* met the compact Zeros group, lost eight aircraft immediately and more during the dog-fights which followed. Then the Japanese dive-bombers found *Hornet* and hit her with two torpedoes and six bombs, reducing her in ten minutes to a blazing wreck.

Enterprise was hit and her forward lift put out of action, though *Hornet*'s dive-bombers exacted some revenge by putting four 1,000-lb bombs through *Shokaku*'s flight deck before Admiral Kinkaid decided he must withdraw. No US carriers were now left in the Pacific, though *Enterprise* would be quickly repaired; but the Japanese had lost another 100 experienced and totally irreplaceable pilots, while US training programmes were gathering pace.

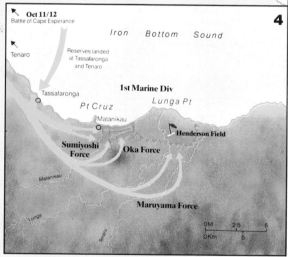

Oct 11/12 Battle of Cape Esperance

Iron Bottom Sound

Tenaro

Reserves landed at Tassafaronga and Tenaro

1st Marine Div

Tassafaronga

Pt Cruz   Lunga Pt

Matanikau

Sumiyoshi Force   **Oka Force**   Henderson Field

Matanikau

Maruyama Force

Lunga

3   Papua/New Guinea. By the beginning of the month the leading Australian troops had pushed the Japanese back past Ioribaiwa as far as Nauro, and the advance continued. Japanese supply difficulties were so great that the advancing Australians came across evidence of cannibalism among them, though they still fought tenaciously in such prepared positions as the 'Gap' and Templeton's Crossing which was reached on Oct 28, just before the drive on Kokoda itself.

But General MacArthur now had more troops and aircraft. The 126th US Infantry Regiment had landed at Kapa Kapa and on Oct 2 their 2nd Battalion moved north up a rugged trail which rose 8,000 feet above Rigo before beginning its drop on the northern side of the Owen Stanley Range. They had only natural obstacles to overcome at first, but these were such that it was the end of the month before they were past Jaure and edging towards the Japanese enclaves at Buna and Gona.

At the same time, information of a possibly usable airstrip at Wanigela in Collingwood Bay was found to be correct.

Engineers were flown in, quickly to be followed by two battalions of the US 128th Infantry Regiment, 2/6th Australian Independent Company and miscellaneous artillery units. They attempted an overland march to Pongani further west along the coast but found the Musa river impassable, so transports were brought up and the journey was made by ferry, again unopposed. By Oct 20 engineers were constructing another airstrip there, more troops and supplies were coming in from Port Moresby, and by the end of the month almost the whole of the 128th US Infantry Regiment were deployed in the area.

From Milne Bay communications with Wanigela and Pongani were established, and then on the night of Oct 22 an Australian infantry battalion with support troops sailed in two destroyers for Goodenough Island, landing in Mud Bay and Tabela Bay. They chased a small, isolated Japanese garrison away on to Fergusson Island, then began the construction of another airstrip near Mud Bay.

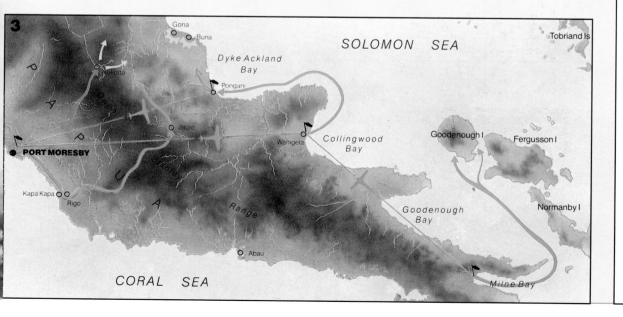

Gona
Buna
Kokoda
SOLOMON SEA
Dyke Ackland Bay
Pongani
Tobriand Is
Jaure
Wanigela   Collingwood Bay
Goodenough I   Fergusson I
PORT MORESBY
Goodenough Bay
Normanby I
Kapa Kapa
Rigo
Range
Abau
Milne Bay
CORAL SEA

4   Guadalcanal. The first half of the month was spent by both sides consolidating their positions and bringing in reinforcements. The 'Tokyo Express' brought Japanese strength up to 20,000 men, the 7th US Marines were brought in with artillery and support units to take US strength up to 23,000. In the process two naval battles were fought, one off Cape Esperance on Oct 11/12 and one off Santa Cruz islands on Oct 24/26. The first was a confused night action during which one Japanese destroyer and one cruiser were sunk, one US destroyer sunk and one damaged, and the Japanese fleet was forced to turn back; but during the following nights it returned and so severely shelled Henderson Field that for a while it was out of action. More Japanese reinforcements and supplies were then landed just west of Lunga Point.

With his army up to strength, General Maruyama decided on a three-pronged assault on Henderson Field, and on Oct 16 his main force began their march through the jungle from Tenaro. His plan was to attack from the south, while eight battalions with tanks in support under Colonel Sumiyoshi and a flanking attack under Colonel Oka, closed in from the west to launch a simultaneous attack on the Matanikau river line on Oct 23. But the long march through the jungle for the main force was slower and more arduous than expected, they had been forced to abandon their artillery and mortars, communications failed and Maruyama arrived 24 hours late.

As a result, both the Sumiyoshi and Oka attacks were brought to a bloody halt by US artillery, Vandergrift was given time to switch forces to meet the threat from the south, and after two days' bloody fighting the Japanese forces withdrew into the jungle, exhausted, out of ammunition and food, leaving some 3,500 dead around the perimeter.

85

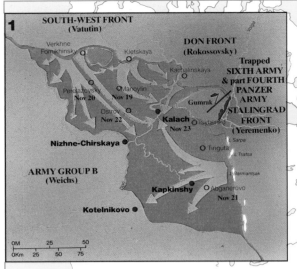

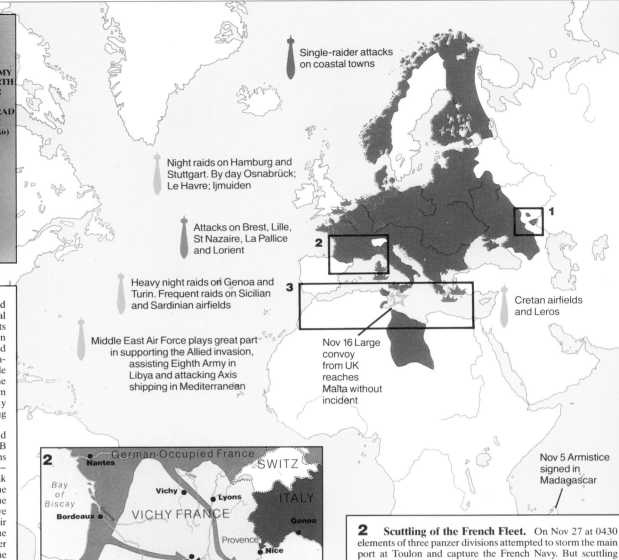

1 South-west Front (Vatutin)

Don Front (Rokossovsky)

Trapped SIXTH ARMY & part FOURTH PANZER ARMY

STALINGRAD FRONT (Yeremenko)

ARMY GROUP B (Weichs)

Single-raider attacks on coastal towns

Night raids on Hamburg and Stuttgart. By day Osnabrück; Le Havre; Ijmuiden

Attacks on Brest, Lille, St Nazaire, La Pallice and Lorient

Heavy night raids on Genoa and Turin. Frequent raids on Sicilian and Sardinian airfields

Middle East Air Force plays great part in supporting the Allied invasion, assisting Eighth Army in Libya and attacking Axis shipping in Mediterranean

Cretan airfields and Leros

Nov 16 Large convoy from UK reaches Malta without incident

Nov 5 Armistice signed in Madagascar

1 Stalingrad. Whatever the sufferings of men of 62nd Army fighting so desperately inside Stalingrad, General Zhukov at the beginning of November was watching events with grim satisfaction. Chuikov's magnificent defence had been sucking Paulus's Sixth Army into an ever-more concentrated maelstrom, with Fourth Panzer Army hovering on the south-west edge. And in the meantime, under an impenetrable security screen, Zhukov had built up three massive fronts on the flanks – Stalingrad Front under Yeremenko stretching down south of the city for 80 miles, Don Front under Rokossovsky and South-west Front under Vatutin between them stretching 130 miles westward along the line of the Don.

On Nov 19 the storm burst on the unfortunate Third and Fourth Rumanian Armies which were all that Army Group B could spare alongside the main conflict. More than 3,500 guns and mortars opened fire – after salvoes from rocket-launchers – along the 14 miles of breakthrough positions, and the tank corps of two Red armies ground forward from Verkhne Fomikhinsky and Kletskaya while from the Don Front one army flanked the drive out of Kletskaya and another drove south-west out of Kachalinskaya with the Don bend to their right. The prime objective for both these fronts – apart from the destruction of the Rumanian armies – was the vital bridge over the Don at Kalach across which all Paulus's ground-borne supplies and reinforcements must pass, and this too was the main target for Yeremenko's IV Tank Corps driving up from the Lake Barmantsak area.

The Rumanians, despite their second-rate weapons and comparative lack of commitment, fought gallantly for most of the first day, but then were overwhelmed. Russian tanks stormed into Manoylin on the first day of the attack, Perelazovsky the day after, Ostrov on Nov 22, while to the south, Yeremenko's men were at Abganerovo Station on Nov 21 and driving down the line towards Kotelnikovo. From both north and south, tank units reached Kalach on Nov 23 though the vital bridge had in fact been captured by a brilliant *coup de main* at 0600 the previous day – and held against fierce counter-attack by a single German motorised rifle battalion. The ring around Paulus's Sixth Army had been formed; now it must be strengthened, forged into an impenetrable steel band.

3 Operation Torch. North Africa. On Nov 8 the Anglo-American army of over 100,000 men in three task forces landed on the North African coast between Safi to the west of Casablanca, and Algiers 800 miles to the east. By evening, General Patton's forces around Casablanca held a wide bridgehead although signs of growing resistance were evident; further west Oran had been surrounded and French resistance was hardening, while at Algiers the landings had been fiercely resisted at first but now the port was in Allied hands and troops were swarming ashore.

2 German-Occupied France

Nantes · Vichy · Lyons · SWITZ

Bay of Biscay · Bordeaux · VICHY FRANCE · ITALY · Genoa

Provence · Nice · Montpellier · Sète · Marseilles · Toulon · Corsica

Barcelona · Sardinia

2 Scuttling of the French Fleet. On Nov 27 at 0430 elements of three panzer divisions attempted to storm the main port at Toulon and capture the French Navy. But scuttling charges had already been laid in all ships and were immediately fired.

Seventy-three ships, including a battleship, 2 battle-cruisers, 7 cruisers, 29 destroyers and 16 submarines, went to the bottom of the harbour, to remain there until the war was over – and not to fight on either side.

Fortunately for the Allies, the French Admiral Darlan was in Algiers, and although he was at first unwilling to cooperate, by noon on Dec 10 he had ordered an end to all French resistance – an order more willingly obeyed the following day when news arrived of the German invasion of the Unoccupied Zone.

But Casablanca is over 1,000 miles from Tunisia where the real objectives of the *Torch* operation lay, so on Nov 12 British airborne forces dropped at Bône to capture the airfield there and by Nov 17 had advanced to Souk el Arba, while on Nov 15 American paratroops dropped 100 miles south and within two days had taken Gafsa. Behind them the main forces were shaking out and trying to organise transport forward on the rudimentary road system; but in front of them the German forces were rallying with breath-taking efficiency. Quickly they threw a bridgehead perimeter around the vital area of Bizerta and Tunis, and other forces flooded ashore in the south to protect Sfax and Gabes. Long before the bulk of the Allied forces could close up to support the frail airborne thrusts, German defences were solid; and soon the Allied advance was to be stalled by torrential rainfall.

At the eastern end of the North African theatre, however, matters went better for the Allies. *Operation Supercharge* had been launched on Nov 2 under a barrage similar to that which had opened the battle, and with similar results; Eighth Army infantry and engineers fought their way implacably forward, their artillery pounded the known Panzerarmee positions, the Sherman and Valentine tanks milled about in the sand-fog behind them, trying desperately to find the channels through which they were to pass. On the second morning they attempted a dawn break-out over Aqqaqir Ridge which, though not successful, shook the nerve of the German defences, already strained by the previous days' fighting. The following morning, a gap was opened in the south-west corner of the deep salient which had now been driven into the German positions; by the afternoon Eighth Army infantry and armour were pouring through, and the Afrika Korps divisions were in full flight. But Rommel conducted a masterly retreat, and when at the end of the month Eighth Army arrived at Agedabia, they faced a well planned defence line running south from El Agheila, around the bend of the Gulf of Sirte.

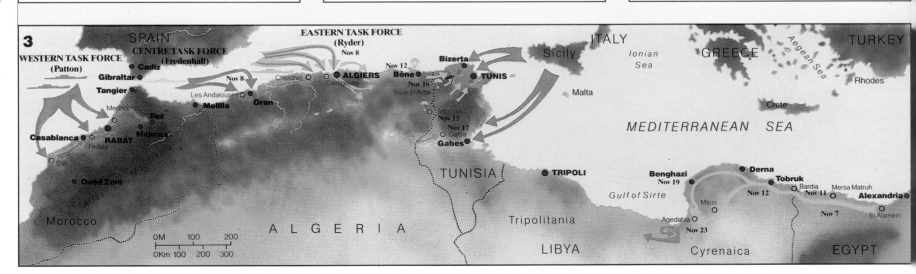

3 SPAIN · ITALY · GREECE · TURKEY

EASTERN TASK FORCE (Ryder) Nov 8

CENTRE TASK FORCE (Fredenhall)

WESTERN TASK FORCE (Patton)

Gibraltar · Cadiz · Nov 8 · Cherchel · ALGIERS · Bône · Bizerta · TUNIS · Sicily · Ionian Sea · Aegean Sea

Tangier · Les Andalouses · Oran · Souk el Arba · Nov 16 · Malta · Rhodes

Medina · Melilla · Tebessa · Nov 15 · Crete

Fez · Meknès · Nov 17 · Gafsa · Gabes · MEDITERRANEAN SEA

Casablanca · RABAT · Fedala

Safi · Oued Zem · TUNISIA · TRIPOLI · Benghazi Nov 19 · Derna · Tobruk · Bardia · Mersa Matruh · Alexandria

Morocco · Gulf of Sirte · Nov 12 · Nov 11

A L G E R I A · Tripolitania · Msus · Nov 7 · El Alamein

Agedabia · Nov 23 · LIBYA · Cyrenaica · EGYPT

NOVEMBER
1942

Burma targets include Rangoon, Akyab, Kalemyo, Pakokku, Meiktila, Mandalay, Magwe and Katha; Bangkok attacked

Japanese attack on N bank of Yangtze river

Attu and Kiska

Chief targets are Kupang; Gasmata and Rabaul; Kavieng; Lae and Salamaua; Munda and Kahil (Solomons)

Light raids on Port Moresby and Darwin

☆ **The Battles in the 'Slot'.** Throughout November, under orders from Imperial General Staff who refused to accept that the price of expelling the Americans from Guadalcanal might be too high, the Japanese Navy ran in supplies and escorted transports full of reinforcements. This meant that the US Navy too had to supply and reinforce the hard-pressed marines and infantry at Henderson Field, and clashes were inevitable.

During Nov 11 US transports arrived and began offloading troops and supplies, but on the 12th came news of strong Japanese naval forces approaching. The transports withdrew, but the escort of 2 heavy cruisers, 3 light cruisers and 8 destroyers turned to meet the enemy force of 2 battleships, a light cruiser and 14 destroyers. The only advantage the Americans had was that one light cruiser was fitted with radar, but in the event, Japanese night-fighting efficiency more than compensated. The fleets met south-east of Savo Island at 0145 on Nov 13 and in the ensuing shambles four US cruisers and three destroyers were crippled, four destroyers were sunk, and the following morning the remaining cruiser was torpedoed and sunk; Japanese losses during the action were two destroyers, but the battleship *Hiei* had been badly damaged and the following morning was found by torpedo-bombers from Henderson Field and finally scuttled. Moreover, an attempt to shell Henderson Field by a Japanese cruiser squadron the following night was only partly successful, and the following day aircraft from the Field caught the squadron south of New Georgia, sank one of the cruisers and damaged two more.

Nov 14/15 brought another attempt to shell Henderson Field out of existence, this time with a fleet consisting of a battleship, three cruisers, a light cruiser and nine destroyers; it was met by a US fleet of two battleships and four destroyers – in the waters south of Savo Island again – and within thirteen minutes all four US destroyers were out of action and three of them sinking. As for the battleships, the Japanese *Kirishima* was reduced in seven minutes to a rudderless wreck when she came under fire from the *Washington's* 16-inch guns, and although the *South Dakota* was badly damaged she was not sunk. The Japanese lost one destroyer, but their fleet was turned back and Henderson Field was spared another bombardment.

Under the cover of this action Admiral Tanaka had tried to run a convoy of 11 transports encircled by 11 destroyers down the 'Slot' to Tassafaronga, but with Henderson Field unneutralised, several of the transports were damaged by torpedo and dive-bombers, and although nightfall helped Tanaka, when dawn broke on Nov 15 they were still offshore and were caught again by US aircraft. All 11 transports were sunk or beached, and only some 2,000 troops with 250 cases of ammunition and 1,500 bags of rice got ashore, quickly to disperse into the jungle. This was the last serious Japanese attempt to run in stores and men; from now on high-speed destroyers only would make the run, releasing strings of buoyant drums of stores which it was hoped would float ashore for the Japanese troops to salvage.

4 Papua/New Guinea. By Nov 2 the Australians had pushed on past Templeton's Crossing and reached Kokoda where their engineers quickly put the landing-ground back into operation; supplies and reinforcements could now be brought up more quickly. By Nov 10 the infantry had pushed the Japanese off well-defended heights at Oivi and Gorari, then advanced to Wairopi where they bridged the Kumusi river and sent two brigades straight on towards Popondetta. The greatest obstacle to their progress was now the jungle and the swamps, as after being driven out of Gorari, the bulk of the Japanese retreated along the Kumusi river and then swung around towards Gona.

Meanwhile, to the east, the American and Australian troops on Hydrographer's Range and at Pongani had been further reinforced by air, and on Nov 16 they began their drive towards Buna and Sanananda. As with the Australian drive from Kokoda, their greatest problem was with the nature of the ground they had to cover, as Japanese intentions by now were to form a strong defensive position from Buna to Gona, with another strong box just to the south of Sanananda. Work on these defences had been in progress almost since the Japanese had landed there in July, and now with practically all the Japanese survivors of the fighting in Papua withdrawing into the bridgehead, it was obvious that a great deal of hard fighting lay ahead.

By the end of November, the defences were all manned, while opposite them the Australians and Americans closed up and prepared for the next stage.

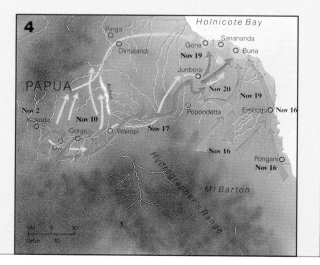

5 Guadalcanal. With the defeat of the Maruyama attacks, General Vandergrift felt that the time had come for him to try to expand his bridgehead in both directions. During the night of Oct 31/Nov 1 engineers threw bridges over the Matanikau and early next morning the three battalions of the 5th Marines crossed and drove west towards Japanese artillery positions beyond Point Cruz. By Nov 3, they had effectively trapped the Japanese against the sea and that day they mounted successive bayonet charges and wiped out the entire Japanese force there. The next day, reinforced by another marine battalion and a battalion from the US 164th Infantry, they drove half a mile further west, when they were ordered to dig a defensive line, man it with the minimum, and then withdraw to help deal with a suddenly discovered threat from the east.

In addition to sending the battalions over the Matanikau, Vandergrift had sent another battalion eastwards towards Koli Point where on Nov 2 they saw a considerable force of Japanese, complete with artillery, unloading at Tetere. The following morning a Japanese patrol discovered the Americans and a battle opened along the beaches and, realising that he was outnumbered and outgunned, the marine commander ordered a withdrawal. During the afternoon he was attacked from the south by a Japanese outflanking movement, but when he signalled his situation back to Henderson Field, Vandergrift immediately sent two battalions of infantry and one of artillery out in support. By Nov 10 the Japanese had all been dispersed into the jungle, where for the rest of the month they were pursued and hunted down by two battalions of marine raiders who had just been sent to Guadalcanal.

Dictatorship in Crisis

'A decision on the Eastern Front in 1942', Hitler had declared before the launch of his great Summer Offensive, 'is mandatory!' – and he had invited his allies to take part in the final drive to eliminate Bolshevism and all forms of Soviet power from the face of the earth. Not only must the Axis have the oil of the Caucasus, but the Wehrmacht (with whatever assistance those allies might contribute) must defeat the Red Army in the field and push the boundaries of German domination at least as far as the Urals. After all, in the six months of active operations in 1941, they had reached at least halfway; 1942 must see the completion of the ultimate *Barbarossa* objective.

At the end of October it looked to many as though these aims would be realised. The drive into the Caucasus had opened with as spectacular an advance as that of the first days of *Barbarossa*, the foothills of the Caucasian Mountains had been reached within two weeks on a front nearly 300 miles wide, and if the pace since then had slowed so that only another 125 miles had been covered, there were excellent tactical reasons for this. An extra 150,000 square miles of Soviet territory now lay behind the advanced German lines, so in all it could be reckoned that nearly 50% of the population of the Soviet Union as it was constituted in 1939 was at the disposal of the conquerors, together with the most highly industrialised areas of the empire. All this booty had to be exploited, administered and controlled.

There were also some minor – and one major – problems still to be solved to the north, where it had not been possible to hold all the gains won during the great victories of 1941. From Yelets up to Demyansk and further north between Lakes Ilmen and Ladoga, Red Army pressure had been sufficient to force the line back in places as much as 200 miles, but these were losses which could easily be afforded – and indeed won back in due course. They had in great part been caused by the necessity for strengthening the vitally important drive in the south at the expense of the northern, less important Army Groups. As for Leningrad, it was unfortunate that von Manstein had been unable to capture the city and carry out his orders that it was to be razed to the ground, but the matter could wait. The capital of the Tsars would still be there when other, more important tasks had been carried out. Perhaps then he would go and oversee its annihilation himself.

Here in the southern sector was where the war would be won – and at this moment Hitler was sure that Fate had focused the destiny of the world in one comparatively small location. On July 23 he had issued Directive No 45 and in one section had ordered Army Group B 'to develop the Don defences and, by a thrust forward to Stalingrad, to smash the enemy forces concentrated there, to occupy the town and to block the land communications between the Don and the Volga as well as the Don itself. Closely connected with this, fast-moving forces will advance [south-east] along the Volga with the task of thrusting through to Astrakhan and blocking the main course of the Volga in the same way.'

Once Army Group B were there, and Army Group A were at Baku, the decision to swing north-west to the Urals or north-east up behind Moscow (or even on south

into Persia) could be taken. In any case, the collapse of the Red Army during those operations would probably leave those issues wide open – no matter what irritating objections the Wehrmacht generals might raise.

In this regard, Hitler had already taken steps to limit criticisms and avoid time-consuming arguments. During early September he had had a furious argument with Jodl (Chief of OKW Operations Staff) with whom he had until this moment always maintained at least polite relations, and he had used the event to isolate himself from the Wehrmacht Command. Briefings now took place in his own hut with only the smallest number of reporting officers, he never attended meals in the Officers' Mess which before he had visited at least once a day, a dozen shorthand typists had been brought from Berlin, put into uniform, ordered to take a personal oath of allegiance to Hitler and from then on recorded every word spoken between Hitler and his military advisers – thus constituting a considerable dampener on anything approaching free discussion.

He had dismissed Field Marshal von Bock in July for hesitation and lack of faith during the drive across to Voronezh, von List in September for refusing to follow exactly his instructions for the drive into the Caucasus, and on Sept 24 Hitler had at last rid himself of that continual thorn in his flesh, the long-time Chief of Staff of the Army, Col-General Halder. The replacement was General Zeitzler, whose take-over address to his senior staff had contained the following passage: 'I require the following from every Staff Officer: he must believe in the Führer and in his method of command. He must on every occasion radiate this confidence to his subordinates and those around him. I have no use for anybody on the General Staff who cannot meet these requirements.'

With such an acolyte at the head of the Army, he should at least be able to curb the more independently minded of the Army Group and Army Commanders, who at one time or another had all exhibited tendencies to behave more like robber barons of the Middle Ages than responsible servants of a political system. Now he would be able to make his own will prevail throughout all ranks, and would himself ensure that the General Staff developed a fanatical belief in the National Socialist ideal which, in view of the tasks now facing them, was more important than mere technical competence.

In any case, the power and weight of his Wehrmacht had made the possession of technical competence, as understood by the General Staff, a matter of far less significance. When the Summer Offensive had opened, Hitler had launched 74 divisions into the attack of which 9 were panzer and 7 motorised infantry, equipped with 1,495 panzers and covered by 1,500 aircraft; the bulk, in fact, of the 6,000,000 men Hitler had deployed along the Eastern Front, with the best of the arms his factories had produced

Although they had undoubtedly suffered some casualties, he had also been able to feed in some reserves – and by comparison the losses suffered by the enemy reduced Wehrmacht losses to minuscule proportions. Upheld by faith and driven by the force of his will, his armies would smash their way forward to victory – the

first important step on the way being the capture of Stalingrad.

By now, one of Hitler's few remaining favourites, Col General von Paulus (to whom it had already been hinted that he was destined for further promotion and Halder's position as soon as Stalingrad had fallen) had fed nearly the whole of his Sixth Army into the battle in the Stalingrad salient together with a large part of Hoth's panzer army which Hitler had directed to his support. Some quarter of a million men with between them five panzer divisions and an almost complete establishment of artillery was concentrated there, and must inevitably succeed in destroying the city bearing the name of Hitler's most hated adversary.

'I will remain on the Volga!' Hitler stated publicly on Nov 8, and he was confident that no force which Stalin's army could produce would ever prise him away from the river. The Führer's will would prevail.

Not surprisingly, Stalin contested this. In August he had signalled Yeremenko: 'I am not going to discuss this question [the suggested evacuation of Stalingrad] at all. It should be understood that if evacuation of industry and the mining of factories starts, then that will be taken as a decision to surrender Stalingrad. For that reason GKO forbids any preparation for the demolition of industrial installations and any preparations for their evacuation.'

With those words he committed the Red Army to one of the fiercest battles of the war, perhaps of the whole history of warfare.

If Hitler's attitude to his generals at this time was sceptical to the point of hostility, it was warm and friendly by comparison with the contempt Stalin held for the Red Army generals, the soldiers of the Red Army, the Russian people as a whole and, one suspects, all mankind.

Hitler sacked his generals; Stalin had them shot. Having developed the practice during his purges of 1937 he had vented his fury over the losses of 1941 (and at the same time stifled any criticism which might have been levelled at his handling of affairs) by wholesale courts martial which had resulted in at least ten major-generals and one army general losing their lives and many more their freedom. During the brief period of Russian counter-attack in December and January the atmosphere of harsh disapproval had eased slightly, but when the Wehrmacht Summer Offensive burst through the Barvenko Salient and thwarted his ambition to recapture Kharkov, his fury mounted again. Events since then, as the Red Army were flung back into the Don bend and driven south in the Caucasus, raised his scorn for Soviet soldiers at all levels – and in all branches – to white heat.

Even the existence of large partisan forces, especially in the area to the north-west of Army Group Centre from the Pripet Marshes up towards and past Vitebsk, did nothing to assuage his contempt, principally because at heart he feared such organisations. After his purge of the military command in 1937 he had in fact specifically prohibited the experimentation or even the planning for use of such forces, officially because it had been decreed that all Red Army planning must be directed to fighting any wars which came about on enemy territory, in reality because to encourage guerrilla tactics meant also encouraging the initiative and independence of mind which such operations necessitate.

Though partisan brigades had operated behind White Russian lines during the early phases of the Revolution and during the Civil War, there had been times when the Red Army had had to turn on them and shoot their leaders for revealing too much of the essential individualism of the guerrilla; Stalin wanted no such trouble in the future and would give no credit for achievement now. However useful they might be, partisans were beyond his immediate control and were thus more objects for suspicion than praise or encouragement.

Like all absolute rulers, Stalin had long since reached the stage of paranoia whereby any disagreement with his own opinion was criminal or stupid, any evidence which supported a contrary view rubbish. Before the German onslaught across the Donets, Red Army intelligence had built up quite an accurate picture of what was likely to happen – but it did not accord with Stalin's ideas as he was sure the Germans intended to attack in the centre. When the presentation was made to him, he swept the papers off the table and poured abuse on those 'who could come up with nothing better than this' – but there was, of course, no attempt to conciliate or apologise when the intelligence predictions proved to have been correct. Instead, there were sweeping condemnations of those who now fell back before the forces which he had himself ordered should be ignored, an immediate hunt for scapegoats was started and all blame was laid on the soldiers; some were demoted, some were disgraced (although none was shot for the moment) and even his old comrade of the 1920s, Marshal Timoshenko, was moved to a lesser post, commanding just the North-west Front as opposed to holding the overall command of the three Fronts along the Volga.

From the fall of Rostov, Stalin decided to make a huge propaganda appeal to the Russian people, representing it as a deliberate abandoning of positions by the Red Army without orders, instead of a well executed withdrawal and escape from a German encirclement to rival those massive scoops of 1941 – which it was. In a flood of passionate anti-German oratory and literature (not unjustified in view of the atrocities being committed behind German lines) he had himself projected across the Soviet Union as the wise, paternalistic Father of the People in whose sympathetic but firm guidance they could place their full trust. Nevertheless, the message he had to give them was that already too much Soviet territory had fallen into the hands of the invaders, and now 'not a step backward' was the cry, each Red Army soldier must fight to the last drop of his blood, and every retreat must be compensated for by a rooting out of 'panic-mongers', 'traitors' and 'cowards'.

Whatever effect all this may have had in the long run, it could do little to stem the vast sweep forward of Hitler's Offensive, and when Stalingrad itself was threatened – the city which not only bore his own name, but had been the scene of his and Voroshilov's triumph 20 years before against the White armies (giving birth to the myth that here the Revolution had been saved) his anxieties increased tenfold and his demands upon the military more exorbitant.

But at least he never panicked or lost his head; instead he abandoned any personal or ideological preferences he held, and picked commanders for proven military competence however much he had belittled it in the past. Col-General Vasilevsky was sent to the Stalingrad Front to take all necessary measures to ensure the defence of the city, and early in August General Yeremenko joined him and the political representative there, Lt-General Nikita Krushchev.

Unfortunately, Yeremenko had arrived only a few days before the Luftwaffe raid which devastated the Stalingrad suburbs and Weitersheim's lance-thrust which had reached the banks of the Volga; and for two days, until reports proved that the industrial heart and centre of the city was still in Soviet hands, Stalin vented

his anger on his generals with curses and threats to have them disgraced and shot.

Then he had a better idea. On Aug 27 he sent for the commander of the West Front, Col-General Georgi Zhukov, informed him that he had been appointed Deputy Supreme Commander of the Red Army, and sent him down to Stalingrad with orders that he was to stop Paulus by mounting massive attacks from the north. (Even Zhukov was not to be allowed to use his own initiative.)

Zhukov arrived about noon on Aug 29, discussed the situation with Vasilevsky who then returned to Moscow, then with some of the other front commanders. As neither the men nor the fuel which Stalin had promised had arrived, he postponed the attack until Sept 3, reported its predictable failure that night, listened to the customary diatribe – 'Do you think that the enemy will wait while you get organised?' etc etc – and launched a new and heavier attack on Sept 5.

It was the most powerful Soviet attack yet mounted in the area, but it was ill-conceived, after five days had hardly advanced at all, had used up an immense quantity of ammunition and made little difference to Paulus's main attack on Stalingrad. On the evening of Sept 12 Zhukov flew back to Moscow to report in person, and with the backing of Vasilevsky endeavoured to

impress on Stalin the impossibility of stopping a huge army with inadequate resources and ill-planned strategy. To Stalin's enquiry as to what more was required, Zhukov replied at least an extra full-strength army, a tank corps, three tank brigades, 400 howitzers and an air army – and while Stalin was studying the maps and lists of reserves he had available, Zhukov and Vasilevsky moved to the other end of the long room. It was, the two generals agreed, necessary to find another way out.

'What other way out?' Stalin asked, looking up and revealing an unsuspected ability to hear at a distance.

They told him, briefly then, in detail 24 hours later. And two of the essential ingredients would be patience on Stalin's part, and some degree of confidence that Vasilevsky and Zhukov knew what they were doing.

From that date – Sept 14 – the fate of Stalingrad and of much else besides, lay in the hands of the Deputy Supreme Commander.

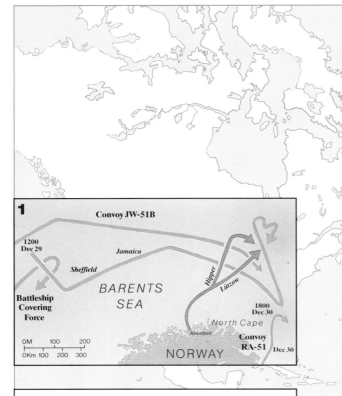

Daytime attacks on Germany, industrial and communications targets, Eindhoven radio factory; shipping

No large-scale raids

Attacks on Lille, Abbeville, Rouen and Lorient

Dec 11/12 'Cockleshell' raid on shipping in Bordeaux by Royal Marine Commandos

Minor raids only – 14,000 tons of bombs dropped on Malta during 1942, 1,468 civilians killed

Night raids on Frankfurt Karlsruhe and Munich

Dec 25 Admiral Darlan assassinated

1 **Battle of the Barents Sea.** Convoy JW-51-B, consisting of 14 merchantmen carrying over 200 tanks, 2,000 trucks, 120 aircraft and 80,000 tons of fuel and stores left Scotland on Dec 22, and ran into a gale on Dec 28 which drove it so far south that by Dec 30, when it could turn east again, it was only 200 miles from Altenfjord. Here lay the pocket-battleship *Lützow* and the heavy cruiser *Hipper* with their destroyers, awaiting just such a chance. Under Admiral Kummetz they sailed late on Dec 30, and by morning were in position with *Hipper* to the north and *Lützow* to the south to trap the convoy.

But in the haze and snow flurries, the captains of both German ships hesitated whereas the captains of the escorting British destroyers attacked *Hipper* at once, determined to drive her away by threat of torpedo attack. Although two of the British destroyers were damaged and one sunk, the *Hipper* was kept at bay until just before noon when two cruisers, HMS *Sheffield* and HMS *Jamaica,* the convoy's covering force, arrived and drove both *Hipper* and *Lützow* with five destroyers (one had been sunk) back to Altenfjord. The humiliation to the Kriegsmarine was so great that Hitler immediately ordered the scrapping of the German Battle Fleet.

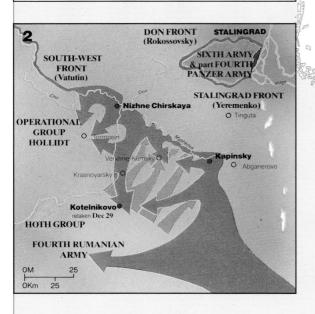

2 **Stalingrad.** When the seriousness of the situation brought about by the encirclement first became clear to Hitler on Nov 23, he agreed for a few hours with all his military advisers from von Paulus to the new Chief of Staff, Col-General Kurt Zeitzler, that Sixth Army should turn away from the Volga and break out to the south-west. But the following morning Reichsmarschall Göring gave categorical assurances that the Luftwaffe could fly in the necessary 750 metric tons of supplies per day which was sufficient to sustain the encircled army (this in defiance of the opinion of every senior Luftwaffe officer to whom he had spoken) and the fate of Sixth Army was sealed. They would stay where they were, Hitler ordered, and a new Army Group commanded by Field Marshal von Manstein would drive up from the concentration area around Kotelnikovo to relieve them.

Operation *Winter Storm* was launched on Dec 12 by Fourth Panzer Army along the Kotelnikovo–Stalingrad axis, with another powerful panzer group, Group Hollidt, on the left flank aimed for Kalach to the north. What could be spared from Sixth Army still battling inside Stalingrad would drive down to meet Manstein's Army Group Don, probably in the neighbourhood of Tinguta.

STAVKA's plans by this time had reached the stage of preparing to launch a huge sweep by South-west and Voronezh Fronts across the Chir, through Tormosin and on down to Rostov and Taganrog – having, of course, first eliminated all

German forces trapped inside the Stalingrad cauldron. It was this problem which posed the first difficulties, for instead of the estimated 90,000 men which STAVKA had forecast, there were in fact some 250,000 men with 100 panzers and 2,000 guns caught in the trap. During the closing days of November the three Soviet armies most closely concerned – 57th, 62nd and 64th – had driven forward as valiantly as possible, and though by the end of the month they had almost halved the encirclement area, they had not – to Stalin's annoyance – totally annihilated von Paulus's men. A new army – 5th Shock – was set up to tighten the ring and new tactics were decided upon; and then the sudden threat from Manstein's Army Group Don 75 miles away developed and attention switched to it.

By this time Red Army units had developed the techniques of extraordinarily stubborn defence and, after recent events, were of high morale. Despite intense artillery opening barrages and the onslaught of two panzer divisions, two Red Army rifle divisions held the main attack until a mechanised corps could come to their aid, so that in two days Army Group Don had only been able to reach Verkhne-Kumsky, while Operational Group Hollidt was stuck fast. By Dec 18 Manstein's forces had only reached the Myshkovka – and they never crossed it; by Dec 23 they knew their losses were too great to continue.

Then on Dec 25, two Soviet armies launched a counter-attack and were at Kotelnikovo by Dec 29. Army Group Don had failed to relieve Stalingrad.

3 **Libya.** Deliberately, Montgomery made no attempt to rush Rommel's defences at El Agheila. There were too many members of Eighth Army who had been there twice before and been thrown back by the Afrika Korps – once into Egypt, once to Gazala. Now the recent landing of First Army threatened Rommel's back, though by the end of November the force was apparently stalled – blocked by German defences and by supply and communication problems.

Montgomery intended to advance towards Tripoli with three divisions – 7th Armoured, 51st Highland and the New Zealand Divisions – grouped together into XXX Corps under General Leese. The remaining Eighth Army Divisions became X Corps under General Horrocks, acting almost entirely as transport for the forward corps.

The greatest problems were those of supply. Everything had to come forward from the Delta, and the railway line only

reached Tobruk. And the roads from there were either ruined by bombing, mining and two years' heavy wear without proper maintenance, or desert tracks; very quickly the trucks and lorries began to break down. Benghazi harbour had to be cleared.

By mid-December, XXX Corps were ready. On the night of 14th/15th the Highlanders and the armour drove forward along the coast under a solid barrage, while away to the south the New Zealanders executed a 150-mile wide hook intended to catch Rommel's divisions at Marble Arch. But Rommel had foreseen the move and withdrawn, leaving only rearguards to face the attack, slowing it further by mines and ingenious booby-traps. The Highlanders were at Marble Arch by Dec 17, but rearguards and booby-traps reduced the advance to a snail's pace and XXX Corps did not reach Sirte until Christmas Day, or the Buerat line until Dec 31.

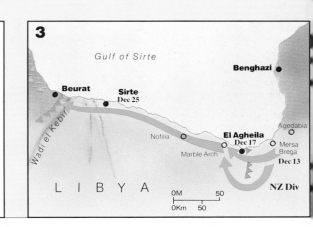

Burma targets include Rangoon, Mandalay, Akyab, Toungoo, Magwe, Monywa and Lashio

India targets are Calcutta and Chittagong

Targets include Lae and Salamaua; Rabaul and Gasmata; Kavieng; Munda

Port Moresby

☆ **The Battle of Tassafaronga.** Despite the losses suffered by the Japanese throughout November – which unlike the Americans they could ill afford – despite also Tanaka's advice that Guadalcanal should be evacuated, Imperial Headquarters still insisted on attempting to wrest the island and its vital airfield from the US marines. So on Nov 30, Tanaka again sailed from Bougainville, this time with nine destroyers, seven of which were loaded with supply drums stacked around the torpedo tubes, to be discharged off Tassafaronga.

Against them, steaming up the 'Slot' from the south-east, was a US fleet of five cruisers and four destroyers, two of which were fitted with radar which should have given the US commander an enormous advantage. He was to throw it away. When the two lines of ships passed each other off Tassafaronga, the Japanese crews were occupied unleashing the supply drums and had no idea that a hostile force was watching them from less than a mile out to sea. In vain the senior US destroyer captain asked for permission to launch his torpedoes, but Admiral Wright hesitated for a fatal four minutes by which time the destroyers had passed their prime targets; even then, a more fateful mistake was made when the admiral ordered the guns to open fire thus alerting the Japanese who reacted immediately, easily turning out of the path of the American torpedoes and launching their own, the flash of the American guns providing the aiming marks.

The Japanese 'Long Lance' oxygen-fuelled torpedoes sped in five flights into the American line of ships, and at 2327 the first flight struck home, in *Minneapolis*'s boiler-room and forecastle and in *New Orleans*'s forecastle, while the second flight hit *Pensacola* amidships. Ten minutes later, *Northampton* was hit by two torpedoes which blasted her open and set her ablaze.

Meanwhile, Tanaka's flotilla with the loss of only one destroyer was speeding away up the 'Slot', leaving Ironbottom Sound lit up by the flames engulfing four US cruisers, of which one, *Northampton*, was soon to sink. Although the other US cruisers and the destroyers were able to reach Tulagi and after basic repairs limp away to Australia, this was undoubtedly Tanaka's victory. But it was his last. Although more battles were to be fought in December, Imperial Headquarters were beginning to see that Tanaka had been right and that Guadalcanal was not worth the price they were paying for it.

5 Papua. Through the last days of November the 25th Australian Brigade drove forward against the Japanese defences around Gona, gradually levering the Japanese away from the central positions, out into the swamps in which they either drowned or starved to death. But it was almost as hard on the attackers, and the drive slowed as exhaustion made itself felt until quite early in the month a fresh brigade – the 21st – arrived, just in time to tip the balance. Gona was entered on Dec 9, and although more Japanese reinforcements landed to the west soon afterwards, by the end of the month they had been wiped out.

To the east, however, the American 126th Infantry were having a rough and frustrating time. Flanked by Australian companies, they managed to drive through Japanese positions along the Soputa–Sanananda road and form a road-block, but the Japanese realised the threat this formed and for the rest of the month only fierce resistance under Captain Huggins kept the road-block in position.

Around Buna, the deadlock remained for the first week of December while the new commander, General Eichelberger, reorganised his forces. Then during the second week, one force drove north along the east bank of the Girua and at last took Buna village on Dec 14, then inched its way towards the Buna Mission while the second force, helped by the Australian 18th Brigade with a squadron of tanks, drove along the coast past Duropa Plantation and the airstrip. Even with the help of tanks (all of which were knocked out by the end) it was Jan 2 before the last Japanese soldier was killed and the way open for a powerful converging attack on Sanananda.

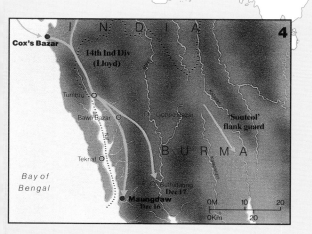

4 Arakan. For reasons of both politics and morale, General Wavell had begun planning for a return of British troops to Burma almost as soon as the long retreat had finished. By September his directives were issued and that month 14th Indian Division left Chittagong on a journey south intended to take it through Cox's Bazar and eventually down to the bottom of the Mayu Peninsula.

But the only road was a four-foot-wide track, and although it was possible to send heavy supplies by sea part of the way, much had to be carried by the troops and progress was almost imperceptible. Thirteen inches of rain fell on one day in November and monsoon conditions reigned in the Bay of Bengal; nevertheless by the beginning of December the division were slogging their way south from Cox's Bazar towards Tumbru and Bawli Bazar where the two constituent brigades separated, one holding to the coast and reaching Maungdaw, and the other driving parallel on the left for Buthidaung. A flank guard of irregulars led by Lt-Colonel J. H. Souther operated well inland to provide intelligence.

On arrival, the brigades found Japanese units holding strong defences along the line of the road between Maungdaw and Buthidaung, and were then instructed to await the arrival of two more brigades, 123rd and 47th Indian, who arrived on Dec 17. It was then discovered that the Japanese had withdrawn into the Mayu Peninsula itself, but it was January before 14th Indian Division were ready to move forward again.

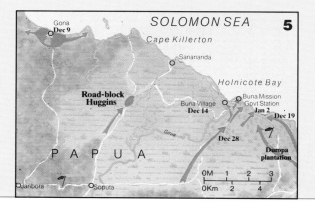

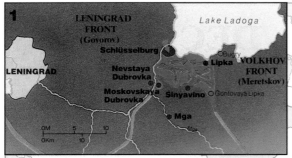

1 **Leningrad: the siege is pierced.** From mid December the units of the 67th Army (Leningrad Front) had trained for an assault across ice against fixed defences. By early January the assault teams had practised following close behind the Red Army artillery 'fire-walls', and on Jan 11 they moved into position along the west bank of the Neva between Moskovskaya Dubrovka and Schlüsselburg. At 0900 on Jan 12 the barrage opened, lasted for 140 minutes and was concluded by salvoes from Katyusha rocket-launchers – and the assault teams moved forward onto the ice. At the same time 2nd Shock Army of Volkhov Front struck westwards under a similar barrage between Lipka on the shores of Lake Ladoga and Gontovaya Lipka five miles to the south.

It took six days of brutal conflict, breaking through German strongpoints immured in frozen bog and forests carpeted in deep snow, before the two forces met to the north of Sinyavino, and during Jan 18 they linked up across the whole width of the corridor. At last Leningrad was linked directly by land with the rest of Russia, a railway between Schlüsselburg and Polyany could be opened (the first train ran on Feb 6) and the Ladoga 'ice road' was no longer the sole supply line.

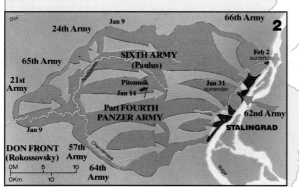

2 **Stalingrad.** As a result of the Red Army drive down past Kotelnikovo, by the beginning of the New Year the outer front of the band around Stalingrad was anything from 100 to 150 miles west of the inner band, the latter tightening all the time around Paulus's entrapped forces. Seven Soviet armies now faced towards the centre of the city and Red Air Force bombers dominated the skies, their fighters shooting down the transport planes that Göring had promised would sustain Sixth Army to the end. German soldiers now huddled for shelter from incessant artillery fire in the holes that Red Army soldiers had dug only two or three weeks before.

On Jan 8 General Rokossovsky sent in a formal proposition that in view of their hopeless situation Sixth Army should surrender but, as expected, Paulus rejected it and at 0805 on Jan 10 the artillery of 24th, 65th and 21st Armies began a powerful barrage augmented by bombers and ground-attack aircraft. At 0900 the infantry of all three armies advanced and the liquidation of the Stalingrad pocket commenced.

As always, the German troops fought back efficiently and bravely. It was the evening of Jan 13 before the Russians reached the western banks of the Rossoshka, but then the Don Front armies to the south fought their way over the Chervlenaya, and on Jan 14 the main German airfield at Pitomnik was captured. Now not only could no more food or ammunition come in, but the wounded could not be flown out. Three days later the last German airfield at Gumrak was taken, and in seven days of battle the 550 square miles held by Sixth Army at the beginning had been reduced to 250.

On Jan 21, the final great attack was launched on a 14-mile stretch of front, with 21st, 57th and 64th Armies aiming now for the Red Oktyabr factory complex. By Jan 25 they had reached the centre of Stalingrad and reduced the German occupied area to 36 square miles, while on Mamayev Kurgan the forces of General Chistyakov from the west and General Chuikov's valiant 62nd Army from the east, at last met. It was an historic moment, and several senior German officers announced that, whatever the attitude of the High Command, they were willing to surrender their units to the Red Army.

There were still a few more days of bitter fighting to be endured by both sides, but on the morning of Jan 31 Soviet troops took the Central Department Store in which Paulus had positioned his HQ, and by noon he was a prisoner of 64th Army. By Feb 2 all German resistance had ceased. The Battle of Stalingrad, one of the most significant in history, had ended with a resounding victory for the Red Army.

Daylight raids on Cherbourg; Copenhagen; Ijmuiden and Hengelo

Night raids on Essen, Cologne, Berlin, Düsseldorf, Hamburg and the Ruhr; Lorient, Brest and Bordeaux

Raids increase over London

Targets include Wilhelms-hafen; St Nazaire, Lorient and Brest

Jan 1 Russians retake Velikiye Luki

Jan 12 Free French forces under Leclerc complete conquest of Fezzan by occupation of Murzuk (capital) and Sebha (military base)

Continuous offensive operations in support of Eighth Army

☆☆ **Casablanca Conference.** Between Jan 14 and 23 President Roosevelt and Mr Churchill held a series of conferences at Casablanca, both men accompanied by their chief military advisers and several important decisions were made, including one to concentrate immediately all naval forces on the defeat of the U-boats, another that the defeat of Germany should take precedence over that of Japan, and a third that Sicily should be invaded as soon as the North African campaign ended.

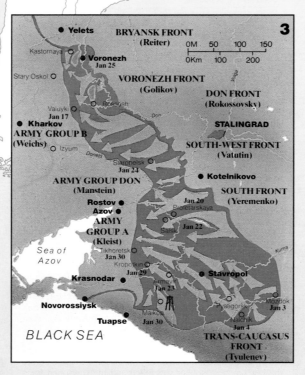

3 **Eastern Front.** While the fate of Sixth Army was being sealed on the inner face of the ring, four Soviet fronts on the outer face were poised to exploit the disarray in the German ranks. Voronezh and South-west Fronts were to be aimed at Kursk and Kharkov respectively, while the newly formed South Front would drive on for Rostov, its left wing aiming for Tikhoretsk and link up with 'Black Sea Group' – the left wing of Trans-Caucasus Front. In this way the German Army Group A would be cut off, and the whole of the German southern wing smashed in.

The overall plan was foiled, to some extent, by quick reaction by Manstein and Kleist who both withdrew the bulk of their forces and evaded the trap, and by the weather. Fog and torrential rain bogged down the main assaults shortly after they had been launched, but in spite of this by the end of the month Voronezh in the north and Mozdok, Maikop, Tikhoretsk and Salsk in the south had been relieved, and German formations were racing back through the rapidly narrowing gap at Rostov.

4 **Libya.** The problems facing Eighth Army at Buerat were exactly the same as those at El Agheila, and the solution had to be the same. Montgomery judged that he could not amass sufficient supplies at the front to launch a three-division attack until Jan 15 at the earliest, and only the most determined efforts by the transport companies of both XXX and X Corps managed it by then, for a devastating storm early in the month had wreaked havoc in the newly cleared Benghazi harbour.

Nevertheless, on Jan 12 the Desert Air Force began sustained bombing attacks on the Axis positions, and three days later 7th Armoured Division led the New Zealand Division in a wide hook to the south around the end of the Wadi el Kebir, while 51st Highland Division drove forward along the coastal strip.

Both advances were soon in trouble. Rommel's demolitions experts had destroyed 6 bridges, blown 177 craters in the roads and laid uncounted mines and booby-traps – along a road bordered on one side by salt marshes and very rough country on the other. As for 7th Armoured, they came up against well sited anti-tank defences and until they could be destroyed little movement could take place. However, under pressure Rommel began withdrawal to the Homs Defences; 7th Armoured reached them on Jan 19, and the following day the Highlanders, spurred on by Montgomery and supported now by 22nd Armoured Brigade, arrived and after bitter fighting broke through on the last stretch to Tripoli on Jan 21.

The Germans pulled out on Jan 22 after destroying most of the port installations at Tripoli, and at 0500 on Jan 23, the first Highlanders rode in on their escorting tanks. By the end of the month, forward patrols had reached Zuara.

Meantime, 3,200 French and colonial troops under General Leclerc had marched up from Equatorial Africa to join Montgomery and the Eighth Army.

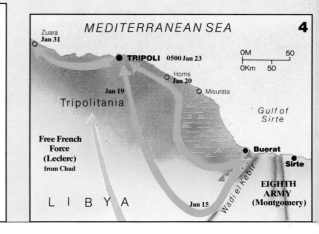

Day and night raids on Burma almost continuous

West of Guadalcanal US cruiser *Chicago* sunk by Japanese torpedo bomber

Main targets are Solomon Islands and New Guinea. Seventy-five thousand tons of shipping sunk at Rabaul

7 Iron Bottom Sound — Lunga Pt — Pt Cruz
Jan 30 — Jan 23 — Kokumbona — Matanikau — Lunga
Jan 17 — **2nd MARINE DIV**
Jan 19 — Jan 10 — **25th INFANTRY DIV**
Jan 18 — Austen — 0M 1 2 / 0Km 1 2

5 Arakan. When the Japanese had retired from the positions between Maungdaw and Buthidaung, they had in fact merely dropped back into strong defences around and just south of Kondan, protecting the important town of Rathedaung. There they waited – and watched; on Jan 1 they even allowed a patrol from 47th Indian Brigade to reach Foul Point. But when, a week later, first a company and then a battalion of Inniskillings attempted to follow up, they ran into a maze of well sited fox-holes hidden in the scrub; they had in fact run into a well laid trap.

But the advance of 14th Indian Division was pressed forward. While more battalions from 47th Brigade followed on down the Mayu Peninsula and vainly attempted to storm Donbaik and the Japanese defence lines, units from 123rd Brigade split on both sides of the Mayu river, one battalion attempting a direct attack on Rathedaung itself, the rest trying to take Kondon from the north.

It was to no avail. The Japanese positions were as stoutly defended as always, and while the two Indian brigades were battling fiercely but making little headway, a new Japanese division was being assembled under an expert commander to take advantage of the extended positions of the Indian units. Throughout February and March, the Kondan, Donbaik, Rathedaung triangle was to be the scene of bitter fighting.

6 Cape Killerton — Jan 16 — Holnicote Bay
Sanananda Pt
7th Aust Div (Vasey) — Jan 22 — Giruwa Jan 22
Jan 16 — Jan 10
Jan 18 — **US 32nd Div (Harding)**
Jan 8 — Buna
Jan 9 — **Road-blocks Rankin, Huggins & Fisk**
0M 0·5 1·5 / 0Km 1

6 Papua. The completion of the attacks against Buna and Gona released troops for a converging drive on Sanananda. From the south, the success of the Huggins Road-block led to the setting up of two more – Fisk and Rankin – and then to the release of Australian fresh battalions from their 7th Division, to push first out to Cape Killerton, then to swing east towards Sanananda.

At the same time another regiment of US infantry was flown forwards from Port Moresby to strengthen the 18th Brigade which had taken Buna, and by the middle of January all three prongs of the attack were grinding their way forward. It was still very tough fighting against desperate Japanese resistance and through very rough and difficult country, but by Jan 20 the defences were visibly crumbling and on Jan 22 Australian troops reached Sanananda Point and the village; and American troops had taken Giruwa.

The only Japanese troops left in Papua, as apart from New Guinea, were either starving to death in the swamps and jungle, or fleeing – and sometimes swimming – along the coast in efforts to reach their base at Salamaua.

7 Guadalcanal. During December General Vandergrift and his 1st Marine Division had been replaced by General Patch and the 2nd Marines, and much of the month had been spent gaining experience of the very particular sort of fighting which the Guadalcanal terrain demanded. Repeated attempts to take the positions on Mount Austen proved unsuccessful though as a training area it was to prove valuable; and early in January the 25th Infantry division arrived to move into that area. By this time, too, Henderson Field was safe and every day the US air strength built up.

On the Japanese side, although the decision had been made at Imperial Headquarters to evacuate the island, the orders did not arrive at the forward HQ until mid-January, when the senior staff officer present replied that the Japanese survivors now left lacked the physical strength to withdraw. But they still possessed the strength to resist, as the US marines and infantry found when General Patch set them off westwards, the marines across the Matanikau and along the coast past Point Cruz, the infantry against the horseshoe ring of defences at the foot of Mount Austen.

Yard by yard the advances pushed forward, past mounds of emaciated bodies of Japanese soldiers – which still had to be watched carefully lest they contain even one man with still a spark of life to enable him to turn and shoot the Americans from the rear. It was Jan 18 before the last survivor on Mount Austen was killed, the 19th before the Marine line was clear over the Matanikau, and Jan 23 before they reached Kokumbona.

Slowly, the Japanese pulled back, and with great skill the Japanese Command cloaked their intentions by building up a picture of an imminent large-scale landing of a new army to replace the one which had been so nearly destroyed.

The threat was enough to slow the American progress even further.

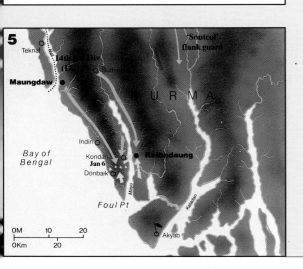

5 'Soutcot' flank guard
Teknaf — 14th IND DIV — Buthidaung
Maungdaw — B U R M A
Indin
Rathedaung — Kondan — Jan 6
Donbaik
Bay of Bengal — Mayu — Kaladan
Foul Pt
Akyab
0M 10 20 / 0Km 20

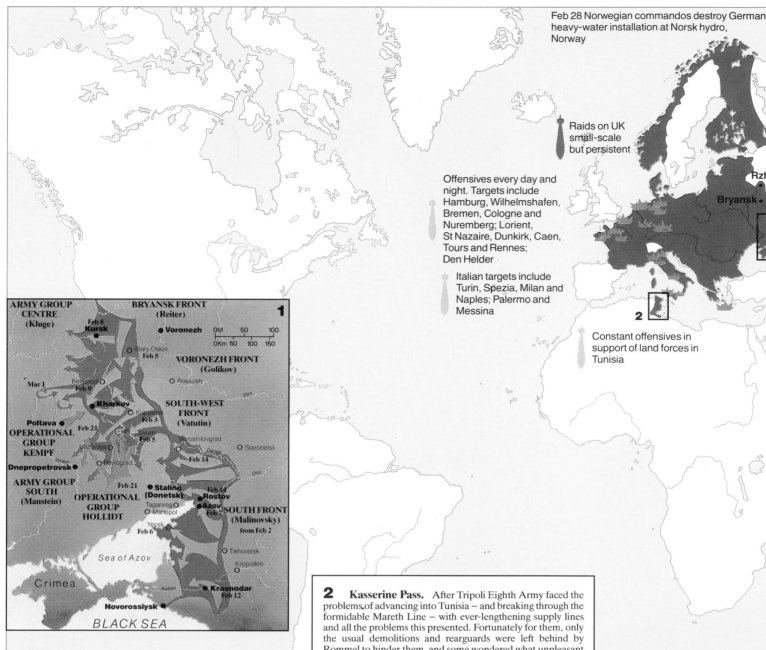

Feb 28 Norwegian commandos destroy German heavy-water installation at Norsk hydro, Norway

Raids on UK small-scale but persistent

Offensives every day and night. Targets include Hamburg, Wilhelmshafen, Bremen, Cologne and Nuremberg; Lorient, St Nazaire, Dunkirk, Caen, Tours and Rennes; Den Helder

Italian targets include Turin, Spezia, Milan and Naples; Palermo and Messina

Russian offensive increases pressure on Rzhev and in Orel–Bryansk area

Rzhev
Bryansk • Orel **1**

Shipping; Cretan airfields

Constant offensives in support of land forces in Tunisia

Inset map 1

ARMY GROUP CENTRE (Kluge)
BRYANSK FRONT (Reiter) **1**
Feb 8 Kursk
Voronezh
0M 50 100
0Km 50 100 150
Stary Oskol Feb 5
VORONEZH FRONT (Golikov)
Rossosh
Belgorod Feb 9
Mar 1
Kharkov
Kupyansk
Feb 3
Poltava Feb 21
Izyum Feb 5
Voroshilovgrad
Starobelsk
OPERATIONAL GROUP KEMPF
Lozovaya
Pavlograd
Feb 14
SOUTH-WEST FRONT (Vatutin)
Dnepropetrovsk
ARMY GROUP SOUTH (Manstein)
OPERATIONAL GROUP HOLLIDT
Feb 21
Stalino (Donetsk)
Taganrog
Mariupol
Feb 14 Rostov
Azov Feb 7
SOUTH FRONT (Malinovsky) from Feb 2
Yeysk Feb 6
Tikhoretsk
Kropotkin
Sea of Azov
Crimea
Kuban
Krasnodar Feb 12
Novorossiysk
BLACK SEA

Inset map 2

2 Bizerta
Mateur
TUNIS
Béja
Cape Bon
Fr XIX Corps
Le Kef
Br 6th Armd Div
Feb 17
Enfidaville
US II Corps
Thala Sbiba
Feb 19–22 Kairouan
Sousse
Feb 21/22 Fondouk
Feb 21
Tebessa
Bou Chebka
Sbeitla Feb 18
Feb 18 Feb 14 Faid Pass
Kasserine Feb 14
Feriana Feb 17
10th & 21st Pz Divs (Arnim)
Sfax
Gafsa Feb 16
Maknassy
Sened
Gulf of Gabes
Chott el Djerid
AFRIKA KORPS (Rommel)
Gabes Djerba
Mareth
Mareth Line
Medenine Feb 16
0M 25 50 75
0Km 25 50 75 100
Zuara
ALGERIA
TUNISIA

---

1 Eastern Front. With the Stalingrad victory the Red Army had annihilated a huge and famous enemy army, grinding down a whole segment of the Wehrmacht to unparalleled defeat. It is hardly surprising that morale throughout the whole military organisation of the Soviet Union was at peak level, that expectations of further successes were nationwide however tired the victors of Stalingrad might be; in any case, the time for further action was *now*, while the enemy were still in disarray and some degree of shock, while the ground was still frozen and hard enough for heavy traffic. In March would come the thaw, and the war would be glued in mud until it dried out.

Not altogether surprisingly Stalin now repeated the errors he had made a year previously – and it must be said that he was supported in his error by the Voronezh and South-west Front commanders, Golikov and Vatutin, who would be most closely concerned with the next stage of the war against the German army. Golikov's armies were to drive west for Kursk and Kharkov, Vatutin's south-west for Mariupol to trap all the German forces still in the Caucasus as they were chased out through the Rostov gap by Malinovsky's South Front.

The drive began in January, slowed at the end of the month by rain, but in February gained pace and seemed set to achieve all that was hoped for. Kursk was liberated on Feb 8, Kharkov on the 16th; to the south Vatutin's men were into the Donbass to take Voroshilovgrad by Feb 14 and go on to threaten Stalino, Malinovsky's units entered Rostov on the 14th. And to STAVKA's gratification, on Feb 27 Red Army units entered Pavlograd, only 25 miles from the Dniepr – and forward patrols actually reached the bank of the river. The only question to arouse doubt in Russian minds was – where were the German prisoners? All that had been captured so far – several hundred thousand – had been Hungarian, Italian or Rumanian.

The Germans were, in fact, concentrated around Poltava in the north and near Stalino in the south, and on Feb 20 the man who had grouped them there, Field Marshal von Manstein, launched them in a counter-attack which bore strong similarities to the one which had blasted Soviet hopes the previous May – and over much the same ground. By Feb 27 they had retaken Lozovaya and the next day had reached the Donetz west of Izyum, while the rest of Manstein's southern force flooded up to the river to strip clear the left flank of Golikov's drive. Kharkov was again under German threat and the front commanders were frantically trying to extricate their forces from yet another successful German onslaught.

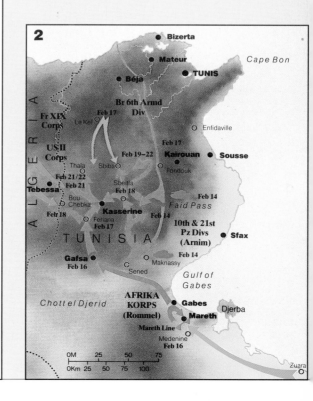

2 Kasserine Pass. After Tripoli Eighth Army faced the problems of advancing into Tunisia – and breaking through the formidable Mareth Line – with ever-lengthening supply lines and all the problems this presented. Fortunately for them, only the usual demolitions and rearguards were left behind by Rommel to hinder them, and some wondered what unpleasant shocks the Desert Fox was preparing. It was with some relief that they learned that Rommel had, in fact, turned his attention northwards.

By now the German reinforcements which had flooded into North Africa had built up into a powerful army – under General von Arnim – and Rommel was gaining the advantages of short supply lines. Together the Axis forces might exploit their central position between the two converging Allied armies by striking and crippling them separately and successively. The US II Corps was the first target of Rommel's plan.

Its front covered the three main passes through the mountains at Gafsa, Faid and Fondouk, and these were so narrow that the holders felt secure. But in the last days of January, 21st Panzer Division had struck at Faid Pass and before help could be rushed to the French defenders were through and holding a sally-port. Then on Feb 14, in a well executed manoeuvre, they tempted an American attack forward onto their usual line of concealed 88mm anti-tank guns, annihilated a tank battalion and captured 44 tanks, 50 half-tracks, 22 trucks and over 20 guns.

Then 10th Panzer Division joined in chasing the Americans back towards Thala, while the Afrika Korps detachment raced up through Gafsa and Feriana towards Kasserine, through which was flooding the chaos of an Allied retreat with American, British and French units all intermingled; and by then a second, relieving attempt by the American 1st Armoured Division had suffered the same fate as the first so that in two days they had lost 100 tanks. They rallied to hold Sbeitla for a day, then withdrew to Kasserine to join the retreat.

The situation was saved by disagreement between Rommel and his superiors on the practicality of Rommel's plans for an immediate thrust north-west towards Tebessa. By the time it was resolved General Alexander had arrived to exert overall command, and had ordered the British 6th Armoured Division southwards to defend Thala and Sbiba; and it was against these positions that Rommel had been ordered to direct his thrust. The result was that when his eager but now tiring units arrived they found far more Allied tanks and infantry than had been bargained for – though with their usual efficiency they were making solid ground when the US 9th Division artillery arrived and tipped the balance.

By Feb 22 Rommel judged that he could go no further north and that he would need all he had left to deal with Eighth Army back on the Mareth Line. The Battle of Kasserine Pass could not be called Rommel's victory; but he had given the Allied Command a nasty jolt.

Task Force of 2 cruisers and
4 destroyers shells Attu

Burma attacked
continuously,
especially
Rangoon. Seaborne
raids on Myebon

Main objectives are Solomons,
New Guinea and Japanese shipping

Russell Is

Feb 21 US 43rd Div makes unopposed landings

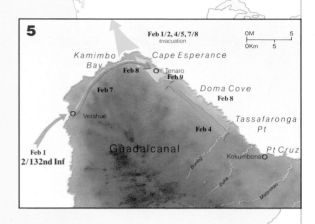

5   Guadalcanal. The Japanese plans worked perfectly. Convinced that yet another huge Japanese army was sailing for Guadalcanal, General Patch held the bulk of his 2nd Marines back around Henderson Field, only patrols out probing the trails leading west towards Cape Esperance. Along them the hungry and ill-clad Japanese survivors made their way to meet the last run of the Tokyo Express, now coming down from Rabaul. At 2130 on the night of Feb 1/2 the first 2,000 men climbed aboard the landing barges which took them out to 22 destroyers; by midnight they were on their way. Two days later a similar operation took place and on the night of Feb 7/8 the last 3,000 Japanese soldiers – in conditions of health which horrified the sailors who helped them aboard – were rescued. In a week the Japanese Navy had lifted off nearly 12,000 men.

3   Chindit I. Orde Charles Wingate was at this time a 40-year-old brigadier, a spiritual descendant of those puritan, deeply religious soldiers who have played such an important part in Britain's imperial history. In 1940 he had been sent to Ethiopia to organise a guerrilla campaign against the Italians and had so impressed General Wavell that in 1942 Wavell had sent for Wingate, to attempt to repeat his Ethiopian adventures beyond the Chindwin against the Japanese.

By the beginning of 1943 Wingate had made his plans and trained his men. Now he proposed to take his Long Range Penetration Groups deep into Japanese-held territory in order to block their lines of communication and supply, wreck their administration centres and persuade the local population that their present oppressors were not invincible.

He divided his force into two groups – Northern Group which he would lead in himself consisting of five columns and a headquarters – in all 2,200 men and 850 mules – Southern Group of two columns – 1,000 men and 250 mules. Every man had been trained in jungle fighting to a pitch Wingate considered higher than that of the Japanese, and every man had an extra specialisation such as demolitions, signals, medical or navigation. Every column also contained a strong air-to-ground co-operation team, for once across the Chindwin and

into enemy territory it would depend solely upon air support for supply and evacuation of wounded.

Wingate's intention was that his forces should eventually cross the Irrawaddy and there form a large base camp from which they would operate for two or three months – and if all proceeded well, by the end of that period perhaps the original force would be flown out and replaced by a second wave.

On Feb 12 Wingate sent his men off through Tamu on the first stage of the operation and on the night of Feb 14/15 he led the Northern Group across the Chindwin at Tonhe, the Southern Group crossing 35 miles south, having turned east at Aukfaung. Neither crossing was contested by the Japanese, but on the 18th the Southern Group hit an enemy post near Maingnyaung where they made a detour and thus lost time. But the air drops were successful and Southern Group pressed on to reach the rail head at Yindaik by the end of the month.

Meanwhile, Wingate had led his Northern Group as far as his first Bivouac area just west of Pinbon, on the way receiving air drops and detaching one column at Tonmakeng for a raid on Sinlamaung, where they found no enemy but collected a little useful information.

The stage was now set for a series of attacks on Japanese positions, and an advance to the Irrawaddy.

4   New Guinea. Having decided at the end of 1942 to give up Guadalcanal and realising by the end of January 1943 that they were being driven out of Papua, the Japanese Command felt that if they could not menace Australia directly, they must at least try to hold the northern Solomons, New Britain and, perhaps most vital of all, northern New Guinea.

They therefore landed fresh forces along the New Guinea coast, built up their strength and fortified their air bases at Lae and Salamaua, and sent in a new division – the 51st – to extend their hold on the entire area. With this extra strength they quickly concluded that they must attack and take the small town and airfield at Wau, occupied by the Australians since March 1942. In Australian hands it threatened Lae and Salamaua, in Japanese hands it would protect those positions and thus the eastern flank of the Japanese perimeter.

Early in the New Year they despatched a force of brigade strength through the jungle and on Jan 27 launched their first

attack on the position; only the fact that a part of the Australian 17th Brigade had arrived a few days before prevented its fall. Bad weather had halted the arrival of the rest of the brigade and during the next two days the position was critical, the defenders forced back to within 400 yards of the vital airstrip. Then late on Jan 29 the weather cleared, plane after plane flew in (57 landings on the first day, all under Japanese fire) and on Feb 3 the Australians mounted a powerful attack which shattered the besieging force to such an extent that the survivors fled in disorder along the jungle trails to their outpost at Mubo.

On Feb 6 the Japanese Air Force attempted to bomb the Wau airstrip out of existence, but they ran into strong fighter defences which had just arrived, the bombers were driven off and never came back; Wau was safely in Australian hands, and by the end of February Australian infantry were closing up to the next objective – the Mubo outpost.

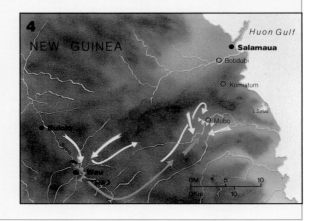

1 Eastern Front. By March 3 Vatutin had been forced to withdraw the bulk of the right wing of South-west Front to the Donets, abandoning nearly 6,000 square miles of his most recent gains. To his north, Golikov, who had reacted to danger slightly more rapidly than Vatutin and swung his left wing towards Vatutin's right in an admirable attempt to help, was therefore now in a thoroughly unenviable situation. His front covered almost 250 miles, his lines of supply were so extended by the recent advances as to be in serious danger of complete breakdown – and an early thaw was giving his supply lines more trouble than it was giving von Manstein's panzer divisions. With some trepidation he signalled STAVKA that Kharkov would have to be surrendered, and the panzers were in fact back in the city by March 15 and into Belgorod by the 19th. By the end of the month, Voronezh Front too was behind the Donets.

Golikov's right flank armies, however, were not so badly affected. They had protected the southern wing of the drive by Bryansk Front which recaptured Kursk and were thus north of Manstein's drive towards Belgorod – and by the time Manstein's forces had consolidated on the Donets, the thaw had arrived in strength and mud engulfed the entire area. Thus a huge salient jutted west above Kharkov, with Kursk its central point, Voronezh Front armies holding the southern face, and Bryansk Front holding the main area and the northern face, running some miles south of Orel.

Above Orel the Rzhev salient had at last gone, though more by default than by conquest. A drive westwards by the Red Army had liberated Velikiye Luki and by March 1 had also recaptured Demyansk, but the build-up of Soviet forces in the pocket south of Demyansk had been noticed which, together with the need for strengthening the German forces in the south for Manstein's counter-offensive, had forced the decision at German Supreme HQ to relinquish the Rzhev salient before it was cut off and the holders encircled.

At the end of February the German Ninth Army had received orders to pull back southwards, and as they did so they were followed by units from both the Kalinin and West Fronts. As the Russian troops advanced they uncovered a horrible tale of destruction, mass killing and slave-labour deportations. Rzhev itself was a devastation, uncounted villages had been reduced to rubble, their populations shot or burned alive. For three weeks the Russian units marched forward across ground littered with the debris of war and deliberate havoc, and the fact that the thaw had coated it all in glutinous mud could barely make it worse. There seems to be in German accounts of these, and other withdrawals they were to conduct upon the same lines, no conception of the wind they had sown from which they would reap such a terrible whirlwind.

On March 12 Vyazma, a horrific shambles, was reached, and by the end of the month the front line ran from Novgorod in a sweep west of Velikiye Luki, then south-east just short of Vitebsk, Smolensk and Roslavl, past Bryansk and Orel, then abruptly west again with the Kursk salient out to the south.

The lines were in place for the vast summer battles of 1943.

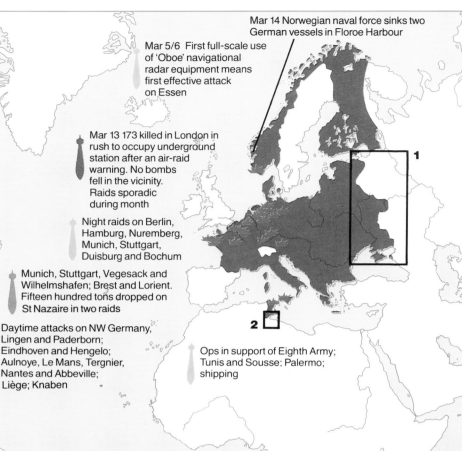

Mar 14 Norwegian naval force sinks two German vessels in Floroe Harbour

Mar 5/6 First full-scale use of 'Oboe' navigational radar equipment means first effective attack on Essen

Mar 13 173 killed in London in rush to occupy underground station after an air-raid warning. No bombs fell in the vicinity. Raids sporadic during month

Night raids on Berlin, Hamburg, Nuremberg, Munich, Stuttgart, and Bochum

Munich, Stuttgart, Vegesack and Wilhelmshafen; Brest and Lorient. Fifteen hundred tons dropped on St Nazaire in two raids

Daytime attacks on NW Germany, Lingen and Paderborn; Eindhoven and Hengelo; Aulnoye, Le Mans, Tergnier, Nantes and Abbeville; Liège; Knaben

Ops in support of Eighth Army; Tunis and Sousse; Palermo; shipping

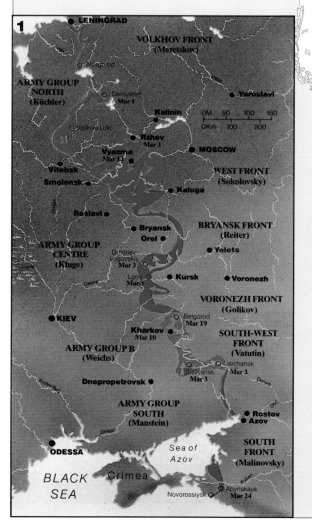

1 LENINGRAD

VOLKHOV FRONT (Meretskov)

ARMY GROUP NORTH (Küchler)

Novgorod · Demyansk Mar 1 · Yaroslavl

Kalinin   0M 50 100 150 0Km 100 200

Velikiye Luki · Rzhev Mar 3

Vyazma Mar 12 · MOSCOW

Vitebsk   WEST FRONT (Sokolovsky)

Smolensk · Kaluga

Roslavl

Bryansk · BRYANSK FRONT (Reiter)
Orel · Yelets

ARMY GROUP CENTRE (Kluge)   Dmitriev Logovskiy Mar 3

Lgov Mar 3 · Kursk · Voronezh

VORONEZH FRONT (Golikov)

KIEV   Belgorod Mar 19

Kharkov Mar 10   SOUTH-WEST FRONT (Vatutin)

ARMY GROUP B (Weichs)   Slavyansk Mar 3 · Lisichansk Mar 3

Dnepropetrovsk

ARMY GROUP SOUTH (Manstein)   Rostov · Azov

ODESSA   Sea of Azov   SOUTH FRONT (Malinovsky)

BLACK SEA   Crimea   Abynskaya · Novorossiysk Mar 24

2 Medmenine and Mareth. As he turned away from Kasserine Rommel learned that Montgomery had moved the bulk of his army into the area around Medmenine, with a large supply base at Ben Gardane back where the Tunisian frontier met the coast. Rommel's only hope was to hit Eighth Army before it could consolidate, so he ordered his three panzer divisions – 10th, 15th and 21st – down to the south. They arrived far too late. By the time they attacked on the morning of March 6 their every move had been foreseen, and Eighth Army infantry, artillery and tanks were awaiting them.

Neither infantry nor armour were, in fact, much engaged. As the German panzer columns approached, they ran first into well sited anti-tank batteries, and those panzers which survived were then blanketed under massed artillery bombardment. By the end of the second attack during the evening, the Afrika Armee had lost 53 of its 150 panzers while Eighth Army had lost nothing but a few anti-tank guns. Three days later, Rommel left Africa for good.

Montgomery's original plan for the Mareth Line attack was to send the New Zealand Division, reinforced by 8th Armoured Brigade and General Leclerc's Free French Force, in a wide hook across the Matmata Hills to the Tebaga Gap, and then across towards Gabes in order to divert Axis attention up there; but the main drive would be by X and XXX Corps divisions straight through the Mareth defences and along the coast to Gabes and beyond.

As it happened those defences were too strong, the attack division – 50th – was held fast in a small bridgehead for the first two days, and Montgomery reacted by sending 4th Indian Division on a short hook through Ksar el Hallouf to Ben Zelten, and the whole of 1st Armoured Division as fast as possible out behind the New Zealand Corps. By March 22 the hook was being challenged by panzer and infantry hastily withdrawn from the Mareth flanks while by March 27 the rest of the defenders were escaping back towards Gabes.

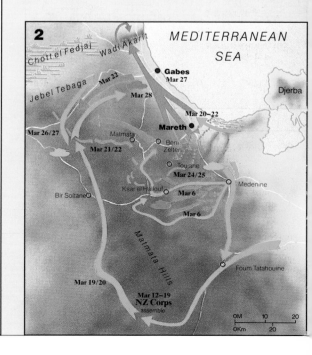

2   MEDITERRANEAN SEA

Chott el Fedjaj · Wadi Akarit

Jebel Tebaga   Mar 22   Gabes Mar 27   Djerba

Mar 28   Mar 20–22

Mareth

Mar 26/27   Matmata   Mar 21/22   Ben Zelten

Touane   Mar 24/25   Medenine

Bir Soltane   Ksar el Hallouf   Mar 6

Mar 6

Matmata Hills

Foum Tatahouine

Mar 19/20   Mar 12–19 NZ Corps assemble

0M 10 20   0Km 20

Komandorski Is

Kiska

Mar 26 Jap convoy and escort attacked by
US naval force. Battle involves ships only,
fighting until ammunition exhausted.
Both sides sustain damage, convoy turns back

Burma targets
include Rathedaung,
Akyab, Gokteik,
Mandalay,
Rangoon and
Toungoo

3

Mar 8 Japanese forces cross Yangtze
between Yichang and Yoyang
Mar 13 Chinese counter-attack and throw
them back

Naval Task Force under Admiral Merrill
shells Vila and Munda in Solomons,
sinks two destroyers

Aru

Nauru

4

Darwin;
Wau (N Guinea);
Russell Is

Mar 15 Allied aircraft damage
troop convoy proceeding towards
Aru Is. Convoy retires

3   Chindit Operations. Having established a bivouac
area close to Pinbon, Wingate sent off two columns on March 1
to sabotage railway lines and another three to ambush roads
and attack Japanese posts. One of these ran into far superior
enemy forces and was scattered, many of the men making their
own precarious ways back to the Chindwin. Column 5 reached
the railway near Bongyaung, drove off the Japanese guards and
blew the bridge with a spectacular explosion, while column 3
blew two more bridges nearby, one with a span of 300 feet.

Meanwhile Southern Group had wrecked sections of the
railway near Kyaikthin, but the next day their headquarters
and one column were themselves ambushed and scattered.
Nevertheless, by March 10 three of the columns had reached
the banks of the Irrawaddy and air drops were proceeding
satisfactorily, so Wingate expanded his ideas to encompass the
larger scheme, ordering the columns across to concentrate in his
chosen area beyond.

By March 19 the northern columns were across, though one
of them had lost all their mules swept away by the current, and
Wingate ordered two columns off to find the huge Gokteik
Gorge viaduct which carries the road between Lashio and
Mandalay. But now when the bulk of his forces had reached the
concentration area, Wingate found to his horror that although
he had chosen from the map a position ideal for air drops, it was
in fact a hot, trackless and totally waterless belt of land in which
his men would die of thirst within days unless he moved them.

Moreover, HQ back in India were becoming anxious about
the distances the supply aircraft were having to fly, and on
March 24 they ordered Wingate to withdraw. It was, in the
circumstances, the only intelligent course to follow, and
Wingate reluctantly agreed, but when at the end of the month
his column returned to the Irrawaddy, they found their crossing
points guarded by strong Japanese patrols and almost all the
local boatmen under arrest and their boats confiscated. General
Mutaguchi, commander of the Japanese army in Burma, had
learned of their presence and reacted quickly.

Boats and rafts were found, stolen or built, and some of the
men actually waded across the Irrawaddy, making their way
between the huge sandbanks – and during April and May,
small, desperate groups of men, all suffering from malaria,
dysentery and starvation to some degree, made their way back
and across the Chindwin. Of the 3,000 men who had
accompanied Wingate, 2,182 got back, though many of them
were in such a poor state of health that they never went into
action again.

This first Chindit operation bore one strong similarity to
Rommel's attack at Kasserine; it could not be claimed as a
victory, but it gave the Japanese occupation troops and their
commander a severe shock.

4   Battle of the Bismarck Sea/New Guinea.   At the
same time as the Japanese brigade launched the attack on Wau,
a convoy of eight transports and eight destroyers left Rabaul, *en
route* to Lae with the remainder of the Japanese 51st Division
on board. Its assembly and movements had all been accurately
reported to Allied Headquarters, and its arrival off Cape
Gloucester on March 1 brought about the first air attack. Bad
weather protected the convoy that day, but on March 2 B-25
Mitchell bombers sank one transport and damaged others
despite mist, rain and thick cloud.

By March 4 the weather had cleared and by now the convoy
was about 30 miles south-east of Finschhafen. Here they were
caught by a large force of Fifth Air Force aircraft, including
Flying Fortresses, Liberators, Mitchells, Beaufighters and
Lightnings, while low-flying Bostons attacked Lae airfield and
effectively kept the Zeros on the ground. In less than an hour all
the remaining transports had been sunk with considerable loss
of life and all the destroyers damaged, and dawn on March 4
revealed just one lone Japanese destroyer still in the area, and
this was quickly sunk.

The Battle of the Bismarck Sea was undoubtedly a unique
battle, for no Allied vessel had been engaged, and all the enemy
transports and half the escorts had been sunk.

With the loss of the transports and so significant a part of their
naval strength, there was little the Japanese could now do to
supply or reinforce their garrisons at Lae and Salamaua, or to
prevent the build-up of American and Australian strength in
the area. Already an auxiliary Australian supply dump was
being formed – Bulldog, at the junction of the rivers Lakekamu
and Eloa – and during March work was carried out widening
the track forward to Wau, at the same time moving forces up
towards Mubo and the Salamaua defences.

As for American forces, by the middle of the month one
battalion of US 162nd Infantry had moved unopposed up from
Gona as far as the mouth of the Mambare river, and at the end
of the month another battalion landed at Morobe at the mouth
of the Waria.

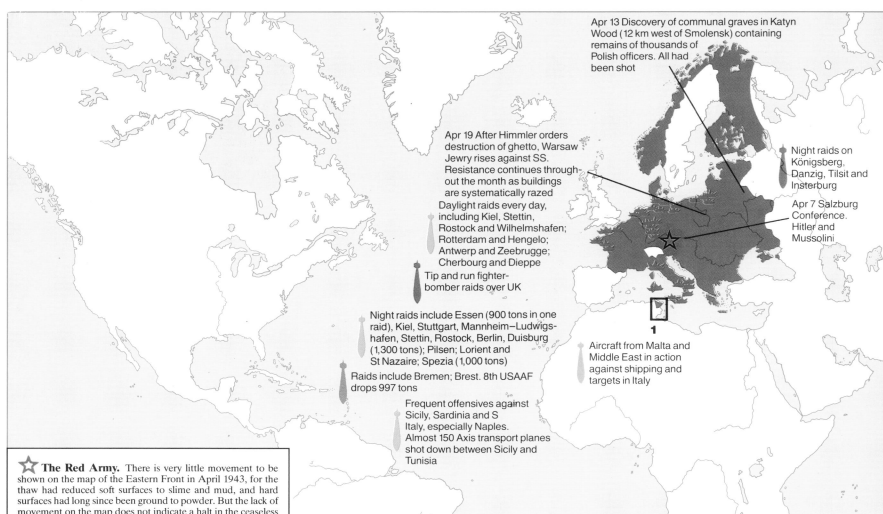

Apr 13 Discovery of communal graves in Katyn Wood (12 km west of Smolensk) containing remains of thousands of Polish officers. All had been shot

Night raids on Königsberg, Danzig, Tilsit and Insterburg

Apr 7 Salzburg Conference. Hitler and Mussolini

Apr 19 After Himmler orders destruction of ghetto, Warsaw Jewry rises against SS. Resistance continues through-out the month as buildings are systematically razed

Daylight raids every day, including Kiel, Stettin, Rostock and Wilhelmshafen; Rotterdam and Hengelo; Antwerp and Zeebrugge; Cherbourg and Dieppe

Tip and run fighter-bomber raids over UK

Night raids include Essen (900 tons in one raid), Kiel, Stuttgart, Mannheim–Ludwigs-hafen, Stettin, Rostock, Berlin, Duisburg (1,300 tons); Pilsen; Lorient and St Nazaire; Spezia (1,000 tons)

Raids include Bremen; Brest. 8th USAAF drops 997 tons

Aircraft from Malta and Middle East in action against shipping and targets in Italy

Frequent offensives against Sicily, Sardinia and S Italy, especially Naples. Almost 150 Axis transport planes shot down between Sicily and Tunisia

The Red Army. There is very little movement to be shown on the map of the Eastern Front in April 1943, for the thaw had reduced soft surfaces to slime and mud, and hard surfaces had long since been ground to powder. But the lack of movement on the map does not indicate a halt in the ceaseless fighting, especially at both ends of the line. Heavy fighting and major air battles took place above and around Leningrad, while down in the Kuban the fighting around Novorossiysk and for the Taman Peninsula was desperate, as the Germans fought for a way out of the trap and the Red Army for the clearance of the Caucasus and a return to the Crimea.

The Red Army was now completely revitalised, for from the furnace of Stalingrad had emerged a force as hard and bright as newly forged steel. The spectacular victory had not only inspired the Allies and spread despondency throughout the Axis, but it had wrung concessions from Stalin to the military arm on an undreamt-of scale. Not only were weapons of excellent quality now reaching the soldiers in vast numbers, but in place of the continual criticism and scorn which had greeted their efforts and sacrifices up to the end of 1942, now they were laden with new decorations, uplifted with promotions. Four new Marshals of the Soviet Union were proclaimed in early January, and to advertise his identification with Red Army victories, on the first 'Red Army Day' – Jan 23 – Stalin appointed himself one as well.

Moreover, to the astonishment of many, badges of rank were introduced, reinstating the *pogon* – the hard shoulder-boards which in 1917 soldiers had torn from the uniforms of the Tsar's officers.

The Red Army, in fact, was now on its way back to becoming a model professional army in which military efficiency was to take precedence over political orthodoxy. No longer must a colonel look over his shoulder to ensure that he had the agreement of his *commissar*, though Party organs were not totally to disappear; they merged into the background – in fact awaiting their moment of rehabilitation once the military battles had been won.

The final modification of Soviet military philosophy was also shortly to take place. In July, ranks from corporal to lieut-colonel were formally acknowledged, and reinstatement made of that historically most disparaged concept, that of the 'officer'.

Stalin, however, was not prepared to grant all this without a price. If discipline throughout the Red Army had been draconian before – when in theory some rights might be allowed to soldiers – now that military competence was the supreme arbiter, discipline was tightened to levels undreamed-of in Western armies. Social mixing between different ranks – even at the level of soldier and corporal – was expressly forbidden, the principle of absolute obedience based on absolute fear was if anything reinforced, and it became widely understood that any Red Army soldier who allowed himself to be taken prisoner would upon liberation have to answer the blistering question 'Why aren't you dead?' It makes, in military terms, for very high morale.

This was the army which would await the next German onslaught, for upon the advice of his marshals reinforced by the intelligence now provided – and believed – from Switzerland by the 'Lucy Ring', Stalin had agreed that the Voronezh and Central Fronts in the Kursk salient and the Reserve (Steppe) Front immediately behind, should be built up to enormous defensive strength, await the German offensive and allow it to smash itself to pieces. Then, when the crucial moment arrived, they would go over to the offensive themselves and achieve the final destruction of the hated Wehrmacht.

1 **The Battle of Wadi Akarit.** At Akarit the Eighth Army faced a problem in one way similar to that at Alamein five months before – a wide frontage to break through, the sea on the right flank and an apparently impregnable natural obstacle on the left. But that obstacle was not a depression with a quagmire at the bottom, but a jumble of half a dozen ridges with apparently vertical rock-faces.

Montgomery's first plan was for a repeat of the Alamein tactics with artillery bombardment, an infantry break-in action in the centre of the position, with X Corps armour lying up close to race through the moment the infantry had made a gap. However, at the close of the planning conference, the commanders of the two infantry divisions most closely concerned – 4th Indian and 51st Highland – approached their corps commander, General Leese, with another plan based upon the long experience of the 4th Indian Division of night fighting in the mountains of the North-west Frontier of India.

As a result, immediately after dusk on April 5 and in total silence, 7th Indian Infantry Brigade with a battalion of Gurkhas in the lead crept into the western foothills. By midnight they had reached the nearest commanding height, a second brigade came in on their right rear to take the inner ridges, and by 0200 on April 6 all the important positions had been captured. The artillery then moved up as close as they could, to protect the forward infantry from inevitable counter-attack at dawn when the enemy realised the situation. There had been plenty of close fighting in the hills, but as surprise had been complete, speed and silence had reigned throughout. At 0900 General Tuker, commanding 4th Indian, reported that a gap was now open for the armour to go through, and although the announcement might have been premature there is no doubt that an excellent opportunity awaited exploitation.

Unfortunately, as had happened before, the armour reached the gap but then waited in it throughout April 6, despite urgent pleas that they should race on through from both General Tuker and General Wimberley of the Highland Division. When eventually they moved off on the morning of April 8 they found the Germans and Italians had gone, leaving just their dead, the badly wounded, a few rearguards – and the usual belts of mines and booby-traps. There is no doubt that a great chance had been missed of trapping a considerable proportion of the Axis forces.

Rommel's absence in no way affected Panzerarmee efficiency in rearguard actions and Eighth Army progress north of the Wadi Akarit was as slow and frustrating as always, rarely making more than ten miles a day. Sfax was reached after a brisk action with panzers of their old antagonists, 15th Panzer Division, Sousse on April 12 and on April 19 the forward troops of Eighth Army closed up to Enfidaville on quite a narrow front, to find themselves at last beside the right-hand corps of First Army, now preparing for the wide assault which would take them to Tunis and finally expel the Axis from North Africa.

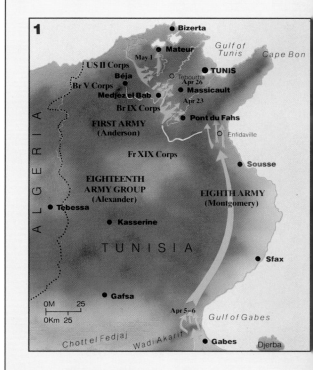

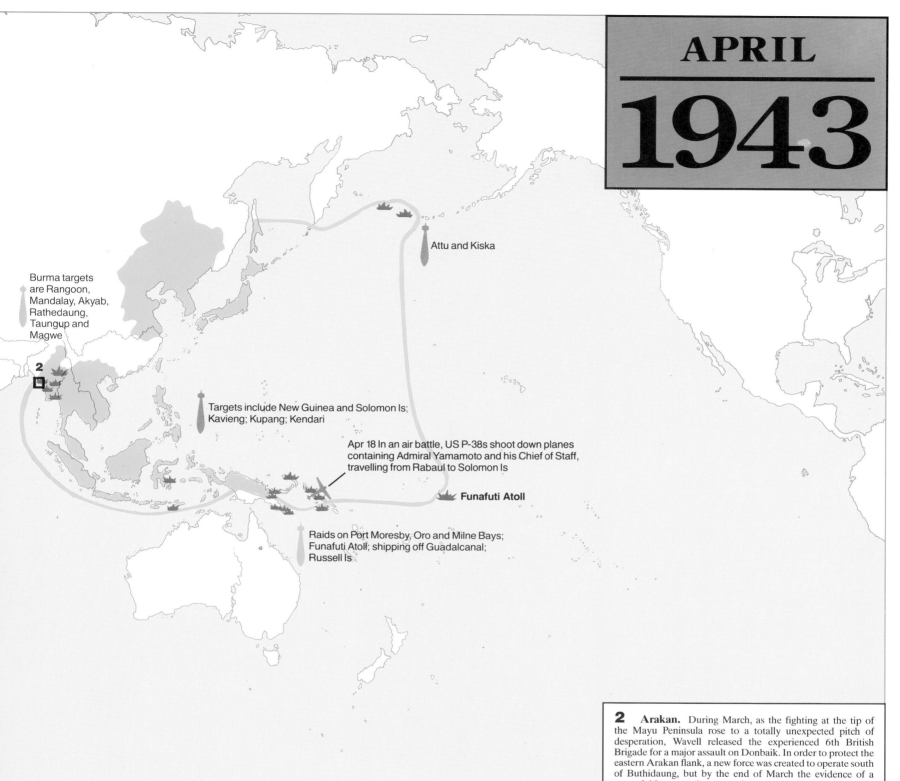

APRIL
1943

Attu and Kiska

Burma targets
are Rangoon,
Mandalay, Akyab,
Rathedaung,
Taungup and
Magwe

2

Targets include New Guinea and Solomon Is;
Kavieng; Kupang; Kendari

Apr 18 In an air battle, US P-38s shoot down planes
containing Admiral Yamamoto and his Chief of Staff,
travelling from Rabaul to Solomon Is

Funafuti Atoll

Raids on Port Moresby, Oro and Milne Bays;
Funafuti Atoll; shipping off Guadalcanal;
Russell Is

2 **Arakan.** During March, as the fighting at the tip of the Mayu Peninsula rose to a totally unexpected pitch of desperation, Wavell released the experienced 6th British Brigade for a major assault on Donbaik. In order to protect the eastern Arakan flank, a new force was created to operate south of Buthidaung, but by the end of March the evidence of a powerful Japanese threat growing across the Kaladan, together with the loss of over 300 killed or wounded during the gallant but abortive attacks on Donbaik, convinced all close observers that this whole Arakan operation was ill advised from the start.

Wavell, however, did not yet agree. He rejected the advice of the commander of 14th Indian Division – General Lloyd – and sent him on leave, replacing him with General Lomax who seemed more optimistically inclined. Exhorting the units east of the Mayu Range to 'stick it out' and the survivors of the 6th British Brigade to hold on fast around Donbaik, both Wavell and Lomax seemed to feel that the approach of the monsoon would enable the brigades to build up their strength for success when the monsoon ended. No notice was to be taken of the rising toll malaria was exacting in those pre-mepacrine days.

Then on April 1, 47th Brigade commander realised that the Japanese were infiltrating between his positions to press on through towards the coast, and his only hope of survival lay in abandoning his heavy equipment and getting there himself as quickly as possible.

But a Japanese column was well ahead of him, and by April 3 had reached and set up a road-block at Indin. This was destroyed by 6th Brigade units, and the orders were at last given for a complete withdrawal from the peninsula back to the Buthidaung–Maungdaw line; but two nights later a strong Japanese force surrounded Indin, and captured the brigade commander and his staff, all of whom were to die in a reportedly barbaric fashion not far off in the jungle.

British and Indian troops who could still march now made their painful way northwards, while the victorious Japanese commander laid his plans for the occupation of the 'Tunnels' of the Buthidaung position, and the pursuit of the British back out of the Arakan. The only hopeful event for the Allies was the appointment on April 14 of Lt-General W. J. Slim to all troops in the area and the resultant realistic appraisal of the situation.

☆ **Battle of the Atlantic.** The convoy system and the new defensive measures against U-boats now began to take effect. Comprehensive air surveillance by long-range aircraft was now available, and the specially formed Hunter–Killer Groups equipped with centrimetric radar were gaining experience. In May 41 U-boats were sunk, and the German naval command were forced to abandon attacks on North Atlantic convoys.

Major night assaults on Dortmund (2,000 tons), Duisberg (1,500 tons), Bochum, Düsseldorf, Essen and Wuppertal (1,500 tons)

Heavy daylight raids. 2,865 tons dropped in all over Kiel, Flensburg, Emden and Wilhelmshafen; St Nazaire; Antwerp

Small forces attack Berlin on 6 nights

Raids on 9 days, 3 nights on UK

Other daylight raids include Cherbourg; Jena; Flushing

Support for land ops in Tunisia until May 12; in one day 2,500 sorties flown, 1,250,000 lbs dropped

Washington

May 12 Trident Conference. Roosevelt, Churchill and heads of Combined Staffs discuss Anglo-American strategy

After surrender of Tunisia offensives directed against Sicily, Sardinia and S Italy

May 16 Demolition of Synagogue ends resistance in Warsaw Ghetto

Round-the-clock bombing of Pantellaria

May 27 First group of British officers parachuted into Yugoslavia to make contact with Partisan movement

1 **The Dambusters Raid.** On the night of May 16, 19 Lancaster bombers of the newly formed 617 Squadron commanded by Wing-Commander Guy Gibson, took off on what was to become one of the most famous bomber operations of the war. They each carried a specially designed bomb which the inventor, Barnes Wallis, believed would be capable of smashing the walls of the huge dams of the Möhne, Sorpe and Eder reservoirs, thus flooding the valleys below and at the same time dispossessing German heavy industry of its essential water supply.

The squadron flew in three waves – the first of nine aircraft to attack the Möhne, the Eder and finally, if they still had bombs left, the Sorpe dams; the second with five aircraft to go straight to the Sorpe dam; the third five aircraft to act as reserve, and either complement the attacks on the first targets or if these had already been destroyed, go on to attack dams at Lister and Ennepe.

The first wave despite losing one aircraft on the way brilliantly attacked the Möhne dam and with the fourth bomb, dropped at 0056 on May 17, breached the dam. They then flew

on to the Eder and at 0154 breached that as well. The following waves were dogged by bad luck. Of the ten aircraft in the two waves, four were shot down, three were forced to turn back, two dropped bombs on the Sorpe and one on the Ennepe, but neither dam was breached.

The resulting floods covered huge areas (see map) and necessitated the diversion of thousands of men from the task of building the 'Atlantic Wall' – Hitler's pet defence project against invasion. The effect on industry was not so great as had been hoped, partially due to the failure of the attack on the Sorpe. Had that dam been breached, according to Reichsminister Albert Speer, Ruhr production would have suffered a crippling blow.

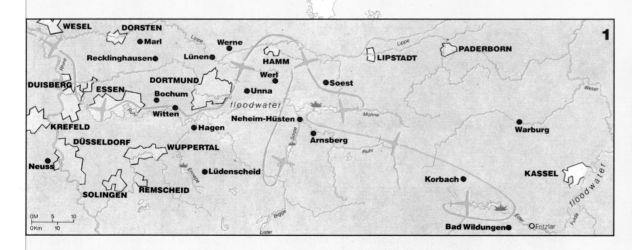

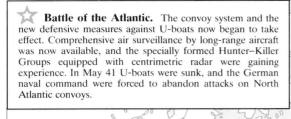

2 **The End in Africa.** Once the Mareth Line had been broken, the war in North Africa had taken on an entirely different aspect. Not only was it no longer a duel between the Eighth Army and the Afrika Korps, for newcomers on both sides swamped the old hands, but the Tunisian terrain forced upon the combatants a different type of tactic. Gone were the opportunities for wide, sweeping attacks and in their place came cautious, probing reconnaissance through steep-sided gully or rock-strewn mountain pass.

For the veterans of Eighth Army it came as an unpleasant shock to realise their experience counted for little; the First Army despite its comparatively recent baptism of fire could operate as effectively as the old desert hands in these closely confined valleys, with limited fields of fire and vertical rock-faces which no tank or jeep driver, however expert, could bounce over.

During the closing days of April, Eighth Army had tried unavailingly to break through the Enfidaville position where

even the 4th Indian Division could make little headway in the opposing hills. It now became quite evident that the main axes for advance lay in the north, from Medjez el Bab towards Tunis, and along the coast to Bizerta – all in First Army ground. Reluctantly, Montgomery accepted that his most important task was now to plan for the invasion of Sicily and that the capture of Cape Bon must lie in other hands. But to ensure that at least a part of Eighth Army would be present, he suggested to General Alexander that he hand over to him 4th Indian Division, 7th Armoured and 201st Guards Brigade – an offer gratefully accepted.

Already, First Army was fighting bitter battles for the hills overlooking the Medjez Gap through which they must pass to reach Tebourba and then Tunis, while US 1st Armoured Division and 34th Infantry ground their way forward towards Mateur, and US 9th Division drove along the valley of the Sedjenane towards Bizerta.

April had thus been a month of unspectacular but bitter fighting; the battles for Longstop Hill overlooking the Medjez Gap were perhaps the grimmest of the whole campaign. May was to reap the profits of that grinding conflict.

On the first day of the month, the Americans in the north under General Bradley broke through along the coast and cut Bizerta off from the south, and by the next day the threatened German forces were pulling back from Mateur, south of the lakes. Then on May 6 Alexander unleashed a massive attack through the central position, by 0900 the way was open for the armour to go through to Massicault, from dawn on May 7 the advance rolled faster and faster and that afternoon to the astonishment of the inhabitants the first armoured cars drove into Tunis. Within hours US tanks were in Bizerta and the next day they met First Army units at Protville; on May 12 General von Arnim surrendered.

The war in North Africa was over.

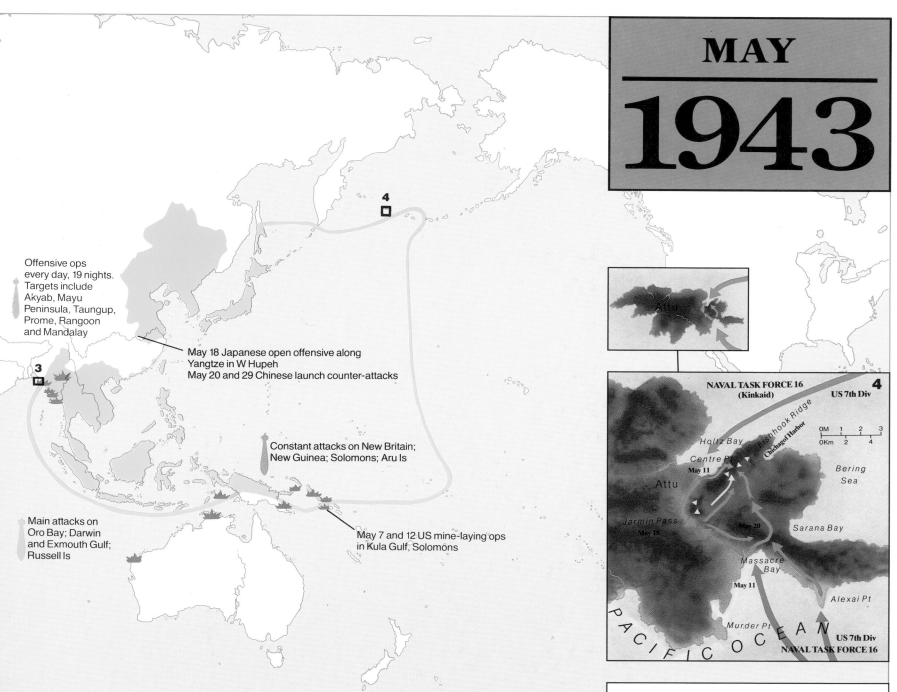

Offensive ops every day, 19 nights. Targets include Akyab, Mayu Peninsula, Taungup, Prome, Rangoon and Mandalay

May 18 Japanese open offensive along Yangtze in W Hupeh
May 20 and 29 Chinese launch counter-attacks

Constant attacks on New Britain; New Guinea; Solomons; Aru Is

Main attacks on Oro Bay; Darwin and Exmouth Gulf; Russell Is

May 7 and 12 US mine-laying ops in Kula Gulf, Solomons

NAVAL TASK FORCE 16 (Kinkaid)   **US 7th Div**   **4**

Holtz Bay · Fishhook Ridge · Chichagof Harbor
Centre P.
May 11
Attu
Bering Sea
Jarmin Pass
May 18
May 20
Sarana Bay
Massacre Bay
May 11
Alexai Pt
Murder Pt
US 7th Div
NAVAL TASK FORCE 16
PACIFIC OCEAN

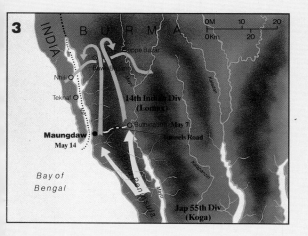

3 **The End in Arakan.** By the beginning of May the survivors of 14th Indian Division were back into and behind the Maungdaw–Buthidaung line, though well aware that the Japanese 55th Division were pressing them hard. General Slim, in the hope of salvaging something from the débâcle, sent down two fresh brigades but once he realised the physical condition of the men of 14th Division he made plans for a further gradual withdrawal.

But on May 3 a battalion of Lancashire Fusiliers was attacked in their positions on the left flank; the Japanese drove through and across the Tunnels road and there was no practical alternative to a hasty withdrawal to the new line curving up from Nhili to Bawli and Goppe Bazars, then down across the Mayu. There, for the moment, the Japanese were content to leave the British almost undisturbed.

The first Arakan Campaign had been a failure for many reasons, the chief being, as Wavell was to admit, that 'a small part of the Army was set a task beyond their training and capacity'. Slim would see to it that such a situation did not arise again.

Later, Churchill was to comment that fighting the Japanese in swampy jungle was 'like going into the water to fight a shark' – but after the war examination of Japanese documents revealed that the British advance down the Mayu Peninsula at the end of 1942, did forestall plans they had been making to occupy Northern Assam.

4 **The Battle for Attu.** The Japanese had occupied the Aleutian island of Attu since the Battle of Midway. On May 11 in thick mist, Admiral Kinkaid's Task Force 16 landed units of the US 7th Division in both Massacre and Holtz Bays, and by early evening both forces had advanced some way towards Jarmin Pass. However by this time the surprise afforded by the morning's mist had gone, Japanese counter-attacks were fierce, and despite the landing of more companies of infantry during the night, junction between the two forces was not achieved.

It was not in fact achieved until May 18, for the Japanese held dominating positions overlooking the valleys and the main pass, and fought off every attempt to dislodge them with efficiency and stubbornness. However, fortunately for the Americans, there were only 2,380 Japanese soldiers on Attu (over 11,000 GIs were to be landed by the end of the month), and gradually the numbers were whittled away. On the night of May 16/17 the Japanese had been withdrawn to concentrate around Chichagof Harbor, which now became the main objective for the Americans.

On May 19 US companies from Massacre Bay and Alexai Point began a drive over the mountains to reach the Sarana Valley and two days later those landed in Holtz Bay attempted to storm Fishhook Ridge. Both attacks ran into strong defences held with fanatical zeal; only massive bombardment from the guns of Task Force 51, which had now joined the naval strength, weakened them sufficiently for US troops to reach the valley leading north to Chichagof Harbor by May 22. On May 25 a converging attack was mounted on Fishhook Ridge from both sides.

For three days the battle raged for the ridge, amid a complex series of trenches and tunnels dug into the hillside; and every Japanese soldier in them had to be killed. When the last of them was dead, leaflets were dropped to the survivors now squeezed into the Chichagof Harbor area, and in reply, at dawn on May 29 the Japanese emerged from their defences and delivered a murderous assault into the US positions in which savage fighting occurred all day.

But by the morning of May 30 it was over. Except for 28 badly wounded, the Japanese defenders were all dead, 500 of whom had committed suicide with their last hand grenades. American losses on one day alone were 550 dead and 1,140 wounded, including a number of men who had gone mad during the frenzy of their first battle with the Japanese.

June 22–July 12
commando raid on Crete

June 18
Announcement
that Field Marshal
Wavell to be Viceroy
of India, General
Auchinleck to take his
place as C-in-C, India

1   The Sicilian Channel. During April and May there had been long discussions on the proposed invasion of Sicily, and in the end General Eisenhower decided that it should at first take the form of a concentrated landing on each side of the Pachino peninsula.

Both naval and air advisers pointed out, however, that the landing-ships and escorts would be extremely vulnerable unless all enemy airfields and bases nearby had been eliminated, so the decision was taken to attempt the destruction by bombing of the vital Italian base at Pantellaria, together with those at Lampedusa and Linosa. If successful, the operation would not only eliminate both submarine and air threats from these bases, it would also demonstrate whether bombing on its own could neutralise a fortress.

Pantellaria is five miles by eight, with sheer cliffs rising out of the sea, and Mussolini had intended that it should be the Italian equivalent of Malta. Twelve thousand troops garrisoned it, its airfield could handle up to 80 fighters, underground hangars and reinforced concrete shelters apparently made the island invulnerable. Lampedusa and Linosa were reportedly as well protected.

As so often, Italian propaganda exaggerated. Bombing began during May and with the end of the campaign in Tunisia, rose to unprecedented heights in the early days of June. More than 3,500 British and American aircraft dropped 5,000 tons of bombs on Pantellaria during the first ten days, and by that time the port was in ruins, the town destroyed, the electric plant wrecked. Shortages of water, food, supplies and ammunition affected the morale not only of the civilian population, but also of the elderly and untried garrison. Nevertheless, the commander, Admiral Pavasi, rejected suggestions that he surrender the island, and assured Rome that 'Pantellaria will continue to resist.'

On the morning of June 11 the invasion fleet bearing the British 1st Division arrived off Pantellaria harbour, and after a 30 minute shelling from the guns of the escorting cruisers and destroyers, the landing-craft proceeded inshore. There was no resistance at all, in fact several Italian soldiers ran down the shore to help the offloading. White flags flew everywhere, the only obstacle to progress was the sad chaos of the Allied bombing.

On Lampedusa, despite Rome's proclaimed confidence that the garrison would 'inflict the greatest possible damage on the enemy!' the invaders were again greeted with white flags and offered any help they needed. By June 20 RAF fighters were operating from the airstrip there, and six days later US P-40 fighters were flying from Pantellaria.

The Air War. Pantellaria was by no means the only target area to feel the weight of Allied bombing during June. The arrival in Europe of B-17 Fortresses in large numbers from the USA, and of Lancasters from British factories at RAF airfields meant that the bombing campaign against Germany could be stepped up and June brought such an increase that for the moment German air defences were overwhelmed.

The Ruhr especially suffered. Düsseldorf, Bochum, Oberhausen, Krefeld, Gelsenkirchen and Wuppertal received over 10,000 tons of bombs during the month, while Cologne, Friederichshafen radar factories and the Schneider works at Le Creusot shared another 5,000 tons between them, all in night raids by the RAF. During daylight hours the USAAF hit Wilhelmshafen, Cuxhaven, Kiel, Bremen and Hüls, dropping altogether 2,458 tons, and although the USAAF lost a number of B-17s the lesson was well learned that daylight raids must be protected by strong fighter escorts.

During June the 'Shuttle Service' was instituted. After bombing the radar factories at Friederichshafen on June 20/21, the Lancasters flew on south and landed in North Africa. Three nights later they returned home, bombing the Italian naval base at La Spezia on the way.

The air war in Russia also rose to new heights of fury. The fiercest battles so far were fought over both the Kuban and Kursk as both sides strove for air superiority for the huge conflicts due to open the next month. In addition, the large centres behind the German Front at Kiev, Roslavl, Orel, Briansk, Gomel and Pskov were hit by the Red Air Force bombers, while the Luftwaffe in turn attacked Volkhov, Yaroslavl and Saratov.

The raids this month were soon to be outclassed in weight and numbers of aircraft, but they gave the first warning of the destruction that could be wreaked from the air.

Destroyers shell Kiska every day, preventing the landing of all supplies except those brought in by submarine

Burma. Raids nearly every day, targets include Maungdaw– Buthidaung area, Mayu Peninsula, Kalemyo, Akyab and Mandalay

Chinese retake Itu, June 3, and break into Ouchinkow and Hwajung, June 30

New Guinea; New Britain; Solomons; Kupang and Lautem; Kendari and Makassar; Waingapu (Someba Is); Tarawa (Gilbert Is)

June 16 Ninety-four Japanese aircraft destroyed for loss of six US planes over Solomons

Bulldog, Port Moresby; Darwin; Russell Is

Trobriand and Woodlark Is occupied without opposition June 22–30

2 New Guinea. Though the Battle of the Bismarck Sea had virtually put an end to Japanese offensive operations in the South Pacific, a combination of weather, lack of craft for amphibious landings and the appalling difficulties of fighting across such country, prohibited any rapid advances by the Allies. General MacArthur's plans for 1943 once Papua and Guadalcanal had been wrested from Japanese control, envisaged twin drives through New Guinea on the left and the Solomons on the right, which would eventually converge on the Bismarck Archipelago and capture the important Japanese bases at Rabaul and Kavieng.

Early in May MacArthur directed the commander of the New Guinea Force, General Blamey, to seize and occupy the Huon Gulf and Peninsula area centred around Salamaua, Lae and Finschhafen, but it was June 29 before the coastal arm of the operation was landed in Nassau Bay south of Lake Salus. From the landing place they moved up to the Bitoi South river before turning west towards Mubo, while one detachment moved south along the coast to secure the area for future landings.

Meanwhile, the 17th Australian Brigade were conducting a holding operation in front of Mubo, awaiting junction with the Americans and the addition of their heavy artillery before mounting a major attack to push the Japanese back towards Salamaua.

3 New Georgia. The drive on the right flank was also delayed until the end of the month, and took the Japanese defenders by surprise. The main garrisons were at Munda on New Georgia and Vila on Kolombangara and these were not immediately threatened by the American first landings.

On June 21 a detachment of US marines was put ashore by ships of Eastern Force near Segi Point, and over the next week these made their way inland towards Viru Harbor. Here on June 30 they were reinforced by more marine units, while at the same time detachments of the 43rd Infantry Division went ashore at Wickham Anchorage on south-east Vanganu island and at Rendova Harbor opposite Munda.

Though the landings were virtually unopposed on land, Japanese aircraft attempted fiercely to hinder them, and several naval actions were fought during the following days.

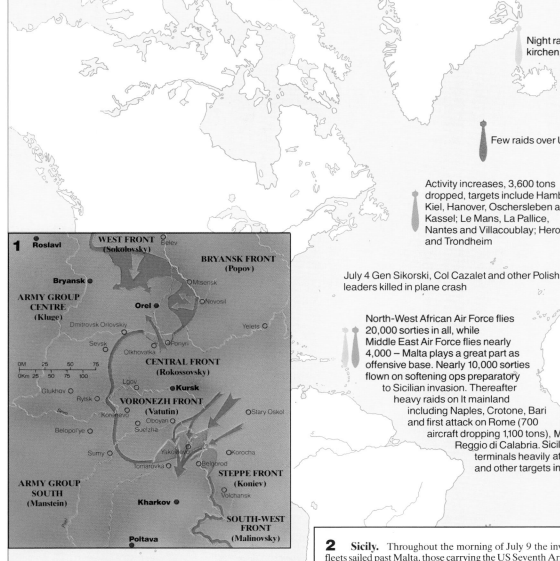

Night raids on Cologne, Gelsenkirchen, Aachen, Hamburg (7,000 tons in raids), Essen (2,000 tons) and Remscheid; Turin (750 tons); Montbéliard

Few raids over UK

Major raids on Gomel, Unech, Roslavl and Orel, NW of Kursk salient and Kerch, Taman and Sennaya to the south

Activity increases, 3,600 tons dropped, targets include Hamburg, Kiel, Hanover, Oschersleben and Kassel; Le Mans, La Pallice, Nantes and Villacoublay; Heroya and Trondheim

July 4 Gen Sikorski, Col Cazalet and other Polish leaders killed in plane crash

July 4–5 Br land forces raid Cretan airfields and withdraw successfully

North-West African Air Force flies 20,000 sorties in all, while Middle East Air Force flies nearly 4,000 – Malta plays a great part as offensive base. Nearly 10,000 sorties flown on softening ops preparatory to Sicilian invasion. Thereafter heavy raids on It mainland including Naples, Crotone, Bari and first attack on Rome (700 aircraft dropping 1,100 tons), Messina and Reggio di Calabria. Sicilian ferry terminals heavily attacked. Shipping and other targets including Crete

1 WEST FRONT (Sokolovsky) — Roslavl, Belev, BRYANSK FRONT (Popov), Bryansk, Mtsensk, ARMY GROUP CENTRE (Kluge), Orel, Novosil, Dmitrovsk Orlovskiy, Yelets, Ponyri, Sevsk, Olkhovatka, Oboyan, CENTRAL FRONT (Rokossovsky), Lgov, Glukhov, Rylsk, Kursk, VORONEZH FRONT (Vatutin), Korenevo, Stary Oskol, Belopol'ye, Suedzha, Sumy, Yakovlevo, Korocha, Tomarovka, Belgorod, STEPPE FRONT (Koniev), Volchansk, ARMY GROUP SOUTH (Manstein), Kharkov, SOUTH-WEST FRONT (Malinovsky), Poltava. 0M 25 50 75 / 0Km 25 50 75 100

1 The Battle of Kursk. Since March all German attention had been focussed on the huge bulge on the map which represented the Kursk Salient. It positively invited attack, and its removal would not only flatten the line, it would also provide a solid strategic base for a drive deep into the Russian heartlands which would prove to the world that the German Wehrmacht was still the most potent factor in the world.

The plan for *Operation Zitadelle* was quite simple. Ninth Army from Army Group Centre would drive down from the north through Ponyri, to meet Fourth Panzer Army from Army Group South coming up from the Belgorod area. Fifty divisions containing 900,000 men would form the original strike force, 20 more divisions would wait in reserve; 10,000 guns, 2,700 tanks and assault guns – including all Tigers and Ferdinands available – would go forward on the ground, while 2,000 Luftwaffe aircraft would ensure total domination above it. 'Victory at Kursk will be a beacon for the whole world,' announced Hitler.

During the early days of July the men, tanks and guns moved to their concentration areas, crowding closer and closer as zero hour approached – 0300, July 5. They were thus extremely vulnerable when at 0200 the massed Soviet artillery and Katushka rocket batteries opened up and blanketed those areas exactly, killing hundreds of waiting soldiers, wrecking signals networks, blasting ammunition dumps and revealing quite clearly that they knew of the German plans in some detail. For the troops thus caught, there was only one escape – forward through the barrage, and into the main Red Army defences.

Ninth Army in the north ran headlong into Soviet Thirteenth, Forty-eighth and Seventieth Armies, Fourth Panzer Army hit the Soviet Sixth and Seventh Guards Armies, all well dug in behind belt after belt of anti-tank defences which first channelled the attackers into killing grounds, then destroyed them.

Over 200 panzers were knocked out on the first day, 25,000 men were killed in the north alone; from the skies 220 German aircraft were shot down. Day followed day as the German divisions battled their way through the defence belts – and when they at last broke clear they ran onto the waiting Red Army infantry and armour. By July 12 Ninth Army had hardly reached Ponyri, while in the south the panzers were still only 20 miles from their start-lines.

On July 15 Central and Voronezh Fronts launched massive counter-attacks which rolled over the devastation of two German armies and within two days had retaken all the lost ground, re-established the lines of the salient, then pushed on towards Orel in the north and Kharkov in the south.

The Battle of Kursk was undoubtedly the greatest tank battle in history; and *Operation Zitadelle* was a disastrous failure of German arms.

2 Sicily. Throughout the morning of July 9 the invasion fleets sailed past Malta, those carrying the US Seventh Army on the west, those carrying the British Eighth Army on the east. Two thousand five hundred ships and landing-craft escorted or were carrying 160,000 men, 14,000 vehicles, 600 tanks and 1,800 guns in what was to that date the biggest amphibious operation in history. They would face an enemy force of nearly 300,000 of whom 40,000 were German veterans of the 15th Panzer Grenadier and the Hermann Göring Divisions.

During the day a typical Mediterranean summer storm blew up to reach gale force by the evening; sea-sickness claimed victims at every rank aboard the transports. Yet despite the weather, in the early evening General Eisenhower decided that the invasion must go ahead and on crowded airfields in Tunisia nearly 150 aircraft began taking off, each towing a glider bearing the officers and men of the British 1st Air-landing Brigade. Two hours later, another 222 C-47s followed them, carrying 3,400 US paratroopers.

Weather conditions wrought havoc among the airborne forces. Only 54 of the British gliders reached Sicily, 40 of the tows wisely turning back, the rest going down into the sea, the men mostly drowned; of the US paratroops, only some 200 landed anywhere near their objective, the rest were scattered over the Sicilian hinterland. Shortly after the last men had dropped and the last glider been released, the wind dropped as quickly as it had arisen, calmness reigned – and the transport fleets approached their landing-beaches.

The British assault waves landed without opposition as the Italian defenders had decided that the weather ruled out any possible danger, but further west the US landing-craft came under fire immediately they approached the beaches. Heavy guns and anti-aircraft fire from the escorting battleships quickly silenced the defences, and both US and British forces were soon probing inshore. They were quickly in touch with the airborne forces who had landed, the US paratroops coalescing into groups to attack Italian posts and all inland traffic, the British force taking the bridge over the river south of Syracuse and hanging grimly on until the main force came up. By the end of the first day the port was in British hands and the coast from Syracuse around and past Licata was firmly held.

When the German troops moved down they were hindered by the airborne forces, and by the time they arrived the Allies had consolidated and were driving north, British up the eastern coast towards Messina, Americans aiming for San Stefano. Within ten days Eighth Army troops reached Enna, two days later Seventh Army had reached the north coast and on July 22 had taken Palermo, taking prisoner thousands of Italian soldiers and welcomed everywhere by delighted Sicilians. On the east coast British units had taken Augusta on July 13, that night commandos and airborne troops captured the bridge over the Simeto and during the rest of the month the combined Allied armies swept the central core of the island clear of Axis troops. By July 31 only the triangle Messina–Catania–San Stefano was still in Axis hands.

2 PALERMO July 22, Tyrrhenian Sea, Termini Imerese July 23, Cefalu, San Stefano, Messina, Trapani, Marsala, Mt Etna, It SIXTH ARMY, Sicily, Enna, Catania July 31, Caltanissetta, Agrigento, July 18, Licata, Gela, Augusta July 13, Syracuse July 10, Ragusa, Modica, Scoglitti. 15th ARMY GROUP (Alexander), US SEVENTH ARMY (Patton), Br EIGHTH ARMY (Montgomery). 0M 25 / 0Km 25. Strait of Messina

☆ **The Fall of Mussolini.** The Italian people had never been enthusiastic about the war, but before Alamein they had at least the hope that their country would emerge from it as well off as when Mussolini took them in. Since Alamein and the series of defeats which followed they had known that if anything was to be salvaged Il Duce and his regime must go. On the evening of July 24 a meeting was convened of the Fascist Grand Council – which had not met for three and a half years – and at it, to Mussolini's discomfiture, the resolution was passed by 19 votes to 9 that all military power, which Mussolini had long since abrogated to himself, should revert to the Crown.

For a few hours, Mussolini was not unduly upset as he was sure that when he took the result of the vote to the King it would be rejected, and he would be told to 'deal with the matter as you think best'. To his astonishment, however, Victor Emmanuel nodded at the news, said he supported it and that he was sure that the Italian people would too. A shocked Il Duce was then led out into a courtyard where he was promptly arrested and driven away in an ambulance.

The next day a new government was formed under the life-long anti-fascist Marshal Badoglio, a new Cabinet sworn in which did not contain a single member of the Fascist Party, and 21 years of dictatorship were at an end.

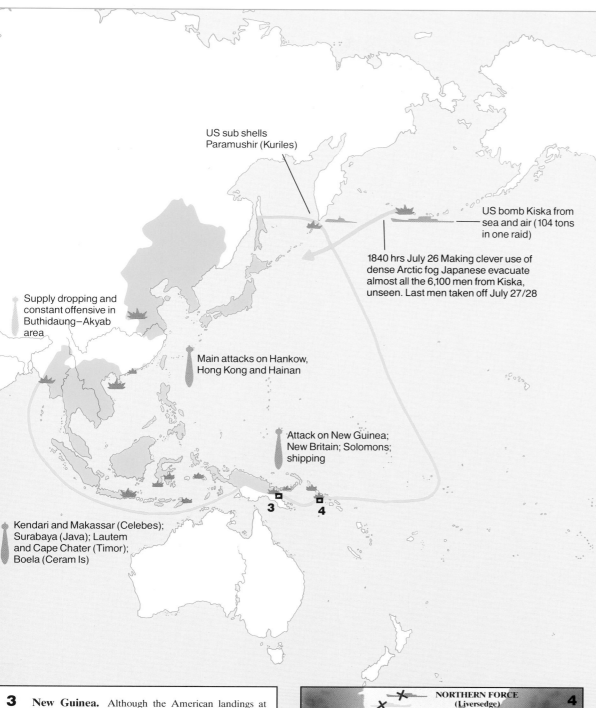

US sub shells Paramushir (Kuriles)

US bomb Kiska from sea and air (104 tons in one raid)

1840 hrs July 26 Making clever use of dense Arctic fog Japanese evacuate almost all the 6,100 men from Kiska, unseen. Last men taken off July 27/28

Supply dropping and constant offensive in Buthidaung–Akyab area

Main attacks on Hankow, Hong Kong and Hainan

Attack on New Guinea; New Britain; Solomons; shipping

Kendari and Makassar (Celebes); Surabaya (Java); Lautem and Cape Chater (Timor); Boela (Ceram Is)

3   New Guinea. Although the American landings at Nassau Bay were virtually unopposed, rough surf and a lack of landing-craft combined to make it a very slow job, so at the beginning of the month a battalion of Australians made their way along the Lababia Ridge and along the Bitoi South to lend assistance. Within a few days matters improved, the battalion began its return accompanied by US infantry and, more important, some units of heavy artillery. With their aid, the attack on the Japanese defences at Mubo was launched and after a week's bitter and grim fighting in the mountainous and unhealthy country, the 17th Australian Brigade forced their way through the Japanese positions, pushing the survivors away towards the next line of defences at Komiatum. Companies from the US 1st/162nd infantry moved on their right flank and by the end of the month the Australians and Americans had closed up to the Komiatum line.

Meanwhile, other battalions of 1st/162nd Infantry moved along the coast, some on foot others by sea, from Nassau Bay to Tambu Bay and by the end of the month were encircling the Japanese positions from the rear and threatening their lines of communication. Once they could get their artillery up on to the Tambu mountains, Salamaua itself would be under fire.

NORTHERN FORCE (Liversedge)
July 4

Kolombangara
Kula Gulf
July 5/6
July 18
July 9
Jap 13th Inf Regt
4th Raider Btn
Vila
Rice Anchorage
Bairoko
Enogai
Tamoko
July 7
New Georgia
July 9
Arundel
July 20-2
Bairoko
Dragon Peninsula
Zaeta
July 17
Zanana
July 7
July 13
Sasavele I
Lulu Lagoon
Laina
Ndume I
Munda
Kia
Llangana
0M 5
0Km 5
July 25
Roviana I
Hathorn Sound

3
Namling
July 24
July 22
Tambu Bay
Huon Gulf
July 25
July 21
Komiom
July 16
July 27
0M 1 2
0Km 2 4
July 12
July 6
L Salus
July 6
July 15
July 3
Bitoi Ridge
Lababia
Bitoi North
Bitoi South
Lababia I
17th Aust Bde
NEW GUINEA

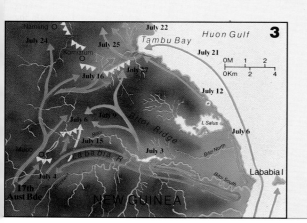

4   New Georgia. During the first few days of July, the US bridgehead on Rendova Island was built up despite continual harassment by Japanese aircraft. Heavy artillery was positioned here and also on Roviana Island just to the north, and on July 3 a concentration of shelling opened from both islands on Munda airfield and the stretch of coast between there and Llagana Point. On July 4, fierce air battles were fought above the entire area, especially over Munda, but so far as American plans were concerned, these were primarily a diversion. That evening US marines landed at Zanana, to be followed the following day by the bulk of the infantry from Rendova.

By now the Japanese Command had begun to appreciate the aims of US forces on New Georgia, and determined to resist them. Their first attempt to reinforce the Munda garrison from Rabaul was turned back by a US naval task force during the night of July 4, but on the next night a force containing ten escort destroyers set out. As they entered Kula Gulf, they were intercepted by a task force of three US cruisers and four destroyers, and in the ensuing battle one US cruiser and three Japanese destroyers were lost, and again the transports retired, though they had managed to put 850 Japanese troops ashore on Kolombangara.

While this battle was being fought, however, some 2,200 US marines and infantry from Guadalcanal had been landed in Rice Anchorage, and despite terrible conditions of rain, mud and tangled undergrowth made their way along trails leading around to Enogai and Bairoko where it was believed Japanese defences existed. By July 7 they had reached the Tamoko river and Enogai, while on the same day to the south, US marines from Zanana had reached the Barike river just north of Laina, having fought off a Japanese company sent out from Munda. Here too the conditions were appalling and exhaustion was taking its toll; not until July 13 was Laina reached and more marines and infantry were brought into a hastily formed bridgehead to give impetus to the flagging advance. They moved out the following day, but again the conditions were dreadful and little advance could be made.

By now more Japanese reinforcements had arrived. On the night of July 9/10, 1,300 Japanese troops crossed from Kolombangara to Bairoko and crossed the Dragon Peninsula to Munda during the next few days. On the same night another 1,200 were landed on Kolombangara and these followed to Bairoko, while on July 12/13 another 1,200 troops were landed on Kolombangara by a convoy which then met US Task Force 18, and lost its flagship *Jintsu* at the cost of one US destroyer sunk, three Allied cruisers damaged.

The troops which had arrived at Munda set out on July 14 on a march to turn the American right flank. It took three days of slogging through the forests to reach the area above the Zanana beachhead, and only the concentrated and miraculously accurate fire of the guns on Roviana and Sasavele held back the Banzai charges. By the morning of July 18 the ground around the base was carpeted with Japanese dead, and later the fringes of the forest were found to be full of Japanese who had died of their wounds.

But Munda was still firmly held by the Japanese in apparently impregnable defences, so more US infantry were brought into Zanana to bring the strength up to two divisions. Marine tank units also arrived to make their laborious ways through the jungle towards the defences, but by the end of the month, although the advance had crept forward along the coast as far as Kia, and inland was driving forwards towards the Lulu Lagoon, Munda and its airfield were still held by the Japanese.

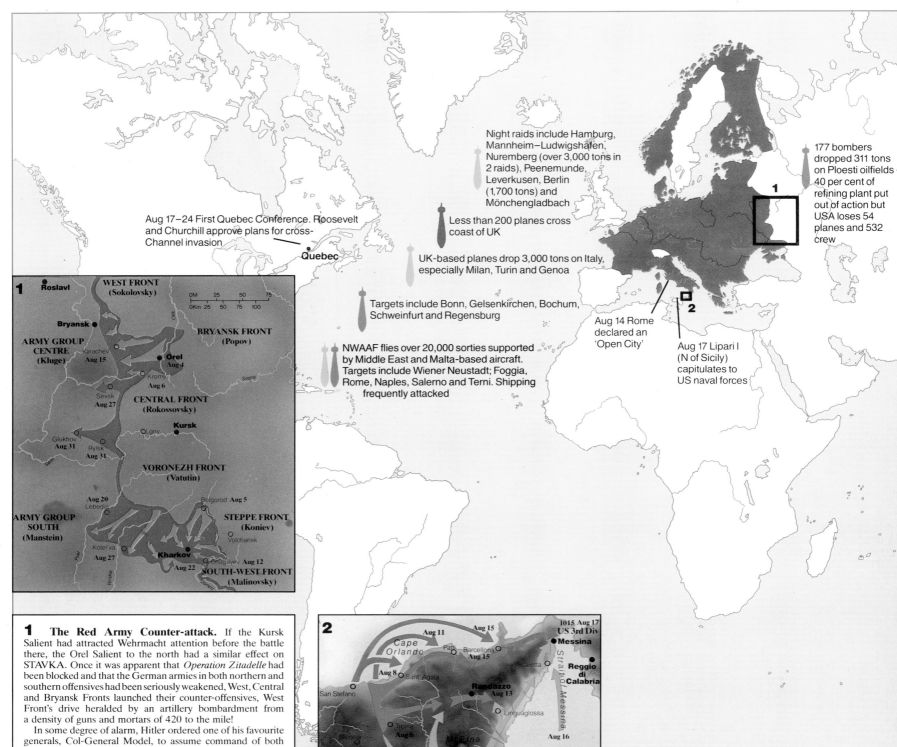

Aug 17–24 First Quebec Conference. Roosevelt and Churchill approve plans for cross-Channel invasion

Night raids include Hamburg, Mannheim–Ludwigshafen, Nuremberg (over 3,000 tons in 2 raids), Peenemunde, Leverkusen, Berlin (1,700 tons) and Mönchengladbach

Less than 200 planes cross coast of UK

UK-based planes drop 3,000 tons on Italy, especially Milan, Turin and Genoa

Targets include Bonn, Gelsenkirchen, Bochum, Schweinfurt and Regensburg

NWAAF flies over 20,000 sorties supported by Middle East and Malta-based aircraft. Targets include Wiener Neustadt; Foggia, Rome, Naples, Salerno and Terni. Shipping frequently attacked

177 bombers dropped 311 tons on Ploesti oilfields – 40 per cent of refining plant put out of action but USA loses 54 planes and 532 crew

Aug 14 Rome declared an 'Open City'

Aug 17 Lipari I (N of Sicily) capitulates to US naval forces

1 **The Red Army Counter-attack.** If the Kursk Salient had attracted Wehrmacht attention before the battle there, the Orel Salient to the north had a similar effect on STAVKA. Once it was apparent that *Operation Zitadelle* had been blocked and that the German armies in both northern and southern offensives had been seriously weakened, West, Central and Bryansk Fronts launched their counter-offensives, West Front's drive heralded by an artillery bombardment from a density of guns and mortars of 420 to the mile!

In some degree of alarm, Hitler ordered one of his favourite generals, Col-General Model, to assume command of both Second Panzer and Ninth Armies on the northern flank – but the Red Army could not now be checked by German orders or promotions. More tank, infantry and guards formations were expertly fed into the battle, by Aug 4 Orel had been emptied of German troops and on the evening of Aug 5 an artillery salute boomed out in Moscow, the first of a long series of such celebrations marking the liberation of major cities from German occupation.

On Aug 5, Central Front units captured the important road junction and supply base of Kromy, and Field Marshal von Kluge reported on the exhaustion and reduced fighting capacity of the Army Group Centre, ending 'It is now a question of getting out of the Orel Salient as fast as possible.' As usual, German rearguard actions were efficiently conducted but by the end of the month the Orel Salient had been flattened, the city of Bryansk now just beyond the main advance.

To the south of the Kursk Salient, Voronezh, Steppe and South-west Fronts had co-ordinated their advances in an exemplary fashion. Having regained the southern line of the Kursk Salient by July 24, they paused to regroup, then on the morning of Aug 3 launched drives down from north of Belgorod towards Kharkov, with a wide flanking move on the right aimed to clear as much as possible of the Psel river-bank.

Belgorod fell early in the attack but German defences here had been well constructed, and the realisation that the loss of Kharkov again would not only be a blow to Wehrmacht prestige but would also severely threaten all German forces left in the Donbass, led to the swift arrival there of three SS panzer divisions – 'Das Reich', 'Totenkopf' and 'Viking'.

But against the Voronezh and Steppe Front formations, now joined by South-west Front units driving in from the Chuguyev district, even this proved of little avail. By Aug 22 the Steppe Front commander, Marshal Koniev, could report his men inside Kharkov and by noon the following day what German forces remained in the city were taken prisoner.

To the west Kotel'va fell on Aug 27 and the line of the Psel was cleared well down past Lebedin. The way was now open for a massive advance to the Dniepr, Kiev and the Ukraine.

2 **The End in Sicily.** It was not to be expected that the final drives towards Messina would be so easy for the Allies as had been the earlier stages of the Sicily campaign. The Axis forces were not just being compressed into the north-eastern corner; following the same tactics as had been followed in Tunisia, the Wehrmacht sent in reinforcements in the shape of the 29th Panzer Grenadier Division and more parachute division formations. Their task was to hold the bridgehead for as long as possible in order to allow the defences in the toe of Italy to be built up, to deny the Allies the ground in which quickly to construct new airfields – and in the end to cover the obviously inevitable evacuation across the Straits of Messina.

As a result, the fighting along the whole line of the Allied advance intensified in ferocity, and in the centre of the island each picturesque little hillside village exacted a high price in German and Canadian lives. The fighting for Centuripe from Aug 1-3 was typical, and after it the left flank of Eighth Army was taken over by 1st US Infantry Division. Even then it needed heavy artillery and air bombardment during four more days for the stubborn panzer grenadiers to be forced out of Troina, and the same measures were necessary to bring about the capture of Adrano. These were the objectives of the left flank of Montgomery's sweep around Mount Etna. Along the coast road, Catania was taken by 50th Division on Aug 5, the XIII Corps advance up and past Acireale was slowed by a trail of minefields, booby-traps and demolitions, and it was Aug 14 before the Highland Division arrived at Linguaglossa.

Meanwhile, General Patton was driving his Seventh Army eastwards along the northern edge of the island. 11 US Corps, reinforced with the newly arrived 3rd and 9th Divisions took part in the heavy fighting for Troina on their right flank, then drove eastwards to arrive at Randazzo on Aug 13, unhinging the German defence and making the British advance along the coast easier.

Along the coast, Patton's 3rd Division took the brunt of the land advance and was greatly helped by a number of seaborne advances which attacked their objectives from the rear. Sant' Agata was the first and was entered on Aug 8, then a more ambitious sweep on Aug 11 outflanked strong German defences running inland from Cape Orlando. Patti fell to 3rd Division and then the widest seaborne sweep gave them Barcellona on Aug 15 – and the following day a seaborne landing on the eastern side of the narrowing corner gave Eighth Army Scaletta; the race between Montgomery and Patton was now very close to the finishing line.

Patton won. At 1015 on Aug 17 he roared into Messina at the head of a motor cavalcade (one of his brigadier-generals and several of his soldiers were already there) and took the surrender of the city and, by inference, of Sicily. 'It was,' announced the first senior British officer to arrive on the scene, as he shook Patton's hand, 'a jolly good race. I congratulate you.'

Montgomery himself was not quite so effusive.

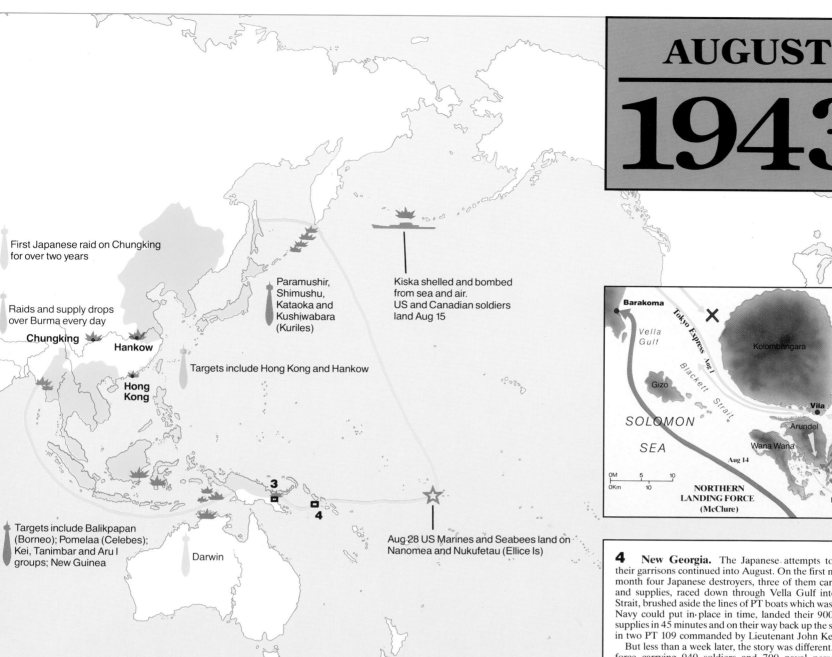

First Japanese raid on Chungking for over two years

Raids and supply drops over Burma every day

Chungking

Hankow

Hong Kong

Targets include Balikpapan (Borneo); Pomelaa (Celebes); Kei, Tanimbar and Aru I groups; New Guinea

Darwin

Paramushir, Shimushu, Kataoka and Kushiwabara (Kuriles)

Targets include Hong Kong and Hankow

Kiska shelled and bombed from sea and air. US and Canadian soldiers land Aug 15

Aug 28 US Marines and Seabees land on Nanomea and Nukufetau (Ellice Is)

NORTHERN LANDING FORCE (McClure)

Barakoma · Vella Gulf · Tokyo Express Aug 1 · Kolombangara · Kula Gulf · Gizo · Blackett Strait · Vila · Arundel · Bairoko · SOLOMON SEA · Wana Wana · Dragon Peninsula · Aug 14 · Aug 24 · Munda Aug 5

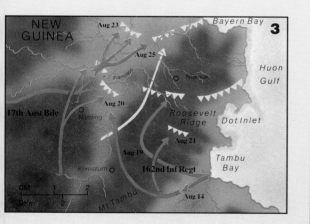

NEW GUINEA · Bayern Bay · Aug 23 · Aug 25 · Huon Gulf · Francisco · Nuknuk · 17th Aust Bde · Aug 20 · Naming · Roosevelt Ridge · Dot Inlet · Aug 21 · 162nd Inf Regt · Aug 19 · Tambu Bay · Komiatum · Mt Tambu · Aug 14 · 3

3   New Guinea. During August the Allied forces brought increasing pressure on the Komiatum line, and as the Japanese defenders became aware of the threat building up in the Tambu Bay area, they tried first to fend it off by hard fighting along Roosevelt Ridge, then as the US artillery reached the top of Mount Tambu, they dropped further back into positions in front of Nuknuk and the maze of tributaries running out from the Francisco river, where they intended to stand and defend Salamaua.

In fact, the Allied commanders had long come to the conclusion that Salamaua was not worth the casualties inevitable in a direct onslaught. With the arrival of the American artillery on Mount Tambu the airfield there would soon be shelled into uselessness, while the town itself had no tactical importance. Lae was the real gateway to the Huon Peninsula, and the sole purpose by mid August of Allied manoeuvrings in front of Salamaua was to lure Japanese troops and supplies forward from the main objective.

Pressure was kept up night and day, but never heavy enough to provoke a main battle. Nevertheless, incessant patrolling edged the Japanese defenders inexorably backwards, threats of seaborne landings – never actually carried out – kept them looking back over their shoulders, and by Aug 25 the line of the Salamaua defences was back to the banks of the Francisco where it ran into Bayern Bay.

4   New Georgia. The Japanese attempts to reinforce their garrisons continued into August. On the first night of the month four Japanese destroyers, three of them carrying men and supplies, raced down through Vella Gulf into Blackett Strait, brushed aside the lines of PT boats which was all the US Navy could put in place in time, landed their 900 men and supplies in 45 minutes and on their way back up the strait sliced in two PT 109 commanded by Lieutenant John Kennedy.

But less than a week later, the story was different. A similar force carrying 940 soldiers and 700 naval personnel was attempting to repeat the previous success, but was hardly into Vella Gulf when it was ambushed by five US destroyers. Within a few minutes the three Japanese destroyers carrying the reinforcement were sinking while their escort fled north and this was the last attempt to reinforce New Georgia. Those Japanese now on the island were on their own.

This had little effect upon their stubborn defence of every post. Along the south coast it was Aug 4 before Munda airfield was in US hands, and although Munda itself was reached the next day, the thousand-odd Japanese troops in overlooking hills had either to be burnt-out of their positions with flame-throwers, or buried alive when the mouths of their caves or dug-outs were blown in. None would surrender.

Along the northern advance, torrential rain and deep swamps had held back the marines and infantry trying to reach Bairoko. A block had, however, been placed across the Bairoko – Munda trail, and on Aug 9 patrols from north and south met there. The main drive then turned north, but for several more days the combination of mud and fanatical defence slowed the advance to a few hundred yards per day. Then with the elimination of the last defences around Munda and the acceptance that no more reinforcements would arrive, the Japanese Command decided upon evacuation. During the nights of Aug 20/22 the survivors of Bairoko garrison were shipped across to Kolombangara, and on the evening of Aug 24 the exhausted and bedraggled marines marched wearily in. The fighting of New Georgia was over.

The next most obvious step would be a landing on Kolombangara, and in preparation for this heavy artillery was emplaced along the western coast of New Georgia and shelling of the area around Vila began. Several days of artillery duels then occurred, and on Aug 27 a battalion of infantry crossed the Hathorne Channel to Arundel, intending to form a small bridgehead from which to advance across the island to the north coast opposite Vila. However, there was a far stronger Japanese force on Arundel than had been calculated and very soon the bridgehead was under tight siege.

Even before this, however, Admiral Halsey had been considering bypassing Kolombangara and landing instead on Vella. Coastwatchers and a reconnaissance patrol confirmed the practicality of this, and in what was very nearly a copybook amphibious operation 6,500 men of Northern Landing Force arrived off Barakoma at 0600 on the morning of Aug 15, and despite several air attacks on the landing beaches during the day, were ashore by the evening. Somewhat to their surprise, they were left in comparative peace for the rest of the month.

1 Advance to the Dniepr. Any doubts the watching world might still have held about the swing in the balance of power on the Eastern Front would surely have been dispelled by the events of this month. By the end of August the Red Army was moving or preparing to move forward along a line over 600 miles long, and its commanders now possessed not only the weapons to arm their cohorts, but the expertise and confidence to guide them into battle, and through the fluctuations of Fortune which would inevitably follow.

Eight Fronts – 3,880,000 men, 70,000 guns and nearly 4,000 tanks covered in the air by 3,750 aircraft, took part in the series of enormous operations which were to take them to the banks of the Dniepr, and back into the Ukraine from which the Red Army had been expelled nearly two years before. And to the south of that gigantic advance, the North Caucasus Front would also drive forward, compressing the survivors of the German Seventeenth Army into the last corner of the Taman peninsula.

If the opening stages of Barbarossa had been the most spectacular military event the world had seen to that date, the Red Army advance to the Dniepr must rank as the most colossal.

The northern flank was held by Kalinin Front under General Yeremenko with West Front under Sokolovsky on his left. At the outset of the advance, West Front would drive for Roslavl, its right wing co-operating with Kalinin Front making for Smolensk whose right flank in turn would drive south to meet them, then swing west to continue the line. Bryansk Front whose first objective was obviously the liberation of Bryansk itself, would then drive across the Desna towards Gomel, Rokossovsky's Central Front on their left driving for Chernigov in the centre, their left wing co-operating with Vatutin's Voronezh Front in the great drive for Kiev.

Steppe Front, South-west Front and South Front were to sweep forward like a huge broom to reach the Dniepr from south of Kiev down to Zaporozhye, while the left wing of Tolbukhin's South Front drove along the shore of the Sea of Azov to reach Melitopol. Beyond the Sea of Azov, Petrov's North Caucasus Front would take Novorossiysk and then drive for Taman and the Kerch Straits.

These blows would fall upon Army Group Centre under von Kluge and Army Group South under Manstein.

The peril in which they stood and the overwhelming force pitted against them was so evident, that Hitler raised few objections to the plans the commanders put forward. These were that while this time every effort would be made to slow the Red Army advance and that every yard of it must be paid for in Russian blood, the retreat to the Eastern Rampart was for the moment inevitable.

This formidable defence line had been under urgent construction since the end of the Battle of Kursk, and its purpose was to ensure that whatever strength the Red Army amassed it would not be sufficient to wrest back from German control the hard-won areas of Western Ukraine and Belorussia. From the north the line ran down along the Narva river, through Lake Chudskoye to Pskov and Nevel, then in front of Vitebsk and Orsha to Gomel and on down along the lines of the Sozh and middle Dniepr to Zaporozhye; then across to Melitopol and the Sea of Azov.

Much of the line had indeed immense natural defences against attack from the east. The Dniepr was deep and fast-running along its middle stretches, in places 1,000 yards wide

Shipping attacked
22 days and 9 nights

Night raids include Berlin (1,000 tons in 20 mins), Mannheim–Ludwigshafen, Munich, Hanover and Bochum; Boulogne, Mont Lucon and Modane

Attacks on UK further diminished

Fortresses and Liberators dropped 5,400 tons on targets including Paris, Nantes and La Pallice; Stuttgart and Emden. US Marauders dropped 2,790 tons on fighter airfields and railway marshalling yards

Sept 19 As a reprisal measure, Boves town burned down by SS. 32 civilians killed

15,000 tons dropped in support of Salerno landings (3,800 sorties in first 4 days) on airfields and communications. Shipping and airfields in Med and Aegean also hit

German garrison in Sardinia embarks for Corsica

with cliff-like west banks rising as much as 300 feet – but with an eastern shore flat, swampy and open. By the time German engineers had been at work (with a considerable force of slave-labour) there seemed good grounds for Hitler's boast 'The Dniepr will flow backwards before the Russians cross it' and in order to deny nothing to its defences he announced that if it were held every man in Army Group South would receive the Iron Cross. Stalin's answer was that the first unit and formation commanders across would become Heroes of the Soviet Union.

Not all fronts opened their attacks on the same date for administrative reasons; obviously not all fronts advanced at the same rate. In the south and the centre important towns were quickly in Red Army hands; in the north Bryansk, though outflanked by Sept 5, did not fall until Sept 17, while it took until Sept 25 to liberate both Roslavl and Smolensk. Chernigov was not in Red Army hands until Sept 21, Poltava until Sept 23; but on Sept 28, to the astonishment and alarm of the German Command, Steppe Front drove in on Kremenchug from north, east and south and despite its garrisoning by the SS divisions 'Das Reich' and 'Grossdeutschland', took it by storm the following day.

The Eastern Rampart had been breached.

2 The Invasion of Italy. By the completion of the campaign in Sicily, the main political and tactical decisions had been taken. The mainland of Italy would be invaded, and the operation would take place in three phases; *Operation Baytown* whereby the bulk of Montgomery's Eighth Army would cross the Straits of Messina on to the toe of Italy, *Operation Slapstick* by which the rest of Eighth Army would land at Taranto on the eastern side of the Italian Peninsula, and *Operation Avalanche* which would put the US Fifth Army consisting of the British X Corps and the US VI Corps, all under command of Lt-General Mark Clark, ashore in the Gulf of Salerno between Amalfi in the north and Paestum in the south. The British corps would land on the left flank, the US corps to the south.

The question which exercised all minds, of course, was the possible strength of the opposition. Would the Italians resist? Would the Germans pull back rapidly to northern Italy if their partners surrendered? Or would every step of the way up the long peninsula be a bitter fight?

High hopes were raised at command level on the morning of Sept 3 when a 'short armistice' was signed in an olive grove near Syracuse with representatives of Marshal Badoglio's government, under which Italian forces would all lay down their arms when approached by Allied soldiers, and the Italian fleet would sail for Malta. As a result, when Eighth Army crossed the Straits of Messina on the same morning they landed without opposition – indeed, some Italian troops even helped unload the landing-craft – while the formations of *Operation Slapstick* occupied Taranto on Sept 9 with only the slightest opposition. By Sept 10 Eighth Army formations were 60 miles along Italy's foot at Nicastro and Catanzaro, the following day they had reached Crotone and raced on to Castrovillari, while on the eastern coast Brindisi had been occupied by Sept 11, and by Sept 22 Bari was taken from the land in order to ensure the safe arrival of 78th Infantry Division by sea. In the meantime the two wings of Eighth Army had met at Potenza on Sept 19.

In front of these Eighth Army drives, the German formations – including some 40,000 men with their weapons and ammunition successfully evacuated from Sicily – had been

steadily and efficiently withdrawing in accordance with orders issued by the newly appointed C-in-C Italy, Field Marshal Kesselring.

He had decided to form his first line of defences to protect Rome, but when the Allied fleets bearing the US Fifth Army arrived off Salerno on Sept 9, the landings threatened the lines of withdrawal at precisely the moment when large forces were drawing level.

As a result, within a few hours Kesselring switched the axis of the retreat and within two days the Salerno bridgehead was virtually sealed in by the German Tenth Army under General von Vietinghoff. By the morning of Sept 13 the Germans had almost split the bridgehead in two, and US staff officers were hastily drawing up plans for evacuation of both corps, but practical difficulties plus the rapid intervention of General Clark put a stop to that. US airborne forces were dropped in, heavy bombing raids were mounted to pound the landward approaches to the bridgehead, and the British 7th Armoured Division was landed. By Sept 16 the bridgehead was safe and expanding to the north, while to the east from Auletta and Potenza in the centre and Bari on the coast, the Eighth Army wings were massing for a drive on the German concentration and supply area around Foggia.

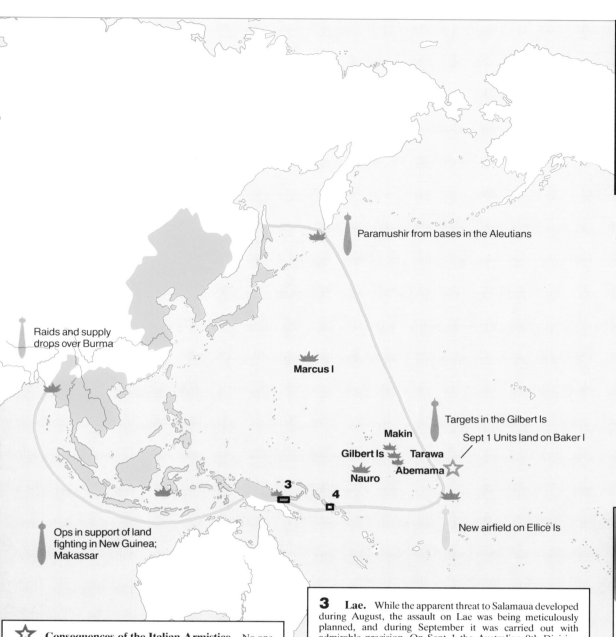

Paramushir from bases in the Aleutians

Raids and supply drops over Burma

Marcus I

Targets in the Gilbert Is

Sept 1 Units land on Baker I

Makin

Gilbert Is   Tarawa

Nauro   Abemama

3

4

Ops in support of land fighting in New Guinea; Makassar

New airfield on Ellice Is

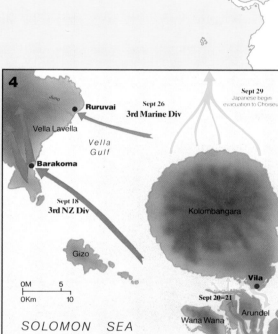

4

Sept 29 Japanese begin evacuation to Choiseul

Juno

Ruruvai   Sept 26 3rd Marine Div

Vella Lavella

Vella Gulf

Barakoma

Sept 18 3rd NZ Div

Kolombangara

Gizo

0M   5
0Km   10

Vila

Sept 20–21

Wana Wana   Arundel

SOLOMON SEA

☆ **Consequences of the Italian Armistice.** No one in the higher reaches of command on either side was particularly surprised when the Italians changed partners. The whole atmosphere of the 45 days of the Badoglio government is perhaps best summed up by Churchill's comment soon after the first, somewhat Machiavellian, negotiations had opened – 'Badoglio knows that he is going to double-cross someone. Let us make sure that it is the Germans, not us!'

The Anglo-American negotiators of the 'Short Armistice' were by no means free of guile. They deliberately gave the impression that they were planning an early descent on the Italian coast north of Rome, with an airborne division dropped on Rome airport, and agreed that they would not announce the Armistice until Sept 12. Badoglio and his staff were thus severely shaken when General Eisenhower released the news on Sept 8, and again when it became obvious that Salerno was the most northern point of the Allied landings – nearly 150 miles short of Rome. Here the German troops, acting with their customary efficiency, were already disarming Italian units and moving in some force to every commanding position.

In Corsica Italian formations held German attempts at bay for a few days before laying down their arms, in Cephalonia (Greece) the Acqui Division resisted fiercely until Sept 23, when the Germans butchered 5,000 of the survivors in revenge, taking their casualty figure to 9,646. Happily, in the majority of cases, the Italian soldiers managed either to give themselves up to the advancing Allies or inconspicuously to slip away homewards.

King Victor Emmanuel and his family, together with Marshal Badoglio and some members of his government, escaped from Rome to Pescara where they were picked up by an Allied corvette, and on Sept 9 the Italian battlefleet sailed from its northern ports for Malta where it surrendered the following day, having lost the battleship *Roma* to Luftwaffe bombing on the way.

By this time, Mussolini had been rescued from his imprisonment on the Gran Sasso by a daring *coup de main* led by Hauptman Otto Skorzeny, and on Sept 23 he proclaimed a new 'Italian Socialist Government' throughout German-occupied Italy, giving over Trieste, Istria and the Alto Adige to direct German control.

Beyond the bounds of the Italian mainland too, the Armistice had its effects. Across the Adriatic the Germans fought a seven-day battle against Mihailovitch's Patriot Army in the Split area while in the Aegean British Special Forces were endeavouring to take control of the Dodecanese Islands around Rhodes. Rhodes itself eluded them, but by the end of the month token forces were on Simi, Stampalia and Ikaria, and quite sizeable formations had arrived on Cos, Leros and Samos.

3   **Lae.** While the apparent threat to Salamaua developed during August, the assault on Lae was being meticulously planned, and during September it was carried out with admirable precision. On Sept 1 the Australian 9th Division (lately back from North Africa) left Milne Bay in massed landing and assault craft, called briefly in at Buna for re-supply and reinforcement, and went ashore on Sept 4 west of the Buhem river and less than 20 miles east of Lae. Within hours they were driving along the coast towards the port while a second brigade fanned out eastwards towards Finschhafen.

The following day the assault developed from the opposite direction. The US 503rd Parachute Regiment was dropped at Nadzab to capture and clear a pre-war emergency landing strip, and the following day the first transports bearing the Australian 7th Division arrived, the first brigade plus the paratroops immediately driving down the Markham valley to attack Lae from the west. Allied planes constantly hammered the area and the Australians around Salamaua switched their pressure to the north. On Sept 11 the Francisco river line was breached and the Australians drove into Lae from all sides, finally to enter the wrecked and dishevelled port on Sept 16.

Immediately, plans for the capture of Finschhafen and the rest of the Huon Peninsula were activated. One brigade of the 9th Division boarded their transports at Lae and by Sept 22 had rounded the Huon Peninsula to land north of Finschhafen, to join in its assault on Oct 2.

Away to the west the Japanese were helplessly fleeing into the mountains, north-west from Kaiapit which a 7th Australian formation had taken on Sep 20, or north across the main range towards Sio.

4   **Vella Lavella.** During the last half of August the men of the Northern Landing Force concentrated on clearing the jungle along the shoreline in order to construct an airfield, and on sending out patrols to find out exactly where the Japanese posts were. They were in fact along the north coast of the island, and the garrisons there were neither large enough to take aggressive action against the landing force, nor likely ever to be reinforced. The only danger to the Allied bridgehead was therefore from air attacks, which occasionally caused damage and casualties.

But Admiral Halsey now decided that Vella Lavella could be transformed into a useful Forward Operating Base, so on Sept 18 the 3rd New Zealand Division under Maj-General Barrowclough was landed at Barakoma, and three days later began a two-pronged drive to the north intended to drive the Japanese into the north-west corner of the island. Though pockets of resistance were encountered, the New Zealanders advanced quite steadily through the rest of the month.

To their north at Ruruvai a mixed formation under 3rd US Marine Division command was put ashore, with the solely constructional purpose of establishing an administrative and communications organisation for the embryo base.

Although the Japanese units in Vella Lavella, Kolombangara and still on Arundel, were ordered to harass the Allied forces as much as possible and to delay any advance they might attempt, Imperial Headquarters had in fact already decided upon evacuation, drawing back all forces in the area to form the strongest possible defence for Rabaul. On Sept 20/21 the last Japanese troops crossed from Arundel to Kolombangara and made their way to the north coast, and on Sept 29 the main evacuation to Choiseul began.

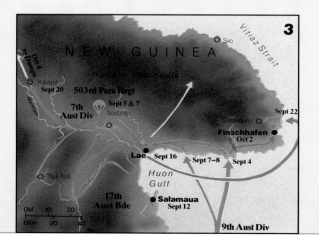

3

Sio

Vitiaz Strait

NEW GUINEA

Kaiapit   Sept 20

503rd Para Regt

7th Aust Div   Sept 5 & 7   Nadzab

Sept 22

Finschhafen   Oct 2

Lae   Sept 16

Sept 7–8   Sept 4

Huon Gulf

0M 10   20
0Km 20   40

17th Aust Bde

Salamaua   Sept 12

9th Aust Div

United States in the Pacific

Since before the First World War American defence staffs had wrestled with the problems of how to defend their interests in the Philippines against an attack by Japan. Since then they had drawn up a series of plans, code-named *Orange*, which envisaged a drive by their Pacific Fleet through the Japanese-mandated islands of the Central Pacific to relieve a beleaguered army garrison, the Philippines, and at the same time to establish US naval control throughout the area.

When war came in December 1941, however, these plans were immediately jeopardised by two unexpected factors. The first was the decision agreed between President Roosevelt and Mr Churchill at their first meeting after Pearl Harbor, that the first priority of the newly united western Allies would be the defeat of Germany, that of Japan to be undertaken later. This in early 1942 apparently predicated a long period of purely defensive measures in the Pacific, holding the Japanese back west of a line running Alaska–Hawaii–Panama.

The second factor was the reality of the astonishing Japanese military expansion which in six months extended the area of Japanese control from the borders of India to Midway, and from the Aleutians to Papua/New Guinea to brush the north coast of Australia. Within weeks of the attack on Pearl Harbor the forward defensive positions which had been earmarked in the *Orange* plans – Wake, Guam, Hong Kong, Manila, Singapore, Burma and the Dutch East Indies – had all been taken by the Japanese while at Pearl Harbor itself, the main implement of the projected American policy – the Pacific Fleet – had been virtually destroyed. A further ingredient of this factor which gave the American planners in 1942 and afterwards much pause for thought was the extraordinary fanaticism and bravery with which the Japanese rank and file, in all three services, would defend their recent conquests, demonstrated for the first time during the epic battle for Guadalcanal.

For a long time the second factor had the effect of negating the first, for however strongly Washington and Whitehall might wish to implement the 'Germany First' policy by transferring men and material across the Atlantic, the sheer immediacy of the danger in the Pacific sucked American resources westwards in order to hold the lines of supply and communication to Australia, the only possible base from which a military – as apart from naval – onslaught could be launched, first to liberate the Philippines, then to invade the Japanese home islands. And once the trend of bulk supplies to the Pacific instead of to Europe had begun it proved very difficult to reverse it, especially in the face of arguments from such powerful personalities as Admiral Ernest J. King who although prepared to pay lip service to the 'Germany First' principle, did not agree with it, or General MacArthur who did not even pay it lip service, except insofar as it affected the direct orders he received from his superiors. For a short time, while it seemed possible that an early invasion of Europe across the English Channel would take place, the US Chief-of-Staff, General George C. Marshall, exercised some curb on the exorbitant demands of his executives in the Pacific, but once it became evident that this was an impracticability at least until the end of 1943, his arguments lost force and more men and material flooded westwards.

In March 1942, it had been agreed between Roosevelt and Churchill that, although Australia and New Zealand would undoubtedly play a part, the war in the Pacific would be an American war. (Britain's war would be the one fought in the Middle East and the Indian Ocean area; the Atlantic and Europe would be shared between them.) As a result of this decision and of the agreed priorities, the islands along the route from Hawaii to Australia – the Phoenix Islands, Ellice Islands, New Hebrides, New Caledonia, and behind them the Samoa and Fiji Islands – were quickly garrisoned and to a small extent fortified, and the ports and cities of the Australian eastern seaboard became the assembly areas for the projected military drives up through New Guinea towards Mindanao and MacArthur's prime target, Luzon.

General MacArthur and his soldiers, however, were by no means to be granted over-riding primacy in the Pacific War. Admiral King and the United States Navy had no intention of yielding the central role they had been allotted in the *Orange* plans, a determination in which they were solidly supported by that highly motivated and prestigious service, the United States Marine Corps. Marching over jungle-clad mountains and island-hopping might be one way to the Philippines, but the route through the Central Pacific still existed and once the crippling factor of Japanese air and naval superiority had been overcome, that way would be open. There was even a third route – and one to take the navy direct to Tokyo itself; from the Aleutians down perhaps through the Kuriles first to Hokkaido and then to Honshu.

By the end of March 1942, the different areas of interest had been recognised, the areas of command delineated. South-west Pacific Area would include Australia, the Philippines, the Solomons, the Bismarck Archipelago, Borneo and the Dutch East Indies east of and including Java, its Commander-in-Chief (CINCSWPA) General Douglas MacArthur. The remainder of the broad expanse of the Pacific in which engagements with the Japanese enemy might take place was named the Pacific Ocean Areas, and its Commander-in-Chief (CINCPOA) would be Admiral Chester W. Nimitz.

However, there were inevitable areas of overlap. Although General MacArthur's area of command was essentially over land, many of the operations which must take place there would require not only amphibious craft, but also naval escort and air cover provided from carriers – and the navy was most unwilling to risk precious carriers and battleships in the dangerous seas north of Australia, especially under command of a soldier; Nimitz, insisted Admiral King, must have command over all naval units, wherever they operated. All services throughout history have had such disagreements with sister services, and this one was ultimately solved in the way all such arguments are – by compromise.

Admiral Nimitz's command was divided into three areas – North, Central and South Pacific. Over the first two he would exercise direct command; over the South Pacific Area – the one most likely to have to act in co-operation with formations under MacArthur's command – he would exercise it through a subordinate area commander, by mid-1943 Admiral William E. Halsey. Admiral Halsey's brief was to act in close liaison with General MacArthur.

So much for the structure. After the Battle of Midway, the turning point in the Pacific War, which caused such losses in Japanese aircraft and surface vessels that she could never again contemplate expansionist tactics that new structure would be subjected to the acid test of converting plans into actuality.

MacArthur's forces in the South-west Pacific Areas were the only ones in actual contact with the enemy in the months immediately after Midway, so the campaign there of necessity took immediate priority. There were several staff discussions and eventually it was agreed that Rabaul should be the main objective for the first phase of the drive back to the Philippines, to be approached by converging attacks through the Solomons and from Australia up through New Guinea/Papua. The first directives issued to MacArthur therefore instructed him to seize the Santa Cruz Islands, Tulagi and Guadalcanal, then the rest of the Solomon Islands and the north-west coast of New Guinea, then to gain control of the whole area of the Bismarck Archipelago.

In the event, the problems presented to MacArthur and his formations in New Guinea so occupied them that the campaign on Guadalcanal was taken over perforce by the South Pacific commander, a development which began to bring home to the planners in both the Pacific and in Washington some realisation of the size of the tasks they had set themselves. As the difficulties presented by the appalling nature of the country over which the fighting would have to take place became apparent, plus the awful climatic conditions and the undreamt-of tenacity of the enemy, so did the extent to which the Pacific theatre would demand ever-greater resources in manpower, aircraft and, even more important, naval transport and shipping.

Moreover, so far as the aircraft and shipping were concerned, plans for the North and Central Pacific Areas as they developed would increase the demands fourfold. Even the ousting of the small Japanese garrisons from the Aleutians entailed the transport of a complete US infantry division to Attu and its supply during a bitter campaign for a whole month. When the campaign through the Central Pacific began, it envisaged an immediate advance through the Marshalls to the Truk–Guam line, with a probable progression north to the Marianas. What would develop after that was at this time still undecided, but there could be no doubt that marines and sailors would be needed in vast numbers, plus the ships to carry them, the aircraft to shield them and the weapons and ammunition to allow them to conquer.

But first Guadalcanal had to be taken against an enemy operating from nearby bases in Rabaul and Truk, throwing reinforcements in with far greater ease than could the United States. During the second half of 1942 Washington was beset by frantic calls for more men, more ships, more aircraft and more weapons and ammunition, and by the end of the year 150,000 more troops had been sent to the Pacific than had been envisaged in April, while half the products of the US aircraft factories had gone there, despite the commitment to the bombing campaign in Europe. And still Japanese troops were fighting on Guadalcanal!

By the time of the Casablanca Conference in January 1943, the US Chiefs-of-Staff had revised their estimates of the strengths they must concentrate for their planned advances towards the Philippines, and despite British fears that their intentions would jeopardise the progress of the war against Germany, they returned to Washington with their programmes virtually intact. Even now, however, they were faced with the fact that in the light of the bitter experience on Guadalcanal and New Guinea, both General MacArthur and Admiral Halsey were demanding more men and more material than ever, and both were disinclined to present any firm timetable for their advance on Rabaul. It was to take some time before either of them felt confident enough of either the strength or the experience of the forces under their command to commit themselves.

However, by April progress was being made and a schedule worked out which the Chiefs-of-Staff accepted as practicable. It would take the rest of 1943 for the drives through the Solomons and along the north coast of New Guinea and Papua to isolate Rabaul, which would then presumably fall early in 1944; after which MacArthur certainly envisaged a progression on through Manokwari to Halmahera or the Celebes and on to Mindanao.

In the meantime, Admiral King was determined to press on with the Central Pacific drive, his plans assisted by the rapid recovery of the strength of the Pacific Fleet as aircraft-carriers slid down the launching ramps of the west coast ports. As for the manpower to crew them and the hundreds of escort ships, he filled the naval

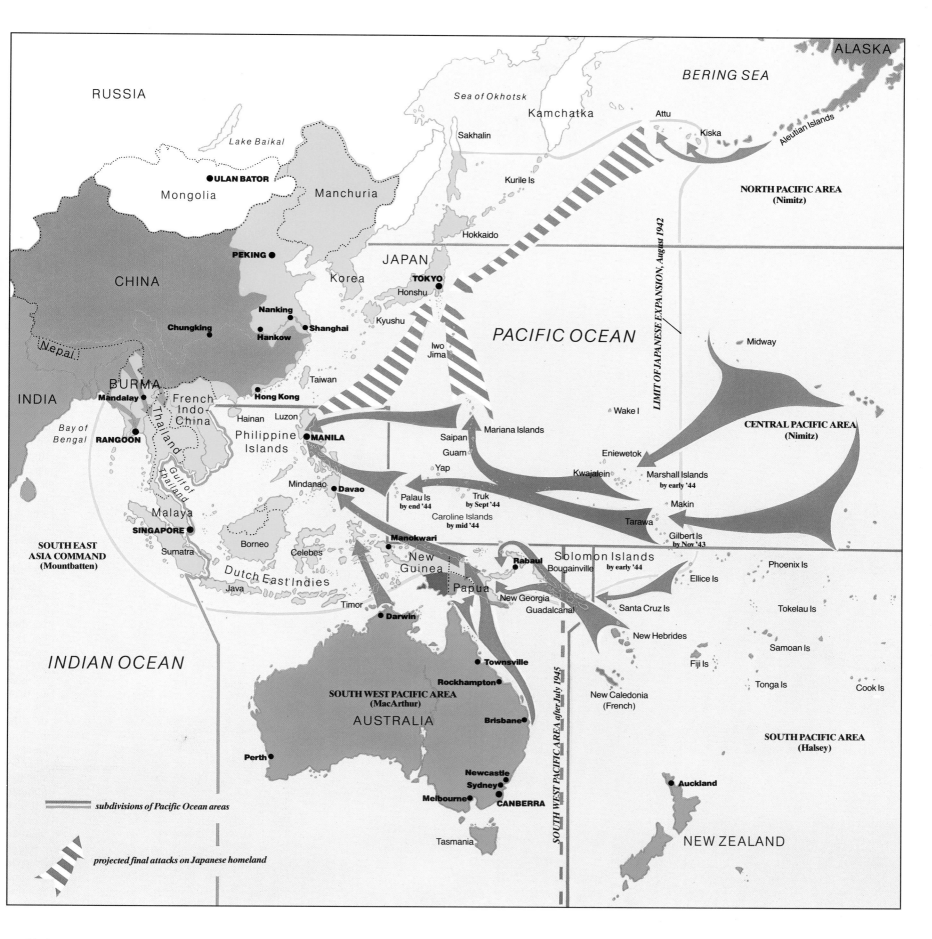

RUSSIA

Lake Baikal

ULAN BATOR
Mongolia

Manchuria

PEKING

CHINA

Nanking

Chungking

Hankow

Shanghai

Nepal

BURMA

Mandalay

INDIA

Bay of
Bengal

RANGOON

Thailand

French
Indo-
China

Hainan

Hong Kong

Taiwan

Luzon

Philippine
Islands

MANILA

Gulf of
Thailand

Malaya

SINGAPORE

Mindanao

Davao

SOUTH EAST
ASIA COMMAND
(Mountbatten)

Sumatra

Borneo

Celebes

Dutch East Indies

Java

Timor

INDIAN OCEAN

Darwin

Sea of Okhotsk

Kamchatka

Sakhalin

Kurile Is

Hokkaido

JAPAN

Korea

TOKYO

Honshu

Kyushu

Iwo
Jima

BERING SEA

ALASKA

Attu

Kiska

Aleutian Islands

NORTH PACIFIC AREA
(Nimitz)

PACIFIC OCEAN

Midway

Wake I

Mariana Islands

Saipan

Guam

Yap

Palau Is
by end '44

Truk
by Sept '44

Caroline Islands
by mid '44

Manokwari

New
Guinea

Rabaul

Papua

New Georgia

Guadalcanal

Eniewetok

Kwajalein

Marshall Islands
by early '44

Makin

Tarawa

Gilbert Is
by Nov '43

Solomon Islands
by early '44

Bougainville

LIMIT OF JAPANESE EXPANSION, August 1942

CENTRAL PACIFIC AREA
(Nimitz)

Phoenix Is

Ellice Is

Santa Cruz Is

New Hebrides

Tokelau Is

Samoan Is

Fiji Is

Tonga Is

Cook Is

SOUTH WEST PACIFIC AREA
(MacArthur)

AUSTRALIA

Townsville

Rockhampton

Brisbane

Perth

Newcastle

Sydney

Melbourne

CANBERRA

Tasmania

New Caledonia
(French)

SOUTH WEST PACIFIC AREA after July 1945

SOUTH PACIFIC AREA
(Halsey)

Auckland

NEW ZEALAND

subdivisions of Pacific Ocean areas

projected final attacks on Japanese homeland

establishments with draftees and laid down training programmes to turn them into sailors with a ruthlessness and thoroughness which would have won the admiration of generations of naval commanders, from Lord Jervis to Lord Jellicoe.

At the Quadrant Conference in Quebec in August 1943, he laid down his timetable for his plans. An assault on the Gilbert Islands would take place in November that year, while the liberation of the Marshalls would occur at the beginning of 1944. Six months later his ships would reach the Carolines, the vital Japanese base at Truk would be taken on Sept 1, 1944, and the Palaus would be in American hands by the end of the year. During the discussions which followed, it became evident that Admiral King had the support of the Joint Chiefs-of-Staff and that, in their opinion, the operations in the Central Pacific held promise of a more rapid advance than those in the South-west Area.

General MacArthur did not agree.

The British representatives at the Quadrant Conference also had grave doubts on some of the aspects of the proposed strategy. Whether or not General MacArthur's historic promise that he would return to the Philippines constituted an All-American pledge, Germany for the British was still the prime enemy, and 'Germany First!' still an Allied commitment. But on this occasion the opinions of both Admiral King and General Marshall were in agreement, and the Pacific operations schedule for 1943/44 was accepted.

Whether they were both fully aware of it at the time, one developing factor was to prove their decision justified, and was also to dissolve the bargaining and bickering between all the opposing factions.

As was already happening in the Soviet Union as a result of the immense industrial and administrative efforts of the early months of the war, the huge potential

of the North American continent was gathering pace towards its apogee. By early 1944, 7,000,000 Americans would be wearing service uniforms, fighters and bombers were pouring from the factories, naval and merchant vessels, from PT boats to aircraft-carriers were joining the fleets in both oceans in ever-greater numbers, and no Allied serviceman would thenceforth go into action inadequately armed.

Japan was about to feel the weight and power of the greatest industrial force the world had seen to that time.

111

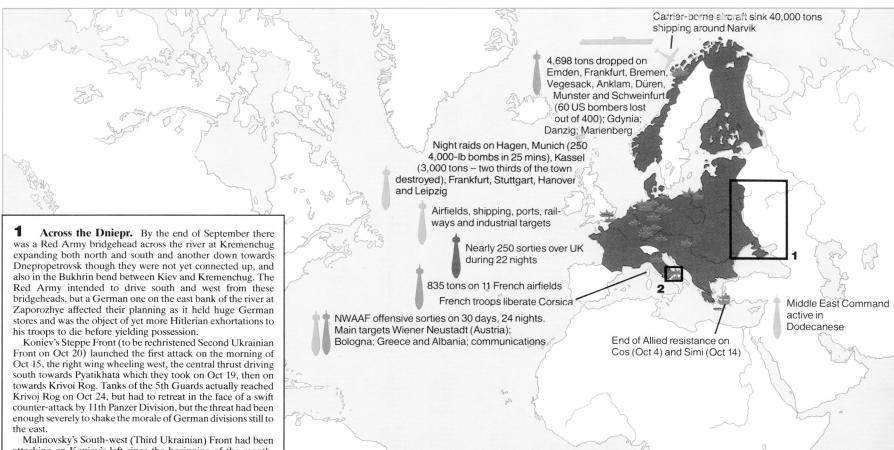

Carrier-borne aircraft sink 40,000 tons shipping around Narvik

4,698 tons dropped on Emden, Frankfurt, Bremen, Vegesack, Anklam, Düren, Munster and Schweinfurt (60 US bombers lost out of 400); Gdynia; Danzig; Marienberg

Night raids on Hagen, Munich (250 4,000-lb bombs in 25 mins), Kassel (3,000 tons – two thirds of the town destroyed), Frankfurt, Stuttgart, Hanover and Leipzig

Airfields, shipping, ports, railways and industrial targets

Nearly 250 sorties over UK during 22 nights

835 tons on 11 French airfields
French troops liberate Corsica

NWAAF offensive sorties on 30 days, 24 nights. Main targets Wiener Neustadt (Austria); Bologna; Greece and Albania; communications

End of Allied resistance on Cos (Oct 4) and Simi (Oct 14)

Middle East Command active in Dodecanese

1 Across the Dniepr. By the end of September there was a Red Army bridgehead across the river at Kremenchug expanding both north and south and another down towards Dnepropetrovsk though they were not yet connected up, and also in the Bukhrin bend between Kiev and Kremenchug. The Red Army intended to drive south and west from these bridgeheads, but a German one on the east bank of the river at Zaporozhye affected their planning as it held huge German stores and was the object of yet more Hitlerian exhortations to his troops to die before yielding possession.

Koniev's Steppe Front (to be rechristened Second Ukrainian Front on Oct 20) launched the first attack on the morning of Oct 15, the right wing wheeling west, the central thrust driving south towards Pyatikhata which they took on Oct 19, then on towards Krivoi Rog. Tanks of the 5th Guards actually reached Krivoj Rog on Oct 24, but had to retreat in the face of a swift counter-attack by 11th Panzer Division, but the threat had been enough severely to shake the morale of German divisions still to the east.

Malinovsky's South-west (Third Ukrainian) Front had been attacking on Koniev's left since the beginning of the month. Zaporozhye was to prove as difficult a nut to crack, and after the first unsuccessful attempts Stalin released Chuikov's Eighth Guards Army (as 62nd Army had been titled since Stalingrad) to help. During Oct 10 another main assault was opened on the bridgehead which ground on until the evening of Oct 13, and that night Eighth Guards smashed their way in. Blowing up the road along the dam and the railway bridge behind them, the German armour and infantry withdrew, and with them went all hope of holding Dnepropetrovsk and Dneprodzerzhinsk to the north, both of which fell on Oct 25. By the end of the month the Red Army had a bridgehead across the Dniepr from Cherkassy down to Zaporozhye, over 200 miles long and in places 50 miles wide.

It did not end there. Between Zaporozhye and the Sea of Azov, Tolbukhin's South (Fourth Ukrainian) Front had been ordered to advance and empty the sack of land between the lower Dniepr and the Black and Azov Seas, at the same time seizing the Perekop Isthmus and cutting off the escape of the German Seventeenth Army. The operation progressed, but slowly in comparison with those to the north. It was not until Oct 23 that Tolbukhin's forces entered Melitopol, whereupon the German Sixth Army retreated north into a heavily-fortified bridgehead around Nikopol, which was later to prove as difficult a nut to crack as Zaporozhye.

Even further south, Petrov's North Caucasus Front completed their operational task. On Oct 9 they chased the last of the German Seventeenth Army out of the Taman peninsula, and the Caucasus was at last completely free of the invader.

2 Italy: the slow drive north begins. The first British troops entered Naples on Oct 1 and the US 82nd Airborne followed them in and took over the city, to be quickly followed by engineers to tackle the extensive demolitions and get the port back into operation. By Oct 6 Fifth Army had closed up to the Volturno river, the British X Corps on the left between Capua and the sea, US VI Corps on the right.

On the night of Oct 12/13 under a powerful artillery barrage, both Corps stormed the river-crossings and by the evening of Oct 14 were across, though on the left the British were held back by the Herman Göring Panzer Division and it took them until the end of the month to reach Teano by which time the Americans were well past Piedimonte d'Alife and driving for Cassino.

On the Adriatic coast, however, the British Eighth Army had had some unexpected success. Foggia, which they had thought would be tenaciously held, was in fact abandoned almost without a fight, the German 1st Parachute Division withdrawing to the line of the Biferno river as they found themselves outflanked by British units driving along towards the coast, Canadians driving for the central positions at Campobasso and Vinchiaturo.

Even before the Parachute Division could reach the Biferno, however, or the XVI Panzer Division which Kesselring was rushing across to help, British commandos of the 2nd Special Service Brigade had landed at Termoli, held the port against every effort to dislodge them until they were reinforced by infantry from 78th Division driving up from Foggia, and thus turned the Biferno line almost before it was formed. The next natural defence line was behind the Trigno river, where Kesselring hastily regrouped his forward units.

The weather and the perpetual problems of supply now imposed a series of checks on the Allied advance. The rain began in mid-October and hardly slackened before the end of the month, reducing roads to swirling rivulets and everything else to swamps. In the centre, the Canadians climbed mountainous waterfalls but by the end of the month had only reached Cantalupo, while despite Termoli being in British hands by Oct 3, it was Oct 22 before Eighth Army formations reached the Trigno – though they did cross it almost immediately, forcing yet another withdrawal on Kesselring's forces.

This withdrawal, however, did not unduly worry the German C-in-C, Italy. Even while the fighting had still been taking place in Sicily, strong defence lines across the Italian peninsula had been reconnoitred and one of these lay just to the north – the 'Gustav Line'.

This was a wide zone in places nearly eight miles across which ran from the mouth of the Garigliano, through Cassino and along the line of the Rapido river, over the heights of the Abruzzi, across the upper Sangro and then along behind it as far as the Adriatic; and during these crucial days when rain had held back the Allied advance, his engineers had completed its defence construction while more German divisions came down from the north to man it, and the hard-pressed troops in front steadily and efficiently dropped back into its protection.

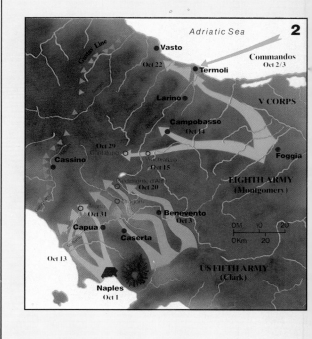

1

KALININ/FIRST BALTIC FRONT (Yeremenko)

MOSCOW

Nevel
Oct 7

Vitebsk

WEST FRONT (Sokolovsky)

Orsha

Mogilev

BRYANSK FRONT (moved north of Nevel to become SECOND BALTIC FRONT) (Popov)

ARMY GROUP CENTRE (Kluge)

Pripet Marshes

Gomel

Loyev
Oct 17

CENTRAL/BELORUSSIAN FRONT (Rokossovsky)

Kursk

VORONEZH/FIRST UKRAINIAN FRONT (Vatutin)

KIEV

Bukhrin

STEPPE/SECOND UKRAINIAN FRONT (Koniev)

Kharkov

ARMY GROUP SOUTH (Manstein)

Cherkassy

Ukraine

Kremenchug

SOUTH-WEST/ THIRD UKRAINIAN FRONT (Malinovsky)

Pyatikhata
Oct 19

Dneprodzerzhinsk Oct 25

Dnepropetrovsk Oct 25

Krivoi Rog

Nikopol

ARMY GROUP A (Kleist)

Zaporozhye
Oct 14

SOUTH/ FOURTH UKRAINIAN FRONT (Tolbukhin)

ODESSA

RUMANIA

Melitopol
Oct 23

Sea of Azov

Oct 9

NORTH CAUCASUS FRONT (Petrov)

BLACK SEA

Crimea

SEVENTEENTH ARMY

Sevastopol

2

Adriatic Sea

Gustav Line

Vasto
Oct 22

Termoli

Commandos Oct 2/3

Larino

V CORPS

Campobasso
Oct 14

Cassino

Oct 29

Oct 15

Oct 20

Oct 31

Foggia

EIGHTH ARMY (Montgomery)

Benevento
Oct 3

Capua

Caserta

0M 10 20
0Km 20

Oct 13

Naples
Oct 1

US FIFTH ARMY (Clark)

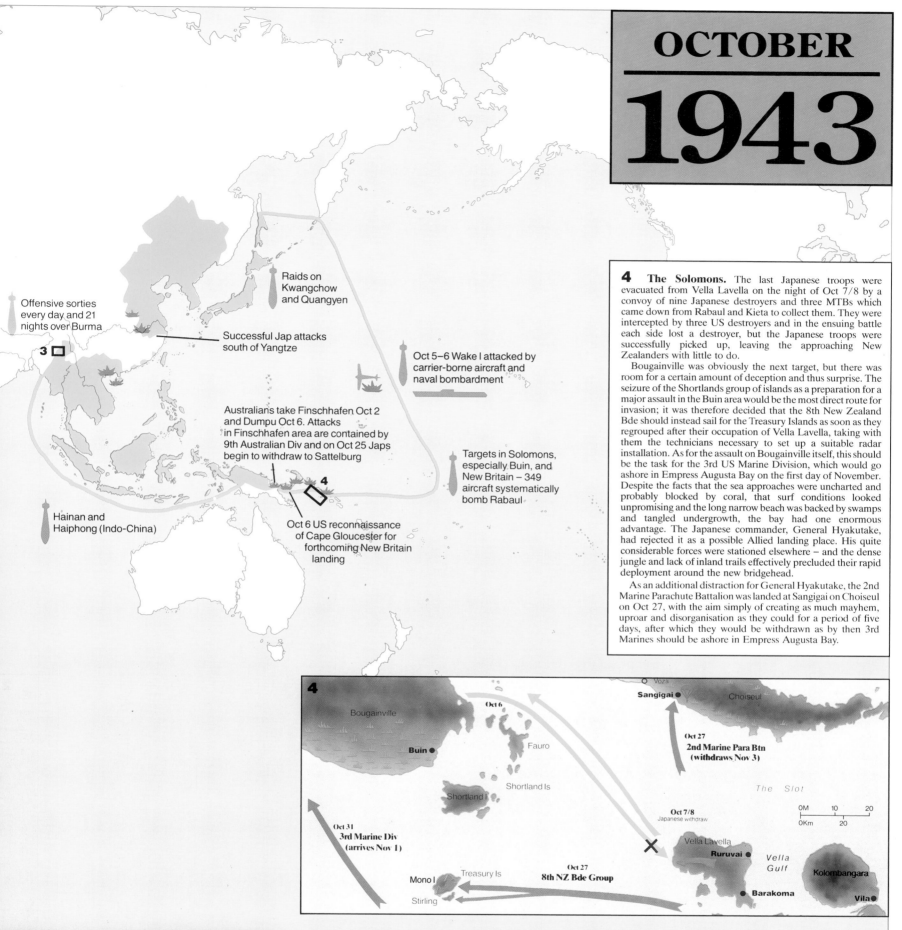

Offensive sorties every day and 21 nights over Burma

3

Raids on Kwangchow and Quangyen

Successful Jap attacks south of Yangtze

Oct 5–6 Wake I attacked by carrier-borne aircraft and naval bombardment

Australians take Finschhafen Oct 2 and Dumpu Oct 6. Attacks in Finschhafen area are contained by 9th Australian Div and on Oct 25 Japs begin to withdraw to Sattelburg

Targets in Solomons, especially Buin, and New Britain – 349 aircraft systematically bomb Rabaul

4

Oct 6 US reconnaissance of Cape Gloucester for forthcoming New Britain landing

Hainan and Haiphong (Indo-China)

4   The Solomons. The last Japanese troops were evacuated from Vella Lavella on the night of Oct 7/8 by a convoy of nine Japanese destroyers and three MTBs which came down from Rabaul and Kieta to collect them. They were intercepted by three US destroyers and in the ensuing battle each side lost a destroyer, but the Japanese troops were successfully picked up, leaving the approaching New Zealanders with little to do.

Bougainville was obviously the next target, but there was room for a certain amount of deception and thus surprise. The seizure of the Shortlands group of islands as a preparation for a major assault in the Buin area would be the most direct route for invasion; it was therefore decided that the 8th New Zealand Bde should instead sail for the Treasury Islands as soon as they regrouped after their occupation of Vella Lavella, taking with them the technicians necessary to set up a suitable radar installation. As for the assault on Bougainville itself, this should be the task for the 3rd US Marine Division, which would go ashore in Empress Augusta Bay on the first day of November. Despite the facts that the sea approaches were uncharted and probably blocked by coral, that surf conditions looked unpromising and the long narrow beach was backed by swamps and tangled undergrowth, the bay had one enormous advantage. The Japanese commander, General Hyakutake, had rejected it as a possible Allied landing place. His quite considerable forces were stationed elsewhere – and the dense jungle and lack of inland trails effectively precluded their rapid deployment around the new bridgehead.

As an additional distraction for General Hyakutake, the 2nd Marine Parachute Battalion was landed at Sangigai on Choiseul on Oct 27, with the aim simply of creating as much mayhem, uproar and disorganisation as they could for a period of five days, after which they would be withdrawn as by then 3rd Marines should be ashore in Empress Augusta Bay.

3   North Burma. Despite the failure of the Arakan offensive and the cost of the first Chindit operation, the decisions had been taken at both the Casablanca and Trident (Washington) Conferences that offensive operations should be opened in North Burma as soon as possible. Then in August Mr Churchill took Orde Wingate to the Quebec Conference where the young brigadier made a strong impression on the American soldiers he met, who now accepted that the British were serious in their intentions of beating the Japanese in Burma.

The help of the Chinese armies would certainly be essential for this, and supplies to them must be maintained. The air route over the 'Hump' from Assam to Yunnan went some way to help, but had obvious shortcomings in that it was vulnerable to Japanese fighters if the planes flew the shortest route, and if they flew far north to avoid them the necessary fuel load cut down the supply tonnage.

An overland route would ease – if not fully solve – the situation, and the simplest solution would be to establish a connection between the Ledo road and the old Burma road

which the Japanese had so successfully cut when they drove north to Lashio. The route for this connection would be across the Patkai mountains, down through the Hukawng valley and on into the Mogaung valley and Myitkyina – and, somewhat to the surprise of the American General Stilwell, the Chinese leader Chiang Kai-shek agreed to release two Chinese divisions – the 22nd and 38th – to pioneer the operation. They would cross the Patkai mountains through the Pangsan Pass and move on down to the Tarung Hka where they would separate and continue southwards in two prongs. Behind the Chinese armies would follow the road-builders, led by American engineers.

The leading formations marched out of Ledo at the beginning of October and met little opposition until the last days of the month, when both prongs came up against the well entrenched Japanese defences on the Tarung river at Ningbyen and Yupbang Ga, and 20 miles to the west at Ngajatzup.

It would need the arrival of Stilwell – at that moment away in Cairo at yet another conference – to get them moving again.

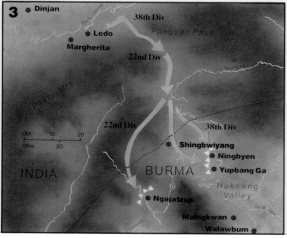

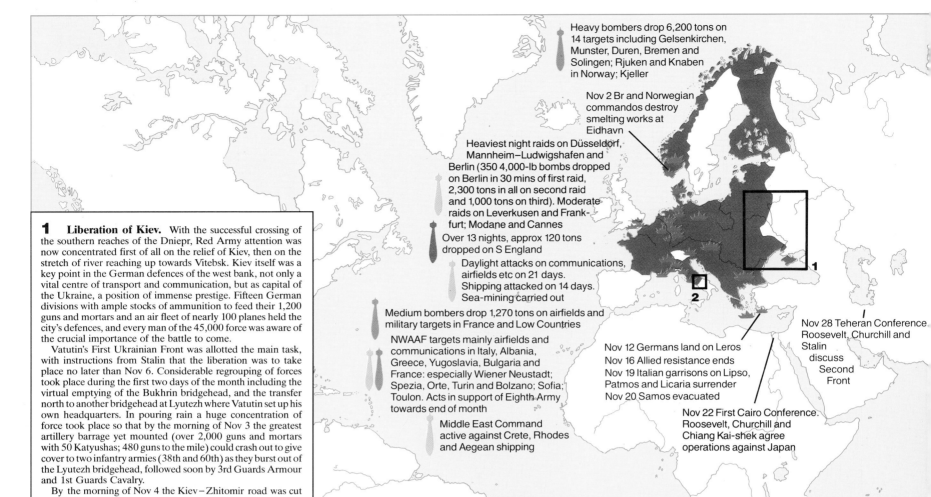

Heavy bombers drop 6,200 tons on 14 targets including Gelsenkirchen, Munster, Duren, Bremen and Solingen; Rjuken and Knaben in Norway; Kjeller

Nov 2 Br and Norwegian commandos destroy smelting works at Eidhavn

Heaviest night raids on Düsseldorf, Mannheim–Ludwigshafen and Berlin (350 4,000-lb bombs dropped on Berlin in 30 mins of first raid, 2,300 tons in all on second raid and 1,000 tons on third). Moderate raids on Leverkusen and Frankfurt; Modane and Cannes

Over 13 nights, approx 120 tons dropped on S England

Daylight attacks on communications, airfields etc on 21 days. Shipping attacked on 14 days. Sea-mining carried out

Medium bombers drop 1,270 tons on airfields and military targets in France and Low Countries

NWAAF targets mainly airfields and communications in Italy, Albania, Greece, Yugoslavia, Bulgaria and France: especially Wiener Neustadt; Spezia, Orte, Turin and Bolzano; Sofia; Toulon. Acts in support of Eighth Army towards end of month

Middle East Command active against Crete, Rhodes and Aegean shipping

Nov 12 Germans land on Leros
Nov 16 Allied resistance ends
Nov 19 Italian garrisons on Lipso, Patmos and Licaria surrender
Nov 20 Samos evacuated

Nov 28 Teheran Conference. Roosevelt, Churchill and Stalin discuss Second Front

Nov 22 First Cairo Conference. Roosevelt, Churchill and Chiang Kai-shek agree operations against Japan

1 Liberation of Kiev. With the successful crossing of the southern reaches of the Dniepr, Red Army attention was now concentrated first of all on the relief of Kiev, then on the stretch of river reaching up towards Vitebsk. Kiev itself was a key point in the German defences of the west bank, not only a vital centre of transport and communication, but as capital of the Ukraine, a position of immense prestige. Fifteen German divisions with ample stocks of ammunition to feed their 1,200 guns and mortars and an air fleet of nearly 100 planes held the city's defences, and every man of the 45,000 force was aware of the crucial importance of the battle to come.

Vatutin's First Ukrainian Front was allotted the main task, with instructions from Stalin that the liberation was to take place no later than Nov 6. Considerable regrouping of forces took place during the first two days of the month including the virtual emptying of the Bukhrin bridgehead, and the transfer north to another bridgehead at Lyutezh where Vatutin set up his own headquarters. In pouring rain a huge concentration of force took place so that by the morning of Nov 3 the greatest artillery barrage yet mounted (over 2,000 guns and mortars with 50 Katyushas; 480 guns to the mile) could crash out to give cover to two infantry armies (38th and 60th) as they burst out of the Lyutezh bridgehead, followed soon by 3rd Guards Armour and 1st Guards Cavalry.

By the morning of Nov 4 the Kiev–Zhitomir road was cut and Red Army infantry were into the outskirts of the city with units of the Czechoslovak Independent Brigade alongside them. The main railway station was in Russian hands by the evening; during the night the German VII Corps HQ pulled out and at 0400 on Nov 6 the message was signalled to Moscow that Kiev, blasted by battle and shamefully ravaged during the months of occupation, was clear of the enemy.

During the next ten days, Vatutin's forces drove west to widen the bridgehead, while to their north Rokossovsky's Belorussian Front strove to keep level. Fastov was taken on Nov 7, Zhitomir on Nov 12, Korosten on Nov 17, Ovruch two days later, Gomel on Nov 26. But soon it became obvious that the advance was spreading out on too wide a front for the forces available – and also that Manstein was concentrating for a counter-attack.

STAVKA warned Vatutin of the dangers, so when the blow fell his defences were strong enough to hold everywhere except at Zhitomir and Korosten, and Kiev was never in danger of renewed German occupation.

By the end of November not only was the west bank of the Dniepr in Russian hands from opposite Mogilev down to Zaporozhye, but the 'sack' between the mouth of the river and the Black Sea had been emptied of the occupiers, the German Seventeenth Army was sealed in the Crimea, and Red Army units had crossed from the Taman peninsula and were threatening Kerch.

2 Approach to the Gustav Line. On the Adriatic coast V Corps continued their slow but persistent drive, the Canadians and British 5th Infantry Division of XIII Corps on their left, clambering along the mountain ridges which constitute the spine of Italy, all still in appalling weather.

With the Trigno river safely behind them British infantry were in Vasto by Nov 5, and on the same day Indian units took Palmoli while, between the two, New Zealanders drove on towards Perano which they reached on Nov 14. In the mountains the Canadians helped by US paratroops forced their way into Isernia on Nov 5, then swung right towards Castel di Sangri, the Sangro river and the deep defences of the Gustav Line behind.

General Montgomery now decided that all his strength would be needed on the coast to force a crossing of the Sangro so he brought the Canadians across to help. On Nov 20 under massive artillery and air cover British, Canadian and New Zealand infantry stormed across to take Mozzogrogna on Nov 28 and Fossacesia on the last day of the month.

But on the western coast of the Italian Peninsula, Fifth Army was already battering against a solid line of defences. From Castel di Sangri in a curve in places as much as ten miles in front of the main Gustav Line, German engineers had constructed a series of forward defences they had dubbed the Reinhard Line.

The centre and commanding position was the Mignano Pass, with the dominating heights of Mount Camino behind it.

During the last days of October General Clark had regrouped the US VI Corps on the right flank of his army, and on Oct 31 he launched a fierce attack which captured Venafro on Nov 2 and threatened to turn the flank of the defences. On the left flank, however, the British X Corps which since Salerno had already lost nearly 40% of its infantry strength, though it managed to take Roccamonfina on Nov 1, then found every route forward totally dominated by German artillery skilfully deployed upon the *massif* of Mount Camino. Throughout the rest of the month, in bitter cold and seemingly unending rain and sleet storms both corps of Fifth Army strove to break the grip which a combination of weather, mountains and German ingenuity had taken on the battle.

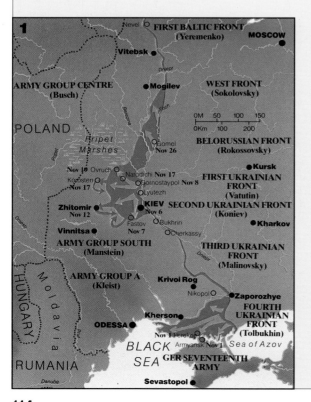

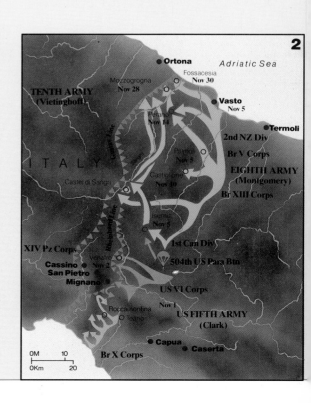

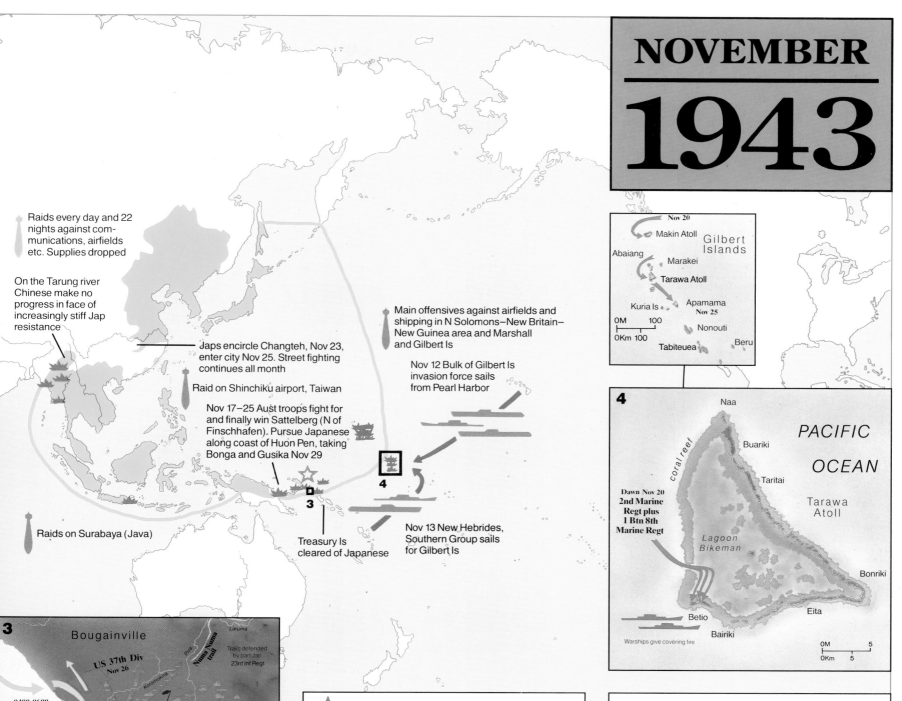

Raids every day and 22 nights against communications, airfields etc. Supplies dropped

On the Tarung river Chinese make no progress in face of increasingly stiff Jap resistance

Japs encircle Changteh, Nov 23, enter city Nov 25. Street fighting continues all month

Raid on Shinchiku airport, Taiwan

Nov 17–25 Aust troops fight for and finally win Sattelberg (N of Finschhafen). Pursue Japanese along coast of Huon Pen, taking Bonga and Gusika Nov 29

Main offensives against airfields and shipping in N Solomons–New Britain–New Guinea area and Marshall and Gilbert Is

Nov 12 Bulk of Gilbert Is invasion force sails from Pearl Harbor

Raids on Surabaya (Java)

Treasury Is cleared of Japanese

Nov 13 New Hebrides, Southern Group sails for Gilbert Is

Gilbert Islands — Nov 20 Makin Atoll, Abaiang, Marakei, Tarawa Atoll, Kuria Is, Apamama Nov 25, Tabiteuea, Nonouti, Beru

4 — PACIFIC OCEAN — Naa, Buariki, Taritai, Tarawa Atoll, Lagoon, Bikeman, Betio, Bairiki, Eita, Bonriki

Dawn Nov 20 2nd Marine Regt plus 1 Btn 8th Marine Regt

Warships give covering fire

3 Bougainville — US 37th Div Nov 26, Laruma, Numa Numa trail, Trails defended by part Jap 23rd Inf Regt, Koromokina, 0400-0600 Nov 7, Part Jap 17th Div Nov 1, Puruata I, US 3rd Marine Div Nov 1, Part Jap 23rd Inf Regt Nov 5, Cape Torokina, US 3rd Marine Div Nov 1, Eastr.-West trail

3 Bougainville.

By dawn on Nov 1 the USN Northern Force ships were off the Empress Augusta Bay shore, and by 0720 the first waves of the 3rd US Marine Division were going ashore while the 3rd Raider Battalion landed on Puruata Island.

To the north-west of the mouth of the Koromokina river, the only hindrance to activities – though it was severe – came from the surf, which wrecked 86 landing-craft that morning. Further east, however, around Torokina, 3rd Marines ran into violent opposition from Japanese strongpoints manned by units which, although astonished by the landings of which they had had no warning, fought with customary Japanese fanaticism. It was mid afternoon before they were all dead, their bunkers flattened or burnt.

Japanese reaction was rapid and soon fighters and bombers were overhead, and a naval force despatched from Rabaul (see Naval Actions).

Ashore the marines gradually forced their way inland through appalling country. A weak Japanese force landed on their left flank on Nov 7 but was easily beaten off as was an attack by part of the Japanese 23rd Infantry Regiment, and by the end of the month the bridgehead was some 7,000 yards deep on a 5,000 yards base.

The Naval Actions.

As soon as news of the landings in Empress Augusta Bay reached Rabaul, a force of two heavy and two light cruisers escorted by six destroyers left to attack the US transports. Their movements were quickly reported by Coastwatchers; shortly after midnight their approach was detected on the radar screens of Rear-Admiral Merrill's Task Force 39, and at 0230 Merrill gave the orders to open fire having achieved total surprise. In the short but violent battle which followed one Japanese light cruiser and one destroyer were sunk, two heavy cruisers and a destroyer badly damaged and the rest chased away. Of 70 Japanese planes which arrived over the bridgehead the following day, 17 were shot down by aircraft from US carriers under command of Rear Admiral Sherman.

As part of the programme to isolate Rabaul, Sherman's force, which included the carriers *Saratoga* and *Princeton*, now deployed for a massed air attack on the port, and on Nov 5 sent 97 aircraft over. They scored hits on six cruisers (including the ones which had escaped from Augusta Bay) for the loss of ten US aircraft, and six days later another attack on Rabaul was mounted. This time 185 planes from the carriers *Essex, Bunker Hill* and *Independence* under Rear Admiral Montgomery took part, and although they only damaged two more ships, the Japanese sent up a large aerial counter-attack and suffered heavy losses in the air battle which followed. From then on the Japanese command realised that Rabaul was too insecure to act as a safe naval base.

November was also the date for opening the Central Pacific drives through the Gilbert and Marshall Islands. Vice Admiral Spruance, with a fleet which contained 6 aircraft carriers, 5 light carriers, 5 battleships, 6 cruisers and 21 destroyers undertook this task and from Nov 19 its 700 aircraft attacked all Japanese airfields within range of Tarawa and Makin Islands – the first objectives for the landing forces.

By dawn the following day, Admiral Spruance's force was deployed in a wide shield to protect the entire operation, and yet another fleet of 8 escort carriers, 7 battleships, 6 heavy and 2 light cruisers and 38 destroyers – all under command of Rear Admiral Hill were in close attendance to the landing force, providing air cover and artillery support.

The days of Japanese naval and air supremacy in the Pacific were over.

4 The Gilbert Islands.

Tarawa consists of a submerged coral reef in the rough shape of an archer's bow which encloses a lagoon into which there is only one channel, near the apex of the bow. Close to this channel is an islet, Betio, upon which the Japanese had constructed the only airstrip in the Gilberts.

Before dawn on Nov 20 the battleships of Hill's fleet opened fire, while marines of 2nd and 8th Marine Regiments clambered down into LVTs (Landing Vessel Tracked), the following waves into LCVPs which, although they held more men and were better armoured, might not clear the reefs. Led by minesweepers and escorted by two destroyers the lines made for the narrow channel, and as dawn broke they were through and turning for the run-in. Carrier-borne aircraft strafed the narrow beaches in front of them, the heavy naval guns pounded the foreshore, shrouding Betio in clouds of coral dust.

A scouting and sniper team were first to land – at a pier they captured and held until supply vessels could come in. On each side the first LVTs clambered across the reef and swanned up the beach, the marines rolling over the sides and racing for the shelter of a coconut palisade. As they reached cover, more shells crashed down in front obliterating two Japanese machine-gun posts, while marine snipers took out the others.

Still at sea the heavier LCVPs grounded on the reefs, the marines slid down into the water and began the awful, slow, open walk to the heavily defended beaches. Despite the mounting casualties, more and more men came over the reefs and through the water. And as the morning passed, then the long afternoon until dusk arrived, it became obvious that more marines than defenders were now ashore, and as supply vessels arrived alongside the pier and discharged heavy weapons and ammunition the initiative inevitably passed to them.

Pack Howitzers were ashore by next morning, destroyers offshore were pin-pointing their targets, two companies of marines broke clean across the airstrip and reached the ocean where they dug in, and now the whole of the western end of Betio was in American hands.

The battle lasted three days and on the last morning 500 Japanese suddenly boiled up out of underground casemates and in 20 minutes of desperate fighting with bayonet and grenade, sacrificed themselves. But by 1312 on Nov 23, Betio was securely in US hands, Tarawa and the whole Gilbert chain soon to follow.

Sinking of the *Scharnhorst*. With the intention of attacking convoy JW 55B to Russia, the German battle-cruiser *Scharnhorst* with five heavy destroyers left her base at Altenfjord on the evening of Dec 25 and by morning was closing on her prey. But from the east three British cruisers were approaching while from the west Admiral Fraser aboard the battleship *Duke of York* with one cruiser and four destroyers was racing in. After an exchange of fire with the three cruisers, *Scharnhorst* turned back but was caught by Fraser and then sunk by a combination of heavy guns from the battleship and torpedoes from the destroyers.

Few raids over UK

7,000 tons dropped in 4 major attacks on Berlin, other major attacks on Leipzig and Frankfurt

Attacks on airfields, railways, industrial and military objectives – especially Pas de Calais

Heavy bombers carry out 10 major operations, drop 12,000 tons – main targets are Solingen, Emden (1,000-bomber raid) Kiel, Bremen (1,200 tons) and SW Germany; Pas de Calais and Paris

Over 1,000 sorties flown on 10 days, targets include Turin, Bolzano, Padua, Dogna and Rimini; Innsbruck; Augsburg

Damaging raid on Bari

Middle East Command bombs airfields in E Med, including Elevsis

Dec 4 Second Cairo Conference. Roosevelt, Churchill and Pres Inönü of Turkey discuss possibility of Turkey entering war

1   The Russian Front. After the enormous exertions of the past three months it would not have been surprising if the Red Army had now to take time for rest and recuperation. In fact, what lull did take place was required for redeployment and the marshalling of even larger forces, not for any form of convalescence. Having smashed their way across the Dniepr, the front commanders were now enjoined by STAVKA to surge on westwards and clear the Western Ukraine completely, sweeping on to the Dniestr and the borders of Moldavia and Rumania, destroying the German Army Groups South and A in the process.

The Four Ukrainian fronts would undertake this mammoth task and as some indication of the forces to be committed, Vatutin's First Ukrainian Front in early December numbered 452,000 men, with 1,100 tanks, almost 6,000 guns and mortars and an air army of 750 fighters and bombers. Altogether 169 rifle and 9 cavalry divisions were deployed from Kiev down to the Black Sea, with over 2,000 tanks in the supporting armoured divisions.

Before they moved, however, there were diversionary manoeuvres to the north. From Nevel down to Korosten the Baltic, West and Belorussian fronts went into action from the beginning of the month, though they had neither the reinforcements nor the weapons replacement which had gone to the Ukrainian fronts. In addition, the weather proved fickle. By December, northern Russia should have been in the grip of fierce frost and ice, rivers and lakes solid, roads and tracks hard as concrete. In fact, the early days brought only a glancing frost, intermittent thaw, slush, mud and sleet. As a result, the swamps, the small rivers and little lakes with which the country between the Dniepr and the Vitebsk-Mogilev line was peppered, were easily defended by the forward units of Army Group Centre, now commanded by Busch as Kluge had been injured in a car accident. At the end of the year, both cities were still beyond the Red Army grasp.

The offensive in the south began in the middle of the month with Malinovsky's front launching attacks towards Kirovograd and Krivoi Rog both of which were for the moment held by Army Group A, committed to defending the metallurgical works at Krivoi Rog and the manganese mines and huge stores at Nikopol.

Then on Christmas Eve, Vatutin's First Ukrainian Front opened their onslaught with a crashing fifty-minute barrage, and three infantry armies swept forward. The same weather conditions as were reigning further north slowed their advance, but by the end of the year Korosten, Zhitomir and Kazatin had been taken and Berdichev outflanked on both sides.

Further south Cherkassy had fallen to Koniev's Second Ukrainian Front, while Tolbukhin's forces had strengthened their positions along both the southern bank of the Dniepr and the approaches to the Crimea.

2   Italy. In addition to the appalling problems posed to both Eighth and Fifth Armies by the weather and the Italian mountains, a decision taken soon after the capture of Naples to move the main USAAF strategic bombing force from Tripolitania to Southern Italy added to their difficulties. Some 300,000 tons of shipping were employed transporting the men and materials needed to instal the US 15th Strategic Air Fleet on the Apulian airfields, mainly around Foggia, and during that period there could be no build-up of land forces to tackle the problems presented them by the Gustav Line.

Nevertheless, Montgomery was determined to try to break through that year. The weather had let him mount a massive artillery and air assault to cover the attacks on Mozzogrogna and Fossacesia at the end of November, and in the next week the Canadians and Indians on the right flank and the British and New Zealanders on the left edged their way forward against comparatively weak but well emplaced defences. Their objectives were Ortona on the coast, Arielli and Orsogna on the left, but every move they made was overshadowed by peaks and every few hundred yards they had to cross streams swollen by rain into small rivers, small rivers raging like big ones.

The New Zealanders reached the centre of Orsogna on Dec 8 but were thrown out again and the town was to remain in German hands for another five months, the Canadians reached Ortona on Dec 20 but then faced a week of ruthless and at times desperate street fighting against German paratroops who had learned their craft on every battlefield from Stalingrad to Sicily. When the Germans withdrew on Dec 27 they left a web of booby-traps, and then took up strong positions only two miles north from which to renew the battle.

On the Fifth Army front matters were no better for the Allies. The Garigliano, the Reinhard Line and then the main belt of the Gustav Line lay in front of them, and every route towards them passed between peaks, all held with skill and determination by German veterans. Mount Camino, Mount la Difensa, Mount Maggiore, Mount Lungo, Mount Sammucro; every one of them would have to be stormed, and if the Allies had on their side an overwhelming superiority in artillery, a powerful supporting airforce and at least numerical superiority in tanks, ammunition had to be brought up along broken and flooded roads, the aircraft could only give useful support if the weather allowed, and tanks were shot to pieces as soon as they entered the passes. Only infantry could move forward in such country and in such conditions, and General Clark could have been forgiven if he had decided to await better weather.

But instead on Dec 3 under the heaviest artillery bombardment that could be mounted, Mount Camino was stormed by British from the south and Americans from the east and by Dec 7 the peak was in Allied hands. Two days later the northern pillars of the Mignano Pass, Mount Sammucro and the neighbouring Mount Lungo overlooking the main road, were both assaulted by divisions of the US 11 Corps, ten days later Mount Lungo was taken, and on Dec 26 Mount Sammucro was in Allied hands.

The Mignano Pass leading towards Cassino was now open to Allied traffic.

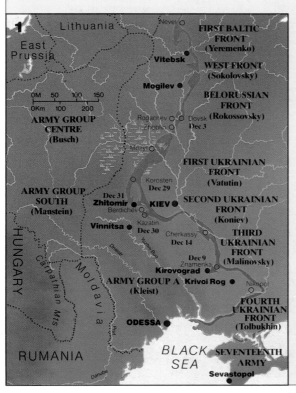

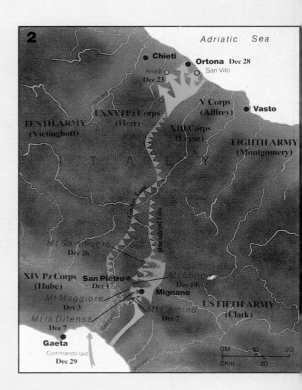

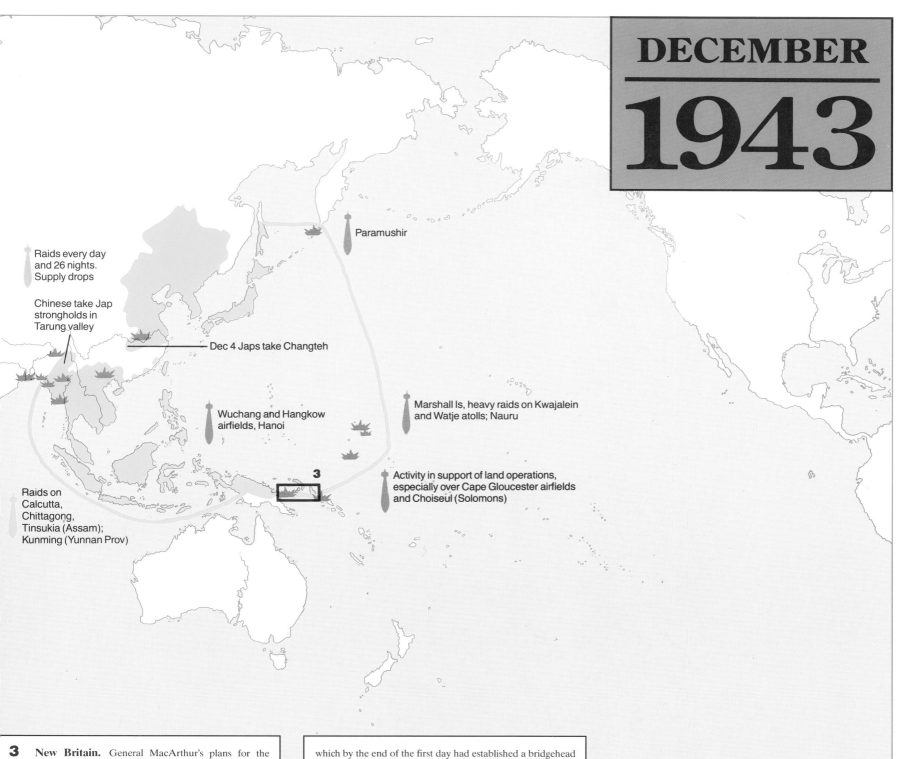

Raids every day and 26 nights. Supply drops

Chinese take Jap strongholds in Tarung valley

Paramushir

Dec 4 Japs take Changteh

Wuchang and Hangkow airfields, Hanoi

Marshall Is, heavy raids on Kwajalein and Watje atolls; Nauru

Raids on Calcutta, Chittagong, Tinsukia (Assam); Kunming (Yunnan Prov)

Activity in support of land operations, especially over Cape Gloucester airfields and Choiseul (Solomons)

3 New Britain. General MacArthur's plans for the isolation of Rabaul were now reaching fulfilment. In addition to the air attacks carried out on the port and surrounding airfields through early November by aircraft from carriers, heavy daylight strikes had also been mounted by the land-based USAAF forces under MacArthur's direction, gradually weakening the Japanese strength available against the amphibious attacks to be launched against the New Britain coast.

For these, control of the Vitiaz and Dampier Straits would be essential, and the clearance of the Huon Peninsula the first step. Having taken Finschhafen in early October, the Australians of 9th Division took Sattelberg after a bitter fight on Nov 25 then moved north to take Wareo on Dec 8 and push on along the coast towards Sio. Inland, the 7th Australians having seized Kaiapit, had moved on to Gusap and Dumpu, thus making it possible for airfields to be constructed in an arc from Tsili Tsili westwards from which air cover could be provided.

Despite all this, however, by mid-December when the first transports left Milne Bay with the US 112th Cavalry Regiment aboard, coast-watchers and intelligence agents were warning of the arrival from Japan and the Philippines of concentrations of bomber and fighter squadrons. There was no doubt that once the landing-beaches for the American forces became evident, they would be subject to fierce air attack.

The objective for the cavalry regiment was Arawe, and on the morning of Dec 15 the men went ashore there against little opposition and by noon the bridgehead was consolidated. But then the Japanese aircraft arrived overhead, and over 100 planes took part in some 400 sorties against the landings. However, warning of their approach from the network of agents made certain that US fighters were there to meet them, and in every strike the Japanese suffered losses. Within ten days the small port at Arawe was sheltering flotillas of motor torpedo-boats, which scoured the waters between New Britain and New Guinea to clear them for the main convoy.

This came up from Milne Bay on Christmas Day, and on Dec 26 landed two combat teams of the US 1st Marine Division

which by the end of the first day had established a bridgehead with a 900 yard perimeter just south-west of Cape Gloucester. Before the end of the year and despite furious air battles fought overhead more 1st Marine Division units and some from 7th Marine Division joined the bridgehead, and the vital airstrip was in US hands, ready for use.

Japanese forces still in New Guinea, New Britain and the Solomons were now isolated, unable to communicate or support each other, subject to increasing starvation of every type of supply, as American control of the air above and the seas around tightened with every day that passed.

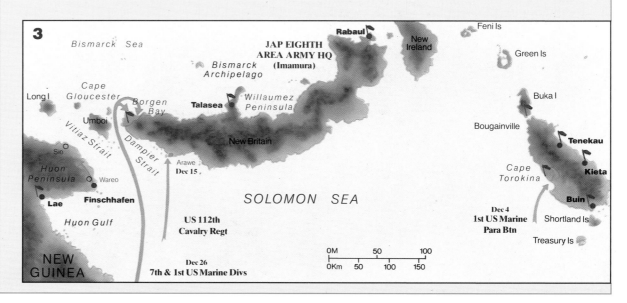

1 **The Russian Front.** Despite the poor conditions, Vatutin's onslaught crashed forward during the first half of January, taking Berdichev on Jan 5, Novgorod Volynsky two days before, threatening Rovno at the end of the month, capturing Sarny to the north and expanding across the Pripet river and taking Mozyr. To the south, they faced a problem. Powerful German forces had been concentrated at Kanev, almost on the border between First and Second Ukrainian Fronts and their destruction could only be carried out by co-operative action by both fronts. But General Koniev at the beginning of January was initially concerned with reaching Kirovograd and then with holding it against furious German counter-attacks; it was Jan 25 before his right flank could launch a drive to meet Vatutin's men attacking from Belaya-Tserkov, which they had taken on Jan 5. Four days later the two wings of the attack met, the German pocket was encircled, reinforcements and heavy artillery arrived to tighten the ring while the Red Air Force pounded the hapless Wehrmacht units unmercifully.

During January, advances had therefore been made from the Pripet down to Kirovograd of between 25 and 75 miles.

Further south, attempts by Malinovsky's Third and Tolbukhin's Fourth Ukrainian Fronts to eliminate the deep salient still existing in the Dniepr bend had petered out in the face of the fierce German determination to hold on to Krivoi Rog and Nikopol, and the eventual Soviet realisation that their capture would necessitate another well planned, massive onslaught.

In the north there had been further advances by Second Baltic Front but far more significant – the siege of Leningrad had been raised and the city, after its 900 days' ordeal, was at last beyond the range of German artillery.

On the night of January 13/14 armies from both Leningrad and Volkhov Fronts attacked under massive bombardments, the first towards Chudovo and then west towards the mouth of the Luga river, the second towards Novgorod. Altogether 375,000 Red Army soldiers with 14,300 guns and mortars and 1,200 tanks covered by ample air fleets drove into positions long held and fortified by Army Group North divisions; but however strong and deep those positions were, they suffered one severe disadvantage. During the previous months – and years – their best and most experienced soldiers had all been bled away to fight in the more important theatres to the south, and now the defences were manned either by elderly soldiers many of whom had been wounded at least once, or by young and inexperienced troops.

The result was that although the strength of the defences held back the flood of Red Army units at first, once the crust was broken and other onslaughts were launched on each side of the first ones – and on the western flank the ships of the Baltic Fleet could contribute over 200,000 heavy shells to the battle – the advance gathered momentum.

Novgorod was occupied on Jan 20 and ten days later Russian spearheads were 50 miles on; Chudovo fell on Jan 29 and two days later the Luga river south of Kingisepp was reached. In Moscow a battery of 324 guns saluted the end of one of the epic sieges of all time.

2 **Italy.** With the way now apparently open for the Allies to advance through the town of Cassino towards Rome, three corps were deployed for the initial attack. Along the coast the British X Corps, reinforced and to some extent rested, would strike north-west through the Aurunci mountains into the Liri valley, while on the right flank the French Expeditionary Corps of Moroccans and Algerians, well skilled in mountain fighting, would drive westwards on a course converging with the British. In the centre the US II Corps would close up to the Rapido river, cross and bridge it for their 1st Armoured Division, who would then break out from the far bank and capture Cassino and the heights above, probably aided by the French coming in on their right.

The French, determined to re-establish the legend of 'La Gloire' advanced without waiting for any zero hour, and had swarmed over the German positions on the flanking mountain-tops to reach the Rapido before the Americans were ready. On the coast, the British were across the Garigliano and into Minturno by Jan 18 and driving for Castelforte on the right, while the 36th (Texas) Division closed up to the Rapido and prepared for the assault.

On the night of Jan 20/21, the Texans launched their attack – but by this time the German defenders had foreseen Allied intentions and were ready. Shell-fire and heavy machine-guns decimated the Texan ranks as they approached the river-bank; those who reached the river boarded the boats – though a quarter of these had already been holed – but few even reached the middle of the river before being sunk. By morning only three platoons were across and although engineers behind them bridged the river, their efforts were soon shot to pieces and the tiny bridgehead wiped out.

Nonetheless, despite both the casualties and the conditions, attempts to press forward continued and by Jan 24 US tanks were across the Rapido, while on the right flank the French launched another spirited attack which took them across the river, on and across the Melfa, then in a curve down between the rivers towards Cassino.

But this pressure along the western flank of the German defences now had a secondary purpose to that of breaking through towards Rome. This was, of course, the main objective, but thoughts of 'Rome by Christmas' had long been abandoned by Allied leaders in the face of such expert and determined German resistance, so a new – or at least different – tactic had been proposed by Mr Churchill. A hook by sea around the western end of the Gustav Line was envisaged, the hurling ashore of a fierce assault force which would drive inland and rampage across the German lines of communication and supply.

By the evening of Jan 21 the fleet of transports and naval escorts was sailing from the Bay of Naples, by midnight the first ships were off the beaches on each side of Anzio, and by the evening of Jan 22 some 45,000 men and 3,000 vehicles were ashore – against negligible opposition, so complete had been the surprise. It seemed that the Alban Hills and then Rome could be theirs for the taking.

Unfortunately, the expedition was commanded by the wrong men. In overall command was General Mark Clark who was still so affected by the crises which had attended the Salerno landings that he warned the Anzio commander, Maj-General John Lucas, 'not to stick his neck out'. As for General Lucas himself, he lacked all enthusiasm for the operation, and as a result, though both the British and US forces at Anzio quickly reached their first objectives and by the end of the month were probing forward, they were then ordered to await 'consolidation' and not advance too far. Thus a great opportunity was lost.

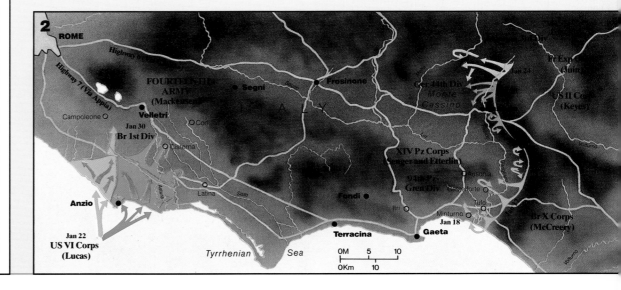

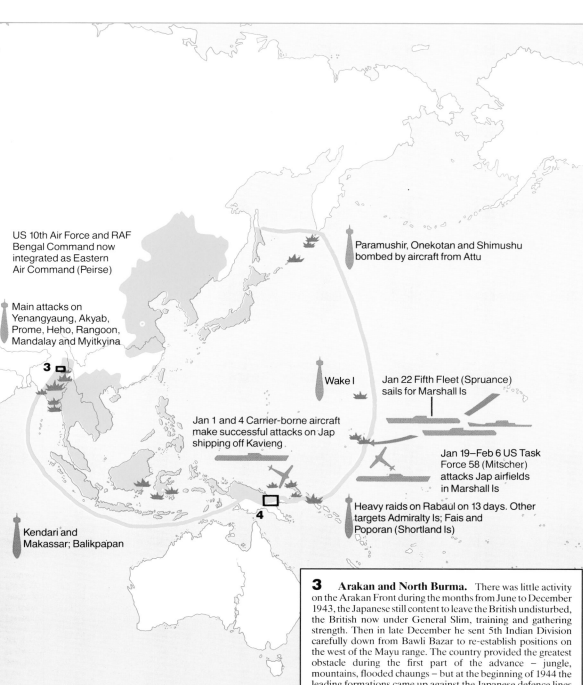

US 10th Air Force and RAF Bengal Command now integrated as Eastern Air Command (Peirse)

Paramushir, Onekotan and Shimushu bombed by aircraft from Attu

Main attacks on Yenangyaung, Akyab, Prome, Heho, Rangoon, Mandalay and Myitkyina

3

Wake I

Jan 22 Fifth Fleet (Spruance) sails for Marshall Is

Jan 1 and 4 Carrier-borne aircraft make successful attacks on Jap shipping off Kavieng

Jan 19–Feb 6 US Task Force 58 (Mitscher) attacks Jap airfields in Marshall Is

4

Heavy raids on Rabaul on 13 days. Other targets Admiralty Is; Fais and Poporan (Shortland Is)

Kendari and Makassar; Balikpapan

Changes in Command in Europe.

By the beginning of 1944, all the crucial decisions regarding the Allied invasion of Europe had been taken. These obviously included the choice of important commanders, and they were ordered to London to take up their posts. General Eisenhower was appointed Supreme Commander, but as the North African Campaign was now closed there was no need to appoint a successor; General H. Maitland Wilson was appointed Commander-in-Chief, Mediterranean.

Air Chief Marshal Tedder accompanied Eisenhower home from Africa as his Deputy Commander, Air Chief Marshal Leigh-Mallory, who was to command the Allied Expeditionary Air Force, was already in England as Commander-in-Chief, Fighter Command.

Command of the field armies in the invasion would go first to General Montgomery during the assault phase, then when sufficient area had been captured to allow the deployment of two army groups, General Omar Bradley would take command of the US group, Montgomery retaining command of the British.

General Montgomery's place in Italy as Eighth Army commander was taken by General Leese who had commanded XXX Corps, General Alexander was appointed Commander-in-Chief, Allied Armies in Italy, with General Mark Clark now given command of both Fifth and Seventh US Armies.

3 **Arakan and North Burma.** There was little activity on the Arakan Front during the months from June to December 1943, the Japanese still content to leave the British undisturbed, the British now under General Slim, training and gathering strength. Then in late December he sent 5th Indian Division carefully down from Bawli Bazar to re-establish positions on the west of the Mayu range. The country provided the greatest obstacle during the first part of the advance – jungle, mountains, flooded chaungs – but at the beginning of 1944 the leading formations came up against the Japanese defence lines still running from Maungdaw across to Buthidaung. For nearly a week a series of small but bitter battles were fought just north of Maungdaw, then a pause was called for regrouping and on Jan 9 the Indians mounted a full-scale attack on the port. To their immense relief they found that during the previous night under cover of darkness, wind and teeming rain, the Japanese defenders had slipped away, and the port – now a grim spectacle of derelict confusion – was theirs. But attempts to move further south were fiercely blocked and the line became static again.

Some 300 miles away to the north-east, General Stilwell was by this time urging on the 22nd and 38th Chinese Divisions in the drives down through the Hukawng Valley towards Myitkyina. By the beginning of January, 38th Division had forced their way into Ningbyen, and to the astonishment of the Japanese commander then pressed on down the river to take Yupbang Ga on Jan 14. The new determination of the Chinese troops and the efficiency of the air supply by the USAAF impressed him considerably, and when he realised that a Chinese formation had crossed the Tarung to the west and was about to cut his forces off at Taihpa Ga, he hurriedly withdrew.

Further west, Stilwell had sent the 22nd Chinese Division down the east bank of the Chindwin to reach Taro by the end of the month, expelling the Japanese from the Taro plain.

4 **New Guinea.** With the 9th Australian Division driving along the northern New Guinea coast, General MacArthur decided to cut off as many of the retreating Japanese as possible, and he sent units of 32nd US Infantry Division (Alamo Force) in a 120-mile seaborne hook from Finschhafen to Saidor. They landed on Jan 2 without loss, occupied harbour and airfields against minimal resistance and then turned east to meet the Australians.

After Sattelberg and Wareo, the problems facing the Australians were largely administrative as their lines of communication and supply were lengthening all the time. They reached Sio on Jan 14 and pushed on further, still fighting the interminable series of skirmishes with Japanese rearguards – though once the news of the US landings at Saidor became known, resistance slackened. Caught between the two pincers, the Japanese troops, weary, starving and ridden with sickness, took refuge in the jungle where even more of them died along the ridges and mountain trails.

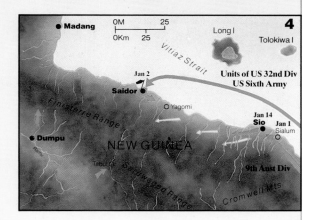

New Britain. The marines' bridgehead at Cape Gloucester had been bitterly contested around the airfield area during the last days of December, but by Jan 2 it was securely in their hands, though its condition rendered it unusable until the engineers could bring in supplies and get to work. In the meantime the marines still faced the prospect of clearing out Japanese defence positions held with their usual fanaticism, amid swamp and jungle and over razor-topped ridges. But slowly, during the rest of January, the bridgehead expanded – the main objective the Willaumez Peninsula and the Talasea airfield, from which the reduction of the Japanese stronghold at Rabaul could be completed.

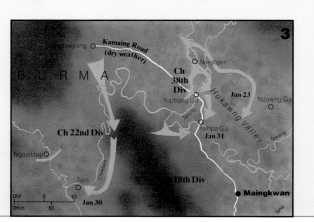

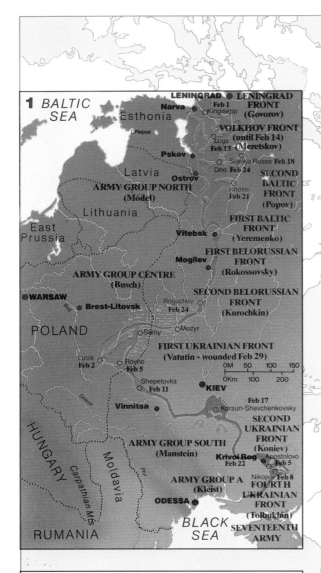

1 BALTIC SEA

Esthonia · Narva · LENINGRAD · LENINGRAD FRONT (Feb 1) (Govorov)

L.Peipus · Luga Feb 13 · VOLKHOV FRONT (until Feb 14) (Meretskov)

Pskov · Staraya Russa Feb 18 · Dno Feb 24 · SECOND BALTIC FRONT (Popov)

Latvia · Ostrov · ARMY GROUP NORTH (Model) · Kholm Feb 21

Lithuania · Vitebsk · FIRST BALTIC FRONT (Yeremenko)

East Prussia · Mogilev · FIRST BELORUSSIAN FRONT (Rokossovsky)

ARMY GROUP CENTRE (Busch)

WARSAW · Brest-Litovsk · Rogachev Feb 24 · Mozyr · SECOND BELORUSSIAN FRONT (Kurochkin)

POLAND · Sarny · Lutsk Feb 2 · Rovno Feb 5 · FIRST UKRAINIAN FRONT (Vatutin - wounded Feb 29)

Shepetovka Feb 11 · KIEV

Vinnitsa · Feb 17 Korsun-Shevchenkovsky · SECOND UKRAINIAN FRONT (Koniev)

ARMY GROUP SOUTH (Manstein) · Krivoi Rog Feb 22 · Apostolovo Feb 5

Nikopol Feb 8 · ARMY GROUP A (Kleist) · FOURTH UKRAINIAN FRONT (Tolbukhin)

ODESSA · SEVENTEENTH ARMY

HUNGARY · Carpathian Mts · Moldavia · RUMANIA · BLACK SEA

0M 50 100 150 / 0Km 100 200

Major night targets are Berlin (2,500 tons – heaviest raid to date), Leipzig (2,300 tons), Stuttgart (2,000 tons) and Schweinfurt

Considerable increase in attacks – bombs dropped on 12 nights, especially on London

24,000 tons dropped during month. Twenty attacks made on 17 major aircraft factories; 22 attacks on airfields. Main targets are Leipzig, Tutow, Bernberg, Gotha, Brunswick, Oschersleben, Halberstadt, and Schweinfurt; Steyr Regensburg

Wilhelmshafen, Frankfurt and Augsburg; Pas de Calais

Marauders drop 3,200 tons on enemy airfields and V-weapon sites

Small-scale raids on 19 German targets and the Gnôme-et-Rhône works at Limoges

Mediterranean ports, railways and airfields in Italy and SE Europe; shipping. Sorties flown in support of Anzio beachhead

Night raids on Finnish targets – Helsinki, Oulu and Kotka

Feb 20 British Admiralty announce air/sea battle lasting 11 days with U-boats attempting to pass through the Strait of Gibraltar

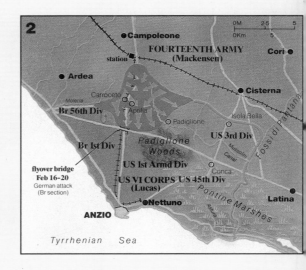

---

1 Russian Front. In the north the advance by Leningrad and Volkhov Fronts, now joined by Second Baltic Front, pressed forward. Kingisepp was liberated on Feb 1, the Luga river crossed, then the Narva river reached and crossed north of Lake Peipus. Luga itself was recaptured on Feb 13, in an administrative move the Volkhov Front was disbanded and Second Baltic closed up to the left flank of Leningrad Front, then to advance and take Staraya Russa on Feb 18 and Dno six days later.

Now the whole northern section of the line moved inexorably westward with the objective of reaching the eastern shore of Lake Peipus, Pskov, the line of the Narva and the extension down to Vitebsk. By Feb 21 Kholm had been retaken, the Red Army held the shore of the lake, Pskov was surrounded and Vitebsk cut off from the north.

To the south, First Ukrainian Front launched another attack, this time from Sarny, which swung south-west in an enormous arc which scythed through behind the German defences to reach Lutsk on the morning of Feb 2 and clear Rovno by Feb 5. Now they were well past the old Polish frontier, almost clear of the Pripet Marshes, the Red Army southern flank threatening the entire area occupied by Manstein's Army Group South and Kleist's Army Group A.

But there were still the matters of the Korsun–Shevchenkovsky pocket based on Kanev, and the point of the huge salient at Krivoi Rog and Nikopol.

All through January the ring around the pocket had been strengthened, the fate of the encircled German formations made more certain. On Feb 8 a formal suggestion that they surrender was rejected, for the next ten days Manstein's panzer and infantry divisions tried unsuccessfully to smash a way through the Soviet ring to the rescue, and the Red Artillery and Air Force continued to pound the encircled men unmercifully. On the night of Feb 16/17 a break-out was attempted in which many senior officers escaped to leave their units to their fate, but the next day resistance ended, 18,200 prisoners were taken. 55,000 Wehrmacht officers and men had been killed or wounded.

Almost as disastrous a defeat overcame the German Army further south. Having paused for regrouping during January, on the last day of that month General Malinovsky's Third Ukrainian Front with Tolbukhin's Fourth launched converging attacks from north-east of Krivoi Rog and south of Nikopol, capturing Apostolovo on Feb 5 and thus splitting the German defending force. Violent counter-attacks were mounted by formations from Kleist's Army Group A, and these blocked further advances southwards by Malinovsky's armies and held open a gap through which most of the Krivoi Rog and Nikopol garrisons escaped. But the vital towns themselves were now liberated by the Red Army – metal works, communication centres and mines back in Soviet hands, though damaged. Another stage in the liberation of the Ukraine had been completed.

2 Anzio and Cassino. Against so expert and imaginative a commander as Marshal Kesselring, the policy of awaiting consolidation invited disaster. While men and material undoubtedly poured ashore at Anzio – and by the end of January 70,000 men were in the bridgehead, with 27,000 tons of stores, 500 guns and 230 tanks – with every day that passed German formations raced closer and not only was an encircling ring clapped around the area, but a counterblow mounted intended to split the Allied force in two, then defeat each in detail.

First of all the British probe towards Campoleone and the US one to Cisterna were blocked and then thrown back, the main area of fighting on the left flank being that between the station and the village of Aprilia. Here on Feb 3 infantry of the British 3rd Brigade found themselves caught between two converging attacks by formations from General Mackensen's Fourteenth Army, pounded by artillery and hammered by violent air attacks.

By mid-morning the German pincers had met, Lucas suggested to the divisional commander that he should pull back, and with the help of the US 504th Airborne Regt and the 1st London Scottish – who had just been landed – a gap was opened through which the survivors withdrew, leaving 1,400 officers and men behind, only 900 of them as prisoners. It was a token of the battles to come.

Showing an awareness of the passage of time sadly lacking in Allied HQ, Mackensen allowed no pause in German attempts to split the bridgehead and reach the sea. Preceded again by air attack and heavy shelling, German panzergrenadiers again attacked the salient from both sides, now driving in towards Aprilia and a farming settlement surrounding a large central building dubbed 'The Factory' by the Guardsmen then holding it.

General Clark visited the bridgehead early on and was worried about the British losses, and as it was now clear that the main German thrust was along the Campoleone-Anzio road, he ordered that a strong defence line should be formed at and around the Flyover Bridge, with US forces moving into and holding the Padiglione area and survivors of the 1st British Division the left flank. Here, on Feb 9, the first German counter-attack was finally halted, but the shell of the Factory was now held by panzergrenadiers, and more and more reinforcements were pouring in from all over Italy to strengthen Mackensen's army. No one doubted that soon another blow would fall on the Anzio defence line.

The strategic position on the Italian Front had now changed. Instead of Anzio relieving pressure on the Cassino Front, extra effort must now be exerted to break the Gustav Line and help the men at Anzio. But the forces at Cassino had now learned the truth behind the basic military maxim that whoever is master of the hills is master of the valleys. Throughout the early weeks of 1944, they strove to push Kesselring's forces off the mountain tops around Cassino, and many mistakenly attributed the bitterness of the task to one factor – a presumed German presence in the vast Benedictine monastery on the very top of Mount Cassino itself.

As a result, after considerable discussion, on the morning of Feb 15, 142 B-17 Flying Fortresses flying in from bases in Sicily and North Africa, dropped 350 tons of high explosive on the monastery of St Benedict, split the building apart and reduced its magnificent interior to ruins.

The following day, the expected German attack fell on the Anzio defences at the Flyover, now held by the US 45th Division with the British 56th on their left. All through the day the fighting increased in ferocity, and the Allied line was pressed back remorselessly. By nightfall it was obvious that the bridgehead itself was in danger and drastic steps must be taken.

On Feb 17, the bombers and fighters which had smashed the monastery deserted the skies over Cassino and appeared over Anzio, concentrating on the area between Campoleone and the Flyover. It was the most concentrated air attack in support of ground forces so far, and although at first its effect was unnoticed, the following day the German assault ceased, the panzergrenadiers withdrew. For the moment, the bridgehead was safe.

2

Campoleone · FOURTEENTH ARMY (Mackensen) · Cori

Ardea · station · Carroceto · Cisterna

Moletta · Br 56th Div · Aprilia · Padiglione · Isola Bella

Br 1st Div · Padiglione Woods · US 3rd Div

flyover bridge Feb 16-20 German attack (Br section) · US 1st Armd Div · Conca

US VI CORPS US 45th Div (Lucas) · Pontine Marshes

ANZIO · Nettuno · Latina

Tyrrhenian Sea · Fossa di Patana

0M 2.5 5 / 0Km 2.5 5

---

3 Arakan. While the 5th Indian Division had been fighting for Maungdaw on the west of the Mayu Range, 7th Indian had prepared to make their own way down from Taung Bazar to Buthidaung to attack the inner end of the Japanese defence line. The advance went quite well until news arrived that as they had advanced, the Japanese 55th Division had cut across behind them to capture Taung Bazar, then drive across to cut the 5th Division's supply routes both in the north and, more crucially, near Ngakyedauk Pass. Quickly and efficiently, an adequate defence force was organised to hold Maungdaw, and the bulk of both Indian Divisions concentrated into an 'Admin Box' near Sinzweya. The engagement then became an exercise in technique.

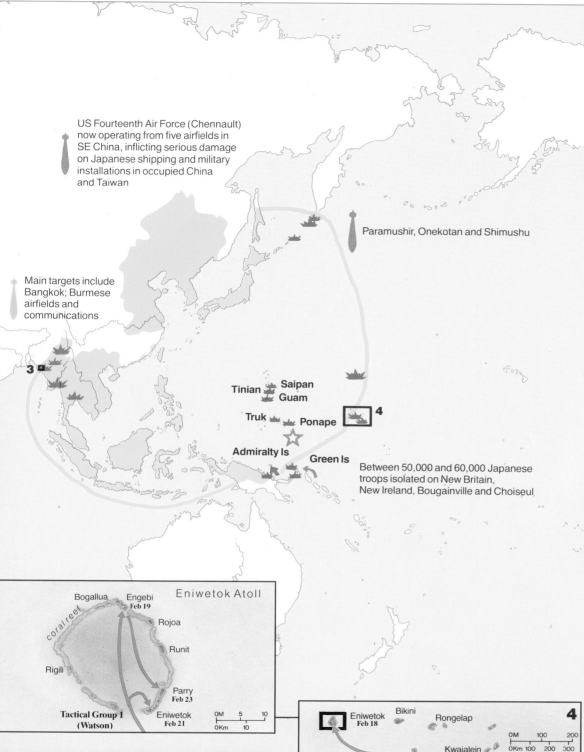

US Fourteenth Air Force (Chennault) now operating from five airfields in SE China, inflicting serious damage on Japanese shipping and military installations in occupied China and Taiwan

Main targets include Bangkok; Burmese airfields and communications

Paramushir, Onekotan and Shimushu

Tinian Saipan
Guam
Truk Ponape

Admiralty Is Green Is

Between 50,000 and 60,000 Japanese troops isolated on New Britain, New Ireland, Bougainville and Choiseul

Eniwetok Atoll

Bogallua Engebi Feb 19
coral reef
Rojoa
Runit
Rigili
Parry Feb 23
Tactical Group 1 (Watson)
Eniwetok Feb 21
0M 5 10
0Km 10

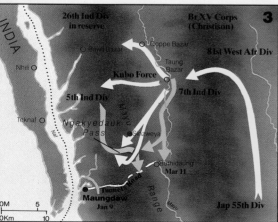

26th Ind Div in reserve
Br XV Corps (Christison)
INDIA
81st West Afr Div
Nhtli
Goppe Bazar
Taung Bazar
Kubo Force
5th Ind Div
7th Ind Div
Teknal
Ngakyedauk Pass
Letwedet
Buthidaung Mar 11
Tuincte
Maungdaw Jan 9
Range
Jap 55th Div
0M 5 10
0Km

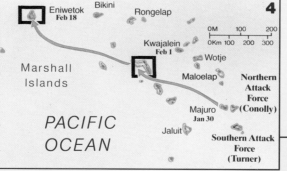

Eniwetok Feb 18 Bikini Rongelap **4**
0M 100 200
0Km 100 200 300
Kwajalein Feb 1
Wotje
Marshall Islands
Maloelap
Northern Attack Force (Conolly)
PACIFIC OCEAN
Majuro Jan 30
Jaluit
Southern Attack Force (Turner)

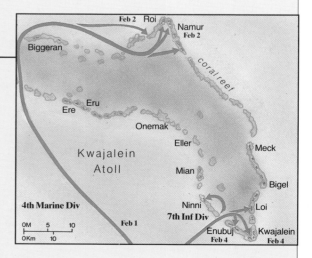

Feb 2 Roi
Namur Feb 2
Biggeran
coral reef
Eru
Ere
Onemak
Eller Meck
Kwajalein Atoll
Mian
Bigel
4th Marine Div
Ninni Loi
7th Inf Div
0M 5 10
0Km 10
Enubuj Feb 4
Kwajalein Feb 4

4 **The Marshall Islands.** There was no doubt in anyone's mind that after the Gilberts, the Marshalls would be the next objective for the US fleets of the Central Pacific Area. There was also a growing confidence that the correct strategy would be to aim for the strongest Japanese garrisons as far west as possible, thus to bypass and isolate the smaller ones and allow them to starve. Moreover, the ever-increasing supply of ships, aircraft, weapons and ammunition – and men to crew and fire them – gave the US commanders a freedom of action not experienced before.

Even before the fleets of transports and escorts left for the Marshalls, all effective Japanese aircraft in the area had been destroyed either in the air or on the ground. Thus when Majuro atoll was attacked on Jan 30 there was no opposition, within days the lagoon was full of US shipping and an airstrip built, and the following day the 4th Marine Division and the 7th Infantry left in a huge convoy for Kwajalein.

Kwajalein atoll surrounds the largest lagoon in the world and consists of countless small islands rising out of the coral reef. Only three were of tactical importance, however: Roi and Namur in the north and Kwajalein island itself at the southern end. Some 297 major vessels carried the two assault divisions, 4th Marines to take the northern islands, 7th Infantry the southern – and during the first hours Task Force 58 would join the preliminary barrage with fast aircraft-carriers and accompanying warships, before sailing westwards to provide a screen against Japanese interference from Truk.

The result was foregone. The dazed defenders of Roi could do little to resist the marines as they landed, or much during their progress across the island; by 1800 the island was taken. On Namur thick jungle absorbed some of the bombardment and hid the defence posts; but overwhelming force and expertise overcame Japanese resistance and both islands were cleared by Feb 2.

On Kwajalein itself a combination of mortar fire, demolitions and flame-throwers blasted the defence away in front of the 7th Infantry, though it took until Feb 4 before they had combed through the entire three-mile length of the island.

Eniwetok lies some 325 miles north-west of Roi and was not scheduled for attack until May I, but with the rapid successes on Kwajalein Admiral Nimitz agreed to a suggestion that there should be no pause in operations. With Japanese interference from Truk virtually ruled out (see below) the attack force left Kwajalein on Feb 17, sailed through the lagoon entrance early the following morning and by 0800 had put two battalions of marines ashore on Engebi. By evening the island was over-run and during the night the last Japanese snipers killed; by next morning the fleets had returned to the south of the lagoon and were plastering Eniwetok and Parry islands. Jungle and defence posts held up the 106th Infantry, but not for long, and by Feb 23 both islands were safely in US hands.

Feb 12. Allied troops occupied Rooke Is between New Britain and Huon Peninsula. US troops took Gorissi, 21 miles east of Cape Gloucester, and reinforcements poured into Cape Gloucester behind them.

Feb 14. 3rd New Zealand Division occupied Green Islands.

Feb 15. Japanese convoy attacked and damaged by US bombers NW of New Ireland. During following days the attacks continued and by Feb 19 the entire convoy was sunk.

Feb 16. Task Force 58 mounted huge attack on Truk, the vital Japanese harbour and base. Within 24 hours US shelling and bombing had destroyed 260 Japanese aircraft, sunk 2 light cruisers, 3 auxiliary cruisers, 4 destroyers, 2 submarine tenders, an armed trawler, a plane ferry and 24 merchantmen. US losses were 25 aircraft and 29 aircrew. This was the most shattering blow yet delivered against the Japanese Navy.

Feb 23. With the Marshall Islands now almost completely under US control and the Carolines rendered impotent by the elimination for the time being of Truk, the temptation to range even deeper into hitherto Japanese controlled waters was irresistible. To the north lay the Marianas, and as Task Force 58 drew away from Truk, its commander accepted the challenge. Within a week of the Truk attack the force was off Guam and

Both Indian divisions were well trained, well led and of sound morale, and fought off every attack with cool success. First attempts to supply them by air were beaten off by Japanese fighters, and two attempts to relieve them were blocked. But every day more Allied aircraft appeared, food and ammunition was dropped in on Feb 11 and from then on quite regularly, and on Feb 25 a relieving brigade broke through 'Okeydoke Pass' as the troops called it, and at the end of the month the Japanese called off the siege and withdrew.

Buthidaung was taken by 7th Indian Division on March 11 and it soon became evident that there was little to prevent an advance down the whole peninsula and on to Akyab. The days of Japanese dominance in jungle fighting were gone.

shelling and bombing the base there, and during the rest of the day the aircraft-carriers cruised implacably northwards, their aircraft bombing and strafing the Japanese installations on Rota, Tinian and Saipan. The US naval plan for the Central Pacific was proceeding very well.

Feb 29. A strong reconnaissance strike force landed at Los Negros on the Admiralty Islands to capture Momote airstrip, and form a small but impregnable bridgehead.

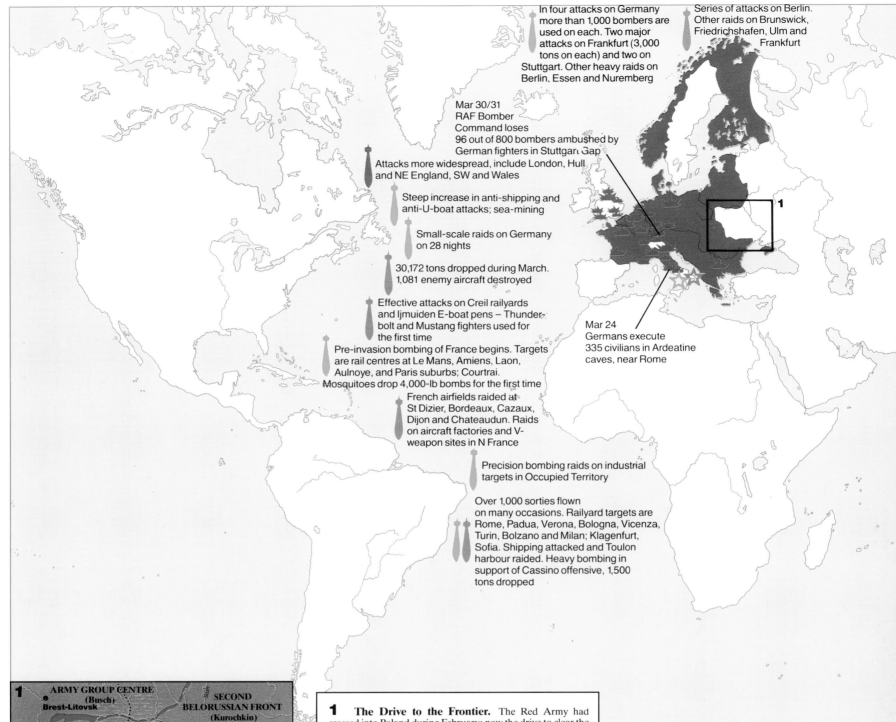

In four attacks on Germany more than 1,000 bombers are used on each. Two major attacks on Frankfurt (3,000 tons on each) and two on Stuttgart. Other heavy raids on Berlin, Essen and Nuremberg

Series of attacks on Berlin. Other raids on Brunswick, Friedrichshafen, Ulm and Frankfurt

Mar 30/31 RAF Bomber Command loses 96 out of 800 bombers ambushed by German fighters in Stuttgart Gap

Attacks more widespread, include London, Hull and NE England, SW and Wales

Steep increase in anti-shipping and anti-U-boat attacks; sea-mining

Small-scale raids on Germany on 28 nights

30,172 tons dropped during March. 1,081 enemy aircraft destroyed

Effective attacks on Creil railyards and Ijmuiden E-boat pens – Thunderbolt and Mustang fighters used for the first time

Pre-invasion bombing of France begins. Targets are rail centres at Le Mans, Amiens, Laon, Aulnoye, and Paris suburbs; Courtrai. Mosquitoes drop 4,000-lb bombs for the first time

French airfields raided at St Dizier, Bordeaux, Cazaux, Dijon and Chateaudun. Raids on aircraft factories and V-weapon sites in N France

Mar 24 Germans execute 335 civilians in Ardeatine caves, near Rome

Precision bombing raids on industrial targets in Occupied Territory

Over 1,000 sorties flown on many occasions. Railyard targets are Rome, Padua, Verona, Bologna, Vicenza, Turin, Bolzano and Milan; Klagenfurt, Sofia. Shipping attacked and Toulon harbour raided. Heavy bombing in support of Cassino offensive, 1,500 tons dropped

1 The Drive to the Frontier. The Red Army had crossed into Poland during February; now the drive to clear the hated enemy out of all Soviet territory seemed to animate every soldier in the army. Despite the spring thaw which now turned every flat surface to mud and every hill into a cascade, the advance ground forward from the Pripet Marshes to the Black Sea.

The northern flank of the advance was held by Second Belorussian Front driving for the Bug to the south of Brest-Litovsk; next came First Ukrainian Front now under Zhukov as Vatutin had been severely wounded at the end of February (he died on April 15). Zhukov's targets were Dubno reached on Mar 17, then Tarnopol, thus deepening the flank overhanging the German forces still battling to save the Dniestr line.

Koniev alongside him with Second Ukrainian Front relieved Staro-Konstantinov on Mar 9, Volochisk a week later, closed a ring around Manstein's forces trapped at Kamenets-Podolsky on Mar 27 and drove down to Chernovtsy two days later. Now the whole front was moving. Uman was liberated on Mar 10, Vinnitsa and Mogilev-Podolsky on Mar 20, while Malinovsky's Third Ukrainians had reached Pervomaisk by Mar 22.

They and Tolbukhin's men of Fourth Ukrainian emptied the Dniepr bend before the end of the month. Novy Bug had been reached by Mar 6, Nikolayev at the mouth of the Yuzhni Bug on Mar 28 and Ochakov on the last day – with Odessa itself less than 50 miles away across the bay.

As for the enemy, Manstein's Army Group South had been repeatedly submerged and only the expertise of its commander extricated those who survived the onslaughts they had tried to stem – needless to say, after prolonged and violent arguments with Hitler. On Mar 25 at a heated interview Manstein threatened to resign if he were not allowed at least to organise escape for the units trapped at Kamenets-Podolsky, and Hitler backed down – but on the last day of March both Manstein and Kleist were summoned to Obersalzburg where the Führer decorated them both with the Knight's Cross with Oak Leaves and Swords – and relieved them of their commands.

It is arguable that the removal of two of the most expert soldiers then serving with the Wehrmacht was as great a triumph for the Red Army as their advances during that month.

☆☆ **Cassino and Anzio.** The bombing of the monastery at Cassino did nothing to help the Allied soldiers. It had turned the huge building from what might have been a strong defensive position had the Germans decided to use it into an impregnable fortress when they did. The Luftwaffe's 1st Parachute Division moved into the debris of the building and turned its mounds of rubble and broken statues into a series of excellent defensive posts. Light and heavy machine-guns covered every possible avenue of advance against them, panzers which could make their way as far as the outskirts were converted into pill-boxes, indeed several Panther tank turrets were removed from their vehicles and set into dug-in steel boxes. And every Allied artillery bombardment or air raid added to the material available to make the place more impregnable, at a fairly minimal cost.

Thus, throughout March, despite gallant attempts by Gurkhas, by Poles, by Frenchmen and by the British and American infantry, the summit of Monte Cassino remained in the hands of the defenders, to loom over and thwart every Allied attempt to get past.

A similar state of affairs existed to the north at Anzio. Kesselring might possess the power and expertise to contain the bridgehead; he did not possess enough of either to destroy it. A second powerful German attack had been mounted right at the end of February, and the US 509th Parachute Regiment was almost wiped out while behind them their 45th Division first held a sagging line, then recovered it. And the next day Liberators, Flying Fortresses, Lightnings and Thunderbolts arrived overhead and so discouraged Kesselring and his men that he sent his Chief-of-Staff, General Westphal, back to Berchtesgaden to tell Hitler that attempts to obliterate the bridgehead at Anzio were pointless.

After three hours of hysterical outbursts against Wehrmacht inefficiency and disloyalty, Hitler agreed. A lull descended upon the Anzio perimeter which, with various degrees of severe discomfort for all those present on both sides, was to last for some weeks.

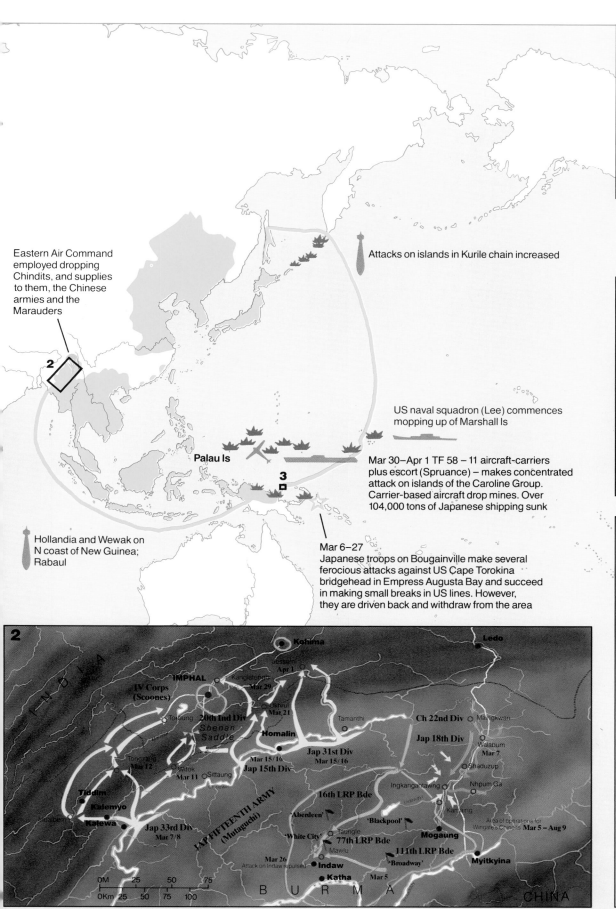

Eastern Air Command employed dropping Chindits, and supplies to them, the Chinese armies and the Marauders

2

Attacks on islands in Kurile chain increased

Palau Is

3

US naval squadron (Lee) commences mopping up of Marshall Is

Mar 30–Apr 1 TF 58 – 11 aircraft-carriers plus escort (Spruance) – makes concentrated attack on islands of the Caroline Group. Carrier-based aircraft drop mines. Over 104,000 tons of Japanese shipping sunk

Hollandia and Wewak on N coast of New Guinea; Rabaul

Mar 6–27 Japanese troops on Bougainville make several ferocious attacks against US Cape Torokina bridgehead in Empress Augusta Bay and succeed in making small breaks in US lines. However, they are driven back and withdraw from the area

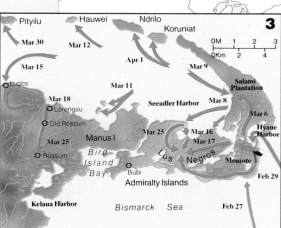

3 **The Admiralty Islands.** Having taken Momote airstrip and secured at least a foothold on Los Negros, MacArthur quickly despatched reinforcements from Finschhafen. They arrived on Mar 2, just in time to beat off a determined 'Banzai' attack which continued through Mar 3/4 and left the bridgehead perimeter littered with Japanese bodies.

But this attack served merely to weaken the strength of the Japanese defenders, while the Americans reinforced their positions every day. By Mar 9, Combat Teams of the 7th Cavalry were landing at Salami Plantation from inside Seeadler Harbor, and hardly a day passed after that without more transports bringing more units into the lagoon and putting them ashore either on Manus Island itself, or on the other islands on the harbour perimeter. By the end of the month the entire Japanese garrison of 4,300 men had been accounted for in dead, wounded or captured (very few) and with the occupation of Manus the isolation of Rabaul was now complete.

Along the New Guinea coast, the Australians of the 9th Division and those of the 7th who had been battling along the Finisterre Ridge converged and met on March 21, another detachment of US infantry of 32nd Div landed 30 miles west of Saidor. Together they forced the Japanese back to Madang.

On New Britain itself, more reinforcements had landed west of Cape Gloucester, marines reached the vital Willaumez peninsula and by Mar 10 had captured Talasea airfield, to push further east to make the holding secure. There was no need for them to advance further as Rabaul was now within easy bombing distance – and not only from Talasea. On Mar 20 a US naval force was put ashore on Emirau island off the tip of New Ireland, engineers followed to construct an airstrip, and by the end of the month Kavieng as well as Rabaul was under air attack.

The whole of the Bismarck Archipelago was now at General MacArthur's mercy – and disposal.

2 **North Burma.** On Mar 7/8 General Mutaguchi launched the forward units of his Fifteenth Army on *Operation U-Go* – 'The March on Delhi'. Its prime objective was the isolation and capture of the huge stores and administration centre which the British had set up at Imphal, from which they intended to launch their own 'March on Rangoon'.

Three Japanese divisions were sent across the Chindwin to accomplish this aim – 33rd that night to reach the Manipur river at Tiddim and Mualbem, then to march north astride the river towards Imphal; 15th Division to cross the Chindwin on the night of Mar 15/16 just north of Sittaung, send one detachment south to meet the right wing of 33rd Division at the Shenan Saddle – and 31st Division also to move on Mar 15/16, cross the Chindwin between Homalin and Tamanthi and drive straight across to Kohima, the settlement through which must pass any reinforcements or supplies sent to Imphal.

By Mar 12 33rd Division were marching along the Manipur, their right flank at Witok. They had met little opposition, for British forces in the area had been instructed to watch and wait – but once it became evident that this was a genuinely serious invasion, the British moved – back into the Imphal plain to

protect the vital stores. By the time the Japanese 33rd Division reached Torbung the first block was in place, while on the right 20th Indian Division were at the Shenan Saddle well before 15th Division reached there.

In the north Mutaguchi's 31st Division made exceptional progress despite the conditions. On the map they had only 75 miles to march; in fact by the time they reached Jessami, still 20 miles from Kohima, they had covered well over 100 miles along tortuous paths over jungle-covered mountains.

In the meantime General Slim had moved. From Arakan the 5th Indian Division had been flown to Imphal, troops were moving down from Manipur and the whole Imphal area was transformed into an armed camp.

Moreover, another threat was already hanging over Mutaguchi's *Operation U-Go*. On the night of March 5/6, 77th Brigade of Wingate's Chindits had been flown into the area south-west of Myitkyina where they had set up a defended perimeter, to be joined by another brigade flown in, and 16th Brigade which had marched in from Ledo. By the time Mutaguchi's divisions were approaching Imphal and Kohima, Wingate's brigades had established themselves in three

strongholds – 'Broadway', 'White City' and 'Aberdeen', from which they intended to take control of the area and cut all Japanese communications.

The original purpose of this second Chindit operation had been in fact to assist the Chinese divisions who had been advancing down through the Hukawng valley and the Taro plain towards Myitkyina, followed by American engineers and now greatly supported by 'Merrill's Marauders', an American formation similar in many ways to the Chindits.

Having forced the Japanese 18th Division out of the Hukawng valley, both Chinese divisions then combined to chase them out of Maingkwan, while the Marauders raced down to Walabum where they cut off the Japanese on Mar 7 and inflicted quite heavy losses.

The pattern was continued for the rest of the month. The Chinese drove on down what was now called the 'Ledo Trace' while the Marauder battalions accompanied by a Chinese regiment, swept around first to Shaduzup, then to Ingkangahtawng. A hard battle was fought here, but Japanese units from the area rescued the 18th Division survivors on the last day of the month.

123

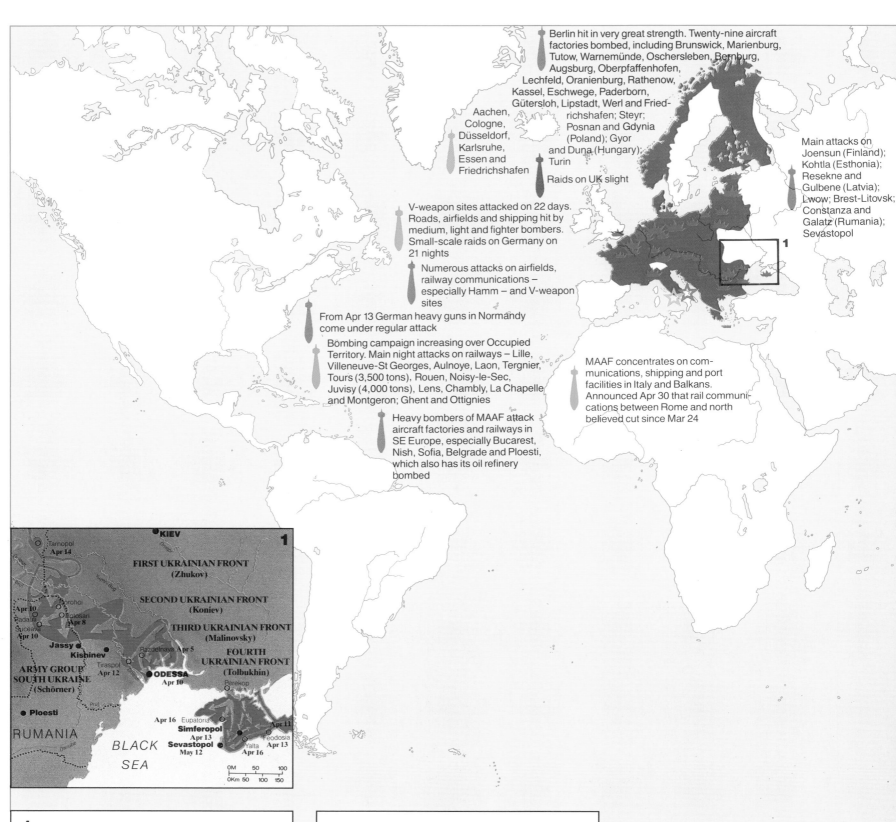

Berlin hit in very great strength. Twenty-nine aircraft factories bombed, including Brunswick, Marienburg, Tutow, Warnemünde, Oschersleben, Bernburg, Augsburg, Oberpfaffenhofen, Lechfeld, Oranienburg, Rathenow, Kassel, Eschwege, Paderborn, Gütersloh, Lipstadt, Werl and Friedrichshafen; Steyr; Posnan and Gdynia (Poland); Gyor and Duna (Hungary); Turin

Raids on UK slight

Aachen, Cologne, Düsseldorf, Karlsruhe, Essen and Friedrichshafen

Main attacks on Joensun (Finland); Kohtla (Esthonia); Resekne and Gulbene (Latvia); Lwow; Brest-Litovsk; Constanza and Galatz (Rumania); Sevastopol

V-weapon sites attacked on 22 days. Roads, airfields and shipping hit by medium, light and fighter bombers. Small-scale raids on Germany on 21 nights

Numerous attacks on airfields, railway communications – especially Hamm – and V-weapon sites

From Apr 13 German heavy guns in Normandy come under regular attack

Bombing campaign increasing over Occupied Territory. Main night attacks on railways – Lille, Villeneuve-St Georges, Aulnoye, Laon, Tergnier, Tours (3,500 tons), Rouen, Noisy-le-Sec, Juvisy (4,000 tons), Lens, Chambly, La Chapelle and Montgeron; Ghent and Ottignies

MAAF concentrates on communications, shipping and port facilities in Italy and Balkans. Announced Apr 30 that rail communications between Rome and north believed cut since Mar 24

Heavy bombers of MAAF attack aircraft factories and railways in SE Europe, especially Bucarest, Nish, Sofia, Belgrade and Ploesti, which also has its oil refinery bombed

1 Into Rumania. Despite the removal of Manstein and Kleist the relief of the German forces trapped at Kamenetz-Podolsky was obviously necessary, and during the first half of April nine panzer divisions and ten infantry divisions strove to break out towards relieving forces driving in towards them from south of Tarnopol. They were not completely to succeed, but while they were trying they effectively blocked First Ukrainian Front's drive to the south. As a result, when Zhukov's men eventually fought their way into Tarnopol on Apr 14, they then faced a desperate and therefore ferocious battle in trying to close with Koniev's Second Ukrainian Front and by the time it was evident that the bulk of First Panzer Army was escaping, First Ukrainian were becoming exhausted. Wisely, STAVKA ordered them to take up defensive positions down as far as the Prut and the Carpathian foothills.

But to the south of them, Koniev's Second and Malinovsky's Third Ukrainian Fronts were smashing their way forward, and crossing on the march rivers which the Wehrmacht had been relying upon as strong defence lines. Koniev's right wing had arrived on the Prut at the end of March, but his left wing had to cross both the Dniestr and the Prut to catch up, while on their left Malinovsky's Third Ukrainian had the Yuzhni Bug to cross, on their way to the Dniestr and the prize objective which Stalin had given them – Odessa.

Another vast heave forward therefore now occurred, comparable in some ways to the prodigious leap which had taken the Red Army to the Dniepr seven months before. The Prut was crossed in the north, Dorohoi and Botosari taken by Apr 8 and Radauti, 50 miles into Rumania, two days later.

Jassy and Kishinev were to remain in German hands for a few days longer, but all Russian eyes were in fact now focused to the south. Malinovsky's armies had burst out of their

bridgehead over the Yuzhni Bug to take Razdelnaya station by Apr 5 and then swing down in a vast sweep, brushing aside what remained of the deposed Kleist's Army Group A (and the Rumanian Third Army) to reach the northern outskirts of Odessa on the evening of Apr 9; and by the afternoon of the next day Soviet forces were standing triumphantly on the famous steps down into the harbour. Two days later, Tiraspol fell and Third Ukrainian Front, too, was across the Dniestr.

Even further south, Tolbukhin's Fourth Ukrainian Front had turned their backs on the conflicts north of the Black Sea. During March they had built up with no attempt at concealment a large force around Perekop, an operation which successfully camouflaged the build-up of an even larger force in the bridgehead they had secured across the Sivash. In addition, the Independent Coastal Army, for the time being under command of General Yeremenko, held a small bridgehead north-west of Kerch, while the Black Sea Fleet and the Azov Flotilla waited offshore.

Altogether some 470,000 men in 30 divisions, with 6,000 guns and mortars, over 500 tanks and 1,250 aircraft were assembled to liberate the Crimea, and on Apr 8 after a two and a half hour concentrated bombardment, Soviet tanks debouched from the Sivash bridgehead and drove south for Eupatoria, Sevastopol and Yalta while from Kerch, Yeremenko's men drove along the coast for Feodosia.

Simferopol was reached by Apr 13, as was Feodosia; Eupatoria and Yalta fell three days later and by Apr 18 the Red Army was occupying the line held 22 months before by Manstein's men around Sevastopol.

The main assault opened with a massive onslaught on May 5 and a week later the port was theirs, the entire Crimea liberated in 34 days.

⭐☆ **Italy.** April at both Anzio and Cassino was a month of stalemate. Both sides regrouped, the Germans strengthening their defences, the Allies building up their forces for the coming onslaught. In front of Cassino was 15th Allied Army Group consisting of the US Fifth Army with the French Expeditionary Corps, and by the end of the month the bulk of the British Eighth Army including the Polish Corps – only two divisions being left on the Adriatic sector.

At Anzio, the rains stopped, the mud dried up, lupins clustered the minefields. For the men on both sides – on both fronts – the battles of mass slaughter lasting only a matter of hours or even minutes, gave way to 'patrolling' – or to lying for hours on end in close proximity to the enemy, awaiting a grenade, a sniper's bullet . . . or relief at the end of the watch.

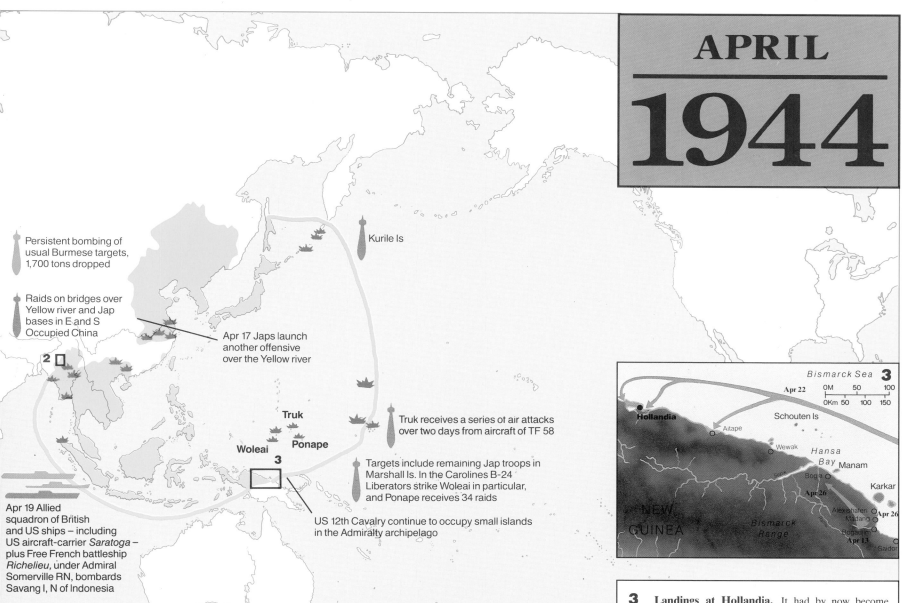

Persistent bombing of usual Burmese targets, 1,700 tons dropped

Raids on bridges over Yellow river and Jap bases in E and S Occupied China

Apr 17 Japs launch another offensive over the Yellow river

2

Truk

Woleai

Ponape

3

Truk receives a series of air attacks over two days from aircraft of TF 58

Targets include remaining Jap troops in Marshall Is. In the Carolines B-24 Liberators strike Woleai in particular, and Ponape receives 34 raids

US 12th Cavalry continue to occupy small islands in the Admiralty archipelago

Apr 19 Allied squadron of British and US ships – including US aircraft-carrier *Saratoga* – plus Free French battleship *Richelieu,* under Admiral Somerville RN, bombards Savang I, N of Indonesia

Kurile Is

Bismarck Sea **3**

Apr 22 0M 50 100
0Km 50 100 150

Hollandia Schouten Is

Aitape

Wewak *Hansa Bay* Manam

Boga Karkar

Apr 26 Alexishafen Apr 26
Madang

NEW GUINEA *Bismarck Range* Bogadjim
Apr 13

Saidor

2   Kohima and Imphal. At 0400 on Apr 5 the leading units of the Japanese 31st Division arrived on the northern outskirts of Kohima and immediately launched into what was to become one of the fiercest battles of the war. They were faced by a hastily organised defence force consisting of one battalion of the Royal West Kents augmented by men of the Assam Regiment, and the faithful and extraordinarily brave Naga villagers.

By the evening of the first day the Japanese had swept around Kohima from the Naga Village to Jail Hill and on the night of Apr 6, as more of their units arrived, they launched a series of attacks across the small stream. They were held, then driven back by the Royal West Kents, but all the time the rest of General Sato's 12,000 men were marching in and he prepared for an overwhelming onslaught which would wipe out the defenders. It was delivered on the night of April 13/14, waves of cheering and shouting infantry and engineers flinging themselves at the rock of a stubborn defence, unexpectedly aided by astonishingly accurate fire from a hitherto silent battery of howitzers at Jotsoma.

The following day, a brigade of reinforcements from 2nd Indian Division arrived at Jotsoma and began the appallingly difficult task of blasting their way over the last two miles into Kohima. Japanese infantry and mountain artillery blocked the way and every man on both sides realised the crucial nature of the battle they were fighting. But on Apr 18 the relieving force got through and the battered survivors of the original defence could make their way back to some form of shelter.

Throughout the rest of April the fighting went on, but now more and more British and Indian troops were coming in from Dimapur, more guns, more weapons of every sort; whereas everything that Sato would get for his task had already arrived.

To the south-west, the defences around Imphal by the end of the first week in April were stiffening. General Scoones commanded IV Corps and had withdrawn 17th Indian Division in front of the Japanese 33rd Division to block them first at Torbung, then further back between the river and the Logtak marshes where they turned the Japanese back. Further east, 20th Indian, after their successful holding action at the Shenam Saddle dropped back to solid defences just to their rear, and the only sign of real danger was in the north. A part of Sato's 31st Division had detached itself at Ukhrul and unexpectedly appeared between Nungshigum Hill and Kanglatongbi. From his reserve 23rd Indian Division Scoones quickly despatched a brigade, and within hours of the danger appearing 5th Indian

Division began arriving in Imphal from the Arakan, swiftly to be deployed to the north.

Thus by mid-April Scoones had four divisions comprising about 60,000 men, plus some 40,000 administrative personnel in Imphal itself, with food, ammunition and general supplies enough to last for weeks. Together they formed an unbreakable ring against which Mutaguchi's gallant soldiers would throw themselves in a succession of fanatical but completely pointless attacks.

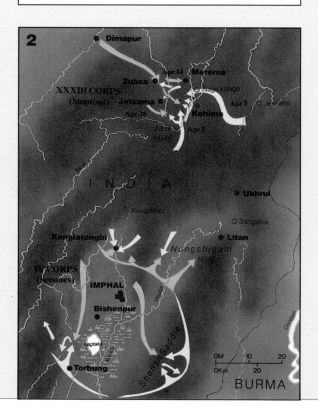

2 Dimapur

Apr 14 Merema
Zubza
XXXIII CORPS Naga Village
(Stopford) Jotsoma Apr 20
Apr 5 Kohima Apr 5 Jessami

Jail Hill Apr 5

I N D I A

Ukhrul

Kanglatongbi Litan
Nungshigum Hill
IV CORPS
(Scoones)
IMPHAL
Bishenpur

Shenam Saddle
Logtak L.
0M 10 20
0Km 20
Torbung

BURMA

3   Landings at Hollandia. It had by now become obvious that the growing power of Allied strength in both man- and strike-power made their advance towards the Philippines and then the Japanese homeland unstoppable. The power lay in the Allied commanders' hands, so did the initiative – and the Japanese had no alternative but to react to Allied moves.

Moreover, as the Japanese forces were so widely deployed and thus in the majority of cases well beyond mutual supporting range, it would not be necessary to destroy them all; they could be isolated and then left to 'wither on the bough'.

This was the strategy General MacArthur now chose to follow, enticing the Japanese forward towards what appeared to be crucial areas, then using the flexibility which naval and air superiority now gave him to land powerful forces in their rear and thus cut them off from supply, communication and even command.

Hollandia was the chief Japanese supply and administrative base on New Guinea, with excellent but undeveloped harbour facilities and three airfields adjacent. US intelligence estimates suggested that some 45,000 troops were stationed between Hansa Bay and Hollandia, but when after the Saidor landing in January the Australians continued their remorseless advance along the coast, the Japanese began to concentrate their forces in the Hansa Bay area, between the Sepik and Wewak rivers. During the last days of April, they focused all their attention there, as the Australians launched an advance from Bogadjim on Apr 13 and by Apr 26 were nearing Bogia.

But while the Japanese had been moving east from Hollandia, a huge US task force was assembling north of the recently occupied Admiralty Islands. It sailed on Apr 19 bearing two infantry divisions and a regimental combat team, proceeded first in a north-westerly direction towards Palau, then abruptly changed course towards New Guinea. On Apr 21 fast carrier planes struck the airfields close to Hollandia while land-based bombers raided Wewak and Hansa Bay, and on Apr 22 after heavy naval bombardment, the two divisions went ashore at Hollandia while the regimental combat team landed at Aitape.

Both landings were virtually unopposed, so effective had been the element of surprise. By Apr 26, all Japanese airfields in both areas had been occupied and US bombers and fighters were flying in, while the whole of the Japanese Eighteenth Army, strung out along the New Guinea coast from Alexishafen (where some units had been bypassed by the Australians) to Hollandia, were now isolated.

According to MacArthur's intelligence staff, there were now some 140,000 Japanese troops cut off from all sources of reinforcement and supply in the Bismarck and Solomon Archipelagoes – 50,000 in New Britain, 10,000 in New Ireland, 20,000 in Bougainville and 60,000 in New Guinea.

Death from sickness and starvation would be the fate of all but the tiny minority prepared to surrender.

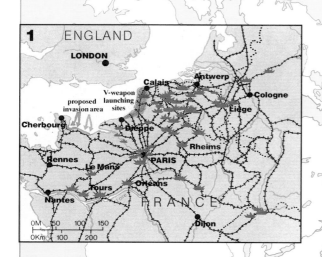

1 ENGLAND

LONDON

Antwerp

Calais

Cologne

V-weapon launching sites

proposed invasion area

Liège

Cherbourg

Dieppe

Rheims

Rennes

Le Mans

PARIS

Orleans

Nantes

Tours

FRANCE

Dijon

0M 50 100 150
0Km 100 200

Night bombing of Duisburg, Dortmund, Brunswick and Aachen, 8,500 tons

Mosquitoes over Germany 26 nights. Intruder aircraft attack 150 airfields

Increased anti-shipping, anti-sub and mine-laying ops in Channel

US Strategic Air Forces based in UK and Italy drop 63,000 tons. Heavy attacks on Berlin, Osnabrück, Münster, Brunswick and Kiel

Oil targets include Leuna, Lutzkendorf, Bohlen, Brux, Politz, Merseburg and Zeitz. Aircraft plants include Tutow, Cottbus, Gorau and Leipzig; Strasbourg; Poznan

Railway targets in Germany include Saarbrücken, Konz, Ehrang, Mannheim, Ludwigshafen, Karlsruhe, Karthaus, Neunkirchen, Hamm, Osnabrück, Schwerte and Soest

US bombers of MAAF attack rail targets including Bucarest, Brasov, Turnu-Severin, Pitesti, Craiova, Belgrade and Nish. Oil installations at Ploesti raided

May 9 End in Crimea

Italian railways, ports and airfields. Support given to ground forces from May 11

1 Air Superiority. By now the combined USAAF and RAF had to all intents and purposes driven the Luftwaffe from the skies – certainly those over the English Channel. It had been recognised from the beginning of planning for a return of the Allies to Europe that the first essential would be command of the air above the invasion areas, and this objective had been pursued for many months.

There had been, however, differences of opinion at the highest levels as to how the objective could best be attained. Even between the 'Bomber Barons', General Carl Spaatz commanding the US Strategic Air Force Europe, and Air Chief Marshal Sir Arthur Harris commanding RAF Bomber Command, there were divergences of opinion, although on one point they were united. They both believed that a land invasion of Europe would be unnecessary and that air power alone could reduce Germany to a condition of abject surrender. General Spaatz believed it would be brought about by the destruction of the concentrations of heavy industry in the Ruhr and Saar valleys, Air Chief Marshal Harris by the smashing of German cities and the breaking of the morale of the German people.

As a result of the US general's opinion campaigns of attacks upon German oil centres, ball-bearing factories and steel mills had been directed; while the Marshal's opinion had led to the widespread destruction of German cities, towns, villages and even hamlets. As by now there was such a profusion of both Lancasters and Flying Fortresses – and bombs of all sizes for them to carry – the differences between them were not of crucial, practical significance and a round-the-clock bombing programme had been in operation for some time.

The first request for a diversion from this joint but divergent policy came with the discovery that German scientists had developed a 'flying bomb' – the V1 – and were in the process of developing 'rockets' – V2 and V3 – which might well affect the prospects for the invasion, if not, indeed, of the whole course of the war. In the face of the evident seriousness of the threat, both commanders modified their own immediate plans, diverted heavy bombers to destroy the German secret weapons base at Peenemunde, while lighter aircraft of the tactical bomber force attacked the 'Flying Bomb' launch sites in the Pas de Calais.

But then a more serious challenge to their intentions arose. General Eisenhower as Supreme Commander for the proposed invasion of Europe, was concerned with the danger in which the invasion force would stand during the crucial period when only a few divisions were ashore awaiting reinforcement across a possibly unfriendly sea. During this crucial period the defenders would be able rapidly to bring up their own reinforcing divisions along interior lines of communication. Therefore, those lines of communication must be destroyed. Eisenhower's deputy, Air Chief Marshal Tedder, who despite his service with the RAF had grown to appreciate the problems of soldiers, saw clearly that the greatest immediate aid the air forces could give to the invasion of Europe – and thus to the defeat of Germany – would be to interdict the movement of German forces towards the Allied bridgehead during the period just before, and as long as necessary after, the landings. But his arguments with two men who thought the landings unnecessary anyway were unavailing. In their view, any interruption of their own bombing campaigns was not only unnecessary, but might give the Germans a respite which could only prolong the war.

The divergence of opinion was such that only some Draconian measure would solve it – and General Eisenhower produced it. If the Air Chiefs would not comply with his wishes, then he was not the Supreme Commander he had been appointed to be and he would have no choice but to return to Washington and place his resignation before the President.

It was sufficient. By March the bomber barons had accepted that among their other tasks such as ensuring air superiority over the landing areas and providing airlifts for airborne forces, they were to direct their strongest efforts to the disruption of the rail and road networks of northern France. The 'Transportation Plan' took precedence over both Spaatz's 'Oil and Industry Plan' and Harris's attack on the German cities.

During the three months to the end of May, 76,200 tons of bombs were dropped on 80 rail and road targets, destroying 51 of them and severely damaging 25 more. Within 150 miles of Le Havre 75% of the rail system was unusable, and what railway stock was left was, according to Albert Speer, held together 'by the last cotter pin'.

2 The Drive for Rome. By the beginning of May General Alexander had grouped both the British Eighth and the US Fifth Armies for the main assault on the Gustav Line between Cassino and the sea. So well concealed had been his preparations that both the German Tenth Army C-in-C, von Vietinghoff, and the commander of the XIV Panzer Corps, General von Senger und Etterlin, were on leave, and the 40-minute barrage from more than 1,600 guns with which the assault was launched took the entire German defence line by surprise.

Nonetheless, the combination of German efficiency and the nature of the country seemed at first sufficient to block the Allied advance. On the right flank the Polish Corps were attempting to storm the Cassino massif, every avenue of advance still swept by accurate machine-gun fire by the entrenched paratroops. Within two hours of the first Polish moves their assault battalions had lost one-fifth of their men, the remainder were pinned down in the open, tanks could not move and by the following evening General Anders had no choice but to halt the attack.

On their left the British XIII Corps lost many men trying to cross the Rapido, assault-boats sunk or swept away by the current. By morning they had formed a small bridgehead on the far bank, but three days later they were still confined there and although slowly deepening the position they had not cracked the Gustav Line or broken through into the Liri valley. Similarly, on the coast the US II Corps seemed stuck and the battle swirled indecisively for three days.

Then, quite suddenly, on May 15 the 2nd Moroccan Division of the French Expeditionary Corps smashed their way through the defence line, the Germans on the US right broke and began to retreat and by the evening of May 14 French, Moroccan and Algerian troops were four miles through it and

Moroccan and Algerian troops were four miles through it and overlooking the Liri valley. This spectacular feat spelled the end of the Gustav Line and of the battles for Cassino, for as the French drove remorselessly forward they dragged the US II Corps along on their left and outflanked Kesselring's defences on the right, forcing him to abandon them.

By May 19 the Americans were at Formia, a seaborne hook took them along the coast to Sperlonga two days later, and on to Terracina the next day. The French had crossed the Aurunci to reach Pico by May 22, the British on their right had reached Pontecorvo, while on May 18 the Poles had taken the monastery. Once it became evident that the German Tenth Army was in retreat, Alexander suggested to General Clark that the time had come for a breakout from Anzio with a powerful drive across to Valmontone to cut both Highways 6 and 7 and thus entrap the retreating Germans.

Unfortunately, Clark's eyes were on Rome, the first capital city to offer possibility of liberation by an Allied general. His first orders were to his British divisions to stage a feint along the coast, then to his three US divisions to advance as far as Cisterna and Highway 7. Both advances ran into strong opposition and it was May 25 before Cisterna was in US hands – the same day that patrols from Anzio met Fifth Army units from Terracina. That evening in direct contravention of his orders, Clark swung the axis of the main attack along Highway 7 towards Rome, only a minor thrust towards Valmontone to give a semblance of obedience.

Within hours, the advance on Rome was stopped dead. At Albano it came up against German defences which had been in position since the Italian armistice, and while Clark's men tried to break through, the German Tenth Army streamed back along Highway 6 through Valmontone, the gap easily held open against the minor thrust. One general's personal ambition had allowed a powerful German force to escape to fight again.

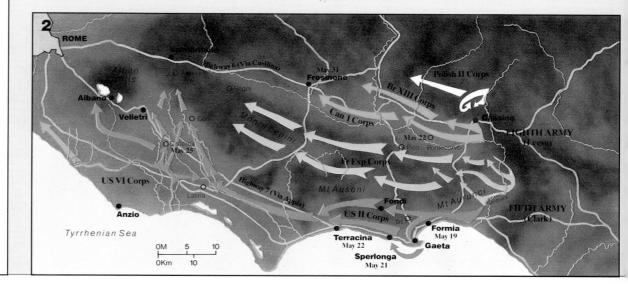

2 ROME

Montecelio

Highway 6 (Via Casilina)

May 31

Frosinone

Polish II Corps

Br XIII Corps

Alban Hills

Albano

Can I Corps

Cassino

Velletri

Monti Lepini

EIGHTH ARMY

Cisterna
May 25

Pico · Pontecorvo

May 22

US VI Corps

Fr Exp Corps

Mt Ausoni

Anzio

Highway 7 (Via Appia)

Latina

US II Corps

Fondi

Mt Aurunci

FIFTH ARMY (Clark)

Tyrrhenian Sea

Terracina
May 22

Formia
May 19

Gaeta

Sperlonga
May 21

0M 5 10
0Km 10

126

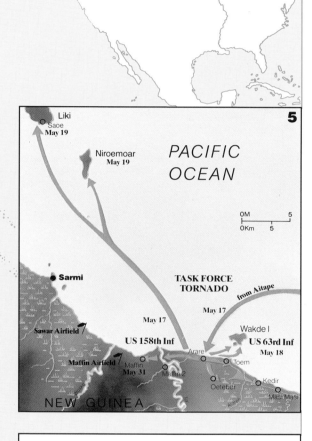

Kuriles

May 31 Start of air drop of supplies to Chinese across Salween river

May 7 Japanese open new offensive towards Hengyang

Marcus I

Wake I

May 19–20 Task Force from Fifth Fleet (Montgomery) bombs Marcus I May 24 Wake I

May 1 Detachment from TF 58 (Lee) bombs and shells Ponape May 23 Wotje Atoll in Marshall Is shelled

May 17 Japanese base at Sourabaya bombed by aircraft of Br Far Eastern Fleet. May 17/18 Liberator bombers continue the attack from bases in SW Pacific

3

Merema Ridge   May 3

Jap 31st Div (Sato)

7th Ind Div

May 15–Jun 1

Naga Village

Kohima tennis court

5

Liki
Saoe
May 19

Niroemoar
May 19

PACIFIC OCEAN

Sarmi

TASK FORCE TORNADO

May 17

US 158th Inf

Sawar Airfield

Maffin Airfield
Maffin
May 31

from Aitape

May 17

Wakde I

US 63rd Inf
May 18

Arare   Toem   Kedir

Oeteber   Masi Masi

NEW GUINEA

4   **The Drives to Mogaung and Myitkyina.** With the capture of Ingkangahtawng in April, General Stilwell split his forces, leaving the Chinese 22nd Division to press on past Kamaing to Seton. Merrill's Marauders withdrew north to Naubum where by the end of April he had assembled both Kachin and Chinese troops to bring them up to a strength of some 7,000 men. These he split into three forces – H, K and M – each to follow mountain tracks down as far as the dry-weather Mogaung–Myitkyina road, after which they would assault Myitkyina.

Despite appalling weather (the rains here were as bad as at Kohima), amoebic dysentery and typhus, they were past Ritpong by May 9 and at Tingkrukawng four days later, while from the other side M Force was driving for Muta Ga and junction with H Force at Arang. Japanese forces along the way had been to some extent by-passed, or forced to withdraw from a defensive post in front of one of the Forces, as they were threatened from the rear by another. By May 16 the leading formations had reached Namkwi, to drive on and occupy the Myitkyina airstrip, while to the west, Chinese 22nd Division formations were near to Seton. The capture of both Mogaung and Myitkyina seemed imminent, though obviously some degree of consolidation would be necessary first.

One area from which they were not to receive reinforcement – much to General Stilwell's fury – was from Yunnan Province. In late April a force of six American-trained Chinese divisions had advanced to the Salween, but apparently under orders from Chiang Kai-shek, proceeded with such caution that one Japanese division was enough to hold them there.

3   **Kohima.** At the end of April the ordeals of the men on both sides at Kohima were intensified by monsoon rains of a weight and ferocity none of them had ever experienced before; diarrhoea and dysentery took a greater toll than bullets.

The fighting was bitter, nevertheless, especially around the District Commissioner's tennis court where the opposing forces were less than 25 yards apart. But the British reinforcements were coming in all the time, they were never short of ammunition and eventually a few tanks made their way in one of which even reached the tennis court and chased out the Japanese. On May 3 and 4 attacks were mounted to try to break across GPT Ridge, at the middle of the month 7th Indian Division began a drive around the north and east of the Naga Village, and on May 25 from the south 2nd Division drove up along both sides of the Aradura Spur. None of these drives was immediately successful, but they all brought pressure on General Sato's men and caused them growing casualties.

As General Mutaguchi's main drive on Imphal was blocked, no men, no food, not a single bullet arrived in Sato's support, and by the end of May he knew that he could not take Kohima and further sacrifice was pointless. After an angry exchange of signals with his superior, he closed down his radio and ordered his men to retire. Thus began for them an agonising walk to the Chindwin, living on grass and roots, their clothing and boots in tatters, using canes or their broken rifles as crutches. It was an epic of endurance no soldier will ever decry.

5   **Wakde Island.** The successful landings at Hollandia and the isolation of large numbers of Japanese troops was no reason, in General MacArthur's eyes, for a delay on his road back to the Philippines. Even while his troops were pouring ashore at Hollandia and Aitape, he was informing the War Department that within 20 days he intended to attack the Japanese positions on Wakde Island, 140 miles further west, with the intention of pressing on towards the Sarmi peninsula as soon as possible afterwards.

As a slightly diversionary move, on May 17 after heavy air and naval bombardment, a regimental combat team went ashore at Arare, and quickly established a base between the Tor river and the marshes to the east between Toem and Oeteber. On the same day a reinforced company landed on a tiny island off Wakde to set up mortar and machine-gun posts, and on May 18 a task force from the beach-head crossed the channel to Wakde Island. Opposition from a well entrenched Japanese garrison held them up at first, but ample air and naval support was available and by May 20 Wakde was completely in US hands.

Moreover, the day before, two other islands to the north-west – Liki and Niroemoar – were occupied and quickly established as radar centres for the next stage in the drive to clear New Guinea completely.

A second regimental combat team was landed at Arare and by the end of the month had crossed the Tor to reach Maffin, its objective being the airstrip there followed by a drive along the coast to Sarmi.

Meanwhile, on the Admiralty Islands, in New Britain and on Buka Island off Bougainville, US forces were tightening the rings around the Japanese forces isolated there, mopping up outposts, confining the areas of Japanese patrolling, cutting off every means of supply which might still exist. The most important aspect of these operations was the gathering of intelligence, and the forestalling of any possible attacks the Japanese commanders might consider mounting. The Japanese troops might all face starvation, but their numbers and fanatical loyalty to their country meant that they could still pose considerable dangers.

4

Ritpong

K Force

Ch...   M Force
May 15

H Force

Ingkangahtawng

Warong

Namyseek

113th Regt

Kamaing

Seton
May 23

Namkwi
May 16

MYITKYINA

Mogaung

127

D-Day

If Hitler's invasion of Russia in 1941 was the greatest military spectacle of all time, the Anglo-American invasion of Normandy was the greatest exhibition of technical ingenuity and organisation. It was not just a question of dropping three airborne divisions (which would require over 1,000 aircraft and some 300 gliders) into France, and then landing another five divisions over the beaches – some 45,000 men from over 4,000 vessels, all of which, like the air transports, must be in the right place at the right time, despite the weather.

These divisions, once ashore, must fight their way through what were believed to be the most impregnable defences ever erected, manned by men of an army which had at one time established dominion over the heartland of the world, stretching from the Pyrenees to Moscow, from North Cape to Libya.

It says much for the springs of human optimism that, as early as the dark days after the Dunkirk evacuation, Mr Churchill had ordered planning to begin for a return across the Channel to confront Hitler's armies, and the British people had accepted that such a gigantic operation would be necessary – though how they expected to raise the necessary forces, let alone produce the weapons with which to arm them, without massive American help and, indeed, intervention only their own blind faith could indicate; but fortunately for them the Japanese attacked Pearl Harbor and thus triggered not only the end of their own imperial ambitions, but of Germany's as well.

Despite pressures from Russia for a Second Front which had grown in force and acrimony since shortly after *Barbarossa* was launched, and American belief that a direct assault on Fortress Europe would be the quickest way of ending Hitler's rule, the vicissitudes of war and the calls of other theatres in the Middle and Far East had caused the postponement of concrete steps towards the operation, until the Casablanca Conference in January 1943. A planning staff was set up under Lt-General F. E. Morgan, and at the Washington Conference the following May it was agreed that *Operation Overlord*, as it was to be named, was to have absolute priority, and that May 1944 was the date towards which all planning should be directed.

By January 1944 the designated commanders were all in England and detailed planning began. Naturally, there were differences of opinion among such powerful personalities, but General Eisenhower's supreme ability to reconcile both people and opinions dealt with most of the problems, and produced acceptable compromises for the rest. Two factors, however, met with unanimous agreement from the beginning – firstly, Allied air supremacy over the beach-heads must be total, secondly every possible measure must be taken to slow the rate of German reinforcement of the defences. The first problem was dealt with, after some argument, by May, the second was partly solved by air power and enormously helped by contact with French Resistance fighters.

As for the armies to carry through the invasion of Europe, agreement was reached that the eight divisions landed by sea and air in the first wave must be followed up by four more within three days, and another 11 by D + 14; 23 divisions, with all their weapons and transport to say nothing of the ships to carry them and aircraft to guard them, must be assembled close to the ports from which they would sail. And behind them must wait many more divisions to be poured into France, once the perimeter of the beach-head had been broken open to allow the armies to sweep deep into the continent. By end of May 1944, Britain had become an armed camp.

There was not one corner of the island which was not occupied by some aspect of preparation for the coming invasion of Europe – the entire coastline was thick with shipping from battleships in the ports down to dinghies pulled up on hards or folboats on beaches. Ships were not confined to shipyards; they occupied

narrow streets and alleyways, constructed like jigsaw puzzles as pre-fabricated parts arrived from factories and sheds all over the country. Every day saw more and more of them splash down into the sea to join the vast concourse of boats which fringed the shore-lines.

The roads inland were packed with tanks, lorries, guns and scout-cars, any large areas of flat ground between Croydon and Plymouth and Winchester and Durham had long since been converted into airfields, now packed with bombers, fighters and gliders – and over everything, everywhere, the soldiers marched, counter-marched, charged and re-formed in every training manoeuvre their instructors could devise.

By the end of May 1944, the whole island knew that the moment when battle would be joined could not be far off, though few knew exactly when or even where the assault would fall. 'When' to some extent depended upon the weather; 'where' was known only to the commanders and their planning staff.

The obvious place for a descent upon Fortress Europe was the Pas de Calais – the shortest route across the Channel, the shortest distance onwards into the heart of Germany. Needless to say, these facts were equally obvious to planners on the opposite side, and the decision had long been taken in Whitehall that instead the assault divisions would go ashore in Normandy between the base of the Cotentin Peninsula and the Orne river some 40 miles to the east.

There would be five landing beaches, two for the corps of the US First Army on the west, three for corps of the British and Canadian Second Army to the east between Arromanches and Ouistreham. At the western end behind the US 'Utah' beach, two US airborne divisions – 82nd and 101st – would be dropped during the dark hours before the landings, while at the eastern end the British 6th Airborne Division would drop to secure the bridges over the Orne to allow the seaborne formations free passage through in their attempt to take Caen on the first day. It was hoped that by that time the Allied bridgehead would be continuous from the Dives to the Vire estuary, and from the Taute estuary up the Cotentin Peninsula as far as Quineville.

By the morning of June 5, 287,000 men and thousands of fighting vehicles had been loaded into ships, which themselves were to become part of a concourse of nearly 5,000 of all shapes and sizes. The weather for the previous few days had been appalling, with unpleasant results below decks, but towards evening there was a break in the clouds and the wind eased. Shortly after sunset the huge convoys which had been approaching the area of the Channel around the Isle of Wight all changed course to the south and began the approach to the Bay of Seine in a wedge widening to over 50 miles. Above them flew some 10,000 aircraft, some bombers, many fighters, and the wallowing gliders and their tugs.

Before midnight of 5/6 June, Pathfinder squadrons of both the US and British airborne divisions had been dropped to guide in the main paratroop forces, and within two hours these were overhead – 20,000 men with the gliders close behind.

At the western end US 82nd Airborne were scattered by the winds over a wide area of marsh and floods in which much of their heavy equipment was lost, though one regiment did keep together to land near Ste Mère-Église which they took and held throughout the day. The winds scattered 101st Division in the area between Vierville and Carentan to such an extent that of its 6,600 men only 1,100 were grouped together during the morning which followed, though another 1,300 were to join up by evening.

Those of both divisions who failed to contact their commanders, however, nevertheless contributed greatly during the days which followed to the chaos and confusion which reigned among the German forces at the base of the Peninsula.

At the eastern end, British 6th Airborne had suffered a similar dispersion of forces, though they had been more fortunate in that their most important objectives, the bridges over the Orne and the Caen Canal, had been quickly taken by glider-borne troops, one section of which had landed less than 50 yards from its target. But formations of 21st Panzer Division reacted quickly and by dawn the paratroops who had reached Le Bas de Ranville were under heavy attack.

Because of the differences in tide, one hour and 25 minutes separated the landing-times of Utah beach on the west from Sword beach on the east, so the men of the US 7th Corps were the first ashore. Under a virtual canopy of shell-fire from escorting battleships, rocket-fire from 17 Support ships and ground attack and bombing of the beaches by 276 aircraft, their assault-craft left their carriers 700 yards out and wallowed in towards the shore, 28 amphibious DD tanks in the water behind them.

They landed amid a pall of sand and smoke – but no enemy. Behind them came the second and third waves, by 1000 six battalions of infantry were moving inland, on the right through deep floods, on the left driving for St Marie-du-Mont and the main Carentan–Valognes road. The two regiments which led the assault on Utah beach lost only 12 men killed that day.

If Utah was the easiest landing, Omaha on its left was the worst and came close to disaster. The beach itself was a narrow arc of steep sand between outcropping rocks, and the Germans had turned it into an ideal defensive position. When the men of US V Corps hit the beach they were unprotected even by DD tanks, as these had been decanted into unruly seas 6,000 yards out and all but two had sunk with their crews. The seas had taken their toll of the landing-craft too and for the first hour ashore – under murderous fire – officers and men of all units were inextricably mixed. It took, in fact, the sheer

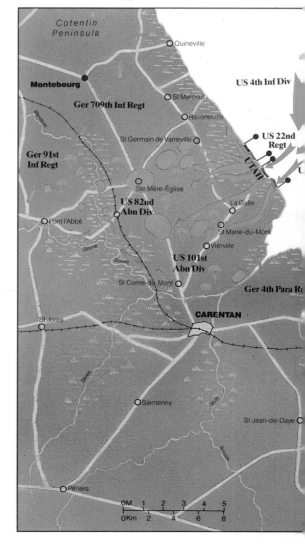

unstoppable tide of men into the beach-head to turn an apparent failure into a grudging success, and as the defenders fell or ran out of ammunition and withdrew the line of the Omaha advance crept southwards until by nightfall the beach-head was nearly two miles deep in the centre and five miles wide along the coast.

The comparative success of the landings on the British beaches – Gold, Juno and Sword – can be ascribed in great part to their use of the specialised armour of their 79th Armoured Division, designed and trained by Maj-General Sir Patrick Hobart. Flail tanks to explode the mines, Bobbin tanks to lay mattresses over mud or clay so that Shermans could follow, Crocodile tanks to burn out opposition with a flame 120 yards long, Bridging tanks to throw a steel arc over craters or ditches to allow the Shermans through – and above all the amphibious DD tanks which swam in with the leading landing-craft and blasted the German machine-gun posts before they could decimate the infantry and engineers debouching from the landing-craft. Why General Bradley had refused Montgomery's offer of specialist tanks to head the US assault on Utah and Omaha will never be known.

The sea conditions imposed the same losses on the British as they did further west, but through the chaos of broken ships and wading men, the LCTs crashed their way, lowered their ramps and let out, first the special tanks and then, once these had cleared the way, the mass of Shermans for the main armoured thrusts. By 1100 seven lanes had been cleared across Gold Beach, twelve across Juno, and both tanks and infantry were off and away, tanks dealing with strongpoints, infantry pressing forward. By nightfall the beaches had linked into a single beach-head twelve miles wide at the coast, five miles deep in places and well across the main Bayeux–Douvres road.

As for Sword Beach and the eastern end of the invasion, commandos who landed on the eastern flank raced through to reinforce the airborne units holding the Orne bridges, while on their right armour and infantry – again led by the specials – landed around Ouistreham and along the coast as far as Lion-sur-Mer, to press inland through Hermanville and reach Biéville on the right, and to cross the Orne to relieve the paratroops and push beyond Ranville towards Troarne on the left.

Nowhere did the lines of the bridgehead actually reach the hoped-for objectives for the first day – and Caen, significantly, remained beyond their reach. But the Allies were back on French soil, and except for Omaha, where over a thousand men had been killed or wounded, the losses had been far less than expected. It had been the weather, far more than the enemy, that had limited the day's achievements.

Ironically, the weather had also been partially responsible for the comparative weakness of the German initial reaction. When the first reports of airborne landings reached German headquarters in both Paris and Rastenburg (where Hitler was asleep), they were greeted with scepticism. 'In this weather?' General Speidel, Rommel's Chief-of-Staff in Paris, is reputed to have scoffed, while General Blumentritt, Chief-of-Staff to German C-in-C, West, von Rundstedt, remained doubtful for some hours, despite the fact that, like Speidel and Rommel himself, he had long felt that his chief's conviction that the invasion would take place in the Pas de Calais was mistaken.

Von Rundstedt's opinions had provoked such an argument with Rommel and Guderian, who both wanted to concentrate panzer divisions south of the Normandy beaches, that Hitler had intervened and taken the four panzer divisions under command of OKW, Supreme Headquarters; which in effect meant that none of them could be moved a yard without his personal consent. And when more reports from the beach-head area at last convinced Speidel and Blumentritt that this really was the long-awaited Allied invasion, Hitler had taken his sleeping tablets and had gone to bed, and no one dared disturb him.

As for the one man who might have risked his career by moving the panzers without that permission, Rommel, he had left for a visit to the Führer's HQ on the morning of June 5, with the specific object of trying to persuade Hitler that he must have at least two more panzer divisions and a Nebelwerfer brigade under his own command in Normandy. He had left, reassured by weather and tidal reports plus those of his reconnaissance aircraft, that there could be no possibility of an Allied landing in the immediate future,

and his absence from the scene, the absence of many senior officers from the German formations in the Cotentin Peninsula at a special conference being held in Rennes, the continual doubts in Rundstedt's mind despite the flood of reports (a week later he was still convinced that the Normandy landings were a bluff and the full weight of the invasion would fall in the Pas de Calais) and the impossibility of contacting Hitler until he awoke in the late morning, all rendered the German military machine uncharacteristically hesitant, its reserves uncommitted, its armour static.

Only the 21st Panzer Division in front of the British airborne forces which had been dropped at Ranville went into action – to a very great extent because they were almost under the paratroops as they came down. But during the morning as they were driving the British back towards Le Bas de Ranville, the corps commander, General Marcks, concluded that their most important duty was to protect Caen or even to drive down from Caen towards Ouistreham to disrupt the seaborne landings; so they drew back and in fact also remained static for the rest of the day.

By nightfall on June 6, therefore, eight infantry divisions of the Anglo-American armies were ashore with all their impedimenta, three armoured brigades, which included many combat Shermans as well as the specialised armour, were there to probe forward, the heavy guns of both British and American battleships and cruisers were close offshore with a perfected technique for helping ground troops, and in the skies above the aircraft of the RAF and USAAF held complete sway.

Moreover, behind the assault fleets and now closing the shore was a fleet of tugs bringing in the 146 caissons and 70 blockships of that truly astonishing engineering phenomena, the Mulberry harbours. They would be assembled off St Laurent in the American sector and off Arromanches in the British, designed and built to float up and down with the tide and protected from the weather by 24,000 feet of breakwater, to allow 12,000 tons of supplies each day to cross to the battle-line. During the next two months it was intended to land 2,000,000 men – 26–30 divisions – 500,000 vehicles and some 3,000,000 tons of supplies over them.

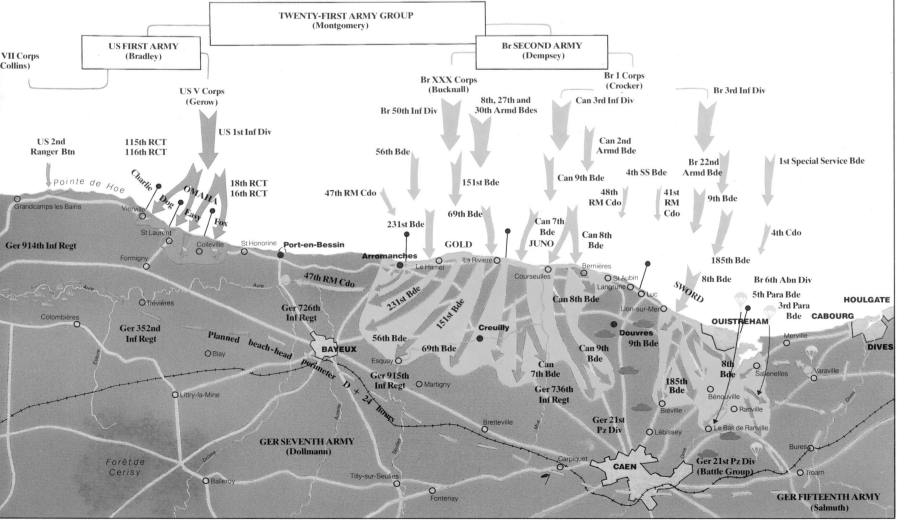

1 The Bridgehead. It took until the evening of June 10 for the five beach-heads to link up from the Douve on the west to the Dives on the east. In places the border ran only five miles from the shoreline, and nowhere was it more than ten, but the flanks were secure and for the moment no major threat seemed to exist along its entire length. The fact that one of the objectives for the first day – Caen – was still in German hands was a disappointment to some of the planners, but not particularly to General Montgomery. Its capture had been intended to create a focal point to which all German forces in the area would be drawn and there destroyed, but a similar effect could now be obtained by concentrating the main weight of Dempsey's Second British Army upon its capture, thereby forcing Rommel to react in defence of such a vital road and communication centre. In doing so, he would have to strip the opposition in front of Bradley's First US Army until these could break out, first to cross the Cotentin Peninsula and then to capture the vital port of Cherbourg.

The battle at the eastern end of the bridgehead therefore grew in intensity as the days passed, one attempt to storm Caen from the airborne bridgehead across the Orne was blocked, so

Flying-bomb attacks on UK commence on June 13 and continue day and night

Bomber Command attacks synthetic oil plants at Gelsenkirchen and Sterkrade

8th USAAF raids oil plants at Emmerich; Hamburg, Magdeburg, Oostemoor, Politz and Bohlen. Other industrial targets are Munich, Sallersleben, Leipzig, Oscherslehen, Bernberg, Aschersleben, Magdeburg and Wittemberg

15th USAAF attacks oil refineries in Rumania, Yugoslavi Austria etc. Makes first shuttle raid to Russia and back. Railways attacked, including Cluj, Simeria, Sznolnok, Szeged, Brasov, Pittesti, Nish, Constanza Budapest and Brod. Galatz airport hit

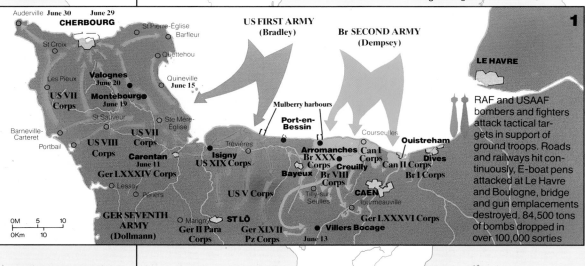

US FIRST ARMY (Bradley)

Br SECOND ARMY (Dempsey)

Main attacks on Italian railways. Support for ground forces

RAF and USAAF bombers and fighters attack tactical targets in support of ground troops. Roads and railways hit continuously, E-boat pens attacked at Le Havre and Boulogne, bridge and gun emplacements destroyed. 84,500 tons of bombs dropped in over 100,000 sorties

Montgomery launched an attack on the town from the west. But on June 19 a summer storm sprang up of such force that the Mulberry harbour at St Laurent was wrecked and the one at Arromanches badly damaged, so for three days reinforcement and supply to the bridgehead were effectively halted.

In the meantime, the two US Corps from Utah and Omaha Beaches had linked up to take Carentan by June 14, while to the north, VII Corps had taken the Montebourg Ridge 13 miles from Cherbourg. By now their western flank was halfway across the peninsula and with the heights of the ridge secure they steamrollered their way on to the coast at Carteret and Portbail, destroying two German infantry divisions on the way.

The newly arrived US VIII Corps now took responsibility for the southern face while VII Corps drove up for Cherbourg. With three divisions driving northwards abreast, they were in and past Valognes on June 19 and closing up to Cherbourg's main defences by June 21. 'Air pulverisation' was called for by General Collins commanding VII Corps, and it began at noon on June 22 with RAF Typhoons delivering rocket attacks followed by waves of Mustangs, more US fighter-bombers and, as the US infantry attacked all along the Cherbourg perimeter, 11 groups of the US 9th Bomber Command arrived overhead – and naval bombardment began from the north.

On Hitler's strict command, the utmost resistance was put up by the Cherbourg garrison and it was June 29 before the last of the forts surrendered – by which time German demolition teams had carried out such a masterly wrecking programme that it was three weeks before the port was open for even the smallest vessels. Fortunately for the Allies, however, the British engineers were as expert at repairing the Mulberry harbour at Arromanches as the Germans had been at destroying Cherbourg and before the end of June the second attack on Caen could begin, its main task that of 'writing down' the German armour.

2 Finland June/July. On June 9 5,500 guns and 880 rocket launchers opened fire on the Finnish defences just north of Leningrad, and two Russian armies began the drive up the Karelian Isthmus towards Viipuri – which they took on June 20. On the same day, another Russian army drove west from the Maselskaya area and the following day yet another drove up between Lakes Ladoga and Onega.

Such was the power of the attack – from nearly 500,000 men with 10,000 guns, 800 tanks and over 2,000 aircraft – that several of the Finnish formations broke and fled to the rear, and even the more stalwart units had little choice but to conduct as respectable a retreat as possible. But by the end of June the Red armies (a third had joined across the Gulf) were at the old frontier, while by mid-July in Karelia they were satisfied to pause at the defence line north of Salmi and, further north, just short of Ilomantsi.

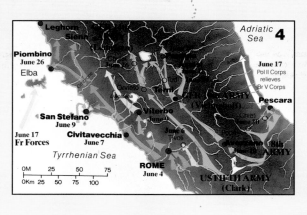

3 Operation Bagration. For some months past the main battles on the Eastern Front had taken place in the south, but Stalin had as early as April decreed a shift of emphasis; Army Group Centre was to be destroyed in a new operation code-named after the Russian General Bagration killed at Borodino. Four new Soviet Fronts would be assembled between Polotsk in the north and Sarny in the south – 1,245,000 men, 2,715 tanks supported by 1,355 self-propelled guns, 24,000 guns and heavy mortars and 2,306 Katyusha rocket-launchers. Four air armies would deploy 5,327 aircraft above the battle, 70,000 lorries would feed it – and with the infantry were 43,500 machine-guns.

At 0400 on June 22 – three years to the day after *Operation Barbarossa* had been launched – the heavy bomber force arrived over Army Group Centre's forward positions and an hour later the barrage opened. By June 27 First Baltic Front under General Bagramyan had encircled Vitebsk and a day later had crossed the Dvina to take Lepel. On their left Third Belorussian Front under the brilliant General Chernyakovsky had provided the southern arm of the Vitebsk encirclement, smashed through Orsha, crossed the Berezina and reached Borisov on the last day of the month, while to their south General Zakharov's Second Belorussian Front took Mogilev and drove on for Minsk.

Meanwhile, on the left flank, First Belorussian Front now under General Rokossovsky had enveloped Bobruisk by June 27, trapped five German divisions and reached Slutsk by June 30. To help the advance, partisan brigades had carried out over 40,000 demolitions on the main railway lines running along the length of the attack front, drawing fierce reaction upon themselves from SS anti-partisan troops.

4 Fall of Rome. With two corps blocked on the Rome approaches, General Clark was fortunate in being able to insert a third into the battle-line. On May 28 he had transferred II US Corps across towards Valmontone, leaving VI Corps at Albano and sending IV Corps along the coast – although at the end of May all three were stalled.

Out on their right flank, the British Eighth Army, their own advance along Highway 7 now pre-empted by II US Corps, moved slowly up the Liri valley, Canadians taking Frosinone on May 31. At the same time, the French Corps were still advancing through the Lepini Mountains – and by a brilliant night movement US 36th Division broke through between Albano and Valmontone, thus outflanking the German defence line.

Kesselring knew when he had been out-manoeuvred – knew in fact that with his immutable weakness in men and

weapons compared with his opponents he always would be – and immediately requested permission to evacuate Rome and drop back to defence lines further north. On June 3 permission was granted, he ordered one last line south of the city to be held while his troops withdrew, and by the afternoon of June 4 only the rearguard of the 4th Parachute Division were still in the city. By evening US troops had closed up to the Tiber – receiving an enthusiastic welcome from the Romans.

By June 6 the sounds of fighting had receded well to the north of Rome as US formations pressed on through the city and British, Canadian and Polish kept abreast to the east. But they were pursuing two veteran German armies – Fourteenth and Tenth – commanded by a master tactician who never missed an opportunity to delay them.

Ironically, the liberation of the first capital city by the Allies was hardly noticed in the clamour of events in Normandy.

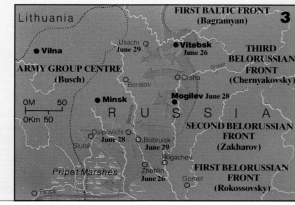

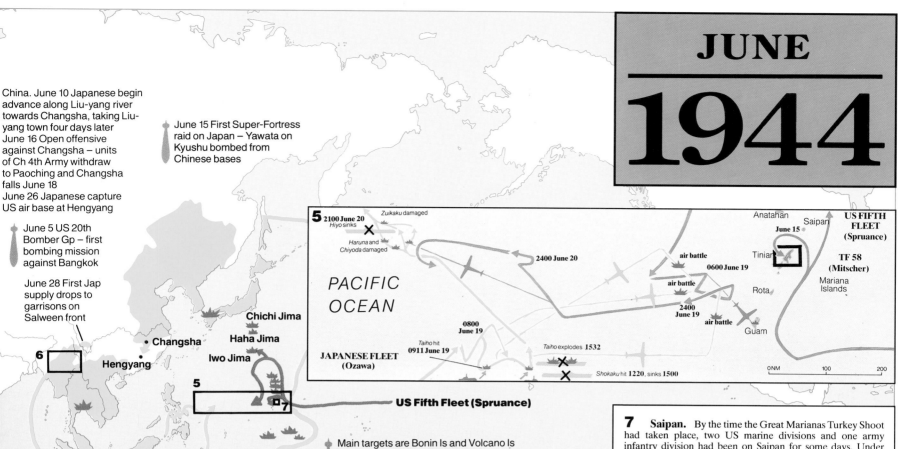

China. June 10 Japanese begin advance along Liu-yang river towards Changsha, taking Liu-yang town four days later
June 16 Open offensive against Changsha – units of Ch 4th Army withdraw to Paoching and Changsha falls June 18
June 26 Japanese capture US air base at Hengyang

June 15 First Super-Fortress raid on Japan – Yawata on Kyushu bombed from Chinese bases

June 5 US 20th Bomber Gp – first bombing mission against Bangkok

June 28 First Jap supply drops to garrisons on Salween front

Main targets are Bonin Is and Volcano Is (just south of Japan), Mariana Is, Caroline Is and Dutch New Guinea; Paramushir in Kuriles

5 The Battle of the Philippine Sea. With Eniwetok in US hands, Truk severely damaged and no longer viable as a powerful Japanese base, the Carolines rendered untenable, and the Marianas already feeling the weight of US Navy shelling and aircraft attack, the Japanese naval C-in-C, Admiral Toyoda, concluded that the best hope his service held for holding the Americans back from his country's last defence line, lay in a decisive confrontation with the US Pacific Fleet in which his own command might inflict sufficient losses to deflect American intentions for at least a year. As quite evidently the US Pacific Fleet was about to launch a major attack in the Marianas, this would provide the opportunity.

It was not a strategic possibility which had escaped the US naval staff, and Admiral Nimitz made the necessary preparations to meet it. On June 8, large naval and marine forces arrived at Eniwetok and Kwajalein en route to Saipan which they were intended to capture, and seven days later they were off the west coast of the islands and the landings commenced. By this time the Japanese command had detected the movements and ordered the concentration of two fleets, then west of the Philippines, to attack the Americans; by June 16 they were together and deploying.

West of Saipan, Admiral Spruance, commanding the US Fifth Fleet and well aware of what was happening, ordered the concentration of the various groups of his Task Force 58 and by June 18 16 aircraft-carriers with in all 896 aircraft aboard were in position and waiting. Then followed 'The Great Marianas Turkey Shoot'.

The fleets themselves never came within 300 miles of each other, but by 0445 on June 19 the first 30 Japanese search planes had been flown off, one aircraft returned with a sighting, and during the morning 236 Japanese aircraft took off. Few of them returned, for they were vastly outnumbered by better aircraft flown by better trained pilots; the hard core of Japanese naval pilots who had wreaked such havoc at Pearl Harbor had long gone. Moreover, during that day two Japanese carriers were sunk and the following day another sunk and three more damaged. On June 19 and 20, 1944, the Japanese Navy went down to ruin.

7 Saipan. By the time the Great Marianas Turkey Shoot had taken place, two US marine divisions and one army infantry division had been on Saipan for some days. Under heavy naval shelling and air cover (which had begun two days before) on June 15 2nd US Marine Division had gone ashore on the west coast of Saipan to the north of Afetna Point, while 4th US Marine Division landed on beaches to the south. Within 20 minutes 8,000 marines were ashore, despite Japanese mortar and artillery support, the heavy shelling and the marines' obstinacy and technique forced the beach-head perimeters inland until by nightfall both were about 5,000 yards wide and 1,300 yards deep.

Counter-attacks inevitably followed, some supported by tanks, but the fire-power of the marines and the overwhelming gun-power of the covering battleships of Task Force 58 (not yet committed to the huge air battle) stopped them and gradually the US beach-heads grew, the space between them narrowing. On June 17 the 27th Infantry Division landed on the 4th Marines' right and pushed with the 4th Marines to the east coast, taking Aslito and its airstrip on the way.

News of the defeat at sea depressed the Japanese commanders but did not affect the resistance of the ordinary soldiers. US forces were still penned in the southern third of the island, when General Holland Smith swung his forces around to the north, with the army infantry between the marine divisions, to begin a slow advance up through the central mountains.

The last frantic Japanese *Banzai* charge took place on July 7 and then the island was in US hands.

6 India and Burma. By June 3 the Battle of Kohima was over, Sato's 31st Division capable of only one more small rearguard action, the bulk of the troops making their painful ways back towards the Chindwin. But Imphal was still under siege and Mutaguchi's men showed no sign of withdrawing, so units of 2nd British Infantry Division began a drive down from Kohima, while up from Imphal came 5th Indian Division. Despite Japanese weakness, it was June 22 before the two divisions met to reopen the main road from Dimapur to Imphal, but then 7th Indian Division followed down from Kohima and drove out to Ukhrul, thus ensuring its safety.

Meanwhile, to their east, the Chinese 22nd Division were still driving down the Mogaung valley, their right-hand brigade taking Kamaing on June 16, linking with the brigade already at Seton, then with Chindit forces still west of the Irrawaddy, taking Mogaung itself on June 26.

But on their eastern flank, despite the fact that Myitkyina airstrip had been in US and Chinese hands since May 19, the road into Myitkyina itself was securely blocked by far stronger Japanese forces than had been expected, and which were in fact being reinforced. Moreover, Merrill's Marauders had now been in the field far longer than had been planned, and their physical and moral strength was fast fading, while figures later revealed that on June 4, out of an original strength of 2,830, 2,394 were either dead or too ill to fight. Engineers who were working on the airstrip were hastily formed into combat formations, a further 2,500 US troops were flown in and during June they tightened the ring around Myitkyina.

Moreover, Chinese armies were now moving slowly forward over the Salween. They had been present for some time, but immobile, but by June 4 some 20,000 men of the Chinese 71st Army were across the river, by June 7 their 88th Division had reached Lungling with the 87th Division closing from the south-east. Ten days later they were forced out by Japanese counter-attacks, but General Chiang Kai-shek sent his Eighth Army up from Indo-China and the whole Japanese position in North Burma now became perilous indeed.

8 Biak. On May 27 units of 41st Division made the first landings on Biak against minimal opposition, but as the troops made their way inland they found themselves ambushed between well dug defensive positions and overlooked from dominating cliff-tops. A Japanese counter-attack supported by tanks drove a block between the beaches and the invaders, necessitating a rapid regrouping and then reinforcement by the rest of the 41st Division.

By June 2 the US troops could begin a drive to their first main objective, the airfield at Mokmer, though it was June 7 before they reached it and a week later before overlooking Japanese artillery was neutralised and US aircraft could begin operations. More reinforcements were brought in, two more airstrips at Borokoe and then Sorido were captured and put into operation, and the Japanese formations gradually forced away towards the centre of the island.

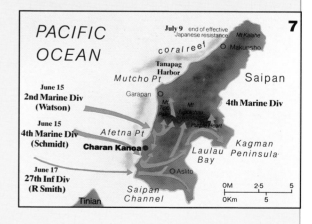

131

1 Cobra and Goodwood. With the wreckage of Cherbourg and control of the Cotentin Peninsula in US VII Corps hands, US VIII Corps with yet another newly arrived corps – XIX – could turn their attentions southwards. At first the confinements of the 'Bocage' country – deep lanes and high hedges behind which German anti-tank guns could hide – made progress slow and costly, but by the evening of July 16, XIX Corps infantry were in the approaches to St Lô, and by the afternoon of July 18 it was in US hands.

On their right, VIII Corps were grinding their way slowly down from the Portbail–Carentan Line to reach Lessay on July 15, where they regrouped after VII Corps came down on their left through Carentan. Then on July 24, with massive air support, General Bradley launched *Operation Cobra*.

It still took four days before the armour could tear itself free of the hedgerows and marshes of the area, but by July 28 they were at Coutances on the right, well past Marigny in the centre and driving down towards Percy on the left, at last to find themselves in the open. Three days later VIII Corps armour swept into Avranches to cross the river and open the way into Brittany and the vital ports of Brest, Lorient and St Nazaire.

Moreover, Lt-General George Patton had now arrived in the district, and with him the XII, XV and XX Corps which, with VIII Corps, would make up his Third Army. General Bradley's US Twelfth Army Group were now into Europe.

The fact that it had arrived safely and, with the US First Army, had now broken out of the Normandy bridgehead, had been due in some measure to the success of General Montgomery's tactics in drawing as much as possible of German strength – especially armour – to the eastern end of the bridgehead, in the fierce battles for and around Caen.

Like Bradley, Montgomery had been receiving considerable reinforcement, but even while the main strength of the Canadian First Army was still coming ashore, converging attacks from the west by Br VIII Corps and from the east out of the airborne bridgehead by I Corps, isolated the XII SS Panzer Division and drove into the ruins of Caen on July 9. Now Montgomery could regroup for a drive, first to encircle the city – for German forces still held the southern bank of the Orne – then further south towards Falaise, the whole movement becoming more urgent when on the evening of July 10 evidence came in that German divisions were being rushed westwards towards the American break-out area.

On July 18 *Operation Goodwood* was launched by three armoured divisions, west of Caen and aiming for Falaise, but still with orders to concentrate on the destruction of the panzer divisions. A week later, as *Operation Cobra* was bursting out of the other end of the bridgehead, *Operation Spring* was launched by the Canadians between Caen and Troarn. Neither *Spring* nor *Goodwood* advanced the line very far towards Falaise, but they held the panzers in position while Bradley's forces raced for Avranches and Brittany beyond.

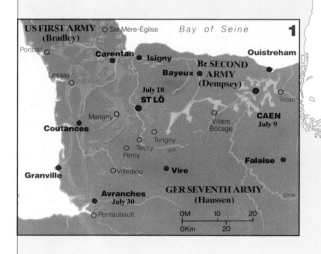

3 Advance to the Gothic Line. After the capture of Rome, the Allies still had good opportunity to cut the German Fourteenth and Tenth Armies apart and destroy the Tenth, but the distraction caused by the fall of the first Axis capital city slowed them up so much that both German armies were able to retreat in their own time. By early July, though the fall of Elba by French forces had hurried the Fourteenth Army retreat up the west coast past Piombino, US Fifth and British Eighth Armies had followed them up to the level of Lake Trasimeno, while on the Adriatic coast the Polish II Corps had relieved the British V Corps and driven up from Pescara to across the Aso.

It was now General Alexander's intention to drive on up the spine of Italy with the left flank of Eighth Army to reach Florence and then break through the Gothic Line – yet another system of defences Marshal Kesselring had built across Italy. Arezzo was taken on July 16 thus levering the Fourteenth Army back out of a line of lesser defences, called the Albert Line.

On Eighth Army's left, the French Expeditionary Corps were still proving themselves the experts at mountain warfare, reached Siena on July 3 and by July 20 had climbed through the mountain to take Certaldo, after which they were withdrawn from the Front to take part in the invasion of southern France in August. The British XIII Corps expanded westwards to fill the gap between them and US Fifth Army, 8th Indian and 2nd New Zealand Divisions driving up towards the Arno river by the end of the month. San Giovanni was taken on July 22.

Coastal Command flies 6,000 sorties – anti-shipping and U-boat ops. Bomber Command hits Le Havre

Mosquitoes make eight attacks on Berlin (250 tons)

London and SE England hit by flying bombs continuously

German oil production. 5,000 tons dropped – Wesseling, Buer, Bottrop, Homburg and Wanne-Eickel; Donges

In five attacks on German industry – three on Stuttgart, one each on Hamburg and Kiel – Bomber Command drops 8,000 tons

Heavy industry hit at Kiel, Mockau, Bernberg, Aschersleben, Leipzig, Halle, Munich (8,700 tons in seven raids), Augsburg, Schweinfurt, Friedrichshafen, Ebelsbach, Regensburg, Linz, Bremen and Ludwigshafen; Peenemunde and Zinnowitz (experimental stations)

8th USAAF bombs Bohlen, Lutzkendorf, Merseburg and Leuna – 15th bombs Blechhammer and Odertal; Vienna; Ploesti; Trieste and Porto Marghere; Pardubice; Berat

July 22 St Gingolph village destroyed in reprisal for Maquisard raid

RAF and USAAF give close support to ground troops in France – Caen, Villers Bocage, Caumont, Jurques, St Lô and bridges over Seine and Loire. Many attacks on communications controlling battle area – Orléans, Paris suburbs, Dijon, Aulnoye, Revigny, Givors, Strasbourg, Metz, Belfort and Saarbrucken; La Roche, Courtrai; Coblenz; and heavy raids on V-weapon sites – 12,000-lb bombs on rocket emplacements: tonnage on some attacks 1,000 – in Pas de Calais

2 Russian Soil Cleared. Throughout July the huge Red Army offensive surged onwards, crossing the original Soviet borders along which the forces for *Operation Barbarossa* had been massed three years before. By July 4 Second and Third Belorussian Fronts had driven forward nearly 150 miles crushing a German pocket left between their joint advances on July 11, Rokossovsky's First Belorussians were driving for Pinsk, and except just west of Minsk the Soviet–Polish border was behind them.

The momentum never flagged. Although desperate resistance was offered by the Germans, Army Group Centre was torn to shreds while above them Army Group North, now commanded by General Lindemann, was forced backwards and in danger of being penned against the Baltic. By July 4 Bagramyan's First Baltic Front had crossed the Dvina to take Polotsk, Chernakovsky's and Zakharov's Belorussian Fronts cut off another 105,000 Germans as they crossed the Berezina and then drove for Vilna and Bialystok respectively, taking the first on July 13 and the second on July 30. 'Army Group Centre', Guderian noted in his diary, 'has now ceased to exist.'

Having taken Vilna, Chernyakovsky's right flank plunged on to take Kaunas and by the end of the month had reached the borders of East Prussia, while on his right Bagramyan's troops swept into both Latvia and Lithuania. Below the wreck of Army Group Centre, Rokossovsky's First Belorussian Front smashed its way on through Pinsk on July 14 to reach Brest-Litovsk on July 28 and cross the Bug, while on his left Chuikov's Guards had captured Lublin on July 13, then reached and crossed the Vistula.

Not surprisingly, matters did not go quite so well for the Red Army in the south, as here was where the main assault had been expected. Field Marshal Model's Army Group North Ukraine (he had commanded both Army Group Centre *and* North

Meanwhile, after occupying Piombino on June 26, US IV Corps had driven into Cecina on July 1, along the coast to Leghorn by July 19, then across the mouth of the Arno and into the city of Pisa four days later. On their right flank Volterra was in their hands by July 9 and Pontadera by July 18 – the Arno and the Gothic Line the next hurdles to cross on their long, hard trudge up the Italian Peninsula.

Ukraine since the end of June when Hitler had sacked Busch) had to a small extent been weakened as Model had drawn off strength to cope with the enormous problems in the centre, but it still held 34 infantry divisions, 1 motorised and 5 panzer divisions. With these, coupled with strong defensive lines along the several tributaries of the Dniestr (and yet more Hitlerian exhortations regarding the necessity to hold Lwow) Model had every hope of protecting the last approaches to southern Poland, Czechoslovakia and Silesia, with all their industrial centres; especially as for the first half of July Koniev's armies of the First Ukrainian Front had remained strangely quiet.

Then, on July 13, the storm burst. Seven Soviet infantry armies, three tank armies and two air armies – over 80 divisions comprising 1,200,000 men with 2,200 tanks and self-propelled guns – took part in the massed assault, and under such tremendous weight of men and fire-power, Model's defences creaked and eventually cracked. Two wide breaches were torn through them in the first week, and Koniev's armies flooded through in two converging movements to cut off 40,000 Germans, reach Yaroslavl on July 23, Przemysl on July 27 – and the same day from north, south, east and west, Soviet infantry and tanks fought their way into the centre of Lwow. Well to the south, Stanislav also fell on July 27. By the end of the month, the Vistula had been reached and crossed, as had the entire length of the 1939 Russo-German border.

The Bomb Plot. On July 20, at Rastenburg in East Prussia – less than 100 miles from the advancing Red Army spearheads – an attempt was made to assassinate Hitler. A bomb concealed in a briefcase was placed by Colonel Count Claus Schenk von Stauffenberg beneath the table upon which Hitler was conducting a staff conference, exactly below the place where he was leaning over a map. Two events combined to save the Führer's life; an officer around the table knocked the briefcase with his foot, bent down and removed it to the other side of one of the heavy plinths supporting the table; and because of reconstruction work at Rastenburg the conference was taking place in a wooden hut instead of the usual concrete bunker, where the blast from the bomb would almost certainly have killed everyone inside. Hitler was deafened, his left hand cut, his clothes singed; otherwise he was unhurt. And he would exact a terrible revenge.

China. July 5 Chinese armies regain Lungmoon, N of Canton. July 11 Jap 11th Army renews attack on Hengyang but is repulsed by Chinese with US air support. Chinese in garrison completely cut off but hold out until Aug 8

May 26–July 31 14th USAAF carries out 4,454 missions in support of Chinese troops in Central East China

July 25 Sabang (Sumatra) severely bombed and shelled by Somerville's Far Eastern Fleet

Super-Fortress raids on industrial targets on Kyushu – Sasebo, Omura and Yawata. Also targets in Occupied China

July 2–4 Two Task Forces bomb and shell Volcano and Bonin Is. Four enemy ships sunk

Guam, Tinian and Rota bombed daily

• Wake I

Main targets Palau Is, Yap and Woleai in Carolines; Timor, Ceram and Halmahera; support of ground forces on New Guinea; isolated Japanese in Kavieng, Rabaul and Bougainville

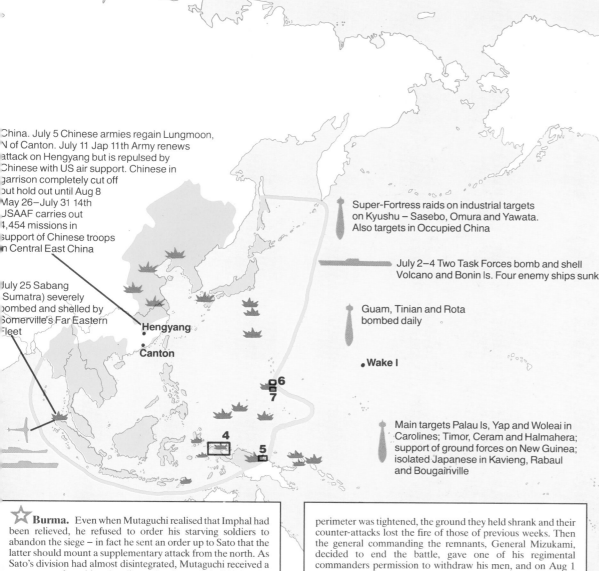

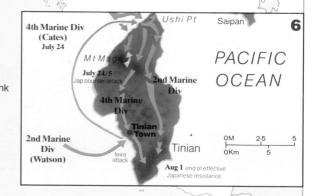

☆ **Burma.** Even when Mutaguchi realised that Imphal had been relieved, he refused to order his starving soldiers to abandon the siege – in fact he sent an order up to Sato that the latter should mount a supplementary attack from the north. As Sato's division had almost disintegrated, Mutaguchi received a curt answer from his subordinate, but it was July 8 before he accepted the position and ordered his own men to join Sato's in the retreat to the Chindwin – one of the most appalling in the annals of warfare. All they had to eat was grass.

Meanwhile to the east the battle for Myitkyina continued, the monsoon rains turning the ground to mud and swamp, men splashing, wading, swimming and sometimes drowning in it. But the US engineers settled down and turned themselves into first-class combat soldiers, and during July the Japanese

perimeter was tightened, the ground they held shrank and their counter-attacks lost the fire of previous weeks. Then the general commanding the remnants, General Mizukami, decided to end the battle, gave one of his regimental commanders permission to withdraw his men, and on Aug 1 committed suicide. Two days later, Myitkyina was in US hands.

Pressure on the Japanese as Chinese troops crossed the Salween was increasing steadily. When the Chinese Eighth Army from Indo-China approached the Seventy-First Army in the north a series of battles took place as the Japanese sought to keep them apart; by the end of July despite the monsoon the two Chinese armies were creeping closer; and with Myitkyina now in US hands with much of northern Burma, supplies would start flooding into the Chinese bases in Yunnan.

6 Tinian. After Saipan, no one doubted that Tinian was the next objective – and Tinian's commander, Admiral Ogata, knew of only one length of coastline where a large enough enemy force could land; the beaches near Tinian Town. But during the nights of July 10 and 11, US Navy swimmers explored the other series of small breaks in Tinian's cliff-ringed coastline, and reported that if the flow ashore of men and material was controlled, they were usable.

On July 24, a spectacular task force appeared off the Tinian Town beaches, shelled and bombed the defences, put marines of the 2nd Division into landing-craft – and later, to Ogata's gratification, withdrew them.

It was some hours before he learned that assault units of 4th Marine Division had landed, under air and artillery cover, on the beaches at the northern tip of the island, and after the first day 15,000 of them occupied a solidifying beach-head.

Japanese suicide attacks were mounted by the next morning, and 2nd Marines had arrived from the feint attack on Tinian Town. Within four days 40,000 Marines were driving southwards, and although on July 24 Ogata mounted a fierce counter-attack lasting two days, the marines' drive down continued until by Aug 1 they had reached the southern tip of the island and real resistance ended. Marine casualties were 394 dead and 1,961 wounded; 9,000 Japanese died.

4 & 5 New Guinea. With Biak in the process of being taken, soon only Noemfoor Island would remain in Japanese hands in Geelvink Bay, and only the Vogelkop Peninsula in all New Guinea. With hardly a halt, MacArthur's drive westwards continued. After a three-week air bombardment of Japanese positions on Noemfoor a regimental combat team landed under a heavy naval bombardment on the north-west coast to capture an airstrip, the next day 503rd Parachute Infantry were dropped in and by July 4 the main positions in the north had been taken. A link around to the south-west by sea on July 6 followed by reinforcement on July 10 resulted in all commanding positions being in US hands by July 12, after which all that remained was the mopping up. By July 31 this was complete.

On July 30, the bulk of the US 6th Division was landed unopposed at the north-west tip of the Vogelkop Peninsula to establish a firm base between Mar and Sansapor, including airstrips. Thus the main Japanese force at Manokwari was by-passed and cut off from escape, reinforcement or supply – as had happened all along the New Guinea northern coast.

But along that coast, east of Hollandia, was General Adachi, once commander of the Japanese Eighteenth Army.

Since first being cut off nearly two months before, he had collected together the equivalent of almost two divisions – near starvation, ragged, disease-ridden, but still with weapons and some ammunition and unsurprisingly in view of Japanese 'Bushido', quite willing to attempt to fight their way out of the trap or die in the attempt.

There was little Adachi could do to give his forces even tactical surprise, for native feeling was pro-US and US planes flew above the area – so when on July 11 he launched the first of a series of fierce, suicidal attacks across the Driniumor river, it was mown down by machine-gun fire, though its initial impetus had taken it across the river. Rebuffed in the centre, Adachi now threw his troops in similar attacks across the river just south of the mouth, and tried to infiltrate them through the foothills of the Torricelli mountains. But every move he made was either reported by native observers or easily predicted by US intelligence, and artillery and heavy automatic fire, preceded by attacks from the air, cut every formation to ribbons and carpeted the ground with Japanese dead.

Finally, at the end of the month, US forces moved forward to drive away the few sick and shattered survivors.

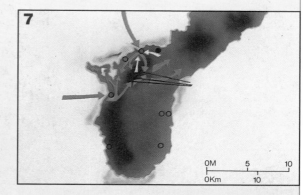

7 Guam. Reasons of prestige and practicality dictated American occupation of Guam. An American possession for over 40 years it had airfields from which B-29s could reach the Japanese home islands, and the best natural harbour in the area.

The forces assembled by the naval and land commanders for its assault were larger and better equipped than usual – 3rd Marine Division, 1st Marine Brigade and 77th Infantry Division with air and sea support – and so were the defending forces, under Lt-General Takeshi. His 11 defence battalions, all his naval battalions, artillery and tanks, plus anti-aircraft batteries and coastal defence units were assembled to combat this attack, made easier because, unlike on Tinian, only one stretch of coastline suited a large amphibious landing. Cliffs, coral reefs, prevailing winds and high surf rendered the rest of the island's perimeter inviolable.

The vulnerable 15-mile stretch covered the island capital Agana, Apra Harbor, Piti Naval Yard, Orote Peninsula and Agat – and after days of heavy bombing four battleships arrived on July 19 and shelled beaches at Asan and Agat continuously and at 0830 on July 21, 3rd Marine Division landed at Asan, 1st Marine Brigade at Agat, with 77th Infantry behind.

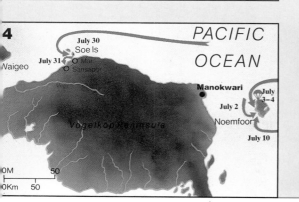

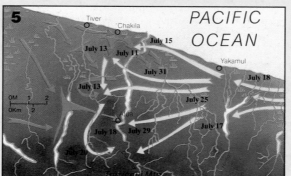

133

1 & 2 Across the Seine. At noon on Aug 1 a delighted General Patton took command of the US Third Army with instructions to liberate Brittany and the vital ports as quickly as possible. Typically, he immediately saw far wider opportunities for his command and although he went through the formalities of requesting permission to exploit them, he did not bother to await reply. Instructing the armoured divisions of his VIII Corps to race straight for Brest, Vannes and Lorient without worrying about their flanks or anything except their speed, he turned the rest of his command eastwards and aimed the bulk at the gap between Chartres and Orléans, 100 miles distant.

He sent XV Corps away on Aug 5 to take Le Mans three days later, while on the right XX Corps reached Angers on Aug 11, to turn and race up towards Chartres, with XII Corps now outside aiming for Orléans. They were advancing at 16–20 miles and using up 250,000 US gallons of petrol per day when suddenly there was a check on the left. Hitler had ordered Hausser's Seventh Army to cut Patton's lines of supply by a drive across the base of the Cotentin Peninsula to Avranches, and it reached within 12 miles before Bradley's First Army stopped it. But the panzer divisions plus the infantry of two German armies were west of a line from Falaise down to Argentan; if that gap was closed they would be trapped.

Patton's XX Corps drove north from Le Mans towards Argentan and the Canadians and British drove down from Caen to Falaise, while US and British bombers and fighter-bombers pounded everything that moved in the pocket; although the gap was not closed, German losses amounted to 60,000 men and practically all the equipment of the entire force. By Aug 20 the pocket was empty and Allied strength was swung east towards the Seine.

Two of Patton's corps cut the Seine both above and below Paris during the next two days while his right-hand corps reached Sens on Aug 22 – and on Aug 25, accompanied by 2nd French Armoured Division under the brilliant General Leclerc, American troops entered Paris.

Meanwhile, from Le Havre up the length of the river to Sens the Allied advance was flooding onwards, and by the end of the

Aug 22–25 German shipping, including *Tirpitz*, attacked in Altenfjord

Attacks become spasmodic towards end of month

Aug 2 First PLUTO – 'Pipe Line Under The Ocean' – becomes operational between Isle of Wight and Cherbourg

Over 48,000 sorties made to drop 79,000 tons in four categories – (a) support of ground troops in France (b) oil production centres in Germany, Poland and Czechoslovakia (c) attacks on V-weapon storage and launching sites (d) strategic bombing of Germany

MAAF flies 10,000 sorties in support of Allied landings in S France, dropping 7,500 tons

Over 73,000 sorties made to drop 122,000 (US) tons in daylight raids over France and Germany. Concentrations on aircraft factories and oil installations. Peenemunde twice heavily attacked. Fighter-bombers fly 24,000 sorties in support of ground troops

Aug 4 For first time, at Russian request, USAAF carries out heavy raid on Rumanian bases and lands in Russia. Returns to England via Italy, bombing Rumania again, Italy and Germany en route

Aug 14 Warsaw – RAF begins supply and ammunition drops to Polish insurgents

Bucarest bombed as reprisal for Rumania's defection

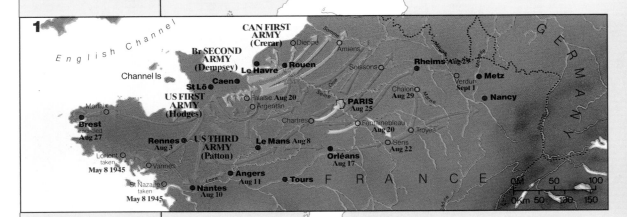

month British and Canadian troops from 21st Army Group were on the Somme from Amiens to the coast, while on their right Patton's corps continued the line on down through Soissons to Rheims and Verdun, with Nancy and Metz threatened further south. In a single month, Allied troops had liberated almost the whole of northern France, from the Atlantic to the Belgian border.

They had also invaded southern France. Aided by French commandos, twelve battalions of US VI Corps had landed east of Toulon on Aug 15 and within a few days had occupied Toulon and Marseilles, then to drive north up the Rhône valley and the Route Napoléon. They were in Grenoble by Aug 23 and by the end of the month approaching Lyons.

The invasion of Europe was now well ahead of schedule.

3 Operation Bagration concluded. It is hardly surprising that by the end of July the pace of the Russian advance was flagging. Not only were their own losses causing some concern, but the number of prisoners the rear administration had now to deal with – however rudimentarily – was itself a large-scale problem, in addition to those inherent in any advance bringing about the lengthening of lines of communication and supply.

Sheer momentum did, however, edge the lines a little further west during August. From Pskov Third Baltic Front hooked around the western side of Lake Peipus to reach Tartu by Aug 25 while away to the south, First Baltic having taken Kaunas, then drove up to the Gulf of Riga, thus apparently cutting off the retreat of a large part of Army Group North in Estonia. Here, however, there was still enough German strength to retaliate, and in the middle of the month four panzer divisions combined to smash open a corridor and form a defence perimeter around Riga.

To the south, weakening advance slowed in the face of strengthening defence. East Prussia, though its borders were crossed, remained unoccupied for a while longer, and the line then continued down the east bank of the Narew as far as the approaches to Warsaw. In the city itself, throughout July the Polish Home Army had listened with growing hope to the

sounds of approaching battle, and at the end of that month in an effort at least to establish their own identity and thus be able to welcome the Red Army as guests into their capital, they rose in revolt against the German occupiers.

At first, surprise and reckless bravery gave the Poles control of large and important sectors of the city, but then to their dismay they heard the sounds of the Red Army approach die away, and by the middle of the month they knew they were on their own – against newly arrived German forces especially chosen, it would seem, for their ruthlessness.

According to Russian accounts, the leaders of the revolt had made no attempt to consult them about their intentions – indeed it would seem that Stalin regarded the Polish Home Army as inimical to his own designs as the Germans themselves. This latter condition combined with the undoubted fact that the Red Army's mighty achievements since June would certainly have tired, and might well have exhausted, them, doomed the Warsaw Rising, and led to the deaths of thousands of brave men and women who had wished to preserve Poland from the two nations who have menaced her for centuries.

South of Warsaw, as to the north, the Russian advances throughout August crept forward, achieving a solid bridgehead over the Vistula at Sandomierz by Aug 18, then continuing down along the line of the Carpathian foothills as far as the

Transylvanian Alps. Here, however, the picture changed. From having played comparatively subsidiary roles throughout June and July, Malinovsky's Second and Tolbukhin's Third Ukrainian Fronts burst into action in August.

On Aug 20 Malinovsky's armies broke through Army Group South Ukraine in the Prut valley opposite Jassy, two days later they had taken Kishinev and on the same day linked up with tanks from Tolbukhin's front, which had driven over the lower Dniestr into Bessarabia. Their basic intention had been to split Army Group South Ukraine into pieces, but political developments intervened; a *coup d'état* took place in Bucarest, Antonescu's Fascist government was overthrown and King Michael promptly appealed for peace.

With the almost immediate disintegration of two Rumanian armies in front of them, Second Ukrainian Front swept down on the right through Focsani and Buzau to Ploesti and its vital oilwells by Aug 30, and on the left through Galatz into Bucarest the following day, while Third Ukrainian Front aided by the Black Sea Fleet, raced along the coast through Constanta and into Bulgaria – where it soon became evident that a similar series of political developments was imminent.

Thus by the end of August, to the west of the Carpathians the Danube valley and Hungary lay open to the Red Army, as did first Sofia and then southern Yugoslavia, further south.

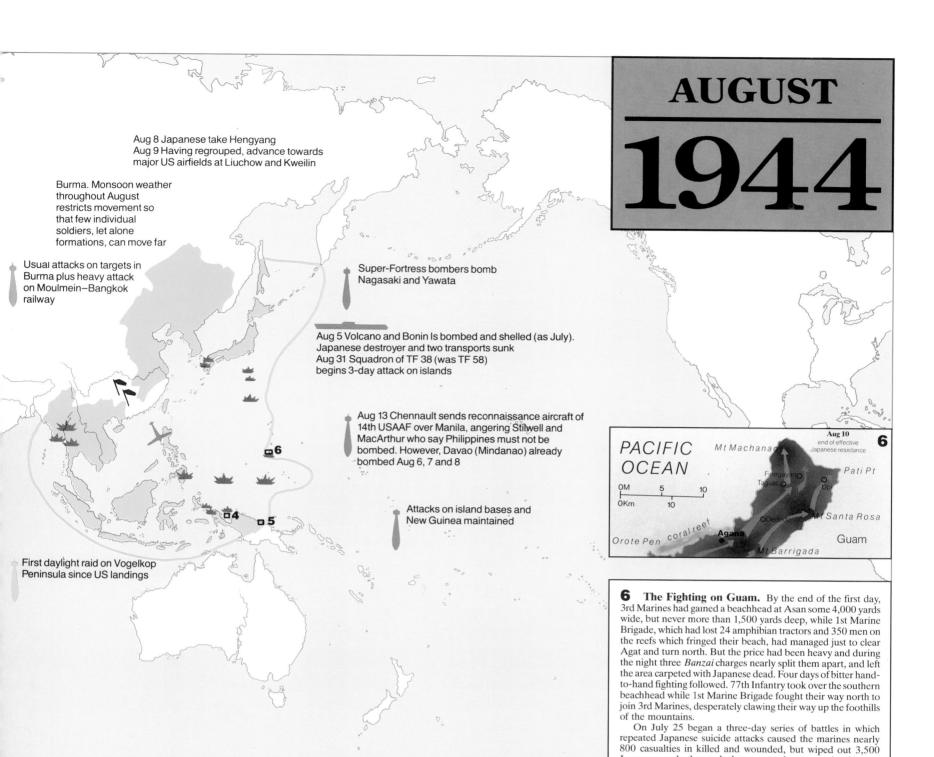

Aug 8 Japanese take Hengyang
Aug 9 Having regrouped, advance towards major US airfields at Liuchow and Kweilin

Burma. Monsoon weather throughout August restricts movement so that few individual soldiers, let alone formations, can move far

Usual attacks on targets in Burma plus heavy attack on Moulmein–Bangkok railway

Super-Fortress bombers bomb Nagasaki and Yawata

Aug 5 Volcano and Bonin Is bombed and shelled (as July). Japanese destroyer and two transports sunk
Aug 31 Squadron of TF 38 (was TF 58) begins 3-day attack on islands

Aug 13 Chennault sends reconnaissance aircraft of 14th USAAF over Manila, angering Stilwell and MacArthur who say Philippines must not be bombed. However, Davao (Mindanao) already bombed Aug 6, 7 and 8

Attacks on island bases and New Guinea maintained

First daylight raid on Vogelkop Peninsula since US landings

PACIFIC OCEAN

6

Aug 10 end of effective Japanese resistance

Mt Machanao
Finegayan
Taguac
Pati Pt
Dededo
Mt Santa Rosa
Agana
Orote Pen coral reef
Mt Barrigada
Guam

0M 5 10
0Km 10

6 **The Fighting on Guam.** By the end of the first day, 3rd Marines had gained a beachhead at Asan some 4,000 yards wide, but never more than 1,500 yards deep, while 1st Marine Brigade, which had lost 24 amphibian tractors and 350 men on the reefs which fringed their beach, had managed just to clear Agat and turn north. But the price had been heavy and during the night three *Banzai* charges nearly split them apart, and left the area carpeted with Japanese dead. Four days of bitter hand-to-hand fighting followed. 77th Infantry took over the southern beachhead while 1st Marine Brigade fought their way north to join 3rd Marines, desperately clawing their way up the foothills of the mountains.

On July 25 began a three-day series of battles in which repeated Japanese suicide attacks caused the marines nearly 800 casualties in killed and wounded, but wiped out 3,500 Japanese; and other such charges cost the same ratio of losses. Inevitably, the two US divisions pushed further and further into the island and on Aug 10 organised Japanese resistance ended. But it was 1960 before the last Japanese soldier came out of hiding.

4 **Biak.** The fighting on the island dragged on sporadically all through July, and it was, in fact, not until July 22 that a concentrated drive north from Borokoe broke completely clear of the bridgehead, though it must be said that physical conditions had delayed the move just as much as Japanese resistance. However, with the delays in movement more naval and ground forces had become available and in order to wind the operation down, combat teams were landed first at Korim Bay on Aug 3, then at Wardo and Warsa Bay, both to drive in and meet the forces coming up from Borokoe and to cut off the retreating remnants of the Japanese forces. Even so, some of them managed to escape to Soepiori and it was January 1945 before the last Japanese resistance was eliminated. In all 7,200 Japanese died – at the end many of starvation.

5 **The Last Resistance.** By the end of July General Adachi's men were so weakened by starvation and battle that even they began to accept the futility of further resistance. On July 31 the US forces had crossed the Driniumor estuary and driven south along the east bank, and by Aug 4 were obviously in a position to cut off the escape routes of any Japanese units still in the Torricelli foothills. Despairingly but efficiently, these therefore disengaged and withdrew; but by Aug 10 most of them had been caught, the remainder dispersing into the rugged hinterland of New Guinea, to die of disease or starvation.

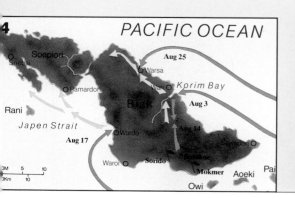

4 PACIFIC OCEAN

Soepiori
Warsa
Pamardon
Korim Bay
Aug 25
Aug 3
Rani
Japen Strait
Aug 14
Aug 17
Wardo
Sorido
Mokmer
Borokoe
Owi
Samardori
Aoeki
Pai

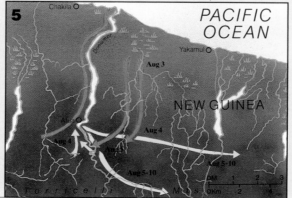

5 PACIFIC OCEAN

Chakila
Yakamul
Aug 3
NEW GUINEA
Aug 4
Aug 4
Aug 5-10
Aug 5-10
Torricelli Mts

1 Seine to the German Frontier. By Aug 31 – a mere 86 days after D-Day and well ahead of schedule – 30 Allied divisions were on or across the Seine. Canadians and British troops had reached the Somme, US First Army was spread between the Oise and the Meuse aiming for Mons and Namur, while on their right Patton's men were on the Meuse, their commander proclaiming that given the fuel and supplies and aided by the US VI Corps and the French commandos coming up from the south, they would be through Metz and into Germany within ten days.

The problem, of course, was that 'fuel and supplies' factor. The only large port yet in Allied hands was Cherbourg and that still hardly operational because of German demolitions. One Mulberry had been wrecked and the other at its fullest capacity

Sept 7 Finnish Peace Delegation arrives in Moscow
Sept 10 Armistice signed

By Sept 30 2,300 flying bombs (of 8,000 launched) reach London
Sept 8 First V2 rocket lands in Chiswick, London

RAF in day and night bombing drops 52,400 tons of bombs and 1,706,000 incendiaries on oil production, supply and communication centres in Germany

Sept 10–16 Second Quebec Conference between Churchill and Roosevelt

French, Dutch and Belgian ports bombed. Mosquitoes and rocket-firing Typhoons support ground operations. Coastal Command flies 4,700 sorties against U-boats and German shipping

USAAF drops 100,000 tons on Germany, Italy and Balkans using Fortresses and Liberators especially over German industrial centres. 1,200 German aircraft destroyed, 530 in air battles

Sept 18 USAAF drops supplies to Polish Home Army in Warsaw and lands in Russia

Germans evacuate garrisons from Aegean islands. 60,000 leave Crete

Tito's Partisans and Br commandos liberate Dalmatian islands

3 The Drive to Riga. The reopening of the corridor from Lithuania to Esthonia in the middle of August was enough challenge to the Baltic Fronts to ensure a massive response. On the morning of Sept 14, 125 Soviet divisions with armoured support and heavy artillery cover opened an assault which stretched from Narva past Lake Peipus and across the Dvina.

At first the German defence lines, as ever, proved difficult to penetrate, but even Hitler could accept that the position of the German forces north of Riga would soon become untenable, and to the surprise of General Schörner, gave permission for them to fall back to the Riga defences.

As a result, Leningrad Front reached Tallinn by Sept 22 and drove on around to take Haapsalu three days later while to the south Second and Third Baltic Fronts broke through south of Tartu to close up to the western face of the Riga line.

In the meantime First Baltic Front had attacked from the south but also been blocked by the defence line, so for the moment STAVKA agreed to a pause while the northern fronts prepared a major assault and First Baltic switched their attention due west for an attack towards Memel.

4 The Drive to Hungary. Rumania had deserted the Axis by the end of August, and by Sept 4 Bulgaria had declared an end to the war with the Western Allies. This did not prevent Tolbukhin's Third Ukrainian Front sweeping across the frontier and driving first down to Varna and Burgas, then in the south across towards Sofia and in the north along the Danube towards Belgrade.

Further north, Malinovsky now divided his front into two – the southern half consisting of one tank and two infantry armies to continue the sweep through Rumania and up towards Budapest, the northern half of two infantry armies and a motorised group to clear the eastern Carpathians. By Sept 7 one arm of his force had driven north from Bucarest to reach Sibiu and then drive on towards Cluj and Oradea, while on their left another arm reached Turnu Severin on Sept 8 and swung north towards Arad. It looked for a few days as though Hungary would be invaded well before the end of the month, but Malinovsky's vehicles and especially the tank tracks had taken a beating, and a halt had to be called to yet another spectacular advance. In the north, too, the physical problems of driving through the Carpathians had hindered a rapid stroke. Nevertheless, Targu Mures was taken before the end of the month, the Germans retreating into Hungary, the Rumanian formations just disintegrating.

This defection of two allies obviously presented problems to the German command, for two army groups – E and F – now seemed likely to be trapped to the south. Army Group F under Field Marshal Weichs was in Yugoslavia and Albania, E under Colonel-General Löhr held Greece. Six hundred thousand men stood in evident danger of being cut off.

would only supply the British, and although by now half a million trucks were ashore, only 15,000 of them were long-distance load carriers. Despite the underwater fuel pipeline, PLUTO, and the 'Red Ball Express' which hurtled along a one-way route from Caen to the rear US bases carrying nothing but petrol, Patton's fuel tanks were empty and there was not enough coming up fast enough for him to lunge forward yet again.

General Montgomery's plans for the advance were for the Canadian forces on the left to invest as quickly as possible the nearer ports, then to press onwards to Zeebrugge and the vital Scheldt Estuary and Antwerp, while the Second British Army drove through Amiens, Arras, Lille and Tournai towards Brussels, the left-hand corps peeling off towards Antwerp once across the Belgian border.

Le Havre was encircled by Sept 1 though it did not fall until the port was a ruin 12 days later; Dieppe fell quite easily, but Boulogne and Calais were stoutly defended on Hitler's orders and rendered almost useless before capture.

But the British drive on the right was swift and spectacular. By Sept 1, XXX Corps armour were on the Scarpe at Arras, the following day both US and British troops reached Tournai and then two brigades of the Guards Armoured Division were ordered to race each other for the centre of Brussels. Despite a couple of sharp actions they both arrived within minutes of each other early on the morning of Sept 3 – to spend the rest of the day mobbed by delighted Bruxellois. On their left 11th Armoured Division reached the outskirts of Antwerp the following day – to an equally enthusiastic welcome which unfortunately lulled everyone into a false sense of security. The Germans along the banks of the Scheldt Estuary were to take full advantage of this.

However, the rapid advance through Belgium gave strength to Montgomery's arguments for a single, powerful drive along the northern flank, with 21st and 12th Army Groups side by side encircling the Ruhr, then smashing on into the heart of Germany before the end of the year. To Patton's fury, for his command would be left well behind down in the south, Eisenhower decided to let at least the first part of Montgomery's plans go ahead – *Operation Market Garden*, the laying of an airborne carpet across the Netherlands to capture vital bridges over which British and US armour would race.

On the morning of Sept 17, three airborne divisions – US 101st and British 1st – were dropped respectively near Eindhoven, Nijmegen and Arnhem. At first all seemed to go well, both US divisions succeeded and by Sept 20 British armour was through to Nijmegen. But at Arnhem the lightly armed paratroops were attacked by two SS panzer divisions, the weather broke and the armour could not get through to their rescue. By the end of the month, the survivors had been withdrawn, and the vital Arnhem bridge destroyed from the air.

2 Through the Gothic Line. For the invasion of southern France, seven infantry divisions – three US and four French (including the North African mountain division) – had been stripped away from Alexander's command; yet he was still expected to break north into the Po valley before winter.

His best chance lay in surprise, followed by a series of 'left and right punches' and with these factors in mind, during August he shifted the main weight of Eighth Army towards the Adriatic coast, where the Polish Corps waited. During the last days of August, they cleared the ground between the Metauro and Foglia rivers, the Germans efficiently dropping back into the main defences behind them. But perhaps because there was no pause in the British attack, some vital positions fell to them before the Germans had consolidated. By Sept 2 on the right they were at Cattolica and hoping to reach Rimini in a single bound, but now the weather broke and torrential rain flooded the area. To give Eighth Army time to regroup, Alexander asked Clark to launch his Fifth Army on the far coast. By Sept 11 they were through the Gothic Line at Pistoia to open the way through the vital Futa Pass on Sept 23. Rain now held Fifth Army in place, but they had given Eighth Army the chance to move on into Rimini and beyond by Sept 21.

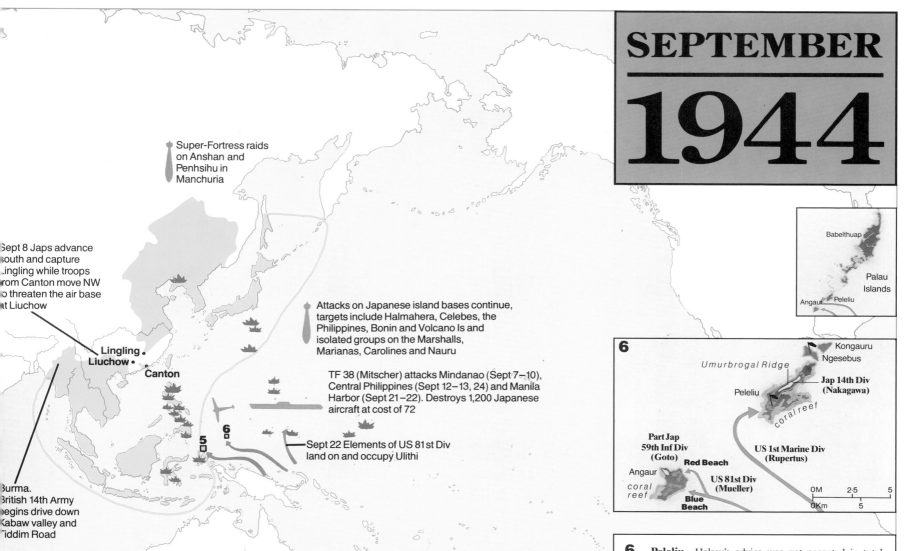

Super-Fortress raids on Anshan and Penhsihu in Manchuria

Sept 8 Japs advance south and capture Lingling while troops from Canton move NW to threaten the air base at Liuchow

Lingling • Liuchow •

Canton

Attacks on Japanese island bases continue, targets include Halmahera, Celebes, the Philippines, Bonin and Volcano Is and isolated groups on the Marshalls, Marianas, Carolines and Nauru

TF 38 (Mitscher) attacks Mindanao (Sept 7–10), Central Philippines (Sept 12–13, 24) and Manila Harbor (Sept 21–22). Destroys 1,200 Japanese aircraft at cost of 72

Sept 22 Elements of US 81st Div land on and occupy Ulithi

Burma. British 14th Army begins drive down Kabaw valley and Tiddim Road

Babelthuap
Palau Islands
Angaur • Peleliu

6
Kongauru
Ngesebus
Umurbrogal Ridge
Jap 14th Div (Nakagawa)
Peleliu
coral reef
Part Jap 59th Inf Div (Goto) — Red Beach
Angaur — US 1st Marine Div (Rupertus)
coral reef
US 81st Div (Mueller)
Blue Beach
0M   2·5   5
0Km   5

5
Sept 19   Cape Sopi
PACIFIC OCEAN
Padangi
Raoe
Tjioe
Sept 18
Morotai
Posiposi
Wajaboela   *Sabatai Mts*
Sept 21
Sept 17
Pilowo
Baroe   Sangowo
Doroeba   Sabatai-Toea   Sept 17
Sept 15   Pitoe
Sept 17
0M   5   10
0Km   10

5   The Halmaheras. With New Guinea now under Allied control, the next obvious step towards the Philippines was into the Moluccas. Growing American power and the implacable advances during the last few months gave the Japanese High Command no choice but to react to Allied threats, so they reinforced the garrison on Halmahera and increased the strength of the squadrons operating from the several airstrips. As for the situation on the island of Morotai to the north, they had little to spare for its protection – a position which quickly became clear to US Intelligence.

As a result, during the early days of September carrier-based aircraft and land-based bombers hit the airfields on Halmahera almost daily, together with airfields on Mindanao, Luzon and in the Visayas between. Fighters attacked defence posts, shipping and troop concentrations, and on the morning of Sept 15 the Third Fleet was off Morotai, heavily shelling all shore positions. A task force of one division plus a regimental combat team went ashore at Pitoe Bay. Two days later Seventh Amphibious Force convoys ferried more combat units to the islands off the south-west coast, then on up to Tjioe and the northern tip of the island, while more troops were put ashore at Sangowo.

The Japanese units on Morotai fought with their customary ferocity, but they were without heavy artillery, and had no hope of support or reinforcement from Halmahera. By Sept 21 all vital positions were in US hands and within 14 days MacArthur could write, 'We now dominate the Moluccas.'

☆ **The Pace Quickens.** By the summer of 1944 it was quite evident that General MacArthur would have his way and return to the Philippines. Admiral Nimitz still argued for an advance from the Marianas to Taiwan, bypassing the Philippines, but MacArthur could claim not only that his route through Halmahera into Mindanao and then on to Luzon was the most feasible approach to the Japanese homeland as his forces could move under cover of land-based air power from start to finish, but could also offer the emotive consideration that the Philippines had been American territory from which they had been ejected by the enemy, and that the Philippine population, despite great hardships, had in the main remained loyal to America. They deserved early liberation.

President Roosevelt held long talks with both Nimitz and MacArthur during the summer and listened carefully to both arguments, deciding tentatively in MacArthur's favour – though postponing a full decision until the Second Quebec Conference, to be held on Sept 11. In the meantime plans entitled 'Musketeer 11', drawn up by MacArthur's staff, envisaged a landing in southern Mindanao on Nov 15, 1944, and on Leyte on Dec 20 – with landings in Lingayen Gulf followed by occupation of Manila and central Luzon scheduled for February and March 1945.

But during early September, a change in the military picture was revealed which led to a drastic revision of the time-scale. On Sept 1 Admiral Halsey had taken command of the US Third Fleet and on Sept 7, as part of the preliminary support for the landings on Morotai, he sent Admiral Mitscher's Task Force 38 of 17 carriers with 340 aircraft to attack Mindanao. A fierce battle had been expected – but very few Japanese planes had been encountered, and investigation revealed that bombings carried out during the previous weeks from bases in New Guinea had severely damaged the Japanese installations. On Sept 12 and 13, attacks on Japanese air bases in the islands between Mindanao and Luzon revealed similar pictures; Japanese air power in the Philippines was at an unexpectedly low level, though how long it would remain so was unclear, for Intelligence sources did indicate that Japanese ground forces in the Philippines were being strengthened.

On Sept 13 Halsey signalled both Admiral Nimitz and General MacArthur that he thought that Leyte could quite possibly be seized immediately – but only if the US Navy dropped plans for extended operations through the Carolines, with the exception of the capture of Ulithi with its deep and wide naval anchorage. This suggestion reached the Joint Chiefs of Staff then attending the Quebec Conference and very quickly resulted in a cable to MacArthur asking by how much he thought he could advance his programme. Within hours a reply came of which the concluding phrase read, 'I am prepared to move immediately to execution of the Leyte landings with a target date of 20 Oct 44.'

He was about to fulfil his famous promise to return.

6   Peleliu. Halsey's advice was not accepted in total. Nimitz still considered that the Palau islands must be taken, both to remove a possible threat to MacArthur's drive up into the Philippines and also to provide a base for further action. His argument was given further strength by Intelligence assessments which suggested that the 25,000 Japanese troops spread throughout the islands would prove no more difficult to defeat than those which had lately been encountered in other islands. In this they were to be proved mistaken.

Lieutenant-General Inoue was an intelligent soldier who had studied recent American tactics, and his 14th Division was one of the finest in the Japanese Army. There would be no useless *Banzai* charges from this division, and its defences, instead of being concentrated on the beaches where they would be annihilated by US air and naval bombardment, lay further back in caves and tunnels through the mass of decayed coral which formed the backbones of the islands, themselves so covered with woods and scrub vegetation that US reconnaissance had seen nothing to indicate their existence.

There was, however, no point in the Americans assaulting the main island, Babelthuap, for there was nothing tactically to justify the cost of capturing it. But on the southern end of the island chain lay Peleliu with a sizeable airstrip, with Ngesebus at its northern end with another, and Angaur to the south. These were the chosen targets for an operation, in the event not unsuitably named *Stalemate*, and carrier-based aircraft from US Third Fleet began airstrikes on Peleliu on Sept 10. Two days later the battleships, cruisers and destroyers of the Fire Support Group arrived offshore to add their weight to the plastering the beaches were taking, to such effect that on the evening of Sept 14 the naval commander reported confidently, 'We have run out of targets.'

D-Day, Sept 15, dawned warm and clear. At 0530 the final three-hour bombardment began and at 0832, under the cover of 50 fighter-bombers, the first wave of 1st Marine Division hit the beaches, followed by successive waves every five minutes. At first all seemed to go well, though a larger number of amphibious vehicles than usual were put out of action, and the left flank of the landing was pinned down by fire from an undiscovered post. But in the centre the marines reached the airstrip and the east coast by nightfall. The following two days were to demonstrate the strength of the defences, but also the aggressiveness of the marines for more and more were landed through the Japanese fire. But by the end of the month, though the beaches and the airstrip were in US hands, the central coral ridge – Umurbrogal – was still in Japanese hands and was to remain so until the end of November.

Angaur was assaulted on Sept 17 by US 81st (Wildcat) Division and the story there was similar. The further inland they penetrated the tougher the fighting became – despite the fact that there were only 1,400 Japanese troops on the island. From well-fortified positions they held the 81st at bay for seven days; even when surrounded they continued to resist. It was not until Oct 23 that the last shots were fired.

The Palaus cost the Americans 1,800 killed and 8,000 wounded. Some 14,000 Japanese were killed.

1 The Scheldt Estuary. By the end of September realisation of Allied failure to secure the vital port of Antwerp was complete and measures had been taken by both sides. Formations of the German Fifteenth Army under General von Zangen were brought rapidly back along the coast to form a pocket around Breskens from Zeebrugge to the Braakman Inlet, then to transfer the bulk across the Scheldt to hold the northern bank from Walcheren along South Beveland to the neck of the isthmus. On the mainland to the east, General Student's First Parachute Army was moved into place.

On the Allied side, Canadians and Poles held positions south of the Scheldt to Antwerp. On their right was now deployed the British I Corps, and Montgomery's orders were that between them they were to open the Scheldt Estuary to

Antwerp, and at the same time advance north-eastwards towards Tilburg.

The Canadian 2nd Division moved first, driving north from Antwerp and by Oct 6 had reached the neck of the South Beveland isthmus, but there they were first blocked and then driven back by Student's paratroops until after Oct 23, when the Canadian 4th Armoured Division came up, with Polish armour and US 104th infantry on their right, and drove both Fifteenth Army and parachute units back through Bergen Op Zoom, allowing the 2nd Division to drive westwards. They were held up by floods but by Oct 26 had advanced 10 miles.

Meanwhile, Calais had fallen and released more troops towards the Breskens Pocket. Early attempts to breach the defence line across the marshes failed, but on Oct 19 the Canadians broke through to reach Aardenburg, then to swing westwards towards Knokke, which fell to them on Nov 1, as did Zeebrugge. This drive had been helped by a second, across the Braakman Inlet by Canadian infantry in Buffaloes from 79th Armoured Division. Surprise was complete, other formations followed into the bridgehead, to break out and take Breskens on Oct 21. Then on Oct 27, Cameronians and Royal Scots of the 52nd Lowland Division crossed the Scheldt from near the Braakman in 137 Buffaloes to land on South Beveland beaches. Two days later they had linked with Canadians at Goes, then crossed into North Beveland. On the same day the causeway leading to Walcheren was reached, but it was known that strong defences here would necessitate a powerful assault, to be mounted the following month.

To the east of Antwerp British troops had reached Venray, while to the south-east, US First Army had occupied Aachen.

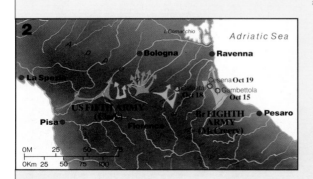

2 Stalemate. For the Allies, this period was the most frustrating of a frustrating campaign. The last week of September had been one long drenching downpour, and so it continued into October. But still the struggle went on, to reach Bologna in the centre and Ravenna on the Adriatic coast, thus to open the way into the Po valley.

Eighth Army was now commanded by General McCreery, and he used his experienced 10th Indian Division to drive along the coast through Gambettola and Cesena, but even they could do little to cross narrow streams swollen to raging torrents without bridging equipment, any example of which was quickly shot to pieces by Kesselring's hard-pressed but efficient formations, almost always outnumbered but equally often holding the higher ground.

The other problem facing both McCreery and Clark was shortage of infantry. Fifth Army's II Corps had lost 15,716 men in killed, wounded or sick since early September, and in this weather and this country, Allied supremacy in armour counted for little. By the end of the month, although they had edged a few miles closer to Bologna, it was still beyond their grasp.

Oct 7–29 Russian Karelian Front pushes German forces from Litsa river positions into Norway

Kirkenes
Petsamo Oct 25
Nautsi Oct 27

Oct 29 *Tirpitz* bombed by Lancasters

Oct 9 Third Moscow Conference. Churchill and Stalin discuss Polish problems

Oct 3 Polish Home Army finally surrenders to German SS

Oct 18 Announced all German males aged 16–60 to be conscripted

Germans continue to launch V1s and V2s at UK

Bomber Command drops 50,000 tons on German cities, 10,000 on Occupied Territories. Communication and oil production centres, Kembs and Sorpe dams hit. Mosquitoes drop 1,500 tons in six Berlin raids. Walcheren and Breskens attacked in support of ground troops. 3,900 sorties by Coastal Command

USAAF drops 99,700 tons on oil plants, rail and industrial centres. Berlin, Kassel, Cologne, Schweinfurt, Bremen and Osnabrück particularly heavily bombed

Oct 18 RN parties land on Scarpanto and Santorini

4 Escape of the German Southern Armies. The flooding advance across the Carpathians in the north, the Transylvanian Alps in the centre, and from the Dniestr well across the Danube in the south had taken its toll of the Red Army.

As a result, Tolbukhin's Third Ukrainian Front, though it had practically occupied the Danube bend during September and by Oct 4 was on the northern bank of the river opposite Belgrade, was stalled there until they managed to slip armour across the river from Turnu Severin and send them up through Nis. There they joined Tito's Partisans in a concentrated attack on Belgrade, which they entered on Oct 19.

Meanwhile, away to the north, Malinovsky's Second Ukrainian Front, suffering from the same problems as those facing Tolbukhin's armies, had attacked northwards on Oct 6, hoping to take Budapest. The Hungarian portion of Army Group South Ukraine melted away rapidly, but when Sixth Guards Tank Army reached Oradea, they were brought to an abrupt halt by strong German panzer forces. Moreover, another panzer division arrived from Budapest, cut through Soviet forces driving up past Debrecen and during the next two days a tank battle was fought out on the flat Hungarian plains, reminiscent in ferocity of the cauldron battles of Kursk.

Even after the Soviet armour had broken clear and resumed their northwards drive towards Nyiregyhaza, they were by no means out of trouble. The panzer forces were now deployed west of the Debrecen–Nyireghhaza line, but to the east lay motorised forces of Friessner's Sixth Army, likely to be trapped. With some of the flair of the old Blitzkrieg days, both forces drove towards each other; their spearheads met after three days, and Sixth Army survivors stormed through the corridor leaving Malinovsky's forces in a state of some shock and disarray.

5 Operation Manna. During the summer it had become increasingly obvious that the German position in Greece was weakening and that it would need little pressure to relieve the long-suffering Greek population of their occupiers. There were not many troops available in view of the commitments in Italy, so only scratch formations could be used. On Sept 23 some 60 Special Service troops had been parachuted on to an airstrip at Araxos, and the following day Dakotas with a mixed force of commandos and men from the Royal Air Force Regiment arrived with jeeps and light weapons. It took them until Oct 4 to take the small port of Patras, the German garrison leaving for Athens by sea, but after that progress quickened. By Oct 7 they had reached Corinth, on Oct 13 more paratroops were dropped into Megara and the following day the Germans left Athens and the British drove in, to a tumultuous reception from the Athenians.

The German withdrawal continued, though as usual they left rearguards and booby-traps to delay pursuit. By the end of the month they were leaving Florina and crossing into Yugoslavia, but in the meantime two seaborne forces had landed to harass them. On Oct 12 British forces had been put ashore on Corfu and in southern Albania, while in the Adriatic a squadron of Special Service troops had visited several of the northern Sporades islands and driven out the remaining German garrisons, then to land at Salonika. There they commandeered transport in which to race into the centre of the city and fight a brisk battle with the last of the German garrison. By the end of the month Greece had been liberated, though a civil war between Communist and anti-Communist parties was obviously imminent.

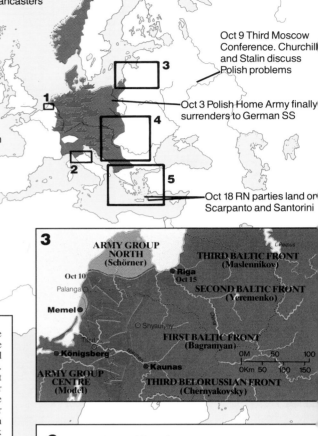

3 The Drive to Memel. First Baltic Front opened their westward drive on Oct 5, and by Oct 10 had reached Palanga on the coast. To the south they reached the Memel perimeter and on down to the line of the Niemen river. Further south, Third Belorussian Front had also driven forward and into East Prussia at the end of the month. More importantly, at the northern end of the line, Second and Third Baltic Fronts launched their main attacks on the Riga defence line on Oct 10, by Oct 13 all the northern section of the city was in their hands and two days later they had crossed the Dvina and occupied the rest of the city. The last Baltic capital had now been liberated from the Germans, as had the larger part of the States themselves.

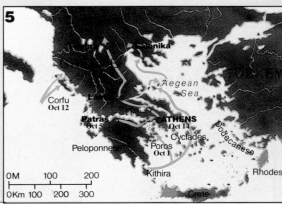

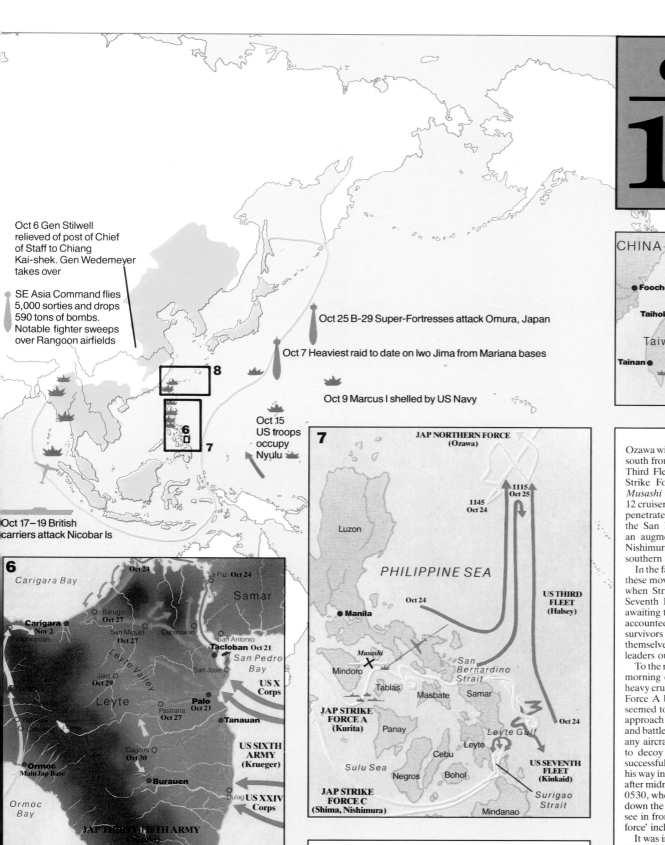

OCTOBER
1944

Oct 6 Gen Stilwell relieved of post of Chief of Staff to Chiang Kai-shek. Gen Wedemeyer takes over

SE Asia Command flies 5,000 sorties and drops 590 tons of bombs. Notable fighter sweeps over Rangoon airfields

Oct 25 B-29 Super-Fortresses attack Omura, Japan

Oct 7 Heaviest raid to date on Iwo Jima from Mariana bases

Oct 9 Marcus I shelled by US Navy

Oct 15 US troops occupy Nyulu

Oct 17–19 British carriers attack Nicobar Is

Map 8 — CHINA / Taiwan
Yellow Sea, Amami O Shima, Tokuno, Foochow, Okinawa Oct 10, Taihoku, Ishigaka, Miyako, Iriomote, Oct 12–14, Tainan, **US THIRD FLEET (Halsey)**
0M 100 200 / 0Km 100 200 300

Map 6 — Leyte Island
Carigara Bay, Samar, La Paz Oct 24, Oct 24, Barugo Oct 24, Carigara Nov 2, Hinunangan, San Miguel Oct 27, Cabalawan, San Antonio, Tacloban Oct 21, San Pedro Bay, Jaro Oct 29, San Jose, Leyte Valley, **US X Corps**, Leyte, Pastrana Oct 27, Palo Oct 21, Tanauan, Dagami Oct 30, **US SIXTH ARMY (Krueger)**, Ormoc Main Jap Base, Burauen, Dulag **US XXIV Corps**, Ormoc Bay, **JAP THIRTY-FIFTH ARMY (Suzuki)**, Leyte Gulf, Abuyog Oct 29, Kilim, Balocawe
0M 5 10 / 0Km 10

Map 7 — Philippine Sea
JAP NORTHERN FORCE (Ozawa), 1115 Oct 25, 1145 Oct 24, Luzon, PHILIPPINE SEA, Manila, Oct 24, **US THIRD FLEET (Halsey)**, Musashi ✗, Mindoro, San Bernardino Strait, Tablas, Masbate, Samar, **JAP STRIKE FORCE A (Kurita)**, Panay, Leyte, Leyte Gulf, Sulu Sea, Cebu, Negros, Bohol, **US SEVENTH FLEET (Kinkaid)**, **JAP STRIKE FORCE C (Shima, Nishimura)**, Surigao Strait, Mindanao

6 Leyte Island – the Landings.

On the morning of Oct 20 the largest concentration of naval and transport shipping yet seen in the Pacific was assembled within the waters of Leyte Gulf. Over 700 vessels had brought the 200,000 men of General Krueger's Sixth Army to redeem General MacArthur's pledge, while scores of aircraft patrolled overhead and hundreds more waited on the carrier decks.

General MacArthur was there himself to watch the first two corps go ashore against negligible opposition along an 18-mile stretch of coast between Dulag and San Jose, and by the end of the day the first vital objective – Tacloban airfield – had been taken by the 1st Cavalry Division, who during the next few days were to drive north to secure the San Juanico Strait between Leyte and Samar, and on to reach Barugo on Carigara Bay.

To the south progress had been as rapid. Two divisions of XXIV Corps had pushed inland and by the end of the month the whole north-east triangle from Abuyog up to Carigara and across to San Juanico Strait was in American hands.

Meanwhile, to the east and north, the greatest naval battle of history had been fought.

7 & 8 Leyte Gulf – the Naval Battles.

On Oct 10, as part of the continuing campaign to reduce Japanese air strength, Admiral Halsey's Third Fleet of new and fast battleships and large aircraft-carriers launched the first of a series of attacks against Okinawa and then Taiwan. On Oct 12 aircraft from Halsey's 17 carriers of Task Force 38 destroyed 160 Japanese aircraft over Taiwan for a loss of 43, while between then and Oct 17, in further battles over northern Luzon, Japanese losses rose to 600 against 90 American. It was an indication not only of American industrial supremacy, but also of the dearth of experienced Japanese pilots compared with the days of Pearl Harbor and Coral Sea.

Halsey then withdrew southwards to take position to the north-east of Leyte Gulf and form a shield for the invasion force against dangers approaching either eastwards through the San Bernardino Strait or down from Japanese home waters. The western and southern flanks of MacArthur's forces were to be protected by Admiral Kinkaid's Seventh Fleet – directly subordinate to MacArthur, while Halsey was now under command of Admiral Nimitz.

With the fall of the Marianas in August the Japanese High Command knew that defeat stared them in the face. They therefore decided upon a bold stroke – a gamble – which might at least win them some time if it came off, and would certainly boost a rapidly falling morale: they would launch their entire naval strength against the next obviously imminent US amphibious assault, hoping not only to wreck it, but also to inflict severe losses on the American fleets. Once it became evident that Leyte Gulf was the target area, they activated Plan *Sho* (Victory), first sending their Main Body under Admiral Ozawa with 4 carriers, 2 battleships, 3 cruisers and 8 destroyers south from the Inland Sea to engage the attentions of Halsey's Third Fleet. Meanwhile under Admiral Kurita the powerful Strike Force A of 5 battleships including the 64,000-ton *Musashi* and *Yamato* (the biggest battleships in the world), 12 cruisers and 15 destroyers, would come east from Borneo to penetrate between Mindoro and Tablas and then through the San Bernardino Strait to attack from the north, while an augmented Strike Force C under Admirals Shima and Nishimura broke through the Surigao Strait to form the southern arm of a crushing pincer.

In the face of US air supremacy there was no chance of any of these movements passing unnoticed. By the evening of Oct 24 when Strike Force C reached Surigao Strait, the entire US Seventh Fleet Bombardment and Fire Support Group was awaiting them. Torpedo attacks from destroyers and PT boats accounted for 2 battleships and 2 destroyers; then when the survivors emerged at the eastern end of the strait they found themselves crossed by the T of the US battle-line which blew the leaders out of the water and chased the rest away.

To the north, Halsey's aircraft had found Kurita's force on the morning of the 24th, sunk the giant *Musashi* and crippled a heavy cruiser – and US submarines had already depleted Strike Force A by 3 cruisers and 2 destroyers! At this point Kurita seemed to turn back, and Halsey switched his attention to the approach from the north of Ozawa's main body with its carriers and battleships. Halsey was not to know that Ozawa had hardly any aircraft and that his movements were expressly intended to decoy the US Third Fleet north; and in this they were successful. After nightfall Kurita turned again, skilfully made his way into and through the San Bernardino Strait, and shortly after midnight on Oct 25 debouched into the Philippine Sea. By 0530, when he learned of Nishimura's defeat, he was speeding down the east coast of Samar towards Leyte Gulf, suddenly to see in front of him what he took to be a 'gigantic enemy task force' including carriers, battleships and cruisers.

It was in fact only the Seventh Fleet Northern Task Force of three slow, old escort carriers with a few destroyers, but Rear-Admiral Clifton Sprague reacted quickly, sending up his aircraft, recalling others and hiding his ships in a providential rain squall, at the same time radioing frantically for help. He was later to claim 'the definite partiality of Almighty God', for though no help could get down from the north and in the desperate manoeuvres carried out by his ships he lost an escort carrier and three destroyers, at 0900 Kurita's forces, only some 40 miles from the Leyte Gulf invasion force, turned and steamed away north.

The explanation for this extraordinary piece of good fortune for the American forces would seem to be that Kurita had been shaken the previous day by the ferocity of the US air attacks which had sunk the *Musashi*, and even more by the news that Nishimura's force had been annihilated. He had also intercepted Sprague's call for help and a reply which seemed to indicate a powerful force coming down from the north, and he was short of fuel. In the circumstances he felt that he had better retreat before he ran out and was caught.

Meanwhile, Halsey's carriers under Admiral Mitscher had found Ozawa's almost defenceless Main Body, and by late afternoon of Oct 25 had sunk all four carriers, a cruiser and a destroyer before Halsey accepted the danger of the situation to the south and turned back – too late as it happened to catch more than one of Kurita's destroyers.

The naval battle of Leyte Gulf spelled the end of Japanese naval power. The Combined Fleets lost 4 carriers, 3 battleships, 6 heavy cruisers, 3 light cruisers and 8 destroyers. Without aircraft or enough fuel, the remaining 12 capital ships could do little but swing at their moorings, awaiting the inevitable air attacks which would sink them.

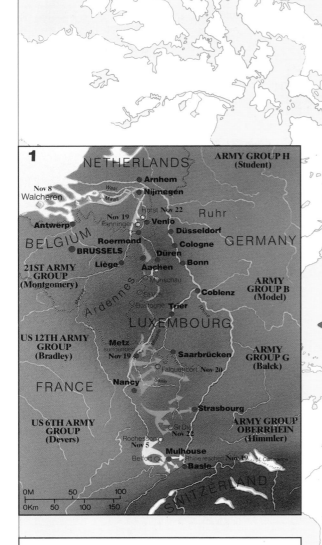

Nov 12 *Tirpitz* finally sunk by Lancasters in Tromsöfjord

Nov 14 Norwegian units land in Norway to operate with Russian Karelian Front against German 20th Mountain Army defences

Bomber Command drops 53,000 tons on German cities and oil production centres, 160 tons on Occupied Territories: Dortmund–Ems canal breached; V2 launching sites in Holland attacked

Army Group North isolated in Courland Peninsula and offshore islands. Hitler refuses permission for them to be evacuated

55,700 tons dropped on German oil production centres and railway marshalling yards. 723 Luftwaffe planes destroyed. Aachen defences hit in support of ground troops

Nov 7 Aegean cleared of Axis shipping

In V1 and V2 attacks on Britain and Low Countries 716 civilians killed and 1,511 injured; V1 and V2 attacks launched against Antwerp

Nov 26 Tito grants permission for use of Yugoslav ports and airfields by RN and RAF

1 Towards the Rhine. Walcheren, the hard block at the entrance to the Scheldt, was known to be well defended and throughout October had been the target of heavy and almost continuous bombing, which although it had demolished vital lengths of the dykes built to keep out the sea, had had little effect upon the well-dug-in German batteries. These covered the sea approaches and the mouth of the Scheldt, and were themselves defended by barbed wire and multiple machine-gun posts.

The main assault on the island took place on Nov 1 and was launched from three directions. Royal Marine commandos of 4th Special Service Brigade landed at Westkapelle on the western beach, an Army commando and a brigade from the 52nd Lowland Division crossed from the Breskens Pocket to land each side of Flushing, and Canadians drove across the causeway linking Walcheren and South Beveland to the east.

Flooded polder land, thick mud, foul weather and above all German tenacity turned the battle into a grim shambles, for tanks could not land and even amphibious Buffaloes could do little but bring up ammunition and food. Otherwise it was a purely infantry battle across bitterly cold mud, and it thus took four days for them to advance the five miles to Middleburg, though drives around the coast were slightly faster.

It was not until Nov 8 that the last German strongpoint was overcome and the vital minesweeping could commence. Two days later the first cargo ship gingerly felt her way up the estuary to Antwerp and some 10,000 tons was unloaded on Dec 1. By Dec 14, despite Luftwaffe, V1 and V2 attacks, 19,000 tons a day were being unloaded. At last the Anglo-American armies could be properly supplied.

Meanwhile, to the east of the Scheldt, British, Canadian and Polish units had continued their advance up to the line of the Maas as far as the bridgehead at Nijmegen, held the line to the south, improving it slightly with a drive towards Venlo and Roermond.

To the south, US forces held the long line down past Aachen through the Ardennes, but below them lay the forces of the increasingly impatient General Patton, determined to break through the Siegfried Line ahead of him and reach the Rhine before anyone else. Despite appalling weather, on Nov 8 he launched his divisions across the swollen Moselle river and country under worse floods than had been known for 25 years. Metz was quickly surrounded though it took 12 days of bloody fighting before it was occupied. Although only one bridge over the Moselle was still sound and the Seille river actually increased from 200 to 500 feet wide while Patton's engineers were trying to bridge it, two armoured and one infantry division were over and driving east by Nov 12, Falquencort was taken by Nov 20, St Die by Nov 22 and Strasbourg reached by the end of the month.

On Patton's right, First French Army – part of General Devers' 6th Army Group – were as eager to get forward as Patton. On Nov 5 they took Rochesson, broke through the Belfort Gap soon afterwards, swept through Mulhouse and reached the Rhine on Nov 19.

☆ **Winter Stalemate.** Despite the appalling weather, the Allies continued trying to edge their way forward through the Romagna. Only McCreery's Indian formations had the expertise to deal with the country, but although Forli was taken by Nov 9, and Ravenna was threatened, all that was happening was the gradual clearance of the front for a Spring Offensive. Nothing else was possible for either the British or the American armies.

2 The Balkan Front. It took a few days for Malinovsky's Second Ukrainian Front to recover from the shock of the armoured battle north of Debrecen, but a sudden signal from Stalin jolted their commander into another bout of activity. Budapest, announced Stalin, must be in their hands within a few days and no logistic figures would be enough to provide excuse. Even the five days suggested by Malinovsky was too long; Budapest must fall within 24 hours – 36 at the most!

Unfortunately for Stalin's requirements, Budapest was another victim of Hitler's *Festung* mania and Malinovsky's armies were still tired and short of supplies – in fact, his first attempt to reach Budapest by a drive west from Kecskemet, taken on Nov 1, reached the city suburbs to the south but then petered out through lack of ammunition and a scarcity of infantry to support the tanks. By Nov 5 the long right-hand flank of the thrust stretched from Szolnok west to the Danube and was immediately attacked by hurriedly assembled panzer formations in the flooded fields to the north. They were fought off, but Budapest was still inviolate.

Malinovsky's second attempt now developed further north, in a drive across the Tisza aimed at skirting the northern suburbs of Budapest, but it was blocked by the same combination of circumstances: shortage of supplies, exhaustion of troops, poor weather and German tenacity. By the end of the month a line from south of Miskolc through Eger to Hatvan had been taken, though the iron and steel centre of Miskolc remained in German hands despite an uprising by the factory workers.

To the south, Tolbukhin's Third Ukrainians, having handed Belgrade over to Tito's Partisans, were ordered to regroup along the middle reaches of the Danube and prepare to drive north-

west on Malinovsky's left flank along a Budapest–Vienna axis. During the second half of the month they bridged the river north of Apatin and drove on up towards Lake Balaton, taking Mohocs on Nov 26 and Pecs, with the support of a miners' rising, on Nov 29.

The redirection of Tolbukhin's armies along the line of the Danube northwards into Hungary considerably eased the pressure on the German Army Groups E and F. General Löhr pulled the last of his forces out of Greece on Nov 1 (though he left 45,000 men – one-third of them Italians – in the Greek islands) and his withdrawal through northern Greece and southern Yugoslavia had been helped by the sudden switch of the attentions of the Allied 'Balkan Air Force' from Yugoslavia to the Peloponnese in aid of the British moves there.

He fought off Russian and Bulgarian drives to cut his escape route at Skopje and further north, then continued up until ordered to turn and stand west of Belgrade. His left-hand formations which had hoped to hold a line eastwards from Scutari – where one of his divisions was held in place until the end of the month by Albanian guerrillas – dropped back to keep level, the German movements harried but not particularly hampered by Partisan formations, who were generally too lightly armed to press them hard.

As for Army Group F, its Second Panzer Army had been badly hit during the fighting in October around Belgrade, but the diversion of Tolbukhin's forces northwards gave it and the rest of the Group time to reorganise in the Drava valley and await the arrival of Army Group E on its southern flank.

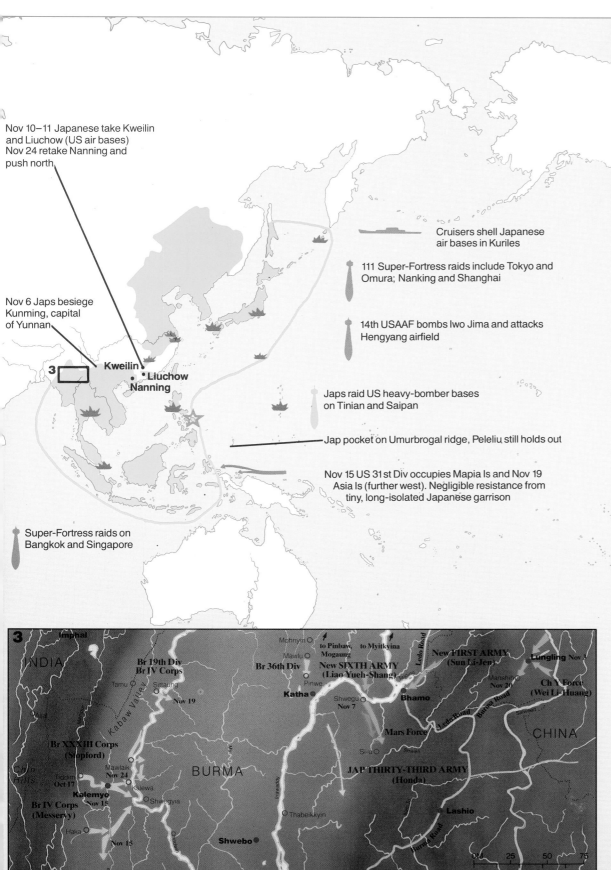

Nov 10–11 Japanese take Kweilin and Liuchow (US air bases) Nov 24 retake Nanning and push north

Nov 6 Japs besiege Kunming, capital of Yunnan

Cruisers shell Japanese air bases in Kuriles

111 Super-Fortress raids include Tokyo and Omura; Nanking and Shanghai

14th USAAF bombs Iwo Jima and attacks Hengyang airfield

Japs raid US heavy-bomber bases on Tinian and Saipan

Jap pocket on Umurbrogal ridge, Peleliu still holds out

Nov 15 US 31st Div occupies Mapia Is and Nov 19 Asia Is (further west). Negligible resistance from tiny, long-isolated Japanese garrison

Super-Fortress raids on Bangkok and Singapore

Naval Actions. Though local gales shut down air operations over Leyte itself, Third Fleet operated away to the north and east. On Nov 5 carrier-borne aircraft attacked shipping in Manila harbour and shot up over 200 aircraft on nearby fields. They destroyed another 600 in various raids on airfields in northern Luzon and outlying islands, and in a fleet action Third Fleet destroyed a complete Japanese convoy including three escort carriers.

They themselves lost 170 planes shot down and a light cruiser torpedoed, and kamikaze attacks sank a destroyer and damaged 4 carriers and 2 light cruisers.

☆ ☆ **The Pause.** Three factors combined to bring action on Leyte itself to a virtual standstill in November. It rained heavily and continuously to wash away tracks and reduce roads to streams, open country to bogs. American forces everywhere had come up against the foothills of the range of hills and mountains which formed the spine of the island. Thirdly, the Allies had to contend with those iron rules of warfare which dictate that the farther one advances from one's base and the longer one's lines of supply, the stronger one's enemy becomes as he falls back.

Nevertheless, in the north, Carigara finally fell to X Corps troops on Nov 2, though strong Japanese defences were obviously building up just beyond, while far to the south XXIV Corps troops crossed a narrow saddle south-west of Abuyog and reach the west coast at Baybay, then to drive nearly 15 miles north along the coast before they hit strong Japanese defences. From Burauen elements of 7th Division probed into the hills, but weather and Japanese patrols slowed progress.

Meanwhile, both sides were bringing in reinforcements. The Americans brought in 32nd Division and 112th Cavalry regimental combat team, both veterans of previous Pacific campaigns, and in mid-November the 11th Airborne Division, who had hurriedly to convert themselves into mountain troops.

As for the Japanese, they flew units from Taiwan and Kyushu into northern Luzon and brought convoys of troops into the main harbour at Ormoc from Mindanao and the Visayas. At the beginning of the month they also brought in the 1st Division from Manchuria and immediately committed it to the defence of the 'Ormoc Corridor'. By using every description of shipping from barges to cruisers and taking advantage of the gales and unceasing rain which held the US planes on the carrier decks, they put ashore over 25,000 troops during November.

By the end of the month, both sides were deployed for the crucial battles.

3 To the Chindwin. Despite the appalling conditions of the monsoon, Fourteenth Army inched their way towards the Chindwin throughout the summer months, passing on their way scenes of horror defying description. The bodies of Japanese soldiers, starved to skeletons, lay everywhere, and those not dead were dying in conditions never imagined before the opening up of the Nazi concentration camps.

Under the Supreme Allied Commander, South-East Asia, Admiral Mountbatten, Fourteenth Army under General Slim and Northern Combat Area Command under General Stilwell were engaged in *Operation Capital* – the advance to the Pakkoku–Mandalay–Lashio line – in order to clear all lines of communication and supply to China. The first requisite for Fourteenth Army was to get bridgeheads across the Chindwin from which, as soon as conditions allowed, they could burst into the central plain and drive for the Irrawaddy.

All through September and October two divisions had been driving south from Tamu, one down the Tiddim Road, the other parallel and down the Kabaw valley. Scrub typhus took a heavier toll of British and Indian lives than did Japanese troops,

though these fought with their customary ferocity when encountered. Nevertheless, by the end of November XXXIII Corps had bridgeheads at Kalewa and Mawlaik, while IV Corps in the north was across the river at Sittaung, poised for the breakout.

To their east, the British 36th Division had been placed under Stilwell's command and in September took up the drive down past Mogaung through Pinbaw and Mohnyin to Mawlu, and in November on to Pinwe. To their left the new Chinese Sixth Army under General Liao Yueh-Shang reached Shwegu on Nov 7 and was there joined by two American regiments with their artillery, to continue the drive on towards the Shweli river and the Japanese Thirty-third Army beyond. East of them the Chinese 38th Division came down from Myitkyina to Bhamo, where they ran into the kind of resistance which had held the Allies back at Myitkyina.

Further east, the Chinese Y Force, which had been fighting around Lungling since July and had twice been forced back to the Salween, could now move slowly forwards as the Japanese were forced to react to the pressures on their left and centre.

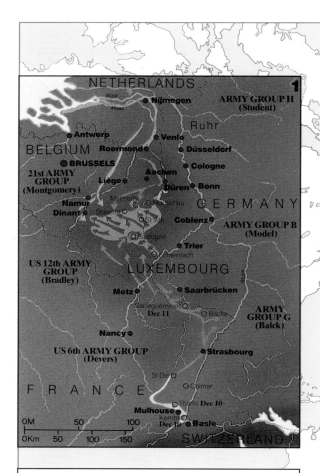

NETHERLANDS

ARMY GROUP H
(Student)

Nijmegen

Antwerp   Venlo   Ruhr

BELGIUM   Roermond   Düsseldorf

BRUSSELS   Aachen   Cologne

21st ARMY   Liège   Düren   Bonn
GROUP
(Montgomery)   G E R M A N Y

Namur
Dinant   Coblenz   ARMY GROUP B
(Model)

US 12th ARMY   Trier
GROUP
(Bradley)   L U X E M B O U R G

Metz   Saarbrücken

Dec 11   ARMY
GROUP G
(Balck)

Nancy

US 6th ARMY GROUP   Strasbourg
(Devers)

St Dié   Colmar

F R A N C E

Mulhouse
Kembs   Dec 10
Dec 11   Basle

0M   50   100
0Km   50   100   150   SWITZERLAND

Bomber Command drops 2,340 tons
on Dutch, Polish and Norwegian
harbour installations and
46,340 tons on German
rail and communication
centres and synthetic
fuel plants

Mosquitoes raid
Berlin and bomb
Gestapo HQ in Oslo

V1 and V2 attacks against
S England and Antwerp cause
367 killed, 847 injured

Dec 22/23 Strong E-boat force routed
off mouth of Scheldt, 2 sunk, 2 more
probably sunk and 5 badly damaged

Support given for ground
troops in Ardennes

Airfields and oil production
centres bombed and, on Dec 24,
2,000 bombers sent over Germany

Weather imposes
stalemate on
Italian front

Dec 3 Communist guerrillas of
ELAS rise in arms in Athens. On
Churchill's orders British forces crush
the revolt. Loyal to agreement with
Churchill in Moscow, Oct 18, Stalin withdraws
support from Greek Communists

1 The Battle of the Bulge. As early as August Hitler had ordered that by November a force of some 25 divisions must be ready to launch a surprise attack on the Anglo-American armies, and to the astonishment of the German High Command (and, later, the Allied Command, too) that force had come into existence. It had been conjured from every corner of German life – from the scouring of the prisons to civil servants and 16-year-old boys. Sometimes these 'recruits' joined the new formations themselves, sometimes other formations in order to release experienced men for the assault.

Three German armies had come into being, and by mid-December they had been marshalled under an exemplary cloak of secrecy opposite that thinly occupied 50-mile strip of line stretching from Monschau in the north to Echternach in the south, held by one comparatively inexperienced US corps – the VII. In the north waited the Sixth Panzer Army under Sepp Dietrich, lately commander of 1st Liebstandarte Adolf Hitler Panzer Division, on his left Fifth Panzer Army under General Hasso von Manteuffel, while to form a 'hard shoulder' against any counter-attack by General Patton's US Third Army, was Seventh Army under General Erich Brandenburger.

Altogether over 200,000 men would take part in *Operation Wacht am Rhein,* equipped with more tanks, guns and ammunition than any German force had been granted for months past. Paratroop units and special commandos dressed in American uniforms were to be dropped well ahead of the advance to cause confusion and disarray.

The objective for the operation was Antwerp, the splitting of the Allied armies moving ever closer to the German frontier and the destruction by starvation of the British, Canadian and American armies, which would be cut off east and north of the German thrust. Morale throughout the bulk of the German force was high, but there were some exceptions. In charge of the entire operation was Field Marshal Gerd von Rundstedt who commented, 'Antwerp? If we reach the Meuse we should go down on our knees and thank God!' while later, Sepp Dietrich who had lost his former admiration for the Führer, wrote, 'All I had to do was to cross the river, capture Brussels, and then go on to take the port of Antwerp. The snow was waist deep and there wasn't room to deploy four tanks abreast, let alone six armoured divisions. It didn't get light until eight and was dark again by four, and my tanks can't fight at night. And all this at Christmas time!'

Nevertheless, the element of surprise and shock gave them some gratifying gains at the beginning. 1st SS Panzer Division swept forward on their northern flank through a gap in the US lines, captured a large petrol dump and reached Malmedy where some of them murdered 150 US prisoners – a piece of self-defeating barbarism, for when rumours of the massacre reached the American positions it produced feelings of both fury and desperation throughout all units and caused them to fight with a commitment which might otherwise not have been present. It also spelt the immediate death of any of the special commandos caught in American uniforms.

To the south Manteuffel's spearheads drove for St Vith but there ran against tank destroyers and heavy artillery which forced them southwards into the gap between St Vith and another vital road junction, Bastogne. Here the bitterest fighting of the operation took place.

The attack had hit General Bradley's 12th Army Group, and as soon as he realised the seriousness of the threat it posed he ordered General Hodge in the north to swing some of his divisions back to hold the flank and then drive down to St Vith.

General Patton was to operate similarly on the southern flank and send up his 4th Armoured Division to Bastogne. 'What the hell,' he said, 'we'll still be killing Krauts!' and in 48 hours with admirable efficiency he swung the bulk of his army through 90 degrees, and drove them north.

General Eisenhower had already released his reserves – 82nd and 101st Airborne Divisions – and they sped northwards from Patton's lines, 101st dropping off to begin their famous stand at Bastogne, 82nd pressing on to St Vith. Mobility was beginning to play a vital part in the battle.

Day by day Manteuffel's spearheads inched farther and farther west towards the Meuse, but as they did so American tank destroyer units and artillery shored up the flanks of the bulge while US infantry drove fiercely into what gaps appeared or held on grimly in isolated positions. For most of the time, however, they had to fight without air cover, for low and dense cloud cover favoured the German advance, though against them deep snow, fuel shortages and traffic jams caused many problems.

As an obviously convenient administrative move, once the pattern of the attack had been perceived, General Eisenhower gave command of the northern flank to Montgomery, Bradley commanding the southern flank, and having given permission for the 82nd Airborne in St Vith to pull out 'in order to tidy up the battlefield' Montgomery then rushed the British 29th Armoured Brigade down towards Dinant and the Meuse crossings, with 2nd US Armoured Division following as quickly as possible – to arrive just in time to halt Manteuffel's 11th Panzer Division short of the river. The next day Patton's armour drove into Bastogne to relieve the battered and weary paratroops, and although it would take several more days to flatten the bulge, the threat to the Allied line had been neutralised. Hitler had also used up a great deal of war material and lost many men who would have been much better employed defensively in the days to come.

2 The Eastern Front. Few people doubted that the comparative quiet along the northern two-thirds of the Eastern Front was anything but the calm before the storm. Stalin had accepted that continual pressure from the Baltic as far south as the Danube would for the moment yield few gains, cause disproportionate losses in both men and material, and hinder the build-up for the vast assault which would be launched into the heart of the Reich in early 1945. By then some 6 million fully equipped Russian soldiers would be deployed in nine fronts along a 1,250-mile line – less than half the length it had been a year before.

Not that there was no action at all in December, for Malinovsky's Second Ukrainians and Tolbukhin's Third Ukrainians were pressing on out of their bridgeheads, with Lake Balaton as the target on the left, Budapest on the right. On the morning of Dec 5, the drive from Hatvan to Eger across the northern suburbs began again, now aimed for Vac, while south of the capital 11 of Malinovsky's rifle battalions crossed the river and fought off every German attempt to destroy the bridgehead formed.

2

P O L A N D

ARMY GROUP
SOUTH
(Friessner)   C Z E C H O S L O V A K I A

Dec 26   FOURTH
UKRAINIAN
VIENNA   Miskolc   FRONT
Bratislava   Eger   Dec 3   (Petrov)
Komarno   Vac   Hatvan
BUDAPEST   Bicske   Jászberény
Dec 24   Adoni   Dec 7   SECOND
Székesfehérvár   L Velencze   UKRAINIAN
FRONT
Ercsing   (Malinovsky)
L Balaton   Dec 7
Pecs   R U M A N I A
Barcs   Szigetvár
Dec 7   Dec 5
Drava   THIRD UKRAINIAN FRONT
(Tolbukhin)
Sava   Vukovar
ARMY GROUP E   Mitrovits
(Löhr)   Dec 4   BELGRADE
Danube

A d r i a t i c   S e a

Meanwhile, Tolbukhin's men drove west from Pecs to reach Szigetvar on Dec 5 and Barcs on the Drava two days later, at the same time edging their way towards Lake Balaton and Lake Valencze on the right. Here on Dec 9 they linked up with Malinovsky's left flank, then planned to take Székesfehérvár and swing around between the two lakes, up to Bicske and then Esztergom on the Danube. Budapest would be surrounded. At the same time, STAVKA ordered Malinovsky to send his two right-hand armies in a wide movement to the north and across the border into Czechoslovakia.

On Dec 20, the wide assault was launched, the junction of Danube and Hron reached on the left, solid progress made on the right. Tolbukhin's assault also began on Dec 20, after three days had broken through the German defences between the lakes and reached Esztergom to link up with Malinovsky's men on Dec 26. Budapest was surrounded, and now the task was to 'thicken the ring'. Third Ukrainians drove west along the Danube for Komarno, Second packing in around the east of the city. But four days of furious attempts to reach the centre of the city only resulted in heavy Russian casualties.

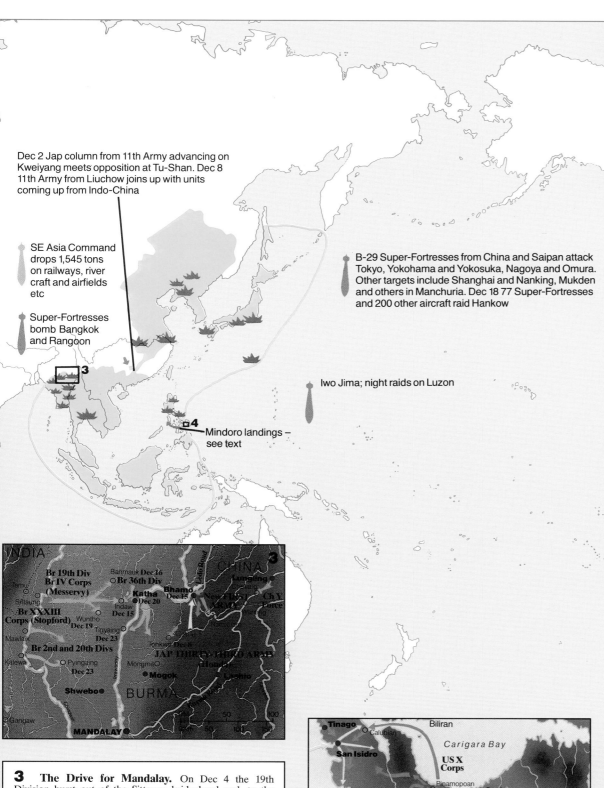

Dec 2 Jap column from 11th Army advancing on Kweiyang meets opposition at Tu-Shan. Dec 8 11th Army from Liuchow joins up with units coming up from Indo-China

SE Asia Command drops 1,545 tons on railways, river craft and airfields etc

Super-Fortresses bomb Bangkok and Rangoon

B-29 Super-Fortresses from China and Saipan attack Tokyo, Yokohama and Yokosuka, Nagoya and Omura. Other targets include Shanghai and Nanking, Mukden and others in Manchuria. Dec 18 77 Super-Fortresses and 200 other aircraft raid Hankow

Iwo Jima; night raids on Luzon

Mindoro landings – see text

3 The Drive for Mandalay. On Dec 4 the 19th Division burst out of the Sittaung bridgehead and, to the astonishment of everyone, knifed through the Japanese positions immediately opposite and by Dec 15 had reached Indaw, 90 miles to the east. Here they linked up with British 36th Division on the right of General Stilwell's Northern Combat Area Command, and so for the first time a connected Allied front existed across north Burma. During the next week other IV Corps formations branched off from 19th Division's route and took Banmauk to the north and Wuntho to the south, cutting the main rail link between Myitkyina and Mandalay.

To the south XXXIII Corps divisions had moved out of Mawlaik to reach the Japanese positions in the Zibyu Taungdan hills, while from Kalewa, 2nd and 20th Divisions drove east towards Shwebo, reaching Pyingaing by Dec 23.

Stilwell's formations were now south and east of the Irrawaddy; after taking Indaw 36th Division had driven down the river to Tigyaing on Dec 23, while on their left Chinese troops had occupied Tonkwa on Dec 8.

Here, however, they had to pause as General Honda commanding the Japanese Thirty-third Army launched a counter-attack with his 56th Division between the two Chinese formations. By Dec 14 the spearheads were close to Bhamo where the Japanese garrison was still fiercely resisting the attacks of the 38th Division. The result might not however have been quite what Honda intended, for on the night of Dec 14/15 the Bhamo garrison, suddenly aware that relief was close at hand and their besiegers' attention had been distracted, cut their way through the ring and escaped – leaving Bhamo to be occupied the next morning, and 38th Division, now augmented by an American combat team, free to drive on down towards Lashio, reaching Namkham not far from the junction of the Ledo and Burma Roads; and from the north-east, Y Force was closing on the same junction.

Slowly but surely Fourteenth Army and Stilwell's NCAC were reaching the objectives of *Operation Capital*.

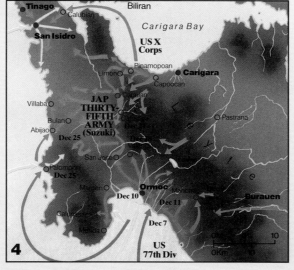

4 End of the Land Battle. At the end of November Japanese reinforcements had come ashore at San Isidro to cross the northern peninsula, and also at Palompon where they drove inland to join the rest of Thirty-fifth Army dug in to protect the Ormoc Corridor.

Japanese paratroops were also landed in attempts to wreck US airfields, but the weather and the unstable soil conditions had already rendered them unserviceable and US air cover was now concentrated on their ubiquitous carriers. The raiders were quickly rounded up and killed.

The final US offensive on Leyte began on Dec 5 when X Corps under powerful air and artillery cover burst through the northern gap and into the Corridor, while XXIV Corps drove across the hills in the centre and up along the coast from Baybay. Two days later 77th Infantry Division landed almost un-opposed near Ormoc which they occupied three days later.

The occupation of Ormoc crucially affected matters to the north by cutting all supplies to the Japanese Thirty-fifth Army, which might otherwise have proved difficult to dislodge. As it was, all Japanese units were now increasingly compressed in the north-west corner of the island, and when formations from US 77th Division were amphibiously hooked around from Ormoc to Palompon, the Japanese were cut off from the sea and any hope of reinforcement.

US artillery and aircraft pounded them day and night, US infantry pressed in upon them from all sides. On Dec 19 the Japanese commander General Suzuki learned officially that no further help or supplies would reach him, and on Dec 25 he received orders to release any units which might be able to make their way to the coast and thence to neighbouring islands. The message also bade him a sorrowful farewell. Of more than 65,000 Japanese troops who had fought on Leyte only some 15,000 were left, though it would take months to complete the dangerous business of mopping them up. Suzuki himself did not leave the island until the end of March 1945, though to all intents and purposes it had been in American hands since Christmas Day.

☆ **Mindoro.** General MacArthur had not, of course, waited for the end of the fighting on Leyte before proceeding with the next step on the way back to Luzon. After much discussion both of objective, and of deception of the Japanese High Command as to where the vital blow was eventually to fall, it was decided that Mindoro should be taken, both to provide airfields for the Luzon operation and also to give the impression that the projected American invasion would take place in the Batangas or Bicol Provinces in the southern half of Luzon – an impression deliberately heightened by organised Philippine guerrilla action there.

On Dec 12 the Western Visayas Task Force with Seventh Fleet escorts sailed from Leyte through the Surigao Strait and set course for Mindoro. The voyage was punctuated by kamikaze attacks, one of which hit the flagship *Nashville* and caused such casualties and damage that she had to return to Leyte. Another check to progress was a quite extraordinary typhoon which caught the convoy while it was refuelling on Dec 16/17. It capsized 3 destroyers, severely damaged 7 others, blew 186 planes overboard and caused the death of nearly 800 men; a fierce naval action with the enemy could hardly have caused more damage.

Nevertheless, by Dec 20 a regimental combat team and the 503rd Parachute Regiment had gone ashore at San Jose, by Dec 23 two airfields were in operation and, despite more suicide attacks, more troops were ashore. HQ Eighth Army was set up and the operation of taking over the whole island was under way.

1 NETHERLANDS
ARMY GROUP H (Student)
Ruhr
Antwerp, Roermond, Venlo, Düsseldorf
21st ARMY GROUP (Montgomery)
Aachen, Cologne
BRUSSELS, Liège, Düren, Bonn
BELGIUM, Namur
Dinant, Coblenz
GERMANY
US 12th ARMY GROUP (Bradley)
LUXEMBOURG
ARMY GROUP B (Model)
Trier, Mainz
ARMY GROUP G (Balck)
Metz, Saarbrücken
Nancy
US 6th ARMY GROUP (Devers)
Strasbourg
FRANCE
Mulhouse
Basle
SWITZERLAND
0M 50 100 150
0Km 50 100 150

11,000 tons dropped on German factories; 7,000 tons on railways and marshalling yards; 2,000 tons on targets in Occupied Territories and 12,800 tons on synthetic fuel plants

Mosquitoes raid Berlin seven times. Fighter Command attacks V2 launching sites and escorts bomber raids

Jan 2 Copenhagen factory making parts for V2 rockets wrecked by saboteurs

Jan 15 First boat-train since 1940 leaves London for Paris

Jan 1 Heavy air battles over Western Front; 800 Luftwaffe planes attack airfields and raid Brussels, losing 188 machines in all

Jan 8 Attica cleared of ELAS troops. Truce agreed with British forces – Cease Fire 0001 Jan 14

V1 and V2 attacks cause 585 killed, 1,629 injured

Fighter-bombers attack German traffic retreating from Ardennes

USAAF sends out 32,539 bomber and fighter sorties. 39,100 tons of bombs dropped on rail and communication centres and oil production plants

☆ **The Italian Resistance.** During the winter months of 1944–45 the weather rendered conditions on the Italian Front impossible for any military activity except artillery duels. The lines therefore remained static. But the German formations – especially the rear echelons – now became conscious of a threat to which little consideration had been given.

The scarcely veiled contempt with which they had long regarded their recent ally was far outweighed by the hatred they received in return. Not only were the Italians now allied to the British, for whom they had a traditional and characteristic liking, and the Americans to whom many of them were related, but now, against the depredations of the retreating German army, they were defending their homes.

They did so with a ferocity and desperate courage which has never been fully recognised – except by the German units who suffered from it. Later when the Allies could take the offensive again, at least some of their success was due to German losses caused by Italian resistance.

1 The Bulge is Flattened. By the end of 1944 Hitler had been told categorically by his three army commanders in the Ardennes that they had no hope of reaching Antwerp, and the only hope of salvaging any sort of gain from *Operation Wacht am Rhein* would be to turn the panzer armies north to drive up west of Liège and then swing in behind Aachen; and before this could even be attempted, Bastogne must fall.

But by this time, Patton had buttressed Bastogne with six of his divisions and was about to attack north towards Houffalize; so Manteuffel's drive eastwards to cut Patton's corridor south of Bastogne ran into a dogged defence – conducted in bitterly cold weather – with fighting as desperate as any in Bastogne itself. It raged on and off until Jan 4, by which time the panzer army was too weak either to cut the corridor or even to delay Patton's drive up to Houffalize, and in the meantime, two US armoured divisions had begun a drive south-east on each side of the Ourthe. The intention was to link up with Patton's armour at Houffalize, then turn and 'flatten the bulge'. Only three badly battered SS panzer divisions barred the way, but aided by deep snow and icy road surfaces, they reduced the US armour to a crawl and it was not until Jan 16 that the two armies met. By then Hitler had accepted that the entire operation had failed – and was also becoming concerned about the imminence of the gigantic assault building up in the east – so he grudgingly gave assent to a withdrawal. Then on Jan 22 the skies at last cleared and the USAAF and RAF could participate, to find German vehicles stalled bumper to bumper in front of the river bridges. Along the ridges of the salient, infantry cheered as they watched the havoc the air forces and the artillery could now wreak.

By Jan 28 the bulge was flattened. The Battle of the Ardennes was over; it had been a great American victory.

The Colmar Pocket. *Wacht am Rhein* was not the only plan Hitler had conceived for an attack on the armies closing in on the Reich from the west. To the south of the Ardennes lay a length of Allied line held by General Devers' 6th Army Group, and after the Battle of the Bulge had begun, held very thinly indeed. When Patton's Third Army swung north towards Bastogne, General Patch's Seventh Army had extended northwards to keep in touch, and the resultant 124 miles of front was held by only seven divisions plus some infantry regiments.

Operation Nordwind was launched on New Year's Eve to take advantage of this by sending eight divisions of Army Group G in drives north of Strasbourg towards the Saverne Gap, and two more up from Colmar. Although General Patch's divisions had held the thrusts to the north by the second day, for some time there was a fear that Strasbourg would have to be abandoned – but the French First Army drove forward and blocked the German advance from Colmar, and by Jan 20, though Patch's front had dropped back nearly 20 miles in places, Strasbourg was held and the line consolidated.

2 The Drive to the Oder. During December 1944 and the early days of January, an enormous Soviet force was built up along a line running roughly south from Memel to eastern Czechoslovakia. Nearly 4 million men concentrated in five fronts – 11 guards armies, 5 shock armies, 6 tank armies, 46 infantry or cavalry armies, all supported by 13 air armies – gave the Red Army commanders superiority in every aspect over the 200-odd German and Hungarian divisions facing them.

The three fronts at the northern end of the line – First Baltic under Bagramyan, Third Belorussian under Chernyakovsky and Second Belorussian under Rokossovsky – were directed to clear the Baltic coast from Memel to Danzig, the Belorussian Fronts aimed particularly at East Prussia. They launched their assault on Jan 12/13.

Chernyakovsky quickly realised that Königsberg would only be won at high cost, and it would take time; strong defence lines blocked the way every few miles and it took his five armies six days to cover only the first 15 of them; he fed in an extra guards army but even then it was Jan 20 before his armies reached Insterburg – only one-third of the way. Fortunately, on his left flank Rokossovsky was having better fortune.

Second Belorussian Front had crossed the Narew, sent two armies between the Masurian Lakes on Chernyakovsky's left flank, and another five armies in a wide sweep aimed at Danzig. They smashed through the hard defensive crust in three days, tank armies followed; by Jan 19 they were aiming through a gap east of Tannenberg and a week later they reached the Baltic each side of Elbing, effectively sealing in the huge German force at Königsberg – about to become as much a victim of Hitler's *Festung* mania as Budapest and Courland.

But the most spectacular advances were made in the central section of the assault front. Marshal Zhukov's First Belorussian Front attacked out of the Magnuszew–Pulawy bridgehead under a bombardment from guns and mortars concentrated at 400 per mile, and backed by rocket batteries; it drove along the main Warsaw–Berlin axis, and was 10 miles along it in the first 24 hours. On his southern flank Zhukov's infantry ripped wide gaps in the defences into which he fed two tank armies, which by the evening of Jan 15 were racing away nearly 30 miles ahead. In the meantime he had encircled Warsaw and directed the First

2
0M 50 100 150
0Km 100 200
BALTIC SEA
Memel Jan 28
FIRST BALTIC FRONT (Bagramyan)
Königsberg
THIRD BELORUSSIAN FRONT (Chernyakovsky)
Gdynia, Danzig
Jan 26 Marienburg
Grudziadz
Bialystok
ARMY GROUP CENTRE (Reinhardt)
Bydgoszcz
SECOND BELORUSSIAN FRONT (Rokossovsky)
Kustrin
Poznan
WARSAW
BERLIN
Lodz Jan 19
FIRST BELORUSSIAN FRONT (Zhukov)
ARMY GROUP A (Harpe)
Breslau
Kielce Jan 15
Katowice
Cracow
FIRST UKRAINIAN FRONT (Koniev)
Gleiwitz
PRAGUE
CZECHOSLOVAKIA
FOURTH UKRAINIAN FRONT
ARMY GROUP SOUTH (Friessner)
Košice (Petrov)
VIENNA
Bratislava
SECOND UKRAINIAN FRONT (Malinovsky)
AUSTRIA
BUDAPEST
THIRD UKRAINIAN FRONT (Tolbukhin)
HUNGARY
YUGOSLAVIA
RUMANIA

Polish Army (which had been part of the Red Army since Stalingrad days) into the ruined capital.

The breach torn in the German defences by the First Belorussians was now 180 miles wide, and Zhukov's tank armies, with as many of his infantry as could keep up, were racing across Poland and into the Reich itself. They brushed aside German formations hurriedly thrown in their path, blocked Poznan and swept past it on Jan 25, reached the Oder on the last day of the month and crossed to form a bridgehead just north of Kustrin. Berlin was just 50 miles away.

Marshal Koniev's armies to the south had done just as well. The bulk of First Ukrainian Front had broken out of the Sandomierz bridgehead on Jan 12/13, under such a massive bombardment that two days later when the Russians entered Kielce the inhabitants were still deafened and half blind, the defenders so stunned and shocked that they could offer little resistance. Then Koniev's armies fanned out. One wing drove down the west bank of the Vistula towards Cracow, the other drove for Czestochowa, and within a week the front was advancing on a 170-mile-wide sweep for, on one axis, over 100 miles; it smashed every sign of resistance on the way.

The leading units raced up past Beuthen and Oppeln towards Breslau, then along the line of the Oder until they joined forces with Zhukov's left flank. By the end of January, the Oder was in Red Army hands from where its headwaters left the Carpathians, northwards to a point just north-west of Berlin. The thunder of Red Army guns could be heard on Unter den Linden.

144

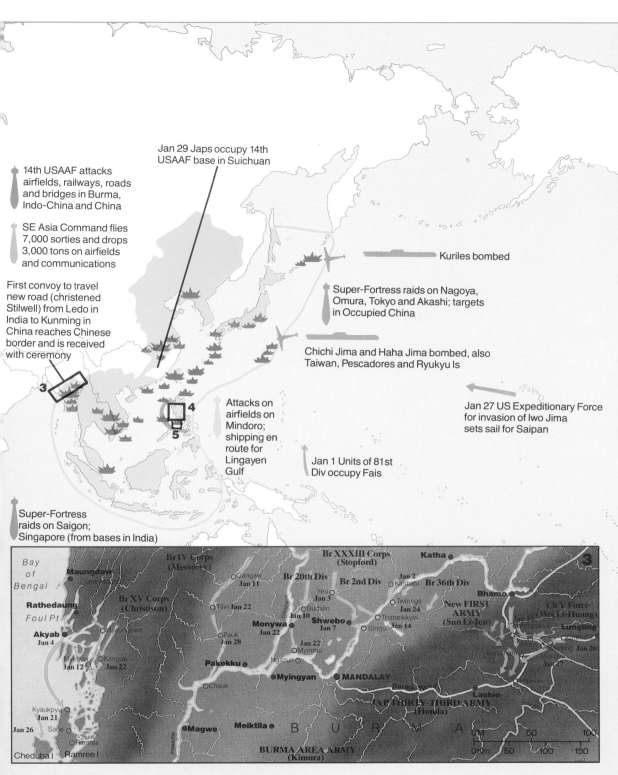

14th USAAF attacks airfields, railways, roads and bridges in Burma, Indo-China and China

SE Asia Command flies 7,000 sorties and drops 3,000 tons on airfields and communications

First convoy to travel new road (christened Stilwell) from Ledo in India to Kunming in China reaches Chinese border and is received with ceremony

Jan 29 Japs occupy 14th USAAF base in Suichuan

Kuriles bombed

Super-Fortress raids on Nagoya, Omura, Tokyo and Akashi; targets in Occupied China

Chichi Jima and Haha Jima bombed, also Taiwan, Pescadores and Ryukyu Is

Attacks on airfields on Mindoro; shipping en route for Lingayen Gulf

Jan 27 US Expeditionary Force for invasion of Iwo Jima sets sail for Saipan

Jan 1 Units of 81st Div occupy Fais

Super-Fortress raids on Saigon; Singapore (from bases in India)

4 Mindoro. On Jan 1 the drive up and along the east coast began. A company of 21st Infantry of 24th Division was shipped north-east to Bongabong, and other companies followed, hooking north by sea or driving along the coastal road, first to Pinamalayan, then up to Calapan, helped all the way by the Philippine guerrillas. On Jan 3 another company landed unopposed at Buenavista on Marinduque while at the same time more infantry were shipped up the west coast of Mindoro to take Mamburao and occupy the north-west tip. Now the final battle for Luzon could be fought.

5 Return to Luzon. Well over 200,000 men of General Krueger's Sixth Army were to be landed in Lingayen Gulf, on the same beaches as those used by the Japanese landing forces during the closing days of 1941. They were then to drive down into the heart of the island, secure the vital airfields and head for Manila. To the north Admiral Halsey's Third Fleet battleships and carriers shielded the area from interference from Taiwan, while from Leyte, Mindoro and further south the Far East Air Forces did the same.

On Jan 9 the huge fleets sailed into the gulf and began putting the troops ashore. They were unopposed, for General Yamashita had concentrated his defences in the hills to the east of Lingayen Gulf, to the south near Clark Airfield, around Manila itself, and lately down in the south.

By evening of the first day 68,000 men were ashore in a bridgehead already 17 miles wide and 4 miles deep. The danger threatening on the left, north-east flank was quickly realised, and US I Corps was given the task of eliminating it.

As a result XIV Corps on their right could press ahead. By Jan 18 they were at Camiling, ten days later at San Fernando, and by Jan 31 they were ten miles north of Manila Bay.

Meanwhile, two divisions of XI Corps had been put ashore at San Antonio on Jan 29, and more troops into Olongapo and Nasugbu on the 30th and 31st.

3 Approach to the Irrawaddy. During December, despite the gratifying advances, General Slim had become uneasy as he realised that General Kimura, now commanding the Burma Area Army in front of his own Fourteenth Army, did not intend to make his main stand north of the Irrawaddy. He had instead withdrawn the bulk across the river and now seemed determined to defend the vital oilfields to the south. General Slim changed his plans.

Some 70 miles south of Mandalay lies Meiktila, the nodal point for all rail and road communications feeding both Fifteenth Army opposite Slim's forces and Thirty-third Army opposite Stilwell. To mount a powerful surprise thrust at Meiktila would completely unbalance Kimura's forces and could result in the clearance of the way to Rangoon. General Slim therefore transferred the northern divisions, including 19th, to XXXIII Corps and instructed General Stopford to continue the drive down towards Monywa, Shwebo and eventually Mandalay, while he switched IV Corps across to the west. He then brought in 17th Division from India who with 7th Division would now drive south through Gangaw, Tilin and Pauk towards Chauk and the western approaches to Meiktila. By the end of January, Pauk had been reached on the right, Myinmu in the centre, Shwebo on the left, with 36th Division still under Stilwell keeping level on the eastern bank of the river.

Beyond them, Chinese First Army and their Y Force, now with more and more American infantry and artillery to help them, were closing in on Lashio.

Arakan. For many months the situation in Arakan had been one of stalemate. Physical conditions here were if anything even worse than elsewhere in Burma throughout the monsoon months, and both sides had transferred many of their formations to the more important areas to the east. But during the last days of December formations of XV Corps under General Christison began probing south through the area of the March–April 1943 defeat, passed through Donbaik and reached Foul Point on Dec 27. Akyab was the next objective and an amphibious attack was being prepared when an air observation officer realised that the Japanese had gone. By Jan 4 Akyab town was in British hands with the port in use, and the next day a squadron of Spitfires landed on the airstrip.

Inland, progress had been just as pleasing. Christison had sent his forces down both sides of the Mayu range and in early January they had crossed the Kaladan and reached Myaungbwe. In a series of amphibious operations aided by 30 motor launches of the Arakan Coastal Forces they closed first on Myebon and then on Kangaw. In all moves they faced little opposition as the main Japanese forces were being pulled eastwards to help resist the greater dangers which faced the Japanese in central Burma.

Nevertheless, it was thought that the Japanese would regard the island of Ramree – potentially a base for wide-ranging air operations once the drive down towards Rangoon began – as being worthy of their customary staunch defence. On Jan 21, therefore, the battleship *Queen Elizabeth* escorted by a carrier, a cruiser and five destroyers, arrived off the northern point of the island and, covered by 85 Liberators of the Strategic Air Force, and Thunderbolts and Mitchells of the RAF, put down the heaviest bombardment yet seen in the theatre. When the first waves of 71st Infantry Brigade touched the shore, no Japanese defences still existed, and by the end of the month formations were probing down the single road along the west coast. Ramree itself was not reached until early February and it took a well-organised assault supported by tanks to break into the town. After the rigours of the Arakan and central Burma, Ramree with its warm days, cool nights and golden beaches seemed paradise to the men who had arrived there.

Another island which received attention was Cheduba off the west coast. It proved to be unoccupied.

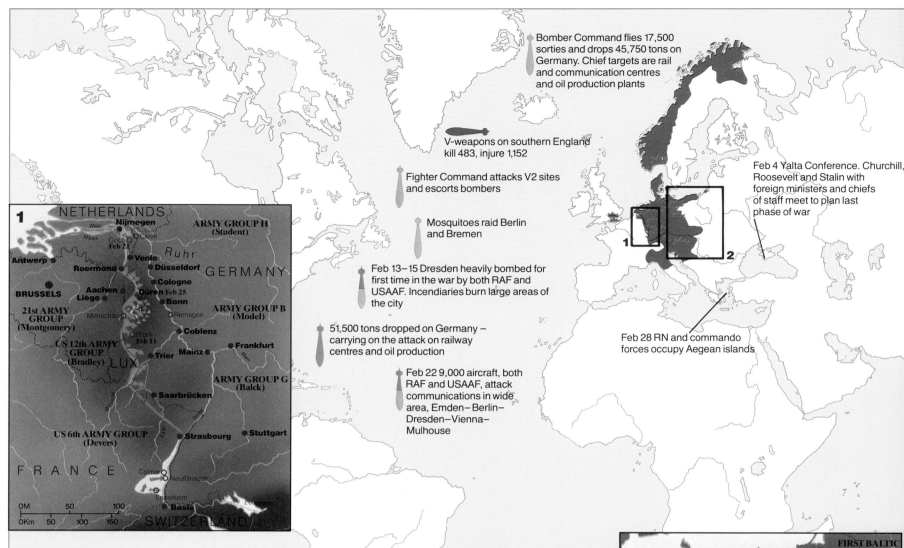

Bomber Command flies 17,500 sorties and drops 45,750 tons on Germany. Chief targets are rail and communication centres and oil production plants

V-weapons on southern England kill 483, injure 1,152

Fighter Command attacks V2 sites and escorts bombers

Mosquitoes raid Berlin and Bremen

Feb 4 Yalta Conference. Churchill, Roosevelt and Stalin with foreign ministers and chiefs of staff meet to plan last phase of war

Feb 13–15 Dresden heavily bombed for first time in the war by both RAF and USAAF. Incendiaries burn large areas of the city

51,500 tons dropped on Germany – carrying on the attack on railway centres and oil production

Feb 22 9,000 aircraft, both RAF and USAAF, attack communications in wide area, Emden–Berlin–Dresden–Vienna–Mulhouse

Feb 28 RN and commando forces occupy Aegean islands

1

NETHERLANDS
ARMY GROUP H (Student)
Nijmegen
Goch Feb 21
Cleve
Antwerp
Roermond · Venlo · Düsseldorf
Ruhr
GERMANY
BRUSSELS
Liège · Aachen · Düren Feb 25 · Cologne
21st ARMY GROUP (Montgomery)
Monschau
Bonn
ARMY GROUP B (Model)
Remagen
US 12th ARMY GROUP (Bradley)
LUX
Prum Feb 11
Coblenz
Trier · Mainz
Frankfurt
ARMY GROUP G (Balck)
Saarbrücken
US 6th ARMY GROUP (Devers)
Strasbourg · Stuttgart
FRANCE
Colmar
NeufBrisach
Ensisheim
Basle
SWITZERLAND
0M 50 100
0Km 50 100 150

BALTIC SEA
Köslin
Gdynia · Königsberg
Danzig · Elbing Feb 10
FIRST BALTIC FRONT (Bagramyan)
Stettin
Neustettin Feb 28
Prechlau
ARMY GROUP VISTULA (Himmler)
Grudziadz
THIRD BELORUSSIAN FRONT (Chernyakovsky until Feb 24)
Kustrin
Arnswalde
Bydgoszcz
SECOND BELORUSSIAN FRONT (Rokossovsky)
BERLIN
Feb 23
Posnan Feb 23
WARSAW
Glogau Feb 13
FIRST BELORUSSIAN FRONT (Zhukov)
GERMANY
Breslau Feb 15
Feb 11
POLAND
FIRST UKRAINIAN FRONT (Koniev)
PRAGUE
ARMY GROUP CENTRE (Schörner)
Cracow
VIENNA
Bratislava
Miskolc
ARMY GROUP SOUTH (Wöhler)
BUDAPEST Feb 18
Székesfehérvár
SECOND UKRAINIAN FRONT (Malinovsky)
THIRD UKRAINIAN FRONT (Tolbukhin)
ITALY
ARMY GROUP E (Weichs)
YUGOSLAVIA
BELGRADE

1 Slow Creep to the Rhine. By the end of January the front line ran from the Scheldt Estuary eastwards as far as Nijmegen on the Waal, across to the Maas, which it followed down as far as Roermond, then the Roer as far as the dams – still held by the Germans who had every intention of using them to turn the river into a raging flood – then down along the line of the Saar.

The task for the Allied armies was to reach the Rhine – Canadian and British in the north, four US armies holding the line from Roermond down to Strasbourg, the French First Army down almost to the Swiss border; and in addition to the resistance they could all expect from German forces, some of whom occupied positions in the long-neglected but still solid Siegfried Line, they all faced problems brought about first by snow and hard ice, then by a prolonged thaw which turned the ground into glutinous mud covered by slush. The soldiers on both sides spent February in conditions of unadulterated misery.

Nevertheless, the battles had to be fought, and the Canadians and British had begun theirs in late January. Two infantry divisions and an armoured brigade attacked two German divisions between Nijmegen and Venlo, but only the units accompanied by specialised armour such as Flails, Crocodiles or Buffaloes could make much headway, and even then at a heavy price.

Then at the end of January, US First Army started for the Roer dams – seven of them, holding back 111 million cubic metres of water increased by the results of the recent thaw. The Germans opened the valves before withdrawing, and when US engineers entered the last one they found that sabotage had been so efficient that there was no way of closing them; until all the water had drained down into the North Sea the river was uncrossable.

But to their north, the Battle of the Reichswald had opened on Feb 8, and under a heavy barrage four infantry divisions rolled forward into one of the bitterest and most depressing battles of the Western Front. Along some parts of the attack, only movement in DUKWs was possible – and they were very vulnerable even to machine-gun fire, let alone light artillery or anti-tank fire. Broken roads caused appalling traffic-jams, sodden tracks made infantry movement – almost all that was possible – a prolonged nightmare.

But gradually they made progress. By Feb 21 Goch and Cleve were in Canadian and British hands, and to the south the river levels at last dropped sufficiently for US Ninth Army engineers to throw bridges over the Roer, and get their armour across to take Duren by Feb 25. Prum to the south had been taken on Feb 11, while by the end of the month Trier was under close threat.

Meanwhile, the French First Army, having entered Strasbourg and taken over from General Patch's Seventh Army, then turned and cleaned out the Colmar Pocket. By the end of February they held the Rhine from Strasbourg down to the northern edge of Basle. Alsace-Lorraine was French again.

2 The Eastern Front. The grinding battles in East Prussia continued on into February, the Königsberg garrison holding firm, the defence lines all requiring strong forces and heavy fighting to overcome. Third Belorussian Front gradually forced their way across the north of Königsberg and into the Samland Peninsula, and it was here that their commander Marshal Chernyakovsky was killed, command then going to Marshal Vasilevsky and the front combined with Bagramyan's First Baltic Front. On the left flank, Elbing was surrounded despite stout defence and violent counter-attacks by Army Group Vistula, now commanded by Reichsführer Heinrich Himmler who had orders to break through to the relief of the Königsberg garrison – themselves under strict orders not to break out to meet them.

But further to the south, the Red Army was finding itself once more in the classic situation brought about by spectacular advance. The soldiers were tired after their tremendous achievements in January, losses had been considerable and not yet made up, and supply lines were long and over-burdened. But the flanks of the deep salient they had driven into German positions were obviously vulnerable and must therefore be buttressed and in places extended.

Along the northern flank, Marshal Rokossovsky's Second Belorussian Front faced Army Group Vistula, stretched between Danzig and the mouth of the Oder with its back on the Baltic coast. But in addition to inexpert command, Army Group Vistula was down to only one substantial force – Second Army – and this was concentrated around Danzig; Rokossovsky therefore launched his attack on Feb 10 between Bydgoszcz and Arnswalde, aimed up towards Köslin. It was a grim, slow advance, for the attack had been planned too quickly, and Red Army strength was not sufficient yet to smash completely the German defences. By Feb 20 the line had only been pushed northwards some 30 miles, and though on the far right the German garrison at Elbing had been finally wiped out, that at Grudziadz still stood, though it had been encircled by Feb 19.

Within the salient, Marshal Zhukov's First Belorussian Front was deliberately holding its fire, building up strength for the final push to Berlin, but to their south Koniev's First Ukrainians were across the Oder and driving for the line of the Neisse. Six Soviet armies burst from their bridgeheads on the morning of Feb 8 after a short artillery barrage, driving between Fourth Panzer Army and Seventeenth Army of Army Group Centre and ignoring for the moment the strong German concentrations in Glogau and Breslau. Within three days they had advanced nearly 40 miles along a 90-mile-wide front and were joined by another guards army on their left flank which swept through Brieg, on north-west to Kanth which they took on Feb 11 to reach the Neisse at Penzig, the rest of the Neisse–Oder line now held up to the Kustrin bridgehead.

In the Carpathian region to the south, Fourth Ukrainian Front were at last able to edge forward from positions in the Dobsina area they had held for some months, blocked from progress by a combination of bad weather, difficult country and lack of reinforcements, the bulk of whom had gone to the more active fronts on each side. As for those fronts, during February Malinovsky's Second Ukrainian still held the line of the Hron down to Esztergom and then on to join with Tolbukhin's Fourth Ukrainians between Lakes Balaton and Valencze. Budapest was still held by nearly 50,000 German and Hungarian troops (though at least 10,000 were wounded); Hitler still regarded Budapest as a vital fortress, which must not be evacuated but must be relieved. During January he ordered two drives by Army Group South, one each side, to relieve the capital, but both failed and by the beginning of February the German troops were penned into a pocket 3 miles wide by 4 miles long in the centre of Pest.

At last, practically out of food and ammunition, their commander gave the orders for an attempted break-out, but few reached even the suburbs and less than 700 reached the German lines.

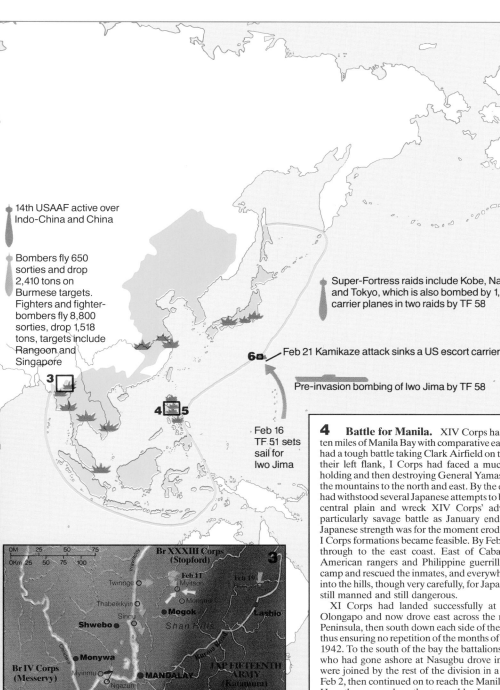

14th USAAF active over Indo-China and China

Bombers fly 650 sorties and drop 2,410 tons on Burmese targets. Fighters and fighter-bombers fly 8,800 sorties, drop 1,518 tons, targets include Rangoon and Singapore

Super-Fortress raids include Kobe, Nagoya and Tokyo, which is also bombed by 1,200 carrier planes in two raids by TF 58

Feb 21 Kamikaze attack sinks a US escort carrier

Pre-invasion bombing of Iwo Jima by TF 58

Feb 16 TF 51 sets sail for Iwo Jima

3 Across the Irrawaddy. During February the main objective was to keep Japanese attention concentrated on the move down towards Mandalay, and away from the flank movement towards Meiktila. Even in the drive towards Meiktila, local application of deception plans was put into operation, and impressions were deliberately created of attempts to cross the Irrawaddy, first at Pakokku itself, then away to the south-west at Chauk.

Opposite the Chauk oilfields lay a small village called Seikpyu, and on Feb 2 an East African Brigade left Pauk, trailing brushwood behind its vehicles to increase the impression of strength, while east of Chauk itself dummy parachute landings and marked maps were dropped. Meanwhile, 7th Division drove in force towards Pakokku as though to take it by force and cross the river there; in fact, the bulk of the division was side-slipped at the last moment to a wide beach a mile upstream from the village of Nyaungu. Here, the river was nearly two miles wide and so at 0400 on Feb 14, under a strong artillery barrage and air cover, the widest river crossing of the Second World War began.

By nightfall one brigade with six tanks, a few mules and three jeeps was across, three days later Nyaungu had been taken and on Feb 21 17th Division and a tank brigade broke out of the bridgehead. They raced forward some 60 miles to Mahlaing where supplies were dropped to them and by the end of the month were just a few miles short of Meiktila where, however, the Japanese were determined to stand. To the north and east, XXXIII Corps and the NCAC had all made their way across the Irrawaddy or southwards towards Mandalay, forcing General Kimura to commit his units to blocking manoeuvres, while to the west of Mandalay itself 20th Division fought its way into Myinmu, crossed the river and formed a bridgehead around the airstrip at Ngazun which became the focus of fierce battles for the next three weeks.

4 Battle for Manila. XIV Corps had reached to within ten miles of Manila Bay with comparative ease, though they had had a tough battle taking Clark Airfield on their right flank. On their left flank, I Corps had faced a much grimmer task in holding and then destroying General Yamashita's main force in the mountains to the north and east. By the end of January they had withstood several Japanese attempts to break down into the central plain and wreck XIV Corps' advance, but after a particularly savage battle as January ended, it seemed that Japanese strength was for the moment eroded; and advance by I Corps formations became feasible. By Feb 11 they had driven through to the east coast. East of Cabanatuan a force of American rangers and Philippine guerrillas reached a PoW camp and rescued the inmates, and everywhere they probed on into the hills, though very carefully, for Japanese positions were still manned and still dangerous.

XI Corps had landed successfully at San Antonio and Olongapo and now drove east across the neck of the Bataan Peninsula, then south down each side of the coast to Mariveles, thus ensuring no repetition of the months of battle there of early 1942. To the south of the bay the battalions of airborne troops who had gone ashore at Nasugbu drove inland for two days, were joined by the rest of the division in a parachute drop on Feb 2, then continued on to reach the Manila suburbs by Feb 4. Here they were abruptly stopped by Japanese defences.

The main advance on Manila was undertaken by two divisions of XIV Corps. A flying column of 1st Cavalry, ordered by MacArthur to break through and rescue the Allied civilians held prisoner in Santo Tomas University, raced over the last bridge in time to stop its destruction and reached the university on the afternoon of Feb 3. Altogether 1,300 Allied prisoners and civilian internees were rescued that day, but the battle for the city was by no means over.

It was held by some 17,000 troops, most of them naval under command of Admiral Iwabuchi, who considered himself independent of Yamashita's command, and thus of his wish that Manila should be declared an Open City. It was therefore to take the US forces until Mar 3 finally to take the city in a battle as tough as that at Stalingrad – though not so prolonged – and at a cost of 6,500 American casualties. Almost no Japanese survived, and as many as 100,000 Philippine islanders may have been killed during the fighting.

5 Iwo Jima. The chief reason for the US capture of Iwo Jima was that it lay only 660 miles from Tokyo and possessed two airfields, one of which would take B-29s immediately.

On the morning of Feb 19 450 vessels of the US Fifth Fleet gathered off the tiny island, and from them 482 LVTs packed with marines began the approach to the beaches, 68 per wave, one wave every five minutes. Continuous air strikes hit the beaches; the navy, having already plastered them, now laid down a creeping barrage in front of the first wave.

At 0902 they landed, 5th Marines on the left, 4th on the right, and for a few minutes were under only scattered fire. Then, as further waves came ashore, a deadly fire from well-concealed positions – light and heavy machine-guns, light artillery and mortars – opened up on them, and the costliest operation in US Marine history opened.

The Japanese defences had been superbly organised and constructed – and if their plans had been as good, the marines would have been defeated. The mistake had been to let the marines ashore at all – for wave after wave flooded in, pressing the ones in front ever forward, and by the end of the first day 30,000 men were ashore with their equipment, and though their casualties had been high, they were across the neck of the island. The following day they had reached the foot of Mount Suribachi which, although only 550 feet high, dominated the island, and on Feb 23 the American flag was raised on the summit.

But there was still a lot of very hard fighting to be done, for a positive lattice of defensive positions had still to be stormed, manned by Japanese troops each of whom had sworn to take ten marines with him.

6 Corregidor. From the end of January tons of explosive and napalm fell on Corregidor, and on Feb 16 a battalion of US paratroops was dropped in the south-west of the island while a battalion of infantry landed on the southern shore of the 'waist'. Surprise gave the Americans quick success but once the Japanese defenders rallied, they streamed out of the underground caves and tunnels and began their usual fierce resistance. US reinforcements poured in, the Japanese were driven back below ground and only flame-throwers, bazookas or close artillery could reach them. Frequently the Japanese would blow themselves and their attackers up, and on Feb 23 they blew up their main ammunition tunnel with a huge explosion which shook the island.

But on the 28th the island was declared secure; of 5,000 Japanese naval troops only 19 were taken prisoner and US casualties amounted to almost 1,000.

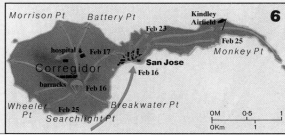

1 **Across the Rhine.** The problem of crossing the last water barrier into the heartland of Germany had exercised the minds of the Allied planners since quite shortly after D-Day. Not only would the Rhine present many problems on its own, but it could obviously be expected that Hitler would demand from his armies a defence of fanatical determination; a great deal of experimentation and specialised training would have to be undertaken, for even the techniques developed for the cross-Channel operation would not necessarily be adequate. Crossing a wide, fast-flowing river was a quite different proposition from landing on a beach, however well defended.

As a result several tank regiments were now converted to the use of Buffaloes (LVTs) to carry the first waves across, the second wave following in assault boats. Close behind the assault troops would come the engineers – so many of them that for the northern crossing in the British and Canadian sector, several American engineer regiments were borrowed. Their job would be to bridge the river, for no one expected any of the existing Rhine bridges still to be usable once the German armies had retreated across them.

There was a vast amount of material to be assembled on the western bank of the Rhine close behind the chosen crossing-points – in the north alone, some 36,000 vehicles including tank transporters, 3,500 pieces of artillery together with the assault boats. All was to be brought up on roads the majority of which had already borne the weight of a retreating army under

Bomber Command drops 28,000 tons on production centres, 5,000 tons on specific rail targets including Bielefeld viaduct, 4,000 tons on harbour installations, 19,000 on oil production centres and 8,500 on tactical targets near the front

Mar 4 Finland declares a state of war with Germany since Sept 15 1944

Mosquitoes continually over Germany, including 29 raids on Berlin

In V1 and V2 raids against England 792 killed, 1,426 injured. Mar 27 1,050th (and last) V2 lands at Orpington, Kent

73,000 tons dropped on rail and communication centres and synthetic oil production, in support of US troops at Remagen bridgehead and at Swinemünde in support of Red Army

Mar 21 Acute food shortages announced in Britain as over 1,000,000 tons given to France, Belgium and Holland

Mar 24 USAAF and RAF in attacks to support Rhine crossings

35,000 sorties flown against targets in Yugoslavia, N Italy and S Austria

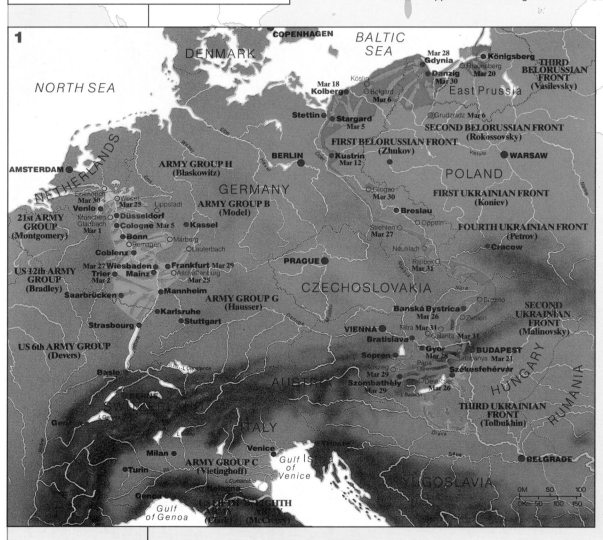

The Eastern Front. By the time February ended not only was Army Group Vistula exhibiting the strains due to command by a man who had never led even a platoon in action before, but Eleventh Army had been fighting for a long time and had suffered considerable losses. Moreover, time had now been given to the Red Army fronts to the south to recover from their tremendous exertions of January, and reinforcements and supplies were arriving.

As Rokossovsky's Second Ukrainians had been unable to break through the German positions in Pomerania to reach the Baltic in February on their own, Marshal Zhukov suggested that his own First Belorussians should support them on the left and that between them his own and Rokossovsky's armies should drive north, splitting Army Group Vistula into sections and destroying them piecemeal. Third Belorussians under Marshal Vasilevsky would block any German attempt to escape to the east, while the Baltic Fleet kept control of all sea communications along the coast.

By the beginning of March the drives were moving out past Neustettin and Pechlau (see February map) and five days later had reached the Baltic at Köslin, its main force now turning east in a drive along the coast towards Gdynia. Strong rearguards were left facing west to prevent damage from a counter-attack. Meanwhile Zhukov's armies were driving for Kolberg which they reached on Mar 18, then turning west and driving along the coast. Here they met other forces of First Belorussian Front which had had a hard fight before breaking through in the Stargard area, and by the end of the month the combined fronts had cleared the Baltic coast as far west as the Stettin Lagoon. They then turned and mopped up all the different pockets they had bypassed on the drives to the coast, and completed the occupation of Gdynia and Danzig.

The only ground now held by German forces east of the Oder was the Courland Peninsula, Königsberg, the Samland Peninsula and the Frische Nehrung – the spit of land protruding across the Bay of Danzig towards Samland.

Battle of Lake Balaton. To the south during March occurred yet another demonstration of Hitler's rapidly diminishing grasp on reality. Having failed in the Ardennes, he now insisted on an attack in the east to redeem it and 'set a blaze to be seen around the world'.

Infuriated by the loss of Budapest, and assuming that the huge salient bulging from its southern edge westwards to Lake Balaton then south and back along the Drava to the Danube would be lightly held, he ordered *Operation Frühlingserwachen* to be launched on Mar 6. I and II SS Panzer Corps would drive south-east from the gap between Lakes Balaton and Valencze with III SS Panzer Corps along the south Valencze shore. South of Lake Balaton Second Panzer Army would attack westwards to meet a corps from Army Group E driving up across the Drava.

Within hours of the launch it became obvious that the Russians had foreseen the attacks and adequately prepared for them. They were all blocked within days, ominous reports came back that now even the SS troops were deserting and making it clear that they considered it not worth dying in a lost war, and by Mar 16 the operation was over.

Meantime Malinovsky's and Tolbukhin's Ukrainian Fronts had opened their drive on Vienna. Almost ignoring the panzer corps to the south, Malinovsky's units crossed the Hron north of Esztergom and drove along the Danube bank, Tolbukhin's sliced through Sixth SS Panzer Army to Pápa and by the end of the month was at Sopron with Vienna but 40 miles away.

shell-fire, and none of which had received much in the way of maintenance for years. Their condition was in no way improved by the recent flooding.

But by the beginning of March, the plans were finalised, Allied air forces were keeping standing patrols over Luftwaffe airfields to ensure that no German eyes could see too much of the preparations. On Mar 1 US Ninth Army, having crossed the Roer, took München Gladbach and five days later reached Cologne, while on the day after, to Hitler's almost maniacal rage, the Remagen Bridge over the Rhine was captured apparently intact. As the US First Army units poured over their engineers threw across auxiliary bridges, so when the main bridge collapsed through over-use on Mar 17, the bridgehead which had been built up was not too badly affected.

On the night of Mar 23/24, under a barrage from the massed heavy artillery that had been assembled, the assault battalions of the British XII and XXX Corps and the US XVI Corps crossed the Rhine on each side of the Lippe river, escorted by DD Sherman tanks, Buffaloes and DUKWs. On the British right flank commandos paddled across and landed opposite Wesel, then approached in darkness to within a mile of the outskirts. Exactly on time RAF bombers arrived overhead and plastered the town for 15 minutes, after which the commandos moved in to capture this important road centre.

Opposition to the crossings was patchy. In some places the artillery barrage had been so heavy that almost no resistance

was encountered and the bridgeheads were quickly built up; in other places the losses while still afloat were heavy and the landings bitterly contested. Nevertheless, by morning there was a sizeable Allied presence on the east bank of the Rhine.

Then about midday the Allied 'Air Armada' arrived. Two parachute divisions were dropped just north-east of Wesel to be quickly followed by gliders bringing in light artillery and stores, all covered by over 2,000 fighters and fighter-bombers keeping the skies clear of the Luftwaffe. By nightfall the paratroops and the men who had made the crossings were linked up and the bridgehead north of the Ruhr was secure.

To the south the crossings made at the same time by the forces of the US 12th Army Group had been just as successful. South of Mainz General Patton had put an assault regiment across the river – there 1,000 feet wide – just before midnight of Mar 22/23, and by the evening of the next day a complete division was across with a firm bridgehead into which was soon to follow a complete armoured division.

During the following days more crossings were made over the stretch of river beween Coblenz and Mannheim, and by the end of the month Wiesbaden, Frankfurt and Aschaffenburg were securely in American hands, Lauterbach and Marburg were encircled, Kassel was under threat while to the north the left-hand flank of US First Army curled up to meet the right-hand flank of US Ninth Army, thus completing the encirclement of the most vital industrial region of Germany, the Ruhr.

148

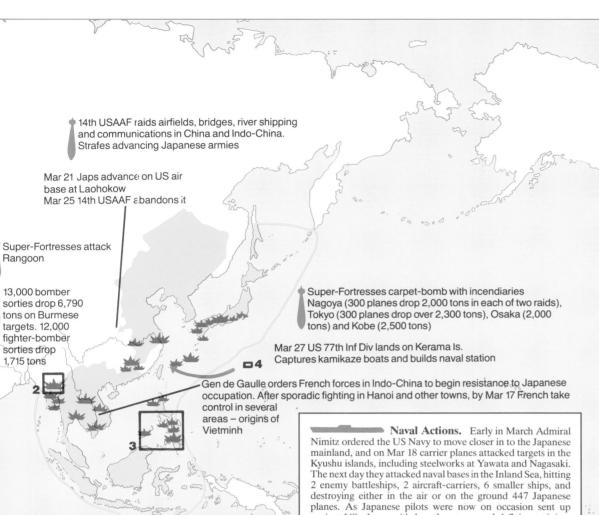

MARCH
1945

14th USAAF raids airfields, bridges, river shipping and communications in China and Indo-China. Strafes advancing Japanese armies

Mar 21 Japs advance on US air base at Laohokow
Mar 25 14th USAAF abandons it

Super-Fortresses attack Rangoon

13,000 bomber sorties drop 6,790 tons on Burmese targets. 12,000 fighter-bomber sorties drop 1,715 tons

Super-Fortresses carpet-bomb with incendiaries Nagoya (300 planes drop 2,000 tons in each of two raids), Tokyo (300 planes drop over 2,300 tons), Osaka (2,000 tons) and Kobe (2,500 tons)

Mar 27 US 77th Inf Div lands on Kerama Is. Captures kamikaze boats and builds naval station

Gen de Gaulle orders French forces in Indo-China to begin resistance to Japanese occupation. After sporadic fighting in Hanoi and other towns, by Mar 17 French take control in several areas – origins of Vietminh

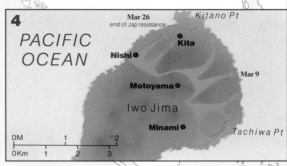

4 PACIFIC OCEAN — Iwo Jima

Naval Actions. Early in March Admiral Nimitz ordered the US Navy to move closer in to the Japanese mainland, and on Mar 18 carrier planes attacked targets in the Kyushu islands, including steelworks at Yawata and Nagasaki. The next day they attacked naval bases in the Inland Sea, hitting 2 enemy battleships, 2 aircraft-carriers, 6 smaller ships, and destroying either in the air or on the ground 447 Japanese planes. As Japanese pilots were now on occasion sent up against US planes with less than two weeks' flying training, these figures are not so remarkable as they look.

By now XXXIII Corps were pressing further south, and by the beginning of the month the 19th Division was driving down from Thabeikkyin towards Mandalay. By Mar 7 the leading units were at Madaya, with Mandalay but 20 miles ahead, and the following day the leading units of 'Stiletto Force' drove into the northern suburbs and began the battle for the second city of Burma. It was to prove a bitter battle, as the Japanese used the pagodas and temples as observation posts, and their artillery reacted swiftly and accurately to every report. In the end, the temples on Mandalay Hill had to be taken by Gurkhas using grenades and satchel bombs and, in the last charge, their *kukris*. By Mar 11, the Pavilion had been taken, but the main objective, Fort Dufferin, remained in Japanese hands.

Another brigade of British and Indian troops was brought in, and at 1100 on Mar 20 Thunderbolts and Hurri-bombers of RAF and USAAF blasted a gap in the north wall. When the infantry stormed in, they found that the Japanese had slipped away through the drains leading under the moat.

Everywhere, the Fourteenth Army and the NCAC were pressing southwards. Myingyan was taken on Mar 20, Ava with its huge and vital bridge on Mar 17, while to the north-east Mogok had been taken by another XXXIII division. The Chinese First Army and Y Force had reached Lashio at last on Mar 7, then to mount a converging attack on Hsipaw on Mar 24. By the end of the month the entire length of the Burma Road from Mandalay eastwards was in Allied hands, and General Kimura's Burma Area Army being pressed ever further south.

4 'The bloodiest month's fighting in the history of the US Marines.' So March 1945 has been described. Iwo Jima is a volcanic island, virtually made of pumice stone. This allowed easy but self-supporting tunnelling – a Japanese speciality – and the northern half of the island had been transformed into a veritable underground labyrinth. In one area 1,000 yards wide and only 200 yards deep, lay 800 separate fortifications, pillboxes and blockhouses. Entire hillocks had been hollowed out and rebuilt to shelter the defenders – and there had been 23,000 when the marines came ashore, each of them fanatically determined to die rather than surrender.

By the beginning of March marine losses had been so high and exhaustion was taking such toll of the survivors that some units had been reduced to 50 per cent efficiency. The 3rd Marine Division had been brought in between the other two, but it was Mar 9 before even these fresher troops had been able to break through to the coast, and in the meantime as 4th and 5th Divisions edged their way yard by yard forward, burning their way into the tunnels, blowing in the entrances with mortars and satchel bombs, they compressed more and more Japanese into an ever smaller area – and as a result had to face the inevitable *Banzai* charges. In one area less than the size of a football pitch they later counted 650 Japanese bodies – and still they came at them, sometimes from behind as they had blown open blocked tunnels in the rear areas. It was not until the night of Mar 25/26 that the last *Banzai* attack took place.

Of the original garrison of 23,000 men, only 1,083, all badly wounded, were taken prisoner; 6,821 US Marines died and 24 Medals of Honor were won on Iwo Jima's eight square miles.

It had taken 72 days of air bombardment, a 3-day naval hammering and 36 days of desperate endeavour by US Marines. How long would Japan herself take? And at what cost?

2 **The capture of Mandalay and Meiktila.** General Slim was to write, 'Road and rail routes from the south-east and west converged on Meiktila, to spread out again to the north like the extended fingers of a hand, whose wrist was Meiktila. Crush that wrist, no blood would flow through the fingers, the whole hand would be paralysed, and the Japanese armies on the arc from the Salween to the Irrawaddy would begin to wither.'

It was thus hardly surprising that the Japanese defended the place strenuously and then, having lost it, launched attacks to retake it. As soon as the Meiktila garrison commander realised that 17th Division was closing fast, he issued every weapon and round of ammunition in his armoury to the troops in the city – even the hospital patients – and organised not only the defence, but also raiding parties to try to cut the British lines of supply. The result was as fierce a battle as had yet been fought in Burma, but administration and service troops, however well led and however brave, are in the end no match for experienced combat troops. By Mar 3 the Gurkhas and West Yorkshiremen of General Cowan's division had pressed the defenders back into a small area in the south of the city, where they slowly but methodically winkled the last snipers and machine-gunners out of the railway yards and buildings.

Four days later, however, the Japanese retook Taungtha in the rear, and then mounted a powerful attack on Meiktila airfield to such effect that another brigade had to be flown in – arriving just as the Japanese began their last dash for the runways. By Mar 22 Japanese pressure was such that any further supplies or reinforcement for 17th Division had to be parachuted in, and it was Mar 29 before the airfield and Meiktila itself was clear of Japanese infiltrators, and a ring of artillery in place to ensure its retention.

3 **The Southern Philippines.** With Leyte, Luzon and Mindoro now effectively under American control, it was necessary to ensure that Japanese formations cut off in the myriad islands in the Visayan, Mindanao and Sulu Seas between Luzon and Mindanao on the east and Borneo on the west, were rendered impotent. This was especially important in so far as the sea passages between the islands were concerned, for nothing must jeopardize the free movement of US shipping throughout the whole area during the crucial weeks ahead.

In this task the US forces would be immensely helped by the well-organised Philippine guerrilla movements which had sprung up in practically every island in response to Japanese oppression. They had already rendered sterling service in Luzon and Leyte, and were at hand to welcome the 'Palawan Force' from 41st Division when it landed on Feb 28. There was little Japanese resistance, for the garrisons had fled into the hills where they were soon hunted down by the combined guerrillas and infantry. By Mar 20 the airfields were operating, the liberation was completed by the end of the month and on Apr 9 the neighbouring island of Busuanga was taken.

Although degrees of resistance were to vary, the same conditions existed and situations developed elsewhere. Lubang had been occupied from Mindoro on Mar 1; Zamboanga and Basilan were occupied on Mar 10 and 16 – both after adequate air and naval bombardment. Landings on Panay took place on Mar 18, on Negros on Mar 29 and on Cebu the day before.

Everywhere the picture was the same. In the face of American initiative, demonstrated by rapid action undertaken with overwhelming force, Japanese morale was dwindling and with it their conviction that victory would be theirs. Even the Japanese soldiers were wondering if a lost cause was worth dying for.

149

Twilight of the Thousand-Year Reich

With the Western Allies across the Rhine and the enormous power of the Red Army lining up along the Oder, Hitler's empire by April 1945 was less than that which he had ruled in 1936. Gone were all the conquered territories he had engulfed into his 'Grossdeutsches Reich', and his Italian ally had dropped away leaving only neutral Switzerland and the mountains of the Alps to protect his southern flank. As for the Far Eastern partner, his feelings for the Japanese had been influenced since his youth by Kaiser Wilhelm's diatribes against the 'Yellow Peril', and nowadays he hardly gave them a thought. They were fighting a different war against a different enemy, and he needed all his attention concentrated upon his personal dilemma and the weakening ability of the Wehrmacht and the German people as a whole to protect him and his Reich.

From each side, gigantic armies pressed in upon him. Along the Rhine from Nijmegen down to Cologne were the Canadian, British and American armies of 21st Army Group, from there down to Mannheim were the two armies of the US Twelfth Army Group and south of them another US army and the French First Army of the US Sixth Army Group. Along the Oder from north to south lay 5 armies of the Second Belorussian Front and the 11 armies of the First Belorussian Front, then 8 armies of the First Ukrainian Front lying along the Neisse with another 11 armies of three more Ukrainian Fronts further south. All these armies were strong and well equipped, up to establishment in manpower, able in places to concentrate artillery to a density of 400 guns per mile and with such an abundance of Sherman tanks along the Rhine and of Stalin and up-dated T-34 tanks along the eastern front, that the probability of their encountering the German Royal, King or Hunting Tiger panzers could be easily accepted. The undoubted quality of the German armour would be overwhelmed by quantity.

This factor of quantity dominated the entire scene. Although on paper three Army Groups – H under General Student, B under Model and G under Hausser – faced the Western Allies across the Rhine, and two – Vistula under Himmler (for the moment) and Centre under Schörner – faced the Red Army, they were all in such a state of disarray as the result of recent defeats that no formation was up to strength in either men or weapons. Old men and boys made up quite a proportion of their complement, and many of the battalions were 'stomach', 'ear and throat' or similarly designated battalions, none of them of the quality to stand long in the path of the forces mounting against them. Kesselring, about to become Commander-in-Chief, West, would inherit a 'bankrupt estate', the shadow of an army which had just lost 300,000 men on the west bank of the Rhine as a result of Hitler's refusal to allow them to cross the river – just as on the eastern front, his refusal to allow the evacuation of Courland had virtually eliminated Army Group North.

On the west his armies had now retreated 500 miles, on the east over 1,000 – in theory, of course, shortening his lines of supply and communication to give him more concentrated strength to resist the powers against him. But Allied air power had negated this advantage, for now if his lines of supply were shorter, they were also in the process of being smashed. Round-the-clock bombing by huge Anglo-American air fleets was at last playing a vital part in the defeat of Germany – not by any effect on the civilian population, which had withstood the nightly rain of fire with a stoic courage which compels admiration, nor by destruction of German manufacturing capacity, which had been far higher in 1944 than in any previous year, and had a momentum to carry on production into 1945 almost until Allied tanks drove through the factory gates. It was the piecemeal destruction of the German hydrogenation plants which converted coal into liquid fuel (with the Ploesti oilfields

gone, almost the sole source of gasoline) and the systematic destruction of the railway complex which was now crippling Germany's power to wage war. Rail stock, lines and especially the junctions and marshalling yards close to industrial centres had been the targets of bombing campaigns of varying concentrations since 1943, but now so complete was Allied air superiority and so massive the air fleets, that Germany's industrial centres were surrounded by transportation wildernesses. The factories might still turn out panzers and aircraft, but there was no petrol for their tanks and no way to move them to the fronts.

Yet the German armies and the people as a whole fought on. For the German soldier the choice might have been easier for he was proud of his uniform, sustained by his comrades in action and held anyway within the laws of military discipline. The civilians were kept under control by a combination of promises and terror.

For many months there had been strong rumours of 'secret weapons' which would turn the war back in Germany's favour – and had not German scientists produced the V-weapons which were bombarding London? More were promised – and for those who might doubt the possibility of technical breakthrough destroying the huge military might now encircling the country, there was the continual political assurance that long before they were themselves overcome, the Western Allies would see the rightness of Hitler's crusade against Bolshevism, and join it.

There were minor strands to this persuasion of German morale, two of them based upon gratuitous contributions by the Western Allies. Roosevelt's assertion to the press after the Casablanca conference that the Allies would accept nothing from the Axis powers but 'unconditional surrender', occasionally repeated by Allied media but trumpeted aloud on frequent occasions by the Nazi Ministry of Propaganda, had recently received added force by what had been called the 'Morgenthau Plan'. Under this, all heavy and much light industry in Germany would be dismantled and the entire country reduced to an agricultural and almost peasant economy – similar in fact to that which the Nazis had tried to establish in Czechoslovakia and other conquered states; as an instrument for strengthening German morale in the face of defeat, this was almost tailored to Goebbels's requirements. However desperate the plight which faced Germany, it was not apparently so dire as the fate which awaited her if she surrendered.

'We shall never surrender!' shrieked Hitler. 'Never! Never! Never!' – and the bulk of his German subjects, sceptical by now of many of his proclamations, saw little with which to disagree in the sentiment; especially if they had served in any capacity on the eastern front and had knowledge of the atrocities committed by their fellow-nationals against the now victorious Slavs. No pity could be expected from that quarter.

Very little pity could be expected either from another large group already within the Reich. Hundreds of thousands of 'Foreign Workers' had been brought in from the Occupied Countries, and if the conditions in which they had existed since arrival were marginally better than in prison-camps, they were still herded about under guard, still expected to work long hours on scanty rations, and of late had on occasion exhibited signs of extreme latent hostility to their hosts.

Moreover, as the Anglo-American and Russian armies drove further into Germany, they would reach the network of concentration camps – and although comparatively few of the German people as a whole knew the full and dreadful details of that system, they knew enough about it to fear the wrath of the liberated inmates – if any survived – and to wonder what effect the discoveries would have on the soldiers of the invading armies.

If the German people lived in justified fear of what would happen to them if and when they capitulated, they were also well aware of the fate which awaited them if they so much as suggested such a course. All knew what had happened to the July 20 conspirators; now the same sentence could be passed on anyone who disagreed with official opinion – which in effect meant disagreement with Hitler's edict. Germany thus lived under two terrors: terror of enemy air attack and the apparently inexorable advance of enemy armies from both sides; and terror from the People's Courts which passed summary judgement on any expression of opinion or act of defiance against Nazi rule. The nation which but a short time before had terrorised Europe now itself lived under terror. And it was a terror which exacted obedience.

The absolute corruption which in Lord Acton's dictum stems from absolute power seems most often to reveal itself in a devastating contempt for those who have granted that power. There had been no weakening of the grip of the National Socialist Party upon the German people as the war entered this period of disaster for them, and no weakening of Hitler's control of the Party. Perhaps because the range of Hitler's command was now geographically circumscribed, it was more complete. The tentacles of the Gestapo reached everywhere, and no one would risk imprisonment in one of the concentration camps, however soon they might be liberated. And the risk did not just entail entertaining treasonable thoughts oneself; punishment could be just as condign for failure to report suspicion of another's possible disenchantment with the regime. Thus a clamp had been placed upon every expression of opinion in an effort to control every opinion; and death could quickly follow any revelation – accidental or not – that the official opinion was not totally accepted.

If the German people as a whole could do nothing to end their condition, their rulers had little desire to do so. The second echelon of power – the senior ranks of the SS – were making arrangements for the transfer of huge sums of money to South America where they hoped to arrive themselves in due course, via escape networks, to live in luxury for the rest of their lives. But the top echelon, the close circle around Hitler, had managed to insulate themselves from reality for so long that they lived in a world of fantasy. Göring had probably the widest knowledge of the outside world, but he was intent upon continuing his life of sybaritic luxury to the end, amassing great wealth with which he might have entertained hopes of buying for himself a comfortable retirement. Bormann was determined to thwart any plan of Göring's and thus increase his own influence in Hitler's court, simply because he had done so now for so long that the habit had become ingrained; Himmler was so out of touch with reality that until the end he believed that when Germany at last surrendered – as he privately accepted that she must – the victors would need him and his organisation to control the country, and he would thus be assured of a high position – if not the highest – in the resulting government. Goebbels, of course, merely continued in his role as Hitler's pale, but vocal and devoted, shadow; and would continue in it to the grave.

As for Hitler himself, he had wielded such great power for so many years that it had become, one suspects, the sole satisfaction of his ego; and capitulation would destroy it all. Food and drink except for minimal requirements had never meant much to him, neither had sex. As for art, music in Wagnerian modes had apparently at times entertained him, painting possibly, architecture so long as it would portray his own consequence. But none of these compared with the satisfaction of the use of untrammelled power, and every day which extended this intoxication was in his mind justified, no matter what the cost in other people's lives.

What were these worth, anyway? When during the

battles on the west bank of the Rhine the presence of civilians seemed likely to impose difficulties on the fighting troops, Hitler had ordered their evacuation 'in a generally south-easterly direction' – and when it was pointed out that there was little or no transportation available, he snapped, 'Then let them walk!' He later added, 'We can no longer afford to concern ourselves with the population.'

He was, in fact, determined that if he fell he would drag Germany down with him. As the enemy closed in from all sides, he issued orders for a 'scorched earth' policy of such stringency that though it might well have hampered the Allied advance, it would even more certainly have robbed the German people of any chance of survival after the war. Destruction carried out on the scale he ordered would have condemned the nation either to starvation soon after the fighting ended, or to an icy death during the following winter.

This was a prospect accepted, apparently, by all the members of his immediate circle except one. Albert Speer, for many years a close friend and indeed favourite, submitted to Hitler a memo remonstrating against his condemnation to such a fate of the people he had so often professed to love and to whose welfare he

had claimed to be devoting his life; to receive in icy tones the reply, 'If the war is lost, the people will be lost also. It is not necessary to worry about what the German people will need for elemental survival. On the contrary, it is best for us to destroy even these things. For the nation has proved to be the weaker, and the future belongs solely to the stronger eastern nation. In any case only those who are inferior will remain after this struggle, for the good have already been killed.'

In effect, the German nation had been unable to obtain for him the world domination he craved; so let it die.

Such callous inhumanity is not historically unknown, of course, in other rulers in other ages, but Albert Speer offers an interesting explanation in one of his descriptions of this last period of Hitler's life. 'He gave the impression of a man whose whole purpose had been destroyed, who was continuing along his established orbit only because of the kinetic energy stored within him . . . There was actually something insubstantial about him. But this was perhaps a permanent quality he had. In retrospect I sometimes ask myself whether this intangibility, this insubstantiality, had not characterised him from early youth . . . It sometimes seems to me that

his seizures of violence could come upon him all the more strongly because there were no human emotions in him to oppose them. He simply could not let anyone approach his inner being because that core was lifeless, empty.'

It probably always had been, but whatever the inner force which had driven him, by the spring of 1945 it was exacting its price. Aged only 56, 'he was shrivelling up like an old man. His limbs trembled; he walked stooped, with dragging footsteps. Even his voice became quavering and lost its old masterfulness. His force had given way to a faltering, toneless manner of speaking. When he became excited, as he frequently did in a senile way, his voice would start breaking. He still had his fits of obstinacy, but they no longer reminded one of a child's tantrums, but of an old man's. His complexion was sallow, his face swollen; his uniform, which in the past he had kept scrupulously neat, was often neglected in this last period of his life and stained by food he had eaten with a shaking hand.'

In view of the suffering Hitler had caused mankind, it is not difficult to suppress any feelings of sympathy Speer's description might evoke. The mills of God might, with advantage, have ground a little faster.

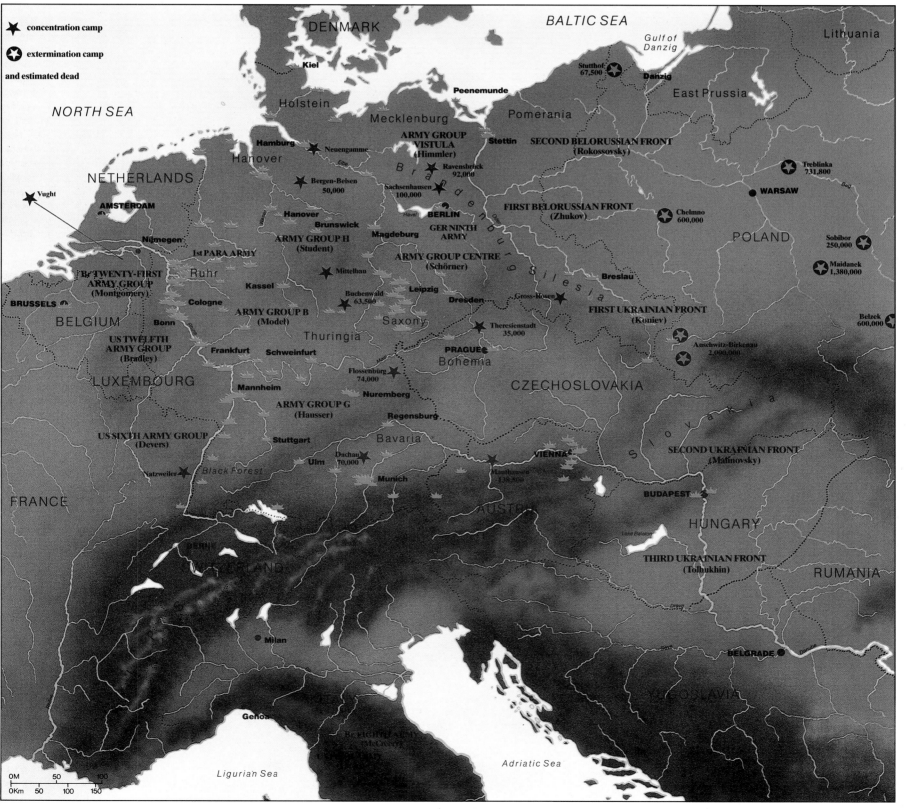

1 The Rhine to the Elbe. In April the strength of the German Wehrmacht finally failed. Since the height of their successes at the end of 1942 they had retreated across thousands of square miles in the west and at least three times as many in the east; their losses in manpower had been a disaster for their nation, in war material incalculable. Now they faced the prospect of battle against powerful – and in the east ferocious and vengeful – enemies, their own divisions shorn of the staunchest elements, mostly by battle though in some instances as the result of incomprehensible political decision; and an alarming lack of weaponry and transport. Pride in past achievement might sustain the older elements, but flesh and blood, even sustained by the highest courage, was not proof against such overwhelming superiority as that possessed by the enemy. No wonder that the defence fronts showed signs of cracking; no wonder that formations which had won glory time after time since 1940 were liable to break apart under the storm which fell upon them once the enemy assaults were launched.

So far as the flooding invasion from the west was concerned, once the Rhine was crossed resistance to the sweep to the Elbe was patchy, for in the minds of many Germans, the faster the Anglo-Americans advanced as far east as possible, the smaller the area of the country to fall into Russian hands. As a result, though in places such as the Ruhr where Model still commanded a formidable force there was some very hard fighting to be carried out by US First Army during the first three

Bomber Command drops 14,000 tons on ports, naval installations and shipping, 6,400 tons on tactical targets ahead of advancing armies, 6,000 tons on rail centres, 5,000 on oil production centres. SS barracks and Hitler's chalet at Berchtesgaden hit

Mosquitoes attack Kiel and Berlin

Apr 1 Large convoy reaches Russia without loss

Lancasters sink pocket-battleships *Admiral Scheer* – Apr 9/10 at Kiel – and *Lützow* – Apr 16 at Swinemünde

Bomber Command drops medical supplies into PoW camps and food into Holland

RAF Liberators attack communications through Brenner Pass

USAAF drops 46,631 tons concentrating on airfields for jet planes, rail and communication centres

Apr 30 British Air Ministry and US Strategic Air Force announce end of strategic bombing campaign in Europe

Apr 12 Death of President Roosevelt at Warm Springs, Georgia

Apr 13 and 24 Belsen, Buchenwald and Dachau concentration camps reached

Drive to Berlin. Three days after Stalin and Eisenhower had agreed that the Anglo-American thrust should be along the Leipzig–Dresden Axis, Stalin held a conference with his two senior marshals, Zhukov and Koniev. The devious and deceitful Western Allies, he informed them, intended to launch a surprise thrust across the North German Plain in order to capture and occupy Berlin before the Red Army could get there: and in view of the achievements of the armies under the command of the two marshals during the past few months, it is hardly surprising that they considered such a development unacceptable.

They had been planning to launch their drive to Berlin early in May, but now, having been given a dividing line between their two operational zones which left open the crucial question of who was to capture the Reichstag and the centre of the city, they rapidly recast their offensives.

At dawn on Apr 16 a tremendous bombardment opened along the Oder and Neisse rivers, and from the Soviet bridgeheads burst the waves of assault troops. Zhukov's thrust reached the Seelow Heights after two days and on his left flank had advanced eight miles, Koniev's storm troops made eight miles in the first day – so he fed in two tank armies and told them to drive north-west, only just avoiding crossing Zhukov's line of advance.

Spurred on by competition, Zhukov now drove his infantry forward with renewed vigour, and by Apr 21 his Eighth Guards Army was into Berlin's eastern suburbs. Thwarted, Koniev now concentrated on reaching the Elbe. Two of his armies drove first to Potsdam where they linked up with Zhukov's Second Guards Tank Army which had come around the north of Berlin – thus between them encircling the city – then the rest of Koniev's Ukrainian Front armies drove westwards. On Apr 25 advanced patrols of his Fifth Guards Army reached the Elbe at Torgau and within minutes were exchanging drinks, buttons and photographs with Americans from the US First Army.

Further south the Second, Third and Fourth Ukrainian Fronts had also swept forward. Austerlitz was taken on Apr 29, Vienna had been in Malinovsky's hands since Apr 18, while Tolbukhin's left wing was driving along the Drava with the rest of Austria open to their occupation as the newly created Army Group Vienna disintegrated in front of them.

The monstrous history of Nazi Germany had only a few more days to run.

Italy. After months of misery and stalemate, the Italian Front suddenly exploded into action on Apr 8. The Allies had now been re-equipped with all the artillery, transport and especially the new 'Fantails' – totally amphibious, well-armoured vessels which could cross mud or shallow water – they would need to break into the Po valley and defeat the German forces there.

On the Adriatic side of the front, Eighth Army commandos, infantry and armour drove forward, the commandos driving along the coastal strip, the infantry and armour driving first for Argenta which they took on Apr 18, then to surge on to Ferrara while their right-hand division swung east across the top of Lake Comacchio to drive for Padua and Venice beyond, which they reached on Apr 28.

Meanwhile the US Fifth Army had attacked on Apr 14 covered by a heavy air attack in front. The US infantry stormed the peaks in front of them and after 48 hours' fierce fighting drove the German forces off, allowing the US armour down into the Po valley. Bologna was theirs by Apr 21, Parma by Apr 25 and they were at Lakes Garda and Como by the end of the month. Along the coast their left-hand forces had driven straight up through La Spezia and Genoa to reach Turin.

During the whole period, Italian partisans had acted as guides and helpers, and on Apr 28 a group of them caught Mussolini and his staff, including his mistress Clara Petacci. The next day they shot them all; Fascism in Italy was finished.

or four days, once the crust was broken resistance faded and in, for instance, Duisberg and Essen, the US forces walked in without firing a shot. By Apr 10 the Ninth Army had taken Hanover and they reached the Elbe south of Magdeburg the next day – while away to the south the US Seventh Army took Schweinfurt. Nuremberg fell on Apr 20, Regensburg on Apr 26 and Munich on Apr 30.

To the Americans' south the French First Army had swung forward in a huge arc to the Swiss frontier, while to the north the British and Canadians of the 21st Army Group had liberated Holland, reached Bremen on April 26, then to race on to the Elbe alongside the Americans, their agreed objectives first the lower Elbe and Hamburg, then Schleswig-Holstein and the Baltic coast as far east as the Lübecker Bight.

There was some argument as to the desirability of 21st Army Group racing for Berlin, but Eisenhower had already agreed

with Stalin that the Anglo-American effort would be concentrated to the south, leaving Berlin to the Red Army. This agreement met strong and vociferous criticism in Whitehall and in some circles in Washington, but Eisenhower was strongly supported by Roosevelt in a belief they both shared – that Russia would prove both amenable and co-operative in all matters concerned with post-war European readjustments, so there was no need to pursue political objectives. Since the Yalta Conference in February Roosevelt had been sure that he and Stalin held very similar views as to the desirability of peace, prosperity and security throughout the post-war world, and the best ways of securing all of them.

Tragically, Roosevelt had died on Apr 12. Truman was sworn in as President the same day to inherit the victories for which Roosevelt had striven so hard; and also the problems his generosity of mind had brought about.

152

Bombers fly 700 sorties, drop 1,300 tons. Fighters and fighter-bombers fly 6,300 sorties and drop 770 tons

Apr 13 Japanese launch large-scale offensive, effectively slowed down by Chinese flank attacks. After fierce fighting Chinese yield Wukang (Apr 25), reinforce Chihchiang and Ankiang air bases

Super-Fortresses constantly over Japan. Apr 4, 6 With first landbased escorting fighters to sweep over Japan, raid Tokyo, destroy 173 Japanese planes; also raid Tokyo Apr 13, 14 (Imperial Palace damaged) and Apr 16 (by 400 planes). Other targets include Kyushu airfields used by kamikaze planes

TF 58 bombs Kyushu

US landings on small islands of Ryukyu group

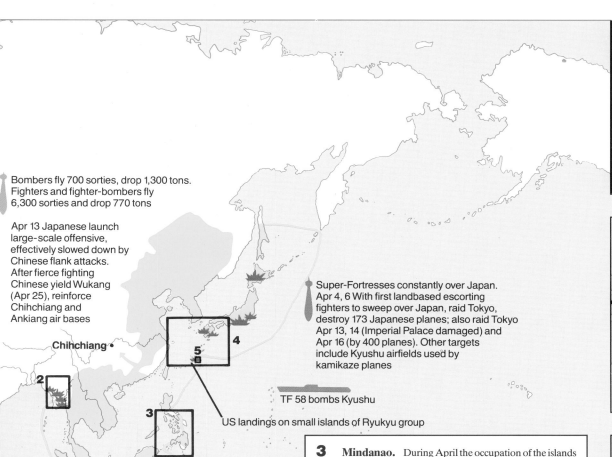

3 **Mindanao.** During April the occupation of the islands continued. In the south the Sulu archipelago was systematically taken under control with only the main Japanese garrison on Jolo giving a great deal of trouble. Further north, American infantry and Philippine guerrillas extended their control in Panay, Cebu and Negros, landed on Bohol – and continued the often grim task of 'mopping up' on Luzon, both in the northern mountains and south of Manila.

Then on Apr 17 and 18, X Corps of Eighth Army went ashore on western Mindanao. By Apr 26 they had crossed to Davao Gulf and were driving up the central valley.

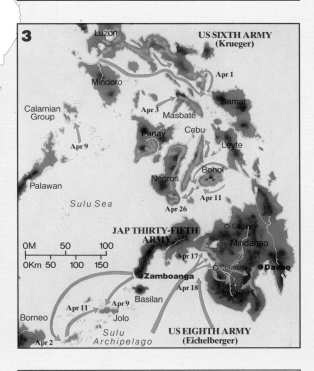

4 & 5 **Okinawa.** The island lies only 325 miles from Japan and the battle for it, lasting from April until June, illustrates both the overwhelming naval and military power developed by America since 1941, and the desperate straits to which this had reduced Japan.

By the morning of Apr 1 (Easter Sunday) 1,457 ships had reached the waters around Okinawa, bearing 183,000 US soldiers and marines or acting as shield for their operations, and one marine and one infantry corps were put ashore immediately. To their astonishment they encountered little opposition and by evening 50,000 men had landed, with their equipment flooding in behind them. General Ushijima had made the decision not to defend the beaches but to fight from his prepared defences; for Japan now had only the creed of the kamikaze to hold their enemies at bay.

They had already struck at the fleet. Before a single US soldier had set foot ashore, 2 escort carriers, 2 large carriers, a battleship, a cruiser, and 4 destroyers had been hit by kamikaze aircraft, and by the end of the operation 1,900 suicide sorties were launched against US forces, sinking 25 ships (none larger than a destroyer) and damaging 254.

But the most spectacular suicide attempt was made by the giant battleship *Yamato*, which left Tokuyama on Apr 6 with only enough fuel to reach Okinawa where it was intended she should run aground and then use her massive guns to wreck the US fleet. But her exit from the Inland Sea was observed and shortly after noon the next day hordes of US planes from the carrier fleet arrived overhead. Bereft of fighter-cover, *Yamato* and her escorts were helpless. At 1423 *Yamato*, hit by 10 torpedoes and 5 bombs, capsized, blew up and sank, and only six of her ten escorts returned to port.

On land, US soldiers and marines continued to flood ashore, taking the vital airfields at Yontan and Kadena at no cost so that within six days 200 marine fighters were operating from them. To the north all the way up to Hedo Point, 6th Marine Division drove steadily on, only encountering some real resistance on Motobu peninsula, which they quickly obliterated. By Apr 19 the northern four-fifths of the island was in their hands.

The southern fifth, from the Shuri defence line, was proving as difficult as Iwo Jima, would cost more and take longer.

2 **The Race to Rangoon.** With Meiktila and Mandalay secure, it became possible that Rangoon could be reached before the next monsoon broke in early May. General Slim had two routes open down which to send his divisions – the Irrawaddy valley down through Chauk and the oil centre of Yenangyaung, then Myingyun and Prome; or the rail route from Meiktila down through Pyawbwe, Shwemyo, Toungoo and Pegu.

He had not enough force to follow both courses in strength, so he gave the main weight to IV Corps to drive down the rail-line, giving XXXIII Corps the task of distracting Kimura's attention westwards, and thus causing a dispersion of Japanese strength. He was helped in the breakthrough by Kimura's deployment, for he had ordered Twenty-eighth and Thirty-third Army commanders to hold the line Yenangyaung–Pyawbwe at all costs, and neither general had the strength to do so.

As a result, although XXXIII Corps in the Irrawaddy valley had a great deal of fierce fighting to do before they bypassed Yenangyaung to reach Magwe (and it took IV Corps 11 days to break through at Pyawbwe, only 30 miles from Meiktila) once

they were both through there was little but Japanese rearguards to hold them back. On the west 7th Indian Division drove down both sides of the river to reach Myingyun on Apr 19, while on their left 20th Indian Division had come down from Meiktila to take Taungdwingyi on Apr 15, cut across and join 7th, together to drive down to Allanmyo by Apr 28.

On the eastern route, 17th Division had broken clear at Pyawbwe and reached Shwemyo by Apr 18, when 5th Indian Division took over and raced on to Puinmana by Apr 20 and Toungoo three days later. As IV Corps was charging south down the main axis, Japanese units which had been driven into the hills on each side were racing after them in an effort to occupy the vital airfields at Toungoo, in the hope of holding them until the monsoon arrived to put them out of action. They failed, and IV Corps were at Payagyi by Apr 29, with Pegu in sight and Rangoon less than 50 miles ahead. They were not, however, destined to be the ones to liberate the port. In order to beat the monsoon, an amphibious force supported by paratroops was already on the way from Ramree.

Battle for the Reichstag

By Apr 25 Zhukov and Koniev's fronts had tightened an iron ring around Berlin. One infantry army, two shock armies, a guards army and three guards tank armies surrounded the city while above it both Anglo-American and Red Air Force bomber fleets dominated the skies and rained their bombs down from above the range of the still considerable anti-aircraft batteries.

The whole world knew that Berlin would soon fall to the Red Army and that no other end was possible. Any responsible government would have declared Berlin an Open City and asked for an armistice. But one prematurely aged, palsied megalo-maniac, in a subterranean bunker under 16 feet of concrete and 6 feet of earth, which not only sheltered him from bomb and shell but also from the dreadful reality surrounding him, could still demand and receive total obedience. The extension of his own life and power for a few more days was far more important than the lives of thousands of men, women and children, despite the devoted support they had given him for the last 12 years.

Hitler's was not the only irrationality, however, to affect the Battle of Berlin, for the Russian dictator had added a touch of his own. May 1 was only six days away, and Stalin's strict orders were that the Red Banner must be flying from the top of the Reichstag in order to make it the most glorious May Day in Soviet history. There could be no question, therefore, of waiting until a combination of continuous shelling and bombing – night and day from every angle – reduced the buildings to rubble and the inhabitants of the city to surrender through shock and starvation. Despite their losses since they had stormed across the Oder, despite their achievements since Stalingrad (and Chuikov's Eighth Guards Army which had held that city were now closing up to Tempelhof Airport) and a very natural reluctance to get killed during the last few days of the war, the Red Army soldiers were now to be launched into the most murderous type of battle – street fighting against an enemy impelled by the fiercest brand of military morale, that of the cornered rat.

There was still a great deal of fighting to take place outside Berlin – against the German Twelfth Army on the Elbe, against a heterogeneous force under SS General Steiner to the north-west and most especially against Ninth Army and Fourth Panzer Army trapped in woods to the south-west of the city. All these forces had to be contained, and their mere existence served to inflame Hitler's imagination with fantasies of massive German armies marching to his relief; the 464,000 Soviet troops supported by 12,700 guns and mortars, 1,500 tanks and 21,000 Katyusha multiple rocket-launchers, which on Apr 26 were launched into the final assault on the core of the battered city, still faced a formidable task.

From the north-west, Second Guards Tank Army would force their way into and through Siemenstadt to reach the banks of the Spree, Third Shock Army on their left driving for Alt Moabit and the Spree, with Charlottenburger Chaussee and the centre of the city beyond. From the east, Fifth Shock Army formations were closing in along both banks of the Spree, while from the south Chuikov's riflemen with tank support were across the Teltow Canal, aiming for the Tiergarten and a swing right to the Reichstag itself. Further west, Twenty-eighth Army and Third Guards Tank Army assaulted the western reaches of the Teltow Canal, then drove further west for the Havel river to cut the lines of communication between Berlin and Potsdam where German troops were still holding out.

Casualties on both sides were horrific. Fire from massed Soviet batteries ploughed up the streets, brought massive buildings crashing down with German snipers and machine-gunners falling with the debris

into streets already carpeted with dead and wounded, now to lie helpless as huge Joseph Stalin tanks crunched their way through the chaos. But the chaos itself provided defence posts amid the rubble, and heavy machine-guns and Panzerfausts – often in the hands of schoolboys anything between 12 and 16 years old – exacted their price in Soviet riflemen and tanks.

By the evening of Apr 27, pressure from north and south had reduced the German-held portion of the city to a sausage-shaped pocket, some 10 miles long and $3\frac{1}{2}$ miles at its widest. On the west the pocket stopped short of the Havel river, on the east it nearly reached the Silesian Station – but its east–west axis was the Kaiser Damm and the Charlottenburger Chaussee, wide avenues which met Unter den Linden at the Brandenburg Gate and, with trees now cut down and lamp-standards removed, was wide enough for small aircraft to land. One – a Storch – had landed on the evening of Apr 25, by a feat of remarkable daring and expertise by the famous woman pilot, Hanna Reitsch.

She had brought in the Luftwaffe General Ritter von Greim, and together they made their way to the Führer Bunker where they entered a world of such macabre fantasy that, had it not been causing such widespread tragedy, would have been comic.

Hitler and his entourage had celebrated the Führer's 56th birthday on Apr 20, Goebbels having delivered the ritual broadcast to the nation the night before, hailing Hitler as the greatest leader of all time and exhorting the German people to continue to believe in him. Hitler himself confidently predicted that the Russians would suffer their worst defeat in Berlin, shook hands with the line of party and military officials who came to congratulate him and refused all suggestions that he should leave the capital. 'I must force a decision here in Berlin – or perish!' he announced, but he sent Göring off to Berchtesgaden to take command in the south if and when the Allies linked up and split Germany in two. Admiral Dönitz should take command in the north.

He had made what was to prove his last public appearance during the afternoon, walking along a line of Hitler Youth in the Chancellery garden, patting them on their shoulders and pinching their cheeks, thanking them for the gallantry they were undoubtedly showing. During the evening he took tea with his two senior secretaries and told them that he was sending them out of the city that night, his last words to one of them, an apparently incoherent mumble, being, 'It is all over.'

The following morning, however, his confidence had returned although by noon, even down in the bunker, the thump of Soviet shells could be heard. But a report had arrived that a sizeable force under SS General Felix Steiner was in position some 25 miles north of Berlin – and immediately more sweeping military miracles were conjured up. Steiner's panzers must counter-attack immediately to the south-west, cut off Zhukov's spearheads, link up with a drive eastwards by formations from Twelfth Army on the Elbe, save Berlin, and take pressure off General Manteuffel's panzer army in the north!

The rest of the day was spent in feverish excitement, which continued throughout the following morning, during which Hitler continued to demand news of Steiner's approach; when about noon it became clear that not only had it not begun, it was not yet even properly organised, the collapse was dramatic. His head jerked, his breath shortened; he shouted that he was surrounded by traitors, lurched wildly back and forth accusing everyone of cowardice and corruption, incompetence and lack of faith, finally collapsing into a chair and crying, 'The war is lost!' One of the factors to

cause him most anguish, apparently, was that the latest traitor, Steiner, came from his beloved SS.

None of his staff had ever seen such a failure of nerve before and they surged around, begging him to continue to have faith, to leave for Berchtesgaden immediately, to assure him of their trust and devotion. Of all of them, he took most comfort from the women – Eva Braun, his secretaries, the cook: 'If only my generals were as brave as you are!' he said, then continued, 'This is the end. I shall remain in Berlin and shoot myself when the time comes. Each of you must make his own decision on when to leave.'

Yet this grotesque farce still had eight days to run – at the cost of thousands more lives ruined or lost. Again and again reports would be given him of troop movements or political developments which would save the situation, save Berlin, save National Socialism, save himself. Wenck's Twelfth Army was marching to the relief having in some way totally disengaged from the Anglo-Americans; Goebbels was about to address the Berlin population again and his eloquence and their courage would throw back the Jewish-Bolshevik hordes. Keitel and Jodl would fly to Berchtesgaden to take command of all forces in the south and bring them north, Göring acting as the Führer's personal representative. But when a telegram arrived from Göring offering to take command in the Reich in view of Hitler's decision to remain in Berlin, he flew into a rage accusing the Reichsmarschall of betrayal and sending back cables stripping him of all ranks and at one time ordering the SS in Berchtesgaden to arrest Göring for treason – though this was later rescinded.

Even after Berlin was completely surrounded and Zhukov's and Koniev's soldiers were driving in towards the centre of the city, he was suddenly galvanised into manic optimism by an entirely fictitious report that when the American and Soviet troops met on the Elbe there were immediate arguments about zones of occupation. '. . . here again is striking evidence of the disunity of our enemies . . . any day – yes, at any hour – war could break out between the Bolsheviks and the Anglo-Saxons . . .'. And always there were the eager enquiries about the advance of General Wenck's Twelfth Army. It would be some days before it became evident that although some of Wenck's formations were indeed driving east, one was aiming only for Potsdam to relieve the German troops encircled there, and the others were trying to reach Ninth Army, trapped to the south-west. None was aiming to reach the centre of Berlin.

In the city itself, conditions now beggared description. Fires raged everywhere, shells and bombs exploded amid toppling buildings and growing mountains of rubble, machine-guns chattered, tanks blew up, women and children screamed in fear and pain at the dreadful searing heat of the flame-throwers. German ammunition was running out, food and water for the population – estimated at $1\frac{1}{2}$ million when the battle opened – were non-existent, as were medical supplies for the growing number of wounded. The terror and misery were exacerbated by groups of hawk-faced young SS officers sent out by Goebbels to make examples of 'deserters or cowards' by shooting them in the back or hanging them from lamp-posts with suitable notices describing their guilt around their necks. By Apr 28 all hope was gone of either reinforcement or resupply, for Soviet guns covered the east-west axis which anyway had been blocked by a crashed Ju-52.

By now the pocket was narrowing fast. Third Shock Army had taken Moabit and crossed Alt Moabit to reach the northern edge of the Tiergarten and beyond it the grim Moabit prison, where they released the prisoners including some Allied prisoners of war, some of whom

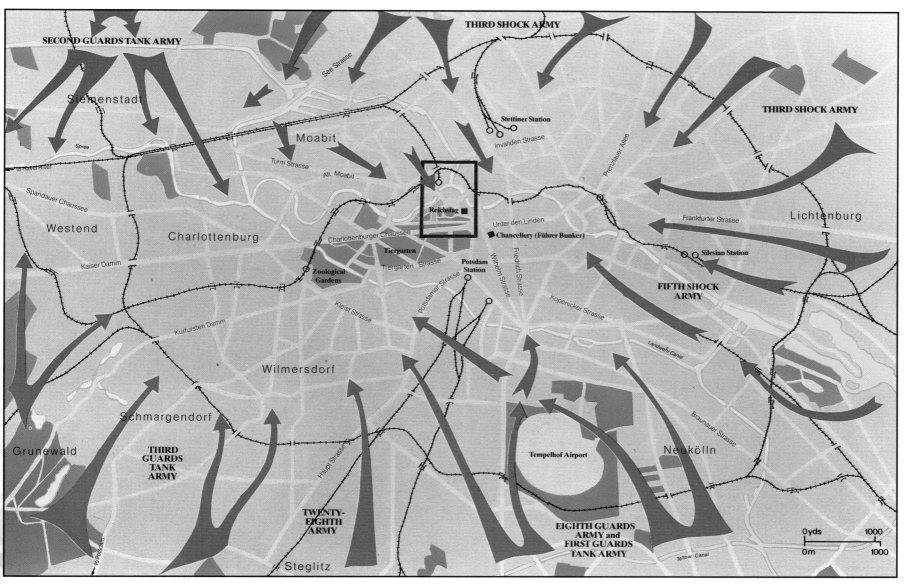

begged for rifles and a chance for revenge. From the south, Chuikov's divisions had crossed the Landwehr Canal, some swimming, some rafting and some, by a subterfuge, getting tanks across the Potsdamer Strasse bridge and into the Tiergarten from the south – then at last to see the Reichstag ahead. This was the great lure for the Soviet troops and from all sides they closed in – Chuikov's men from west and south, Fifth Shock Army from the east and Third Shock Army from the north-west; by the evening of Apr 28, Third Shock were only 550 yards from it, separated only by the Spree and the Königs Platz.

There were, however, serious obstacles in between. The Moltke Bridge was barricaded at both ends, covered with anti-tank obstacles and under multiple machine-gun fire from the nearby buildings. Beyond on the right were the massive stone buildings of the Ministry of the Interior (the 'Himmler Haus' to many unfortunates) and the Kroll Opera, while the areas to the left and centre had been thoroughly barricaded and mined. As for the Reichstag itself, although it had never been properly repaired since the notorious fire of Feb 27, 1933, it was now a bastion of defence, garrisoned by SS units – as were all other main buildings. Some 5,000 fanatics, aware of their predicament and prepared to sell their lives dearly, would have to be put out of action before the Red Banner would fly above the ruins.

Nevertheless, during the night of Apr 28/29 the Moltke Bridge was stormed by two Red Army rifle battalions and by morning four rifle regiments with their artillery, flame-throwers and tanks were across and occupying a large building opposite the Himmler Haus. More troops were fed in, more artillery brought up close to the Spree to fire over open sights, and at 0700 on Apr 30 the attack on the Himmler Haus began.

It lasted all day in a crisis of ferocious battle from floor to floor and room to room, with an intensity comparable on the eastern front only to that at Stalingrad, and equalled for the Western Allies only across the Kohima tennis court. All the time, fire poured down on Soviet troops crossing the bridge or attempting to cross the

Königs Platz, from machine-guns and light artillery emplaced on the Kroll Opera roof.

But by 0430 on Apr 30, the last German in the Himmler Haus was dead, and guns, Katyusha rocket-launchers, tanks and self-propelled guns flooded over the bridge to assault the Reichstag over open sights. The main attack went in at 1300 and the Reichstag seemed almost to disappear under the cloud of smoke and dust; but a hail of fire still swept the square in front and cut down the Soviet riflemen trying to reach the entrances. It was 1400 before the doors were smashed in and Russian troops were inside, 1425 before the first Red Banner was hoisted on the main column by a window on the second floor.

Still the fighting increased in ferocity. At 1800 a second main assault was mounted, more troops rushed across the squares and threw themselves into the building, racing up the central staircase, still having to battle from room to room. 'The fighting became fiercer and fiercer, the barrels of our weapons too hot to touch. There was no water, we were tormented by thirst, the smoke gnawed at our eyes, many men's uniforms were on fire.'

But by 2250 they had broken through to the roof – though there were still many more hours of fighting to come in the rooms beneath – and the victory banner was hoisted proudly over a prostrate city. May Day was still 70 minutes off.

Not long after the Red Banner had waved from the Reichstag second-floor window, Hitler committed suicide. He had spent the morning listening yet again to reports from his staff, completing and correcting his political testament which he had been writing during the last two days, and arranging for it to reach Admiral Dönitz together with the names of those he nominated to succeed as the chief officers of state; Goebbels was to be Chancellor.

He took lunch at 1400 in company with his two secretaries and his cook, then he fetched Eva Braun – now Eva Hitler as he had married her the previous day – from her room, bade farewell to Goebbels, Bormann and

the others who had remained in the bunker and returned to his room. Those outside waited a few minutes, then a shot rang out and when they entered the room they found Hitler lying on a sofa, soaked in blood; he had shot himself through the head. On the right-hand side lay the body of his wife who had taken poison. It was 1530 on Monday, April 30, 1945.

A man of enormous but demonic gifts who had lifted his country from weakness and chaos to unparalleled power only to drop her back into chaos again – all in the space of 12 years – he had possessed the attributes of greatness while remaining destitute of human quality. The world is better for his leaving it.

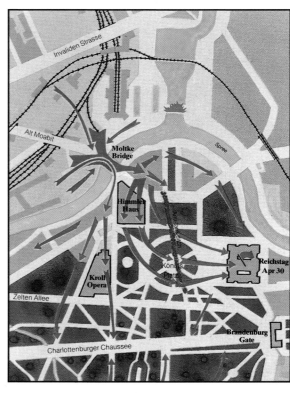

1 The End in Europe. With Hitler's death the whole apparatus of National Socialism began to disintegrate. Not only had his been the creative force behind the whole sinister concept, it had been his energy and manic personality which had held it all together. With him gone it stood revealed as the malevolent but ramshackle edifice it was.

The leading political figures immediately sought to escape the consequences of their misdeeds, either by flight or suicide. The more responsible military leaders, freed at last from the domination of a despotic nihilist, rediscovered their consciences and began attempting to save as much of their country, and as many of their compatriots, as possible from the retribution which the behaviour of such organisations as the SS and the Einsatzgruppen in foreign countries – Russia in particular – seemed likely to have brought upon them.

Hitler had nominated Grand Admiral Dönitz as his successor as Reich President, and it is possible that no one could have executed the few remaining duties of that office any better than he did. His first duty as he saw it was to bring about an end to the fighting, but in such a way that the largest possible number of German soldiers, together with the accompanying host of refugees now running into millions, would be able to cross the Elbe and surrender to the Western Allies. With this in mind he sent envoys to the nearest of those Allies who, as Dönitz was in Flensburg, were the British.

By this time, May 2, British armour had crossed the Elbe and

May 2/3 Mosquitoes bomb Kiel in last attack on Germany. Fighter Command flies 220 sorties in first eight days. Fighter-bombers attack transport and shipping. Coastal Command flies 1,150 anti-U-boat and anti-shipping sorties

Bomber Command drops 5,206 tons of food into Holland and brings out 71,900 released PoWs

May 5 Uprising in Copenhagen. German forces in Denmark surrender

May 6 All German forces in Holland surrender

May 9 German garrisons in Channel Islands surrender

May 8 VE DAY. German forces in Lorient and St Nazaire surrender

May 14 Announcement from Vienna that *Anschluss* null and void

May 23 All members of German Government in Flensburg arrested as PoWs. Himmler commits suicide

May 8–11 All German forces in Dodecanese surrender

May 28 Anti-French riots throughout Syria

May 2 Surrender of all German armies in Italy

May 12 German garrison on Crete surrenders

Map

1 NORTH SEA — BALTIC SEA — Frische Nehrung — Flensburg, Kiel, Rostock, Stralsund May 1, Wismar May 2, Lübeck May 2, Wilhelmshaven, Emden May 2, Bremerhaven, Oldenburg May 2, Hamburg May 3, Wittenberge, Neuruppin

SECOND BELORUSSIAN FRONT (Rokossovsky)

POLAND

Br TWENTY-FIRST ARMY GROUP (Montgomery) — BERLIN, Brandenburg, Magdeburg, Wittenberg

FIRST BELORUSSIAN FRONT (Zhukov)

FIRST UKRAINIAN FRONT (Koniev) — Breslau May 7 surrenders after 82 days

Leipzig — Torgau — Dresden May 8, Görlitz May 8

ARMY GROUP CENTRE (Schörner)

FOURTH UKRAINIAN FRONT (Yeremenko)

Karlsbad — Prague uprising May 5, PRAGUE, Pilsen, Pardubice, Olmütz May 8, Brno

US TWELFTH ARMY GROUP (Bradley)

Regensburg — Ceske Budejovice

SECOND UKRAINIAN FRONT (Malinovsky)

Passau — VIENNA

US SIXTH ARMY GROUP (Devers) — Munich, Linz May 5

THIRD UKRAINIAN FRONT (Tolbukhin)

FRANCE — Salzburg May 4, Graz May 9, BUDAPEST, L. Balaton

SWITZERLAND — Bregenz May 1, Füssen, Innsbruck, Brenner Pass

AUSTRIA — Slovenj Gradec May 15

US FIFTH ARMY (Truscott)

Br EIGHTH ARMY (McCreery) — Milan, Venice, Trieste, Zagreb May 8, Turin

ITALY — L. Comacchio — Adriatic Sea — Ligurian Sea

YUGOSLAVIA

0M 50 100 / 0Km 50 100 150

the Mulde down past Leipzig, and below that point lay not only Czechoslovakia, but also Austria – in which, by repute, lay an 'alpine redoubt' in which fanatical Nazis were reputed to be preparing a 'last stand'. Patton's Third Army had been directed to advance and deal with this threat, with the middle Danube as the axis of advance and Linz the prime objective, while Salzburg, Berchtesgaden, Innsbruck and the Brenner Pass were to be taken by Patch's Seventh Army on the right wing.

As there was no such thing as an alpine redoubt, opposition to the American advance was minimal and almost every town they drove through was decorated with white sheets. Linz was in Patton's hands by May 5 and Patch's troops were at the Brenner Pass the following day. Any prospect of a genuine German Army counter-attack had been negated by lack of fuel.

Patton's left flank crossed the Czechoslovak border and reached Karlsbad in the north, Pilsen and Ceske Budejovice in the centre, then ran on to the Danube east of Linz. On that line by agreement between Eisenhower and the Russians, it stopped. Beyond it lay Prague, nearly a million German soldiers of Army Group Centre (Schörner), plus the remnant of Army Group Austria (Wöhler) still with 2,000 tanks and 10,000 guns – and the Red Army soldiers of Second, Third and Fourth Ukrainian Fronts, with six armies of First Ukrainians streaming down from Torgau to help them.

The position of Army Group Centre had been such that in May it could quite easily have moved westwards out of Czechoslovakia and into the American zone, and on May 4 this is what Dönitz ordered the commander to organise.

But the recently promoted (Apr 10) Field Marshal Ferdinand Schörner had been appointed Commander-in-Chief of the German Army by Hitler – to take effect upon Hitler's death – and he saw no reason to take orders from an admiral, however senior. In addition he claimed that the greatest strength of Army Group Centre at the time rested in the extremely strong defences it now occupied, and that if the Army Group left them, it would disintegrate.

He therefore directed panzer formations into Prague to deal with an uprising which exploded on May 5, and issued an order to his troops beginning, 'Enemy propaganda is spreading false rumours that Germany has capitulated to the Allies.'

As the Red Army in such circumstances was as willing to fight on as he was, another fierce battle broke out on May 8 – and as the Ukrainian Fronts were all provided with overwhelming air cover, they were soon streaming in from every angle towards Prague and Army Group Centre. By May 9 Koniev's armour had broken through defences on the original Czech border and reached the northern outskirts of the capital, and with the aid of the insurgents had cleared the Germans out of the city by that evening – and from the east Malinovsky's Second Ukrainians and Yeremenko's Fourth Ukrainians, after a battle with First Panzer Army at Olmütz, were closing up fast.

But by May 10 the German troops had realised that their commander had lied to them and there was no point in more sacrifice. Despite Schörner's instructions, they began to give themselves up or slip away to the west; by May 11 the Army Group had disintegrated, and 858,000 were Red Army prisoners, including 60 generals. But not Schörner who had flown out – professedly to command the 'alpine redoubt'.

By May 14 the seam between the armies of the Western Allies and the Red Army was joined from the Baltic to deep into the Austrian Alps.

The Third Reich was no more.

reached the Baltic east of Lübeck, and if any of Army Group Vistula were to escape from the Red Army, they must now be allowed through British lines. But Field Marshal Montgomery was perfectly aware of the agreements which had been made between all the Allies regarding the German surrender, and had no intention of making any commitments which might upset them. Moreover, as the armies under his command were already occupying most of north Germany, there was no need for him to make the slightest concession. The envoys had better obtain permission to surrender all German forces in the neighbourhood, unconditionally and immediately, otherwise he would reopen an aggressive offensive – in respect of which, if

the Gauleiter of Hamburg did not immediately surrender the city, it would be subjected to the heaviest raid yet mounted by RAF Bomber Command.

It was enough. On May 4 the first armistice was signed on Lüneburg heath, two days later the Unconditional Surrender of Germany to the Western Allies and Russia was signed by General Jodl at General Eisenhower's HQ at Rheims, and on May 8 a similar surrender was signed in Berlin by General Keitel in the presence of Marshal Zhukov.

The Western Allies had agreed that they would not be unreasonable with regard to refugees; but it was not to be as simple at that. By the end of April the US armies held the line of

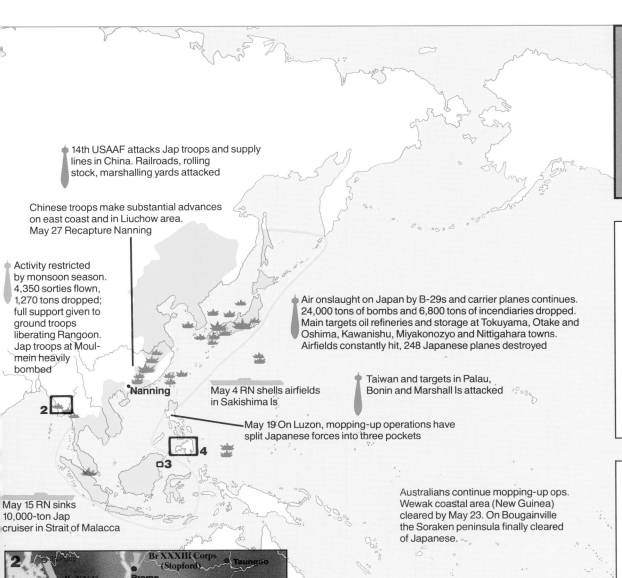

14th USAAF attacks Jap troops and supply lines in China. Railroads, rolling stock, marshalling yards attacked

Chinese troops make substantial advances on east coast and in Liuchow area. May 27 Recapture Nanning

Activity restricted by monsoon season. 4,350 sorties flown, 1,270 tons dropped; full support given to ground troops liberating Rangoon. Jap troops at Moulmein heavily bombed

Air onslaught on Japan by B-29s and carrier planes continues. 24,000 tons of bombs and 6,800 tons of incendiaries dropped. Main targets oil refineries and storage at Tokuyama, Otake and Oshima, Kawanishu, Miyakonozyo and Nittigahara towns. Airfields constantly hit, 248 Japanese planes destroyed

Nanning

May 4 RN shells airfields in Sakishima Is

Taiwan and targets in Palau, Bonin and Marshall Is attacked

May 19 On Luzon, mopping-up operations have split Japanese forces into three pockets

May 15 RN sinks 10,000-ton Jap cruiser in Strait of Malacca

Australians continue mopping-up ops. Wewak coastal area (New Guinea) cleared by May 23. On Bougainville the Soraken peninsula finally cleared of Japanese.

2 Br XXXIII Corps (Stopford) — Taungoo

Br XV Corps (Christison) — Prome May 2

Sandoway May 9

BURMA

JAP TWENTY-EIGHTH ARMY (Sakurai)

Pegu Yoma

Karen Hills

Br IV Corps (Messervy)

Bay of Bengal

Gwa May 13

Pegu May 2

Hlegu May 6

Sittang

RANGOON May 3

Kyauktan

Elephant Pt

26th Ind Div May 2

☆ Okinawa

Okinawa. During April three divisions of the infantry of XXIV Corps had turned south after their landing and immediately come up against the Shuri defence line. When it became obvious that the main Japanese strength lay here, General Buckner organised a powerful offensive but the three divisions still failed to break through. Now General Ushijima mounted a counter-attack supported by kamikaze missions from Kyushu which hit 18 US ships and caused 682 naval casualties, though fresh infantry and marines halted the Japanese breakout.

A second US attack on May 11 again failed to break the Shuri line, and shortly afterwards the monsoons brought 12 inches of rain in 17 days. But by now 1st and 6th Marine Divisions had joined the attacking force, and on May 29 marines at last broke into Shuri Castle; 68,548 dead Japanese had been counted in a very restricted area, and the cream of Ushijima's army had undoubtedly been destroyed. But there was still a hard core left at the end of the month.

4 **Mindanao.** Despite the fact that X Corps had been able to drive the 110 miles from west to east on Mindanao, there was still the matter of large numbers of enemy troops up in the hills to the north and north-west. Davao itself was taken on May 3, but attempts to drive further north to the top of the gulf met ferocious resistance, as did attempts to drive up into the hills from the coast.

In the central region, the drive north continued, and two airstrips at Kibawe and Maramag were the scenes of desperate resistance by the Japanese, but by May 23 the US infantry of X Corps were 20 miles further on.

On May 10 a regimental combat team of 40th Division had been landed in Macajalar Bay, a stretch on the north coast already in guerrilla hands, and the team began their drive down to meet X Corps troops coming up through the centre. The first two days' progress was easy enough but they then found themselves at the entrance to a well-defended canyon and it was May 18 before the team was through, eventually to make contact with X Corps on May 23. Although strategically Mindanao was now under American control, as elsewhere in the Philippines, it would take weeks of grim patrolling and mopping up before the last Japanese resistance ended.

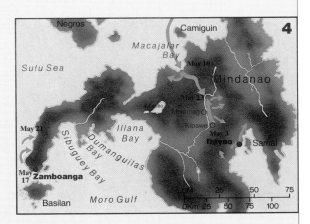

4 Negros — Camiguin — Macajalar Bay — May 10 — Mindanao — Sulu Sea — Illana Bay — Maramag — Kibawe — May 3 — Davao — Samal — May 21 — Dumanguilas Bay — Sibuguey Bay — May 17 Zamboanga — Basilan — Moro Gulf

2 **Rangoon.** During March, General Slim had begun wondering if his drive down central Burma would reach Rangoon in time, especially as there were meteorological indications that the monsoon might break early. Then at the end of the month his Director of Plans produced a paper which demonstrated that unless a port could be obtained through which supplies could be poured, Fourteenth Army would soon grind to a halt. An early – and successful – assault on Rangoon itself would obviously solve both problems; *Operation Dracula* was put into immediate development.

A fleet of warships, troop transports and landing-craft was assembled in the waters around Akyab and Ramree; 26th Indian Division, who had fought in the Arakan, brought down and briefed; and early on the morning of May 1, 2/3rd Gurkha Parachute Battalion loaded into 40 Dakotas and transported through storms of such force that half the escorting fighters had to turn back. The meteorological forecasts had been correct and the monsoon burst the next morning.

By this time the paratroops had dropped just west of Elephant Point and were making their way through driving rain and flooded creeks to the mouth of the Pegu river, where they successfully attacked the Japanese garrison of 37 thoroughly demoralised troops. At 0215 on the morning of May 2 the convoy bringing in 26th Indian Division arrived at the lowering positions, and into the landing-craft clambered the first wave of assault troops – many of them already sea-sick and about to commence a 30-mile trip to the beaches, in darkness, rain and a heavy swell. It was fortunate that the only troops in the vicinity of the landing were the Gurkhas.

Conditions were so bad that there was no chance of landing vehicles or guns, but the infantry squelched their way inland on both banks of the Pegu river and reached Kyauktan by mid-

afternoon, to be told by the villagers that the Japanese had all left five days before. Subsequent investigations revealed that there were no Japanese soldiers in Rangoon either, and as a result, at about 1600 on May 3 two infantry battalions in transports preceded by minesweepers arrived at Rangoon docks and set about re-establishing order, for the Japanese had wrecked electrical, sanitation and water services and looting was prevalent.

Nevertheless, Rangoon had been liberated after 38 months of Japanese occupation, and now transports could bring in not only food and medical aid for the inhabitants and the released prisoners, but also engineers to put the port into working order again, plus arms and supplies for Fourteenth Army to the north.

By May 6, units from 17th Indian Division, having swum the flooded *chaungs* where bridges had been destroyed, arrived at Hlegu where they met units from 26th Indian Division, thereby closing the gap, and all that remained for Fourteenth Army was to round up and trap the remnants of the Japanese armies which had swept so triumphantly through Burma three years before. Disordered, leaderless, starving, many of them so dejected that they were prepared to be taken prisoner, these unfortunates were faced with the task of crossing a flooded countryside, then attempting to cross the Irrawaddy and the Sittang, both patrolled by enemy soldiers waiting to kill them. And what awaited them in Thailand or Indo-China except the hatred they had stirred up against them wherever they went? Their Japanese homeland was a long way away.

3 Cape Djoeata May 27 — Tarakan — May 30–31 — Batagan Strait — Djoeta oilfield — May 30–31 — Cape Binalatoeng — Sadau I Apr 30 — Sesanip oilfield — May 31 — Tarakan Airfield May 6 — Tarakan May 17 — Lingkas May 1 — May 9 — 9th Aust Div — Cape Batoe May 13

3 **Tarakan.** With the Philippines under Allied control Borneo was obviously the next large-scale objective, and as a preliminary the oil-rich island of Tarakan off the east coast. Australian commandos and units of their 9th Division went ashore on May 1 near Lingkas, and drove for the airfield at Tarakan and the Sesanip oilfield near by. Most of the way they were subject to fanatical suicide charges by the defending Japanese infantry, but Australian tanks blasted them from their holes and trenches and infantry divided the defences into small pockets and then wiped them out. As elsewhere the defenders had constructed labyrinthine systems of tunnels which had to be blocked and burnt out, but gradually planes, tanks and flame-throwers gave the Australian infantry the necessary cover. By the end of the month Cape Djoeata had been reached and the Australians were driving along the north coast, they had reached the east coast at Cape Binalatoeng, and were pressing the Japanese further and further back into the central hills. By June 21, all Japanese resistance was at an end.

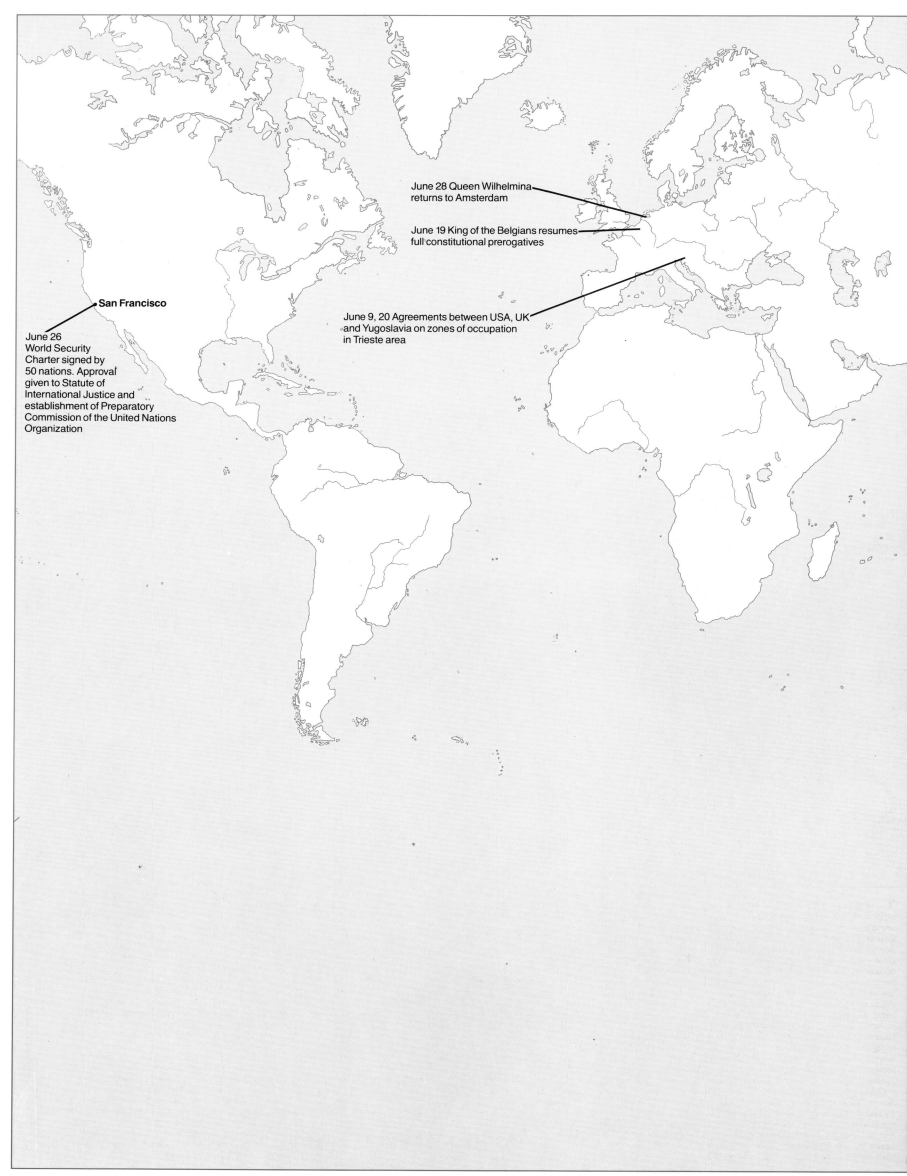

June 28 Queen Wilhelmina returns to Amsterdam

June 19 King of the Belgians resumes full constitutional prerogatives

San Francisco

June 26 World Security Charter signed by 50 nations. Approval given to Statute of International Justice and establishment of Preparatory Commission of the United Nations Organization

June 9, 20 Agreements between USA, UK and Yugoslavia on zones of occupation in Trieste area

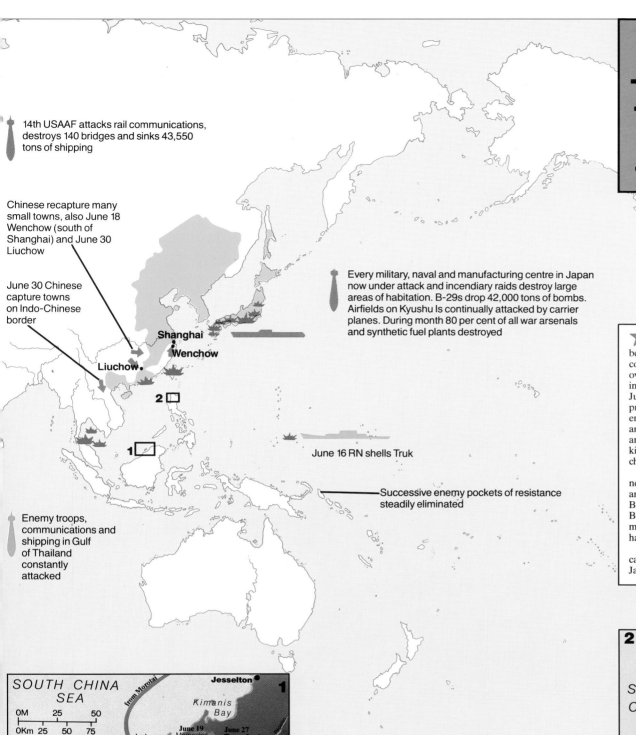

14th USAAF attacks rail communications, destroys 140 bridges and sinks 43,550 tons of shipping

Chinese recapture many small towns, also June 18 Wenchow (south of Shanghai) and June 30 Liuchow

June 30 Chinese capture towns on Indo-Chinese border

Every military, naval and manufacturing centre in Japan now under attack and incendiary raids destroy large areas of habitation. B-29s drop 42,000 tons of bombs. Airfields on Kyushu Is continually attacked by carrier planes. During month 80 per cent of all war arsenals and synthetic fuel plants destroyed

Shanghai
Wenchow
Liuchow

June 16 RN shells Truk

Successive enemy pockets of resistance steadily eliminated

Enemy troops, communications and shipping in Gulf of Thailand constantly attacked

☆ **Okinawa.** A short pause in the battle followed at the beginning of June, and then in the middle of the month the combined US infantry and marines launched an attack in overwhelming strength. General Ushijima had some 11,000 infantry left with 22,000 artillery and service troops, but on June 17 they began to weaken and disintegrate under the pressure. After 80 days of unceasing conflict against a superior enemy equipped with apparently unlimited arms and ammunition, Japanese soldiers, penned into an ever-decreasing area, began to surrender. But the majority still fought until killed, or took their own lives, and on June 21 Ushijima and his chief staff officers followed this course.

Nearly 110,000 Japanese soldiers were killed on Okinawa, nearly 9,000 Japanese aircraft destroyed. US naval casualties amounted to 9,731 of whom 4,907 were killed, while General Buckner's Tenth Army lost 7,613 killed (including General Buckner himself) and some 52,000 wounded or missing – plus many who had suffered so severely from battle fatigue that they had had to be evacuated.

As after Iwo Jima, many were wondering how many casualties would have to be suffered for the occupation of the Japanese homeland.

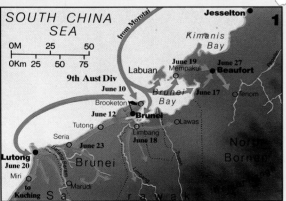

SOUTH CHINA SEA

0M 25 50
0Km 25 50 75

Jesselton ●
Kimanis Bay
from Morotai
June 19 Mempakul June 27 **Beaufort** ●
Labuan
9th Aust Div
June 10
Brunei Bay June 17 ○Tenom
Brooketon
June 12 **Brunei** ●
Tutong ○ ○Lawas
Seria ○ Limbang June 18
June 23
Lutong
June 20
Miri ○ ○Marudi
to Kuching
Brunei
North Borneo
Sarawak

1 **Brunei Bay.** After Tarakan, the Australians supported by the US Navy and the Allied Air Forces were intent upon driving the Japanese out of Borneo and away from their chief source of oil, rubber and minerals. On June 4 the Brunei Attack Group left Morotai and by June 10 were off the great natural harbour and naval base of Brunei Bay. So devastating was the naval bombardment on Labuan that when the first units of the 24th Australian Brigade went ashore only a few dazed survivors were left amid the wrecked Japanese defences; by nightfall the town and airstrip were in Australian hands and all resistance had ended by June 15.

Across the bay at Brooketon, 20th Brigade had landed; by June 13 Brunei airfield and town was occupied and the drive along the coast commenced. Tutong and its oil refinery was taken on June 17, on June 20 an unopposed landing at Lutong secured the oil storage tanks and refineries, and everywhere the Australian infantry were moving inland with little difficulty.

Other landings and movements had taken place in Brunei Bay itself and to the north-east. Mempakul was taken on June 19 and the rail junction at Beaufort on June 27. By the end of the month, the 9th Australian Division was in total control of 135 miles of the North Borneo coastline and almost 5,000 square miles of countryside. The North Borneo campaign was over except – as usual – for the mopping up.

2 **The Closing Campaign.** The tasks for General Krueger's Sixth Army were by no means over when Manila fell. The spectacular successes obtained by XIV Corps in their drive down into the heart of the Philippines had not been mirrored by I Corps in the north, who were to face some of the bitterest fighting of the Pacific war.

General Yamashita, while accepting that his forces faced inevitable defeat, had decided that they would last longest and cause most American casualties by utilising the defensive advantages of the mountains of the Cordillera Central Range, feeding his men from the 'rice bowl' of the Cagayan valley behind. From the ground to the south of Lingayen Gulf, where the invading US forces were concentrated, the only way into the valley was through the Balete Pass to Imugan and on to Bambang, all the way through the worst sort of mountain terrain.

The task of breaking through the formidable defensive positions held in strength by Yamashita's forces fell to the 32nd, 25th and 6th Divisions of I Corps, and during February, March and April they had battled against a strongly entrenched enemy in well-sited positions in ideal defensive country – and since early April in drenching rainstorms. Only the overwhelming technical superiority in artillery, infantry weapons and air power gained them even the meagre advances made each day. It was May 13 before 25th Division units emerged from the northern end of Balete Pass, at last to meet 32nd Division units at Imugan and begin the drive into the Cagayan valley.

The battle for Luzon now entered its final phase. As had

SOUTH CHINA SEA

June 26
Tuguegarao June 25
US 37th Div
June 19 Ilagan ●
Kiangan
Lingayen Gulf
Lingayen **Dagupan** I Corps

happened elsewhere, the Japanese Command had concentrated all their strength in one defensive crust, and once that had been broken through, there was little to check the resultant US advance. At the end of May the exhausted 25th Division had been relieved by the 37th, and by June 6 Bambang was in their hands; four days later they were at Bagabag, 40 miles north of Balete Pass.

This move effectively isolated the main Japanese Command who had established themselves at Kiangan, but except for directing the recuperated 6th Division to mount a drive against them, US I Corps' commander concentrated on 37th Division's drive up the Cagayan valley. By June 19 they were at Ilagan, and by June 25, in co-operation with guerrilla units which had long been active in the area, they arrived at Tuguegarao.

In the meantime, US rangers and guerrilla forces had captured Aparri on the north coast, and on June 23 the US 11th Airborne Division dropped into the airfield just to the south of the port. By June 26, 37th Division and 11th Airborne had met to the north of Tuguegarao, and the only centre of Japanese resistance left in the Philippines was General Yamashita's last stronghold in the Kiangan pocket.

This was under siege by July 12, and the fate of the majority of Japanese soldiers still in Luzon – death from starvation or sickness – became inevitable.

July 5 General Election in UK
July 26 Result gives Labour
overwhelming victory.
Churchill resigns

July 12 Britain and USA take over
full control of Berlin sectors
July 17 Potsdam Conference opens

July 16 FIRST ATOMIC BOMB
test in New Mexico

The Manhattan Project. Arguably, the first step in the production of the atomic bomb was taken in 1895 when radioactivity was discovered by the French scientist, Henri Becquerel. The possibility of using the energy locked inside the atom was, however, of little more than academic interest until 1938, when the German scientist, Otto Hahn, working in the Kaiser Wilhelm Institute and profiting from the work of the British scientists Rutherford, Cockcroft and Walton, discovered that by bombarding uranium with neutrons it would split into barium and krypton, the resultant two nuclei containing between them less energy than the uranium nucleus from which they came. It was as a result of this discovery that physicists around the world began speculating on the possibility of making an atomic bomb.

It was fortunate for the Western Allies that many of the foremost German scientists in the field were Jews, and thus unable to continue working in Germany; several of the most important left for Britain or America, and it was in Washington that some of them persuaded Einstein to write a letter to President Roosevelt, alerting him to the possibilities, and warning him that some progress was being made in Germany. The possibility that Hitler might obtain the atomic bomb thus became the main spur behind what was to become a gigantic scientific and industrial project.

Scientists working in British universities, a French team in Paris and the remarkable Niels Bohr in Denmark, all produced evidence and arguments to the effect that atomic power was a realisable possibility; as far as the bomb was concerned, however, no one was quite prepared to forecast whether the result would be a 'small pop' or a 'big bang'. Although in 1940 Britain was the state most anxious to obtain the bomb, there was neither the industrial potential, manpower – or even space – available for a project of such a size which might or might not produce the required end result.

After Pearl Harbor, however, with America anxious to possess what seemed likely to be the most powerful weapon of all time, those problems were solved. The leading British scientists crossed the Atlantic with their European colleagues, plans were prepared for the huge industrial complex required to separate out the vital uranium 235, to be built eventually at Oak Ridge, Tennessee, and an administrative organisation was set up to co-ordinate all aspects of atomic – soon to be renamed nuclear – activity. In Chicago a team under the Italian scientist Enrico Fermi was working on the construction of a 'reactor' which would produce a self-sustaining chain reaction, and would, in fact, eventually produce the substance now known as plutonium.

Some idea of the size of this project can be obtained from the

information that, in the end, America had gambled some $2,000 million on it – in days when such a sum of money was not envisaged even as a National Debt! Only America could have afforded to risk such investment of time, money and manpower in something which no one could be certain, until the end, would not just produce a 'small pop'.

The test came at 0530 on the morning of Monday, July 16, 1945, on the Alamogordo bombing range, a desolate stretch of desert some 200 miles from Los Alamos in southern New Mexico. More than 250 members of the Manhattan team of scientists and administrators were gathered to observe 'Trinity', the code-name for the testing of the first atomic bomb.

Weather posed some temporary difficulties, for Sunday evening had been wet and windy. But at 0200 on Monday the skies cleared, weather experts became more hopeful and just after 0500 the countdown began; by 0530 the count was down to one-second intervals and eventually the voice pronounced the words, 'four, three, two, one – now'.

'Suddenly,' one of the observers was to write, 'and without any sound, the hills were bathed in brilliant light as if someone had turned the sun on with a switch.'

After the glare came the blast wave, then the thunder – and the scientists knew that it was, indeed, the 'Big Bang'.

The world had entered the age of nuclear warfare.

160

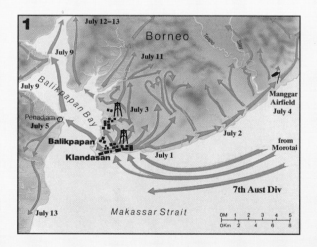

14th USAAF continues attacks on Japanese rail and military targets
July 11 Declaration that Japanese Air Force has been cleared from China's skies. Bombers from Okinawa drop 400 tons on Shanghai

July 14 Third Fleet shells Kamaishi, 275 miles N of Tokyo. *King George V* and *Formidable* join in combined attack on Tokyo with 1,500 planes

Chinese advance in SW. July 27 Enter Kweilin

Kweilin

July 27 60,000 leaflets dropped on Japan warning population of 'destruction from the air'
July 29 Six of the warned cities attacked

Air operations against Japan now reaching a climax. In addition to raids by as many as 600 B-29s, B-25s (Mitchells) attack Japan from land bases and on July 10 raids by 1,000 or more carrier planes begin. July 24 1,500 carrier planes attack Kure naval base and on July 28 2,000 planes sweep over Inland Sea and attack shipping. Estimated 1,023 surface ships and 1,257 Japanese planes destroyed or damaged

Gen MacArthur announces liberation of the whole of the Philippines

July 5–10 RN minesweeping in approaches to Strait of Malacca.
July 24 bombards Japanese installations and troop concentrations on west coast of Malaya

RAF bombers and fighters support ground forces and attack Japanese lines of communication and shipping off Kra Isthmus, Sumatra and Padang. 3,100 sorties flown, 750 tons dropped.
July 10 Nicobar Is bombed

1 Balikpapan. The third and largest amphibious operation to be launched against the Japanese fell upon Balikpapan, in Borneo, probably the richest of all the sources of oil the Japanese had captured during their spectacular expansion in 1942. On June 26 the Balikpapan Attack Group had left Morotai, and three days later were in position to fire over 45,000 shells into the area of the peninsula to the east of Balikpapan Bay, which had already been subjected to 20 days of bombing by Liberators of the US 5th and 13th Air Forces and the Royal Australian Air Force.

On July 1, two brigades of the 7th Australian Division stormed ashore at Klandasan to repeat the successes of their fellow countrymen of 9th Division to the north. By July 3 all the high ground overlooking Balikpapan was in their hands, and 21st Brigade was racing along the coast to take the airfield at Manggar by July 4.

The following day a battalion crossed Balikpapan Bay under naval gunfire and took Penadjam, then hooked further north to take command of the entire area of the vital bay. They were assisted in this by Dutch East Indies forces which landed on the north-east side, further up, and then led the probing drives inland.

By the end of July every objective of the Borneo campaign had been achieved – Brunei Bay, Balikpapan, the important airfields, rich oilfields and vital refineries lost during 1942, all recaptured. The Japanese forces had been defeated and driven into the hills, where little but death from starvation and sickness awaited them.

1 **Plans for Invasion.** In the spring of 1945 a Japanese colonel told General Wainwright, just completing his third year as a prisoner of war, 'You have no chance of beating Japan . . . it took 20,000 American troops to defeat 2,000 Japanese soldiers on Attu . . . there are 100 million people in the Japanese empire. It will take ten times 100 million to defeat Japan . . .'

Even allowing for the officer's hubristic exaggeration, even allowing for the known economic plight of Japan in 1945, even allowing for the fact that of late a percentage of her soldiers had been willing to surrender, there was never any doubt that an Allied invasion of the Japanese homeland would face resistance of a ferocity unmatched in the annals of history. However exhausted and hungry soldiers may be, however poorly armed compared with their antagonists, when defending their homes they will exhibit a bravery and dedication to astonish the world – none more so than the Japanese soldiers of 1945. When asked to estimate the number of casualties the Allied invasion force might expect, the US Secretary of War, Henry L. Stimson, suggested 1 million – and even more optimistically minded military men expected casualties in the range 30,000–50,000 in the first stage alone. The number of Japanese who might be expected to die before resistance ended, from Hokkaido in the north to Kyushu in the south, was something no one was prepared to guess at. It would undoubtedly completely overshadow casualty figures in the West.

Planning began in April, with General MacArthur in command of all land forces, Admiral Nimitz commanding the naval forces, and General Kenney the Far Eastern Air Forces – though after July the vast B-29 bomber force became part of the United States Army Strategic Air Force, under General Carl Spaatz.

The first stage of the invasion – *Operation Olympic* – would be a landing by four corps of General Krueger's Sixth Army on the southern coast of Kyushu with the aim of securing the island as far as the Sendai–Tsuno line, after which supporting corps and indeed armies would follow. Nearly 500,000 men would be involved in this first landing, transported and supported by 2,902 warships of Admiral Spruance's Fifth Fleet, with Admiral Halsey's Third Fleet of 120 capital ships and destroyers supplying strategic cover. The proposed date for D-Day was Oct 18, but 'softening up' the target areas by air attack would proceed immediately, and build up until by D-Day at least 40,000 tons of bombs per month, mainly incendiaries, would be dropped.

The second stage of the invasion – *Operation Coronet* – was given a tentative target date of Mar 1, 1946 and entailed landing two complete armies, one on each side of Tokyo Bay. In the event of continued Japanese resistance – and few considered this unlikely – the two armoured divisions landed on the western side of the bay would drive up towards the Japanese capital, while infantry mopped up behind them and more armour was brought ashore.

What reinforcement would be required for the corps on Kyushu and the armies on Honshu could not, of course, be accurately predicted; but in all the planners counted on the availability of 5 million Allied soldiers and marines, supported by the largest concentration of naval and air power the world had ever seen.

As for the defending forces, Allied Intelligence had calculated that there were 2,350,000 officers and men under arms in 53 infantry divisions and 25 brigades, deployed throughout the Japanese homelands. In support of these regular troops, there were another 3,800,000 service and garrison troops; and according to Japanese radio, the national volunteer militia of 28 million.

How would they fight?

It was with feelings of almost indescribable relief that on Aug 14 Allied servicemen all over the world learned that we were not going to have to find out.

The Decision. It was not until Apr 24 – 12 days after he had been sworn in as President of the United States of America – that Truman learned of the Manhattan Project, and the possibility of the possession in the not-too-distant future of a bomb of hitherto unimagined power. Nothing could be certain, of course, until the projected test at Alamogordo, but the indications were good and Secretary of War Stimson said he was 99 per cent certain of success.

It was obviously going to be President Truman's decision as to whether – and where – the bomb was to be used; in the circumstances, it was hardly a decision at all.

Whatever Japan's industrial, economic or even military situation, there was no sign yet that her rulers were considering surrender on any terms whatsoever, and every reason to believe that the only way to bring her to terms would be by an invasion which would cost hundreds of thousands of Allied – and almost certainly millions of Japanese – lives.

There was also a political reason for using the bomb – if it worked. During his first weeks of office, Truman had been shocked to discover the extent of his predecessor's willingness to accommodate himself to Stalin's views, opinions and wishes on many subjects, including the spheres of interest in eastern Europe and the desirability of holding free elections in the newly liberated countries. Roosevelt's faith that he and Stalin shared a belief in the principles of freedom throughout the world which would bring to it a universal happiness – despite his old friend Churchill's scepticism on the subject – struck Truman as unrealistic. It exhibited, he felt, some of the naivety displayed by Prime Minister Chamberlain when he returned from Munich in September 1938 proclaiming that Herr Hitler was a gentleman whose word could be trusted.

Already there were indications that agreements made at Yalta – especially with regard to Poland – were not being implemented and there seemed to be unnecessary complications about the allocated zones of occupation in Germany and Austria; now the European war was over the only reason for conciliating Stalin was the agreed entry of Russia into the war against Japan. This would undoubtedly spread Soviet influence throughout Manchuria and China, which Truman considered undesirable anyway, and if the Manhattan Project was successful, their help would become unnecessary.

In the circumstances, the President felt that he need no longer continue Roosevelt's conciliatory attitude to Stalin; on the day he heard about the atomic bomb he spoke so sharply to Soviet Foreign Minister Molotov on Polish matters that the latter expostulated, 'I have never been talked to like that in my life!'

Truman was attending the Potsdam Conference with Stalin and Churchill when he learned of the success of the test firing at Alamogordo and, in agreement with Churchill, decided to issue to Japan one last ultimatum which threatened her with prompt and utter destruction but did not mention the bomb; it stated the terms for surrender, made no mention of the Emperor's position and still contained the word 'unconditional' – and when no satisfactory reply was received, the decision was made to drop the bomb. It would serve not only to bring about the Japanese surrender, but also to render unnecessary Russian entry into the war against Japan, with her inevitable occupation of Manchuria.

The Bomb is Dropped. By the beginning of August the component parts of the uranium bomb, known as 'Little Boy', had been shipped to Tinian under conditions of the tightest security, and on the evening of Aug 5 the crew of the B-29 bomber *Enola Gay* were puzzled to find that for the moment they could not enter their plane, which had been surrounded all day by guards.

After a briefing which bewildered them even more, they went aboard to find a huge 'gimmick' resting in a steel brace in the bomb bay, nearly 14 feet long and 5 feet wide. At 0245 on Aug 6 *Enola Gay* took off, followed shortly by two more B-29s carrying scientists to observe the explosion, and as they gained altitude, Captain William Parsons USN began arming the bomb. The risk of *Enola Gay* crashing on take-off, though slight, had been sufficient to make Parsons change the original schedule by which he would have armed the bomb on the ground.

By 0400 all was ready, and the pilot Colonel Paul Tibbetts now informed the other 11 men aboard that from then on all conversation would be recorded ('for history – so watch your language') and that they were carrying an atomic bomb – of which most of the crew had never heard. Down below, through cloudbreaks, they could see the coast of Japan.

Three weather planes were up ahead of them, and they reported that above Hiroshima, the favoured target (the others were Kokura and Nagasaki), was a ten-mile wide stretch of clear sky. At 0800, Colonel Tibbets asked Parsons if he agreed that below them was Hiroshima, and when Parsons agreed he handed control of the plane to Major Ferebee, the bomb-aimer. At 0815 the aiming-point, the centre of a bridge, and the cross-hairs of Ferebee's bomb-sight coincided, he pressed the control, the bomb-doors opened and Little Boy fell out, its drogue parachute opened and it fell nose-first towards its target. *Enola Gay* and the two observer planes turned sharply away and at 0816 they saw a vast explosion exactly over the target, which turned first into a gigantic fireball, then the towering mushroom cloud. Hiroshima had been destroyed.

As the Japanese reaction to Truman's ultimatum sent from Potsdam had been virtually to ignore it, and the only reaction to events at Hiroshima seemed to be indignation at the use of such a weapon, it was now decided to drop 'Fat Man', the plutonium bomb – but after issuing due warning. Leaflets were dropped over Japanese cities, broadcasts were made. But no sign of a willingness to surrender came from Tokyo, so at 0349 on Aug 9 Fat Man left Tinian and was dropped, just before 1100, over Nagasaki.

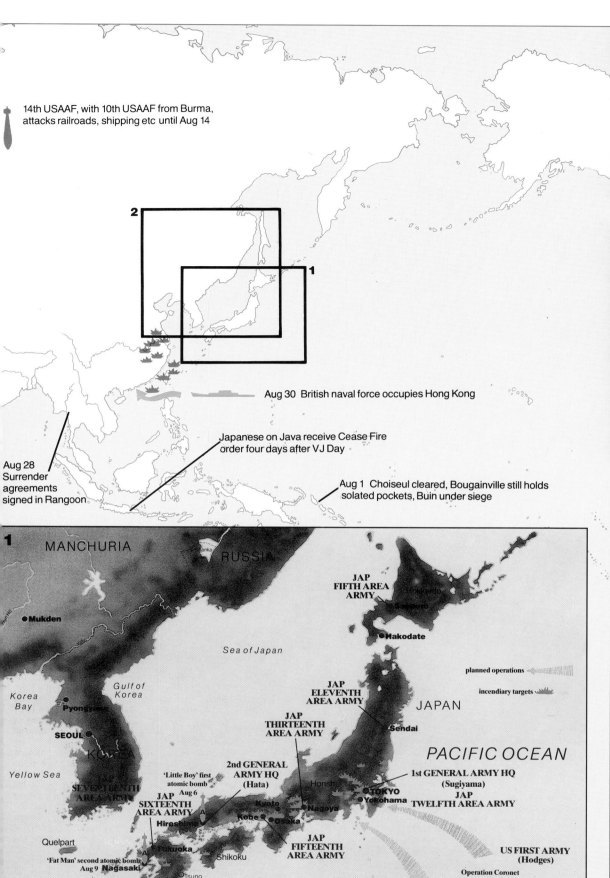

14th USAAF, with 10th USAAF from Burma, attacks railroads, shipping etc until Aug 14

Aug 30 British naval force occupies Hong Kong

Japanese on Java receive Cease Fire order four days after VJ Day

Aug 28 Surrender agreements signed in Rangoon

Aug 1 Choiseul cleared, Bougainville still holds solated pockets, Buin under siege

1 MANCHURIA

RUSSIA

JAP FIFTH AREA ARMY

Mukden

Sea of Japan

Hakodate

planned operations

incendiary targets

JAP ELEVENTH AREA ARMY

JAPAN

JAP THIRTEENTH AREA ARMY

Sendai

Korea Bay

Gulf of Korea

Pyongyang

SEOUL

KOREA

Yellow Sea

JAP SEVENTEENTH AREA ARMY

'Little Boy' first atomic bomb Aug 6

2nd GENERAL ARMY HQ (Hata)

PACIFIC OCEAN

1st GENERAL ARMY HQ (Sugiyama)

JAP TWELFTH AREA ARMY

Honshu

TOKYO Yokohama

Kyoto

Nagoya

JAP SIXTEENTH AREA ARMY

Kobe Osaka

Hiroshima

Quelpart

Fukuoka

Shikoku

JAP FIFTEENTH AREA ARMY

US FIRST ARMY (Hodges)

'Fat Man' second atomic bomb Aug 9 Nagasaki

Tsuno

Operation Coronet Mar 1, 1946

Operation Olympic US SIXTH ARMY (Krueger) Nov 1

Sendai

Kyushu

US IX CORPS (Ryder)

US EIGHTH ARMY (Eichelberger)

US V Amph CORPS (Schmidt)

40th Inf Div

US XI CORPS (Hall)

US I CORPS (Swift)

0M 50 100 150
0Km 100 200

2

TRANS-BAIKAL FRONT (Malinovsky)

MANCHURIA

SECOND FAR EAST FRONT (Purkayev)

OUTER MONGOLIA
Gobi Desert

HINGAN MTS

Hailar

Tsitsihar

Harbin Aug 18

Sungari

FIRST FAR EAST FRONT (Meretskov)

INNER MONGOLIA

Changchun

Kalgan

Chengteh

Mukden Aug 18

Sea of Japan

JAPAN

PEKING
Ch People's
Eighth Army

Port Arthur

Pyongyang

SEOUL

Honshu

CHINA

KOREA

TOKYO

2 Manchuria. At Yalta Stalin had promised Roosevelt that Russia would enter the war against Japan three months after the defeat of Germany; and true to his word, the Soviet Union declared war on Aug 8. The move was obviously not one made solely in selfless friendship and no one expected that it should be; Stalin could remember quite clearly the Russian humiliation of 1905 when Japan had seized the naval base of Port Arthur from the Tsar, and he was glad to take the opportunity to reverse it. The three months' interval had been taken up with the transferral of highly experienced armies, under equally experienced leaders, from the western theatre to the long frontiers between Manchuria and Russia and between Inner and Outer Mongolia.

By the time Little Boy was dropped on Hiroshima, First Far East Front under Meretskov was deployed along the Ussuri north of Vladivostok, Second Far East Front under Purkayev along Manchuria's north-east border, Malinovsky's Trans-Baikal Front along the north-west frontier, with four of its armies in Outer Mongolia.

They crossed the borders on the morning of Aug 9. To the astonishment of the Kwantung Army leaders who had thought the Hingan mountains impassable by armour, Red Army tanks were on the summits by Aug 11, then to drive down into the central Manchurian plain, herding the Japanese along in front at great speed. By Aug 19 the Red Army had reached Tsitsihar, while to the south, one arm was at Chengteh, north of Peking, and another almost at Changchun and Mukden, with Port Arthur beckoning ahead.

Both the Far East Fronts could show comparable successes. Purkayev's right wing met Malinovsky's men in Tsitsihar and his left wing met Meretskov's men in Harbin on Aug 18, though First Far East Front had come up against fierce resistance during the first few days. But, as usual, once the hard Japanese crust was broken, there was little behind it. To the south Kirin fell after heavy air attacks and on the far left flank, Thirty-fourth Army drove straight down the coast into Korea.

But by then, enormous confusion reigned throughout the Kwantung Army, following the Japanese Government's announcement of unconditional surrender to the Allies. Some commanders refused to believe it, some thought it only referred to the Western Allies. It took a direct order brought to the Kwantung Army Commander, General Yamada, by a member of the Japanese Royal Family on Aug 17, to convince him that the war was indeed over, and the surrender to Marshal Vasilevsky was signed the following day.

Port Arthur was in Russian hands again, and Truman's attempt to keep the Russians out of Manchuria had not succeeded.

Capitulation. By the beginning of August, the Japanese leadership was split. Though the vast majority of the Japanese population, despite their hunger, their exhaustion and the destruction of their homes and families, still believed the assurances continually given them of certain Japanese victory, at the highest levels of command and in the Supreme War Council it was realised that this was now impossible.

It was in the attitude to this conclusion that the differences arose. The Foreign Minister, Admiral Togo, felt it his duty to do what he could to save the Japanese nation and in pursuit of this aim was already trying to open negotiations with the Americans, via Russia, to end the war on terms somewhat better than those offered in the Potsdam ultimatum. But the attitude of the War Minister and the powerful military wing he represented was summed up by the announcement by one of them that if the whole Japanese race were wiped out, its

determination to preserve the national polity and obey the Imperial Will would be for ever recorded in the annals of man; it was better to die than to seek ignominious 'safety'.

In the face of such intractable fanaticism, the only course was to ascertain what, exactly, the Imperial Will was. On Aug 9, shortly after news of the second bomb on Nagasaki had been received, and with the realisation that Japan was now also at war with Russia, a meeting of the Supreme War Council was called. During the arguments which followed, both factions held together – and the voting was even; so with some trepidation, a message was sent asking for an Imperial decision.

To the astonishment of all present, Hirohito appeared at the Council chamber himself and softly announced that in order to spare the people further suffering, the terms of the Potsdam ultimatum were to be accepted.

Japan acknowledged defeat.

The World in Autumn 1945

It took several weeks, if not months, for the full significance of the events of Aug 6 and Aug 9 to be appreciated. The statistical details became known quite soon of course but, even after the horrors of six years of a ferociously fought war, it was difficult to grasp that at Hiroshima, in a matter of a second or two, over 50,000 people had been suddenly and comprehensively burned to death.

The existence of such terrifying power had hardly been suspected by anyone except the scientists who had worked in the very specialised fields of molecular or atomic physics, and it took a long time to realise that neither politics nor warfare were ever likely to be the same again. All that the majority of people knew – or cared for the moment – was that the bombs had brought about the end of the war, and now they could begin the task of putting their world back together again. The fact that it would be a very different world from the one they had left behind in 1939 was not immediately obvious, for the costs to the world of the conflict now over had not yet been calculated, let alone assessed.

World War II lasted nearly six years, and was conducted with unparalleled ferocity over a large proportion of the world's surface using weapons of far greater destructive power – even before the atomic explosions – than ever before conceived. It was waged by 56 nations (though some had been far more closely involved than others), it engaged the attentions and energies of vast numbers of people, and in the end, if one includes the deliberate attempts at genocide in Germany and the savage reprisals against dissident populations in Russia, it killed or damaged over 50 million of them.

Even against the traumata of World War I, the war in Vietnam or the Iran–Iraq conflict, World War II thus still constitutes the most violent and prolonged self-inflicted injury on mankind of which history has record. From a purely European point of view it might be thought that World War I was more devastating in human cost, for it was fought in great part in Belgium and northern France, and in the swathe of misery and massacre which stretched from the Belgian coast to Switzerland an average of 2,000 British, French and German soldiers died every day as a result of 'normal activity', while during the vast set-piece battles such as Verdun, on the Somme or at Passchendaele, hundreds of thousands of lives were consumed as with the appetite of Moloch. Other fronts in the Balkans, or in Russia after 1916, were regarded as secondary, and although casualties suffered in these theatres served to drain strength from the main protagonists, these were the 'sideshows' – outside the main arena.

In World War II, the Verduns and Passchendaeles were fought at Stalingrad and Kursk, the naval equivalents of Jutland and Dogger Bank were fought in the Pacific at Midway, Coral Sea and Leyte Gulf, and once the giants, Germany and Russia, Japan and the United States, became fully engaged, Europe was the 'sideshow'.

As a result, the costs to the Europeans were comparatively small. Britain and the Commonwealth lost an estimated half a million soldiers and civilians, France far fewer soldiers but more civilians, Belgian and Dutch losses could be counted in tens of thousands. It was the Soviet Union among the victors who suffered far and away the greatest losses, claiming at least 13 million soldiers killed and 7,700,000 civilians – though of late Soviet historians have adjusted these figures in the light of discoveries that many of the casualties had in fact died in Stalin's own prison camps, and many of the soldiers died at the hands of the Soviet police when it was felt by Stalin or his minions that they had not fought hard enough before allowing themselves to be taken prisoner. None the less, there is no doubt that the heaviest burden of the defeat of Germany had fallen upon the Red Army, who could truthfully point out that

in the battles for the defence of Stalingrad alone they had lost more men than the United States had during the entire war.

The Soviet Union had also suffered 72,000 towns and villages laid waste – and the major pre-war Russian industrial area had been laid waste *twice*, once by the retreating Red Army in 1941–42, then by the Germans as they fell back between 1943 and 1945. The major food-producing areas of the Ukraine and the Kuban had been in German hands for much of the war, feeding Germans and sacked by them as they left, so now Russia faced problems of food shortages and a huge population already hungry. During the war this problem had been considerably eased by aid from America, but one of President Truman's first and most significant acts, once the war with Germany was over, was to end Lend-Lease to Russia.

If Soviet attitudes hardened towards their erstwhile allies once Berlin had fallen and the fighting in Europe ended, those Allies themselves were not entirely blameless. From the point of view of Stalin and his military advisers, the world at the end of 1945 looked just as dangerous for them as it had done during 1941 and 1942. Despite enormous sacrifices, despite the fact that as recently as June 1945 the Red Army had been the finest army in the world – in quality and experience as well as in quantity – the Soviet Union was now at the mercy of the possessors of the atomic bomb – a suddenly and alarmingly hostile United States. In the circumstances, their best – their only – protection would be as wide a buffer zone as could be established between the air bases of Britain and America, and their own borders.

In October 1943 the European Advisory Commission had been set up with a charter agreed by the United States Secretary of State, Cordell Hull, and the British and Soviet Foreign Ministers, Anthony Eden and Vyacheslav Molotov; one of its tasks had been to decide upon the zones of occupation and administration of Germany and Austria once victory had been secured. On October 12, 1944 a protocol was signed dividing Germany into an eastern zone, and north-western and south-western zones, by which the western boundaries of the area to be occupied by the Soviet Union ran close to the western borders of Mecklenburg, Brandenburg, Saxony and Thuringia. The areas between there and the Rhine were to be allocated to Britain and the United States, and eventually General de Gaulle secured a zone under French occupation; but the Soviet Union certainly obtained the largest single area – 85,300 square miles against 96,100 square miles shared between the three Western Allies. On the other hand, the eastern zone had a population of only 24,400,000, while 40,400,000 –

many of them deliberate refugees from Soviet control – lived in the western sector.

There was little argument or dissension between the USSR and the Western Allies about these zones during the weeks and months immediately following VE Day, and by the beginning of July 1945 British and American forces had drawn back from the Elbe to their agreed line of east-west demarcation; only the details of British and American entry into Berlin and the division of that city into its occupational zones caused any bickering or fraying tempers. The demands of General de Gaulle for French participation irritated the Americans somewhat but caused Stalin merely amusement, for as long as no one expected him to part with any of his territory to the French, the West could divide up as they chose.

It was the problems presented by the Soviet occupation of what have since become known as the 'Eastern Bloc' countries, from Bulgaria in the south to Esthonia in the north, which caused arguments and in the end hostility.

At the opening of the Potsdam Conference at the end of July, despite the saddening absence of President Roosevelt, some of the atmosphere of wartime co-operation and even joviality continued, especially between Churchill and Stalin. Stalin had gone as far as to assure Churchill and the newcomer, President Truman, that he was personally against Sovietisation of the countries occupied by the Red Army, and that free elections would be held in all of them; in return, apparently unaware of the paradox, both western leaders had echoed Roosevelt's view that those countries would have post-war governments friendly to Russia.

But by the end of the conference Churchill was no longer Prime Minister, his place having been taken by Clement Attlee, who had brought with him as Foreign Minister Ernest Bevin. As one observer was later acidly to comment, Bevin seemed to regard the Soviet Union as a splinter movement of the Transport and General Workers' Union of which he had himself for many years been General Secretary. Stalin had suffered a minor heart attack just before the conference opened, and in the changed atmosphere engendered by the new men, retired somewhat into the background leaving the main business to be conducted by his intransigent and bellicose Foreign Minister, Molotov. As a result, by Aug 2 when the conference ended, little progress had been made on any significant issue, but those on the Soviet side had concluded that from now on co-operation and friendliness from the West was at an end. The prospect of outright hostility from the powers possessing the atomic bomb seemed a distinct possibility.

It was at the Foreign Ministers' Conference which met in London on Sept 12 that matters came to a head. The first subject upon which Molotov made the Soviet position clear was with regard to reparations. It had been agreed at Yalta that the Allies would demand $20 billion of reparations from Germany, half to go to Russia. In view of the destruction which had been wreaked in her western provinces and now the sudden withdrawal of Lend-Lease, the Soviet Union was removing at top speed $10 billion worth of industrial equipment and food, and also demanding at least one half of all German merchant shipping still afloat. Moreover, from countries such as Hungary and Rumania who had voluntarily fought at Germany's side, she would require comparable reparations, $300 million worth from Rumania to be taken in oil, shipping, locomotives, agricultural produce and timber; and a similar amount from Hungary.

In addition, there was to be no question of Russia handing back to Rumania the areas of Bessarabia and Bukovina she had gained under the Vienna Award, or of Hungary retaining the strip of south Slovakia and Ruthenia sequestered in 1939 from Czechoslovakia. By

164

the same token, Poland would not receive back the eastern provinces she had lost in 1939 when the Red Army had closed up to meet the German Army after the first wartime campaign, though she would be recompensed with large tracts of East and West Prussia, Pomerania and Upper Silesia; Poland's western frontier would now run along the Oder and Neisse rivers.

As for the business of free elections in any of these countries, Molotov confessed himself puzzled by the repeated references of the Western ministers to this absurd matter. It had long been agreed that these countries must be ruled by governments friendly to Soviet Russia, so what was the point of holding free or any other sort of elections when the possibility existed that they might return governments the Soviet Union might deem unfriendly? No! There would be no elections, and whatever governments assumed office in the countries of the Eastern Bloc, they would only do so with complete approval from Moscow.

Two new terms now entered the political dictionary: Churchill's 'Iron Curtain'; and 'Cold War', apparently first coined by Bernard M. Baruch, the United States representative on the United Nations Atomic Energy Commission. They still remain in current usage.

In contrast to the complications which beset the end of the fighting in Europe and the resettlement of the central European communities, the takeover of control by the victors in Japan was simple and smooth. Once the Emperor had issued his edict there was immediate obedience to the orders to surrender as soon as those orders arrived and were believed, though this did take some time in such distant places as Burma, Bougainville and New Guinea. But in Japan itself the acceptance of defeat was total and although the War Minister, the Chief of Staff and a few others felt it incumbent upon them to commit hara-kiri, the expected mass suicides did not occur. Later when the Emperor broke with all

tradition and broadcast to his people, the majority listened on their knees and in wonder, but also with incomprehension as Hirohito spoke in court Japanese, understood by very few.

The first Japanese delegation to come forward to offer official surrender and to make arrangements for the transfer of control arrived at the headquarters of the Supreme Allied Commander, General MacArthur, in Manila on Aug 19 and returned to Tokyo the following day with their instructions. They were on hand to meet the first American troops flown in on Aug 28, to be followed by nearly 5,000 more during the next two days and a complete occupation force as soon as transport could be organised.

On Aug 30 General MacArthur arrived and was driven into Tokyo between serried ranks of immaculate Japanese soldiers, still armed but motionless, while he himself looked neither right nor left and deliberately gave the impression of a man of stone, unmoved by emotion of either mercy or hatred. On Sept 2 he took the formal surrender aboard the battleship USS *Missouri* in Tokyo Bay. The Japanese delegation had deliberately been kept waiting on the quarterdeck for nearly half an hour and when eventually the signing ceremony took place, close to MacArthur stood Generals Wainwright and Percival, taken prisoner at Bataan and Singapore respectively so many anguished months before, recently liberated and both exhausted and emaciated by their ordeals. Japan was not going to be allowed to forget that she had brought the war upon herself, and that many of her soldiers had acted with barbarous cruelty.

Nevertheless, MacArthur ended his speech with the words, 'Nor is it for us here to meet, representing as we do a majority of the people of the earth, in a spirit of distrust, malice or hatred . . . Let us pray that peace be now restored to the world and that God will preserve it always.'

It was a spirit which was to guide the whole of

MacArthur's policy during his rule in Japan, and goes a long way to explain the absence of even sullenness in the compliance with his orders. It was obvious to everyone that his chief and immediate concern was to re-establish order and essential services, and to bring home as quickly as possible some 4 million Japanese soldiers still overseas.

This, of course, did present problems. Luzon, Borneo, Indo-China, Hong Kong, Malaya, Burma, and in particular China, had all been occupied by Japanese troops who had acted at times with varying degrees of barbarity, and a proportion of the newly liberated peoples were, not suprisingly, intent upon revenge; the Japanese forces had to keep their arms for self-protection until they were safely on their way home. But the problems were for the most part overcome, and within two months the bulk of the Japanese army which three years before had dominated the East from Manchuria to New Guinea and from Rangoon across to Guadalcanal, were returning. The most significant ceremony of all was probably that on Sept 9 when an army of a million troops formally surrendered to the Chinese at Nanking.

Not only Japanese troops had to be brought home, of course; there were also the unfortunate British, Commonwealth and American prisoners of war, to say nothing of the plight of native populations displaced throughout the Pacific and decimated by hunger and sickness during the war years.

Both MacArthur and Mountbatten set about solving enormous and urgent problems presented by the reoccupation of huge areas of difficult country, and then relieving the often horrifying conditions found there. British troops reached Hong Kong some two weeks after the capitulation to find civilians and PoWs, despite their own weakness and emaciation, trying to cope with local Chinese worried by the possibilities of takeover either by Chinese Communists or Chiang Kai-shek's Nationalists, and as a result more intent upon looting and escape than establishing any sort of order.

On the other hand, British warships arrived off Singapore on Sept 3 and the takeover from the Japanese had some of the smoothness of the Changing of the Guard. Relations were polite until the British reached Changi Jail and saw the conditions of the prisoners taken three and a half years before – reflected soon afterwards by reports from parachute teams dropped into camps further north. Relations changed abruptly and Japanese soldiers were put to work repairing some of the damage they had done.

But there were very few of the problems of occupation zones or 'occupied countries' which so bedevilled the European situation. Australia and New Zealand felt briefly that perhaps they might have a part to play, but Britain under a Labour Government had no such desires, and Russia's claim to a role in the occupation of Japan was soon rejected; with no force *in situ* to support her claims, there was little that Moscow could do apart from make ritual diplomatic protest. General MacArthur was to remain in almost sole command of the Japanese homelands for some time to come, and to rule them with a wisdom and tolerant discipline which came as a surprise to many who had had cause to question his judgement and pronouncements in the past. It would seem that in many ways his attitude to his country's enemies embodied the precept with which Winston Churchill was to preface his own history of World War II:

In War	:	Resolution
In Defeat	:	Defiance
In Victory	:	Magnanimity
In Peace	:	Goodwill

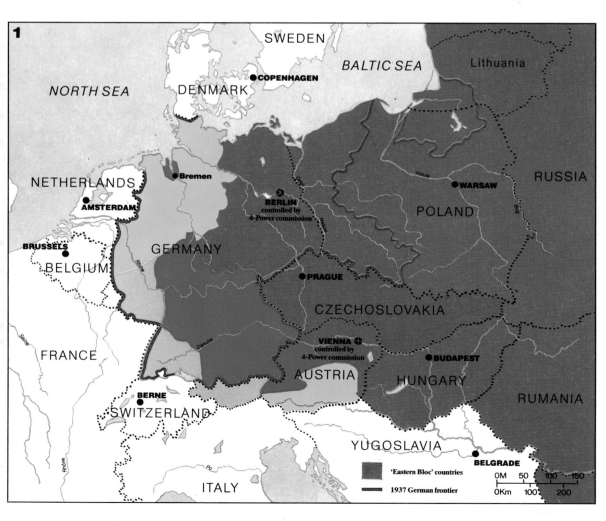

Bibliography

This list of books is not intended as a bibliography of World War II, for such a catalogue would at least double the size of this volume. The list is simply one of books the authors think would be of interest and enjoyment to those readers whose appetite has been whetted by one or more of the necessarily limited essays accompanying the maps in this volume, and who, as a result, would like to know more. It is, in fact, merely a guide to further reading.

General
Carver, Michael — *Twentieth Century Warriors*, Weidenfeld & Nicolson, 1987
Churchill, Winston S. — *The Second World War* (6 vols), Cassell, 1948–54
Colville, John — *The Fringes of Power*, Hodder and Stoughton, 1985
Liddell Hart, B.H. — *History of the Second World War*, Cassell, 1970
Purnell's History of the Second World War (8 vols), BPC, 1964–66

Europe
Ash, Bernard — *Norway, 1940*, Cassell, 1964
Blumenson, Martin — *The Duel for France*, Houghton Mifflin, 1963
Clark, Mark — *Calculated Risk*, Harrap, 1951
Cooper, Matthew — *The German Army, 1933–45*, MacDonald, 1978
Eisenhower, Dwight D. — *Crusade in Europe*, Heinemann, 1948
Gardner, Brian — *1945 – The Wasted Hour*, Cassell, 1963
Horne, Alistair — *To Lose a Battle*, Macmillan, 1969
Kee, Robert — *The World We Left Behind*, Weidenfeld & Nicolson, 1984
Keegan, John — *Six Armies in Normandy*, Cape, 1982
MacDonald, Charles — *The Mighty Endeavour*, Guild Press, 1978
The Battle of the Bulge, Weidenfeld & Nicolson, 1984
Mann, Golo — *History of Germany since 1789*, The Hogarth Press, 1984
O'Neill, Robert — *The German Army and the Nazi Party*, Cassell, 1966
Orgill, Douglas — *The Gothic Line*, Heinemann, 1967
Pitt, Barrie — *Churchill and the Generals*, Sidgwick & Jackson, 1981
Roberts, J.M. — *Europe 1880–1945*, Longman, 1967
Speer, Albert — *Inside the Third Reich*, Weidenfeld & Nicolson, 1970
Stone, Norman — *Hitler*, Hodder and Stoughton, 1980
Toland, John — *The Last Hundred Days*, Barker, 1965
Upton, A.F. — *Finland in Crisis*, Faber & Faber, 1965
Warlimont, W. — *Inside Hitler's Headquarters*, Weidenfeld & Nicolson, 1964
Wilmot, Chester — *The Struggle for Europe*, Collins, 1952
Wiskemann, Elizabeth — *Europe of the Dictators*, Collins, 1966

North Africa
Agar-Hamilton and Turner — *Crisis in the Desert*, Oxford University Press, 1952
The Sidi Rezegh Battles, Oxford University Press, 1957
Barclay, C.N. — *On Their Shoulders*, Faber & Faber, 1964
Carver, Michael — *Tobruk*, Batsford, 1964
Dilemmas of the Desert War, Batsford, 1986
Connell, John. — *Wavell, Scholar and Soldier*, Collins, 1964
Jackson, W.G.F. — *The North African Campaign*, Batsford, 1975
Kennedy-Shaw, W.B. — *Long Range Desert Group*, Collins, 1945

MacIntyre, Donald — *The Battle for the Mediterranean*, Batsford, 1964
Macksey, K.J. — *The Crucible of Power*, Hutchinson, 1969
Rommel; Battles and Campaigns, Arms and Armour, 1979
Mellenthin, von F.W. — *Panzer Battles*, Oklahoma Press, 1956
Pitt, Barrie — *The Crucible of War: Western Desert 1941*, Cape, 1980
The Crucible of War: Year of Alamein 1942, Cape, 1982

Russian Front
Clark, Alan — *Barbarossa*, Hutchinson, 1965
Craig, William — *Enemy at the Gates*, Hodder and Stoughton, 1973
Erickson, John — *The Soviet High Command*, Macmillan, 1962
The Road to Stalingrad, Weidenfeld & Nicolson, 1975
The Road to Berlin, Weidenfeld & Nicolson, 1983
Goure, Leon — *The Siege of Leningrad*, Stanford University Press, 1962
Guderian, Heinz — *Panzer Leader*, Dutton, 1957
Leach, Barry — *German Strategy against Russia 1939–41*, Oxford University Press, 1973
Mackintosh, Malcolm — *Juggernaut*, Macmillan, 1967
Manstein, Erich von — *Lost Victories*, Methuen, 1958
Ziemke, Earl — *Stalingrad to Berlin*, USA Historical Series, 1968

Far East
Calvert, Michael — *Prisoners of Hope*, Cape, 1952
Hoyt, Edwin P. — *Japan's War*, Century Hutchinson, 1986
MacArthur, Douglas — *Reports of General MacArthur (Vol 1)*, Library of Congress, 1966
Slim, Field Marshal W. — *Defeat into Victory*, Cassell, 1956

People
Aron, Robert — *de Gaulle Triumphant*, Putnam, 1970
Blumenson, Martin — *The Patton Papers*, Houghton Mifflin, 1974
Carver, Michael — *Harding of Petherton*, Weidenfeld & Nicolson, 1978
Chalfont, Alun — *Montgomery of Alamein*, Weidenfeld & Nicolson, 1976
Chaney, Otto P. — *Zhukov*, David and Charles, 1972
Clark, Mark — *Calculated Risk*, Harrap, 1951
Hamilton, Nigel — *Monty, 1887–1942*, Hamish Hamilton, 1981
Hunt, David — *A Don at War*, Kimber, 1966
Jackson, W.G.F. — *Alexander of Tunis*, Batsford, 1971
Kesselring, Field Marshal A. — *Memoirs*, Kimber, 1953
Liddell Hart, B.H. (ed) — *The Rommel Papers*, Collins, 1953
Mitcham, S.W. — *Hitler's Field Marshals*, Leo Cooper, 1988
Sixsmith, E.K.G. — *Eisenhower*, Batsford, 1973
Trevor-Roper, H.R. (ed) — *Hitler's War Directives*, Sidgwick and Jackson, 1964

Index

Geographical

Eastern Front

170

European and Middle Eastern Fronts

Pacific Front

Political and Military

How to use the maps

1 Full-colour double-page global maps for each month from September 1939 to August 1945 display ground force and fleet movements, bombing offensives, and shipping losses. On a scale never before attempted, this is the most ambitious military cartographic project ever published.

2 Larger-scale detail maps focus on theatres of conflict, campaigns, operations and individual actions at every level from street-fighting to complete battlefronts. The full extent of *Operation Barbarossa* is mapped for the first time and the maps' positioning on the page enables 'flicker-effect' illustration of the Eastern Front campaigns.

3 Territorial gains and losses and front movements are clearly indicated for each month of the war in detailed campaign maps. Army formation movement indications are accompanied by campaign dates and the names of army commanders. A numerical coding system relates detail maps to the global overview maps.

4 Colour coding for the major combatant powers on the global maps indicates the expanding and declining areas of military influence and strategic initiative. Throughout the double-page spreads, the western theatre is shown on the left-hand page and the eastern and Pacific theatres on the right-hand page.

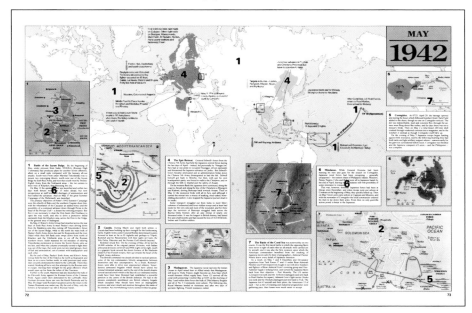

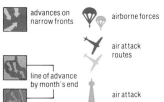

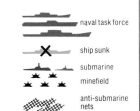

5 Imaginative design and use of graphic symbols provides at-a-glance identification of major airfields, minefields, airborne offensives, surface and submarine fleet positions, aircraft, armour and naval strengths, positions and movement.

6 Barrie Pitt's authoritative essay-captions – totalling some quarter of a million words – explain and expand upon the tactics and strategies, conflicts and campaigns illustrated by the maps and provide a comprehensive and illuminating narrative of the entire conflict.

7 Each map is individually scaled. Terrain, topography, and communications are indicated on the detail maps to provide a clear portrait of each theatre of war. Appendices include a useful bibliography and a fully detailed geographical and military index.

Supplementary map-and-essay features focus on crucial events of the conflict such as *Operation Barbarossa*, the Battle of El Alamein and the D-Day landings and a concluding feature assesses the consequences of six years of global total war.

Key

Geographical features
- major city
- major town
- minor town or village
- fortress
- oil production area
- railway
- important road
- marshland
- desert track

Combatant forces
- British and Commonwealth
- US forces
- German forces
- Russian forces
- Italian forces
- Japanese forces
- French forces
- Australian forces
- Chinese forces
- Polish forces

Forces' movements
- advances on a single broad front
- advances on narrow fronts
- line of advance by month's end

Military features
- armoured forces
- airborne forces
- air attack routes
- air attack
- air raids
- airfields
- fortified line or perimeter
- minefield
- naval task force
- ship sunk
- submarine
- minefield
- anti-submarine nets